LABOR-MANAGEMENT RELATIONS

McGraw-Hill Series in Management

FRED LUTHANS AND KEITH DAVIS, CONSULTING EDITORS

Allen: The Management Profession
Arnold and Feldman: Organizational Behavior
Benton: Supervision and Management
Buchele: The Management of Business and Public Organizations
Cascio: Managing Human Resources: Productivity, Quality of Work Life, Profits
Cleland and King: Management: A Systems Approach
Cleland and King: Systems Analysis and Project Management
Dale: Management: Theory and Practice
Davis and Newstrom: Human Behavior at Work: Organizational Behavior
Del Mar: Operations and Industrial Management: Designing and Managing for Productivity
Dobler, Lee, and Burt: Purchasing and Materials Management: Text and Cases
Dunn and Rachel: Wage and Salary Administration: Total Compensation Systems
Feldman and Arnold: Managing Individual and Group Behavior in Organizations
Finch, Jones, and Litterer: Managing for Organizational Effectiveness: An Experiential Approach
Flippo: Personnel Management
Frederick, Davis, and Post: Business and Society: Management, Public Policy, Ethics
Gerloff: Organizational Theory and Design: A Strategic Approach for Management
Hampton: Management
Hampton: Inside Management: Readings from *Business Week*
Hicks and Gullett: Management
Hicks and Gullett: Organizations: Theory and Behavior
Hodgetts: Effective Supervision: A Practical Approach
Jauch and Glueck: Business Policy and Strategic Management
Jauch and Glueck: Strategic Management and Business Policy
Jauch and Townsend: Cases in Strategic Management and Business Policy
Johnson, Kast, and Rosenzweig: The Theory and Management of Systems
Karlins: The Human Use of Human Resources
Kast and Rosenzweig: Experiential Exercises and Cases in Management
Knudson, Woodworth, and Bell: Management: An Experiential Approach
Koontz, O'Donnell, and Weihrich: Essentials of Management
Koontz and Weihrich: Management
Kopelman: Managing Productivity in Organizations: A Practical, People-Oriented Perspective
Levin, McLaughlin, Lamone, and Kottas: Production/Operations Management: Contemporary Policy for Managing Operating Systems
Luthans: Organizational Behavior

LABOR-MANAGEMENT RELATIONS

FOURTH EDITION

Daniel Quinn Mills

Graduate School of Business Administration
Harvard University

McGraw-Hill Publishing Company

New York   St. Louis   San Francisco   Auckland   Bogotá   Caracas
Hamburg   Lisbon   London   Madrid   Mexico   Milan
Montreal   New Delhi   Oklahoma City   Paris   San Juan
São Paulo   Singapore   Sydney   Tokyo   Toronto

To Joyce, Lisa, and Shirley

This book was set in Palatino by the College Composition Unit
in cooperation with Ruttle Shaw & Wetherill, Inc.
The editors were Kathleen L. Loy, Cynthia L. Phelps, and Linda Richmond;
the production supervisor was Salvador Gonzales.
The cover was designed by Scott Chelius.
R. R. Donnelley & Sons Company was printer and binder.

LABOR-MANAGEMENT RELATIONS.

3 4 5 6 7 8 9 0 DOC DOC 9 3 2 1 0

ISBN 0-07-042429-2

Library of Congress Cataloging-in-Publication Data

Mills, Daniel Quinn
    Labor-management relations / Daniel Quinn Mills. -- 4th ed.
    p. cm.
    Includes bibliographies and indexes.
    ISBN 0-07-042429-2
    1. Industrial relations--United States.   2. Industrial relations.
I. Title.
HD8072.5.M54 1989
331'.0973--dc19   88-13110

ABOUT THE AUTHOR

DANIEL QUINN MILLS holds the Albert J. Weatherhead, Jr., Chair as a Professor of Business Administration at the Harvard University Graduate School of Business Administration. He has taught for many years and is the author of numerous books and articles.

Professor Mills is widely and often quoted in the national media, including *The New York Times, Wall Street Journal, Chicago Tribune, Los Angeles Times,* and *Business Week.* He has appeared on the Today Show on NBC.

CONTENTS

PREFACE

This fourth edition of *Labor-Management Relations* is the result of continuing changes in our economy, in the law, and in research. Students who have used the previous editions of *Labor-Management Relations* and faculty members who have taught from it have been in touch with me suggesting alterations, additions, and improvements in the text.

Also, this edition, like the others, owes a major debt to my continuing experience as a neutral in the practice of labor-management relations. I continue to serve as a mediator and as an arbitrator in labor-management disputes and to have the opportunity to discuss with union officials, managers, and government officials various aspects of their own involvement in collective bargaining, grievance processing, and dispute settlement. A focus on the actors involved in labor-management relations (employees, unions, management, government, and the public) remains a principal feature of this book.

Labor-management relations is the subject of this book. Also included is material from personnel administration, human behavior in organizations, and labor economics. Other books frequently try to treat labor relations with other disciplines, but usually choose to emphasize one set of factors or another. In the past, the most common mergers were of labor relations and labor economics. Today, labor relations are often combined with a theoretical structure derived from the behavioral sciences. But, in my judgment, these combinations, which aim at straightforwardness in presentation, suffer from oversimplification. In an effort to give students a clear presentation, these books give them instead only a half-truth. In our society, labor relations is, in fact, a complex combination of law, human relations, and economics. This book attempts to slight none of these influential factors.

This edition reflects a change in American labor relations practice by including a subtle change in emphasis, accomplished by detailed rewriting, from labor-management relations as a formal, adversarial relationship, typi-fied by written contracts and detailed rules, to a more informal and cooper-ative relationship, typified by working understandings. This is not to say that American industrial relations has accomplished this transition completely, or even in a majority of situations, but that the adversarial system is no longer so dominant that it can be used as a surrogate for the system as a whole.

Unfortunately, sources of data about labor-management relations were richer several years ago than they are now. In particular, agencies of the fed-eral government have reduced the types of data collected and the frequency of publication. As a result, several tables and charts in the text cannot be up-dated and have been removed. Others can be updated only to a limited de-gree.

Organization   Users of the second edition helped to determine the orga-nization of subsequent editions. Essentially, the chapters on the history, phi-losophy, and structure of the American labor movement were moved to the front of the book, permitting students to obtain historical perspective and some acquaintance with American unions before turning to the legal frame-work, which is so important in our country. The chapters on the legal frame-work of collective bargaining remain in the front of the book, so that students obtain at the outset an understanding of how the law prescribes the roles of unions, managers, and government agencies in determining how employees are treated by the companies for which they work. This organization allows the student to obtain an understanding of how unions are chosen by employ-ees before moving on to consider the characteristics of the American labor movement and the collective bargaining process.

Central Theme   Viewed in the context described above, the central theme for the book has not changed. This theme begins with the recognition that at the core of employee-employer relationships is the exercise of authority and the use of power. Labor relations is, in a fundamental sense, about the use of power by managers. When employees suffer from the abuse of authority by managers, unions are a device by which employees establish a countervailing center of power. Collective bargaining is a process by which two centers of power are brought to an accommodation with each other. Because of the threat of overt conflict in collective bargaining, government has the obliga-tion to establish the rules by which the contests of management and labor are played out. Where a collective bargaining agreement exists, grievance proce-dures are a method by which disputes between two powerful protagonists can be resolved with as little disruption to the work organization and the ex-ternal community as possible.

The resolution of contests between management and labor creates rights and obligations for each. It is through the creation of rights for employees that conflict between management and labor is minimized and increased hu-manization is brought to the workplace. And, on the other hand, it is by the creation (or protection) of the rights of managers that economic necessity is recognized and efficiency is advanced. Thus, the theme of power, its exercise and its limitations, is found throughout labor-management relations. Newly vigorous competition in output markets and developments in capital markets give focus to and place constraints on all of this. But they do not change it.

Students of labor-management relations should take away from this book five ideas:

First, an appreciation of the role of management and unions in our society

Second, a framework for analysis of labor-relations problems and their resolution

Third, experience in grievance arbitration and collective bargaining negotiations obtained from exercises provided at the end of this volume

Fourth, increased knowledge and information about labor-management relations

Fifth, a review and reexamination of their own attitudes, based on new knowledge and experience

Students should be free to develop their own attitudes and opinions about labor relations. In order to facilitate independent thinking, I have tried to avoid offering broad judgments about important ideas. Instead, I have attempted to provide a reasonable amount of information, both pro and con, from which students, with guidance from their instructor, can make their own judgments. Above all, this book is intended to ask readers to think hard about questions of labor-management relations, for underlying forces often point to conflicts and contradictions and, therefore, to the problems and opportunities of the future.

I am deeply grateful for the assistance of many reviewers, including: C. Autermiller, Oakland Community College; Barry S. Axe, Trenton State College; Herbert Bienstock, Queens College; Donald Coffin, Indiana University, Northwest; Joan Dahl, Cal-State, Northridge; Jack Fiorito, University of Iowa; Charles Greer, Oklahoma State University; I. B. Helburn, University of Texas, Austin; Christine Hobart, Northeastern University; Nancy Johnson, University of Kentucky; Fred Luthans, University of Nebraska; Ronald Miller, Oregon State University; Harry Mills, East Texas State University; Jonathan Monat, California State University, Long Beach; Stanley Phillips, Tennessee Technical University; Ted Prenting, Marist College; Mark Prous, SUNY-Potsdam; Ali Raza, California State University-Sacramento; Robert Rodgers, University of Texas, Austin; Ronald Seeber, Cornell University; Lee Stepina, Florida State University; William D. Torrence, University of Nebraska; Harold White, Arizona State University; and Ben Workinson, Michigan State University. I hope that this revised edition is responsive to their needs.

Daniel Quinn Mills

PRINCIPLES OF LABOR-MANAGEMENT RELATIONS

CONTEMPORARY LABOR-MANAGEMENT RELATIONS

The work world is a central concern in the lives of most people. Because of its importance, the study of work is interdisciplinary. Some aspects of work are governed by laws administered by various governmental institutions. Other important aspects of work depend on labor-management relations and hinge on an understanding of individual or group psychology, economics factors, sociological trends, and power relationships.

The first section of this book discusses the contours of labor-management relations, what the study is about, and why it is an important subject. An overview is presented through which the reader can begin to integrate its many and diverse facets.

CHAPTER 1

THE INDUSTRIAL RELATIONS SYSTEM IN THE UNITED STATES

MODERN ECONOMIC SOCIETY

The economic and social status of most people in modern economic society depends to a large degree on their occupations. Most adults in our country, both men and women, hold jobs. We all spend a considerable amount of our time at our place of work. Through work we develop many of our personal associations, our attitudes, and other aspects of our lives. Work is crucial to most people's economic security. Jobs provide the mechanism by which each of us contributes to the economic wellbeing of the society as a whole. In return, jobs provide us with an income. The amount of the income a job provides helps to determine an individual's, and a family's, standard of living, especially in terms of the goods and services consumed. Income also provides people with opportunities, such as the opportunity to travel, to engage in hobbies or in recreational activities, or to develop talents, such as those in music, art, or dancing. The income and benefits associated with many jobs also provide protection against weakness, injury, and even, to a degree, loss of the job itself.

There have been many important changes over the years in the work force in the United States and in the types of jobs people have. For example, a much larger proportion of women are now working or seeking work than in the past. Since World War II the percentage of women 16 years of age and older who are in the labor force has grown from 32 to 55 percent. At the same time the proportion of men in the labor force has declined from 87 to 76 percent. In 1948, 28 percent of the people in the American labor force were women. In 1986, that proportion had risen to 45 percent (see Figure 1-1). At the

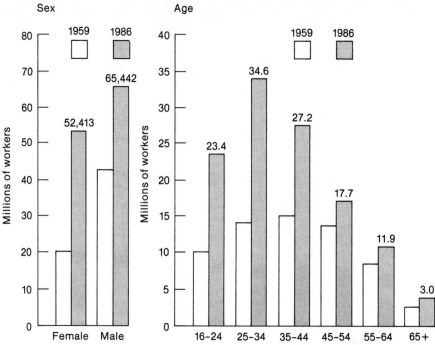

FIGURE 1-1 The labor force has shifted to more women members as well as younger members. (*Source: Bureau of Labor Statistics, Employment and Earnings, 34:1, January 1987, pp. 157–158.*)

beginning of this century people with jobs had completed on average only 8 years of school. Today they have completed more than 12 years, on average. Also at the beginning of this century only one-fifth of the work force held white-collar jobs. Most people earned a living as farmers or as craftspersons and laborers. But today more than half the work force is employed in white-collar occupations of one type or another.[1] These are very significant changes, and in the pages ahead we shall see how our country has coped with them.

As we all know, some jobs are better than others. Good jobs provide higher pay, better benefits, and better working conditions than poorer jobs. And since we spend so much time on the job, the personal relationships at the workplace are important to all of us. But what causes some jobs to be better than others? Who sets the standards that apply to various jobs, and by what process is it done?

Ours is a society of employees and managers. In the past, many more people worked for themselves or for members of their families, but this is no longer the case in industrialized countries. Instead, most people work for or-

---

[1] Clark Kerr, "Introduction," in Clark Kerr and Jerome Rosow, eds., *Work In America: The Decade Ahead* (New York: Van Nostrand Reinhold, 1979), pp. ix–xxvii.

ganizations that vary in size from small to very large.[2] Some private business organizations now have several hundred thousand employees, and some levels of government, like the federal government, have several million employees. Most organizations are smaller, of course, but they also have policies and procedures, and each individual is only a small part of their functioning.

PLAN OF THE BOOK

It is through an interaction of employers and workers that the conditions of employment are determined. This book is about that interaction. It is divided into eight major sections which describe aspects of the relationship of management and labor, and it includes exercises from which the reader can develop some personal experience in handling labor relations problems.

The book is organized as follows:

Part A   examines the American industrial relations system.

Part B   describes the unions and the American labor movement as a whole.

Part C   examines the context which government has established for labor relations in the United States.

Part D   describes the operation of nonunion companies and analyzes why workers might want to join unions.

Part E   describes the process of collective bargaining.

Part F   considers some of the most important subjects which arise in collective bargaining, especially compensation.

Part G   points out the very great diversity which exists in the relationships of unions and companies in the various industries in the private sector.

Part H   examines the equally great diversity of circumstances which now exist in the public employment.

Part I   assesses the consequences of our system of labor relations and takes a look into the future.

Throughout the text runs the theme of the power which is inherent in the relation of employer to employee and the various limitations which are imposed, whether by law, union influence, or management self-discipline, on the ways in which power is exercised.

WHAT IS AN INDUSTRIAL RELATIONS SYSTEM?

Labor-management relations take place within a context that may be described as an industrial relations system. The concept of such a system is a very broad one, so that one may speak of the industrial relations system of a

[2] John T. Dunlop, "Introduction," in John T. Dunlop and Walter Galenson, eds., *Labor in the Twentieth Century* (New York: Academic Press, 1978), pp. 1–10.

nation; and within a nation one may speak of the industrial relations system of a particular industry. An industrial relations system is characterized by having certain active institutions, a context in which they operate, and a certain output. It is important to think of industrial relations as being a system because the concept of a system focuses attention on interrelationships among the system's parts. In fact, the industrial relations system of each country constitutes a method of dealing with certain fundamental problems of labor relations that exist in all countries, but which assume different forms as a result of the peculiar form in which they occur.[3]

How is the term "industrial relations systems" to be defined? First, the system is industrial in nature because we do not include in it the relationships that exist in the agricultural sector, which explicitly involves the growing of crops and husbandry of animals. In most countries these activities still consume most of the labor force. Also, traditional agriculture has its own special systems of organization, which in many countries depend primarily on land ownership and tenancy. The organization and the conduct of agriculture are important topics, but ones which are generally excluded in discussion of industrial relations systems. (However, in the United States the number of persons engaged in agriculture has declined to such a low proportion of the total labor force—only 3 or 4 percent—that some parts of agriculture are now being reorganized on the basis of models taken from the industrial sector.) The distribution, processing, and retailing of agricultural commodities are, of course, industrial activities that are included in our definition of an industrial relations system.

Further, the term "industrial" is meant to include the labor-management relations which exist in service industries and in public service. In this sense, the term "industrial" is not meant to be limited to industry (i.e., manufacturing), but harkens back to an older meaning of industry which refers to the way a person earns a living. Hence, "industrial" in industrial relations systems refers to the workplace—whatever and wherever it is.

"Industrial relations" may be defined as the processes by which human beings and their organizations interact at the workplace and, more broadly, in society as a whole to establish the terms and conditions of employment. The process of relations between persons and organizations is stressed, not just the resulting standards. Finally, a "system" is spoken of in order to emphasize the interrelations among persons, organizations, and standards in the industrial environment.

Each nation may be said to have some characteristic fashion of dealing with the social, economic, and legal problems that arise among its citizens. If each of these areas is conceived to involve a system, then the industrial relations system may be described as an area in which they overlap. Thus, the industrial relations system is seen to involve important aspects of the social, economic, and legal systems of a country as they relate to the industrial

---

[3] John T. Dunlop, *Industrial Relations Systems* (New York: Holt, 1957).

FIGURE 1-2   Identification of an industrial relations system.

workplace and the relationships among employees and managers. Figure 1-2 provides a diagrammatic identification of an industrial relations system. The diagram shows that the industrial relations system is derived from the intersection of the other, more basic systems.[4] It also shows that the other systems overlap two by two outside the industrial relations system. Thus, in the United States, the economic and legal systems overlap a great deal in areas other than industrial relations, such as commercial law. Similarly, the social and economic systems overlap broadly outside industrial relations, including, for example, income maintenance programs like Social Security and welfare assistance. Thus, we see that the industrial relations system is deeply embedded in our country's basic framework and is not a thing apart. In fact, many persons who make their livelihood in industrial relations have been broadly trained as tradespeople, lawyers, or business people and come therefore from the legal or economic system, bringing their attitudes and practices into the industrial relations system. To further illustrate the point, in the United States the federal courts that ordinarily handle labor relations cases are not specialized courts, but instead handle the full range of legal activity that comes before the federal judiciary. (The National Labor Relations Board is not a court, but rather an administrative tribunal. It is much like a specialized court.) Thus, industrial relations matters are not separated from the broad range of legal activities in the United States, but are in fact deeply intermingled with them.[5]

HOW DOES OUR INDUSTRIAL RELATIONS SYSTEM OPERATE?

An industrial relations system involves certain institutions, which we may term "actors" in the system. In the United States the major actors are, broadly defined, three: management and management organizations, employees and their organizations, and the government in its role as a regulator

[4] Dunlop described the economic and industrial relations systems as part of an encompassing social system. The formulation used here is, therefore, not Dunlop's, but a modification.

[5] Nicholas Bain, "Approaches to Industrial Relations Theory: An Appraisal and a Theory," *Labor and Society*. 3:2. April 1978, pp. 199–216.

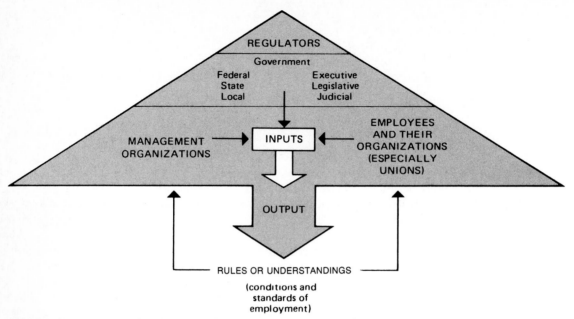

FIGURE 1-3   A diagram of the industrial relations systems in the United States.

and judge. These actors together determine the output of the system, which we may describe as a set of rules about terms and conditions of employment. Described in this way, the system seems simple enough—but unfortunately, there are many complications. For example, there is not one government in the United States, but many governments, with different levels of government (e.g., federal, state, and municipal) and many branches of government (executive, legislative, and judicial). It is a basic characterization of government in America that these different levels and branches are kept more separate than is ordinarily the case abroad. We refer to this separation as the "balance of powers," or "separation of powers," doctrine. Because of this separation, the many agencies of government are each, to a degree, separate actors in our industrial relations system. (In addition, governments are major employers in the United States, so that they also belong in the category of management and management organizations as well as in the category of regulators.)

Figure 1-3 is a diagrammatic representation of the industrial relations systems in the United States. This representation is also accurate for the systems in most Western European countries.[6] In other countries, certain other institutions, such as the church, a particular political party, or a national movement, may serve as independent actors in the system also.

[6] Hugh Armstrong Clegg. *Trade Unionism under Collective Bargaining* (Oxford: Basil Blackwell, 1976).

The actors in the system interact with one another to develop the basic output of the system, including a set of rules or understandings about working conditions and standards of employment. Employees must be compensated, trained, assigned work, and transferred in ways which are mutually understood and accepted by both managers and employees. The most formal method of establishing how actions are to be taken involves the creation of specific rules. For convenience we refer to rules here, but the informal understandings and working relationships between managers and employees are also of great significance. We will have much to say about rules in the next section of this chapter.

When rules have been established, they have an impact on both management and labor, who with government participated in their establishment. Sometimes the impact, or feedback, is what was expected and intended. When this is the case, the actors in the industrial relations system may turn their attention to other problems. However, sometimes the rules which have been created have unexpected consequences. Management or labor may be surprised and upset at the unintended consequences of a rule. In this case, the actor that is aggrieved is likely to seek further changes in the rule, or may go to the regulatory agencies to attempt to get the rule changed. Thus, feedback plays an important role in the operation of the industrial relations system.

Conflict may, of course, occur among the actors in the industrial relations system. Strikes, which are often the product of disputes between management and labor, occur frequently in the United States. Conflict causes considerable public attention, but it is not the primary product of the industrial relations system. To adopt the view that conflict is the primary output of the system, i.e., the most significant thing to be studied and explained, risks the absurd conclusion that when there is little conflict, there is little or nothing to be studied. However, we shall see that rules about how conflict is to be managed and controlled are an important element of the output of the system.

An industrial relations system may also be said to operate within a set of constraints involving both the technology available to the economic system and the ideology of the society as a whole. Technology is very important, for it helps to determine the types of jobs available and the amount of output that can be produced and in turn can support living standards. Improving technology is both a blessing and a curse to the industrial relations system. It creates the capacity to provide higher living standards, but it also generates disputes among labor and management about work assignments, pay levels, and similar matters associated with new processes and equipment.

The ideological direction of a society is also an important constraint on an industrial relations system. In the United States people generally accept privately owned business as a legitimate part of our economic system, and the attempts of management to make a reasonable profit for private stockholders are accepted (although people may argue about what is "reasonable"). In contrast, in many other countries the legitimacy of private ownership of business is far less acceptable. Where government, unions, and managers do not accept each other's legitimacy, very great difficulties can develop for the industrial relations system. Stability in industrial relations requires a degree of correspondence among the actors' views of industrial society, although the specific nature of the views (e.g., favorable or unfavorable to private business or favorable or unfavorable to unions) is less significant.[7]

RULES ABOUT WHAT?

There is much to be said about the rules or understandings that are the product of the industrial relations system. First, they may concern many types of matters, including compensation, discrimination, hiring, workers' rights, and so on. Second, they may be either *substantive* or *procedural*. This is a very important distinction, to which we will return often in later chapters.

Substantive rules establish the matter exactly, as, for example, the amount of compensation, the length of the workday, and the size of the overtime premium (e.g., time and a half).

Procedural rules establish how things are to be done, as, for example, what steps a company must take to set a new rule or to discharge an employee. Procedural rules generally describe how substantive rules are to be made or implemented. We usually think mostly about substantive rules, but procedural rules are equally, or often more, important. When management and labor cannot agree on what the substantive rule will be (e.g., how much a particular employee should be paid), often they can agree on how the rule will be decided (e.g., by reference to an impartial arbitrator, who will issue a decision as to what amount the employee will be paid).

The rules produced by an industrial relations system may be in several different forms. In many instances they are in the form of the personnel policies, practices, and procedures of various companies. In many other instances they are found in the collective bargaining agreements between companies and labor unions. In some instances they are in written form; in other instances they are in the form of tacit understandings and/or unwritten practices.

Some union-management agreements are very brief and treat only a few matters. Other agreements are quite lengthy and involve many provisions. Many agreements are more than 200 pages long. Tables of contents include such headings as:[8]

- Local working conditions
- Contracting out (i.e., subcontracting)

---

[7] A critical review of the concept of an industrial relations system can be found in S. J. Wood et al., "The Industrial Relations System Concept as a Basis for Theory in Industrial Relations," *British Journal of Industrial Relations*, 13, 1975, pp. 291–309. See also A. J. Geare, "The Field of Study of Industrial Relations," *The Journal of Industrial Relations*, 19:3, September 1977, pp. 274–283. See also William K. Roche, "Systems Analysis and Industrial Relations," *Economic and Industrial Democracy*, 7:1, February 1986, pp. 3–28.

[8] Each heading involves a topic that will be treated later in this book.

- Recognition and union membership
- Rates of pay
- Job classifications and incentives
- Hours of work and overtime
- Holidays
- Vacations
- Seniority
- Adjustment of complaints and grievances
- Discharge of employees
- Management functions
- Safety and health

Rules are also drawn from the decisions of arbitrators and courts and from statutes (i.e., laws) passed by legislatures and applying to companies, employees, and unions. Since governments, management, and labor are all deeply interested in the rules of the workplace, it is no surprise that government tries by regulation to affect the rules that management and labor establish, and, conversely, that management and labor try through political activity and lobbying to affect the laws that governments pass concerning the rules of the workplace.

There is very great diversity in the rules that exist within the American industrial relations systems. Few collective bargaining agreements have the same provisions. Agreements within the same industry often show substantial similarity, but those from another industry are likely to be very different. For example, seniority provisions are of great importance in agreements involving railways and in many manufacturing agreements (especially in the steel industry, for example), but collective bargaining agreements in the construction industry are virtually silent about seniority. In most instances, seniority does not even exist in the construction industry. For another example, agreements in manufacturing are virtually silent about supervisors and managers, since these persons are not represented by the unions. But in many industries supervisory personnel are unionized, and the agreements include provisions about supervisory jobs (for example, supermarket agreements commonly cover department managers, construction and utility agreements cover foremen, and maritime agreements cover ships' officers).

Examples of differences in rules may be multiplied many times over. For brevity's sake, only two additional instances are described here:

- Grievance procedures in collective bargaining agreements ordinarily end in binding arbitration by a neutral party, but in some industries (including trucking and electrical construction) the final resolution is made by a joint labor-management committee without the participation of a neutral person (see Chapter 11).
- Incentive pay is common in some industries (e.g., steel, textiles, apparel) but almost altogether absent in others (supermarkets, automobile manufacturing, construction). In industries that use incentives, the incentive pull

(i.e., the amount of earnings beyond base pay accounted for by incentives) may be as much as 70 to 80 percent in steel, but only 10 to 15 percent in textiles and apparel (see Chapter 13).

American labor law has many provisions that differ by industry or class of worker. For example, the garment manufacturing industry is exempt from the general prohibition against secondary boycotts. A secondary boycott is a strike (or other action) directed by a union against employer A in order to bring pressure on employer B, with whom the union has a dispute. The construction industry is exempt from the general prohibition against "prehire" agreements. A prehire agreement involves an employer's recognition of a union as the representative of workers the employer has not yet hired. Railway and airline employees are covered by laws that are different from the laws operative in other private companies. Public employees are covered by still other laws.

What accounts for this diversity? Which differences are appropriate? Which are not? Should there be greater diversity or less? Questions like these are at the heart of the analysis of an industrial relations system and its output. The function of analysis is to discover not only similarity but also difference, and to assist in the explanation and understanding of both.[9]

WHAT ARE THE MOST DISTINGUISHING CHARACTERISTICS OF OUR INDUSTRIAL RELATIONS SYSTEM?

Certain characteristics distinguish the American industrial system from those abroad. The characteristics of our system will become apparent in later chapters, but it is useful to summarize them at the outset to give the reader a sense of the most distinguishing aspects of our system.

1 *The principle of exclusive representation holds that for a given group of workers there shall be one and only one union with the right to represent the workers.* This principle has its origins in the doctrine of exclusive jurisdiction, which developed in the nineteenth and early twentieth centuries in the American Federation of Labor. The doctrine holds that in any given job territory (such as an occupation or an industry) there shall be one and only one legitimate union.

In 1935 an altered form of this doctrine was included in the National Labor Relations Act. The act conveys upon a union certified by the NLRB to represent a group of workers the right and duty to be the exclusive representative of those workers. The employer may not deal with another union, nor may another union interfere with the bargaining relationship (except at certain specified intervals and in certain conditions), and the union cannot decline to represent any member of the unit of workers certified by the board.

---

[9] Peter B. Doeringer, "Industrial Relations Research in International Perspective," International Industrial Relations Association Congress, September 1976 (mimeographed); and Kenneth F. Walker, "Toward a Useful General and Comparative Theory of Industrial Relations," International Industrial Relations Association World Congress, September 1976 (mimeographed).

This principle of exclusive representation is different in significant ways from the doctrine of exclusive jurisdiction from which it emerged. Exclusive representation is founded on the will of the majority of workers in an employee unit as expressed in a secret-ballot election conducted by an agency of the government. The exclusive jurisdiction of a trade union in the old practices of the American Federation of Labor rested solely on decisions of the AFL itself. Furthermore, the AFL based its jurisdictional lines largely upon the craft in which a worker was employed, while the principle of exclusive representation is largely independent of the occupation of employees.

Despite these differences, the principle of exclusive representation had its origins in the practices of the AFL and has been widely accepted by the American trade union movement. Exclusive representation today stands in marked contrast to the multiple unionism (based upon religious or ideological orientation) that is common in much of Western Europe. The principle of exclusive jurisdiction, accepted and enforced both by the courts and by the trade union federation (the AFL-CIO) has given American labor relations a stability that is unusual (though not unknown) abroad.

2 *Bargaining between employers and unions is very much decentralized in the United States.* Collective bargaining agreements tend to be comprehensive, and bargaining tends to involve only one tier of relationships, e.g., between a company and a union, or between a plant and a union.

In Europe, negotiations tend to be more centralized and to involve multiple tiers. For example, industrywide negotiations between a union or group of unions and an employer association are common in Europe, but unusual in the United States. And in Europe it is common for the industrywide negotiations to dispose of certain matters, while others are left to company-level or plant-level negotiations. (Though in some countries, different tiers bargain over the *same* issues as well.)

In some countries the government, together with national union and employer federations, takes a role in determining the outcome of collective bargaining. The United States has no counterpart to this except in unusual periods of national crisis, especially wartime.

3 *There is a direct line of authority or responsibility from a national union to a local union in a particular workplace.* Thus, the unions function fully at the national level and at the plant level. This is in very great contrast to the situation in Europe, where the national union federations may be very weakly organized at the individual workplace. In Germany, for example, the industrywide collective bargaining agreements are negotiated by labor unions, but the plant-level agreements are negotiated by works councils, which are separate from the unions. The United States has no institution which is a counterpart to a works council.

4 *An employer has a much greater opportunity to remain nonunionized in the United States than in Europe or Japan.* American law confers the right to oppose unionism on both employees and employers. Many American employers do oppose the unionization of their employees and actively campaign against unions that are trying to organize at their facilities. Furthermore, an employer able to remain nonunion is not covered by laws which extend the practices and terms of collective bargaining agreements to nonunion companies, in contrast to what is commonly the case abroad.

5 *Unions are relatively numerous in the United States.* There are some 110 national unions in our country, in contrast to 17 in Germany. American unions cooperate in some instances but compete vigorously with each other for membership and political influence.

6 *The ideological orientation of most American unions is more moderate than that of the trade union movement in Europe and Japan.* American unions for the most part accept capitalism as an economic system and have little confidence in or commitment to a socialist alternative. In Germany and Britain, the trade unions are predominately socialist in orientation, while in France and Italy the strongest elements of the labor movement are communist.

7 *Institutions for the resolution of labor-management conflict are highly developed in the United States.* Grievances are handled by binding arbitration by neutrals (see Chapter 12) and disputes over contract terms by mediation and by procedures for negotiation prescribed by law (see Chapter 11). As a result, there is probably less conflict and social disruption in labor management relations than would otherwise be expected in so large and diverse a democracy. The commitment of the unions to centrist political ideologies also contributes to overall political and social stability in the country.

8 *The American industrial relations system is slowly changing over time.* In stressing that there is an industrial relations system, we emphasize that the various parts of the labor relations process in America have a systematic relationship to each other. But this should not be taken to imply that the system is static. It is not. In recent years a series of important developments have occurred in the system. The role of collective bargaining has diminished as the proportion of our labor force in unions has declined (see Chapter 3). In collective bargaining there has been a shift in emphasis away from labor-management conflict toward a broader role for cooperation as management and labor try to preserve profits and jobs against nonunion and foreign competition. Change is occurring slowly in our industrial relations system.[10]

At the workplace the various tasks are divided among the workers. One type of division is according to workers' skill levels. Another relates to supervisory responsibilities and accounts for one of the most general classifications of the members of an organization: the supervisors and the nonsupervisory personnel. It is symptomatic of the changes going on in our society that we do not have a really precise pair of terms representing this

---

[10] D. Quinn Mills and Janice McCormick. *Industrial Relations in Transition* (New York: John Wiley & Sons, 1985), especially chap. 1. See also Thomas A. Kochan, Robert B. McKersie, and Harry C. Katz, "U.S. Industrial Relations in Transition: A Summary Report," *Proceedings*, The Industrial Relations Research Association Annual Meeting in December 1984, published in 1985.

distinction. We might say managers and employers, but managers are also employees. We might say managers and workers, but most employees today are not workers in the sense of blue-collar production workers. Instead, most employees are salespeople, clerks, or professional or paraprofessional people. For example, nurses, and even doctors, are generally employees of some hospital or clinic, often in a nonmanagerial capacity, and it seems inaccurate to refer to them simply as workers. So when we wish to be precise, we should say that there are supervisors and nonsupervisory personnel. When we are talking less precisely, we may follow a common convention in describing supervisors as management and nonsupervisory personnel as labor. Hence, we speak of labor-management relations. As the terms imply, management has essentially a supervisory or leadership role at the workplace and labor has essentially a performance role. Management and labor may be said to constitute the human side of an organization.

Management and labor are not all there is to producing a product or to providing services, however. The economic system also requires other inputs, including energy, materials, machinery, physical facilities (such as a building), technological know-how, and working capital (or cash). These inputs are used in various degrees by different types of organizations, but all, including government agencies, require some of each. Economic society involves the combination of these inputs in various proportions and different ways to produce goods and services, which our population consumes. Management and labor are the human factors that organize and combine these inputs in order to produce goods and services.

Management and labor together determine most of the conditions at the workplace. In some manner or another, wages and salaries are established, benefits are provided, hours of work are set, job assignments are made, and disagreements and disputes are handled. Often in the past, and in some instances today, a single individual owned a business establishment personally and would hire and fire people, setting the conditions of work and inviting employees to "take it or leave it." But that day is largely past. Today managers represent a large and often diffuse group of stockholders who own the company, and policies are set on the owners' behalf. In many instances workers are organized collectively into unions, which bargain with management over the terms and conditions of their employment.

Table 1-1 presents some general examples of elements of the bargaining power of business management and unions. Both strengths and vulnerabilities are listed, since either side's power in bargaining has both its positive and negative elements.

LABOR-MANAGEMENT RELATIONS AND THE CITIZEN

Should each citizen know something about labor-management relations? How do the activities of management and labor affect people? Does it help a person to understand these matters? In what way?

TABLE 1-1 SOME GENERAL EXAMPLES OF THE ELEMENTS OF BARGAINING POWER

Management or business	Unions
Strengths	
Ownership of jobs	Support of employees
Ownership of facilities	Support of other unions
Control over business plans, decisions, and financial resources	Financial resources
	Some management structure
Control over management organizational structure	Legal protection through laws, regulations, and contracts
Shared interests with business community	Communication resources
Communication resources	
Vulnerabilities	
Survival requires economic viability, which depends on:	Union leaders depend on the support of majority of members
Availability, capability, and attitude of workers	Leaders can deliver to employees only what employer will concede
Age, efficiency, and cost of plant and equipment	Activities are subject to legal restrictions in use of strike and picketing
Cost of production	Financial survival depends on maintaining employment and membership
Method of receiving raw materials and distributing product	
Customer satisfaction	
Stockholder control	
Uncontrollable market forces	
Wide-ranging laws and regulations	

Source: E. Robert Livernash, "Note on the Analytical Framework of the Labor Policy Association Seminar on the Dynamics of Power in Employee Relations," Washington, D.C., Labor Policy Association, 1979 (mimeographed).

There are many reasons why each person should make an effort to know something about labor-management relations. Among the most important is the fact that decisions about the workplace affect:

The quality of life   The type of environment that exists at the workplace helps to determine the satisfaction individuals have in their own lives and the attitudes they hold toward others.

Economic wellbeing   The economic health of the working person, of his or her family, and even of whole communities depends upon decisions about the workplace.

Social status   In our society the position of people in the social hierarchy is affected by their occupations. Whether or not this is appropriate, it nevertheless affects all our lives. Decisions by management and labor about jobs therefore affect not only our economic lives but our social lives as well.

Political activity   Management and labor, especially where workers are members of unions, play a very significant role in our political life and affect decisions of government at all levels. Because management and union leaders represent large organizations, they are often able to dispense large sums of money in political activities (although sometimes such activities are illegal) and therefore may affect political decisions more than the individual citizen. As a result, understanding our process of self-government requires some knowledge of the political practices of management and labor.

In summary, in the United States management and labor constitute a kind of private government of the workplace that to some degree affects all our lives, even the lives of those who have no direct dealings with either management or labor. Furthermore, because business organizations and labor unions are large aggregations of people and involve the livelihoods of many individuals, they are able to influence other people and organizations, including government, in substantial ways. They are, therefore, a major factor affecting the economic, social, and political institutions of our society. The citizen who wishes to understand and influence our society and, thereby, his or her own life, needs to know a good deal about management and labor.

LABOR-MANAGEMENT RELATIONS AND THE MANAGER

It is a somewhat bewildering fact that while citizens and employees generally recognize the importance of studying labor-management relations, many managers do not. Instead, managers often assert that they are too busy with other business problems to think about labor relations. But this is simply foolishness, for a major part of any manager's job involves interaction with other people, and the firm's employees as a group are often the largest single cost factor in its operations.

We may list and describe briefly five major reasons why managers need to study and understand labor-management relations.

Profitability

A major factor in whether a company is profitable or not is its labor relations. Not all companies manage labor relations the same way, of course, but when these relations are well managed the company may have a considerable profit advantage. Strikes, low productivity, rapid turnover of key personnel, and similar characteristics of a company with poor labor relations are profit destroyers. Newspapers, commercial magazines, and the trade press are full of articles entitled, for example, "Labor Is Key to Profits for _____ Corporation" or "Strike Causes Losses at _____ Corporation."

Many managers presume that they know how to handle labor relations well, as if somehow they were born with an instinct to manage well. But, in fact, people learn to manage labor relations in the same way they learn to do other things: by experience, thought, and study.

Managements in government and in private, not-for-profit organizations—such as hospitals, museums, and orchestras—must meet budgets and keep from losing money. They, too, must be concerned with labor relations and minimizing any unfavorable impact on their organization. For example, a headline can also read, "New Labor Agreement with Police Causes Increase in Tax Rate."

A Fast Track to the Top[11]

Many managers are ambitious. They want to get to the top of their organization, or at least to obtain as responsible and financially rewarding a position as they are able. In various companies there are certain managerial jobs that lead to the top more quickly and directly than others. In some companies it is a financial background that sets a "comer" apart; in others it is sales or marketing or production. But in many companies, the personnel, or labor relations, specialist also has a good chance.

It was not always this way. A few years ago personnel and labor relations were generally considered specialty areas that did not fit a person for top management. But that has changed. New problems arising from increased employee unrest and more government regulations have caused personnel and labor relations to become top priorities for management. Some companies now regularly rotate their best young managers through the personnel and labor relations departments so that they learn how to handle these problems. And the managers who are able to solve difficulties in this area are increasingly attractive as top managers.[12]

This is also true in areas other than business. Universities, for example, increasingly select their top officials from persons trained in labor-management relations. The national government does the same. In recent years Secretaries of State, Treasury, Defense, and Labor (including George Shultz, James T. Schlesinger, and John T. Dunlop) have each had a background in labor-management relations.

Why has there been this change? What has carried personnel and labor-management relations from a management backwater to a position in the mainstream? There are surely many reasons, but chief among them is that training in labor-management relations involves learning how to accommodate conflicting interests between different groups of people. Problems of accommodation are increasingly important to business and other organizations, and especially so at the top of the organization. People who can

---

[11] "Personnel—Fast Track to the Top," *Dunn's Review*, 105:4, April 1975, pp. 74ff.

[12] Herbert E. Meyer, "Personnel Directors Are the New Corporate Heroes," *Fortune*, 93:2, February 1976, pp. 84ff.

analyze and understand such problems are rare and valuable, and even more so are those who have the capacity to solve them.

Disputes

Among the more obvious advantages that some knowledge of labor relations confers upon an executive is an enhanced ability to cope with labor relations problems in his or her own organization. These problems do occur in all organizations from time to time, regardless of whether employees are represented by a union. A manager who is acquainted with labor relations should be better prepared to understand the context of such a problem and better able to develop a method to resolve it.

Poorly Structured Problems

For many managers, labor relations problems are a source of frustration because they seem so difficult to define and to handle objectively. Indeed, as compared with most other management problems (whether of finance, production, sales, or research and development), labor relations problems are poorly structured. They do not lend themselves readily to unambiguous definition and to optimal solutions. Instead, labor relations problems require solutions in the form of accommodations. Often the specific action taken to resolve a problem is less important than the fact that whatever action is taken must be one on which all those involved can agree. In many instances, managers are not able to find optimal solutions, and the best they can hope for is that they and the company will survive the problem.

Managers often refer to such problems as "people" problems, to distinguish them from more technical difficulties. People problems require a form of "muddling through" and compromise, or bargaining, that executives may find distasteful. But people problems are important. And, although labor relations problems are often poorly structured, they can nevertheless be handled well or ineptly. Study of such problems allows a manager to handle them well. A manager may, by study and experience, develop the capacity to resolve people problems.

Managers so often handle people problems badly that it is useful to examine why this is so. To a surprisingly large degree, managers' problems in labor relations arise not out of the objectives that managers have, but rather out of how managers try to get things done. To put it bluntly, it is not what managers do that causes so much trouble, but how they do it.

Many managers will devote considerable time and effort to discovering a potential solution to a production problem, for example. Often the solution that the manager has worked out requires that other people in the organization carry it out. Yet these same hard-working managers often try to put their solution into effect without giving *any* consideration to *how* the solution should be implemented. When problems arise with other people in carrying out the proposed solution, the managers often invent reasons for the difficulty that absolve them of any responsibility. They describe the people problems as nontechnical, political, or psychological and insist that they, as managers, cannot be expected to deal with such issues. They lack, they say, the conniving, manipulative nature that the resolution of human problems requires. They are, they believe, above such concerns. And, to excuse a failure to implement the technical solution, they blame the shortsightedness, stubbornness, or ill will of others, as if these conditions were complete and acceptable excuses for a manager's failure.

Good managers recognize, however, that human problems are as important a constraint to the solution of a difficult situation as are technical problems. They recognize that a problem is not solved simply when an idea is developed, but only when the idea is successfully implemented. They know that leadership and supervision of employees are critical elements of the manager's role and that to approach people problems in a way that conforms to known principles greatly increases the chances of success. The successful handling of people problems is necessary to get the job done.

Labor relations problems are not the only poorly structured problems a manager may confront. Difficulties with customers, suppliers, government officials, and community groups may be akin to labor relations problems. The knowledge and techniques derived from studying labor relations are likely to be helpful when applied to other areas, just as statistical and quantitative techniques may have a general applicability to the problems that confront a manager.

Professional Management

Management is in many ways assuming the characteristics of a profession. A body of knowledge about management is developing. Graduate schools now award thousands of master's degrees each year in business administration or management. Managers' behavior is increasingly judged by the standards of good behavior established by managers as a whole.

In the area of labor relations the increasing professionalization of management is especially important. This is so because in the past managers often felt free to pursue any tactics in order to repress concerted activity among their employees. Violence, intimidation, bribery, and similar undertakings were once common. They still occur, unfortunately, but on a far smaller scale than in the past.

Managers used to excuse such tactics on the grounds of expediency—it was necessary to keep the union out, or to break a strike, and, ultimately, to make a profit. Today expediency is no longer a very effective justification. Most of the community of managers and teachers of management does not accept such tactics as right and appropriate methods, regardless of their success or of the provocation.

In the area of labor relations there are certain principles emerging as standards of the profession of management that are valued for their own sake. They are not a blueprint for managerial action, but rather broad standards of conduct. Among the more important are:

- Giving personal financial considerations is not an appropriate method of resolving disputes.
- Employing violence, using intimidation, and especially accepting the assistance of organized crime in settling disputes are not appropriate.

Unfortunately, there are still a significant number of situations in the United States in which these methods are in common use both by employers and by labor union officials. On the other hand, there are also many situations in which arrangements can be made on a handshake basis and in which a person's word is his or her bond.

Personal dealings are at the heart of labor relations matters, and the increase in professionalization of the standards applied to labor relations behavior is an important constructive factor in American life.

WHY STUDY UNIONS?

Most American employees are not represented by labor unions or employee associations. Yet in this book about labor-management relations we devote what may seem a disproportionate amount of attention to unions and to union-management relations. After all, if unions represent only about 17.5 percent of all employees, shouldn't they receive only about 17.5 percent of the attention in this book? In fact, they receive considerably more than that amount of attention. Why is this so?

There are three reasons for making a careful and complete study of unions and union-management relations.

Unions Are Pattern Setters

Through collective bargaining, unions are pattern setters in establishing wage levels, fringe benefits, and working conditions. Many nonunion companies, even many of the largest and most profitable ones, simply adopt the standards established by their unionized competitors. Thus, in order to understand the operations of the nonunionized sector of American industry, the student must take a long and careful look at the unionized sector.

Unions Are a Major Political and Economic Force

Unions provide a mechanism through which millions of American employees take action in the general economic and political spheres of their communities and the nation. Unions constitute a separate and significant force in a way which has no counterpart in the nonunionized sector. Thus, in order to understand the environment in which all Americans operate, unions deserve careful study.

Unions Have Intrinsic Interest and Importance

Unions are large and important human institutions that deserve study for their own intrinsic interest. A well-educated citizen must know something about the institutions of our society, including, for example, business corporations, churches, private foundations, governmental organizations, and the communications media. Unions are institutions also. Furthermore, as we shall see below, the activities of unions have an intrinsic interest to anyone who wants to know how human organizations operate and what they do. Again, there are no counterpart organizations of similar interest among nonunionized employees.

MODELS OF LABOR-MANAGEMENT RELATIONS

A "model" is a mental construct with which people organize their thoughts about a topic. When people consider labor-management relations, they usually think about a single company dealing with a single local union. This is, of course, a model. It may be represented diagrammatically as in Figure 1-4 by showing the management of company A dealing with union local No. 100, which represents company A's employees. The line between the company and the union has arrows pointing both ways and indicates that each side influences the other. Also, the absence of any other organizations or lines indicates that the relationship between company A and local No. 100 is all there really is to know about the system of labor-management relations indicated here. Figure 1-4 represents a model, in that it identifies the parties

FIGURE 1-4   A simple model of labor-management relations.

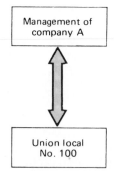

Management of company A

Union local No. 100

involved, indicates their relationship to each other, and excludes other organizations and relationships as insignificant (i.e., extraneous).

Unfortunately, most labor-management relations are not so simple. Instead, both company A and local No. 100 may be found to be at the center of a web of relationships to other organizations, of which their relationship to each other is only a single instance. In Figure 1-5 we examine the web of relationships involving company A. We see that company A has responsibilities to its stockholders and customers as well as to local No. 100. It also has relationships with other companies through an association to which it belongs; it has obligations imposed by governmental regulatory bodies; it has commitments to the communities in which it operates; and it has responsibilities to other unions with which it deals.

This is a more accurate model of the relationship of company A to local No. 100 because it shows that the company must also deal with many of these other groups on issues that affect local No. 100. For example, in considering whether to give in to wage demands by local No. 100 or to take a strike, company A must consider the impact of its choice on its customers, its stockholders, the communities in which it operates, its nonunionized employees, and the other unions with which it deals. Often the strong preferences of one or more of these groups will determine company A's decision.

The local union is also involved in a web of relationships. Figure 1-6 shows that local No. 100 must consider in its own activities the views of its national union, other unions, the community in which it is located, its political friends (whom it should not embarrass by its activities), other companies with which it has contacts (if any), and the management of company A itself.

Figures 1-5 and 1-6 describe an alternative model to Figure 1-4. The alter-

FIGURE 1-5 Company A and its relationships.

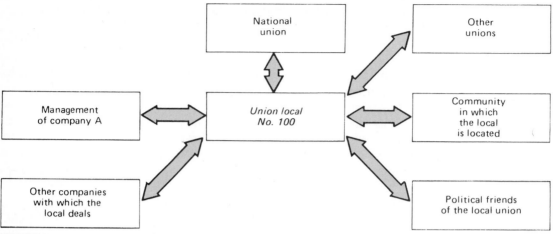

FIGURE 1-6 Union local No. 100 and its relationships.

native is much more complex and shows that there are many more factors involved in the relationship between company A and local No. 100 than just the two organizations alone. As such, the more complicated model is generally a more accurate reflection of reality.

The model in Figure 1-4 may be referred to as a "one-to-one" model. The few situations in which it applies in reality are not difficult ones to analyze. Most often, however, labor relations are of the type diagrammed in Figures 1-5 and 1-6 and are not simple at all.

In the remainder of this book we shall often describe labor relations using the model of Figure 1-4 for convenience and simplicity. But the reader should remember that this is an oversimplification, and in many instances we shall try to reflect reality better by using a model of the type given in Figures 1-5 and 1-6.

The reader will recall that John Dunlop's model of the industrial relations system focused on the development of rules for the workplace as the ultimate outcome. There are other outcomes of significance, however, including the political activity of unions, the decisions by companies about where to locate facilities, and decisions by managers and unions about lockouts and strikes.

A model (see Figure 1-7) offered by Sethi and Dimmock illustrates these additional outcomes, as well as the rules determined to apply at the workplace, and also shows the influences. It stresses, to a greater degree than Dunlop, the ethos (i.e., the values, philosophy, and ideology) of the participants in the system. In part because of the importance of ethos and choices in the model, its authors refer to it as a "transactional model."

In essence, the transactional model implies that management and union are influenced in their actions by other factors than economics. This implication is consistent with much of the psychological and behavioral research now being conducted on labor relations.

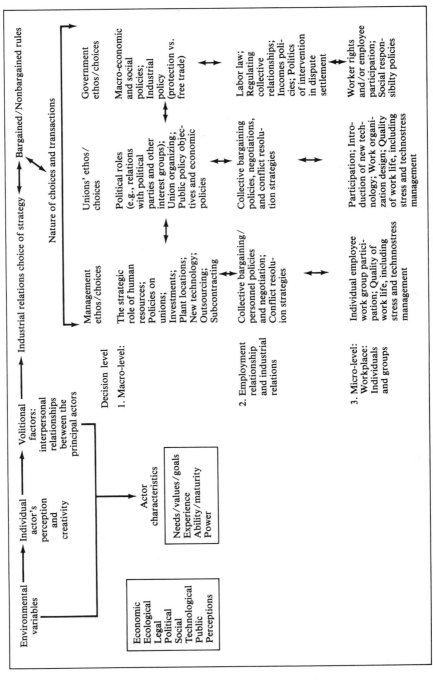

Figure 1-7 Transactional model of industrial relations. (*Source:* Amarjit S. Sethi and Stuart J. Dimmock, "A Transactional Model of Industrial Relations," *Labour and Society,* 12:2 May 1987, p. 180. The figure is adapted from Thomas Kochan, Robert McKersie, and Peter Cappelli, "Strategic Choices and Theory," *Industrial Relations,* 23, Winter 1984, p. 23.)

CHAPTER SUMMARY

Modern economic society is made up largely of organizations such as business firms or government agencies and the people who work for them (i.e., who are their employees). The processes by which the wages, benefits, and other conditions of work are determined may be termed an industrial relations system.

The industrial relations system is composed of numerous organizations of management and employees, and different levels and branches of government. It is deeply embedded in our country's basic social, economic, and legal systems. The processes of the industrial relations system mold the terms and conditions of employment and the rules about how conflict is to be expressed and controlled. There is a great diversity between industries and between classes of workers in the types of rules which apply.

The American industrial relations system has a number of characteristics which distinguish it from those of other countries: (1) There is usually exclusive representation by one union of any given group of workers; (2) bargaining between employers and unions is very much decentralized, although there are direct lines of authority and responsibility between a national union and a local union in a particular workplace; and (3) it is easier for an employer to be nonunionized in the United States than it is abroad. Also, there are a greater number of unions in America than in most other countries, and the industrial relations system here has a more moderate ideological orientation than elsewhere.

It is important for citizens in general to know about labor-management relations because these relations are a significant factor affecting the economic, social, and political institutions of our society. For employees labor-management relations affect the wages and conditions of their jobs. For managers such knowledge and understanding are indispensable. Employees are often the largest cost factor in whether a company is profitable or not. Skill in labor-management relations includes the valuable ability of accommodating the interests and needs of different groups of people.

QUESTIONS FOR THOUGHT AND DISCUSSION

1 What are some of your already-established attitudes about labor, unions, business managers, and government regulation of labor relations? How have these ideas been formed—through personal experiences? Family attitudes? The mass media? Formal education? Keep these answers and, as you go through this book, pay special attention to information which supports or contradicts your preconceptions and current knowledge.

2 In what way does American practice in industrial relations make up a system?

3 What outcomes produced by an industrial relations system are most important, in your opinion?

4 What is the most appropriate role for government in the industrial relations system?

5 Do you think industrial conflict is well-managed in our system? Why or why not? What social and economic factors have influenced the management of industrial conflict?

6 Why is there such a great diversity in the United States in the rules and conditions of work, both between industries and between types of workers? What are some of the differences you are aware of at present?

7 What factors limit management's power in the workplace?

8 What contributes to stability in the American labor relations system?

9 What factors are most important in causing workers to join unions? What factors are most important in causing workers *not* to join unions? Why?

10 Can Figures 1-5 and 1-6 be combined into a single model? What other types of models (or diagrams) of labor-management relations can you develop?

11 How does the transactional model differ from Dunlop's model of the industrial relations system?

SELECTED READING

Dunlop, John T., *Industrial Relations Systems* (New York: Holt, 1957).

Dunlop, John T., and Derek L. Bok, *Labor and the American Community* (New York: Simon and Schuster, 1970). Chapter 1 describes public opinion polls that tell how people in the United States feel about unions.

Somers, G. G., ed., *Essay in Industrial Relations Theory* (Ames, Iowa: Iowa State University Press, 1969).

B

THE HISTORICAL AND INSTITUTIONAL CONTEXT

Management has been hostile to unions during most of American history. Wherever possible, employers have opposed the growth of unions, often with the assistance of the law and the courts. In this environment, isolated local unions of workers at the plant, office, or construction site would not long survive. In order to provide mutual assistance and protection unions have banded together to form large national organizations.

National union organizations have gone beyond assisting the activities of local unions at the plant level. They also conduct lobbying and other political activities at the state and federal levels. Through the activities of national unions, employees have extended their countervailing power against management beyond the work site and into the broader stream of American social and economic life.

CHAPTER 2

HISTORY AND PHILOSOPHY OF AMERICAN UNIONISM

THEMES IN AMERICAN LABOR HISTORY

Unions are not a recent development in American history. Organizations of craftspeople and workers originated at about the time of the American Revolution, which established the independent United States. Nor are strikes a new development, for, as we shall see, associations of skilled tradespeople in American cities conducted strikes as early as the late eighteenth century. However, American trade unionism has not had a simple and straightforward line of development.[1] Rather, the progress of American trade unionism has been accompanied by as much failure as success, by as many false starts as enduring accomplishments, by serious blunders that took generations to rectify, and by sudden and largely unforeseeable achievements.

In the next few pages we review briefly the history of American unionism. It is convenient to approach the history in a generally chronological order. However, there are certain themes that run throughout the story that the reader should bear in mind.

1 *The impact of the business cycle on labor unions*   Early trade unionism arose in periods of business expansion and collapsed during depressions. It was not until the late 1800s that some few unions were able to survive depression and not until the mid-twentieth century that labor organizations as a whole

---

[1] Three general sources for material on the American union movement are Richard B. Morris, *Encyclopedia of American History* (New York: Harper, various editions); Maurice F. Neufield, *A Representative Bibliography of American Labor History* (Ithaca, N.Y.: Cornell University, 1964); and Daniel J. Leab, ed., *The Labor History Reader* (Urbana: University of Illinois Press, 1985).

seemed able to endure the strains of recession. In part, this development is the result of a moderation in the severity of downturns caused by modern governmental economic policy. The development is also a result of the increased size, diversification, and financial and administrative strength of unions as organizations. In the early days of unionism each economic crisis caused the institutional or organizational framework of unionism to collapse. This no longer occurs.

2 *The impact of the growth and development of the American economy on unionism* The rapid industrial expansion of the United States in the last quarter of the nineteenth century and the first quarter of the twentieth century provided both the opportunity for expansion of unions and the threat of a very difficult environment in which to act. Emergent big business was politically and economically powerful. With some few exceptions, American trade unions first gained a foothold in the mass-production industries, then lost it. Violent struggles, costing many lives, characterized the period of union collapse and resurgence many years later. But the union organization of the mass-production industries in the 1930s brought to labor relations a period of relative peace, which has continued to this day.

3 *The ebb and flow of radical and Marxist influence in American trade unionism* Reformist, politically active trade unionism first appeared in the 1830s and later in the nineteenth century became a militant and radical force. Efforts to organize American labor into a Marxist or socialist mold, like so much of European trade unionism, occurred with great regularity. Examples include the socialists' and anarchists' efforts of the late nineteenth century, the formation of the International Workers of the World (IWW) in the early twentieth century, and the emergence of the communist-dominated unions of the CIO in the 1930s. Again and again leftist groups have attempted to capture the American trade union movement and to divert it to a radical political orientation. The 1980s, however, are a period of very little influence for radical leadership within the trade union movement.

4 *The progress of government regulation of trade unionism* Unions have never been free of legal restraint, and much of the history of American trade unions involves their efforts to free themselves of limitations on their activities imposed by courts or legislative bodies. For most of the history of American trade unionism the federal government exerted only a small influence on labor relations between private-sector employers and workers, although federal officials did intervene in important instances in major disputes. The labor turmoil of the 1930s reached such proportions, however, that the federal government intervened by statute to establish a legal framework for unionism and collective bargaining. In consequence, the activities of American unions and employers have become increasingly subject to legal oversight and are now the subject of public regulation to a degree previously unknown in the United States.

5 *The development of the mainstream of the American labor movement* Throughout the turmoil accompanying labor-management conflict in America and the rapidly changing forms of its political manifestations, there has continued the somewhat unspectacular growth of the national trade unions and their central body, the American Federation of Labor (AFL). Founded in 1886, the AFL has weathered repeated depressions and has fought off challenges from both the radicals, who criticize it as too moderate, and those business people who have fought all labor unions. In competition with other forms of unionism, including geographic councils, single big unions, and, finally, industrial unions, the national trade union structure of the AFL has survived and has emerged as the dominant form of American unionism. But the AFL has been much affected by the movements that have challenged it, and its current structure is the result of the absorption of many characteristics of the organizations it has outlasted.

BEGINNINGS OF LABOR UNIONISM, 1794–1886

The First Unions

It is often thought that labor unions are essentially a response by workers to unbearably oppressive employment conditions. Certainly some unions have developed from such a background. But most American labor union activity has been among skilled or semiskilled workers and is the outgrowth of their attempts to regulate in their own interest the trades at which they make a living. Our earliest trade unions appear from today's perspective much like medieval guilds. The distinction between employer and employee was not so sharp then. There were few corporations and few large employers. Craftspeople worked for themselves, or in small shops, and were often in conflict with their customers or with the merchants to whom they sold their products. In order to raise their earnings directly, or to shut out competitors, working people formed organizations, ostensibly for the purpose of regulating a trade by imposing standards of training, quality, and price on those practicing it. In some instances, these organizations came into conflict with the employers, merchants, or potential competitors and conducted work stoppages. For example, the Federal Society of Journeymen Cordwainers (shoemakers) of Philadelphia was formed in 1794 and conducted a strike in 1799. New York City printers struck in 1794, cabinetmakers in 1796, and Pittsburgh shoemakers in 1809. The issues in dispute ordinarily involved hours of work, earnings, the regulation of apprenticeship, and demands that only members of the particular journeyman society should be hired by employers (a so-called closed shop) or patronized by merchants. Some theorists of labor history are of the view that these earliest elements of trade union concern have endured in the American labor movement, and they characterize the movement as "scarcity-conscious" unionism.[2]

Not surprisingly, the associations were often prosecuted as illegal conspiracies under the common law, especially when strikes occurred. The decision

[2] Selig Perlman, *A History of Trade Unionism in the United States* (New York: Macmillan, 1929); and Perlman, *A Theory of the Labor Movement* (New York: Macmillan, 1928).

of state courts often went against the associations until 1842, when Chief Justice Lemuel Shaw of Massachusetts ruled in *Commonwealth v. Hunt* that trade unions *were lawful and strikes for a closed shop were legal.* Although not binding outside of Massachusetts, Justice Shaw's decision was accorded substantial weight as a precedent by judges in other states and marked an important liberalization of judicial tolerance for union activities.

The first unions did not arise for the purpose of collective bargaining with employers, either in the United States or in England, from whose unions American workers drew much of their leadership. "The object of trade unionism used to be to uphold the price of labor against the encroachments of the employers," wrote one historian of the British labor movement. "'Collective bargaining' is an afterthought, forced on capital and labour alike because of the straining after industrial peace and the apparent necessity for securing it for lengthened periods."[3]

Printing and textile manufacturing were two of the first economic activities to be practiced on a large scale. Businesses hired labor for work in plants, and disputes developed over earnings and conditions in the plants. In 1824, for example, the first recorded strike by women workers occurred among weavers at a Pawtucket, Rhode Island, factory. Labor organization advanced to such a degree that by 1836, some 13 cities had central trade association councils. Political participation by workers was accelerated by the removal of property qualifications for voting in various states in the period from 1818 to 1843, and so-called labor parties became active in Philadelphia, New York, and Boston. In 1834 President Andrew Jackson intervened with federal troops to put down a strike by Irish laborers trying to obtain a closed shop on construction of the Chesapeake and Ohio Canal in Maryland; this was the first such use of federal troops against workers but not, as we shall see, the last.[4]

The oldest local union now operating in the United States is local No. 101 of the International Typographical Union. The local was established in Washington, D.C., on January 7, 1815, as the Columbia Typographical Society. Although other labor organizations were formed earlier, as noted above, no other earlier union has functioned continuously to the present.[5]

The National Trades Union

This yearly trade union activity culminated in the formation of the National Trades Union in 1834 by delegates from central trades councils of various cities meeting in New York. A New York City congressman from the Tammany Hall political organization, Ely Moore, became the chief officer of the organization. In a remarkable demonstration of political effectiveness, Moore and the NTU prevailed upon President Andrew Jackson to establish the 10-hour

[3] Fred Knee, "The Revolt of Labour," *Social Democrat*, November 1910; reprinted in K. Coates and A. Topham, eds., *Industrial Democracy in Great Britain*, vol. 1 (Nottingham: Spokesman Books, 1975), pp. 44–47.

[4] Arthur M. Schlesinger, Jr., *The Age of Jackson* (Boston: Little, Brown, 1945).

[5] "Oldest Local," *AFL-CIO News*, Feb., 5, 1977.

day in the Philadelphia Navy Yard and on President Martin van Buren to extend the 10-hour day to all workers on federal public works. At this time most manufacturing workers were on an 11- or 12-hour day. This cooperation between labor officials and a national Democratic administration has caused some historians to see great parallels between the 1830s and President Franklin D. Roosevelt's administration a century later. Attempts to form national associations in various trades were also begun at this time, but the panic of 1837 (an early depression) brought the collapse of most of the local associations and eventually of the NTU itself.

National Unions Emerge in Various Trades

The 1850s and 1860s saw the emergence of a group of national trade unions. The National Typographical Union was formed in 1852, the Hat Finishers in 1854, the Stone Cutters in 1855, the United Cigarmakers in 1856, and the Iron Molders (i.e., steel and iron workers) in 1859. The panic of 1857 shattered the weaker organizations, but some survived. The National Typographical Union still exists today, while the cigarmakers and stone cutters have been absorbed into other organizations (the cigarmakers, for example, numbering 2500, merged with the Retail, Wholesale, and Department Store Union in 1974). Attempts at trade union organization continued during the Civil War, and in 1865, for example, delegates from several Midwestern cities formed the Bricklayers National Union. The railway brotherhoods also originated in this period, including the Locomotive Engineers (1863), the Conductors (1868), and the Firemen (1873). By 1866 enough trade associations existed to form the National Labor Union, with the immediate objective of an 8-hour working day. The failure of the 8-hour campaign led to a concentration on political reform, and in 1872 the National Labor Union became the National Labor Reform Party with a nominee for President of the United States. The nominee was unsuccessful, and the movement collapsed. However, in 1868, largely as a result of National Labor Union influence, Congress established the 8-hour day for government laborers and mechanics.

In the early 1870s there were about 30 national unions, and total union membership was perhaps 300,000. In the depression of the 1870s, starting about 1873, the number of unions and membership fell by 80 percent or so. The depression generated radical labor activity, including riots in New York City, the formation of the Molly Maguires, a radical organization of Irish coal miners (ten members were hanged for murder in 1875), and, finally, the general railway strike of 1877 against wage cuts. The strike was broken by federal troops and state militia in battles at Pittsburgh and in West Virginia, with 35 people killed.

Knights of Labor

Out of the turmoil of the 1870s emerged the most substantial labor organization yet seen in the United States, but in a form that appears very strange to those familiar with the modern American labor movement. Called the Knights of Labor, this organization was a sort of fraternal organization of working people. It began among tailors in Philadelphia in 1871 as a secret fraternal order and grew to national prominence under the leadership of Terence V. Powderly in the period from 1879 to 1886. The Knights grew to a membership of more than 700,000 in the mid-1880s, organized in some 6000 local assemblies, and the organization exerted considerable political influence. In the Eastern states, assemblies were primarily of industrial workers; in the Western states, of farmers. Assemblies could be organized on a trade or industrial basis, and the Knights were so significant that many local trade unions affiliated as assemblies. In the depression of the mid-1880s the assemblies of industrial workers and trade unionists turned to strikes to protect their earnings and jobs. A series of strikes against various railway companies was successful, even against the opposition of financial magnate Jay Gould. Gould is said to have boasted at the time that "I could hire one half of the working class to kill the other half."[6]

However, the Knights' success did not continue. A strike against the Southwest Railroad System failed, and a general strike for the 8-hour day in Chicago collapsed. On May 4, 1886, in Chicago, a bomb was thrown at police breaking up an Anarcho-Communist rally at Haymarket Square. The bomb exploded, killing 7 police officers and wounding 70 others. A trial of alleged conspirators resulted in the execution of several radical leaders, although the actual bomb thrower was never identified.[7] In a general wave of public reaction against strikes and labor agitators, the Knights began to lose membership. As membership among workers declined, the farmers' assemblies seized control of the Knights. Thereafter, the Knights rapidly declined as a workers' movement and in 1893 disappeared into the agrarian movement entirely.

TRADE UNIONS, 1886–1905

Formation of the AFL

The American Federation of Labor was formed in the aftermath of the 1886 debacle. Meeting in December 1886 in Columbus, Ohio, some 25 groups representing perhaps 150,000 members established another central trade union federation. Largely, the delegates represented and were committed to labor organization on a trade basis. Many of the groups involved had been cooperating previously through the Federation of Organized Trades and Labor Unions (founded in 1881), which was now abolished. The AFL selected Samuel Gompers, a leader of the Cigarmakers Union, as president.[8]

---

[6] Sidney Lens, *The Labor Wars* (New York: Doubleday, 1974), p. 7.

[7] Leon Stein and Philip Taft, eds., *The Accused, the Accusers, the Famous Speeches of the Eight Chicago Anarchists in Court, 1887* (New York: Arno, 1969).

[8] Lee M. White, "The Founding Convention," *AFL-CIO Federationist*, 88:11, November 1981, pp. 1–5.

Gompers was to be president of the AFL for 37 of the next 38 years (until his death in December 1924, at 74 years of age). He was an Englishman by birth, apprenticed in London as a cigarmaker, and came to the United States in 1863. He is probably the single most important individual in American trade union history, for he kept the AFL together despite internal divisions and external opposition. He maintained a commitment to principles that we now perceive to be fundamental to American unionism, including organization by trade, the primacy of the national union, and business unionism. He was particularly influential in opposing socialist ideology (though originally a socialist himself) and in insisting that the AFL remain unaffiliated with any political party.

Problems in the 1890s

The AFL experienced very difficult times in the great depression of the 1890s, but thereafter made rapid gains. At this time it was the only effective national organization of workers in the United States. As such, it began to encounter substantial opposition from the business executives who controlled the rapidly expanding manufacturing sector of the economy. In 1895 the National Association of Manufacturers was formed, and it engaged the AFL in a struggle that the AFL itself was never able to resolve successfully (though the CIO did so in the 1930s).

Nonetheless, the AFL prospered and by 1904 claimed almost 2 million members.[9] Membership was concentrated among railway and building trades workers and in the coal industry. Organization in manufacturing was much more spotty and in fact was being weakened. In 1892, for example, a strike against Carnegie Steel Corporation at Homestead, Pennsylvania, was broken by private police (of the Pinkerton detective agency) and state militia. Another steel strike, in 1901, was beaten by the newly established United States Steel Corporation so effectively that steelworkers remained largely non-unionized until 1937 (although an unsuccessful attempt was made in 1919 to organize the industry).

The Pullman Strike

In 1894 a strike against the Pullman Company (a railway car manufacturer), in opposition to a wage cut, began among nonunionized workers at a company-owned town outside Chicago. Eugene V. Debs was a leader of the Brotherhood of Railway Firemen and organizer (in 1893) of a multitrade, industrial-type union, the American Railway Union (not affiliated with the AFL). Debs felt obliged to assist the strikers. A nationwide rail strike was called and was particularly effective in the Midwest. Alleging violence, the railways

[9] Leo Wolman, *Ebb and Flow in Trade Unionism* (New York: National Bureau of Economic Research, 1936).

sought federal assistance in keeping the trains running. The attorney general of the United States was a former railway corporation legal counsel. He supplied 3400 men as federal deputies to help the railways maintain operation. When violence ensued, President Grover Cleveland sent federal troops to Illinois to break the strike, over the protest of the governor of Illinois. A federal court injunction (i.e., a court order to cease and desist certain activities) was issued against the strike, and Debs was jailed for contempt of court. The strike was broken.[10] Debs' American Railway Union collapsed, and he left trade unionism to become the longtime head of the Socialist party in America (five times a candidate for President of the United States).[11] The AFL, however, was relieved that it had resisted overtures to join the strike. Once again the AFL had confirmed its view that general social crusades or assistance to oppressed workers when they lacked the capacity to defend themselves was a dangerous sort of idealism that would likely result in the destruction of the AFL itself (as the Pullman strike had resulted in the destruction of the American Railway Union). The AFL continued its moderate course, emphasizing collective bargaining by its affiliates and the achievement of gains by political activity.

RADICAL UNIONISM IN THE UNITED STATES, 1905–1920

Did violence and repression by employers spawn radical unionism? Or did radical unionism require such a response? Perhaps this issue is debatable, but certainly the two went hand in hand. By the early twentieth century employers in many industries had crushed labor union activity, and the federal government and, in some instances, state governments had become their willing accomplices. In 1902, for example, federal courts began to apply the Sherman Antitrust Act (passed in 1890) to the activities of trade unions, further increasing the extent of federal resistance to unions (see the so-called Danbury Hatters case[12]). Injunctions obtained from federal courts under the Sherman Act soon became an especially powerful tool for employers in resisting union organization.

A radical response to the success of employers in repressing unions, and to the supposed moderation of the AFL, was already developing by 1900. In the mines of the far West radicals had formed the Western Federation of Miners, and in 1895 a federation to rival the AFL had been formed, the American Labor Union. Finally, in 1905 in Chicago, these two groups established the Industrial Workers of the World (IWW), or "Wobblies," as they came to be called. The IWW stood for abolition of capitalism, the end of the wage system, and industrial unionism. In the West the IWW organized unskilled and migratory workers in lumber, agriculture, and shipping; but they also made

---

[10] Leon Stein and Philip Taft, eds., *The Pullman Strike* (New York: Arno, 1969).

[11] Irving Stone, *Adversary in the House: The Life of Eugene V. Debs* (New York: Doubleday, 1947).

[12] *Loewe v. Lawler*, 208 U.S. 274 (1908).

some headway in organizing large-scale industrial strikes, as in the Lawrence, Massachusetts, textile mills in 1912. The IWW lived a short and violent existence. Its leaders preached revolution, but in action it was possibly as sinned against as sinning. For example, in 1906 government authorities from Idaho virtually kidnapped Bill Haywood, the IWW's leading organizer in Denver. He was tried for murder, but the state failed to get a conviction. Haywood was released. Meanwhile, however, the IWW had dissolved into internal bickering.

The struggle for the allegiance of workers was waged between the AFL and the socialists (who were deeply involved in the IWW) continually in the years around the turn of the century. The AFL repeatedly rejected the revolutionary rhetoric of the socialists. In 1903, speaking at the Federation convention, AFL President Gompers replied to his socialist critics:

> I want to tell you Socialists that I have studied your philosophy, read your works upon economics....I have heard your orators and watched the work of your movement the world over. I have kept close watch upon you, and know what you have up your sleeve. And I want to say that I am entirely at variance with your philosophy....Economically, you are unsound; socially, you are wrong; and industrially you are an impossibility.

But the AFL was not always able to extricate itself from the situations created by the agitation of leftists, and sometimes this inability led to disastrous results.

During World War I the AFL supported the war effort and joined in government-sponsored committees to keep production going. The IWW, however, opposed the war effort. The AFL, in consequence, grew and prospered during the war, while the IWW suffered increasing prosecution. In 1919, following the Bolshevik revolution in Russia, a communist party was established in the United States. In the ensuing public scare, the federal government's Department of Justice conducted nationwide mass arrests of political and labor agitators, and hundreds were deported from the country. On a single day, January 2, 1920, federal agents carried out raids in 33 cities and arrested 2700 persons for radical political or union activity. The IWW was destroyed as an active force in the process. (In the 1980s the IWW exists as a small organization committed to its traditions and to the objectives of its founders.)[13]

The AFL attempted to distinguish itself from the radicals. With some governmental support, it attempted to retain the gains in membership and collective bargaining that had been achieved during the war. But in 1919 the communist labor organizer William Z. Foster provoked the AFL into urging a strike in the nation's steel industry. The strikers sought union recognition, collective bargaining, a shorter workday, and wage increases. Thousands of workers supported the strike, which continued for 3 months before collapsing. Organization of the steel industry was still 2 decades away, and both the

---

[13] Mary Williams, "For the 'Wobblies' A Shaky Economy Aids in 'Comeback,'" *Wall Street Journal*, Aug. 17, 1983, pp. 1, 9, 17.

AFL and its steel industry affiliate, the Amalgamated Association of Iron, Steel and Mine Workers, were badly damaged by the struggle.[14]

SETBACKS IN THE ROARING TWENTIES, 1920–1932

A sharp recession in 1921 and 1922 and strong opposition from employers weakened the unions in the 1920s. In the aftermath of the recession economic conditions improved steadily, but most large companies were unwilling to deal with unions. Manufacturing remained unorganized, and industrialists supported efforts by unionized employers, especially in the building and printing trades, to abrogate their collective bargaining agreements. AFL membership fell from about 4 million in 1921 to 3 million in 1929, and the unions, in order to remain in existence, often resorted to wage-cutting and similar devices.[15] It was the first prolonged period of prosperity in which the unions did not expand. American business seemed to have won its battle to restrict unionism.[16]

In 1924 Gompers died and the presidency of the AFL passed to William Green, a Mine Workers official. Green held the position for 28 years, and at his death it went to George Meany. Green was not a strong leader like Gompers, however, and during his presidency the AFL was governed in practice by a small group of leaders of several of the larger national unions, who met periodically to play poker and to discuss AFL policy. It was this group that in 1940 chose George Meany to become secretary-treasurer of the AFL. It was not an imaginative or farseeing group, and under its leadership the AFL all but lost its first position in the American labor movement.

The twenties were the period in which mass production first came into its own in the American economy. The bulk of employees involved in mass production were not skilled workers and were not the targets of AFL organizers. Management spent considerable sums on industrial welfare work—housing, flower beds, parks and libraries, elementary schools, teachers, medical clinics and staff—to make workers' lives more pleasant. There were often also company unions; a subtle objective of this movement was undoubtedly to convey the sense that management would look out for workers without independent unions.[17] This sort of activity continued vigorously up until the stock market crash of 1929.

The great depression began late in 1929 and deepened without letup until 1933. By that year AFL membership had shrunk to about 2 million. The United

---

[14] See David Montgomery, *Workers' Control in America* (Cambridge: Cambridge University Press, 1979), and David Brody, *Labor in Crisis: The Steel Strike of 1919*, 2d ed. (Urbana: University of Illinois Press, 1987).

[15] Vertrees S. Wyckoff, *Wage Policies of Labor Organizations in a Period of Industrial Depression* (New York: Arno, 1926).

[16] Robert N. Zieger, "Herbert Hoover, The Wage Earner and the New Economic System, 1919–1929," *Business History Review*, 51:2, Summer 1977, pp. 161–189.

[17] David Brody, "The Rise and Decline of Welfare Capitalism," in his *Workers in Industrial America: Essays on the Twentieth Century Struggle* (New York: Oxford, 1980).

Mine Workers, the AFL's largest affiliate, shrank from 500,000 to 150,000 in that period. For the first time since the depression of the 1890s there was cause to fear that the national unions would not survive. In 1932, however, a Democratic presidential candidate, Franklin Roosevelt, was elected and in 1933 a slow economic recovery began.

THE EMERGENCE OF THE INDUSTRIAL UNIONS, 1932–1939

Formation of the CIO

The decade of the 1930s was the most turbulent in American labor history. In the economic turmoil that followed the great depression, the moral authority of American business was discredited and the seemingly stable industrial relations of the 1920s disappeared. Labor agitation increased as workers were recalled to factories in the aftermath of the depression. In 1934 the government began to sponsor collective bargaining as part of a program for national recovery. In 1935, when that program was declared unconstitutional by the Supreme Court, Congress passed the National Labor Relations Act to establish a mechanism by which workers could form unions. By 1935 AFL membership had recovered to 3 million or so and total union membership (excluding company-dominated unions) to 4 million or so. But this was only the beginning.

Some labor leaders foresaw the possibility of enormous gains in the organization of workers in mass-production industries. John L. Lewis, president of the United Mine Workers, became an advocate of a major organizing campaign. The leaders of the AFL did not oppose an organizing campaign but did insist that workers be allocated by trade to the national union representing that occupation. Thus, carpenters working as maintenance employees in steel foundries were to be enrolled in the United Brotherhood of Carpenters, and so on. Lewis argued that this policy was so divisive and expensive that it would not work. Instead, Lewis proposed to organize workers on an industry basis (much as the Mine Workers themselves were organized). The AFL would not agree, and at one time Lewis and William Hutcheson, president of the Carpenters, came to blows over the issue on the floor of the AFL convention.

Lewis and several associates began to support organizing on an industrial basis late in 1935, acting as a committee on industrial organization (CIO). In 1936 the CIO began to organize the steel and motor vehicle industries, employing mine workers as organizers to supplement workers in the industries directly involved and using Mine Workers' funds. In December 1936, workers seized several General Motors plants in Flint, Michigan, beginning a 44-day sit-down strike. The tactic was an illegal seizure of private property (that of General Motors), but feelings were high, and the state government was now in hands friendly to the unions and did not intervene against the workers. Sit-ins spread to other industries and, unable to recapture their plants, corporations accepted the formation of industrial unions. (The sit-down was found illegal by the Supreme Court in 1939 after years of litigation and has largely been abandoned by organized labor since.)

Organizing Steel

The most dramatic events of the struggle were in the steel industry. In 1937 the highest officials of the United States Steel Corporation met with John L. Lewis to discuss recognition of the CIO's Steel Workers' Organizing Committee. Suddenly, and under no apparent duress, the corporation signed an agreement recognizing the union as the representative of its employees. There was no election and not even a sit-down stike. This peaceful recognition of the CIO by United States Steel must, in the words of one of the foremost historians of this period, "surely rank as one of the critical junctures of American economic history. Not only did it ensure the existence of unionism in basic steel, but it provided inestimable assistance to the CIO in its drive to organize other industries."[18]

Nonetheless, continuing the policy of most manufacturers,[19] other steel companies resisted the CIO, and on Memorial Day in 1937, police defending a Republic Steel plant in Chicago fired on union demonstrators, killing 4 and wounding 84. It was not until 1941 that the other steel companies recognized the union.

Similarly, an NLRB election in 1941 at Ford Motor Company was won by the CIO (though unsuccessfully contested by the AFL). The company did not accept defeat graciously. I. A. Capizzi, general counsel for Ford, stated, "The Ford Motor Company must now deal with a Communist-influenced and -led organization. . . . The NLRB is an exact replica of the so-called courts by which Communist, Nazi, and Fascist partners purge the men who resist their tyrannies. It is a dictatorial concept imported from Europe."[20] There was little or no truth to these charges, but they indicate the bitterness and extreme feelings characteristic of the times.

A New Federation

By 1941, the CIO had organized the steel, auto, rubber, and meat-packing industries on a virtually exclusive basis and was challenging the AFL in many other industries. In the process the CIO had broken completely with the AFL. In May 1938 the AFL expelled the CIO unions from membership, and they established a rival federation, the Congress of Industrial Organizations (also CIO), under the leadership of John L. Lewis and Sidney Hillman of the Amalgamated Clothing Workers. Lewis, meanwhile, had been suc-

---

[18] Walter Galenson, *The CIO Challenge to the AFL* (Cambridge, Mass.: Harvard University Press, 1960), p. 93.

[19] Edward Levinson, *I Break Strikes! The Technique of Pearl L. Bergoff* (New York: Arno, 1935). This book describes Bergoff's assembly of an organization of ruffians, which he leased to employers to defeat strikes.

[20] Galenson, *The CIO*, p. 183.

cessful in substantially increasing the membership of the United Mine Workers. Perhaps Lewis's success blinded him, because he now acted in a way that split the CIO and weakened it substantially. In 1940 Lewis opposed President Roosevelt's bid for election to a third term. When Roosevelt was reelected, Lewis resigned from the CIO and Philip Murray, a vice president of the Mine Workers, became CIO president. Lewis later engaged in disputes with Murray and withdrew the Mine Workers from the CIO in 1942. In 1946 he reaffiliated with the AFL but left it again 2 years later.[21] Lewis retired from the presidency of the Mine Workers in 1960 and died in 1969. Without its largest affiliate union and its strongest leader, the CIO after 1940 was a less dynamic organization than before.[22]

What were the causes of the success of labor's great organizing drives in the 1930s? The passage of the National Labor Relations Act is often credited with a substantial role,[23] but there were other factors as well. It must be remembered that in most major manufacturing industries CIO organizers were able to obtain NLRB-ordered elections only after sit-downs and other forms of strikes had opened the door to organization. Also, in some important instances, employers granted union recognition without a struggle and without NLRB compulsion, although perhaps in the belief that the law made resistance useless. Still, it cannot be imagined that the law alone would have brought about the rapid expansion of unionism that occurred. Instead, the law channeled labor agitation into a particular framework, helping to limit violence, and in the end, because the labor organizers exploited its provisions cleverly, helping to extend unionism in the 1930s to a greater degree than would probably otherwise have been possible.

EXPANSION AND RIVALRY, 1940–1955

What was happening to the AFL during the period of CIO growth? It was noticed so little by the public during much of this period that most observers of the labor-management relations scene were predicting its demise. Industrial unionism was to be the wave of the future and was expected to transplant the discredited craft union structure. The AFL's weak and failing attempts to challenge the CIO in several industries, especially autos, reinforced this view. But it was wrong.

In fact, the AFL emerged from World War II larger than the CIO. Using the threat of the CIO to persuade employers of the wisdom of dealing with the AFL and citing the NLRA to help persuade workers to join, the AFL unions expanded rapidly. Table 2-1 shows that in the 1940s the AFL added membership at a much more rapid rate than the CIO.

[21] Saul Alinsky, *John L. Lewis* (New York: Putnam, 1949).
[22] Melvin Dubofsky, *John L. Lewis: A Biography* (New York: Quadrangle/New York Times Book Co., 1977).
[23] Neil Sheflin, Leo Troy, C. Timothy Koeller, "Structural Stability in Models of American Trade Union Growth," *Quarterly Journal of Economics*, 96:1, February 1981, pp. 77–88.

TABLE 2-1 TRADE UNION MEMBERSHIP (In Thousands)

	AFL	CIO	Independent	Total
1934	3045	—	683	3,728
1938	3623	4038	604	8,265
1941	4569	5000	920	10,489
1943	6564	5285	1793	13,642

Source: U.S. Department of Labor, Bureau of Labor Statistics, *Handbook of Labor Statistics* (Washington, D.C.: U.S. Government Printing Office, December 1980), Bulletin No. 2070, p. 411.

World War II brought a return of full employment to the economy and permitted the unions to consolidate their position. Yet throughout the war, rivalry continued as two national labor federations sought to represent trade unionism in the political and economic arenas. In the aftermath of the war, a wave of strikes brought substantial economic gains as the industrial conflict, which had been largely abandoned during the war, resumed. The Congress elected in 1946 was the first since 1930 with a Republican majority, and in 1947 it passed a law (the Taft-Hartley Act) amending the NLRA to place greater restrictions on unions' behavior. The AFL and the CIO both bitterly opposed the law but were unable to prevent its enactment. The period of labor's political ascendancy, which had accompanied President Roosevelt's New Deal, was at an end.

The great organizing period having ended, the two federations turned their attention inward. The CIO, particularly, had welcomed assistance from communist groups during its organizing campaigns. In consequence, many CIO unions were heavily influenced by radical groups.[24] With the onset of the cold-war rivalry between the United States and the Soviet Union, the communist involvement became a liability. Congress in the Taft-Hartley Act required a noncommunist affidavit from labor union leaders, under penalty of denying to the union involved the protection of the law. The law alone did little to remove communists from union offices or influence—it simply drove them underground, i.e., into secrecy and deception—but the noncommunist officials of the CIO seized it as an opportunity to wrest control of many unions from the communists.

In some instances, noncommunist leadership within a national union was able to wrest control from the communists directly. For example, in the Transport Workers Union, Mike Quill used the communists' political support for the 1948 Presidential campaign of Henry A. Wallace (against Harry S. Truman, Democrat, and Thomas E. Dewey, Republican) to brand the communists as more interested in politics than in the needs of the workers. "So far as 42,000 transit workers are concerned, I say wages before Wallace," Quill argued in a bid for the presidency of the union. Winning office, Quill

---

[24] Benjamin Stolberg, *The Story of the CIO* (New York: Arno Press, 1938).

and his supporters stripped the union's high command of 19 supposed communists, and 16 national organizers were dismissed. Left-wing publicity people, secretaries, and clerks were fired. And the union's national convention adopted a constitution prohibiting communists and their supporters from holding office in the union. About the communists, Quill said, "We had a lot of help from the communists. They worked for us night and day. I'm sorry they didn't continue to help. I'm sorry they loused it up...but they showed allegiance to the Soviet Union and not to the American labor movement."[25]

In other national unions it was not possible to wrest control from within. In consequence, in 1949 and 1950 the CIO expelled 11 national unions with 900,000 members on grounds of communist control. After expulsion, the CIO chartered new national unions in the same industries and supported organizing campaigns in which the new CIO unions sought to capture the membership and collective bargaining rights held by the old unions. In most instances the CIO was successful in creating viable new, noncommunist unions to replace those expelled. But many of the communist-dominated organizations still exist today as remnants of their former selves.[26]

CONSOLIDATION, 1955–1972

In 1952 both William Green, president of the AFL, and Philip Murray, president of the CIO, passed away. George Meany became president of the AFL, and Walter P. Reuther (the president of the UAW) became president of the CIO. Discussions about a merger between the two federations began in earnest. The passing of the men who had been participants in the early struggles between the two federations had removed a major impediment to merger. Another had been removed when the CIO destroyed the communist influence within its organizations.

In 1955 the merger was completed, and the AFL-CIO was formed, a combination of the two federations with its own constitution. The AFL, the larger of the two federations, had absorbed its rival, but only by adopting features that it had rejected in expelling the CIO some 20 years earlier. The principle of exclusive jurisdiction was modified to accept the industrial unions and was now accompanied by a principle of respecting established bargaining units, whatever the conflicting claims of national unions to the jurisdiction might be. Furthermore, the new federation's constitution provided for considerable oversight of the affairs of national union affiliates. A strong provision against domination of unions by communists or other totalitarian groups was included, as well as provisions against corruption in the leadership of national union affiliates. The executive council of the Federation also bound itself to seek to remove overlapping or conflicting jurisdictions between affiliated na-

[25] L. H. Whittemore, *The Man Who Ran the Subways: The Story of Mike Quill* (New York: Holt, 1968), p. 3.
[26] Bert Cochran, *Labor and Communism* (Princeton, N.J.: Princeton University Press, 1978). See also Thomas R. Brooks, "Rewriting History," *AFL-CIO Federationist*, 85:5, May 1978, pp. 11–15.

tional unions by encouraging mergers between former AFL and former CIO affiliates. In the years since 1955 there have been a number of such mergers, including unions in the metals, food, and paper industries.

The AFL-CIO has worked as a federation probably better than reasonably could have been expected. Conflict among the national unions in the Federation has been kept to tolerable levels. There has been no organizing surge of the type that occurred in the 1930s and 1940s, but millions of additional workers have been brought into the Federation.[27]

Perhaps what is most interesting in a human sense about the merger is that two groups of such different styles could be successfully combined. The CIO had been founded upon a core of idealistic organizers, largely leftist in political orientation, who sought to live among the workers. Pay scales for CIO officials tended to be considerably lower than those in the AFL. The AFL's propensity for holding conventions at such places as Miami Beach offended the CIO adherents strongly. The AFL, on the other hand, regarded most CIO representatives as impractical, radical individuals and reciprocated their disapproval. Despite these personal divisions, the merger has somehow worked, and the labor movement today is relatively united and without serious internal ideological or life-style cleavages. But the criticism from the left that the AFL is too conservative has continued even into the late 1980s.

TRANSITION 1972–1989

Beginning about 1972 (the date has not been exactly determined by researchers) the American labor movement began a profound transformation. Union organization among the blue-collar workforce in manufacturing and construction declined substantially. But union organization in the public sector (i.e., among the employees of state, local, and federal governments) continued a period of substantial growth that had begun in the 1960s (see Table 2-2).

The result was that the American labor movement began to shift away from its predominantly private-sector orientation. By 1988 one in three union members was a government employee.[28]

George Meany headed the AFL-CIO for 24 years. In 1979 he resigned, and died soon after (on January 11, 1980). Lane Kirkland, the secretary-treasurer of the AFL-CIO, was selected to replace Meany as president, and Thomas R. Donahue, Meany's assistant, replaced Kirkland as secretary-treasurer. Kirkland was born in South Carolina and served in the merchant marines in World War II as a member of the International Organization of Masters, Mates, and Pilots, an AFL union. He studied foreign affairs at Georgetown

---

[27] Joseph C. Goulden, *Meany* (New York: Atheneum, 1972), p. 173.
[28] Richard B. Freeman, "Contraction and Expansion," Cambridge, MA, National Bureau of Economic Research Working Paper No. 2399, February 1988. Also, R. B. Freeman "Contraction and Expansion: The Divergence of Private Sector and Public Sector Unionism in the United States," *Journal of Economic Perspectives*, 2, 2 (Spring 1988), pp. 63–88; and Melvin W. Reder, "The Rise and Fall of Unions," *Journal of Economic Perspectives*, 2:2 Spring 1988, pp. 89–110.

TABLE 2-2 UNION MEMBERSHIP AS PERCENT OF U.S. LABOR FORCE: PRIVATE AND PUBLIC SECTORS; SELECTED YEARS, 1900–1984

Year	Total labor force	Private sector	Public sector
1900	3.0		
1914	6.8		
1917	7.5		
1920	12.0		
1921	11.3		
1922	9.4		
1929	7.0		
1933	5.8		
1937	11.7		
1939	13.4		
1940	14.6		
1945	23.6		
1950	22.1		
1953	26.8		
1960	22.3	31.9	10.8
1962	23.9	31.6	24.3
1970	25.4	29.1	32.0
1971	24.5	28.2	33.0
1972	24.4	27.3	35.4
1973	24.5	26.6	37.0
1974	24.1	26.2	38.0
1975	23.7	26.3	39.6
1976	23.0	25.1	40.2
1977	21.8	23.6	38.1
1978	21.3	22.5	36.7
1979	21.0	22.0	36.4
1980	19.6	20.6	35.1
1981	19.0	19.9	35.4
1982	17.8	19.0	35.1
1983	16.6	17.8	34.1
1984 (p)	16.1	16.6	33.1

Source: Total labor force: 1900–53 (Bernstein, 1954); 1960–84 (Troy and Sheflin, 1985), Table 3.41; Public Sector. Melvin W. Reder, "The Rise and Fall of Unions," *Journal of Economic Perspectives,* 2:2, Spring 1988, p. 106.

Note: Since they are from different sources, Column 1 is not strictly comparable to Columns 2 and 3. Also, these are the most recent data available as of the fall of 1987 when the article was prepared.

University in Washington, D.C., and in the late 1940s became an assistant to George Meany. He was elected secretary-treasurer of the AFL-CIO in 1969.

In the years immediately following Kirkland's election to the AFL-CIO presidency, the American labor movement encountered very difficult times. Its membership eroded rapidly as workers lost jobs due to foreign and non-union competition. By 1988 its proportion of the American work force had fallen to a post-World War II low, but the first signs of stabilization and renewed growth and influence were to be seen. There were signs of stabilization and renewed growth and influence in the numbers; and in the mass-production industries—the ones hit hardest by competition from abroad—these signs seemed firmly rooted in a fundamental rethinking of shopfloor relations and productivity.

CHARACTERISTICS OF THE LABOR MOVEMENT IN AMERICA

The United States now has one of the largest organized labor movements in the world. American unionists are proudest of the freedom of their organizations from interference or control by the government. American unions are "free" trade unions, they point out, in that these organizations of workers were created by the workers themselves and are controlled by them. Workers have many interests, and unions in the United States reflect those interests, which include representing workers in their relations with employers, providing certain benefits and insurance for workers, assisting in educational activities, and serving as a mechanism to advance workers' desires through the political process.

The American labor movement is not homogeneous. Although it is possible to identify certain basic characteristics of American unions, especially as contrasted with those abroad, internally the American labor movement has many variations and divisions. These divisions include those between industrial, craft, and service unions, between skilled and unskilled workers, between large and small organizations, and between centralized and decentralized organizations. Periodically the movement is splintered into opposing factions, and although the 1980s have been, by comparison to other years, a period of relative unity in the labor movement, it is a fragile unity, possibly subject to sudden and substantial change.

Principles of Structure

The basic structural principle of the American labor movement is that each major, identifiable group of workers is entitled to its own labor organization. This is in contrast to other principles of organization, such as the suggestion that all workers should be members of one big union. Instead, groups of American workers have ordinarily formed and governed their own independent organizations. These organizations are related to each other, if at all, through the device of a general federation.

In trade union doctrine, the right of each group of workers to its own union is accompanied by another principle: that there should be one and only one union for each group. There should not be "dual" unionism. Adherence to this principle is necessary to preserve the labor movement from what is felt would be excessive fragmentation, with corresponding rivalry and weakness. The group of jobs in which a union purports to have rights to represent workers is referred to as its "jurisdiction" (or "trade jurisdiction"). The term "jurisdiction" is also used with the preface "geographic" to indicate the geographic area to which a particular union lays claim or to refer to the geographic coverage of a collective bargaining agreement. The principle of only one union for each group of workers is referred to in trade union parlance as "exclusive jurisdiction," meaning that only one union has a right to represent workers doing a particular group of jobs.

The principle of exclusive jurisdiction has not been simple to apply. In an economy as complex and changing as that of the United States, there are always conflicts among workers and among unions as to who should be represented by what organization. Initially (in the nineteenth and early twentieth centuries), the American Federation of Labor tried to establish unions on a craft (or occupational) basis and was substantially successful in doing so. Among these craft unions were such groups as shoemakers, cigar wrappers, printers, and bricklayers. However, some crafts were too small to support unions and were combined with a paramount craft into a form of enlarged craft union. For example, the United Brotherhood of Carpenters and Joiners of America, for many years the largest union in the American Federation of Labor and generally referred to as a craft union, in fact includes in its trade jurisdiction not only carpenters (who are the paramount craft in the union) but also piledrivers, dock builders, millwrights (i.e., machinery installers), sheetrock installers (i.e., installers of gypsum wallboard), and soft-floor (i.e., carpet and linoleum) layers.[29] And in some industries, trades could not be distinguished fully enough without undue confusion and rivalry, so that the AFL established so-called craft unions that were largely industrial unions. Among these modified craft organizations were the United Association of Journeymen and Apprentices of the Plumbing and Pipefitting Industry, whose very name betrays an industrial basis,[30] as does that of the United Mine Workers (in the coal industry). In later years, it became apparent that in some industries not even a modified craft union could survive against employer resistance, and, over the objections of the AFL, unions were established on a strictly industrial basis in such manufacturing industries as automobiles, steel, and aluminum.

Thus, the result of a historical process has been that unions in America reflect craft, modified craft, and industrial orientations in defining their jurisdiction. Nonetheless, the principle that there should be only a single organization for each group, however defined, remains alive and in fact has, in a much modified form, been incorporated in federal labor legislation, as we shall see below. The resolution of disputes between contending unions over what organization is entitled to represent which workers remains a function of the central federation, the AFL-CIO.

What explains the structural principles of American unions? "It is the primacy of collective bargaining," say two American researchers. "Other goals

---

[29] Robert A. Christie, *Empire in Wood* (Ithaca, N.Y.: New York State School of Industrial Labor Relations, Cornell, 1956).

[30] Martin Segal, *The Rise of the United Association: National Unionism in the Pipe Trades, 1884–1924* (Cambridge, Mass.: Harvard University Press, 1970).

that have been hypothesized as primary to unions include revolution, job consciousness, business union, maximizing (or satisficing), power accumulation, monopoly, organizational and a 'front for capitalism.'"[31] But other goals fail to explain American union structure as well as does the need to be so structured as to perform bargaining well. In the theory of union behavior offered by Jack Barbash, the bargaining goal prevails in clashes with other goals, historical evidence shows collective bargaining to be the basic working principle of union structural government and administration, and the concept of revolution as a union goal is invalid because of its fundamental inconsistency with collective bargaining.[32]

Principles of Administration

The American trade union movement is a decentralized movement. National unions, which have the jurisdiction to represent certain groups of workers, are "sovereign" bodies, meaning that they alone make policy for the union. National unions may choose to be affiliated with a central federation or not, or to participate in concerted activities with other unions or not. The central federation of national unions, the AFL-CIO, is more a place for cooperation than a governing body.

The national unions differ considerably as to how they organize themselves. Some national unions have a policy of "local autonomy," which grants to local unions considerable freedom from intervention in their affairs by the national union unless there are irregularities, generally of a financial nature, in the administration of the local. Local autonomy ordinarily extends to the financing of the local, to its activities in the political process in the state or city in which it is located, and to relations with local employers. In the national unions that operate in the printing industry, in local cartage trucking and warehousing, and in construction, for example, autonomy is a jealously guarded right of the local unions.

Other national unions grant far less discretion to their local unions. Instead, the constitutions of the national unions rather rigidly limit the authority of the locals, so that the national unions themselves may be said to be far more centralized. This is especially true of the United Steelworkers of America.

Nonetheless, in all national unions, at any time, a struggle continues as to the relative authority of the national union versus its local affiliates. Ordinarily this struggle is muted, but sometimes it breaks into open internal dis-

---

[31] Rudy Oswald and Rick Kraehevski, "Union Structure" in James L. Stein and Barbara D. Dennis, eds., *Trade Unionism in the United States* (Madison, Wis.: University of Wisconsin Industrial Relations Research Institute, 1981), pp. 5–6.

[32] Jack Barbash, "The Union as a Bargaining Organization," *Proceedings* of the 28th Annual Meeting of the Industrial Relations Records Association, Madison, Wis., 1975, pp. 145–153 (esp. pp. 149–150).

sension (as, for example, in the unions in the paper manufacturing industry in the 1960s and in the United Mine Workers in the 1970s).

A Moderate Trade Unionism

The trade union movement in the United States has as its primary professed objective the improvement of the welfare of working people. This commitment it shares with labor movements abroad, except in some of the totalitarian states. Yet the American labor movement and those in Western Europe, in particular, differ considerably as to what direction improvement should take and how it can best be achieved. American unions have generally sought to obtain better wages and working conditions for workers in as direct and immediate a way as possible. Concerns about broadly based political and social change have been, if not forsworn, at least subordinated to attempts to ameliorate conditions as quickly as possible for the workers directly represented by the union.[33]

This emphasis on achieving improved wages and conditions as soon as possible, without regard to broader social aims, has been termed "business unionism" and is said to represent the central type of American trade union activity.[34] Its emphasis is on self-help, generally through collective bargaining with employers. It is often contrasted to revolutionary unionism, in which unions are perceived primarily as agencies in the attempt to alter substantially the form of government and economic society. This distinction is sometimes overdrawn. American labor's emphasis on business unionism should not obscure its use of other methods to improve the condition of working people. For example, the unions are deeply involved in political activity in the United States (as we shall see below). Furthermore, unions engage in educational and social activities, the objective of which is to uplift the worker. To cite only a few examples, unions publish magazines with articles of general interest, send out special informatory pamphlets on public issues, provide training programs, and sometimes provide scholarships to school.

The support of American unions for business unionism is in contrast to the philosophy of most labor movements abroad. Basically, European trade unions have sought to advance the entire working class by transforming the total society. The European labor movement developed country by country

---

[33] Many studies support these generalizations. For example, a survey of the membership of five local unions in Ohio in the early 1960s demonstrated that a majority of the workers wished their union to concentrate its efforts on improving wages, benefits, and working conditions, and were less concerned or less enthusiastic about political or social objectives. Robert W. Miller, Frederick A. Zeller, and Glenn W. Miller, *The Practice of Local Union Leadership: A Study in Five Local Unions* (Columbus, Ohio: Ohio State, 1965).

[34] Robert F. Hoxie, *Trade Unionism in the United States* (New York: Appleton, 1921). Hoxie identifies four types of unionism: business, uplift (i.e., educational), revolutionary, and predatory (i.e., corrupt). A fifth type, reform unionism, may also be said to exist.

out of three sources: the trade unions, the socialist or communist political parties, and workers' cooperative movements. The resultant European labor movements place a much greater emphasis on achieving substantial change in the social system through political ends than does American labor. Where it has seemed impossible to achieve such change, elements of the European labor movement have sought a total substitute society made up of workers' organizations, a concept so remote from American labor philosophy that it is hard for an American to grasp.[35]

It is interesting to speculate on the reasons why the American trade union movement developed so differently from the one in Europe, despite historical ties between them. Probable reasons involve differences in basic characteristics of economic society on the two sides of the Atlantic and different historical experiences in different nations. Among the characteristics of American economic society that distinguished it, at formative stages in the development of the labor movement, from that of the European countries are:

1 The absence of previously existing feudalism with its rigid set of class attitudes and practices

2 The extension of full citizenship and voting rights for the white, male, urban working class at a relatively early date

3 Free public education

4 The possibility for workers to raise their standard of living and to move into managerial and entrepreneurial positions[36]

These characteristics of American society contributed to the development of a labor movement that was relatively free of class-consciousness, politically active *within* the existing system of government, somewhat less concerned with achieving social goals, and more concerned with obtaining immediate advances in wages and working conditions.

Perhaps the most generally recognized formulation of labor's overall goals is from a statement attributed to Samuel Gompers. But did he ever say it? As explained by AFL-CIO President Lane Kirkland to students at Dartmouth College, the matter is as follows:

> Let me address a canard that has dogged American labor for many years. It has found its way into textbooks, learned papers and baser prose, and may be no stranger here. That is the legend that our founder, Samuel Gompers, when asked what labor wanted responded simply: "More." That has become a synonym for our alleged innocence of ideals, if not unbridled avarice in the accepted wisdom.
>
> A university group from the University of Maryland recently completed the task of copying and indexing all of Gompers' recorded papers and works. I asked them to find that quote and was informed that it did not exist. The only source

[35] Everett M. Kassalow, *Trade Unions and Industrial Relations: An International Comparison* (New York: Random House, 1969).

[36] Ibid. See also Walter Galenson, "Why the American Labor Movement Is Not Socialist," *American Review*, 1:2, Winter 1961, pp. 1–19.

from which it could have been derived was an item dated 1893, when Gompers declared:

"What does labor want?...We want more schoolhouses and less jails; more books and less arsenals; more learning and less vice; more constant work and less crime; more leisure and less greed; more justice and less revenge...."[37]

The dominant philosophy of the American labor movement has traditionally gone beyond business unionism to a general defense of American capitalism. In its defense of American free enterprise, the labor movement distinguishes itself from most trade union movements abroad, which are avowedly socialist or communist in ideology, and opens itself to considerable criticism from the left in the United States.[38] But the enthusiasm with which the American trade unions have supported American free enterprise has been lessening in recent years.

In 1969 in a speech to the ministers of labor of the governments which make up the Organization of American States (an organization of most of the nations of the Western Hemisphere), George Meany endorsed American capitalism, saying in part:

We accept without question the right of management to manage, with reasonable consideration, of course, for the rights of workers to a fair share of the wealth produced.

We accept without question the right of management to adequate compensation for its efforts.

We accept without question the right of the investor for a return on his investment in an enterprise.

But by 1980, the AFL-CIO was more cautious. In its proposals to the Democratic and Republican parties for their platforms in a presidential election year, the Federation chose not to endorse free enterprise, but to stress the democratic element of American society:

The AFL-CIO believes the American dream has currency; workers have the right to continue to seek a better life. In a democratic society, it is wrong for one group to impose lower expectations on another group, to demand a degree of sacrifice not demanded of all, to permit exploitation of some for the profit of others....

Resolving the inevitable conflicts between employer zeal for profits and the determination of workers for fair compensation is never easy in a democratic society. The quick solution, of course, is government compulsion, but democracy is not designed to be convenient; it is supposed to give the participants the opportunity to live their own lives.

Smarting under legislative defeats at the hands of the business community[39] and frustrated by business opposition to union organization attempts, the lead-

---

[37] Lane Kirkland, remarks at Dartmouth College, October 4, 1982, text printed in *AFL-CIO News*, Oct. 16, 1982, p. 2.

[38] Lawrence Lader, *Power on the Left: American Radical Movements Since 1946* (New York: Norton, 1979).

[39] D. Quinn Mills, "Flawed Victory in Labor Law Reform," *Harvard Business Review*, 57:3, May-June 1979, pp. 92–102.

ers of organized labor in the United States have begun to shift slowly away from their largely unqualified support of American capitalism. In May 1978, Lane Kirkland, then secretary-treasurer of the AFL-CIO, reminded a management audience that U.S. management's role and status have not been under serious attack by any ideology espoused by labor. But he accused management of fomenting "class warfare" against workers and unions in recent years. The unions would not continue to deal as they had in the past with management on a basis of mutual acceptance if this continued, he said.[40]

POLITICAL ACTIVITY OF AMERICAN LABOR

Only in a relative sense, that is, in comparison to some labor movements abroad, may American unions be said to have neglected political activity. Indeed, within the United States unions are credited with being one of the most active, and perhaps one of the most effective, political interest groups. But there are, as we shall see, limits to labor's political success.

Labor's Political Goals

What do the unions seek to achieve through political activity? In general, unions may be said to have both positive and negative goals. Positive goals involve the enactment of legislation favorable to organized labor. Negative goals involve preventing the enactment of unfavorable legislation. In much of the history of the trade union movement, negative, or defensive, political activity has been the more important activity for the unions. Particularly in the case of the American Federation of Labor, unions have not ordinarily sought legislation that would affect the collective bargaining process. Instead, the unions have sought to keep the government outside the process. The major example of this political activity by unions was the long campaign, which began in the 1890s and ended with apparent success only in 1932, to relieve collective bargaining from the application of the antitrust statutes.

There have been exceptions, of course. In 1926 the railway unions joined in support of the Railway Labor Act. And in 1935 the AFL supported the enactment of the National Labor Relations Act. But since that time, union political activity has largely been directed at preventing legislation that would restrict the gains labor has made. For example, the unions opposed the Taft-Hartley Act in 1947, labeling it a "slave labor act." In 1959 the unions opposed the Landrum-Griffin Act as well. In both these instances the unions were unsuccessful in preventing further legislative restrictions of their activities. But in other years bills introduced by opponents of organized labor in Congress have been successfully opposed by union lobbyists.

It should be noted that unions have a twin purpose in much of their de-

---

[40] "Kirkland Speeches," Bureau of National Affairs, *Daily Labor Report* No. 194, Oct. 4, 1979, p. C1.

fensive political activity: both to keep antiunion forces from using legislation to restrict union activity and to keep the government out of collective bargaining and out of the internal affairs of unions to as great a degree as possible. Labor often looks to the business community for support for the latter proposition. For example, reviewing the experience of the National War Labor Board of World War II, George Meany wrote, "there is a moral in this story of 'wage stabilization' by government that should appeal equally to American business and American labor—keep politicians out of the field of labor relations."[41]

In areas other than collective bargaining the unions have sought to make advances through political activity.[42] Unions have supported legislation on minimum wages, overtime provisions, equal employment opportunities, pension reform, national health insurance, and other such generally applicable social welfare measures, some of which have been enacted and others not. Unions have not been the only groups in support of such measures, but, because the unions are often more politically effective than other liberal groups, they have had an influence on American social welfare legislation out of proportion to their size and membership. "There is simply no avoiding the conclusion," one liberal observer has said, "that, considering its power as well as its views, labor has been the chief force for progressive domestic legislation in America."[43]

AFL-CIO Secretary-Treasurer Thomas R. Donahue has stressed that the labor movement "is literally in the business of assuring people fair and equitable treatment in the workplace."[44] But labor does not limit its methods to collective bargaining with employers. Instead, it turns to lobbying and other political activities as well. In 1983, for example, the AFL-CIO reported with pride that it had been identified by academic researchers as a major influence in American health care policy in the 1970s.[45]

Yet even here, in the opinion of some liberals, there is a paradox in the political objectives of organized labor. For reasons that are unclear to these liberals, the unions support certain progressive pieces of legislation, but not others. This behavior results in bitter denunciations of the unions as supporters of the status quo by the same liberal groups who rely upon union support to obtain passage of whatever liberal legislation is enacted. This pattern of political behavior was very characteristic of the AFL. In 1923 Mollie Ray Carroll studied the political attitudes of the AFL and found that it supported proposals for workers' compensation legislation but steadfastly opposed campaigns for health and old-age insurance (i.e., Social Security legis-

---

[41] George Meany, "The National War Labor Board," *American Federationist*, 53:4, April 1946.
[42] John T. Dunlop, "Past and Future Tendencies in American Labor Organizations," *Daedalus*, 107:1, Winter 1978, pp. 79–96. See also Peter Gourevitch, Peter Lange, and Andrew Martin, "Industrial Relations and Politics," in Peter B. Doeringer, ed., *Industrial Relations in International Perspective* (New York: Macmillan, 1981), pp. 401–416.
[43] Andrew Levinson, *The Working Class Majority* (New York: Coward, McCann, 1974).
[44] Susan Dunlop, "Equity in Paychecks," *AFL-CIO News*, May 14, 1983, p. 3.
[45] "A Healthy Influence," *AFL-CIO News*, May 14, 1983, p. 1.

lation).[46] In the 1930s, partly because of the example set by the CIO, the AFL began to support a wider range of social legislation, a practice which the AFL-CIO continues today. Nevertheless, the Federation continues to favor reliance on collective bargaining to achieve many elements of security for workers, so that in the United States, unions have not supported, and Congress has not enacted, legislation dealing with layoffs, severance pay, discharges, vacations, holidays, and other such employment standards, which are generally subject to government regulation abroad.

There has been resistance to labor's support for social reforms. In the mid-1970s members of the Chevrolet unit of United Auto Workers local No. 25 in St. Louis went to court charging that union officials improperly contributed union funds to organizations "espousing and promoting ideological doctrines and causes totally unrelated to, and in many instances antithetical to, the interests and welfare of the union and its members." The doctrines and causes to which the members objected were largely those supported by liberal and pacifist groups, including Students for a Democratic Society, the New Mobilization for Peace, Americans for Democratic Action, and the United States Committee for Democracy in Greece. The lawsuit argued that the union should be restricted from making contributions to causes unrelated to collective bargaining. In 1979, the Eighth Circuit Court of Appeals dismissed the lawsuit, saying that the court "should not take on itself the role of deciding which causes a union can or cannot support."[47]

Labor and American Political Parties

The American labor movement has tended since the 1930s to be considerably closer to the Democratic party in national, state, and local politics than to the Republican party. However, the labor movement is not a part of either political party. Unionists who serve in the councils of either party do so as individuals, not as representatives of trade unions. And in an important sense labor has built its own national political organization independently of the parties.

The formal position of the AFL-CIO is, in the words of its president, Lane Kirkland, that "the only approach that makes sense [is] to support our friends, irrespective of party, on the basis of their records." Further, Kirkland said, "The American trade union movement...has no desire to be an integral part of the [political] parties as such, and we will not be influenced or guided in our role in society by party politics."[48]

The fundamental elements of this position, set forth in 1980, are the same as those enunciated by Samuel Gompers for the AFL three-quarters of a century earlier and expressed in the slogan "reward our friends, and punish our

[46] Mollie Ray Carroll, *Labor and Politics: The Attitude of the American Federation of Labor toward Legislation and Politics* (New York: Arno, 1923).

[47] *Gaubauer et al. v. Woodcock et al.*, 1979.

[48] Lane Kirkland, quoted in *AFL-CIO News*, Dec. 13, 1980, p. 7.

enemies."[49] By this formulation, Gompers suggested that the labor movement would provide electoral support to public officials friendly to its interests and attempt to defeat others.

Dunlop and Bok characterize the political strategy of the AFL-CIO as having three elements:

1 An independent and nonpartisan stance toward political parties

2 Active support to only a narrow set of legislative goals at any particular time

3 Utilization of the lobbying tactics of a special-interest group with the federal and state legislatures[50]

Perhaps the first of these elements is the most surprising to readers in light of the substantial degree of union support for the Democratic party that has been evidenced since the 1930s. In fact, from its inception in 1955 until 1972, the Federation regularly endorsed the Democratic party's nominee for President of the United States, and the chief political activists of the AFL-CIO were deeply involved in the internal activities of the Democratic party. It seemed to many that the Federation and the Democratic party were becoming so closely linked that they resembled the structure of labor parties in Europe. However, in 1968 a bitter political division opened within the Democratic party and a Republican candidate, Richard Nixon, was elected President. In the period prior to the 1972 election the division within the Democratic party widened, and in 1972 the AFL-CIO broke two long-standing policies. First, for the first time it endorsed a candidate (Senator Hubert H. Humphrey) for the Democratic party's presidential nomination prior to the nominating convention. Second, when Senator George McGovern was nominated instead, the Federation for the first time in its history failed to endorse the Democratic candidate. Instead, the Federation remained formally neutral, while many of its national union affiliates endorsed one candidate or another. The Republican candidate, President Nixon, was reelected.

In 1976 the unions returned to the Democratic fold, endorsing the Democratic candidate, Jimmy Carter, for election. In 1979 the AFL-CIO and the Democratic administration headed by President Carter negotiated a wide-ranging "national accord" by which the government agreed to consult with the unions on matters of national economic policy. The AFL-CIO and the administration thereafter cooperated closely. The AFL-CIO endorsed Carter for reelection in 1980 and worked strongly on his behalf. The Republican candidate, Ronald Reagan, received the endorsement of the Teamsters Union and of only one affiliate of the AFL-CIO, the small National Maritime Union. Probably the AFL-CIO and the Democratic party had never been so closely con-

---

[49] "Letter of Gompers to All Trade Unionists in America, Apr. 7, 1906," *The American Federationist*, vol. 13, 1906.

[50] John T. Dunlop and Derek Bok, *Labor and the American Community* (New York: Simon and Schuster, 1970), pp. 386–387.

nected as in 1980. The Republican candidate was, however, the victor in the 1980 election.

Following the 1980 election, the AFL-CIO abandoned its policy of staying out of the presidential primary election process. The unions noted that the primary elections had become a major element in selecting presidential candidates, so that if the AFL-CIO wished to influence the choice of these candidates, it had to participate in the primaries. Further, the Federation sought and obtained the election of a number of trade unionists to the Democratic party's National Committee. In 1984 the AFL-CIO made the most substantial effort ever made by American labor on behalf of a presidential candidate. The AFL-CIO endorsed former Vice President Walter Mondale of Minnesota for president before the primaries. The unions provided support for Mondale in hard-fought primary battles and were credited by many political observers with being instrumental in his nomination for president by the Democratic Party. However, Mondale's union support also became an issue in the campaign as Mondale's opponents argued that he was too close to organized labor.[51]

Mr. Mondale was resoundingly defeated by President Reagan, a Republican, in the 1984 presidential election. In the aftermath of the election the AFL-CIO defended its efforts on behalf of Mondale. Labor's polls showed that its members voted by a large majority for Mondale (a statistic disputed by Republicans), and the president of a major AFL-CIO union wrote in the *New York Times,* "If the race were to be replayed tomorrow, we'd all do the same thing, only harder."[52]

At the state and local levels, unions continue to support Democratic candidates for office in far greater numbers than Republicans. There are exceptions, however, in which liberal Republicans receive union political support. If the labor movement were to become part of the Democratic party in a formal way, such alliances between labor and certain Republicans would be foreclosed. This is a result that the AFL-CIO does not want now.

Labor's Political Activity

Unions provide two major types of support to candidates for public office: financial contributions and direct campaigning. In 1936 the CIO made the first substantial financial commitment to a political party, a gift of $770,000 to the Democratic National Committee. By 1984 union contributions to candidates totaled many millions of dollars, and total election-oriented spending

---

[51] "Review of Mondale Record Reveals Number of Policy Differences with Labor Federation," *Daily Labor Report* No. 83, Apr. 30, 1984, pp. C1-C3. This is the most careful and dispassionate analysis of the Mondale–AFL-CIO record on public issues.

[52] Gerald W. McEntee, "Labor Strategy Next Time," *The New York Times,* Nov. 11, 1984, p. A-31. McEntee is president of the American Federation of State, County, and Municipal Employees. See also the statement of AFL-CIO President Lane Kirkland, *AFL-CIO News,* 29:5, Nov. 10, 1984, p. 1.

was considerably more. In defense of this practice, the unions cite even larger totals contributed by business people, bankers, and corporations. Election law reform restricted union political contributions in 1976, but not expenditures for voter registration and similar purposes.

How does labor raise and spend money for political purposes? The unions, like employers, are prohibited by federal law from using members' dues (or corporate funds in the case of employers) for most political activities. Instead, the unions establish separate organizations, like the AFL-CIO's COPE, which solicit and collect contributions from individuals and are then free to use the money as they desire. National unions separately have similar organizations, such as the Machinists Non-Partisan Political League, the Railway Clerks' Political League, the Steelworkers' Voluntary Political Action Fund, and the Teamsters' DRIVE. These organizations as a whole supply more financial support for political activities than does COPE. Most of these funds are not used as contributions to candidates, however. Most are used to support such activities as registering voters and taking them to the polls.

What does labor receive for this political activity? Sometimes nothing. Labor often supports a candidate only to prevent him or her from being solely dependent on business support. In other instances, labor supports candidates who are friendly to organized labor's position on legislation, and who are susceptible to influence from the unions.[53] In still other instances, union leaders may expect special favors (sometimes illegal or unethical) from the politicians they have helped elect. However, organized labor is not alone in seeking to influence politicians in each of these three ways—business and professional societies do the same. Controlling the degree of influence exercised by interest groups through financial support for politicians is a persistent problem in all democracies, including our own.[54]

How Politically Effective Is Organized Labor?

Because of the unions' substantial political efforts, it is easy to overestimate their effectiveness. Unions do not control the American political process. They do not control a major political party. Despite union endorsements, the Democratic presidential candidates have failed to be elected in six of the nine national elections since the start of the 1950s, and in a seventh the AFL-CIO endorsed no candidate. At the congressional level, many senators and representatives are elected with labor support, but again, labor is often ineffective in influencing their actions. In 1974, for example, a Congress was elected with such large Democratic majorities that the AFL-CIO touted it as a "veto-proof" Congress and prepared to seek enactment of its own legislative pro-

---

[53] Philip Taft, *Labor Politics American Style: The California State Federation of Labor* (Cambridge, Mass.: Harvard University Press, 1968).

[54] J. David Greenstone, *Labor in American Politics* (Chicago: University of Chicago Press, 1977).

gram over the expected objections of the Republican President. The result was devastating to the unions. A whole series of union-backed measures were passed by Congress, vetoed by the President, and the vetoes sustained in the Congress.[55]

What are the limitations on labor's political power? First, in election campaigns the unions are often unable to deliver the votes of union members for candidates whom the leadership endorses. Many public opinion polls over a long period have demonstrated that not only do union members often ignore the suggestions of their leaders as to whether or not to vote, but many workers and other voters simply use union endorsements as a guide to tell them for whom *not* to vote. A study of AFL-CIO affiliated members conducted in Pennsylvania showed that in the 1984 presidential election, unions were unable to influence their members' decisions about whether or not to vote but had "surprisingly strong influence on the Presidential choice of those who did vote."[56] Second, in congressional lobbying (or in lobbying in the state legislatures) the disunity of labor organizations hinders their efforts. It is not uncommon for the AFL-CIO to be lobbying for a particular piece of legislation while its member unions are, in some cases, supporting alternative bills, or even opposing the measure altogether. In part, the frequent disunity of the labor movement reflects its complexity in terms of interests, with different unions having different industrial and occupational orientations. In part, also, the frequent disunity arises from conflicts between unions over jurisdiction, or internal politics and personality clashes. As a consequence of these factors, the labor movement (like the American business community) rarely operates cohesively and thereby exercises considerably less influence than might be imagined in light of its financial and organizational strength.

Labor unions as a group are generally not cohesive in the political process, except perhaps in presidential elections. A study of the involvement of individual unions in the political process in 1978–1982 demonstrated the large extent of differences between unions in political activity. The study found that the demographic characteristics of its membership, its economic situation, and the union's own internal political processes affected its external political activity. Among the study's more interesting findings were that the higher the proportion of a union's members who were female, the greater its involvement in politics. Also, the more democratic the union, the greater its external political activity, suggesting that union leaders are not out of touch with their members' political preferences.[57]

---

[55] See, for example, "Labor's Losing Battle on Capitol Hill," *Business Week,* July 14, 1975, p. 56.

[56] Donald E. Stokes, "Voting Research and the Labor Vote," in Charles M. Rehmus and Doris B. McLaughlin, eds., *Labor and American Politics* (Ann Arbor: University of Michigan Press, 1967), pp. 384–391; and Tom Juravich and Peter R. Shergold, "The Impact of Unions on Voting Behavior of Their Members," *Industrial and Labor Relations Review,* 41:3 April 1988, p. 374.

[57] John Thomas Delaney, Jack Fiorito, and Marick F. Masters, "The Effects of Union Organizational and Environmental Characteristics on Union Political Action," *American Journal of Political Science,* 24 May 1988.

In the 1980s American unions have dealt at the national level with a President largely unsympathetic to them. As a result, the political power of organized labor has seemed to be at a low ebb. Yet a careful study of the union's record during the first term of President Ronald Reagan indicates some substantial political successes.[58] This should remind us that the unions are an ongoing political influence in America with some reverses in what appear to be favorable settings (as in 1974–1975) and some successes in what appear to be unfavorable settings (as in 1981–1984).

CHAPTER SUMMARY

Certain themes run throughout the history of American trade unionism. Both the cyclical expansion and depression of business and the long-term growth and development of the American economy have affected the size and strength of labor organizations. There has been a continuous and often dramatic struggle for control within the trade unions between the mainstream on one side and Marxist and other radical groups on the other. At the same time, the moderate mainstream has grown steadily. Finally, government regulation of trade unionism has expanded despite the unions.

The first unions, in the early 1800s, were an outgrowth of the desire for workers to regulate and control the trades at which they made a living. As early as 1834, a National Trades Union had been formed, but depression in 1837 brought about its collapse. By the early 1870s, there were 30 national unions and a total union membership of 300,000, which dropped by 80 percent in the depression of the 1870s. The American Federation of Labor, which was committed to organization by trade and to business unionism, was established in 1886. Although it encountered strong opposition from manufacturers, it prospered and grew to nearly 2 million members by 1904. The period from 1905 to 1920 was characterized by violent struggles between employers intent on repressing unions and radicals who wanted to abolish capitalism. A recession in the early 1920s and employer opposition weakened the unions, and the great depression in the early 1930s devastated the labor movement.

The 1930s was the most turbulent decade in labor history. Labor agitation increased, and the government endorsed collective bargaining as part of the program for national recovery and industrial peace. Labor unions expanded rapidly, and there were great organizing drives in the steel, auto, rubber, and meat-packing industries. World War II and the return to full employment permitted the unions to make even greater organizing gains and to consolidate their position. In the late 1940s and early 1950s communist control and involvement in unions, particularly in the CIO, was largely ended, and in 1955 the AFL and the CIO formed a merged federation. The AFL-CIO has operated for the most part without serious internal ideological cleavages.

---

[58] Marick F. Masters and John Thomas Delaney, "Union Legislative Records during President Reagan's First Term," *Journal of Labor Research,* 8:1, Winter 1987, pp. 14–17.

In the 1970s and 1980s the labor movement entered a long transition, in which unions declined in manufacturing and construction and grew among government employees.

The U.S. labor movement, which is now one of the largest and best financed in the world, is very heterogeneous, involving many divisions and factions. There are, however, basic structural principles of American labor organization which are important in understanding labor relations. These include (1) the principle of exclusive jurisdiction, the doctrine that there should be one and only one union to represent each group of workers; (2) the principle of local autonomy, which gives local unions the right to run their own affairs with minimal control by the national union and thus contributes to strong local, or workplace, unions; and (3) the emphasis on business unionism, the concentration on obtaining better wages and working conditions for union members. The emphasis on business unionism is in contrast to the philosophy of labor movements abroad, which have sought the advancement of the working class through revolutionary transformation of the total social structure.

American unions have been active and effective political interest groups. They have tried to block antiunion forces from using legislation to restrict union activity, and they have tried to keep government out of collective bargaining and the internal affairs of unions. The political strategy of the AFL-CIO has been to remain independent in terms of party, although there has been fairly consistent support of Democratic party candidates. The unions have not been as politically effective as their financial and organizational strength warrants, largely because there is such a diversity of interests in the movement.

QUESTIONS FOR THOUGHT AND DISCUSSION

1 What impact did business cycles have on the labor movement before World War II? Why? Has the impact of recessions on the unions changed since World War II? Why or why not?

2 Why haven't socialists and communists been more influential in the American labor movement?

3 What were the advantages and disadvantages of industrial unionism? Of craft unionism?

4 Is the American labor movement becoming more like labor movements in Europe? If so, how and why?

5 Will the enactment of legislation on such issues as pensions and health and safety undermine collective bargaining? Why or why not?

6 Is the American trade unions' philosophy too conservative? Is it too liberal?

7 What are the traditional differences in philosophy between the AFL and the CIO? Which had a "better" platform and for whom?

8 Why has there been (and is still) such strong opposition to the trade union movement by business management?

9 What are the goals, or objectives, of the labor movement? Were unions necessary to achieve better working conditions and fairer compensation for workers?

10 What is the relationship of the trade union movement to the political parties and the political process? How much political influence would you say the trade unions have? What are the pros and cons of the political influence or involvement of the unions?

11 What have been some of the strongest pressures at work in the formation of the trade unions?

12 Despite its financial and organizational strength, the American labor movement has exercised considerably less influence than it might. Do you agree? If so, why?

13 What are the internal and external factors that have limited the power and influence of the unions?

14 Were government support and protection necessary for the development of the American labor movement? Was government intervention appropriate?

SELECTED READING

Ashenfelter, Orley, and John Pencavel, "American Trade Union Growth: 1900–1960," *Quarterly Journal of Economics*, 83, August 1969, pp. 434–448.

Barkin, Solomon, *The Decline of the Labor Movement* (Santa Barbara, Calif.: Fund for the Republic, Center for the Study of Democratic Institutions, 1961).

Gompers, Samuel, *Seventy Years of Life and Labor*, 2 vols. (New York: E. P. Dutton, 1925).

Gordon, David M., Richard C. Edwards, and Michael Reich, *Segmented Work, Divided Workers* (New York: Cambridge University Press, 1982).

Goulden, Joseph C., *Meany* (New York: Atheneum, 1972).

Grossman, Jonathan, and William T. Moye, "Labor History in the 1970's: A Question of Identity" in Thomas A. Kochan et al., eds., *Industrial Relations Research in the 1970's* (Madison, Wis.: Industrial Relations Research Association, 1982, pp. 283–310).

Larson, Simeon, and Bruce Nissen, eds., *Theories of the Labor Movement* (Detroit: Wayne State University Press, 1986).

Lens, Sidney, *The Labor Wars* (New York: Doubleday, 1974).

Lieberman, Sima, *Labor Movements and Labor Thought: Spain, France, Germany and the United States* (New York: Praeger, 1985).

Livesay, Harold C., *Samuel Gompers and Organized Labor in America* (Boston: Little, Brown, 1978).

Neufeld, Maurice, Daniel J. Leaband, and Dorothy Swanson, *American Working Class History: A Representative Bibliography* (New York: R. R. Bowker, 1983).

Schacht, John N., *The Making of Telephone Unionism, 1920–1947* (New Brunswick, N.J.: Rutgers University Press, 1985).

Schnapper, M. B., *American Labor: A Pictorial Social History* (Washington, D.C.: Public Affairs Press, 1972).

Stone, Irving, *Adversary in the House: The Life of Eugene V. Debs* (New York: Doubleday, 1947).

CHAPTER 3

MEMBERSHIP AND STRUCTURE IN THE AMERICAN LABOR MOVEMENT

MEMBERSHIP OF THE LABOR MOVEMENT

Statistics do not give a comprehensive picture of the labor movement, but they help to provide a framework in which an evaluation can be made. We are fortunate in the United States to have extensive and reasonably reliable data about labor unions. These data are collected periodically by the federal government and permit us to assemble a quantitative portrait of unions in the United States.[1] However, not all the relevant information is published regularly, and there is a lag time between data collection and the subsequent publication. Consequently, the most up-to-date information available may be several years old. The figures in these chapters represent the most current information available.

Membership of National Unions

In 1985 there were 200 major labor organizations headquartered in the United States. These unions reported a membership of 19.8 million, of whom almost 1.5 million were in Canada. Because of their Canadian membership, many American unions refer to themselves as "international" unions. Ordinarily, however, the terms "national" and "international" are used synonymously in the United States. As a proportion of the total labor force in the United States (both employed and unemployed persons), union and employee association membership was 17.5 percent in 1986. Recent estimates suggest that in 1987-1988, union membership slipped further to about 17 percent.

[1] Bureau of National Affairs, *Directory of U.S. Labor Organizations, 1986–87* (Washington, D.C., October 1986).

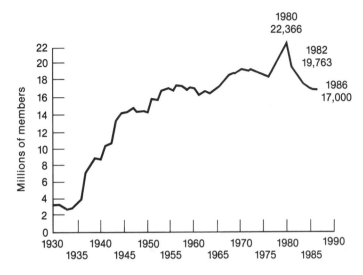

Excludes Canadian membership, but includes members in other areas outside the United States. Members of AFL-CIO directly affiliated local unions are also included. For the years 1948-1952, midpoints of membership estimates, which were expressed as ranges, were used.

FIGURE 3-1 Membership of national unions, 1930 to 1986. (*From Bureau of Labor Statistics, Directory of National Unions and Employee Associations, 1976, Washington, D.C., U.S. Government Printing Office, 1977. Data for 1977–1982, Bureau of National Affairs, Directory of U.S. Labor Organizations, 1984–1985, Washington, D.C., p. 2. Data for 1983–1986, Bureau of Labor Statistics, Employment and Earnings, 32-34:1 January 1985–1987, p. 219.*)

Figure 3-1 shows the membership of national unions in the United States from 1930 to 1986, the last year for which comprehensive data are available. The reader will note the steep growth of membership in the late 1930s and early 1940s, its moderate growth through the 1950s, and its resumed growth in the 1960s. Figure 3-2 shows membership as a proportion of the nonagricultural labor force through 1984. This chart tells a different story. Although total membership increased in the period from 1935 to 1980, the proportion of the labor force in unions has been declining irregularly since its last peak in the mid-1950s. Furthermore, in recent years union membership has declined in manufacturing, largely because of a general decline in manufacturing employment. However, union membership has grown among government employees until, by 1972, the proportion of public employees organized in unions was approximately the same as the percentage of all employees (private and public) who are union members. By 1982 the percentage of public employees in unions exceeded the percentage of private employees.

In recent years the Canadian membership of many United States-headquartered international unions has withdrawn to form separate unions for Canadians only. In the major such event in the 1970s, the Canadian members of the United Paperworkers left the international union. In the fall of 1984, the Canadian members of the United Automobile Workers withdrew to form

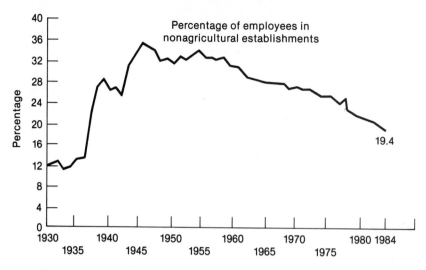

Excludes Canadian membership

FIGURE 3-2 Union membership as a percentage of employees in nonagricultural establishments, 1930–1984. *(From Bureau of Labor Statistics, Directory of National Unions and Employee Associations, 1979, Washington, D.C.: U.S. Government Printing Office, 1980. Data for 1979–1982 from Bureau of National Affairs, Directory of U.S. Labor Organizations, 1984–1985, Washington, D.C., and Bureau of Labor Statistics, Handbook of Labor Statistics, December 1983, Bulletin 2175. Data for 1983–1984 from Leo Troy and Neil Sheflin, U.S. Union Sourcebook, West Orange, N.J.: Industrial Relations Data and Information Services, 1985.)*

their own organization. It appears that slowly the international character of American-based unions is disappearing.

Employee Associations

In addition to the nation's 200 national labor unions, there are 30 major professional and state employee associations, which in 1986 had approximately 2 million members. These employee associations are not labor unions per se, and in the past they were generally reluctant to espouse unionlike aims or to endorse union methods (such as strikes). In the 1960s, however, this changed, so that many of the employee associations are now very much like unions in their behavior and may fairly be considered "quasi-unions." The largest of these associations is the National Education Association (NEA), with a membership of 1.7 million. Interestingly, there also exists an AFL-CIO–affiliated union of teachers, the American Federation of Teachers (AFT), with a membership of 610,000. There have been merger discussions between the professional association, NEA, and the union, AFT, but without success to date. If the total membership of employee associations is added to that of labor unions, then in 1986 total membership was 17 million and constituted 17.5 percent of the total labor force in the United States.

Membership of the AFL-CIO

The AFL-CIO does not include as affiliates all American labor unions. In 1987, there were 90 national unions affiliated with the AFL-CIO. AFL-CIO affiliates included in 1987 a total of 14.2 million members[2] (and 84 percent of total union and association membership). In the 1970s both the largest national union (the International Brotherhood of Teamsters) and the third largest national union (the United Automobile Workers) were not affiliated with the Federation. But in 1981 the UAW rejoined the AFL-CIO, raising its U.S. membership to 17,076,000 and 75 percent of total union and association membership in that year. In 1987 the Teamsters rejoined the AFL-CIO, boosting its membership by approximately 1.6 million, thus increasing its total of union and association membership by nearly 10 percent.

In recent years there has been a rapid pace of mergers of national unions. Between 1978 and 1987, for example, the number of national unions affiliated with the AFL-CIO declined from 108 to 90, primarily through mergers. By and large mergers represented attempts of unions to consolidate resources as economic conditions deteriorated.[3]

Size of National Unions and Employee Associations

National unions and employee associations vary greatly in size. In 1983 some 60 national unions and employee associations had fewer than 1000 members, and an additional 158 unions and employee associations had fewer than 10,000 members. In contrast, four national unions and employee associations had more than 1 million members, and 15 had more than 400,000 members. The 10 largest national unions and employee associations included almost 50 percent of total membership.[4] Since the effective operation of a national union requires the capacity to support full-time salaried officers, to place representatives in the field, to provide staff services, and to obtain legal counsel, all of which is increasingly expensive, many smaller national unions have been engaged in mergers.

Women, Minority, and White-Collar Membership

Labor unions are often thought of as primarily organizations of blue-collar, male workers, and in fact many labor union members have these characteristics. Unions also include many female, minority, and white-collar members, however. After years of discrimination, and in some instances legal proceedings, these groups have formed an increasing proportion of union mem-

---

[2] Included in the AFL-CIO total are 55,000 members of local unions affiliated directly with the Federation, not with any national union.

[3] Larry T. Adams, "Labor Organization Mergers, 1979–1984: Adapting to Change," *Monthly Labor Review*, October 1984, p. 39.

[4] Leo Troy and Neil Sheflin, *U.S. Union Sourcebook: Membership, Structure, Finance, Directory* (West Orange, N.J.: Industrial Relations Data and Information Services, 1985), pp. 3–18.

bership.[5] In 1986 women constituted 33 percent of union membership, a smaller proportion than they form of the work force as a whole. Minority workers constituted in 1986 some 20.5 percent of union membership, a larger proportion than they represented in the work force. White-collar workers constituted 19.8 percent of union membership in 1978 (the last year for which data are available) a substantially smaller proportion than their part of the total work force.[6]

Women, minorities, and white-collar workers are not evenly distributed among national unions, but they reflect in their union affiliation their distribution among industries and geographic regions. The following unions have a substantial number of women members:

The Amalgamated Clothing and Textile Workers International Union
The International Ladies Garment Workers Union
The United Food and Commercial Workers
The International Brotherhood of Electrical Workers

Minority membership is especially large in the following unions:

The Laborers International Union
The United Steelworkers
The United Automobile Workers

White-collar membership is more diverse and includes substantial proportions of the memberships of unions of actors, musicians, retail clerks, office and professional employees, and government employees.

As the proportion of Hispanics in our work force has grown, the AFL-CIO has made special efforts to contact them and try to interest them in unions. The AFL-CIO has a Hispanic advocacy arm called the Labor Council for Latin American Advancement. When the 1986 Immigration Act offered amnesty to persons who had been living in the country illegally, the Labor Council developed video tapes and other information in Spanish to inform Hispanics of their rights.

In recent decades the participation of women in the nation's labor force has continued to rise. By 1987 more than 46 percent of all adult women were full-time workers, and about 44 percent of all full-time workers were women. As women have come to play a more important role in the labor market, their relationship to the unions has become a more significant matter.[7] Although some unions have long represented many women, others have been made up primarily of men. The leadership of the trade unions has also been largely male, as has been that of the business community.[8] Several years ago a group of women in the trade unions formed

[5] Ray Marshall, *The Negro and Organized Labor* (New York: Wiley, 1965); and Ray Marshall, *The Negro Worker* (New York: Random House, 1967).

[6] William B. Gould, *Black Workers in White Unions* (Ithaca, N.Y.: Cornell, 1977).

[7] Linda H. LeGrande, "Women in Labor Organizations: Their Ranks Are Increasing," *Monthly Labor Review*, 101:8, August 1978. See also U.S. Department of Labor, Employment and Training Administration, *Women and Work* (Washington, D.C.: U.S. Government Printing Office, Monograph No. 46, 1977).

[8] James J. Kenneally, *Women and American Trade Unions* (Boston: Eden Press, 1978).

an organization called the Coalition of Labor Union Women. The coalition supports the increased participation of women in unions and in political activity. Joyce Miller, a vice president and social services director of the Amalgamated Clothing and Textile Workers Union has been the president of the coalition. In 1980, Miller was elected to the executive council of the AFL-CIO, the first woman to serve on that body. By 1988, three women served on the 35-member executive council.

Large numbers of women are employed in American industry as clerical workers.[9] Unionization among these employees is relatively low. In recent years, however, several associations of clerical employees have emerged, and these groups are now developing relationships with various elements of the labor movement. Among these associations are Working Women, the National Association of Office Workers, and Nine to Five. Clerical employees of banking institutions and insurance companies play an especially important role in these organizations.[10] Several women's organizations have developed relationships with labor unions, and in the 1980s unions increased their efforts to organize large numbers of clerical workers, many of whom are women.[11]

For a number of years there have been projections that union organizing among white-collar employees—most of whom are unorganized—would increase. This has not occurred, however. Instead, in the early 1980s white-collar union election activity declined 75 percent, and the proportion of union victories in elections declined from 54 percent to 42 percent.[12] Nonetheless, a substantial increase in union organizing among white-collar workers may be likely in the future, given the large numbers of potential members in white-collar jobs.

Union Organization by Industry

The industrial distribution of union membership is also uneven. Table 3-1 lists 31 industries or sectors of the economy and groups them into four categories by proportion of union membership to total employment. These statistics are useful to indicate relative standing, but they should not be considered fully reliable. This is because of problems of definition and measurement and currency. For example, in some industries the work force size and geographic distribution are constantly changing (especially in construction and agriculture) so that the proportion of the work force that is unionized varies constantly, and to a degree about which there is little or no information. Data for manufacturing industries

[9] Nancy S. Barrett, "Women in the Job Market: Occupations, Earnings and Career Opportunities," in Ralph E. Smith, ed., *The Subtle Revolution: Women at Work* (Washington, D.C.: The Urban Institute, 1979), pp. 31–62.

[10] Robert Jackall, *Workers in a Labyrinth: Jobs and Survival in a Bank Bureaucracy* (New York: Universe Books, 1978).

[11] See Linda McDonnell, "Women and Unions," a series of articles published by the Minneapolis *Star* in the summer of 1980. See also David Wagner, "Clerical Workers: How Organizable Are They?" *Labor Center Review*, 2:1, Spring–Summer 1979, pp. 20–50.

[12] John G. Kilgour, "White-Collar Organizing: A Reappraisal," *Personnel*, 63:8, August 1986, pp. 14–19.

TABLE 3-1 INDUSTRIES BY PROPORTION OF UNION ORGANIZATION

75 percent and over	50 to 74 percent
Transportation	Transportation equipment
Mining	Primary metals
Paper	Apparel
	Tobacco manufacturers
	Federal government

25 to 49 percent	Less than 25 percent
Telephone and telegraph	Printing and publishing
Petroleum refining	Chemicals
Food and kindred products	Textile mill products
Stone, clay, and glass products	Instruments
Fabricated metals	Service
Electrical machinery	Trade
Leather	Agriculture and fishing
Furniture	Finance
Electric, gas utilities	
Machinery	
Lumber	
Rubber	
Contract construction	
Local government	
State government	

Source: Bureau of Labor Statistics, *Directory of National Unions and Employee Associations,* 1979 (Washington, D.C.: U.S. Government Printing Office, 1980), with some adjustments by the author.

and government service are more reliable. Also, in recent years the government has cut back expenditures on data collection, so that more recent reliable estimates do not exist.

Richard Freeman and James Medoff compared estimates of union membership by industry drawn from various surveys made by the federal government for other purposes. These data show major differences between union representation figures based on different definitions. For example, in the period from 1973 to 1975, members of labor unions constituted 36.1 percent of all production workers and 23.7 percent of all employees (production and nonproduction both). But employees who were covered by the provisions of a collective bargaining agreement, whether or not they were members of a union, made up 45.0 percent of production workers and 29.8 percent of all employees (1968 to 1972). The researchers also showed that the percentage of persons covered by a collective bargaining agreement who were union members was highest outside the South (94 percent) and lowest in the South (80 percent).[13] These data, though now almost 15 years old, are the most recent available in published form.

Union membership in most of the manufacturing, transportation, and construction industries shown in Table 3-1 has been declining. For example, a recent study shows that union membership in construction declined from one-half in 1966 to less than one-third in 1983.[14] In the paper manufacturing industry, in contrast, union membership has slowly increased since the 1960s according to industry officials.

Union Organization by Geographic Region

Finally, union membership is concentrated in certain geographic regions (see Figure 3-3). Generally, union membership as a proportion of the labor force is highest in the Middle Atlantic, North Central, and far Western states. (The most recent data for all states are from 1982.) The most highly unionized states are New York (with 35.8 percent unionized, mainly in the manufacturing industry), Michigan (33.7 percent), Washington (32.9 percent, largely in lumber and milling), Hawaii (31.5 percent, mainly agricultural workers), Alaska (30.4 percent), and West Virginia (28.9 percent, largely in the bituminous coal industry). Other states with a high proportion of union membership are Illinois, Oregon, Ohio, and Pennsylvania. The Southeastern states are the least unionized. South Carolina has only 5.8 percent of its work force organized, North Carolina, 8.9 percent, and Mississippi, 9.3 percent. Some Western and Midwestern states also have little unionization, including South Dakota (10.3 percent), Texas (12.5 percent), and Oklahoma (12.9 percent). Over the past several years, unionization has been decreasing throughout the country.

Where Have All the Members Gone?

What has caused the decline in union membership as a proportion of the work force in the United States? There are several factors, including:

• The decline in employment of blue-collar workers (who have been highly unionized); blue-collar workers have declined from more than 50 percent of all employees in the 1920s to 32 percent in the 1980s.

• The growth of nonunion firms.

• The provision by government of many services and protections for employees which in the past were available primarily from unions. Since

---

[13] Richard B. Freeman and James L. Medoff, "New Estimates of Private Sector Unionism in the United States," *Industrial and Labor Relations Review*, 32:2, January 1979, pp. 143–174. See also A.J. Thieblot, Jr., *An Analysis of Data on Union Membership* (St. Louis: Washington University, Center for the Study of American Business, Working Paper 38, October 1978).

[14] Steven G. Allen, "Declining Unionization in Construction: The Facts and the Reasons," *Industrial and Labor Relations Review*, 41:3, April 1988, p. 343.

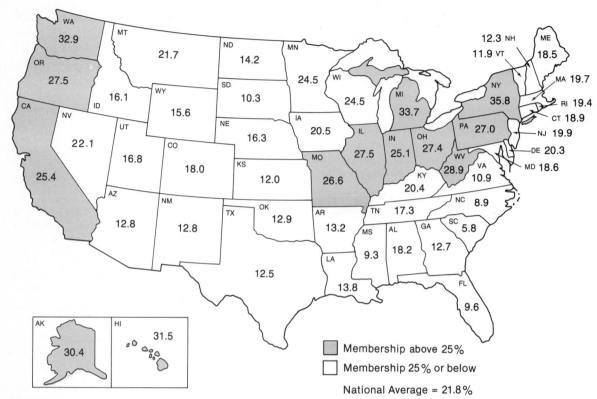

FIGURE 3-3 Union membership as a percent of states' total labor force, 1982. (*Source: U.S. Union Sourcebook, 1985. West Orange, N.J.: Industrial Relations Information Services.*)

government now provides protection, employees have less need of a union, and because unions have by and large supported increased government protection, they may be said to have contributed to their own decline.[15]

• The decline of the rate of growth in the nation's economy.[16]

• Increased employer hostility to unions, possibly because with greater competition, especially from foreign firms, the cost of being unionized is now more difficult for companies to bear.

• "A decreased desire for unionization by nonunion workers who

[15] George R. Neumann and Ellen R. Rissman, "Where Have All the Union Members Gone?" *Journal of Labor Economics*, 2:2, 1984, pp. 175, 192. See also "Unions in Decline: Causes and Consequences," *The American Economic Review*, 76:2, May 1986, pp. 92–108; and Lee P. Stepina and Jack Fiorito, "Toward a Comprehensive Theory of Union Growth and Decline," *Industrial Relations*, 25:3, Fall 1986, pp. 248ff.

[16] William T. Dickens and Jonathan S. Leonard, "Accounting for the Decline in Union Membership, 1950–1980," *Industrial and Labor Relations Review*, 38:3, April 1985, pp. 323–334.

are…more satisfied with their jobs and have less faith that a union would benefit them." In support of this proposition Henry Farber notes that two extensive surveys of American workers showed a dramatic increase in non-union workers' satisfaction with their jobs between 1977 and 1984.[17]

• Limited effectiveness and resources of unions in organizing.[18]

THE NATIONAL UNION

In the United States we often think that labor unions exist primarily to perform the functions of collective bargaining and contract administration for their members. And, of course, this is a very important part of their role. But each union also has an ongoing life as an institution or organization, with its own internal political affairs, procedures, financial structure, and concerns for its survival as an organization. In this section we will briefly examine unions as organizations. We begin with the national union, which is the sovereign body in the American labor movement. We shall then turn to the local union, closest of the organizational entities to the union member. Last, we will examine the federation of national unions, the AFL-CIO.

Organizational Structure

A national union is composed of local unions, which it charters, and is ultimately governed by a national convention of the local unions. The functions of the national union, the duties of its officers, and the relationship between the national union and its local affiliates are set forth in a constitution of the national union. National conventions are held every 1 or 2 years by most unions, but a period of up to 5 years between conventions is common. At the convention, the constitution may be amended, resolutions proposed for adoption, officers elected, budgets reviewed, dues changed, and other similar business conducted. The conventions of some large unions are very elaborate and costly affairs, with invited speakers and entertainers, reports of resolution committees, speeches by officers, electioneering on behalf of candidates for office, and similar activities. In some national unions the locals pay the expenses of delegates to the conventions. In others, the national union defrays all or part of the cost in order to permit small locals to be represented.

When the convention is not in session, a national union is governed by its general president and general executive board, usually made up of the

---

[17]Henry Farber, "The Decline of Unionization in the United States," National Bureau of Economic Research, Cambridge, Mass., Working Paper No. 2267, August 1987.

[18] Paula B. Voos, "Trends in Union Organizing Expenditures, 1953–1977," *Industrial and Labor Relations Review*, 38:1, October 1984, pp. 52–63. See also Paula Voos, "Union Organizing Expenditures," *Journal of Labor Research*, 8:1, Winter 1987, pp. 19ff.

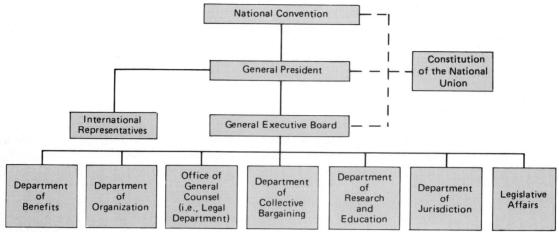

FIGURE 3-4 Organizational structure of a national union.

president, secretary-treasurer, and vice presidents of the national union.[19] The actions of the president and the board are subject to the provisions of the national union's constitution. Figure 3-4 describes the governance of an idealized national union (the specific structure varies, of course). Larger national unions now possess, in one organizational arrangement or another, the range of staff functions listed in Figure 3-4. Benefits of some type, whether strike funds, pension or welfare funds, or death benefits, are provided, and records of eligibility maintained (increasingly by the use of electronic computers); information is prepared for organizing activities; a legal department assists the union in litigation and interpretations of the law; a file of collective bargaining agreements and provisions is maintained; research and education programs are set up; the jurisdiction of the trade is overseen and defended (especially by the craft and modified craft unions), and lobbyists are employed to represent the union's views to government officials and legislators.

In addition to these staff functions, attached to the office of the general president is a group of full-time salaried representatives of the national union. Generally, these representatives are hired, or appointed, by the general president (although in some unions they are elected by the convention). The function of these international representatives is, in large part, to serve as intermediaries between the national and local unions. The "rep" assists the locals in collective bargaining negotiations and in handling grievances and renders assistance in the administration of the locals. Reps are also responsible for efforts to organize the unorganized workers in their area, and,

[19] In at least one major union, the International Brotherhood of Electrical Workers (IBEW), the general executive board is made up of elected persons (other than the union's vice presidents) who represent the various industries in which the union has members.

in craft unions, for protecting the jurisdiction of the union. Furthermore, reps keep the national union informed about developments in the locals.[20]

Financing

A national union is supported financially by a "tax" paid by each local on the basis of its membership size. The tax is generally referred to as the "per capita." Its amount is specified in the constitution of the national union and may be set in either dollar or percentage terms. In some few national unions (including the United Steelworkers, United Mine Workers, the Communication Workers, and the Airline Pilots Association) the national receives dues directly and remits a share to the locals. Ordinarily, the reverse occurs. The amount of money received by unions in the United States is large, by international standards, and the assets of American unions are substantial. For example, in 1976 (the most recent year for which data are available), United States unions reported $4 billion in assets, about evenly distributed among local unions and national unions. If the labor movement in the United States were to be conceived of as a corporation (Labor, Inc.), then in 1976 it would have ranked in assets as the thirty-third largest United States industrial corporation.

Union revenues are spent primarily on recurring operating expenses, especially salaries for officers and employees (43 percent in 1976). Strike benefit payments, pension benefit payments, and the like constituted 17 percent of expenditures in 1976.[21]

Selecting Leaders

The choosing of union leaders is a political process instead of a process of promotion through merit or selection by senior officers, as is common in corporations. National unions in the United States generally elect officers at their conventions. Since by federal law an election for national officers must be held at least once in a 5-year period, conventions must be held at least that frequently. A number of unions (36 in 1972), however, elect national officers by a referendum of the membership. Elections ordinarily involve opposing candidates and are often between opposing slates of officers running as a group. There are, however, a significant number of instances in which officers are unopposed for reelection. Sometimes union

---

[20] See Morris A. Horowitz, *The Structure and Government of the Carpenters' Union* (New York: Wiley, 1962); Jack Stieber, *Governing the UAW* (New York: Wiley, 1962); and Lloyd Ulman, *The Government of the Steelworkers' Union* (New York: Wiley, 1962).

[21] Leo Troy, "American Unions and Their Wealth," *Industrial Relations*, 14:2, May 1975, pp. 134–144. Also Leo Troy, "The Finances of American Unions, 1962–69," in National Bureau of Economic Research, *Explorations in Economic Research*, 2:2, 1975, pp. 217–251; and Neil Sheflin and Leo Troy, "Finances of American Unions in the Seventies," *Journal of Labor Research*, 4:2, Spring 1983, pp. 149–158.

general presidents serve for many years; in other instances they are defeated after only one or two terms.

The political process in national unions is not very much like that in the United States as a whole. Organized parties that contend for election to office exist only in the International Typographical Union.[22] National union leadership is rarely particularly tolerant of opposition, although both self-restraint and federal regulation limit the suppression of dissenting views. In most instances, the individuals who succeed in being elected general presidents of major unions are men 40 years of age or older who have become very skilled in the handling of people. They almost invariably have worked their way up through various local and national offices in the union and ordinarily began their careers as workers. This is in contrast to union leadership in many countries abroad, where lawyers or other professionals are officers of the unions.[23] There are exceptions, however, to this pattern of development of national union leaders. In some instances, especially in the building trades, general presidents have groomed their sons to follow them as general presidents, and the sons have been elected in turn. There are certain disadvantages to this process if the result is an inept and undemocratic leader. Generally, however, in recent decades at least, the quality of leadership so obtained has been high, and the unions involved have benefited from continuity of policy and from leaders carefully trained for the job.

Turnover among national union officers is low, and there have long been concerns that they may be too firmly entrenched in their positions to need to be responsive to the membership.[24] However, recent research indicates that the performance of union leaders in their positions affects the likelihood that they will retain their office.[25]

THE LOCAL UNION

Number and Size of Locals

We may summarize certain aspects of our review of the local union, since many characteristics of the nationals apply to the locals, though on a different scale. There are in the United States some 71,000 local unions, most of which are af-

[22] Seymour M. Lipset, Martin Trow, and James Coleman, *Union Democracy: The Internal Politics of the International Typographic Union* (Glencoe, Ill.: Free Press, 1956).

[23] A study in the United States of national union presidents, secretaries, and vice presidents showed that 17 percent had completed college, fewer than half had any college training, and more than 25 percent had not completed high school: Abraham Friedman, "Characteristics of National and International Union Leaders," unpublished manuscript, 1967, cited by John Dunlop and Derek Bok in *Labor and the American Community* (New York: Simon and Schuster, 1970), p. 181.

[24] Shulamit Kahn, Kevin Lang, and Donna Kadev, "National Union Leader Performance and Turnover in Building Trades," *Industrial Relations*, 25:3, Fall 1986, pp. 276–291.

[25] See Seymour Martin Lipset, Martin Trow, and James Coleman, *Union Democracy* (New York: Doubleday, 1962); and J. David Edelstein and Malcolm Warner, *Comparative Union Democracy* (New York: Wiley, 1976).

filiated with national unions. Locals hold their charters at the pleasure of the national union, although some locals predate their national. Generally, locals guard their separate existence carefully, and union constitutional provisions limit the capacity of the national union to abolish or merge local unions.

Locals vary greatly in size, averaging about 200 members. But many are much larger. Some locals, with as many as 30,000 to 40,000 members, are larger than some national unions. In manufacturing and services, a local union ordinarily represents the workers in a single plant or facility. In other industries, however, a local ordinarily has a geographic jurisdiction and represents the employees of many employers and at many working places.

Administration of Locals

Locals are governed in much the same way as national unions. Membership meetings are the chief executive body, and the officers of the local union govern in accordance with bylaws adopted by the local. The officers of a local union ordinarily include a president, vice president, secretary, treasurer (sometimes these last two offices are described as recording secretary and financial secretary, respectively), and a sergeant at arms. Officers are chosen by election from the membership and are ordinarily not paid by the union. Stewards are also elected, or named by the officers, to represent the union in grievance handling and in the administration of collective bargaining agreements. Stewards are usually paid by the employer and are workers designated by the union and detailed on occasion from duty as workers to represent the union (see Figure 3-5).[26]

A local union ordinarily does not have the same staff structure that a national union has. Locals do not have research and education directors, general counsels, legislative aides, and so on, although most locals retain legal counsel from a law firm.

A local union in the construction, retail trade, and transportation industries, for example, not only has the organizational structure shown in Figure 3-5, but has additional officials as well (see Figure 3-6). The membership elects a business agent (or business representative) who is a full-time, salaried official of the local union (except in very small locals, where limited finances prevent engaging a salaried official). Larger locals will also elect (or allow the business agent to appoint) assistant business agents, who are also full-time, salaried officials of the local. Some of the largest construction locals hire as many as 35 assistant business agents. The principal duty of the business agent is to enforce the local's collective bargaining agreements. He or she is expected to travel a great deal in order to visit the various workplaces

---

[26] Eric Bastone, Ian Boraston, and Stephen Frenkel, *Shop Stewards in Action: The Organization of Workplace Conflict and Accommodation* (Forest Grove, Ore.: ISBS, 1977). Also, Allan N. Nash, *The Union Steward: Duties, Rights, and Status* (Ithaca, N.Y.: New York State School of Industrial and Labor Relations, Cornell, 1977). Also, Tony DeAngelis, *Basic Steward Training*, revised (Minneapolis, Minn.: University of Minnesota Industrial Relations Center, 1983).

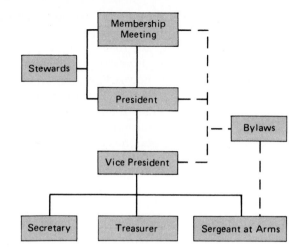

FIGURE 3-5 Organizational structure of a local union in manufacturing or services.

where members of the local are employed (in fact, many years ago the business agent was called the "walking delegate" of the local). Figure 3-6 also includes the position of "apprentice coordinator," which increasingly exists as a full-time salaried position of a skilled craft local union. Thus, the local has full- and part-time officers and salaried and nonsalaried officers. The whole structure is held together by a set of bylaws that define the duties of the various officers.[27]

[27] George Strauss, "Union Government in the United States: Research Past and Future," *Industrial Relations*, 16:2, May 1977, pp. 215–242.

FIGURE 3-6 Organizational structure of a local union in the construction, transportation, and retail trade industries.

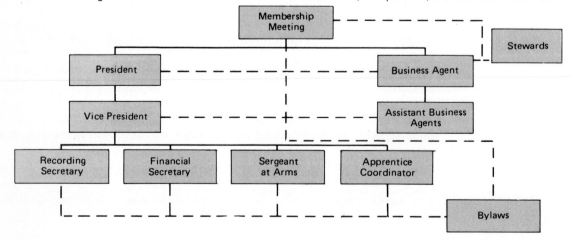

TABLE 3-2 FUNCTIONS OF A LOCAL UNION

---

1 Collective bargaining, the "bread and butter" of any local union
2 Contract administration to ensure the agreement is lived up to
3 Establishment and administration of fringe benefits
4 Organization, which is the life-blood of the union and ultimately makes the first three essential points possible
5 Ensuring a continuing supply of jobs
6 Protection of the union's supply of jobs
7 Apprentice training to ensure a steady supply of well-trained workers
8 Political action to protect negotiated gains, both locally and nationally
9 Community relations so that the union can help shape public attitudes toward the union
10 Information and education so that union members are up to date and aware of what is happening around them
11 Management of legal affairs, which have today become an integral part of every union
12 Maintenance of good relations with all other labor and management
13 Internal administration of the union to ensure that it runs efficiently, giving the members the most for their dues dollars

---

Source: General Secretary John T. Joyce, Bricklayers International Union, *St. Louis Labor Tribune*, Aug. 30, 1974, p. 7.

Functions of Locals

The functions of a local union are remarkably varied. One list developed by the general secretary of a craft union included 13 items, and is given in Table 3-2. In addition to duties to its own membership, a local union has duties to its national union and to other locals of its national. An international officer of the United Steelworkers once described a "good" local union as one that:

1 *Supports the political activities* of the national union
2 *Supports other steelworker locals* that are on strike
3 *Attends the convention* of the national union and participates in its activities[28]

Election of Officers

Local union officials are elected for a period of 1, 2, or 3 years. Federal law requires elections at least every 3 years, but most locals hold them more frequently. In some local unions the political process is very stable, with few contests for office and with officials serving many terms. In others, factions exist that compete for office and turnover is very frequent.

Local union memberships are rarely homogeneous. Instead, a local union is a mixture of conflicting interest groups. For example, in an industrial local union these groups might be older versus younger workers or skilled versus unskilled or semiskilled workers. Conflicts arise because, for example, older workers might desire improvements in a pension plan or be very strong supporters of a seniority system as a method of allocating benefits, while younger workers might prefer a wage increase over improved pensions and might

[28] Statement of James Smith, assistant to the president, United Steelworkers of America, Oct. 25, 1974.

feel little loyalty to a seniority system. Since union officials must get elected frequently, they often tend to let their political interests overrule their better judgment.[29] This often occasions bitterness and anger in employers and national union officials about the behavior of local union leadership. Other observers, however, may applaud it as reflecting the changing will of the democratic majority of the local union.

Compensation of Officers

Compensation of local union officials varies greatly. Many local officials receive no compensation from the union, as we have seen. Others receive a salary. Ordinarily salary levels are commensurate with the earnings of the workers, although generally above the average level of earnings of the local's members. In some trades and large locals, however, salary levels may be much higher. Some large locals of the Teamsters, especially, pay substantial salaries to union officials. And there has developed in recent years the questionable practice of union officials receiving more than a single salary. It has even been reported that some union officials are able to collect more than three salaries.[30] Often there is nothing illegal about this process, but it does permit the establishment of substantial incomes for some few union officials through the pyramiding of salaries.

Participation of Members

The participation of members in the affairs of local unions has been investigated several times. Most studies indicate that there is both an active and an inactive segment of membership. Union meetings ordinarily attract only a small proportion of the local's total membership. However, if a major issue, such as a strike vote or a ratification vote on a proposed new collective bargaining agreement, is scheduled, a very high proportion of the membership may turn out.[31] While it may be regrettable that there is not ordinarily greater participation by members in local union affairs, it cannot be said to be unusual in our society. Voters often turn out in small numbers in governmental elections: town meetings are often conducted in virtually empty halls; and corporation stockholder meetings are often poorly attended. Union members are no different from the general public in this aspect of their behavior.

Unions try by various devices to encourage participation by members in the affairs of the local. Some unions distribute to local officers guides which describe

---

[29] Address by General President Hunter P. Wharton, International Union of Operating Engineers, to the South Atlantic Conference of the International Union, Oct. 21, 1974 (mimeographed).

[30] Jerry Landauer, "Wearing Many Hats," *Wall Street Journal*, Aug. 17, 1973, pp. 1 and 19. Similar pyramiding sometimes occurs in the business and educational worlds. See also L. Appelbaum and H. R. Blaire. "Compensation and Turnover of Union Officers," *Industrial Relations*, 14:2, May 1975, pp. 156–157.

[31] Arnold S. Tannenbaum and Robert L. Kahn, *Participation in Union Locals* (Evanston, Ill.: Row, Peterson, 1958).

methods of assisting union members in meeting family health and welfare needs. It is thought that if the union goes beyond the workplace to meet the needs of members, it will be likely to attract greater participation and loyalty from its members. The United Steelworkers once had a rule that a member had to attend at least half of the local union's regular meetings for the 3 years prior to an election in order to be eligible to run for office in the local. But in 1977 the U.S. Supreme Court found that this was not a reasonable qualification for union officers. The Court pointed out that 96.5 percent of the membership of the local union which complained about the meeting attendance rule would have been ineligible to run for office if it had been enforced.

Financing of Local Unions

The financing of local unions is by dues paid by the membership. The amount of dues varies, but averages perhaps 1 percent of union members' annual income. A rule of thumb often used is that dues average 1 or 2 hours' pay per month per member. When a local union must collect monthly dues from each member, the administrative expense and loss of income from members who do not pay are substantial. While sanctions may be placed by the union on members who do not pay, such measures are sometimes ineffective (or even counterproductive). Unions often seek, therefore, to obtain the employers' agreement to deduct the dues of union members from their paychecks and forward the money directly to the union as a lump sum. This is called a "checkoff" and can be done only if (1) the employer agrees and (2) each worker individually signs a document authorizing the deduction to be made from his or her pay. Various local unions also handle their financial affairs, in terms of balancing revenues and expenditures and the amount of borrowing by the local, very differently. Some are conservative fiscal managers; others are not.[32]

Ordinarily unions establish dues as a fixed dollar amount to be paid each month. But some unions have recently begun to set dues as a percentage of a member's earnings. A complaint by some members of the Air Line Pilots Association went to court because of this. In 1980, a federal circuit court of appeals ruled that the union could lawfully set dues as a percent of a member's earnings (*Bagnall v. Air Line Pilots Association*, 1980).

THE FEDERATION

The American Federation of Labor–Congress of Industrial Organizations (AFL-CIO) is the central trade union federation in the United States. Its lengthy name is a result of its establishment by merger of the AFL and the CIO in 1955. Not only its name but also its organizational structure reflects the merger, as we shall

---

[32] Elisabeth Allison, "Financial Analysis of the Local Union," *Industrial Relations*, 14:2, May 1975, pp. 145–155. See also Gary N. Chaison, "Local Union Mergers," *Journal of Labor Research*, 4:4, Fall 1983, pp. 325–338.

see below. Since the merger, the Federation has achieved a degree of internal cohesion and external influence in American society unparalleled in labor's history, and perhaps never matched by any other single nongovernmental institution in the United States. Whether the influence of the AFL-CIO can remain at this high level is a matter we shall explore below.

Functions of the Federation

The Federation is a device by which national unions in the United States may cooperate with each other to pursue certain common objectives and to attempt to resolve certain problems internal to the affairs of organized labor. The most important of its functions are:

1 *Improving the image* of labor in American society
2 *Conducting political activity,* both by participating in elections and by lobbying with elected officials
3 *Resolving disputes* between national unions
4 *Strengthening weak links* in the labor movement
5 *Policing the internal affairs* of particular unions whose actions threaten the good name or influence of the labor movement as a whole[33]

The items not included on this list are as important to an understanding of the AFL-CIO as the points that are enumerated. Collective bargaining is the major omitted item. The Federation does not ordinarily become involved in negotiations with employers in the United States; collective bargaining is the province of the national and local unions. Collective bargaining is at the heart of the concerns of "business unionism," and American trade unionism is characterized as the world's preeminent example of business unionism. Thus, the AFL-CIO's exclusion from collective bargaining both suggests the substantial degree to which its role is limited in the activities of the American labor movement and demonstrates the primacy of the national union.

It would be difficult to distinguish among the five functions of the Federation listed above in terms of importance. But among the most difficult tasks of the Federation is the resolution of disputes among national unions. In 1962 concern about the potentially disruptive impact of internal disputes was so great that a special procedure was set up under article XX of the AFL-CIO constitution, which provided for the resolution of such disputes. Complaints can be filed by one affiliated national union against another where a union thinks it has an established relationship with a group of workers and another union is trying to raid its members. There follows a process of mediation and eventual arbitration before an impartial umpire, in which a decision is rendered. An appeal may then be filed by an affected union to the executive council of the AFL-CIO. Sanctions are provided against a national union that

[33] Dunlop and Bok, *Labor,* p. 190. See also Victor Reisel, "Last Giant," Sept. 24, 1976, syndicated newspaper column.

refuses to accept an award under article XX. On February 18, 1986, the Federation extended the article XX procedure to provide a mechanism to settle disputes between national or international unions that were attempting to organize the same workers—that is, where no established collective bargaining relationship yet existed.

From 1962 to 1982 (the most recent data available), some 2217 cases were filed under article XX, of which 56.3 percent were settled by discussion and mediation. In that period, 15 national unions were placed in noncompliance. Eleven eventually complied, and in 1983 only three unions, the International Typographical Union, the Graphic Arts International Union, and the National Association of Broadcast Employees and Technicians, were under sanctions.[34]

This record of resolving disputes among national unions is remarkable in light of the history of bitter divisions within the American labor movement. It is even more remarkable as the achievement of a federation established by the merger of two groups of rival national unions. George Meany said that the plan was "working wonderfully...beyond my wildest dream."[35] Whether or not the article XX procedure will continue to compile such a record remains to be seen, but its current success is clearly a major contributor to the relative unity of the American labor movement.

The major provisions of the Internal Disputes Plan (article XX) and two cases describing its operation are to be found in the experiential exercises at the end of this volume.

In recent years the AFL-CIO has become concerned with what appears to be a decline in the public's opinion of unions. By doing public opinion polling the unions discovered that their members held a much more favorable view of unions than did nonmembers. This "image gap," as the union termed it, became a target for union advertising.[36] In an effort to enhance labor's image, the AFL-CIO in 1983 began a nationwide television series showing unions and their members at work and in community services.[37] In May 1988, the Federation launched its largest advertising campaign, "Union Yes." The goal of the presentations was to talk directly to American workers about the value of unions.

Authority

How does the AFL-CIO compare with trade union central bodies abroad? Is it stronger or weaker, more centralized or less centralized? Most Western in-

---

[34] "Mediation Proves Successful in Settling Internal Disputes," *AFL-CIO News*, March 2, 1983.

[35] "Most Internal Disputes Settled by Mediation," *AFL-CIO News*, Mar. 1, 1975, p. 2.

[36] James A. Craft and Suharl Abboushi, "The Union Image: Concept, Programs and Analysis," *Journal of Labor Research*, 4:4, Fall 1983, pp. 299–304; Carol Keegan, "How Union Members and Nonmembers View the Role of Unions," *Monthly Labor Review*, 111:8, August 1987, p. 50.

[37] "New Season Opens for TV Series of Labor," *AFL-CIO News*, Jan. 7, 1984, p. 6; and Lane Kirkland, "Using Television to Reach Workers," *AFL-CIO News*, 33:20, May 14, 1988, p. 3.

TABLE 3-3 ESTIMATE OF AUTHORITY OF CENTRAL UNION BODIES IN SELECTED COUNTRIES

	Percentage of total union revenues received by central bodies	Intervention in internal union affairs	Involvement in collective bargaining	Percentage of industrial labor force in unions
Highly centralized				
Austria	80	H*	H	65
Norway	18	M	H	65
Sweden	18	M	H	80
Moderately centralized				
Belgium	40	M	M	71
Denmark	9	M	M	58
France	21	M	M	22
Decentralized				
West Germany	12	L	L	38
Great Britain	2	L	M	48
United States	3	M	L	30

*H = high; M = moderate; L = low.
Source: John P. Windmuller, "The Authority of National Trade Union Confederations: A Comparative Analysis," in D.B. Lipsky, ed. *Union Power and Public Policy* (Ithaca, N.Y.: Cornell University Press, 1975), tables 2 and 3. Data are from various years in the period 1964-1973, and data for France are from the CFDT.

dustrial countries have a federation of national unions. The number of nationals affiliated with the central body varies by country; there is a low of 16 in West Germany (where the trade union movement has virtually no fragmentation) and a high of more than 100 in the United States and Britain. In all Western countries except Israel and Austria, the trade union central body is a federation of legally separate national unions; but in those two countries, the national unions are simply subdivisions of the central body, without separate legal identity.[38]

Table 3-3 presents estimates of the authority of central union bodies in certain selected Western European countries and the United States. It will be noted that the Federation in the United States is described as decentralized, with only a moderate authority to intervene in the internal affairs of national unions, and only low involvement in collective bargaining. The table also shows that the percentage of the industrial labor force that is unionized is low in the United States (only France is lower) and that the Federation receives a relatively small percentage of total union revenues (only Britain is lower). This table does not suggest that the AFL-CIO is a weak or insignificant organization. It indicates only that the AFL-CIO's authority with respect to the national unions is relatively more limited than in many countries

[38] John P. Windmuller, "The Authority of National Trade Union Confederations: A Comparative Analysis," in David B. Lipsky, ed., *Union Power and Public Policy* (Ithaca, N.Y.: Cornell University Press, 1975), pp. 91–108.

abroad. On an absolute scale, however, the AFL-CIO is wealthier and more influential in American society than many federations abroad.

Structure

The AFL-CIO is a federation of about 90 national unions. Its supreme governing body is a national convention, which is held every 2 years. At the convention each national union is represented according to the size of the membership for which it pays a per capita tax to the AFL-CIO. The convention elects two top officers, the president and the secretary-treasurer. The president interprets the AFL-CIO constitution and directs its staff (totaling more than 100 people) between conventions. The secretary-treasurer is responsible for financial matters. The Federation has an executive council of 33 vice presidents (who are ordinarily general presidents of national unions), which meets at least three times a year to adopt policy and oversee the internal operations of the Federation. In 1980 the AFL-CIO set aside 2 of the 33 seats on its executive council, one to go to a woman and one to a member of a minority group.

The 90 unions which in 1987 made up the AFL-CIO vary greatly in size. According to one careful estimate, in 1977–1978 some 70.7 percent of the total membership of the AFL-CIO was contributed by the 10 largest national unions affiliated with the Federation.[39] An important element of the AFL-CIO's function is to seek to bring about mergers that will strengthen the trade union movement as a whole. In recent years there have been several significant mergers, which created larger organizations and lessened competition among national unions.[40]

There is also a general board, consisting of the officers of the Federation, the executive council, and a principal officer of each affiliated national union and department. The general board meets only occasionally, at the request of the president, and acts on matters referred to it by the executive council. (For example, a meeting of the general board was called in 1975 to consider the deepening economic recession of that year and to propose policies to the government to expand the economy.)

The AFL-CIO has a very complex administrative structure. The Federation has central bodies in all 50 states and Puerto Rico, and over 700 local central bodies. It is a characteristic complexity of AFL-CIO structure that, although a national union may be an affiliate of the AFL-CIO, the national union's local unions in a particular state may not be affiliated with the state AFL-CIO body. The Federation also has a group of eight trade and industrial depart-

---

[39] John P. Windmuller, "Concentration in the Union Structure: A Comparative Analysis," Cornell University, unpublished, 1980.

[40] Gideon Chitayat, *Trade Union Mergers and Labor Conglomerates* (New York: Praeger, 1979). See also John Freeman and Jack Brittain, "Union Merger Process and the Industrial Environment," *Industrial Relations*, 16:2, May 1977, pp. 173–185; "Union Mergers in the 1970's," *Monthly Labor Review*, 101:10, October 1978, pp. 13–23; and Gary N. Chaison, *When Unions Merge* (Lexington, Mass.: Lexington Books, 1986).

ments. An industrial union department is composed of the national unions that were the old CIO. The national unions affiliate with the departments that represent their interests. The trade and industrial departments have local and state bodies also. The Federation also has staff departments, of which the most important is the department of organization and field services, which supervises regional offices of the AFL-CIO. This department was created in its present form at the 1973 convention of the Federation.

Activities

The AFL-CIO attempts to organize craft and industrial unions, to assist its affiliated national unions in their organizing work, to supply legal assistance in some litigation, and to represent its affiliates in governmental and nongovernmental agencies. It maintains research, information, publicity, and educational services as well. AFL-CIO publications include a weekly newspaper, *The AFL-CIO News,* and pamphlets and organizing information. In civic affairs, the AFL-CIO encourages and promotes the involvement of union members in such community projects as campaigns for voter registration, better schools, more hospitals, and the elimination of slums.

The AFL-CIO has for a long time had an interest in the education of union members and officers. By 1970, for example, Federation President George Meany reported that some 15,000 members of AFL-CIO unions were enrolled in summer school programs on the nation's campuses. Many universities conduct labor education programs on a year-round basis.[41] But the labor movement has never developed the same close affiliation with the universities that the business community has evolved (reflected in part by the growth of graduate schools of business at the nation's universities and by the development of undergraduate business administration courses). Instead, the labor movement has grown more disenchanted with the universities. Meany voiced labor's disenchantment as follows:

> It is unfortunate that there seems to be a view in certain parts of the academic world that labor's problem is smugness and self-satisfaction, and that it needs a great deal of abrasive criticism to open its eyes. In this arrogant conviction, from time to time we see academic facilities turned over to labor's enemies to use as a forum for attacking labor.[42]

(Incidentally, Meany's reference to "labor's enemies" was probably not directed to the business community, but to left-wing and radical critics of the unions.)

Reflecting this discontent with American universities, the AFL-CIO has es-

---

[41] Lois S. Gray, "Academic Degrees for Labor Studies," *Monthly Labor Review,* 100:6, June 1977, pp. 15–20.

[42] Remarks of AFL-CIO President George Meany at the 25th anniversary dinner of the New York State School of Industrial and Labor Relations, New York City, Dec. 11, 1970. The remarks were reprinted in Bureau of National Affairs, *Daily Labor Report,* No. 240, Dec. 11, 1970, pp. F1-F2.

tablished its own university at a suburban campus in Silver Spring, Maryland, just north of Washington, D.C. The AFL-CIO Labor Studies Center is an incorporated, nonprofit educational institution governed by a board of trustees composed of labor and public members. It was established in 1969 at a cost of several million dollars. In 1974, a college degree program was established at the center, offering bachelor's degrees in labor studies.[43]

The AFL-CIO also takes a strong interest in American foreign policy. From the earliest days of the AFL under Samuel Gompers, and continuing through the period of the two federations (AFL and CIO), the American labor movement has remained substantially independent of governmental foreign policy.[44] In recent decades, the position of the labor movement as expressed by the AFL-CIO has been strongly antitotalitarian, opposing both communist and fascist regimes. This position often places the American labor movement in opposition both to the position of foreign labor movements and to that of our own government. The AFL-CIO has consistently opposed the policy of the United States government to establish a detente (i.e., understanding) with the Soviet Union. For example, on October 1, 1974, Meany testified before the Senate Foreign Relations Committee. He quoted complimentary comments by Don Kendall, president of Pepsi-Cola Corporation, about Leonid Brezhnev, chief of the Communist party of the Soviet Union, and then proceeded to reiterate the AFL-CIO's opposition to the detente policy, characterizing it as "building castles of sand on the watery foundations of petty greed, wishful thinking, irresponsibility, self-indulgence, and plain old ignorance...[as well as] the inability to...understand clearly the nature of freedom's enemies."[45]

These statements demonstrate the continuing threads of the AFL-CIO's foreign policy position: (1) opposition to totalitarianism and (2) fear that the American government and business community will reach accommodation with totalitarian regimes that will threaten the existence of free labor movements.[46] So sensitive is the AFL-CIO to the threat of totalitarian advance that the U.S. Congress has repeatedly declared, in the Foreign Assistance Act, that aiding the development of free and democratic trade unions is an objective of U.S. foreign policy.[47] The AFL-CIO supports an organization named The American Institute for Free Labor Development which has been active in Latin America in opposition to communist regimes.[48]

[43] Carolyn J. Jacobson, "An Expanding Role for Labor's College," *American Federationist*, 81:10, October 1974, pp. 13–19.

[44] Arnold Beichman, "American Labor and U.S. Foreign Policy," *American Federationist*, 81:10, October 1974, pp. 20–24. Also, Lane Kirkland, "Free Trade Unions—Force for Democracy," *American Federationist*, 85:4, April 1978, pp. 1–5.

[45] Statement of AFL-CIO President George Meany to the Senate Foreign Relations Committee, Oct. 1, 1974. The text is in AFL-CIO *Free Trade Union News*, 29:9, October 1974, pp. 1–8.

[46] Roy Godson, *American Labor and European Politics* (New York: Crane, Russack, 1976).

[47] Memorandum of the Secretaries of State and Labor to all U.S. Ambassadors, reprinted in *AFL-CIO News*, Aug. 12, 1978, p. 5.

[48] See Donald Robinson, "Bill Doherty's Blue-Collar Freedom Fighters," *Reader's Digest*, September 1985, pp. 141–144.

LABOR UNITED?

In 1955, the most recent year for which data are available, at the time of the AFL-CIO merger, Steelworker general counsel Arthur J. Goldberg (later secretary of Labor, Supreme Court associate justice, and ambassador to the United Nations) wrote an account of the merger, entitled *AFL-CIO Labor United*.[49] Yet labor remained united only very briefly. In 1957 the AFL-CIO expelled its largest affiliate, the Teamsters, after the Teamsters' leaders were accused of unethical practices and when an agreement to reform the practices could not be obtained.[50] In 1968 the United Automobile Workers, then the largest AFL-CIO affiliate, withdrew in a dispute with the Federation. In 1981, the UAW rejoined the AFL-CIO, and the Teamsters, the largest union in the United States, rejoined in 1987. (The Teamsters and the UAW briefly formed a rival federation, the American Labor Alliance, in the late 1960s, which did not survive.)

The reaffiliation of the UAW and the Teamsters makes it fair to say that the labor movement is today as cohesive as it has been at virtually any time in its long history.

CHAPTER SUMMARY

In 1985, the most recent year for which data are available, there were 200 major labor organizations in the United States with a total reported membership of almost 17 million, or 17.5 percent of the total labor force. Of these, 90 national unions, or 84 percent of the total union membership, were affiliated with the AFL-CIO. Although total union membership has grown in the years since 1935, the proportion of the labor force in unions has been declining since the 1950s. Also, the number of women, minority, and white-collar workers in unions has been rising.

Unions are ongoing organizations, each with its own internal political affairs, procedures, financial structure, and concerns for survival. It is important to understand unions as organizations. In the United States, there are local unions, national unions, and a federation of national unions—the AFL-CIO. A national union is composed of local unions and is governed by a national convention of the local unions, which is held every few years. Its functions, the duties of its officers, and its relationships to affiliates are set forth in a constitution. The national union has a general president and an executive board made up of the president, a secretary-treasurer, and several vice presidents. There is also a group of full-time salaried representatives attached to the general president's office who serve as intermediaries between the national and local unions.

Union leaders are elected to their posts, but the political process in national unions generally does not involve organized parties. Financial support

---

[49] Arthur J. Goldberg, *AFL-CIO Labor United* (New York: McGraw-Hill, 1956).
[50] Gary N. Chaison, "Federation Expulsions and Union Mergers in the United States," *Relations Industrielles*, 28:2, 1973, pp. 343–360.

for the national unions comes from taxes paid by the locals, and this revenue, which is substantial, is spent on officers' and employees' salaries, governmental lobbyists, a legal department, the national convention, strike benefit payments, pension and welfare plans, and many other functions.

There are some 71,000 local unions in the United States, most of which are affiliated with national unions. Locals vary greatly in size (from 200 to 40,000 members) and in the units of jurisdiction which they represent. Many of the organizational characteristics of the locals are similar to those of the national unions. They are governed through their membership meetings and financed by membership dues. The officers are elected to office, but not ordinarily paid by the unions. Some local unions elect full-time salaried business agents, or representatives, who enforce the local's collective bargaining agreements. In addition to its responsibilities to the national union, the local union's basic functions include collective bargaining, contract administration, union organizing and recruiting, apprentice training, education, political action, and management of legal affairs.

The AFL-CIO is the central trade union federation in the United States. Through the Federation, about 90 national unions cooperate with each other to pursue common objectives and resolve the internal disputes and problems of organized labor. The Federation does not engage in collective bargaining, which instead is the province of the national and local unions. In relation to the trade union federations in other countries, the AFL-CIO is considered to be decentralized, possessing only moderate authority to intervene in the affairs of national unions. Nevertheless, it has had a remarkable record for resolving disputes in national unions. The governing body of the Federation is a national convention, held every 2 years, which elects the president and secretary-treasurer. An executive council of 33 members meets at least three times a year to adopt policy and conduct other business. The administrative structure of the AFL-CIO is very complex and includes over 700 local central bodies and trade, industrial, and staff departments, which also have local and state offices. The Federation maintains legal, research, information, publicity, and educational services and has had a strong interest in American foreign policy as well.

QUESTIONS FOR THOUGHT AND DISCUSSION

1 How is a national union different from an employee association (such as the National Education Association)? Will the differences widen or narrow in coming years? Why?

2 Why are there not more women and minority members of labor unions? Are they too few now? Too many? Do businesses have a better record in treating women and minorities fairly than unions have? Does government have a better record?

3 Why are local unions in construction structured differently from those in manufacturing? Does the difference in structure make a difference in how effective they are in representing their members? Why or why not?

4 Does the AFL-CIO have enough authority with respect to its affiliate national

unions? How should its role be expanded? Contracted? Should the AFL-CIO be involved in collective bargaining?

5 Local unions often seek to obtain agreements with employers to deduct the dues of union members from their paychecks and forward these monies to the union as a lump sum—the checkoff. Do you think this is a fair and reasonable arrangement? Argue the question from the point of view of the union's officers, the employer, and a union member who did not initially vote for the union.

6 Do you believe that the size of the labor movement in general will expand or contract in the coming decade? What industries and areas are now most unionized? What industries or sectors of the economy will show increased unionization in the future?

7 How do people become leaders in national unions? Do you think the election of officers in local and national unions is better than selection by merit or professional expertise? Why? Is the union political process truly democratic? Why or why not?

8 What are some of the functions of a local union? Of the national union?

9 Is the size of union membership in this country at all surprising? Why or why not?

10 Why do you think the AFL-CIO has taken such a strong position against communist and fascist regimes abroad?

11 One of the functions of the AFL-CIO is to improve the image of labor. If you were in charge of publicity for the AFL-CIO, how would you approach this task? How would you promote "big labor"? How would you design a television advertising program for labor?

12 How does understanding unions as organizations help to illuminate some of the actions and reactions of unions and union leaders?

SELECTED READING

Brill, Steven, *The Teamsters* (New York: Simon and Schuster, 1978).

Cook, Alice, et al., eds., *Women and Trade Unions in Eleven Industrialized Countries* (Philadelphia: Temple University Press, 1984).

Estey, Martin, *The Unions: Structure, Development and Management*, 2d ed. (New York: Harcourt, Brace & World, 1976).

Herding, R., *Job Control and Union Structure* (Rotterdam: Rotterdam University Press, 1972).

Herling, John, *The Right to Challenge: People and Power in the Steelworkers Union* (New York: Harper & Row, 1972).

Marshall, Ray, *The Negro Worker* (New York: Random House, 1967).

Roomkin, Myron J., and Hervey A. Juris, "A Critical Appraisal of Research on Unions and Collective Bargaining," in Thomas A. Barocci et al., eds., *Industrial Relations Research in the 1970's* (Madison, Wis.: Industrial Relations Research Association, pp. 311–354).

Sayles, Leonard R., and George Strauss, *The Local Union* (New York: Harcourt, Brace & World, 1967).

Stieber, Jack, *Governing the UAW* (New York: Wiley, 1962).

Wallihan, James, *Union Government and Organization in the United States* (Washington, D.C.: Bureau of National Affairs, 1985).

C

LABOR-MANAGEMENT RELATIONS AND THE LEGAL SETTING

Work is performed in our society by persons who are specialized by function into different occupations and industries, permitting us to accomplish work more efficiently. With specialization, however, come differences in the status and authority of people in the workplace. In consequence, work is ordinarily performed by some persons under the supervision or direction of others.

Labor-management relations are concerned with the relationships that exist between those persons who perform work and those who direct and supervise it. Supervisory relations involve the exercise of authority and the use of power. Therefore, labor-management relations involve the use of power by managers and employees.

When there are disagreements and disputes, the unrestrained use of power can result in very disruptive conflicts. In some instances, the conflict imposes actual harm only on the employer and the workers immediately involved. In other instances, the broader community may also suffer losses. As a result, the broader community often restricts the use of power through law.

Matters which might otherwise result in conflicts involving a contest of power are often settled by the creation of legal rights for individuals, companies, and unions. Also, companies and unions often jointly agree to establish rights for each other so that work may proceed unhindered by disputes. Rights place limits on the unbridled use of power.

Labor-management relations in the United States involve both the exercise of power by employers and unions and the limitations which the creation of rights places on the use of power.

CHAPTER 4

STATUTORY AND JUDICIAL REGULATION OF LABOR RELATIONS

LAW AND LABOR RELATIONS

Citizens of the United States live in a free country. However, in the area of labor relations the activities of workers, unions, and employers are very much regulated and restricted by law. This has not always been the case. Many years ago there was little government interference in labor relations. However, disputes between labor and management were often taken to the courts or the legislatures by one side or the other in an attempt to gain some advantage. Other disputes threatened to disrupt society through violence or through interrupting vital public services, and these, too, brought about government intervention. As a result, there has developed a network of law and regulatory agencies that oversees most aspects of labor relations.

American labor law has certain fundamental characteristics that make it different from labor law in other countries. Some of these characteristics it shares with American law generally, and these we shall explore below; but others are unique to labor law itself. Perhaps the two most distinctive features of American labor law are these:

1 *Different procedures and standards* exist for different sectors of the economy.

2 *Most American law* regulates the procedures followed in the relations of labor and management but leaves the substantive rules of the workplace (e.g., the amount of wages, fringe benefits, layoff provisions) to the action of management alone or management and labor jointly.

American labor law is now very extensive and complex. When Congress published the texts of the federal statutes that pertained to labor relations, labor standards, and employee benefits, the complete text consumed 3 volumes and 1060 pages.[1] In addition to the statutory language, there are thousands on thousands of pages of administrative regulations issued by government agencies applying the laws and even more pages of court decisions interpreting them. The result is that labor law has become a field for experts. Many lawyers specialize in the practice of labor law, and most large law firms now have labor lawyers on their staffs. In most major cities a number of smaller law firms practice in this branch of the law exclusively. Union organization campaigns, collective bargaining negotiations, and the handling of grievances all find labor and management increasingly bringing lawyers in to represent or advise them. Our major law schools provide courses in labor law and even permit students to specialize in the area. A wide variety of textbooks in labor law are also now available.[2] The field is both sizable and growing.

The result of the growth of labor law is that the average business person, worker, or labor leader is not ordinarily able to comprehend fully his or her own rights and responsibilities. Instead, these people must rely on expert legal advice. It is common for articles or books about labor relations to begin by advising the reader to see a labor lawyer, and this is sound advice. Nonetheless, there is much about the law that the nonlawyer must know, including its basic features, how it has developed, and some of its major provisions. Detailed questions cannot, however, be answered except by specialists.

CHARACTERISTICS OF AMERICAN LAW

What Is Justice?

A primary function of law is the settlement of disputes between citizens. When such a dispute exists, as for example between a union and a company, the complaining parties want either to win the dispute or at least to receive justice. The law has the function, it may be said, of dispensing justice. Unfortunately, justice is not a simple concept or one that all of us define in the same way. As a result, laws that appear to some to be fully just appear to others as the height of injustice. Such division of opinion has been especially common with respect to labor disputes.

In order to provide a framework for the evaluation of labor law as it has developed in this country, it is useful to begin with a brief examination of the concept of justice. In essence, different theories of justice devolve into different rules for deciding whether to do one thing or another, i.e., how to make a choice. A study of justice[3] lists three different principles of justice (Table 4-1):

---

[1] U.S. Congress, Senate Committee on Labor and Public Welfare, Subcommittee on Labor, *Compilation of Selected Labor Laws Pertaining to Labor Relations*, 3 vols. (Washington, D.C.: U.S. Government Printing Office, committee print, Sept. 6, 1974).

[2] See, for example, Julius G. Getman and John D. Blackburn, *Labor Relations: Law, Practice and Policy*, 2d ed. (Mineola. N.Y.: Foundation Press, 1982).

[3] John Rawls, *A Theory of Justice* (Cambridge, Mass.: Harvard University Press, 1971).

TABLE 4-1 THEORIES OF JUSTICE

Justice is found in serving:
- The greatest good for the greatest number
- The needs of the disadvantaged
- A balancing of various principles of fairness

- *The greatest good (utilitarianism)* Justice is the greatest good for the greatest number.
- *Equality or fairness (egalitarianism)* Justice is equality in duty and rights among individuals, and inequality is justified only if its existence causes all, especially the least favored (i.e., the disadvantaged), to benefit.
- *Balancing among principles (intuitionism)* Justice involves the accommodation of several diverse principles of justice, including equality, liberty, property rights, and human rights.

These three different theories of justice may lead to very different conceptions of what the law ought to be as it applies to conflicts between labor and management. The first theory suggests that the law ought to favor the interests of society as a whole; the second suggests that the law ought to favor the weak, poor, and disadvantaged; the third theory suggests trying to find a balance between the other two. The history of American labor relations law is full of the debate among proponents of each of these theories.

Types of Law

The United States has four distinct types of law (Table 4-2), and all are involved in labor relations.

- *Constitutional law* The Constitution of the United States is a written document that is our highest form of law. All other law must conform to its provisions.
- *Statutory law* Congress, state legislatures, and other representative bodies may enact "laws," or statutes.
- *Common law* The actions of courts and the customs of the people constitute a body of law that is called common law. Common law rests primarily on decisions of courts and upon the willingness of one court to follow what

TABLE 4-2 TYPES OF LAW

- Constitutional
- Statutory
- Common
- Administrative

another has done (i.e., to follow "precedent"). Common law is especially important in the area of procedure.

• *Administrative law* Agencies of government are often set up to apply particular statutes, and the regulations and decisions issued by these agencies constitute administrative law.

The following examples of each type of law may be found in the field of labor relations:

Constitutional

• The Fourteenth Amendment to the U.S. Constitution prohibits involuntary servitude and so rules out certain types of relationships between companies and workers.

• The First Amendment to the U.S. Constitution guarantees freedom of speech and so ensures that both union and management have a high degree of latitude in voicing their opinions in labor union organizing drives.

• The First Amendment does not protect employees of a private company from discharge or other disciplinary action if they complain to supervisors. A union contract may protect them, or in some instances, the National Labor Relations Act may protect them; but the freedom of speech guarantee in the U.S. Constitution does not. However, the First Amendment prohibits government from abridging freedom of speech, and so does apply to public agencies acting as employers. Therefore, if a public employee complains to a supervisor about working conditions, that employee is protected from discipline by the First Amendment to the Constitution.[4]

Statutory

• The National Labor Relations Act establishes rules and procedures for unions and management in most of the private sector of our economy.

• The Employees Retirement and Income Security Act establishes certain standards that employers must meet in providing pension coverage for workers, if any coverage is provided at all.

Common

• Courts in various states, operating under different statutes, will still often honor decisions of courts in other states when the same or a similar issue was in dispute.

• The practice of labor and management in an area, unless clearly contrary to statutory law, will often be upheld by a court simply because it is the prevailing practice.

---

[4] *Givhan v. Western Line Consolidated School District*, 77 U.S. 1051 (1979).

Administrative

• The National Labor Relations Board hears and issues rulings in disputes arising under the National Labor Relations Act.

• The Labor-Management Services Administration of the U.S. Department of Labor acts on cases arising under the Landrum-Griffin Act.

Functions of Labor Law

Law as it is applied to labor relations in this country has three primary functions:

1 *To facilitate and protect private voluntary arrangements,* such as private contracts.

2 *To resolve disputes.*

3 *To establish minimum standards* for employment, as, for example, the minimum wage and health and safety standards.

The Federal Court System

The federal government, by passing statutes about labor relations, has directed most litigation involving private companies and unions into the federal court system. Briefly, there are three levels of courts: district, appeals, and the Supreme Court. Efforts to enforce contractual provisions between a company and a union are made in federal district courts. (Complaints about violations of various statutes are taken first to federal administrative agencies. Thus, an unfair labor practice charge goes first to the National Labor Relations Board. A charge of racial discrimination in employment goes first to the Equal Employment Opportunity Commission.)

Appeals from decisions of the district courts and from actions of the administrative agencies are taken to the courts of appeals. Finally, appeals from decisions of the courts of appeals are made to the Supreme Court. The Supreme Court is unlike the other two levels of the federal court system in that it does not have to consider cases filed with it, but uses its own discretion to decide which cases to hear (a process involving the issuance of a *writ of certiorari*).[5]

The Supreme Court ordinarily receives many appeals each term involving labor relations cases and usually accepts several for decision. It is interesting that labor relations cases are sometimes of such significance as to receive special treatment. For example, only three cases have been accepted by the Supreme Court for its own decision without first having been decided by a court of appeals. Two of these cases involved labor relations. The first involved the 1947 Mine Workers strike. The second involved President

[5] Alvin L. Goldman, *The Supreme Court and Labor Management Relations Law* (Lexington, Mass.: Lexington Books, D.C. Heath, 1976).

Truman's seizure of the basic steel industry from its owners in 1952 as part of the President's efforts to settle the steel strike of that year. The third instance involved the Special Prosecutor's subpoena of the Watergate tapes from President Nixon.[6]

THE NATURE OF LAW

Whether it be labor or another form of law, there are certain basic characteristics of the legal process in this country. Among the most important are the following:

1 *The law is a result of a process of historical evolution.* It is changing constantly, but it also contains many vestiges of the past.

2 *The law is an often paradoxical combination of unchanging principles and common-sense adjustments to changing conditions.*[7]

3 *The role of judges in making the law what it really is at any given time is very important.* In fact, judges may read into the law very different meanings than those of the parties who sought or even drafted the legislation itself.[8]

4 *Legal thinking is essentially classification (i.e., a process of inclusion and exclusion) and analogy.* What may be legal behavior for one type of organization (like a union) may be illegal behavior for another (like a corporation). Alternatively, what may be legal in one industry may be illegal in another. Much of the practice of law involves determining into what category a particular event falls and then looking up the rule that applies to it. When there is a question regarding classification, the issue is likely to be settled by argument using analogy (i.e., this situation is very like another situation and should therefore be treated as the other was treated).[9]

5 *Our system of law places considerable reliance on advocacy, or the adversary system, as a method of jurisprudence.* Rather than the court itself (i.e., the government) investigating a dispute or alleged violation of the law (in order to determine the truth), each side brings its own advocates (usually attorneys, lawyers) and witnesses. The court hears each side and attempts to determine the case on the record that is compiled. Elsewhere in the world much more reliance is placed on active investigation by officers of the court to get at the facts. Surprisingly, in the United States many federal administrative agencies, especially the NLRB, operate much like courts abroad, in that the agency investigates the dispute itself.

6 *Law may be divided into two categories: substantive and procedural.* Substantive law involves rules about topics, such as what the minimum wage is to

---

[6] Leon Jaworski, *The Right and the Power* (New York: Simon and Schuster, 1977), p. 175.

[7] Oliver Wendell Holmes, Jr., *The Common Law* (Boston: Little, Brown, 1938, first published 1881).

[8] John R. Commons, *Legal Foundations of Capitalism* (Madison, Wis.: The University of Wisconsin Press, 1957, first published 1922).

[9] Harold J. Berman and William R. Greiner, *The Nature and Functions of Law,* 3d ed. (New York: Foundation Press, 1972).

be. Procedural law includes rules about how things are to be done. Procedural law includes such matters as rules of pleadings, process, evidence, jurisdiction, rulings, and appeals. Ordinarily we are much more interested in substantive law than in procedural law, but the latter can be very important, as when cases are dismissed because of procedural irregularities (so-called technicalities). An undue regard for the niceties of procedure is called "legalism," a term that suggests a legal system more interested in its own activities than in justice for citizens.[10] In recent years charges have been made that labor relations law has become increasingly legalistic.[11]

7 *There are two broad standards in American law: (1) specific rules, and (2) equity (i.e., adherence to generally accepted principles).* Detailed rules arise from legislation and court decisions. The equity standard is applied by courts where rules are lacking. Most labor litigation is decided via detailed rules, but issues of equity sometimes arise.

THE DEVELOPMENT OF LABOR LAW

Unions as Conspiracies   As early as the first decade of the 1800s, unions had gained enough importance in some trades to cause employers to go to courts for relief from union activities. In 1806 Philadelphia shoemakers' employers charged that unions were conspiracies to do them harm, and as such, that unions were illegal combinations. The court agreed and was followed by other courts in some 17 trials between 1806 and 1842. While unions continued to operate in this period, the courts, employing the common-law doctrine of conspiracy (imported from Great Britain), often found the unions' very existence to be in violation of law.[12]

In 1842 a Massachusetts case changed this. Chief Justice Lemuel Shaw of the Massachusetts Supreme Judicial Court ruled that a union was not per se an illegal conspiracy. For a union to be in violation of the law, the court ruled that it must be shown that the union's objectives or the means it was employing were illegal (*Commonwealth v. Hunt*). This decision did not put an end to conspiracy trials against labor unions,[13] but it did begin the process of legalizing their existence and activities. Furthermore, as the nineteenth century continued, juries became less willing to convict unions of conspiracy charges, and the value of the legal doctrine of conspiracy to employers declined.[14]

The Labor Injunction   In 1895 the Supreme Court of the United States upheld the issuance of an injunction by a federal court against Eugene Debs

[10] Judith N. Shklar, *Legalism* (Cambridge, Mass.: Harvard University Press, 1964).
[11] Douglas V. Brown, "Legalism and Industrial Relations in the United States," *Proceedings* of the Industrial Relations Research Association, 1970, pp. 2–11.
[12] John R. Commons and Eugene A. Gilmore, *A Documentary History of American Industrial Society* (Cleveland: A. H. Clark, 1910).
[13] Edwin E. Witte, "Early American Labor Cases," *Yale Law Journal*, 35, 1926, p. 827.
[14] Benjamin J. Taylor and Fred Whitney, *Labor-Relations Law*, 3d ed. (Englewood Cliffs, N.J.: Prentice-Hall, 1979), pp. 22–23.

and the American Railway Union in the Pullman strike. The injunction had been sought by the attorney general of the United States on grounds of interference with the delivery of the mail by train. In the years thereafter, labor injunctions were commonly issued. Prior to 1931, some 1845 injunctions were issued by state and federal courts in labor disputes.[15]

The injunction was a court order to an individual or an organization to cease certain activities (or, conversely, but much less frequently in practice, to perform certain activities). Failure to obey the order rendered the person or organization subject to summary punishment for contempt of court. The labor injunction was, therefore, a very powerful legal tool, and one which, unlike the conspiracy charges, involved no need for a lengthy, and possibly unsuccessful, trial by jury.

When union organizers appeared at a plant, or a strike was threatened, employers would send lawyers to a court seeking an injunction. The employers argued that irreparable harm was threatened to the company as a result of the union activity, and they sought an order to the union and its activists to cease their efforts. Often the process of seeking an injunction was full of abuses. For example, injunctions were issued on a "John Doe" basis, i.e., against no one in particular but anyone in general, even persons not involved in the dispute itself. Injunctions also sometimes made acts illegal that otherwise were legal. Finally, injunctions were commonly issued without giving their objects any chance to be heard by the judge issuing the order.

The Yellow-Dog Contract   The labor injunction was not the only legal tool used by management to oppose unions. Another such tool was a contract between the workers and the employer, by which the workers bound themselves not to become members of a union while they worked for the company. This sort of contract was labeled by the unions a "yellow-dog" contract, because, they said, only a yellow dog would sign it. The combination of the labor injunction and the yellow-dog contract became a virtually insurmountable barrier for the unions.

In 1917 the Supreme Court of the United States not only upheld the legality of the yellow-dog contract, but permitted federal courts to issue injunctions to enforce it (*Hitchman Coat Company v. Mitchell*). The result was that employers could insist that workers sign a contract not to join a union, or they would be fired, and the federal courts would enforce the contract by issuing injunctions against union organizers who tried to persuade workers to join the union and thereby violate the contract.

The Antitrust Laws   In 1890 the Congress passed the Sherman Antitrust Act, and employers found in this statute a new weapon against union activity. The law made combinations in restraint of trade illegal. Presumably

---

[15] Edwin E. Witte, *The Government in Labor Disputes* (New York: McGraw-Hill, 1932), p. 234.

aimed against big corporations, the "trusts," the Sherman Act was soon applied against union activities. The advantage of the act was that it provided for the issuance of injunctions for enforcement, with additional provisions for fines, jail terms, and treble (i.e., tripled) damages for violations of the act.

In 1902 the United Hatters, an AFL union, undertook to organize Loewe and Company, a hat manufacturer located in Danbury, Connecticut. A strike against the company failed, and so the union turned to a product boycott. The boycott was effective enough to cause the company to file suit under the Sherman Act. In 1908 the U.S. Supreme Court found against the union and ordered a judgment of $252,000 against the union and its members, an enormous sum for those days (*Loewe v. Lawlor*, or, more commonly, *Danbury Hatters*).

This and the *Hitchman* decision constituted the high-water mark of the federal courts' intervention against union activities. During World War I the unions, with Presidential support, gained members, but they lost these gains completely in the aftermath of the war. The 1920s were a largely antiunion period, buttressed by legal support.

MAJOR LABOR LAWS

After the First World War, Congress became increasingly involved in labor relations through the passage of legislation. Table 4-3 lists the major pieces of legislation that have affected the private sector in the United States. These statutes regulate union organization and collective bargaining. It is interesting that the last three acts listed were passed in 1935, 1947, and 1959, at 12-year intervals from each other. The year 1971 passed without a major piece of legislation, and there is no indication of the immediate likelihood of further major legislation.

Table 4-3 lists the acts by their general description and includes the designation of the congressional sponsors of the bill where the designation is widely used. Thus, the Labor Management Relations Act of 1947 was cosponsored by Senator Taft and Representative Hartley and is customarily referred to as the Taft-Hartley Act. Of the five acts listed in Table 4-3, only the Norris-LaGuardia Act applies to all private industry. The Railway Labor Act applies to the railway and airline industries. The National Labor Relations Act (NLRA) and the acts that amended it (Taft-Hartley and Landrum-Griffin) apply to the private sector excluding airlines and railways.

TABLE 4-3 MAJOR FEDERAL LEGISLATION DEALING WITH LABOR RELATIONS

1926	Railway Labor Act
1932	Anti-Injunction Act (Norris-LaGuardia Act)
1935	National Labor Relations Act (Wagner Act)
1947	Labor Management Relations Act (Taft-Hartley Act)
1959	Labor Management Reporting and Disclosure Act (Landrum-Griffin Act)

The Railway Labor Act Following a particularly difficult strike, railway unions and the carriers cooperated in developing legislation that was enacted by Congress in 1926. This and the passage of the health-care amendments to the Taft-Hartley Act in 1974 are the only times in U.S. history when such co-operation has occurred. Ordinarily, labor legislation has been passed in an atmosphere of extreme conflict. For example, in 1935 employers bitterly opposed the NLRA, and in 1947 the unions labeled the Taft-Hartley Act a "slave labor bill" and vowed to get it repealed.

Collective bargaining under the Railway Labor Act differs in several important respects from that which was later to be established under the National Labor Relations Act. There are three fundamental differences. First, whether or not an obligation exists between the employer and the union to bargain about a specific issue is determined on a matter-by-matter basis, not, as under the National Labor Relations Act, on the basis of a broad statement (specifically, "wages, hours, and conditions of work") in the law. Second, arbitration of grievances is statutory rather than on the basis of the collective bargaining agreement between the employer and the union. Third, policies under the Railway Labor Act are interpreted not by an administrative agency of government (like the National Labor Relations Board) but by the federal courts. State courts may also be involved in deciding disputes between airlines or railways and the unions, but only in order to apply the federal law.[16]

The Railway Labor Act is an extensive piece of legislation. Among its major provisions are mechanisms for dealing with labor disputes. Grievances can be submitted to the National Railway Adjustment Board. An unresolved grievance may go to an arbitrator appointed by the National Mediation Board. Under the act, therefore, arbitration is paid for by the government. Elsewhere in American labor relations, the parties bear this financial cost. As a partial result of the parties' facing no costs, the arbitration mechanism of the Railway Labor Act has had tremendous backlogs.

Disputes over the negotiation of collective bargaining agreements are subject to a different set of procedures. These provisions may best be presented in the fashion of an outline:

Collective Bargaining Under the Railway Labor Act

Scope

1 Since 1926, all railroads and subsidiaries; since 1936, all U.S. flag air carriers that operate within or from the United States.

---

[16] Henry H. Perritt, Jr., "Control of Economic Activity under the Railway Labor Act," in *Strikes, Stoppages and Boycotts 1980* (New York: Practicing Law Institute, 1980). See also National Mediation Board, *The National Mediation Board at Fifty* (Washington, D.C.: U.S. Government Printing Office, 1985).

2 All employees and subordinate officials as defined by the Interstate Commerce Commission.

3 Airline pilots specifically included.

Purposes

1 Avoid interruptions to interstate commerce.

2 Protect employee and employer freedom of self-organization and representation.

3 Provide prompt, peaceful settlement of major and minor disputes.

Negotiation

1 30 days' written notice of intended changes required.

2 Conferences to be held within 10 days after notice.

3 Strikes not permitted during these conferences or for 10 days after conferences are terminated.

Mediation

1 Either party may request mediation from the National Mediation Board after direct negotiations have begun and failed or there is a refusal to negotiate.

2 NMB may impose mediation in the case of a "labor emergency" without a request from either party.

3 The status quo (no strike and no change in conditions) is preserved during mediation.

4 No prescribed time limit or cutoff for mediation.

Arbitration

1 If mediation fails, NMB must proffer voluntary arbitration.

2 If arbitration is accepted, the award made is final and binding.

3 If either party refuses, NMB withdraws from the case and the status quo is preserved for a 30-day "cooling-off" period.

Emergency

Statutory Provisions

1 President of United States may set up an Emergency Board if:

a No settlement is reached under the foregoing provisions.

b The NMB judges the dispute could "threaten substantially to interrupt interstate commerce to a degree such as to deprive any section of the country of essential transportation service" and so informs the President.

2 Emergency Board investigates and makes recommendation only—not binding.

3 Creation preserves status quo for up to 60 days:
a 30 days maximum for board to submit report.
b 30 days after report.

Presidential Action (Nonstatutory)

1 Convince parties to accept Emergency Board recommendations or his own recommendations.
2 Seek special legislation from Congress.

Some provisions of the Railway Labor Act anticipated those of the NLRA. For example, management was not to interfere with labor in its choice of representatives and vice versa. Also, "the majority of any craft or class of employees" was to determine a representative for all that craft or class. Finally, the determination of which union should represent a class of workers is the responsibility of the National Mediation Board, by means of a secret-ballot election or other appropriate method. But this does not mean that the law promotes union organization. For example, in 1987, Delta Air Lines, which is largely nonunion, purchased Western Airlines, which was largely unionized. The unions at Western attempted to block the acquisition by charging that it would extinguish the unions' representation rights and nullify their contracts with Western. But Supreme Court Justice Sandra Day O'Connor permitted the acquisition to go ahead.[17]

Unlike the later NLRA, however, the Railway Labor Act permitted penalties to be assessed against carriers or unions not following the requirements of the act. Under the NLRA the courts have held for only *remedial*, not punitive, actions. Thus, a company that violates the NLRA (or Taft-Hartley, which amended the NLRA) can be ordered to make restitution of damages caused others by its acts, but cannot be fined for its illegal actions as a punishment. Under the NLRA, the only time a penalty may be assessed is for a willful failure to cooperate in investigations or proceedings under the act.

Under the Railway Labor Act unions are granted a wider range of activities directed against employers than under the NLRA. For example, unions are allowed by the Railway Labor Act to picket employers who are not directly involved in a labor dispute in order to try to force the noninvolved companies to bring pressure on directly involved employers to settle the dispute. When the Maine Central Railroad decided to abolish the jobs of 300 of the 400 members of the Brotherhood of Maintenance of Ways Employees (BMWE), the union decided to picket other railways which interchanged traffic with the Maine Central. This action, labeled secondary picketing, would be illegal under the NLRA, but the Supreme Court found it to be legal under the Railway Labor Act.[18]

---

[17] *Teamsters v. Western Airlines, Inc.*, U.S. Supreme Court, A-716, Apr. 1, 1987.
[18] *Burlington Northern Railway Company v. Brotherhood of Maintenance of Way Employees*, U.S. Supreme Court, No. 86–39, Apr. 28, 1987.

The Norris-LaGuardia Act   The Norris-LaGuardia Act was the first of several statutes enacted in the 1930s in which Congress actively favored union organization and collective bargaining. The act began with a statement by which the public policy of the United States was declared as follows:

> Whereas under prevailing economic conditions, developed with the aid of governmental authority for owners of property to organize in corporate...forms of ownership association, the individual unorganized worker is commonly helpless ...wherefore...it is necessary that he have full freedom of association...for the purpose of collective bargaining or other mutual aid or protection....

Therefore, the law established a series of limitations on the rights of federal courts to issue injunctions and provided a series of procedural steps that must be followed prior to issuing an injunction. The most important procedural requirement was that a hearing be held to determine whether or not an injunction should be issued. At this hearing the union could challenge the alleged need for an injunction. The procedure has been especially effective in reducing the use of the labor injunction in the years since 1932. The act also made unenforceable in the federal courts the yellow-dog contract, which then passed from the labor relations scene.

The National Labor Relations Act   The National Labor Relations Act was passed in 1935. It is the most important single piece of labor-management relations legislation. It established the basic obligations of companies in dealing with unions and also established the National Labor Relations Board, a federal administrative agency, to adjudicate and enforce the law. So significant is this statute and its various amendments that the following two chapters deal with it in detail.

The Landrum-Griffin Act   A union exercises considerable power, potentially, over the persons it represents, both its members and nonmembers. The legal source of this power is the provision of the National Labor Relations Act which provides that a union selected by the majority of employees in a bargaining unit shall be the sole, or exclusive, representative of all the employees. An American union, therefore, does not legally represent only its own members. The right, or obligation, of a union to represent all employees in a bargaining unit delegates to the union the authority to take actions that will substantially affect the welfare of individual employees. Among these actions are such things as processing or not processing grievances, calling strikes, and deciding to accept one type of wage-and-benefit offer in collective bargaining rather than another.

Because a union can and does exercise authority over employees, there has grown up in the United States a substantial body of law about how that authority can be exercised. Underlying this body of law is an analogy which seems to view the relation of an employee to the union which represents him or her as similar to the relation of a citizen to the government. The rights conveyed by law to the individual with respect to the union are therefore somewhat similar to those conveyed to the citizen with respect to the government.

In 1959, the Landrum-Griffin Act was passed as an amendment to the Taft-Hartley Act. The Landrum-Griffin Act made some changes in the provisions of Taft-Hartley which applied to the relations of employers and unions, but it also placed restrictions on the activities of unions with respect to the people they represent. These provisions of the act are the result of a public debate and a congressional review of the internal affairs of unions in which the central issue was the impact of the union on the freedom of the worker. Title I of the act is entitled a "Bill of Rights" for union members. It provides that every member of a labor organization is to have certain enumerated rights and privileges. Included are the following:

- Equal rights to nominate candidates for union elections, attend membership meetings, and vote on union business
- Freedom of speech and assembly in and out of union meeting
- Right to sue in court against the union (but prior to initiating a suit union members must exhaust reasonable hearing procedures within the union)
- Right to have a copy of the collective bargaining agreement with the employer that directly affects the union member

Furthermore, the law provides that dues and initiation fees of a local union can be increased only by a secret ballot of the members.[19]

The law also establishes procedural safeguards for union members. No member may be disciplined by a union without being served with specific written charges, given a reasonable time to prepare a defense, and afforded a full and fair hearing by the union. Final judgment remains, however, within the union. Usually the final step in an internal disciplinary procedure in a union is an appeal by the member to the general president of the national union or to its general executive board. The United Auto Workers, virtually alone among American unions, provides for a final appeal to an outside, independent panel.[20] In about one-fourth of cases, the panel, called the public review board, has overruled the union's decision.

This provision of the law has generated some interesting court cases. One in particular found its way to the Supreme Court. George Hardeman, a boilermaker, was a member of the International Brotherhood of Boilermakers Lo-

---

[19] Janice R. Bellace and Alan D. Berkowitz, *The Landrum-Griffin Act: Twenty Years of Federal Protection of Union Members' Rights* (Philadelphia: The Wharton School, University of Pennsylvania, 1979). See also Clark Kerr, "Unions and Union Leaders of Their Own Choosing," *The Next Twenty Years in Industrial Relations* (Cambridge, Mass.: MIT, 1958).

[20] Jack Stieber, *Democracy and Public Review: An Analysis of the UAW Public Review Board* (Santa Barbara, Calif.: Center for the Study of Democratic Institutions, 1960). See also "Union Power to Discipline Members who Resign," *Harvard Law Review*, 86:8, 1973, pp. 1536–1569.

cal Lodge 112. On October 3, 1960, he went to the union hiring hall to see Herman Wise, business manager of the local lodge and the official responsible for referring workers for jobs. Hardeman had talked to a friend of his, an employer who had promised to ask for him by name for a job in the vicinity. He sought assurance from Wise that he would be referred for the job. When Wise refused to make a definite commitment, Hardeman threatened violence if no work was forthcoming in the next few days.

On October 4 Hardeman returned to the hiring hall and waited for a referral. None was forthcoming. The next day, in his words, he "went to the hall...and waited from the time the hall opened until we had the trouble. I tried to make up my mind what to do, whether to sue the local or Wise or beat hell out of Wise, and then I made up my mind." When Wise came out of his office to go to a local job site, as required by his duties as business manager, Hardeman handed him a copy of a telegram asking for Hardeman by name. As Wise was reading the telegram, Hardeman began punching him in the face.

Hardeman was tried for this conduct on charges of creating dissension and working against the interest and harmony of the local lodge and of threatening and using force to restrain an officer of the local lodge from properly discharging the duties of his office. The trial committee found him "guilty as charged," and the local lodge sustained the finding and voted his expulsion for an indefinite period. Internal union review of this action, instituted by Hardeman, modified neither the verdict nor the penalty.

Five years later, Hardeman sued the union, alleging that it had violated the Landrum-Griffin Act by denying him a full and fair hearing in the union's disciplinary proceedings. A federal district court in Alabama found the union guilty, and a jury awarded Hardeman damages of $152,150. The Supreme Court reversed the decision. The question, said the Court, was "whether the evidence in the union disciplinary proceeding was sufficient to support a finding of guilt." And, the Court concluded, "We think there is no question that the charges were adequately supported."[21]

In the Hardeman case, the courts ultimately upheld the validity of the union's actions. But in other instances, violations of the law have been found. For example, on December 2, 1976, Dave Newman, a steward in Local 1101 of the Communications Workers, was removed from his post after he had condemned the leadership's tactics at a membership meeting. Newman called for a nationwide strike unless the telephone company agreed to a 32-hour work week at 40 hours' pay and no layoffs. This position by an official of the union was at variance with the official position of the union, and so Newman was removed from his position as a union official, but not as an employee of the telephone company. Newman sued the union, seeking reinstatement. After lengthy litigation a federal district court ordered Newman reinstated as a steward. The judge held that the views of the local union's

---

[21] *Boilermakers v. Hardeman*, 123 U.S. 516 (1971).

president—that no member could serve as a union steward without renouncing the right to express opposition to the local's policies—constituted a violation of the Landrum-Griffin Act.[22]

Other sections of the Landrum-Griffin Act deal with trusteeships and union elections. A trusteeship involves a process by which a national union sets aside the duly elected officers of a local union and appoints trustees to administer the local's affairs and finances. Ordinarily, the trusteeship power is vested in the general president of a national union (or the general executive board) by the constitution of the union. The trusteeship provision of the constitution of one major national union reads as follows:

> For the purpose of correcting corruption or financial malpractice, assuring the performance of collective bargaining agreements or other duties of a bargaining representative, restoring democratic procedures, or otherwise carrying out the legitimate objectives of the international union, including the observances of the ritual, obligation, laws, rules or decisions of the organization or its duly constituted authorities, [the general president] shall have full power to suspend or remove such local officers, suspend or revoke charters of such local unions or place such local unions and their officers and members under international supervision.

There was evidence submitted to Congress of the abuse of this procedure by certain national unions. They were accused of looting the treasuries of local unions and suppressing democracy in the locals. To prevent such abuses, Congress included in the act limitations on the application of the trusteeship's power.

The act requires national unions to hold elections at intervals of not more than 5 years and locals to hold them at not more than 3-year intervals. These provisions were intended to see that union officers did not perpetuate themselves in office indefinitely, as a few had done, by not calling elections. Incidentally, when the law was passed, many local union officials who ran for election each year successfully persuaded their members to extend their term of office to 3 years on the grounds that Congress favored a 3-year term. The act also provides safeguards regarding the fair conduct of elections. Charges that union elections were unfairly conducted can be filed with the Secretary of Labor of the United States. If an investigation indicates that the election was improper, the Secretary may invalidate the election and cause a new one to be held. There has not been great use of this power by the Secretary. Only a relatively few national elections have been rerun. By far the largest case of a court-ordered rerun was the election in the United Mine Workers in 1972, in which hundreds of government personnel supervised balloting in 1200 local unions at a cost of several million dollars to the government.

The act provides safeguards for the handling of union funds by union officers, including bonding requirements. Finally, unions are required to file periodic reports with the Bureau of Labor Management Reports of the De-

---

[22] *Newman et al. v. Communication Workers Local 1101*, 597 F.2d 833 (1979).

partment of Labor regarding the internal operations and finances of the unions. These files are open to the public and have become an excellent source of information and research data about unions.

The law as it applies to the relationship of employees and unions makes some important distinctions. One is that although the union represents all employees in a bargaining unit, it may apply discipline under its bylaws only to those employees who are members of the union. Thus, if union members decide to work during a strike called by the union or to violate a rule against banking too much in extra earnings under an incentive pay plan, the union may take action against them according to its own internal procedures. The courts will, of course, look over the union's shoulder, so to speak, to be sure that the procedures used are legal. But some researchers believe that allowing the union to discipline its members unduly restricts the freedom of the individual. In particular, some observers wish to permit employees to resign from union membership when the employees are in substantial disagreement with a union policy and thereby avoid fines or other possible disciplinary action by the union.[23]

Further, the union member is in a sense subject to two sets of rules, both of which the union is involved in enforcing. One set involves the bylaws of the local union and the constitution of the national union of which it is a part, if any. A second set of rules encompasses those created by the collective bargaining agreement between the union and the employer. This twofold system of rules has been referred to as the process of "dual governance" in unions.[24]

Are unions democratic enough? It is sometimes said that unions are probably less democratic than governmental units. But this view ignores important differences between unions and governmental units. For example, an employee who wishes to escape union discipline may resign from the union. A citizen cannot escape the law of a municipality by resigning from it. Even where there is a union security clause in the collective bargaining agreement (see Chapter 16), an employee's obligations to the union do not ordinarily extend beyond a willingness to pay dues and assessments as uniformly levied on all members of the union. Thus, it is possible to be represented by a union and yet be free of obligations to it to a greater extent than to governmental units.

On the other hand, the internal processes of unions are not subject to the full range of procedural safeguards that exist for citizens in their dealings with government, nor are the processes under a collective bargaining agreement (for example, the grievance arbitration procedure, see Chapter 12) subject to the full requirements of due process as present in our courts.

---

[23] Harry H. Wellington, "Union Fines and Workers' Rights," *Yale Law Journal*, 85:8, July 1976, pp. 1022–1059.

[24] Alice H. Cook, "Dual Governance in Unions: A Tool for Analysis," *Industrial and Labor Relations Review*, 15:3, April 1962, pp. 323–349.

The internal decision-making procedures of unions are subject to considerable regulation and therefore compare favorably with democratic procedures in governmental units. Elections must be held at specified times and conducted in a specified manner. This does not prevent abuses from sometimes occurring in some unions, just as abuses of the governmental political process occur that sometimes require redress in the courts or in Congress.

Other Legislation

The legislation listed in Table 4-3 is the major federal legislation dealing with labor relations, but it is not the only legislation that has an effect on labor and management. There are many statutes that have done so, and it is not possible to list them all here. However, in order to provide some familiarity with the types and range of these statutes, following is a list that includes dates of enactment, titles, and brief descriptions of the more significant pieces of legislation:

- *The Antikickback Law (Copeland Act)* makes it a crime to induce or accept payments from workers ("kickbacks") for getting them jobs on construction financed with federal funds. (1934)
- *The Interstate Transportation of Strikebreakers Act (Byrnes Act)* makes it a crime to transport or travel in interstate commerce for the purpose of interfering by force or threats with peaceful picketing by employees or with other rights of employees. (1936)
- *The Prevailing Wages Law (Davis-Bacon Act)* requires that on all federal and federally assisted construction (of above a certain size) the wages and fringe benefits paid to workers shall not be less than those found by the Secretary of Labor to be prevailing in the area. (1936)
- *The Overtime Law (Walsh-Healy Act)* requires payment of overtime at one and a half times the base hourly rate for all work in excess of 8 hours per day on federal nonconstruction contracts. (1936)
- *The Fair Labor Standards Act* requires all private employers subject to federal law (and above a certain small size) to pay at least a minimum level of wages ($3.35 per hour in 1981) to employees and to pay one and a half times the worker's regular hourly wage for work beyond 40 hours in a week to certain categories of employees. Employees subject to the overtime provision are called "nonexempt" employees, and those not covered are called "exempt" employees.[25] (1938)
- *The Farm Labor Contractor Registration Act* requires persons serving as contractors for migrant farm laborers to register with the federal government and to meet certain standards. (1963)
- *The Equal Pay Act* provides that employers cannot pay different rates of pay for the same job on the basis of sex or race. (1963)

[25] Rudolf A. Oswald, "Fair Labor Standards," in Joseph P. Goldberg et al., *Federal Policies and Worker Status Since the Thirties* (Madison, Wis.: Industrial Relations Research Association, 1976), pp. 107–134.

- *The Civil Rights Act, Title VII,* concerns employment practices and makes it illegal for an employer to discriminate against any person because of race, color, religion, sex, or national origin. Similar provisions apply to unions and employment agencies. The Equal Employment Opportunity Commission (EEOC) is established by the act to enforce Title VII. (1964) (Substantial amendments were made in 1972, and Title VII was renamed the Equal Employment Opportunity Act of 1972.)
- *The Services Contract Act (McNamara-O'Hara Act)* requires payment of one and a half times base hourly rate for all hours of work in excess of either 8 hours per day or 40 hours per week in any federal contract for services not covered by Walsh-Healy. (1965)
- *The Age Discrimination Act* makes it illegal for an employer to discriminate in employment practices among employees for reasons of age. It is intended to protect the rights of older workers. In 1978, the act was amended to make it unlawful for a private employer to force workers to retire before age 70. (1968)
- *The Health Industry Amendments to Taft-Hartley* extend coverage of the Taft-Hartley Act to approximately 1.4 million employees working in private nonprofit hospitals and apply special notice and mediation procedures designed to minimize work stoppages in contract disputes at all health-care institutions (except publicly operated hospitals). (1974)
- *The Employees Retirement Income Security Act (ERISA)* protects the pensions of employees of private concerns, in part by insuring pensions against business failure. (1974)
- *The Labor-Management Cooperation Act* encourages the formation of labor-management problem-solving groups. It also amends Taft-Hartley to permit such joint programs to be funded by employer payments made pursuant to a collective bargaining agreement. Previously, U.S. courts, citing Taft-Hartley, had barred unions from the management of such funds. (1978)

The Labor-Management Cooperation Act reflects the increasing emphasis being placed on cooperation between management and labor, rather than the emphasis of previous statutes on settling disputes. The purposes of the law are:

(1) to improve communication between representatives of labor and management;

(2) to provide workers and employers with opportunities to study and explore new and innovative joint approaches to achieving organizational effectiveness;

(3) to assist workers and employers in solving problems of mutual concern not susceptible to resolution within the collective bargaining process;

(4) to study and explore ways of eliminating potential problems which reduce the competitiveness and inhibit the economic development of plant area or industry;

(5) to enhance the involvement of workers in making decisions that affect their working lives;

(6) to expand and improve working relationships between workers and managers; and

(7) to encourage free collective bargaining by establishing continuing mechanisms for communication between employers and their employees through federal assistance to the formation and operation of labor-management committees.

• *Bankruptcy legislation* was passed by Congress to preserve collective bargaining agreements from being set aside by the courts when a company declared bankruptcy. The Supreme Court had permitted a company to cancel its agreement with a union as soon as it filed for reorganization under the bankruptcy laws. Soon several companies had availed themselves of the opportunity afforded by bankruptcy to avoid collective bargaining contract obligations. Congress then passed a law requiring a company that files for bankruptcy to bargain with a union over any changes it wants to make in the contract. (1984)

EQUAL EMPLOYMENT OPPORTUNITY

Title VII of the Civil Rights Act has had a special impact on labor relations.[26] In response to suits by blacks and women's groups, the courts have found in many instances that employers and unions, together and separately, have discriminated against minority groups and/or women. The companies involved have sometimes settled the court cases in advance of decisions by agreeing to certain conditions. At other times the courts have fashioned remedies to rectify past discrimination and to attempt to prevent it in the future.

Various types of actions have been directed by the courts. Awards of back pay to people who were discriminated against have been common. Courts have sometimes established preferential hiring lists for minorities, or the courts have virtually taken control of apprenticeship programs to see that minorities are recruited and trained for skilled jobs.

Impact on Seniority Systems   A special group of problems has attended the discriminatory impact of seniority systems established by collective bargaining agreements. The maintenance of separate seniority lists for blacks and whites has been found illegal, but separate departmental seniority, under which blacks have been confined to certain departments, has in some cases been found to result in restricting minorities to lower-paying jobs. The rearrangement or merger of seniority districts in the basic steel industry to attempt to eliminate such discrimination has been an especially important result of civil rights legislation.[27]

[26] Arthur B. Smith, Jr., "The Impact on Collective Bargaining of Equal Employment Opportunity Remedies," *Industrial and Labor Relations Review*, 28:3, April 1975, pp. 376–394.
[27] David Ziskind, "Retroactive Seniority: A Remedy for Hiring Discrimination," Industrial Relations Research Association, *Proceedings* of the Spring Meetings, May 1976, pp. 480–489.

In 1977 the U.S. Supreme Court considered the degree to which Title VII required changes in seniority systems. The specific case which the court reviewed involved practices under collective bargaining agreements in the trucking industry. In that industry it has been common for many years, going back to before the passage of the Civil Rights Act in 1964, to have separate bargaining units for city drivers and for over-the-road, or long-distance, drivers. The over-the-road drivers ordinarily get better pay and benefits. As a result of the dual structure of bargaining units, a driver who wished to transfer from city driving to an over-the-road job had to give up his or her entire seniority and start at the bottom of the list in the over-the-road unit. The federal government and a group of minority persons challenged this practice in court, arguing that it tended to perpetuate a pattern of racial discrimination by causing minority employees in the city-driver units to stay out of the largely nonminority over-the-road units in order not to give up their seniority.

The Supreme Court, however, found that the practice of dual seniority units in the trucking industry was not illegal, even though it did, indeed, perpetuate a system of past racial discrimination. The Court reached this conclusion by finding that when it passed the Civil Rights Act in 1964, Congress had intended to leave existing seniority systems untouched, even "where the employer's pre-Act discrimination resulted in whites having greater existing seniority rights than [blacks]."[28]

In 1982, the Supreme Court broadened the immunity of *bona fide* seniority systems (those without an intent to discriminate). It ruled that the exemption from Title VII of the Civil Rights Act was not limited to seniority systems in place prior to the effective date of the statute. Instead it extends to seniority systems established since the act.[29]

Could a city ignore a *bona fide* seniority system in its labor agreement with a firefighters' local union to preserve the employment of black firefighters who had less seniority than their white counterparts? The city of Memphis did so. The Supreme Court, however, determined that the city had acted illegally, saying that only individual and identifiable victims of real discrimination are entitled to special consideration, not whole classes of people.[30]

Why this continuing concern for protecting the rights of minorities? The answer is that despite progress in racial relations in our country, there is still serious discrimination. In 1984, for example, the Michigan Civil Rights Commission issued a report describing in detail 9 years of harassment suffered by the first black person to be hired into a skilled job at a Michigan steel plant. The welder was ostracized and threatened, and he lived in constant stress and fear. When he complained to management about his treatment by other

---

[28] *T.I.M.E.—D.C., Inc., v. United States, International Brotherhood of Teamsters v. United States* 431 U.S. 324 (1977), and *East Texas Motor Freight System, Inc., v. Rodriguez*, 97 S. Ct. 1891 (1977).
[29] *American Tobacco Company v. Patterson, No. 80–1199*, April 5, 1982.
[30] *Fire Fighters Local 1784 v. Stotts*, 1984.

workers, he was told that management could do nothing about it. A complaint to a government agency finally brought relief via state equal employment opportunity laws.[31]

Impact on Grievance Procedures　A further set of problems with which the courts are now grappling is the effect of civil rights legislation on the collective bargaining relationship. For example, if a group of minority employees decides to disregard the grievance process in the collective bargaining agreement and strike in a dispute over alleged discrimination, does the law protect them from discipline by the employer? A federal appeals court said that it does: "Concerted activity regarding racial discrimination enjoys a special status." The court was reading the Civil Rights Act with the National Labor Relations Act to reach this conclusion. But the Supreme Court disagreed. If the union was fairly representing the minority employees, it said, then they could not go outside the grievance procedure with impunity.[32]

Impact on the NLRA　To what degree should the National Labor Relations Board consider equal employment opportunity in the application of the National Labor Relations Act? For example, should an employer's objection that a union discriminates against women and/or minorities be investigated by the board before it certifies the union as an exclusive collective bargaining representative for the company's employees? In several cases decided in 1977 and 1978, the NLRB held that the U.S. Constitution does not require and the NLRA does not permit the NLRB to withhold certification from unions that allegedly practice racial, sexual, or other discrimination.

A second question involves the obligation which the NLRA imposes on unions to represent all employees fairly. Does this obligation entitle the unions to insist that employers furnish the union with detailed data concerning the demographic composition of the employer's work force? In a series of recent decisions, the NLRB has said that the employers must give the unions otherwise confidential data about hiring practices, applicants for jobs, employees, and the employer's status with respect to the Equal Employment Opportunities Commission.[33]

---

[31] *Michigan Dept. of Civil Rights v. Firestone Steel Products*, Nos. 12190-EM and 15378 EM, May 1984.

[32] *Emporium Capwell Co. v. Western Addition Community Organization*, 420 U.S. 50 (1975).

[33] Betty Southard Murphy, "Today's Concerns," *Proceedings* of the Thirty-Second National Conference on Labor (New York: New York University Press, 1980). The cases cited are *Handy Andy, Inc., Bell and Howell, Co.*, and *Murcel Manufacturing Corp.* with respect to the issue of certification; and *Westinghouse Electric Corp.* and *East Dayton Tool and Die Co.* with respect to the employer's obligation to provide data.

Comparable Worth On average in the United States, women make about 65 percent of the earnings that men receive from their jobs;[34] this figure has increased by an average of about 1 percent per year over the last 5 years. Some of this disparity is explained by the fact that women frequently receive less pay for the same jobs than men receive. This is illegal under both the Equal Pay Act and the Civil Rights Act, Title VII, and perhaps it will be eliminated over time as the laws are more closely adhered to. But the great bulk of the difference in the average rates of pay of men and women lies in two other factors. The first is that women often move in and then out and then back in the labor force again. In this process they forgo training opportunities, promotions, and the accumulation of seniority. Each of these lost opportunities may adversely affect women's earnings as compared with those of men. A major reason why women leave the labor force, of course, is to raise families. Also, many young women, believing that they will work only a short time before quitting to raise families, do not look for jobs with long-term potential that pay good wages. These are factors cited by Nancy Barrett from her research into the behavior of women in the labor market.[35]

These factors are important, but much less so in quantitative terms than another factor: the uneven distribution of women and men among job classifications, or occupations. Over all, women are concentrated in occupations that pay considerably less than occupations in which men predominate. For example, in 1982, clerical workers were 78 percent female, service workers were 52 percent female, teachers were 67 percent female, and textile workers were 72 percent female. During 1982 women made up approximately 43 percent of all persons employed in the United States.[36]

During the 1970s the American labor force grew rapidly, and women made up 57 percent of the growth. The most striking shift in the distribution of the sexes among occupations occurred among managers, where women held 18.5 percent of managerial positions in 1970 and 30.5 percent of managerial positions in 1980.[37] Despite this progress, however, most of the occupations in which women are disproportionately represented are among the

[34] James P. Smith and Michael P. Ward, *Women's Wages and Work in the Twentieth Century* (Santa Monica, Calif.: Rand Corporation Publications Division, 1984). According to these authors the increase in the percentage of women's hourly wages as a percent of men's from 60 to 64 percent (1980 to 1983) was the largest and swiftest gain in this century. See also Bureau of National Affairs, *Daily Labor Report* No. 121, June 22, 1984, p. A-8, where Janet Norwood, Commissioner of the Bureau of Labor Statistics, describes the trend of women's relative pay as up; and U.S. Bureau of the Census, *Statistical Abstract of the United States 1987*, 107th ed. (Washington, D.C., 1986).
[35] Nancy S. Barrett, "Women in the Job Market: Occupations, Earnings and Career Opportunities," in Ralph E. Smith, ed., *The Subtle Revolution: Women at Work* (Washington, D.C.: The Urban Institute, 1979), pp. 31–62.
[36] Earl F. Mellor, "Investigating Earning Differences in Weekly Earnings of Women and Men," in *Monthly Labor Review*, 107:6, June 1984, pp. 20–23.
[37] N. F. Rytina and S. Bianchi, "Occupational Reclassification and Distribution by Gender," *Monthly Labor Review*, 107:3, March 1984, pp. 11–17 (esp. pp. 14 and 13 for the data cited in the text).

lower-paying jobs in the country. The result is that, on average, women earn considerably less than men.

But does this fact demonstrate that there is illegal discrimination against women in the job market? Increasingly, women's organizations insist that it does, and recently some federal court judges have begun to find merit to their argument.

Are women's jobs paid less than men's, on average, not because of differences in the job or skill content of the work, nor because of working conditions, nor because of the availability or nonavailability of persons who can do the work, but simply because most of the people in the jobs are women? This is the issue that lies at the heart of the emerging controversy over what has come to be called the *theory of comparable worth*. According to this theory, jobs should be compensated according to their value to the organization, not according to who holds them. Thus, in companies where floor sweepers (predominantly male) are paid more than clerical workers (predominantly female) the rates of pay should be realigned—the rates of clerical workers might then be higher than those of sweepers. As a practical matter, it often happens that male sweepers in manufacturing plants are represented by labor unions and receive higher pay than clerical workers, who are often unrepresented by unions. But it is hard to argue that the sweepers' jobs are more highly skilled, more valuable to the company, or more difficult to fill than the clerical workers' jobs.

The theory of comparable worth becomes a legal doctrine when it becomes the basis of an assertion that jobs in which women predominate are undervalued because women are in those jobs and that this is discrimination in violation of the law. When this argument has been put to federal courts, the courts have given varying and contradictory answers. Some federal courts have dismissed the comparable worth theory as without merit. But others have not agreed. In August 1980, the Third Circuit Court of Appeals ruled that sex-based wage discrimination is illegal under Title VII of the Civil Rights Act even when the jobs in question are different from one another. The suit involved was brought not by a women's organization, per se, but by the International Union of Electrical Workers against Westinghouse Electric Company.[38]

Other litigation has involved public employees. In a case involving some 15,000 employees of Washington State, the Ninth Circuit Court of Appeals in effect required the state to equalize pay among men and women in jobs that require equivalent skill, education, and effort, even where the jobs are different.[39] Other cases have not been as favorable to the concept of comparable worth. The Supreme Court held in another case from Washington State that nursing teachers complaining that they were paid less than other teach-

---

[38] *IUE v. Westinghouse*, 631 F.2d 1094 (1980).

[39] "Washington State Employees to Get First Comparable Worth Pay Raises," Bureau of National Affairs, *Daily Labor Report* No. 114, June 13, 1984, pp. A6-A7.

ers at the University of Washington had to show they were victims of sex discrimination, not simply paid less because of market forces.[40]

It appears that litigation and legislative contests over comparable worth will continue. In November 1984, six members of Congress (both Senators and Representatives) asked the General Accounting Office (an agency of Congress) to study the federal pay system to determine if there is pay equity among jobs held predominately by women and among those held predominately by men. About 40 percent of the 2 million federal work force are women. Women earn an average of 60 percent of men's earnings in federal jobs.[41]

This action by Congress is significant because an issue like comparable worth often gets significant push to action at the federal level, which sets informal standards for other employers, both state and local governments, and private companies.

Sexual Harassment at Work One of the most difficult problems that many women face in the workplace is the unwelcome attention of male co-workers or supervisors. For many years the problem was largely hidden. But in recent years several surveys, and a generally more candid public discussion of such matters, have brought it into the open. In the spring of 1980, the Equal Employment Opportunity Commission issued guidelines which specified that sexual harassment at work is, in many instances, a violation of Title VII of the Civil Rights Act. Specifically, unwelcome sexual advances become a matter of illegality when the employee's acquiescence is a condition of employment or becomes a basis for employment decisions by the employer or the employer's agent. The guidelines apply to men as well as to women, although it is expected that the primary application will be to women. Complaints by injured parties can be made to the commission, and if the matter cannot be worked out with the employer, the commission may go to court against the employer.

Affirmative Action Statute law is not the only source of protection of the rights of minorities, women, and other groups in the workplace. The federal government, and some state and local governments, also have imposed obligations of an affirmative nature on companies which do business with the governments. Affirmative obligations are distinguished from the requirements placed on employers by the Civil Rights Act and other statutes in that the statutes essentially prohibit discrimination against affected groups, whereas affirmative obligations go beyond nondiscrimination.

Employers with federal government contracts of $50,000 or more and 50 or more employees are obligated to prepare and maintain a written affirmative action program. The plans provide goals and timetables by which the em-

[40] Stephen Wermiel, "High Limit," *Wall Street Journal*, Nov. 27, 1984, p. 12.
[41] Bureau of National Affairs, *Daily Labor Report* No. 226, Nov. 23, 1984, pp. A8-A9.

TABLE 4-4 ELEMENTS OF AN AFFIRMATIVE ACTION PLAN

- Establishment of quantitative (statistical) objectives for representation of women and minorities in all jobs, levels, and functions
- Inclusion of equal opportunity issues in regular management training
- Specific training in equal opportunity, including:
  (a) Knowledge-focused training (i.e., legal issues, company policy, benefits, changes)
  (b) Attitude-focused training
  (c) Behavior-focused training (i.e., training dealing with managerial expectations of behavior with an emphasis on behavior changes in recruiting, selecting, training, work assignment, and career development of employees)

---

ployers will attempt to seek out minority and other target-group persons for hiring into job opportunities or for promotion, training, and similar advancement. Failure to meet the affirmative action obligations may cause companies to be barred from receiving federal contracts. Table 4-4 shows the elements of a typical business affirmative action plan.

Do affirmative action plans discriminate in favor of minorities and women against white males? A white male who was employed at a plant in the South raised this issue in a lawsuit that found its way to the Supreme Court. The United Steelworkers represented employees at the plant. The union and the company had negotiated a new on-the-job training program to replace a prior-experience requirement for entry into better-paying craft jobs in the plant. The objective of the plan was to achieve a representation of blacks in craft jobs equal to the 39 percent representation of blacks in the labor force in the community surrounding the plant. To achieve this, the union and the company agreed to admit blacks and whites to the new training program on a one-to-one basis. At the time the plan was implemented only 1.83 percent of the skilled crafts workers in the plant were minority group members. A white male who failed to be admitted to the program challenged its ratio for white-black admissions. The Supreme Court found that even though neither the company nor the union had been found guilty of discriminating against minorities in regard to the skilled jobs, nonetheless, where the goals and timetables for the purpose of eliminating racial imbalance were voluntarily adopted by the union and the company, the affirmative action plan was legal. In this case the Court seemed to say that goals and timetables for minority advancement were not illegal reverse discrimination, even though some white male employees might thereby be passed over for training and promotion.[42] In cases decided subsequently, the Supreme Court has permitted unions and companies to negotiate affirmative action plans that override seniority when determining which employees are to be laid off in a company that has to reduce its work force.[43] But in other cases the Court has seemed

---

[42] *United Steelworkers of America v. Weber*, 443 U.S. 193 (1979).
[43] *Tangren v. Wackenhut Services, Inc.*, 81 U.S. 1540 (1982).

to rule that too great a dependence on quotas based on race could result in illegal discrimination against white males.

Reverse Discrimination   Reverse discrimination occurs when a minority, woman, or member of another affected group is hired, promoted, transferred, etc., in preference to another person, including a white male, solely on the grounds of the sex, race, age, etc., of the individual who receives the advantage. When an employer gives preferential treatment solely on the basis of sex, race, etc., he or she is in danger of violating the law. The Supreme Court, in a decision involving preference given to racial minorities for admission to medical school, has apparently held that preference given solely on the basis of race is illegal.[44]

From this discussion it should be clear that, in the area of employment practices, Congress and the courts are trying to steer a careful course between protection of the rights of minority members and women, which have long been infringed, and those of the remaining members of the work force.[45] The area of civil rights law is still in a period of rapid change.[46] The protections of the law are being extended to new groups. The answers to such questions as what behavior by an employer or a union is illegal, what sort of evidence is necessary to prove guilt, and what kinds of remedies can be created by the courts are each in continuing evolution.

Law Protecting Other Groups

Racial minorities and women are not the only groups receiving protection from employment discrimination under federal law. Table 4-5 lists the major protected groups and the principal statutes (and dates) which protect them. Many of these statutes, or other policies of the federal government, require not only that an employer not discriminate against members of these groups, but that positive actions be taken to remedy the continuing effects of past discrimination. Thus, firms with federal government contracts are required to take affirmative action with respect to the hiring and promotion of members of protected groups identified in Table 4-5.[47]

The Occupational Safety and Health Act (OSHA) protects the safety and health of workers employed by private industry. It is the most comprehensive piece of industrial safety and health legislation passed anywhere. OSHA's enactment followed decades of cooperative effort between some managements and some unions to improve occupational health and safety.

---

[44] *Bakke v. Regents of the University of California,* 438 U.S. 265 (1978).
[45] Kenneth T. Lopatka, "Developing Concepts in Title VII Law," in L. J. Hausman et al., eds., *Equal Rights and Industrial Relations,* pp. 31–70.
[46] Arthur B. Smith, Jr., "The Law and Equal Employment Opportunity: What's Past Should Not Be Prologue," *Industrial and Labor Relations Review,* 33:4, July 1980, pp. 493–505.
[47] Phyllis A. Wallace, *Black Women in the Labor Force,* Cambridge, Mass.: MIT Press, 1980.

TABLE 4-5 PROTECTED GROUPS UNDER FEDERAL ANTIDISCRIMINATION LAW

• Persons over 40 years of age	Age Discrimination in Employment Act (1967)
• Racial and ethnic minorities	Equal Pay Act (1963)
	Civil Rights Act (1964)
	Equal Employment Opportunity Act (1972)
• Women	Civil Rights Act (1964)
	Equal Employment Opportunity Act (1972)
	Education Act Amendments (Title IX) (1972)
• Handicapped	Rehabilitation Act (1973)
• Vietnam-era veterans	Vietnam-Era Veterans Readjustment Assistance Act (1974)

But it largely replaced the cooperative efforts with a generalized process of regulation by a government agency.

Under OSHA the government establishes standards for workplace health and safety. In the years since its enactment, the government has issued a great number of these standards. Employers have complained vigorously that the standards are in many cases impractical and unduly expensive in application. These complaints have caused some members of Congress to propose legislation restricting the government's authority to impose regulations, especially on small businesses. Responding to this criticism, the Occupational Safety and Health Administration of the Department of Labor, which administers the act, in December 1977 announced plans to revoke more than 1000 job-safety standards which the agency agreed were of little value in protecting worker safety and health.[48] Nonetheless, efforts to further restrict government activities under OSHA continue in the Congress, where they are supported by employer lobbyists and opposed by union lobbyists.

Section 8(f)1 of OSHA gives any employee or union the right to complain to the Secretary of Labor when the employee or the union believes there is a violation of a safety or health standard which threatens physical harm. And if the Secretary believes there are reasonable grounds for the complaint, he or she is required to order a special inspection for the alleged hazard as soon as possible.

These provisions of the act sometimes conflict with employee desires and union behavior on the job. One company tried to comply with OSHA regulations that required persons working over water to wear life jackets by disciplining employees who refused to wear jackets. But the employees did not like the jackets and struck in refusal to wear them. The employer then asked a federal court to order the employees to return to work.[49]

Many industries in the United States have a long tradition of joint management-labor safety committees. And in Europe, safety legislation in

---

[48] "Labor Agency Acts," *The Wall Street Journal*, Dec. 6, 1977.

[49] Leo Teplow, "Comprehensive Safety and Health Measures in the Workplace," in Joseph P. Goldberg et al., eds., *Federal Policies and Worker Status Since the Thirties* (Madison, Wis.: Industrial Relations Research Association, 1976), pp. 209–242.

many countries requires such committees generally and encourages resolution of workplace health and safety problems by these committees. But the American law, OSHA, makes no provision for such committees. The AFL-CIO has recently asked employers to support such committees as an alternative to the excessive government regulation of which the employers complain.[50] The employers have not yet supported that position, however.

The Return of the Antitrust Laws

As was pointed out above, the first part of the twentieth century saw the high-water mark of the use of the antitrust laws against unions. In the 1940s a series of decisions by the Supreme Court virtually granted the unions an exception from the application of the antitrust statutes. But in the 1970s employers again sought to restrict union activities through suits filed under the antitrust laws, and the courts received the suits with considerable sympathy.

In 1975 the Supreme Court considered a case involving the plumbers' union in Dallas, Texas. The union had picketed a general construction contractor, Connel Construction Company, for the purpose of obtaining an agreement that the contractor would subcontract all plumbing and mechanical work only to firms having an agreement with the plumbers' union. The appellate court had upheld the union's action on the grounds that it advanced a legitimate union interest in organizing nonunion subcontractors. But the Supreme Court reversed the appellate court. The Court held that this effort by the plumbers went beyond legitimate union goals and had the effect of restraining competition. Therefore, it was in violation of the antitrust laws, the Court said.[51] In consequence, as the 1980s continue, it has again become common for employers to file antitrust suits against unions, and litigation continues in an effort to define how far the courts will now go in restricting union activity by application of the antitrust laws.

Smarting under the renewed application of the antitrust laws to prohibit certain of their activities, the unions tried to turn the antitrust weapon against employers. In 1974 the Associated General Contractors of California, an employer association with collective bargaining agreements with the carpenters' union, held a seminar in which member companies were told how to operate nonunion. Soon thereafter, the carpenters' unions in California brought suit under the antitrust laws against the AGC charging that AGC was engaged in a conspiracy to undermine and destroy the union. The Ninth Circuit Court of Appeals upheld the unions' complaint, saying that it was virtually the reverse image of the situation that confronted the Supreme Court in the Connel Construction case. Yet the Supreme Court in reviewing the California carpenters' allegations held that "the union's most specific

---

[50] Matt Witt, "Learning Job-Safety and Health from Europe," *The New York Times*, May 5, 1979.
[51] *Connel Construction Company v. Plumbers Local 100*, 421 U.S. 616 (1975).

claims of injury involve matters that are not subject to review under the antitrust laws."[52]

THEORIES OF THE LEGISLATIVE PROCESS

In the preceding pages we charted the development of the major features of American labor relations law. But how should we attempt to understand the process as a whole? Has legal regulation evolved as a logical response to the developing problems of our industrial society? Or does it represent instead a series of historical accidents? There is a surprising degree of dispute among the country's most outstanding scholars with respect to these issues. With respect to labor law, it may be said that the more fundamental the question that is asked, the more uncertain the answer.

Law as the Perfection of Reason The development of American labor law may be viewed as the adjustment of the rules of society to the experience of management and labor in the context of changing economic, social, and political circumstances. Thus, in the 1930s, when companies exploited the workers too much, the government intervened on behalf of the unions by passing first the Norris-LaGuardia Act and then the National Labor Relations Act. Later, when a wave of strikes following World War II demonstrated that unions had become too powerful, Congress enacted Taft-Hartley to restore the balance. When revelations in the late 1950s demonstrated corruption in unions, Congress responded by placing controls on the internal behavior of unions (the Landrum-Griffin Act).

Labor legislation is viewed by the proponents of this theory as the vehicle by which a national labor policy is devised. They believe the process to be largely rational and characterized by public debate and by decisions based on the preponderance of the testimony placed before Congress. The legislative process is conceived as a quasi-judicial process, in which advocates for management and labor make their case and Congress, influenced by an intelligent and informed citizenry, makes its own decision on how best to proceed in the national interest. The procedure is legitimate because it is democratic in nature and is one by which problems are met and solved.[53]

The proponents of this view do not deny that the system has imperfections. They admit that it sometimes is very slow to react, that crises may be necessary to stimulate action,[54] and that as a result the pendulum of the law may swing too far in one direction for a time. But as the nation becomes

---

[52] *Associated General Constructors of California, Inc. v. California State Council of Carpenters,* U.S. Supreme Court No. 81–334, Feb. 22, 1983. See also Bureau of National Affairs, *Daily Labor Report* No. 36, Feb. 22, 1983, pp. AA1-AA2.

[53] David Ziskind, "Standards for Evaluating Labor Legislation," *Cornell Law Quarterly,* 51:3, Spring 1966, pp. 517–518.

[54] Archibald Cox, *Law and the National Labor Policy* (Los Angeles: University of California Press, Institute of Industrial Relations Monograph Series, No. 5, 1960).

aware of an imbalance, the legislative process will respond, and the passage of new statutes will cause the pendulum to return to a moderate position.

The imperfections that exist are believed to be short-term and subject to correction. They do not gainsay the essential rationality of the process. For example, Taylor and Whitney conclude their text on labor law with the observation: "Repeated examination of government regulation of the collective bargaining process is evident.... The policies forthcoming depend and have depended largely upon the public's view of the type of economic system it desires.... The citizen should become more informed...since he will determine the ultimate status of unions."[55] In this observation, written in the 1970s, one can hear the echo of Sir Edward Coke, writing in the early 1600s: "Reason is the life of the law, nay the common law is nothing else but reason.... The law, which is perfection of reason."[56]

Law as the Reflection of the Society   What is most characteristic of the view of the legislative process as one of reason is a rather uncritical attitude toward its results. This view tends to presume that if a problem exists, it will eventually be dealt with in a constructive fashion. But others do not hold this view. Instead, it may be argued that the law is not so much a method of correcting the abuses in society as it is a reflection of those abuses. Legislation is still viewed as a process of reason, but not as one that necessarily results in benign outcomes.

For example, Derek Bok contrasted American labor law with that of several European countries, asking the question "[how did] our labor laws come to take...a shape that is so different from the labor laws in other industrial democracies?" The answer, he concludes, has to do "with the nature of our unions, our employers, and our working people and the peculiar ways in which they organize and deal with one another." The result is a system of law that "permits great flexibility...and provides abundant opportunities for initiative." But "these national traits have also produced a system of labor law that is uniquely hard on the weak, the uneducated, the unorganized and the unlucky."

But these are not, in Bok's view, "haphazard oversights." Instead, "they are part of a long series of...choices that weigh against the weak and the unorganized."[57] Thus, the system is rational but deeply imperfect.

Furthermore, the system is paradoxical. "The pressures engendered by a decentralized, competitive system of labor relations have led to a web of regulation that is highly complex and extremely litigious. As a result, the United States—so identified with free enterprise and so skeptical of bureaucracy—paradoxically emerges with a regulatory system that is much more intricate

---

[55] Taylor and Whitney, *Labor-Relations Law*, pp. 582 and 586.

[56] Sir Edward Coke, *Institutes*, Commentary upon Littleton, First Institute, Section 138.

[57] Derek C. Bok, "Reflections on the Distinctive Character of American Labor Laws," *Harvard Law Review*, 84:6, April 1971, pp. 1458–1460.

and burdensome than that of Sweden, home of welfare socialism."[58] In this view, the legislative process and the law itself are not fundamental devices by which wrongs are righted in society and the weak protected, although law sometimes performs this function. Law is rather a further process, in addition to economic and political means, by which the powerful institutions of society, including business and labor unions, conduct their relations with each other.[59] Labor relations law, rather than establishing the rules of the game, is itself a part of the game.

Law as Accommodation to Pressure Groups   There is yet another theory of legislation and law that departs still further from the conception of law as the perfection of reason. In the place of a rational choice among alternatives, each designed to resolve a problem, this view substitutes the largely political and expedient response to the clash of narrow and parochial interests. The legislation that results is subject to inordinate influence by current events, although the legislation itself may endure for decades. It is often inconsistent with itself, a result of impulsive congressional action.[60] It reflects no underlying consensus about how the country should conduct its labor relations and so is characterized by formal compromises in statutory language, when no underlying agreement exists, a process that "assures unending litigation."[61]

Far from being a process in which management and labor jointly influence Congress to a set of views consistent with their own objectives, "the responsibility of organized management and labor in shaping the legislative framework and in the administration of the statutes is virtually nil; it is confined to making formal and highly extreme public statements."[62] The legislative framework of collective bargaining is now regulated by a highly partisan political process. Politicians enact legislation with little regard for its relation to the actual needs of business and labor, but with great regard for its political consequences.[63] The result is not an intelligent structure of law adapted to the resolution of real problems, but instead a crazy-quilt pattern of regulation that creates as many problems as it solves, and serves little or no constructive function on the whole. "The government is seeking to impose on parties to collective bargaining by statute and administrative rulings a set of standards of conduct which in many respects is highly unrealistic...and leads to impractical and unreal policies and to mass evasion and disrespect."[64] Labor re-

---

[58] Ibid., p. 1460.

[59] John R. Commons and J. B. Andrews, *Principles of Labor Legislation* (New York: Harper, 1927).

[60] Douglas V. Brown and Charles A. Myers, "Historical Evolution," in Joseph Shister, Benjamin Aaron, and Clyde Summers, eds., *Public Policy and Collective Bargaining* (New York: Harper & Row, 1962), pp. 1–27.

[61] John T. Dunlop, "Consensus and National Labor Policy," *Proceedings* of the Industrial Relations Research Association, 1960, p. 6.

[62] Ibid., p. 5.

[63] David R. Mayhew, *Congress: The Electoral Connection* (New Haven: Yale University Press, 1974).

[64] Dunlop, "Consensus," pp. 6–7.

lations law, rather than establishing the rules of the game, or even being a part of the game, is, in this theory of law, an alien imposition that simply hampers the performance of the players.

Are the Laws Enforced?

If a person is to understand American labor-management relations, he or she must be willing to consider the possibility that Congress passes laws which it does not intend to have enforced. This is a highly controversial matter, but to the extent that it is true, it explains why even when laws exist, workers may wish to be represented by unions.

After observing the process of government regulation for years, John T. Dunlop concluded that except where unions exist, laws "are not generally enforced, save in larger enterprises.... The Congress will never appropriate the money and staff required [for] enforcement...and the inevitable game between the regulator and the regulatee goes to the persistent and the well-heeled."[65]

CHAPTER SUMMARY

American labor law is extensive and complex. Increasingly, both labor and management depend on legal specialists for guidance in their disputes and negotiations. Nonetheless, it is very important for managers, employees, and intelligent citizens to know some of the basic characteristics of the law in general and, in particular, how labor law developed and some of its major statutes and provisions.

Within the general legal framework, there are three different theories of what type of justice the law should seek: utilitarian, egalitarian, or a balance of principles. There are also three conflicting theories of the nature of the legislative process: (1) that the law is a product of the rational, intelligent adjustment of the rules to social changes, (2) that the law reflects, rather than corrects, the attitudes and abuses of society, and (3) that the law has developed haphazardly in accommodation to pressure groups. Each theory of the legislative process leads us to view labor legislation in a very different way.

Labor relations exist within the province of four types of law—constitutional law; statutory, or legislative, law; common law; and administrative law. Labor laws function basically to protect collective bargaining contracts, to resolve disputes, and to establish minimum standards for employment. American labor laws involve different procedures and standards for different sectors of the economy.

Labor law developed from an antiunion position in the early 1800s toward the search for peaceful means of settling disputes to an active support for

---

[65] John T. Dunlop, "The Legal Framework of Industrial Relations in the United States," Bureau of National Affairs, *Daily Labor Report* No. 194, Oct. 7, 1985, p. E1.

union organizing in the years after the great depression of the 1930s. Legal tools that were used against emerging unions in the nineteenth and early twentieth centuries included the labor injunction, yellow-dog contracts requiring workers not to join unions, and antitrust laws. The Railway Act of 1926 was the first major piece of legislation which established procedures for collective bargaining. It was enacted with the cooperation of both unions and carriers. The Norris-LaGuardia Anti-Injunction Act was enacted in 1932. It was followed by the National Labor Relations Act of 1935, also called the Wagner Act, which has been the most important single piece of labor-management relations regulation. The Taft-Hartley Act of 1947 modified the NLRA. The Landrum-Griffin Act in 1959 regulated the internal workings of unions and established a bill of rights for union members.

In addition to major federal legislation there are many other statutes which affect labor-management relations. The more significant legislative acts include the Fair Labor Standards Act, which establishes the minimum wage; the Equal Employment Opportunity Act of 1972; and the Age Discrimination Act. The Equal Opportunity Act has engendered new practices in relation to seniority systems, to collective bargaining procedures, and to applications of the National Labor Relations Act. More recent new issues with a legal aspect include equal pay for jobs of comparable worth, protection against sexual harassment at work, affirmative action, and reverse discrimination.

QUESTIONS FOR THOUGHT AND DISCUSSION

1 What are the major types of law in the United States? How does each apply to labor relations? Give examples.

2 What were the major stages in the development of labor law in the United States?

3 What is the labor injunction? How was the injunction used to control union activities? What impact did the Norris-LaGuardia Act have on the labor injunction?

4 What are the major features of the Landrum-Griffin Act? Think about and discuss some aspect of the Landrum-Griffin Act from the perspective of a manager, a union member or official, or a citizen/consumer.

5 How does the concept of equal pay for the same job differ from the concept of equal pay for jobs of comparable worth?

6 What are the implications of the courts again applying the antitrust laws to some union activities? Should this be done?

7 Which theory of the legislative process do you think is most applicable to labor law? Why?

8 Why is it important to understand the legal setting of labor-management relations, not only the major pieces of labor legislation but also the nature and characteristics of the legal process in which they are rooted (e.g., the evolving nature of the law, its adversarial nature)?

9 What is distinctive about American labor law and in what ways could these characteristics have importance for management and union officials?

10 What impact has the equal employment opportunity clause (Title VII) of the 1964 Civil Rights Act had on seniority systems?

SELECTED READING

Bellace, Janice R., and Alan D. Berkowitz, *The Landrum-Griffin Act: Twenty Years of Federal Protection of Union Members' Rights* (Philadelphia: Industrial Research Unit, Wharton School, The University of Pennsylvania, 1979).

Berman, Harold J., and William R. Greiner, *The Nature and Functions of Law*, 3d ed. (New York: Foundation Press, 1972).

Cox, Archibald, *Law and the National Labor Policy* (Los Angeles: University of California Institute of Industrial Relations Monograph Series, No. 5, 1960).

Gohmann, John W., ed., *Air and Rail Labor Relations: The Railway Labor Act* (Dubuque, Iowa: Kendall/Hunt Publishing, 1979).

Goldberg, Joseph P., et al., eds., *Federal Policies and Worker Status Since the Thirties* (Madison, Wis.: Industrial Relations Research Association, 1976).

Gould, William B., *A Primer on American Labor Law* (Cambridge, Mass.: MIT Press, 1984).

Justice, Betty W., *Unions, Workers and the Law* (Washington, D.C.: BNA Books, 1983).

Keeline, Thomas J., *NLRB and Judicial Control of Union Discipline* (Philadelphia: Industrial Research Unit, Wharton School, The University of Pennsylvania, 1976).

McAdams, Alan K., *Power and Politics in Labor Legislation* (New York: Columbia University Press, 1964).

Morris, Charles, *The Developing Labor Law* (Washington, D.C.: The Bureau of National Affairs, rev. ed., 1981).

The Railway Labor Act at Fifty; Collective Bargaining in the Railroad and Airline Industries (Washington, D.C.: U.S. Government Printing Office, 1977).

Summers, Clyde W., and Robert J. Rabin, *The Rights of Union Members* (New York: American Civil Liberties Union, 1980).

Taylor, Benjamin J., and Fred Whitney, *Labor Relations Law*, 3d ed. (Englewood Cliffs, N.J.: Prentice-Hall, 1979).

Wallace, Phyllis A., ed., *Equal Employment Opportunity and the AT&T Case* (Cambridge, Mass.: MIT Press, 1976).

CHAPTER 5

THE NLRB AND UNION ORGANIZATION

ORIGINS

The National Relations Board (NLRB) is an independent federal agency. It was created in 1935 by Congress to administer the basic law governing relations between labor unions and business enterprises in the private sector. It was established by the National Labor Relations Act (NLRA) and administers that act as it has been amended. The law bestows on employees certain rights, which are set forth primarily in section 7 of the act. Section 7, entitled "Rights of Employees," reads as follows:

> Employees shall have the right to self-organization, to form, join or assist labor organizations, to bargain collectively through representatives of their own choosing, and to engage in other concerted activities for the purpose of collective bargaining or other mutual aid/or protection, and shall also have the right to refrain from any or all such activities....

These rights of employees are not self-enforcing. It was in order to ensure that employees could exercise these rights and to protect them and the public from certain unfair labor practices (which are spelled out in section 8 of the act) that Congress established the NLRB.

The stated purpose of the nation's labor law is to serve the public interest by reducing interruptions in commerce arising from industrial strife. It seeks to do this by providing orderly process for protecting and implementing the respective rights of employees, employers, and unions in their relations with each other. The NLRB has been given two principal functions by the law: (1) to determine through secret-ballot elections the free, democratic choice by employees of whether they wish to be represented by a union in dealing with their employer, and if so, by which union, and (2) to prevent unlawful acts, i.e., unfair labor practices, by employers or unions and to remedy the unlawful acts. The board does not act on its own initiative in either function; it processes charges of unfair labor practices and petitions for employee elections that are filed in the board's various regional offices.

The NLRB was established by the Wagner Act in 1935, but it had an immediate predecessor. Under the National Industrial Recovery Act (NIRA), a broad piece of legislation dealing with recovery from the great depression, a National Labor Board (NLB) had been established in 1933. The NLB had as its mission the protection of rights granted employees under the NIRA, which were similar to those rights later set forth in section 7 of the National Labor Relations Act. Senator Robert F. Wagner of New York was appointed chairman of the NLB. The board was largely ineffective, however. Employers were unwilling to accept unionization of unorganized employees, and the board had no enforcement powers. The NLB tried to hold elections to see if employees wanted to be represented by unions, but in some cases the companies simply refused to permit the elections. Early in 1934 President Roosevelt tried to strengthen the NLB through a presidential executive order, but was unable to provide it with enforcement powers. In late 1934 Congress passed a joint resolution attached to the NIRA legislation establishing the National Labor Relations Board in place of the NLB. The NIRA was declared unconstitutional in 1935, and the NLRB was thereby abolished. During this 2-year period, 1933 to 1935, union membership increased by almost one-third, but most of this increase was achieved by strikes, without the use of the NLB or NLRB machinery which, as we have seen, was opposed by employers and lacked enforcement powers.

Following the termination of the NIRA, Senator Wagner proposed the reestablishment of the NLRB by means of a statute dealing only with labor relations. Congress thereupon passed the National Labor Relations Act in 1935, establishing another National Labor Relations Board. However, once again employer opposition made it impossible for the NLRB to function until the act was reviewed by the Supreme Court. In 1937, some 19 months after the passage of the Wagner Act, the act was declared constitutional by the Supreme Court. The first year and a half of the board had been spent formulating strategy for the Supreme Court test. The board began to function in 1937.[1]

ORGANIZATION AND STRUCTURE

The National Labor Relations Board involves a five-member board that has quasi-judicial functions and an administrative agency. The five-member

---

[1] James A. Gross, *The Making of the NLRB*, vol. 1 (Albany: State University of New York Press, 1974), pp. 3 and 229.

board itself acts as a judicial body in deciding cases submitted to it. There is also an office of the general counsel of the board that is largely independent of the five-member board. The general counsel is responsible for the issuance and prosecution of formal complaints about violation of the law. The general counsel has supervision of the NLRB's regional offices. The board's chairperson is the chief executive officer of the NLRB as a whole and is a member of the five-member board.

Each of the five members of the board is appointed by the President for a term of 5 years, and the appointment must be confirmed by the Senate. The 5-year terms are staggered, so that one member's term expires each year. The President appoints one of the five members of the board as chairperson.

Figure 5-1 describes some aspects of the structure of the NLRB. It shows the five-member board as separate and distinct from the office of the general counsel. The general counsel's office has several divisions, including a division of litigation, which handles court cases; a division of operations, which administers the regional offices; and a division of administration, which handles personnel, budgetary, and similar functions. The board itself is shown to include the staffs of administrative law judges. Administrative law judges hear cases and issue decisions. They are attached to the board for administrative purposes, but are stationed in either San Francisco or Washington, D.C. They are assigned cases, conduct hearings, and issue decisions. ALJs, as they are called, are appointed under the Civil Service regulations of the federal government. They are not subject to removal by the board. In the

FIGURE 5-1   NLRB organization chart (simplified). (*Source: Chairman's Office, National Labor Relations Board.*)

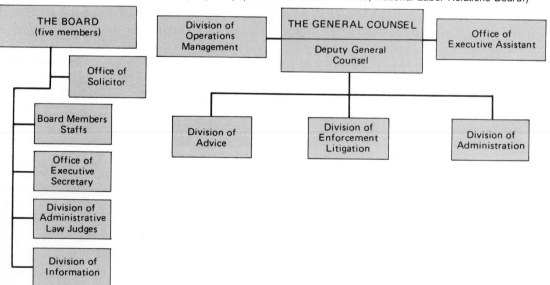

process of hearing cases and making decisions, they are fully independent of the board. There are 95 ALJs, headed by a chief administrative law judge.

The arrangement between the board itself and the general counsel's office is somewhat unusual for agencies of government. Ordinarily, the general counsel's office is simply the legal department (so to speak) of an agency. But at the NLRB the general counsel exercises a substantial degree of independent, in fact, separate, judgment regarding matters that come before the agency. Why is this so? In the period from 1935 to 1947 the organization of the agency was not as it is now. In that period the general counsel's office was an agent of the three-member board, taking its direction from the chairperson of the board. But employers complained about this arrangement. The NLRB was, they said, both prosecutor and judge. With respect to unfair labor practices, the board investigated charges, issued complaints when it thought the law had been violated, and prosecuted the employers (until 1947 only an employer could commit an unfair labor practice). The five-member board was the tribunal, i.e., the judge, before whom the case was heard. Agents of the board were thus both the prosecutor and the judge. This, the companies argued, was contrary to American judicial tradition and was unfair.

In 1947 Congress, in the Taft-Hartley amendments to the Wagner Act, separated the office of the general counsel from the board. Because of this organizational change, the role of prosecutor was separated from that of judge in the activities of the NLRB. The Taft-Hartley Act also established unfair labor practices as they applied to unions. These two reforms—the separation of the functions of the agency and the establishment of union unfair labor practice categories—were viewed as major factors increasing the impartiality of the board. The unions unsuccessfully opposed these reforms, believing they would weaken the board in its capacity to promote collective bargaining and to protect the rights of employees.[2]

Through decisions of the board and of the federal courts, the law as administered by the NLRB has become very complex. As a result, there has developed a group of lawyers working for both labor and management who are expert in the interpretation of the nation's labor laws. Also, membership on the board itself requires considerable experience in the meaning and application of the law. As a result, the NLRB is filled not with persons who have had experience in labor-management relations but rather with lawyers who have had experience in the federal government. For example, in 1980 the average length of service in the federal government of the members of the NLRB was 35 years.

Case Handling

In fiscal 1983 (running from October 1982 through September 1983), the NLRB received 49,436 cases of all types. Of these, 40,634 cases involved

[2] James A. Gross, *The Reshaping of the National Labor Relations Board: National Labor Policy in Transition, 1937–1947* (Albany: State University of New York Press, 1982).

charges of unfair labor practices affecting workers and 8078 were petitions seeking union representation elections. During fiscal 1983, the five-member board issued 1122 decisions in contested unfair labor practice cases. A contested case involves a dispute over the application of the law which is resolved by the board. How does it happen that with more than 40,600 cases filed with the NLRB, only about 1120 decisions were issued by the five-member board?

In fiscal 1983, about 82 percent of all cases filed dealt with unfair labor practices. Of these, not all were disposed of in 1983. But in 1983 the board and its agents took final action on 38,041 unfair labor practice cases (some filed prior to fiscal 1983). Of these cases disposed of in fiscal 1983, 33.0 percent were dismissed by the office of the general counsel without the issuance of a formal complaint. An additional 33.8 percent were withdrawn by the charging party, and 28.3 percent were settled or adjusted by the parties involved. Only about 2.8 percent of all the charges filed led to the issuance of a complaint which necessitated a decision by the board. Also, only a small proportion of representation cases reach the five-member board. Thus, most cases filed with the regional offices never reach the board itself.

OPERATIONS

How does the NLRB process its case load? Representation cases are treated differently from unfair labor practice charges. We shall consider each in turn.

Representation Cases   The NLRB can conduct an election only when a petition has been filed requesting one. A petition for the certification by the board of a bargaining representative can be filed by an employee or a group of employees or a union, or it can be filed by an employer. The petition must be signed, sworn to, or affirmed under oath and filed with the NLRB's regional office in the area involved. If filed by or on behalf of employees, the petition must be supported by a showing that a substantial number (30 percent or more) of employees wish to be represented by a bargaining representative, and the petition must state that the employer refuses to recognize their representative for the purposes of collective bargaining. If an employer files the petition, it must state that employees or a union have made a claim for recognition as the exclusive representative of the particular group of employees involved.

When a petition is filed, a regional office of the board must investigate to see if a question of representation actually exists. If a question is found to exist, then the regional office may hold a hearing if necessary, at which the employer and the persons seeking the representation appear to present their respective positions. The investigation is to determine:

1 *If the board has jurisdiction to conduct an election.* Some employees and employers are outside the coverage of the NLRA. Among groups not covered are agricultural laborers, domestic servants, government employees, supervisors, and independent contractors.

2 *Whether there is enough showing of employee interest* in a collective bargaining representative to justify an election.

3 *Whether there actually is a question* about representation.

4 *Whether the election is sought in an appropriate unit of employees.* (This is an especially important question, to which we will return later.)

5 *Whether the representative (ordinarily a union) named in the petition is qualified.* (This is also an important matter to be discussed later.)

6 *Whether there are any legal barriers to an election.* Often such a barrier takes the form of a *bona fide* existing collective bargaining agreement covering the employees in question. Such an agreement may constitute a *contract bar* to an election. Another legal impediment involves the certification by the NLRB of a bargaining unit within the previous year. Such a certification bars an election, as does a previous election held within the prior 12 months.

If the regional office of the board finds that the circumstances with respect to these six matters are such as to permit a question of representation to be resolved, then the board must conduct a secret-ballot election. If a union wins a majority of the votes in the election, it will be certified by the board as the exclusive collective bargaining representative of the employees in the bargaining unit, which was found by the board to be appropriate. A union that is certified is entitled to be recognized by the employer. If the employer fails to bargain with the union, it commits an unfair labor practice.

The five-member board has delegated much of its authority in representation cases to the regional directors of the NLRB. Appeals from decisions of the regional directors with respect to bargaining unit determinations and objections on how elections are conducted can be taken to the five-member board, however.

Unfair Labor Practice Cases The basic procedures in cases involving charges of unfair labor practices are described in Figure 5-2. These procedures are initiated by the filing of a charge. A charge may be filed by an employee, an employer, a labor organization, or any person other than a board employee. Like representation petitions, charge forms are available from regional offices of the NLRB and must be signed, sworn to, or affirmed under oath and filed with the regional office in the geographic area in which the alleged unfair labor practice was committed. The regional office must investigate the charge, ordinarily by sending a representative to interview the person complaining and the company or union against which the charge was brought. The regional office, with such guidance from the general counsel's office in Washington as is appropriate, may issue a complaint if its investigation shows that there is cause to believe a violation of the law has occurred. The issuance of a complaint by the general counsel's office is a formal legal act, in which charges of violation of the law are set forth and the

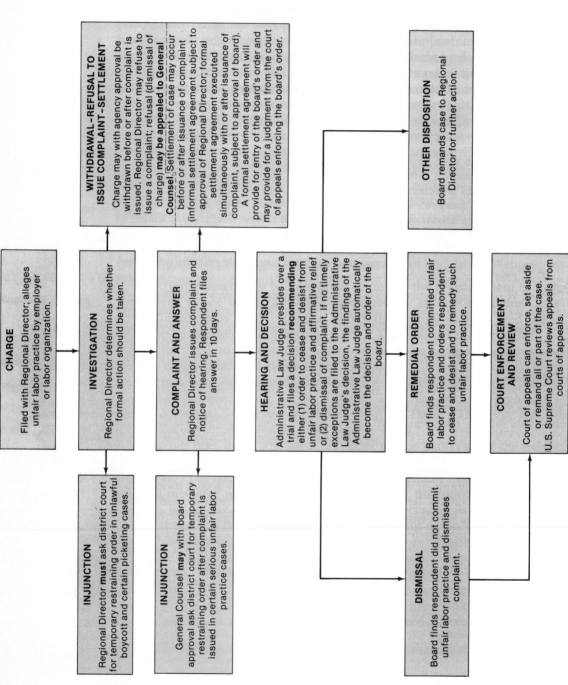

CHARGE

Filed with Regional Director; alleges unfair labor practice by employer or labor organization.

INVESTIGATION

Regional Director determines whether formal action should be taken.

COMPLAINT AND ANSWER

Regional Director issues complaint and notice of hearing. Respondent files answer in 10 days.

HEARING AND DECISION

Administrative Law Judge presides over a trial and files a decision **recommending** either (1) order to cease and desist from unfair labor practice and affirmative relief or (2) dismissal of complaint. If no timely exceptions are filed to the Administrative Law Judge's decision, the findings of the Administrative Law Judge automatically become the decision and order of the board.

REMEDIAL ORDER

Board finds respondent committed unfair labor practice and orders respondent to cease and desist and to remedy such unfair labor practice.

COURT ENFORCEMENT AND REVIEW

Court of appeals can enforce, set aside or remand all or part of the case. U.S. Supreme Court reviews appeals from courts of appeals.

WITHDRAWAL–REFUSAL TO ISSUE COMPLAINT–SETTLEMENT

Charge may with agency approval be withdrawn before or after complaint is issued. Regional Director may refuse to issue a complaint; refusal (dismissal of charge) **may be appealed to General Counsel.** Settlement of case may occur before or after issuance of complaint (informal settlement agreement subject to approval of Regional Director; formal settlement agreement executed simultaneously with or after issuance of complaint, subject to approval of board). A formal settlement agreement will provide for entry of the board's order and may provide for a judgment from the court of appeals enforcing the board's order.

OTHER DISPOSITION

Board remands case to Regional Director for further action.

INJUNCTION

Regional Director **must** ask district court for temporary restraining order in unlawful boycott and certain picketing cases.

INJUNCTION

General Counsel **may** with board approval ask district court for temporary restraining order after complaint is issued in certain serious unfair labor practice cases.

DISMISSAL

Board finds respondent did not commit unfair labor practice and dismisses complaint.

FIGURE 5-2 NLRB basic procedures in cases involving charges of unfair labor practice charges. (*Source: Chairman's Office, National Labor Relations Board.*)

charged party is informed of a hearing to be held regarding the complaint. Once a formal complaint is issued, the office of the general counsel becomes the prosecutor and the government bears the costs of the further legal proceedings. The person or organization that initially filed a charge is usually not formally involved except perhaps to give evidence. Occasionally a charging party may have its own lawyer, but the general counsel's office plays the major prosecuting role. The party against which the complaint was filed (either a union or an employer) must defend itself with its own legal counsel against the allegations of the government (i.e., the office of the general counsel) that it has violated the law.

The regional director may refuse to issue a formal complaint after investigating the charges filed. The director would refuse to issue a complaint if no merit were found to the accusation that a company or a union had violated the labor law. If the regional director refuses to issue a complaint in any case, the person who originally filed the charge is entitled to (1) a statement of findings and reasons from the regional director, (2) a decision not to issue a complaint, which shows precedents for the decision, (3) a right to take an appeal to Washington to the office of appeals in the general counsel's office and to people who are wholly independent of the officers in the regional office. The general counsel may choose to issue a complaint or not to do so. If the decision is not to do so, the office of appeals issues a letter setting forth the reasons why a complaint was not issued. This lengthy procedure provides as complete a review and response to a charge filed with the board as any federal agency provides in any matter before it. Ordinarily, if the agency decides to take no action on a charge or a matter of any nature brought to it, the charging party is unlikely to be successful in any court appeal of that decision or an opinion giving the reasons for it.[3]

When a formal complaint is issued, a hearing is held before an administrative law judge. The representatives of the regional office of the NLRB serve as prosecutors, and counsel for the company or union defends it. The regional office, on behalf of the board, has power to examine and copy any evidence of any person being investigated that relates to the matter under review and may issue subpoenas and obtain federal court orders to compel the production of evidence or giving of testimony. Based on the record of the hearing, the judge makes findings and recommendations. All parties to the hearing may appeal the decision of the ALJ to the five-member board.

The five-member board, on appeal, reviews the decisions of the ALJs and may affirm, alter, or amend their decisions. However, approximately 80 percent of the decisions are issued by three-member panels, with only the more difficult cases going to the full five-member board.

---

[3] J. Davis, *Discretionary Justice: A Preliminary Inquiry* (Baton Rouge, La.: Louisiana State University Press, 1969). The advice given to NLRB regional offices by the general counsel's office in Washington is generally available publicly as a result of a Supreme Court decision (*Sears Roebuck*, 1975) and is published by Labor Relations Press at Fort Washington, Pa. NLRB decisions are published by the board and are circulated by several reporting agencies, including the Bureau of National Affairs and the Commerce Clearing House, both in Washington, D.C.

The National Labor Relations Act is not a criminal statute, but a civil one, and it is entirely remedial. It is intended to prevent and remedy unfair labor practices, not to punish the people responsible for them. Therefore, if a company or union is convicted of an unfair labor practice, it is not fined, nor are its officers jailed. The board fashions a remedial order that attempts to make up for the infraction of the law. In determining the remedy in any particular case, the board has considerable discretion.

If an employer created a union that it dominated, a violation of the law, the board might order the company to disestablish the union. If a union illegally collected dues from employees, the board might order the union to refund the dues, plus interest. If a company refused to bargain with a union, in violation of the law, the board would issue an order compelling the company to bargain with the union.

In fashioning remedial orders, the NLRB often requires companies to make restitution to employees for wages lost as a result of the employer's action in violation of the law. Thus, companies sometimes are required by the board to pay sums of money to employees against whom they have taken action found by the board to be illegal. But these payments are not technically penalties. For example, if employees were unlawfully discharged by an employer, the board would require the employer to reinstate the employees and pay them for working time missed plus interest. In the largest such payment required by the NLRB, a major American chemical company agreed in December 1979 to pay $12 million in back pay to 405 Louisiana chemical plant workers unlawfully locked out of their jobs by the company for 3 years. Such a financial requirement may seem to the company like a penalty, but it is legally different from the award of damages by a court. The NLRB's remedial power, for example, is limited to the financial losses which the workers can be shown to have actually sustained. Back pay for time lost at work is reduced by the amount an employee earned at any job he or she was able to get during the time the employer denied the employee the right to work. Damages would not be limited in this fashion.

COURT ACTIONS

Appeals If a company or union fails to comply with an order of the NLRB, the board may petition a U.S. circuit court of appeals for a court order enforcing the board's directive. Thus, the NLRB cannot enforce its own orders, but must make application to a federal court to do so (see Figure 5-3). An employer or a union against which the NLRB's order was issued may oppose the NLRB's request for a court order. This is one method by which an employer or a union may obtain court review of NLRB actions.[4]

A company or union may also simply petition a circuit court of appeals to

---

[4] Douglas S. McDowell et al., *NLRB Remedies for Unfair Labor Practices* (Philadelphia: Industrial Research Unit, The Wharton School, University of Pennsylvania, 1976).

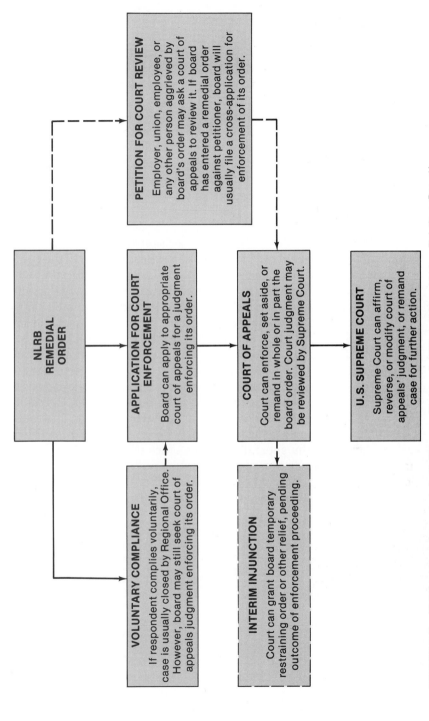

FIGURE 5-3 NLRB order enforcement chart. (*Source: Chairman's Office, National Labor Relations Board.*)

review any decision or final order of the board. The court of appeals may approve the board's order and enforce it, or it may remand the order to the board for reconsideration. It may also change the board's order or even set it aside entirely. If the court enforces a board order, failure by a company or union to comply with the order may be punished by fine or imprisonment for contempt of court. In some cases the U.S. Supreme Court is asked to review decisions of the circuit courts about NLRB orders. The Supreme Court decides on its own which cases it will hear and which it will not hear, looking for a substantial question of law or a conflict between the decisions of circuit courts of appeal in deciding to hear a case.

A great number of disputes involving labor law find their way into the federal courts of appeals. The National Labor Relations Board conducts more extensive litigation in the United States courts of appeals than any other federal agency. In fiscal 1983 there were 338 appeals court decisions in NLRB-related cases. In these rulings the NLRB decision was fully affirmed by the circuit courts of appeals in 81.7 percent of the cases. Since 1935 the courts of appeals have reviewed 7217 decisions of the NLRB, fully affirming 63.4 percent of them and setting aside 14.7 percent. Litigation of board decisions in the Supreme Court is less extensive. In fiscal 1983 the Supreme Court decided five cases involving NLRB decisions, fully affirming three, partially affirming one, and setting aside one. Since 1935 the Supreme Court has ruled on 226 NLRB decisions, fully affirming 60.2 percent of them and setting aside 16.0 percent.

The mill of justice grinds slowly, and in recent years more slowly yet. Table 5-1 shows the average number of days between successive stages in NLRB and court review of unfair labor practice charges. In 1980, for example, a charge took an average of 46 days to go from filing to the issuance of a complaint by the general counsel's office of the NLRB, another 155 days to the close of the hearing by the NLRB; another 158 days until an administrative law judge rendered a decision, another 133 days till a decision was made by the NLRB. If the case went on appeal from the board to a circuit court of

TABLE 5-1 DAYS IN PROCESSING UNFAIR LABOR PRACTICE CHARGES, 1960–1983 (All Times in Days)

Year	Filing to complaint	Complaint to close of hearing	Close of hearing to ALJ decision	ALJ to board decision	Board decision to court of appeals opinion
1960	52	66	88	149	—
1965	59	67	123	122	—
1970	57	58	84	124	—
1975	54	55	72	134	359
1980	46	155	158	133	485
1983	43	156	118	324	N/A

Source: Paul Weiler, "Promises to Keep," *Harvard Law Review*, 96:8, June 1983, p. 1796. Also, 48th Annual Report of NLRB.

appeals, another 485 days were added to the process. The process is so slow that unions and management often complain.

Enforcement in District Courts In certain instances the law requires the NLRB to ask federal district courts to grant injunctions against certain types of activities. Section 10(1) of the act requires that whenever a charge is filed alleging a violation of certain sections of the act relating to boycotts, picketing, and work stoppages, the preliminary investigation of the charge must be given priority over all other types of cases in the regional office where it was filed. A second priority must be given to charges alleging violations by employers or unions that involve discrimination against employees with respect to membership in a union. If the preliminary investigation of the first-priority cases shows there is reasonable cause to believe that the charge is true and that a complaint should be issued, the board is required to ask a federal district court to grant an injunction against the offending party, pending final resolution of the matter. Section 10(j) of the act permits the board to petition a district court for an injunction in connection with any unfair labor practice complaint after a formal complaint has been issued.

Through these provisions of the law, as well as in other ways, the injunction, issued by a federal district court, has found its way back into labor relations. But in these procedures at least, the injunction is granted at the behest of a governmental agency, not of the employer or union.[5]

In fiscal 1983 the NLRB sought district court injunctions in 110 cases in which it was required to seek an injunction if it had cause to believe a violation of the law had occurred. It also sought 39 injunctions in connection with complaints that it had issued or pursuant to section 10(j) of the act, where it is given the discretion to enforce one of its orders.

Representation Proceedings The National Labor Relations Act requires that an employer bargain with the representative of its employees, but it does not require that the representative be selected in any particular fashion, as long as the representative is clearly the choice of the majority of the employees. The act also provides that the employees' representative for collective bargaining can be any individual or labor organization. A supervisor or any other management representative cannot be an employee representative.

UNIT DETERMINATIONS

How Determinations Are Made Section 9(b) of the NLRA authorizes the NLRB to decide in each representation case whether "in order to assure to employees the fullest freedom in exercising the rights guaranteed by this Act,

---

[5] Frank W. McCulloch and Tim Bornstein, *The National Labor Relations Board* (New York: Praeger, 1974).

the unit appropriate for the purposes of collective bargaining shall be the employer unit, craft unit, plant unit, or subdivision thereof." This section of the NLRA is regarded as one of the broadest grants of discretion that Congress has entrusted to any federal administrative agency.[6]

A unit can thus be all the employees of a company in however many plants it has, all the employees in a single plant, or even separate groups of employees within a plant. The board will certify a multiemployer unit if the employers and the union agree to set up such a unit, but it will not establish a multiemployer unit in any other case.[7]

There are certain limitations placed on this grant of discretion by the act itself. Among the most important limitations are:

1 *The board is not permitted* to approve a unit that includes both professional and nonprofessional employees unless a majority of the professional employees involved vote to be included in a mixed unit.

2 *The board is prohibited* from including plant guards in the same unit with other employees.

3 *Supervisors are excluded* from the coverage of the act, and therefore from inclusion in a bargaining unit, by virtue of not being included in the term "employee" to which the act applies. Whether an individual is a supervisor in the board's view depends on his or her authority over employees and not merely on the person's formal title.[8]

The exclusion of supervisors from coverage by the act is important. The exclusion was entered into the act by the Taft-Hartley amendment of 1947. Prior to that time there was a national union of foremen (the Foremen's Association of America) that was active in many industries, especially in the automobile industry. The passage of the Taft-Hartley Act removed the prohibitions against employers discharging supervisors for union activity. Thereafter, in the face of overt employer opposition, the foremen's unions declined.

How has the board exercised its discretion in establishing bargaining units? The board has generally sought to determine the appropriateness of a bargaining unit on the ground of the common employment interests of the employees involved. Those who have the same or substantially similar interests concerning wages, hours, and working conditions are grouped by the board into a bargaining unit. The following factors are also considered:

1 *Any history* of collective bargaining by the employees involved
2 *The desires* of the employees
3 *The extent* to which the employees are organized into a union

---

[6] Ibid., p. 125.
[7] John E. Abodeely, *The NLRB and the Appropriate Bargaining Unit* (Philadelphia: Industrial Research Unit, Wharton School, University of Pennsylvania, 1971).
[8] Robert B. Allen, "Status of Supervisors under NLRA," *Louisiana Law Review*, 35:4, Summer 1975, pp. 800–812.

Section 9(c)5 of the act prohibits the board from giving the third factor controlling weight. That is, the board cannot determine that an appropriate unit is simply whoever the union has gotten to support it.[9]

The determination of bargaining units can have a major impact on the likelihood of the unionization of a group of employees. For example, until the early 1970s the employees of one subsidiary of a major corporation were represented by an independent union. The independent union began to lose its support, however, and several national unions became interested in seeking recognition rights. The company employed some 40,000 persons in several states at 200 or so facilities. The unions sought NLRB decisions establishing several separate units, involving each major facility or the major facilities in each metropolitan area. So defined, the cost to the unions of the election campaigns would be minimized and the unions would not incur the cost of servicing small, isolated facilities with few employees, since they would not be in the established units. The company, however, sought a unit consisting of all its nonsupervisory personnel in all states in which it operated and in all its facilities. The company argued that since it used a single personnel system for all employees, the unit should conform to its administrative procedures.

The NLRB's regional office held hearings to determine the appropriate unit and decided in favor of the employer's proposal. The unit was established to cover all the company's nonsupervisory employees. The subsequent election campaign was beyond the financial capability of all but one of the interested unions. That union assigned more than 100 full-time organizers and spent several million dollars in the election campaign (which it ultimately won). In a similar instance involving another company, the union obtained authorization cards from about 70 percent of the employees at one of the employer's major facilities. When the NLRB decided that the appropriate unit was companywide, the union abandoned the effort to organize the employees as too costly.

The employer and the union may, of course, agree on the appropriate unit and thereby expedite an election, but when there is a dispute over the appropriate unit, the delay involved in scheduling an election can be substantial. Hearings must be held and a decision prepared by the NLRB's regional director. Then either side, union or management, may appeal to the five-member board, which may at its discretion review the regional director's unit determination. The unions object to the delay often involved in this process, maintaining that it weakens their ability to get a favorable vote from the employees.

Craft versus Industrial Units   A major issue in the matter of unit determinations involves craft versus industrial units. Craft unions have

[9] Editors, "The Board and Section 9(c)(5)...," *Harvard Law Review*, 79:5, February 1966, pp. 811–840.

charged the NLRB with favoring industrial units. By including the few craft workers in industrial facilities with the large numbers of production workers, the board virtually guaranteed that in any election an industrial union would prevail. To prevent this, the craft unions in the old AFL tried to get a provision included in the Wagner Act to protect craft unions. They were unsuccessful. In the Taft-Hartley Act, however, Congress wrote into the law a provision that the NLRB may permit workers to vote on a craft unit even if an industrial unit already exists. The board had ruled in the *General Electric* case (1944) that it would accept a petition from craft workers to leave a larger industrial bargaining unit when it could be shown that the craft employees involved were a "true" craft and not merely a dissident faction and that the craft members had maintained their identity. This doctrine permitted so-called craft severance elections.

After the passage of Taft-Hartley, however, the board decided, in the *National Tube* case (1948), to prohibit craft severance in certain industries involving allegedly "integrated" production processes. Criticism of this decision led the board to limit it in the *American Potash* case (1954). The prohibition of craft severance in integrated industries had been limited to the basic steel, aluminum, lumber, and wet milling industries. Under the *American Potash* doctrine the board held that outside the industries just cited, craft units would be permitted to break out of industrial units irrespective of their importance to the total production process.

In 1955 the board again reviewed the craft severance question and again changed its policy. The board reasserted its discretion to find craft unions inappropriate for collective bargaining. In *Mallinckrodt* (1966) the board set out a group of factors that it would consider in granting or refusing craft severance petitions. In a major application of the *Mallinckrodt* doctrine, the board in 1976 refused to permit craft severance for skilled trades in the rubber industry. In rubber, the existing bargaining units are industrial units in which the United Rubber Workers (URW) represent both skilled tradespeople and production workers. The International Society of Skilled Trades filed a petition with the NLRB for severance of skilled tradespeople from the industrial units represented by the URW. In *Firestone Tire and Rubber Co.* (1976) the board refused to sever the skilled trades from the broader unit. The board found that the skilled trades employees had the same working conditions and received essentially the same fringe benefits as the production workers. The skilled tradespeople also had their interest actively pursued by the URW via the contractual grievance and arbitration procedure. The separate community of interests that the skilled tradespeople had enjoyed by reason of their skills was found to have been largely integrated into the broader community of interest shared with the production workers in view of (1) the long and stable 28-year history of collective bargaining between the company and the URW; (2) the high degree of integration of production processes in the employer's operations, which might make a separate work stoppage by a craft unit damaging to all; (3) the active participation of the skilled trades in the administration of the URW and in negotiations by the URW with the company; and (4) the likelihood that craft severance would have a disruptive effect on the rubber industry as a whole.

In the area of craft severance the NLRB can be observed dealing with a difficult problem of conflicting interests. Companies and industrial unions prefer the stability in a bargaining relationship that a single, large unit seems to create.[10] But craftspeople and craft unions object to their special interests being submerged in those of the more numerous production workers. The board, whose membership changes in the course of time, periodically reconsiders the issue of craft severance as it arises in cases presented to the board and not infrequently changes its policies toward the issue.

Bargaining Units versus Bargaining Structure   The law requires the NLRB to establish bargaining units, but it does not require unions and employers to utilize the units as the actual elements of the bargaining process. Many do not. In the oil industry, for example, NLRB certifications are issued to locals of the Oil, Chemical, and Atomic Workers union (OCAW) at particular refineries belonging to the various oil companies. But bargaining itself is very much centralized and coordinated among the locals and companies. Similarly, in much of the electric manufacturing industry, NLRB certifications are issued on a single-union, single-plant basis, while bargaining takes place on a companywide, multiunion basis. Thus, the NLRB may be said to make decisions about bargaining units but not about certain important aspects of bargaining structure. To put it differently, the NLRB tells unions and management if they must bargain but does not necessarily specify the form in which negotiations occur. If the union and the employer agree to negotiations on a broader basis than the NLRB has certified, the board will permit it. But if either party refuses to agree, the NLRB will require that bargaining be on the basis of the board-certified unit.

Should the NLRB be more concerned with bargaining structure? Certainly the NLRB has concerned itself with a major aspect of bargaining structure in its decisions with respect to the craft severance issue. With respect to the other aspects of bargaining structure, it has been less direct. NLRB decisions often affect bargaining structure, but ordinarily those decisions have been made on the basis of other considerations.[11] An important aspect of bargaining structure involves the level at which various issues are negotiated. In the steel and auto industries, for example (see Chapter 18), economic issues are negotiated at the industry- and companywide levels, respectively, but many working conditions are negotiated at the plant level and are included in local

---

[10] Peter Henle, "Union Policy and the Size of the Bargaining Unit," in Arnold R. Weber, ed., *The Structure of Collective Bargaining* (Chicago: Graduate School of Business Administration, 1961), pp. 107–140.

[11] Douglas V. Brown and George Shultz, "Public Policy and the Structure of Collective Bargaining," in Arnold R. Weber, ed., *The Structure of Collective Bargaining* (Chicago: Graduate School of Business, 1961), pp. 300–324.

supplements to the national agreements. The NLRB does not normally recognize such matters in making unit determinations. The board's reluctance to involve itself in many questions of bargaining structure is probably appropriate, since it leaves the parties free to develop such arrangements as they wish.

In some situations, however, disputes over bargaining structure become the occasion for unfair labor practice charges. The board may then be drawn into disputes over bargaining structure independently of unit determinations. For example, the board once upheld the legality of an interunion agreement that no single union would sign a contract providing for less than certain agreed-upon provisions without the consent of the other unions (*Standard Oil*, 1962). And in the *General Electric* case (1968) the board permitted a union to include representatives of other unions on its negotiating committee. The other unions involved were required to have contracts with the company and were not allowed to vote on decisions by the union directly involved in the negotiations. The company had objected to bargaining with a union committee so constituted. These cases, and others like them, took the board into the heart of questions about the structure of bargaining.

In 1975 White Consolidated Industries purchased five Westinghouse appliance manufacturing plants. The five plants contained six bargaining units, which before the takeover were part of 42 separately certified (by the NLRB) bargaining units of Westinghouse employees. Although each unit was separately certified, the International Union of Electrical Workers and Westinghouse had bargained on a multiplant national basis through a union-elected committee called the Westinghouse conference board. At the time that White Consolidated took over the five plants, it accepted virtually all terms of the current Westinghouse agreement with the Electrical Workers. One year later, however, White-Westinghouse (a unit of White Consolidated) informed the union that it would bargain thereafter only on a plant-by-plant basis. When the collective bargaining agreement expired on July 11, 1976, the union struck. The strike continued for 3 months and ended only when the company agreed to a new contract covering a multiplant unit of all five plants. Meanwhile, the union had charged that the company had committed an unfair labor practice when it refused to bargain for all five plants as a single unit. The NLRB agreed. And in July 1979, a federal court of appeals upheld the NLRB's finding that White-Westinghouse had been guilty of an unfair labor practice in refusing to bargain on the multiplant basis.

HOW AN ELECTION IS CONDUCTED

When the NLRB finds that a question of representation exists, it must, by law, hold a secret-ballot election among employees to see if the employees want to have a bargaining representative. In such an election, employees who are in the bargaining unit are given a choice of one or more bargaining representatives or of no representative at all. To be certified as a bargaining representative, an individual or a labor union must receive a majority of the valid votes cast. If a majority of employees votes for a bargaining representative, that representative is certified as the exclusive bargaining agent for all employees in the unit. This is a critical aspect of American labor law. It prevents more than one union from having the right to speak for a single group of employees (i.e., a single bargaining unit). It adds great stability to our labor relations but continues to seem to some people to be an unreasonable infringement of the freedom of individuals.[12]

Elections are usually conducted within 30 days after the regional director of the board directs that an election is to be held. To be entitled to vote, an employee must have worked in the bargaining unit during an eligibility period set by the board and must be employed in the unit on the date of the election. Sometimes elections are conducted while a strike is under way. If the strike is legal, strikers may vote in the election. If the strikers have been permanently replaced, they may nevertheless vote up to 12 months after the strike began; but their permanent replacements may also vote.

The NLRB prepares ballots, selects voting places, and has representatives who observe the election and tabulate the votes (see Figure 5-4). A ballot may say:

Do you wish to be represented for the purpose of collective bargaining by:

	Yes	No
The United Metalworkers	_____	_____
The Union of Workers	_____	_____
No union	_____	_____

If any category gets a majority of ballots cast, no runoff is held. If no category gets a majority, there is a runoff between the two categories receiving the largest number of ballots. The category getting the majority of votes cast in the two-way election prevails.

Some elections involve large numbers of employees. In 1974, for example, the NLRB conducted an election involving 16,000 employees of Cannon Mills Company in North Carolina. The election was conducted at 31 separate polling places and was overseen by 30 agents of the NLRB. Of 16,256 employees eligible to vote, 8473 voted against the union and 6801 for the union. Other elections have involved up to 40,000 employees and more than 100 polling places in several states.

NLRB elections are conducted in accordance with strict standards de-

---

[12] George Schatzki, "Majority Rule, Exclusive Representation, and the Interests of Individual Workers: Should Exclusivity Be Abolished?" *University of Pennsylvania Law Review*, 123:4, April 1975, pp. 897–938.

1 You see sitting at a desk union representatives, the U.S. government's NLRB agents who conduct the election, and a company representative.	**6** After you have marked your ballot, you fold it so no one can see how it is marked, and you leave the voting booth.
2 You give your name and employee identification number.	**7** You drop the folded-up ballot into a locked ballot box which no one but the government agents can open. Your ballot is mixed in with all the other ballots cast by your fellow workers.
3 The representatives check your name off the official list of eligible voters so no one else can vote under your name and no one can vote twice.	**8** After the polls are closed, the government agents open the ballot box and the counting begins.
4 A government agent gives you a ballot. It does *not* list your name or number or have any other means of identification.	**9** The government agents count the ballots while union and company representatives watch.
5 You go into the voting booth which is curtained to give you privacy and to prevent anyone from seeing how you mark your ballot.	**10** After announcing the results, the government agents seal up the ballots.

THE U.S. GOVERNMENT GUARANTEES THAT YOUR BALLOT IS CAST IN SECRET.

FIGURE 5-4   You are ready to vote in an NLRB election. (*Source: Adapted from a pamphlet issued by the United Steelworkers of America.*)

signed to give the employees an opportunity to make a free choice. For example, it is unlawful for either employers or unions to make any election speeches, statements, or comments during working time to massed assemblies of staff members within 24 hours before the scheduled time for conducting an election. These speeches, statements, and comments constitute "captive audience speeches," and the making of any such speech is grounds for setting aside an election.

A manager or a union official may speak to groups of employees during the 24-hour period before the election *only* so long as attendance at the meeting or gathering is voluntary and it occurs on employees' own time.

Prior to the last 24 hours before an election, an employer may legally attempt to persuade employees not to vote for a union, just as a union may attempt to persuade them to vote for a union. But should an employer act in this fashion?

If the employer or a union doesn't believe the standards for a fair election were met, it may file an objection with the regional director and thereafter may appeal any decision to the board in Washington.

An election will be set aside if it was accompanied by conduct that the NLRB considers created an atmosphere of confusion or fear of reprisals and thus interfered with the employees' freedom of choice. In any particular case the NLRB does not attempt to determine whether the conduct actually interfered with the employees' expression of free choice, but rather asks whether the conduct tended to do so. If it is reasonable to believe that the conduct would tend to interfere with the free expression of the employees' choice, the election may be set aside. Examples of conduct the board considers to interfere with employee free choice are:

- Threats of loss of jobs or benefits by an employer or a union to influence the votes or union activities of employees.
- Misstatements of important facts in the election campaign by an employer or a union when the other party does not have a fair chance to reply.
- An employer's firing employees to discourage or encourage their union activities or a union's causing an employer to take such action.
- An employer's or a union's making campaign speeches to assembled groups of employees on company time within the 24-hour period before the election.
- The incitement of racial or religious prejudice by inflammatory campaign appeals made by either an employer or a union.
- Threats or the use of physical force or violence against employees by an employer or a union to influence their votes.
- The occurrence of extensive violence or trouble or widespread fear of job losses that prevents the holding of a fair election, whether or not caused by an employer or a union.
- The union is endorsed as a "strong and honest" union by the Commissioner of Labor of the state in which the balloting is conducted. The endorsement is made by a letter written on official stationery to the workers who are

to vote in the representation election and is sent the day before the election is scheduled to take place.

Do Campaign Tactics Affect the Outcome of NLRB Elections?

Representation elections conducted by the NLRB ordinarily involve an extensive campaign carried on both by the union or unions seeking to represent the workers and by the company. In the election campaign, both the unions and the company try to persuade the workers to vote a certain way. The NLRB has, for most of its history, regulated what the unions and employers say and do in the midst of election campaigns. If either side oversteps what the NLRB thinks are appropriate limits under the law, then the election may be postponed or set aside by the board. Thus, a union or employer which wins an election may be deprived of victory if its election tactics were illegal.

The NLRB and its agents spend considerable effort overseeing the conduct of elections. But it is not certain that this effort contributes substantially to the outcome of elections. A study of elections conducted by researchers and published in 1976 indicates that the statements made by union or management representatives in an election campaign, even where these statements were misleading or false, did not substantially affect the outcome of the election. In effect, the researchers argued, employees had their minds made up about how they would vote independently of statements by the union or company.[13]

In 1962 in a decision titled *Hollywood Ceramics,* the NLRB stated:

> We believe that an election should be set aside...where there has been a misrepresentation or other similar campaign trickery, which involves a substantial departure from the truth, at a time which prevents the other party or parties from making an effective reply, so that the misrepresentation, whether deliberate or not, may reasonably be expected to have a significant impact on the election. However, the mere fact that a message is inarticulately or vaguely worded and subject to different interpretations will not suffice to establish such misrepresentation as would lead us to set the election aside.

However, in April 1977, the board abandoned its policy as set forth in *Hollywood Ceramics.* Instead, in the *Shopping Kart Food Market* case, it announced that it would no longer probe into the truth or falsity of statements made by parties during an election campaign and would not overturn elections on the basis of misleading campaign statements.

But the board adhered to this new policy for only 20 months. In December 1978, the board decided a case (*General Knit of California, Inc.*) in which the employees voted in October 1977 to be represented by a union. The union acknowledged that it had distributed shortly before the election a leaflet which stated that the company had had a profit of $19.6 million in 1976, when in fact the company had had a loss of more than $5 million in that year.

---

[13] Julius G. Getman et al., *Union Representation Elections: Law and Reality* (New York: Basic Books, 1976).

Faced with these facts, the board set aside the election and abandoned its *Shopping Kart* doctrine, returning explicitly to the policy set forth in *Hollywood Ceramics*. So now, once again, the NLRB does inquire into the statements made by unions and employers in the course of election campaigns. And in this set of events one can also see that the board is willing to overturn its own precedents as it attempts to fashion its policies to the cases that come before it.[14]

In recent years, the question of what an employer may do in a union organization campaign has moved beyond the issue of individual actions or statements and has dealt with broad patterns of behavior. In particular, the unions charge that there has grown up an industry of consultants whose purpose is to help corporations prevent organization of their employees by unions. Since 1979, a subcommittee of the U.S. House of Representatives concerned with labor-management relations has held hearings in which the unions have argued that federal laws should be tightened to prevent management from using "union-busting" consultants.

In a study of 130 NLRB elections held in retail grocery stores, researcher John J. Lawler found that management consultants did help to turn close votes against the unions. But he also found that other aspects of the election, including the size of the potential bargaining unit and the shortage or oversupply of labor in the area, were more important in determining the election outcome than the involvement of management consultants.[15]

The union's response has not been limited to seeking congressional support for restrictive legislation about such consultants. In collective bargaining negotiations the unions have sought to get management to agree not to oppose unionization by their members in union representation elections. In 1976, the United Auto Workers obtained from General Motors a pledge "to neither discourage nor encourage the Union's efforts in organizing production and maintenance employees traditionally represented by the union elsewhere in General Motors, but [to] observe a posture of neutrality in these matters." In turn, the UAW pledged "to conduct itself in a manner which neither demeans the Corporation as an organization nor its representatives as individuals."

Thus, despite the provisions of the National Labor Relations Act which attempt to provide for a full and fair opportunity for employees to express their preferences about union representation, both labor and management have developed the practice of mounting elaborate campaigns designed to influence these preferences. So widespread has this practice become that now both labor and management must attempt in the collective bargaining process to establish limitations on each other's actions in order to ensure a fair opportunity for workers to express their desires.

---

[14] Stephen B. Goldberg et al., "Union Representation Elections: Law and Reality: The Authors Respond to the Critics," *Michigan Law Review*, 79:4, March 1981, pp. 564–593. Also, Goldberg, "Empirical Research in Labor Law," *University of Illinois Law Review*, 1(1981), pp. 15–31.

[15] John J. Lawler, "The Influence of Management Consultants on the Outcome of Union Certification Elections," *Industrial and Labor Relations Review*, 38:1, October 1984, pp. 38–51.

Decertification Elections

The NLRB conducts elections not only to see if workers who are not presently represented by a union wish to be represented but also to determine if workers who are presently represented by a union wish to continue to be represented. An election for union representation ordinarily begins with a petition (called an RC petition) filed by workers or by a union seeking an election. Similarly, an election to determine if workers want to get rid of a union, called a decertification election, ordinarily begins with a petition filed by employees (called an RD petition) or by an employer (called an RM petition).

Elections to decertify a union are much less common than elections to see if presently unrepresented employees wish to have a union. But decertification elections have been increasing.[16] In 1966, the NLRB conducted about 200 decertification elections. By 1983 the NLRB conducted some 922 such elections. Unions ordinarily lose these elections. In 1983, for example, of 922 RD elections held, unions lost 75 percent. Approximately 23,700 employees gave up union representation as a result of these elections.

The Role of Employers in an Election

There has been a great deal of litigation before the board about what employers may and may not do in the course of an NLRB election campaign. Originally the NLRB tried to require employers to remain outside the election process. However, in the Taft-Hartley Act of 1947 Congress provided that:

> The expressing of any view, argument, or opinion, or the dissemination thereof, whether in written, printed, graphic, or visual form, shall not constitute or be evidence of an unfair labor practice under any of the provisions of this Act, if such expression contains no threat of reprisal or force or promise of benefit.

This provision was intended to ensure that the right of employers to express their views was not unduly restricted by the NLRB. As a practical matter, this statutory language had the effect of putting the employer back into the matter of union organization—usually in opposition to unionization.

In the spring of 1988 a group of technical and clerical workers at Harvard University, who were affiliated with the American Federation of State, County and Municipal Employees (AFSCME), petitioned for and obtained an NLRB election among several thousand Harvard employees. When the union asked Harvard's president to remain neutral during the campaign, and students at Harvard College joined the request, the University's president wrote the following letter to employees and students of the university. Since Pres-

---

[16] William E. Fulmer, "When Employees Want to Oust Their Union," *Harvard Business Review*, 56:2, March–April 1978, pp. 163–171. See also John J. Lawler and Greg Hundley, "Determinants of Certification and Decertification Activity," *Industrial Relations*, 22:3, Fall 1983, pp. 335–348.

ident Bok of Harvard taught labor law before becoming an administrator, the letter represents a particularly knowledgeable response from an employer. It is reproduced below from the *Harvard Gazette,* May 6, 1988, page 4.

Should the Harvard admininistration be "neutral" toward the efforts of the American Federation of State, County and Municipal Employees (AFSCME) to organize our support staff? In other words, should Harvard feel obliged not to disclose its views on the union election nor to present its reasons for opposing union representation?

Since Harvard is an institution dedicated to the free exchange of ideas, it seems odd to suggest that the administration keep silent on an issue that clearly affects the University and the welfare of those who live and work here. Yet this is the view advanced in a petition signed by 3,000 students and endorsed by a number of student organizations, including the *Crimson.* With such backing, the proposition merits a thoughtful response.

Apparently, the argument for neutrality is that the administration is not an ordinary party to the debate over union representation, since Harvard employs the staff members and hence controls the livelihood of those who will vote in the election. As a result, it is said, an expression of Harvard's opposition carries an inevitable threat that dire consequences may befall those who vote in favor of the union.

In weighing this argument, it is important to bear in mind that staff members will decide on representation by secret ballot so that Harvard need never know how any individual votes. Hence, the notion that Harvard's opposition will intimidate staff members and coerce them into voting against the union reflects surprisingly little respect for their independence of mind and seems inplausible on its face.

The argument for neutrality also finds no support in the system of legal rules worked out over many years under the National Labor Relations Act to guarantee fair union elections. In order to insure a free and informed choice, the Act expressly guarantees to the employer a right to communicate to employees about the election and has done so for four decades, through Democratic as well as Republican administrations. The law protects employees against coercion and manipulation by prohibiting acts of intimidation, such as firing or penalizing union supporters; it likewise bans specific kinds of speech that could prejudice a free and informed choice; notably, employer threats, promises of benefits if the union loses, and interrogations. But the law in no way seeks to silence employers from presenting accurate facts and reasoned arguments in opposition to the union.

This framework of rules is not only well established but based on sound democratic principles. In a democracy that guarantees free speech, employers should have a right to communicate on a subject of obvious importance to their organization. In addition, if employees are to make an informed choice on whether or not to be represented by a union, they need to hear relevant facts and arguments on *both* sides of the issue and not merely listen to views in favor of the union. In order to learn the arguments and facts against as well as for the union, they will normally need to hear from the employer. For though individual employees may choose to argue against representation, they cannot begin to match the union's financial resources and organizing expertise. At Harvard, for example, numerous staff members have expressed opposition to the union, but they can hardly muster the hundreds of thousands of dollars, the paid organizers, the legal staff, and the other resources that AFSCME has poured into this campaign.

Some students have argued, nevertheless, that Harvard has an unfair advantage in presenting its case because it can call meetings of the staff during working hours. Yet Harvard has not exercised its legal right to compel attendance at these meetings and the record shows that many staff members do not choose to attend. Morever, it would be hard to argue that the union has been placed at an overall disadvantage in this campaign. The union has had three years to communicate its message in countless different settings, while the University has confined its campaign to less than three months. In addition, the law gives the union various advantages not granted to Harvard, such as the opportunity to decide when to call for an election, the right to promise any gains in wages, benefits or terms of employment, and the right to question employees about their views on union representation. Under the law, employers cannot do any of these things.

Since most people who urge neutrality strongly favor the union, they may feel that employers need not speak since they have no important arguments to make. Such sentiments often animate arguments against free speech. But there is no support for this notion generally nor is there in this case. In fact, there are many legitimate reasons why employees might oppose a union. To mention but a few, employees may find that they are already receiving higher wages and benefits than the union has typically been able to achieve; they may resent the possibility of being compelled to pay substantial dues or agency fees; they often dislike union efforts to abolish merit pay or to secure less flexible work rules; and they may fear that collective bargaining will lead to strikes, resulting in losses of pay and conceivably even the loss of jobs. In no small part because of reasons such as these, unions regularly lose more contested elections than they win.

As is so often the case, then, there are two sides to the question whether to be represented by a union. Before our staff members enter the polling booth to make a decision important to their lives and welfare, they deserve the opportunity to inform themselves fully on all aspects of the subject. Hence, it is not only in keeping with Harvard's commitment to free expression but a matter of fairness to our staff that they be made aware of all the pertinent facts and considerations rather than merely listening to the views of one side. In this spirit, we have done our best to present information and arguments and decide the issue of representation when they cast their ballots on May 17.

It is now common for employers to express their opposition to unionization of their employees by conducting a campaign to persuade employees not to join unions. A substantial group of lawyers and consultants, who offer their services to employers threatened by a union organizing campaign, has grown up. These advisers sometimes offer a preplanned strategy for the employer to follow in opposing unions.[17] Some of the tactics used are very imaginative. For example, in 1974 Dean Witter and Company, a New York stock brokerage firm, was faced with a campaign to organize its employees. The firm distributed to its employees listings of strikes that local affiliates of

---

[17] Lyman Powell, *How to Handle a Union Organizing Drive* (Los Angeles: Libby's, 1968); Louis Jackson and Robert Lewis, *Winning NLRB Elections: Management Strategy and Preventative Programs* (New York: Practising Law Institute, 1972).

the national union involved had conducted in the last year and a half. At another time during the campaign the company paid employees with two checks—one amounting only to union dues that employees would pay if the union won the election and the other check amounting to the employees' regular pay less the union dues. The union lost that particular election by a vote of 469 to 154.[18]

An employer that oversteps the limits of the statutory language quoted above may find itself convicted of an unfair labor practice. But what is illegal and what is not? Specifically, with respect to statements by employers in the course of a union organizing drive, there is a bewildering complexity of NLRB rulings:

• An employer predicted in a speech to employees that if the union came into the plant, the company would face economic disaster.

The NLRB held this not to be a "threat of reprisal" and therefore found the employer's action did not violate the law (Agar Packing and Provision Corporation, 1949).

• An employer in a speech and mailing to employees said that if the union was voted in, the annual wage increases the company ordinarily provided for employees would be delayed.

The NLRB found the employer guilty of an unfair labor practice—a threat not to pay employees a benefit ordinarily provided (Peterson Builders, Inc., v. Boilermakers, 1974).

• Two supervisors for a company suggested to employees about to vote in an NLRB election that the company would be likely to provide more and better job opportunities in the plant if it were nonunion.

The NLRB found the employer guilty of a thinly veiled threat of reprisal (General Electric v. International Union of Electrical Workers Local 676, 1974).

• A representative of the Catholic diocese of Gary, Indiana, read a Bible text to union leaders before an election by lay teachers to choose, or not choose, a bargaining representative. The text read in part, "Cleanse your hands, ye sinners."

The NLRB's general counsel issued an unfair labor practice complaint (Diocese of Gary, Indiana, 1976).

• An employer held a meeting with supervisors, floorladies, and working foremen, instructing them on their proper roles in a current union organizational campaign. Among other things, the employees were told not to talk to NLRB agents outside the presence of company attorneys.

The NLRB found no violation of the law, saying that at the time of the meeting the employer "honestly regarded the floorladies and working foremen" as part of supervision (Cato Show Printing Co., 1975).

• During a union campaign a meeting was held between employees and the employer at the employees' request. A spokesperson for the employees

---

[18] Bureau of National Affairs, *Daily Labor Report* No. 246, Dec. 20, 1974, p. A1.

told the employer that all the employees had decided that they did not want to join the union. The employer asked, "Nobody wants to join the union?" The employees said no. "Well, fine. That's excellent. Is this everybody here? Nobody wants to join the union?"

The NLRB found that there was no violation of the law, since the employer polled the employees only after the employees had openly stated their position to him. The employer merely verified what they had told him (Jerome J. Jacomet et al., 1976).

• An election was scheduled from 2:45 to 4:45 p.m. On the day of the election, the company president spoke individually to every employee on the first shift—approximately half of the eligible voters—urging them to vote against union representation. The talks lasted a few minutes at each employee's work station. The union lost the vote.

The NLRB held that the talks were informal and individual, and as such did not tend to develop a mass psychology and therefore were lawful. The election results were allowed to stand (Electro-Wire Products et al., 1979).

• An employer responded to employee dissatisfaction with a union by initiating a proposal to terminate the collective bargaining agreement and assisting employees to circulate an antiunion petition.

The NLRB held that the company had violated the law. On appeal a federal court held that the employer must maintain complete neutrality of action, though it can express its views, about unionization of its employees. This the company had not done (Texaco, Inc. v. NLRB, Fifth Circuit Court of Appeals, No. 82-4454, 1984).

• An employer met with workers who were considering forming a union. He was asked if a rumor that the plant would be closed if the union won an election was true. "What would you do in my shoes?" the employer replied.

The NLRB held that in the context of threats by other supervisors, the response was coercive and in violation of the law (Rosewood Manufacturing Inc., 269 NLRB no. 140, 1984).

• An employer sent a letter to all employees during a union organizing effort. The letter read in part, "We have been able to work on an informal and person-to-person basis. If the union comes in this will change. We will have to run things by the book, with a stranger, and will not be able to handle personal requests as we have been doing." The NLRB's regional director found that these statements were misrepresentations of employees' rights under section 9 (a) of the act, under which employees retain the right to present individual grievances to their employer. The regional director reasoned that these statements posed a threat to take away existing rights.

The board itself disagreed. It found that the employer's statements in the letter were not threats, but permissible campaign rhetoric (TriCast Inc., 274 NLRB no. 59, 1985).

The examples just cited indicate actions which management can take in a union organization campaign without violating the law. But the unions maintain that management in many instances knowingly violates the requirements of federal law in order to defeat union organization campaigns. Academic research supports the proposition that companies may have something to gain by violation of the law if they are thereby successful in thwarting union organization of their employees.[19] This research does not prove that managements do sometimes knowingly violate the law, since to have an incentive to do something does not necessarily imply that an action is taken.

The remedial powers of the NLRB do not seem adequate, however, to dissuade some employers from violation of the labor laws as a strategy to avoid union organization. In 1977 and 1978, the unions sought to obtain amendments to the Taft-Hartley Act which would, in the unions' view, better protect the rights of workers to organize unions. Specifically, the unions wanted:

- Elections held more quickly
- Preliminary injunctions to prevent employers from discharging union supporters, rather than reinstatement orders by the NLRB following the discharge of union activists
- Authority for the NLRB to enforce its own orders, rather than to have to go to the federal district courts to get board orders enforced
- Government contracts to be denied to companies found in repeated violation of the labor laws

These suggestions for changes in the law were embodied in legislation labeled the labor law reform bill. In 1978 the bill passed the U.S. House of Representatives but was defeated by a filibuster in the Senate.

Who Is Winning NLRB Elections?

The board conducted 4405 representation elections in fiscal 1983, in which 209,918 employees were eligible to vote and 181,308 valid votes were cast. Unions won 43 percent of the elections, involving 90,370 eligible voters, and lost 57 percent of the elections, involving 90,938 eligible voters. In recent years the percentage of elections won by unions has steadily fallen from 57 percent in 1968 to 43 percent in 1983. (Surprisingly, in 1988 the most recent comprehensive data available for NLRB elections were for 1983.)

Table 5-2 shows the percentage of union victories in NLRB elections every 5 years since 1950. The substantial decline in union victories is evident. The table also shows that the proportion of the nonagricultural work force won by unions in elections has fallen dramatically (from 1.92 percent in 1950 to 0.12 percent in 1983).

Why are unions losing more and more representation elections? The unions maintain that the NLRB has tipped the scales in favor of management. Management is now increasingly free to oppose unions and to do so actively and with legal impunity. As a result, unions lose elections. When unions win elections, employers often engage in surface bargaining, i.e., bargaining without any serious intent to reach agreement, so that the union can-

---

[19] Charles R. Greer and Stanley A. Martin, "Calculative Strategy Decisions During Union Organization Campaigns," *Sloan Management Review*, 19:2, Winter 1978, pp. 61–74.

TABLE 5-2 UNION VICTORY RATE IN NLRB ELECTIONS AND FRACTION OF LABOR FORCE IN UNION VICTORIES

	Union victory rate in NLRB elections	Fraction of nonagricultural work force in union victories, %
1950	74	1.92
1955	68	0.87
1960	59	0.62
1965	61	0.64
1970	56	0.53
1975	50	0.33
1980	48	0.24
1983	43	0.12

Source: Paul Weiler, "Promises to Keep," *Harvard Law Review*, 96:8, June 1983, p. 1792. Also, 48th Annual Report of NLRB, p. 13.

not obtain a contract. The effect is to demonstrate the futility of union organization to employees.[20] Finally, the unions charge, the board has imposed unreasonable legal restrictions on the organizing activities of unions. One major example that the unions cite involves the repeated denial by the board of the right of nonemployee (or "outside") union organizers to go onto the employers' property to talk with employees.[21]

Richard B. Freeman has made quantitative estimates of the importance of various factors in the decline of union successes in NLRB elections. In 1950 unions won representation rights for 84 percent of the employees eligible to vote in NLRB elections. By 1980, unions won representation rights for only 37 percent.

- 40 percent of the decline was a result of increased management opposition
- 20 percent was due to reduced union organizing efforts
- 40 percent was due to changes in the economy and other factors[22]

Management opposition to unions takes many forms, some of which are more positive than others. Many companies encourage employee communication and participation programs, including nonunion grievance procedures. In effect, they provide employees with a substitute for

[20] AFL-CIO *News,* Oct. 30, 1976, p. 8.

[21] Max Zimny, "Access of Union Organizers to 'Private' Property," *Labor Law Journal,* 25:10, October 1974, pp. 618–624. See also Stephen I. Schlossberg, *Organizing and the Law* (Washington, D.C.: Bureau of National Affairs, 1967). This board policy was established by decision of the Supreme Court in 1956 (*Babcock & Wilcox Co.*).

[22] Richard B. Freeman, "Why Are Unions Faring Poorly in NLRB Representation Elections?" in Thomas A. Kochan, ed., *Challenges and Choices Facing American Labor* (Cambridge, Mass.: MIT Press, 1985), pp. 45–64.

unions, and appear to be more successful in avoiding unions than are other companies.[23]

One of the most difficult NLRB policies for the unions to accept involves the question of what the law requires when an employer has by unfair labor practices (see Chapter 6) prevented a union from gaining a majority. Should the board order the employer to bargain with the union despite the union's never having won an election?

Conair Corporation is a manufacturer of hair care and grooming products with a plant at Edison, New Jersey. A local of the International Ladies Garment Workers Union tried to organize the plant and received authorization cards from 46 percent of 380 production and maintenance employees. The company acted quickly. The top management threatened to close the plant and move production to Hong Kong if the union won an election. Managers threatened to end benefits if employees voted for the union. Many employees were so afraid of losing their jobs that they went to the union and sought return of the authorization cards. The union then called a strike. The company fired all strikers and promised benefit increases and improved working conditions to employees if they would not strike. The union gave up the strike after 5 months. Meanwhile an NLRB election had been held. The company contributed to profit sharing for nonunion members only and promised other improvements if the employees would abandon the union. In an election held on December 7, 1977, some 9 months after the start of the organizing effort, the union got one-third of the ballots cast.

The NLRB in 1982 held that the management's violations of the labor law were so "outrageous" and "pervasive" that it would be ordered to bargain with the union regardless of the election's outcome, and it issued an order to the company to recognize the union.[24] The Supreme Court had suggested that in an exceptional case marked by flagrant employer violations that preclude a fair election, the NLRB might issue a bargaining order even if the union could not and even if the union had never shown majority support.[25] In 1983 the District of Columbia Circuit Court of Appeals struck down the NLRB order against Conair.

In 1984 the NLRB returned to the same question and announced that it would "under no circumstances" issue a bargaining order where the union had not demonstrated majority support.[26]

---

[23] Jack Fiorito, Christopher Lowman, and Forrest D. Nelson, "The Impact of Human Resource Policies on Union Organizing," *Industrial Relations*, 26:2, Spring 1987, pp. 113ff. See also Kenneth Gilberg and Nancy Abrams, "Countering Unions' New Organizing Techniques," *Personnel*, 64:6, June 1987, pp. 12ff.

[24] "Divided NLRB," Bureau of National Affairs, *Daily Labor Report* No. 106, June 2, 1982, pp. AA-1, AA-2. The case is *Conair Corporation*, 1982.

[25] *Gissell Packing Co.*, 71 LRRM 2481, 1969.

[26] "Board Rejects Bargaining Order," Bureau of National Affairs, *Daily Labor Report*, No. 97, May 18, 1984, pp. AA-1, AA-2. The case is *Gourmet Foods, Inc. and Teamsters Local 503*, May 14, 1984.

To the unions it appears that the policy of the NLRB and the courts means simply that an employer who flagrantly and successfully violates the labor laws will be allowed to enjoy his success. It is this situation, perhaps more than any other, that in the mid-1980s caused union officials to publicly question whether or not the nation's labor laws are of any benefit to workers who wish to organize a union.

There is today considerable ambivalence in opinion about the NLRA. Professor Paul C. Weiler of Harvard Law School has commented:

> If there is any one observation that one can make with some degree of confidence during this, the fiftieth anniversary year of the National Labor Relations Act, it is that the authors of the Act would be mightily surprised to hear who is saying what about their offspring. The business community, which excoriated the Wagner Act as the most radical feature of the New Deal, now praises the balanced and constructive character of our legislation. The "God-damned Labor Board," to use Fortune Magazine's sobriquet of 1938, is now applauded by management attorneys for its moderate and even-handed jurisprudence. Meanwhile, the Democratic supporters of the union movement in Congress have just issued a report entitled "Has Labor Law Failed?": their answer to their question is most emphatically, "Yes!" More and more union leaders—up to and including Lane Kirkland, President of the AFL-CIO—are saying that labor would be better off if the Board were disbanded, the Act repealed, and we were all "to return to the law of the jungle."[27]

In essence, those who support unions believe the NLRA was enacted to foster union organization, and that it has been perverted in recent years. Jay Siegel, a management attorney, described the law's posture in the mid-1980s as follows:

> Fifty years after the passage of the National Labor Relations Act, U.S. labor policy is precisely where the sense of the nation wants it to be: conservative toward the unionization of workers but supportive of their individual rights. However distressful to organized labor this may be, it is a classic example of the democratic process at work.[28]

He writes elsewhere,

> The collectivist approach runs counter to the individualistic trends that have marked our way of life beginning in the 1970s, particularly among the younger people entering the workforce for the first time. Their way of life is to "do their own thing." Thus, they are restless in a work environment that does not allow for easy expression. They recognize, however, that there is a price to be paid for the wages and benefits they receive from a company and so tolerate, in most instances, the employer's rules for conduct and job performance. But they do not see a need for additional structure in the form of a union for which they may not get

---

[27] Paul C. Weiler, "Reflections on the NLRA at 50," Bureau of National Affairs, *Daily Labor Report* No. 112, June 11, 1985, pp. E1–E11. See also James A. Gross, "Conflicting Statutory Purposes," *Industrial Labor Relations Review*, 39:1, October 1985, pp. 7–18.
[28] Jay S. Siegel, "A New Labor Policy Consensus," *The Wall Street Journal*, Sept. 4, 1985, p. 18.

any direct or immediate benefit and have to pay a dues charge, which is simply lost money to them.[29]

In 1987 a personnel consultant studied whether political bias influences decisions by the NLRB. He found a sharp difference between voting of appointees of the two political parties. "Republican members originally appointed by Republican presidents appear to be staunch party-liners who make decisions which are influenced by political party philosophy," he said, adding that such appointees were less likely to decide in favor of unions over employers than nominees of other political stripes.

According to him the same cannot be said of nominees selected by Democratic Presidents. "Results also suggest," he said, "that Democratic members originally appointed by Democratic Presidents are no more likely to decide in favor of employers or unions, but play by the rules and render decisions in an evenhanded manner."[30]

These observers agree that the NLRA has tilted away from unions, but disagree whether this is good or bad. This is a question for the American people to answer.

CHAPTER SUMMARY

The National Labor Relations Board is a federal agency which administers the law governing labor relations. It was created by Congress in 1935 and has two principal functions: (1) to determine through elections whether employees wish to be represented by a union and, if so, what union; and (2) to prevent unfair (i.e., unlawful) labor practices by either employers or unions.

The organization and the structure of the NLRB are complex. The board consists of a five-member board, which acts as a judicial body in deciding cases submitted to it, and as an administrative agency, which has about 95 administrative law judges (ALJs) who hear cases and issue decisions. There is also an independent general counsel's office, which is responsible for the issuance and prosecution of formal complaints. The Taft-Hartley Act amendments of 1947 separated the role of prosecutor (the general counsel) from that of judge (the ALJs and the board) in the structure of the NLRB.

The board does not act on its own initiative, but processes petitions for employee elections and charges of unfair labor practices. In a recent year, the NLRB received more than 50,000 cases, about 75 percent of which involved charges of unfair labor practices. An unfair labor practice proceeding is initiated by the filing of a charge with a regional office of the NLRB, which investigates the charge. If a formal complaint is issued, the office of the general counsel becomes the prosecutor, the government bears the costs, and an ALJ hears the case. Appeals of board decisions go to various federal circuit courts

---

[29] Jay S. Siegel, "Has Labor's Day Passed?" *The Boston Globe,* Sept. 3, 1985, p. 25.

[30] "Consultant...," Bureau of National Affairs, *Daily Labor Report,* No. 2, January 5, 1988, p. A-10.

of appeal, and some ultimately find their way to the U.S. Supreme Court. The NLRB has the largest volume of federal court appeals of any federal administrative agency.

An important aspect of unfair labor practice proceedings is that there are no provisions for the issuing of penalties for violations—only remedial orders intended to prevent and remedy unfair labor practices.

Enforcement of NLRB decisions can also be complicated. In the face of union or employer noncompliance, the board must ask a federal district court to issue an order enforcing the board's decision. The union or company may, in turn, ask the federal district court not to enforce the decision and thus tie up the matter in further litigation and review.

The question of whether a group of employees should be represented by a union is legally determined by majority rule. Usually, this entails an election conducted by the NLRB after a petition has been filed requesting one. First, however, an investigation must determine the appropriate unit in which to conduct the election. The choice of a bargaining unit can have a major impact on the likelihood of unionization of an employee group and frequently involves the question of craft versus industrial units. Through the years, the board has taken (and sometimes rescinded) various positions on this issue.

The NLRB regulates what the unions and employers may say and do in election campaigns. Representation elections ordinarily involve extensive campaigns conducted by both the employer and the union. In the past 2 decades, the proportion of NLRB elections won by unions has steadily declined, and the unions claim that management has been increasingly free to oppose unions and to defeat union attempts to obtain bargaining rights.

QUESTIONS FOR THOUGHT AND DISCUSSION

1 Why is the general counsel's office separated from the five-member NLRB? Does this organizational arrangement help ensure the board's fairness? Why or why not?

2 How does the NLRB's handling of representation cases differ from its handling of unfair labor practice cases? Do you have ideas on how either procedure could be improved?

3 It is sometimes suggested that the NLRB be abolished and all labor law cases be sent directly to the federal court system. Do you agree? Why or why not?

4 What should be the role of an employer when its employees are going to vote in an NLRB election? Should the employer be neutral? Should it be prounion or antiunion? Does the NLRB let the employer take part in the election campaign? Should it do so?

5 Why are unions losing so many NLRB elections? Is the process at fault? Are the unions at fault? Give reasons for your answers.

6 Why are unit determinations important? What factors are involved in judging the appropriate size and type of unit? Do you feel that the NLRB has too much dis-

cretionary power in making these determinations? What would be a better method?

7 What is bargaining structure and how do bargaining units differ from bargaining structure? Should the NLRB be more concerned with bargaining structure? Why?

8 What problems might be associated with the fact that interpretation of the nation's labor laws requires increasingly specialized legal expertise rather than experience in labor-management relations?

9 Do campaign tactics affect the outcome of NLRB elections? What evidence is there to support your answer?

10 How are NLRB decisions enforced? Describe the ways in which a noncompliant defendant can tie up an unfair labor practice case or a representation proceeding. Can you think of ways to improve the procedures for reaching equitable settlements of complaints?

SELECTED READING

Feldacker, Bruce S., *Labor Guide to Labor Law*, 2d ed. (Reston, Va.: Reston Publishing Company, 1983).

Gagoula, Kenneth, *Union Organizing and Staying Organized* (Reston, Va.: Reston Publishing Company, 1983).

Getman, Julius G., et al., *Union Representation Elections: Law and Reality* (New York: Basic Books, 1976).

Goldman, Alvin L., *The Supreme Court and Labor-Management Relations Law* (Lexington, Mass.: Lexington Books, 1976).

Gould, William B., IV, "Fifty years under the National Labor Relations Act: A Retrospective View," *Labor Law Journal*, 37:4, April 1986, pp. 235–243.

Gross, James A., *The Making of the NLRB*, 2 vols. (Albany, N.Y.: State University of New York, 1974) and *The Reshaping of the NLRB* (Albany, N.Y.: State University of New York, 1982).

Murphy, Betty Southard, and Elliot S. Azoff, *Practice and Procedure before the National Labor Relations Board* (Washington, D.C.: Bureau of National Affairs, Corporate Practice Series No. 41, 1985).

Schlossberg, Stephen I., and Judith A. Scott, *Organizing and the Law*, 3d ed. (Washington, D.C.: BNA Books, 1983).

Weiler, Paul, "Promises to Keep," *Harvard Law Review* 96:8, June 1983, pp. 1769–1822; "Striking a New Balance," *Harvard Law Review*, 98:2, December 1984, pp. 351–420; "Reflections on the NLRA at 50," speech to the National Academy of Arbitrators, May 30, 1985, published in Bureau of National Affairs, *Daily Labor Report* No. 112, June 11, 1985, pp. E1–E11; and "Milestone or Tombstone: The Wagner Act at Fifty," *Harvard Journal on Legislation*, 23:1, Winter 1986, pp. 1–31.

6

UNFAIR LABOR PRACTICES

UNFAIR LABOR PRACTICES BY EMPLOYERS

American labor law is not greatly concerned with the substantive results of collective bargaining (i.e., with what wage levels are established, how long the workday is, and so on) in the private sector, but it is very much concerned with the procedures of the parties in labor relations. The NLRB closely regulates activities of unions and employers with respect to each other and with respect to employees. The NLRB has the authority to issue general rules or regulations to implement the provisions of the labor laws, but rarely does so; it prefers to decide individual cases. These case decisions provide guidance to employers and unions involved in a similar situation concerning what is legal and what is illegal activity.

There is a body of NLRB and court decisions with respect to unfair labor practices which is very large. Furthermore, the absence of generally promulgated rules prevents a simple listing of what is and is not legal. All that can reasonably be done in a text is to discuss some of the more significant matters that have arisen under the labor laws.

Types

Section 8(a) of the National Labor Relations Act proscribes certain activities by employers. Specifically, employers are prohibited by the act from:

• Interfering with, coercing, or restraining employees in exercise of their rights to join or assist labor organizations, or *not* to join or assist [section 8(a)(1)]

• Assisting, dominating, or contributing financially to labor unions [section 8(a)(2)]
• Discriminating against employees to discourage or encourage union membership, except as provided by a valid union security clause in a collective bargaining agreement [section 8(a)(3)]
• Discriminating against employees because they have filed charges or given testimony to the NLRB [section 8(a)(4)]
• Refusing to bargain in good faith with the representatives of employees [section 8(a)(5)]

Interference with the Rights of Employees

Section 8(a)(1) involves a broad prohibition on employer interference with employees exercising their rights under the labor laws. The prohibition is so broad that whenever the NLRB finds that an employer has committed any other unfair labor practice by virtue of violating sections 8(a)(2) or 8(a)(5) of the act, it also finds a violation of section 8(a)(1). Employer conduct that is in violation of this section of the act can occur at any time in the course of the relationship between an employer and its employees and their union(s), if any. However, section 8(a)(1) violations are especially common in the course of a union organization campaign. Some examples of what an employer legally can and cannot do under section 8(a)(1) in an election campaign were given in the previous chapter.

Violations of section 8(a)(1), which are not also violations of other parts of section 8(a), include such actions as:

• Threatening employees with loss of jobs or benefits if they should join or vote for a union
• Threatening to close down a plant if a union should be organized in it
• Questioning employees about union membership or activities in a situation that tends to restrain or coerce the employees
• Spying or pretending to spy on union meetings
• Granting wage increases intentionally timed to discourage employees from joining a union

As we saw in the preceding chapter, it is not the intent of section 8(a)(1) to require an employer to be neutral about its employees' decision to join or not to join a union. The law simply prohibits the employer from interfering with, restraining, or coercing employees in their choice. The employer may legally inform, urge, or persuade employees about joining or not joining a union.

The conduct that constitutes a violation of section 8(a)(1) can best be described by an example. On August 23, 1973, three employees of a company in Albany, New York, began a campaign to organize other employees for collective bargaining. The company was a wholesale and retail grocer. The three employees had met with officials of a Teamsters local union and therefore sought authorization cards from other employees indicating a desire to have the Teamsters as a collective bargaining representative. On September 1 a supervisor of the company asked one employee what he thought about the union representing him. The employee replied that he wanted the union to represent him. The supervisor then said that he would remember this remark and that, whether the union got in or not, the employee could lose his job over it. On September 4 two union officers met with the president of the company. The union officials stated that they had signed authorization cards from 43 of the 49 employees in the company's warehouse. They demanded that the employer recognize the union and bargain with it. The company's president refused, saying he preferred to file for an NLRB election. He did not file, however.

On September 5 the company's vice president addressed a meeting of warehouse and office employees. He stated that the warehouse employees were attempting to form a union and that if they voted to strike, they would only hurt the company and the office employees. By such a strike, he said, the company would lose customers and might go out of business. If that happened, all the employees would lose their jobs. The way to prevent this was to deal with the matter in other ways. He asked the employees to give the matter much further thought. After the meeting the vice president asked a particular employee to try to influence other employees in the company's favor. When the employee refused, the vice president told him that if the employees struck, "We aren't going to be friends any more."

On September 8, a group of 39 employees unanimously voted to strike on the following day to obtain union recognition. Later that day the union officials and some employees met with the company's vice president and sought to have him agree to an election conducted by a state mediator. He refused, saying that he was worried about the effects of a strike and that if the employees went on strike he would file a petition with the NLRB the following Monday. No such petition was filed.

The strike began the next day, September 9. The pickets carried signs stating that the employees were "on strike for better wages and benefits, Local 294, Teamsters." The strike continued from September 9 to September 29. During the strike the company's president spoke daily to the strikers, individually and in groups, on the picket line and at the premises, telling them that they might as well go home, that they had ruined his business, that the company was selling out and putting padlocks on the doors, that he would not hire the employees back anyway, and that certain of the employees had no seniority.

On September 29 the employees returned to work after the company's president told them that he would take back all the strikers in accordance with their seniority. This he failed to do. On October 8 the company's president talked to an employee who had both signed a union authorization card and participated in the strike. The president told the employee that the employee had gone about the strike the wrong way. "You are pretty far down on the seniority list," he said. "You will be voting for your job, not for the union." The president said he'd hire the employee back if the employee would try to get other employees who were low on the seniority list to come to work.

The NLRB found several violations of section 8(a)(1) in the company's behavior. Specifically, it found:

- Unlawful interrogation of employees
- Illegal threats of job loss
- Illegal threats of plant closing
- Illegal solicitation to discourage union activity

In consequence of the many serious violations of the law by the employer, the NLRB found that it was unlikely that a fair election could be held. The board dispensed with an election and ordered the company to bargain with the union (*Trading Post, Inc., v. Local 294, International Brotherhood of Teamsters,* 1976).

Another classic unfair labor practice case involved Del Rey Tortilleria, Inc., of Chicago, a family-owned corporation. The company employed some 70 unskilled workers at one facility and 40 unskilled employees at another. Nearly all the employees were of Mexican descent. Some were undocumented aliens, and most were poorly educated immigrants with little working knowledge of English who worked for the minimum wage.

The company's chief operating officer was away in Mexico on business. In his absence, his stepdaughters were left in charge. In late September Luis Maldonada and several other employees asked the owners to establish a regularly scheduled break time to replace what the court calls the arbitrary system then in operation. Replying that the employees were a "bunch of pigs" and that they made a "mess of the lunchroom," the owners refused to give them a regular break and also sent home those employees who requested a break. Shortly afterwards, Maldonado contacted Local 76 of the International Ladies Garment Workers Union.

After an organizational drive and two days before Local 76 filed its representation petition, the union's organizing director sent a telegram to the owners informing them of the organizing drive and identifying the three employees on the organizing committee, including Maldonado.

Thereafter, the company conducted several coercive interrogations. In one case a plant supervisor asked an employee which employees were in the union and why they needed a union at all. In another case, one of the owners called an employee into the office and asked him if he was involved in the union. When the employee denied involvement, the owner told him that if he was involved, he would be suspended for 3 days, just as one of the employees on the organizing committee had been suspended. In the interview of two employees, both were asked about their status with respect to the union. When they admitted to membership, they were each told that they no longer had jobs. One of the employees also was threatened with a visit from the police if he failed to cooperate.

Two days after the company had been notified of the organizational effort, the employees were due to be paid. The company posted a notice which required the employees to present two forms of identification in order to obtain their paychecks, the court relates. Employees were told to present their Social Security cards and their green cards or "Micas," which are issued by the Immigration and Naturalization Service to indicate lawful presence in the United States. In addition, on several occasions discharged employees were informed that they were fired, at least in part, because of their union activities. Several employees were informed that they could be reinstated if they would renounce the union.

Reviewing the NLRB's finding of unfair labor practices by the company, a judge wrote:

> This case presents a classic case of anti-union behavior by a company. The day after the first union meeting, the violations began with a promise of wage benefits in return for rejection of the union. As the union's organizing drive intensified, so did the company's retaliatory measures. Indeed, the company's threatening and hostile posture with respect to employees in the union carried over to the hearing. In fact, at two separate junctures in his decision, the administrative law judge noted that de la Torre was making audible comments from the counsel table thereby affecting the responses of the witnesses.

The court enforced the board's order requiring the reinstatement of three employees whose discharges were motivated by antiunion animus. It rejected the company's argument that two of the employees were fired pursuant to an established "no drinking" rule. It also rejected the company's position that the third employee was fired because she broke a box of tostadas when making room to sit down in the lunchroom. "The company had never before nor after fired anyone for breaking tostadas. Moreover, [the employee] volunteered to pay for the damage. Thus, the breakage argument is clearly pretextual," the court concluded (*NLRB v. Del Rey Tortilleria, Inc., 7th Circuit Court of Appeals, No. 85–1199,* Apr. 2, 1986).[1]

There has been important litigation under section 8(a)(1) about the right of employees to have union representation at meetings with management. For many years the NLRB had not prevented management from holding investigatory meetings with employees while denying the union the right to be present, but by the 1970s the NLRB was ready to change its position. In one case that came to the board, an employee had shut down her machine and was causing a minor disturbance on the floor of an apparel manufacturing firm. The employee was directed by her supervisor to resume production. She refused. The manager then ordered the employee to go to the president's office. The employee refused to go without a union representative accompanying her. In the ensuing 6-day dispute, the employee was not allowed to work, and two union officials who tried to represent her were

---

[1] Reported in Bureau of National Affairs, *Daily Labor Report* No. 94, May 15, 1986, pp. A-1 and A-2.

suspended from work also. When, after 6 days, the employee gave a final refusal to a private interview with the company's president, both she and the union stewards were discharged.

The union filed an unfair labor practice charge with the board. The board found that there were "reasonable grounds to believe that disciplinary action might result from the Employer's investigation" of the employee's conduct. Therefore, said the board, the employee had a right to union representation. The employer was found guilty of an unfair labor practice, specifically a violation of section 8(a)(1) of the act, by virtue of his action in discharging the employee, suspending and discharging one union steward, and suspending a second union steward (*Quality Manufacturing*, 1972).

A federal court of appeals overturned the board's decision in July 1973. The court found that the board's decision represented a departure from existing law and that the board offered no support for it. Further, said the court, "every situation wherein an employee is directed by management to cooperate in an investigatory interview carries the implicit threat of discipline if such direction is not obeyed." But, presumably, the court felt that employees were not entitled to union representation in all such instances.

The Supreme Court ruled on the *Quality Manufacturing* case and a similar case in 1975. The Court reversed the appellate court, holding that the NLRB was correct in finding that the law gives an employee the right to insist on the presence of a union representative at an investigatory interview that might result in disciplinary action. In an interesting aside, the court said that even if some of the board's earlier decisions (i.e., its own precedents) may be read as reaching a contrary conclusion, they did not freeze "the development of this important aspect of the national labor law. The responsibility to adopt the Act to changing patterns of industrial life is entrusted to the Board."[2]

Employees' rights to take concerted action in their own interests are the source of a number of important cases before the NLRB. In one such case five employees staged a brief work stoppage in order to obtain an explanation from the employer of the discharge of their supervisor. Apparently, the supervisor had made extra efforts to meet with the employees for discussions and counseling on matters directly bearing on their employment relationship. When the supervisor was discharged, the employees were concerned that their own situation at the workplace would suffer. The employer discharged the five persons who participated in the work stoppage. The NLRB decided that because the employees held the reasonable expectation that their employment would suffer as a result of the discharge of the supervisor, the employees' action was protected by the law and the employer was required to reinstate the five (*Puerto Rico Food Products Corporation*, 1979).

[2] *International Ladies Garment Workers Union, Upper South Department, v. Quality Manufacturing Co.*, 420 U.S. 276, and *NLRB v. J. Weingarten, Inc.*, 420 U.S. 251. Wallace B. Nelson, "Union Representation during Investigation Interviews," *The Arbitration Journal*, 31:3, Sept. 1976, pp. 181–190.

The National Labor Relations Act can also, with other statutes (such as the Civil Rights Act) and the Constitution, serve as a basis for court action against employers who violate the rights of employees or other union organizers. The Amalgamated Clothing and Textile Workers sued the mayor, police chief, and other officials of Milledgeville, Georgia, for unlawful surveillance of union organizers and employees of J. P. Stevens and Company. According to the suit, the city's police department kept union officials and attorneys under surveillance by stationing police officers in unmarked cars near the Holiday Inn where the organizers stayed and conducted meetings. The manager of the Holiday Inn was alleged to have provided police officers with keys to a room next to the room used by the union officials, so that the police could observe and record the names of all persons entering and leaving the union organizers' room. On April 26, 1979, a federal district court issued an injunction against the mayor, police chief, and other officials of the Georgia city, and also against the manager of the Holiday Inn, prohibiting them from conducting surveillance of the union officials.[3]

Unfair labor practices by employers directed at union proponents apparently affect the outcome of elections.[4] In part, the opportunity for illegal behavior is created by the long campaigns that precede union elections under NLRB auspices. Canada has no such period for campaigns. Instead elections are held very quickly after a petition for an election is received by the labor board. As one observer has pointed out, "In Canada the simple device of dispensing with the protracted campaign eliminates most of the opportunity for illegal intimidation and limits the rate of employer unfair labor practices to a fraction of the American rate."[5]

Discrimination Against Employees

Going Out of Business   Can the labor laws prohibit a corporation from going out of business? This was the central issue in a case, involving section 8(a)(3) of the National Labor Relations Act, that found its way to the Supreme Court in 1965.

Darlington Manufacturing Company was a South Carolina corporation operating one textile mill. A majority of the stock of the corporation was held by Deering-Milliken and Co., a New York "selling house" that markets textile products. Deering-Milliken was controlled by Roger Milliken, president of Darlington Manufacturing Company, and by other members of the Milliken

---

[3] Bureau of National Affairs, *Daily Labor Report* No. 78, Apr. 20, 1979, and No. 83, Apr. 27, 1979.

[4] William T. Dickens, "The Effect of Company Campaigns on Certification Elections," *Industrial and Labor Relations Review*, 36:4, July 1983, pp. 560–575. Also see Herbert G. Heneman III and Marcus H. Sandven, "Predicting the Outcome of Union Certification Elections: A Review of the Literature," *Industrial and Labor Relations Review*, 36:4, July 1983, pp. 537–559.

[5] Paul Weiler, "Promises to Keep: Securing Workers' Rights to Self-Organization under the NLRA," *Harvard Law Review*, 96:8, June 1983, p. 1821.

family. Deering-Milliken operated 17 textile manufacturers involving some 27 mills, all of the products of which were marketed through Deering-Milliken.

In March 1956 the Textile Workers Union of America tried to organize Darlington. The company resisted and threatened to close the mill. On September 6, 1956, the union won a narrow victory in an NLRB election. On September 12 the board of directors of Darlington met and voted to liquidate the corporation. On October 19 the stockholders voted their approval. In November the plant ceased operations, all employees were discharged, and in December all machinery and equipment of the company was sold piecemeal at auction and the property was leased to another tenant.

The union filed a charge of an unfair labor practice. The board's regional office investigated and filed a formal complaint. The five-member board found the company had violated section 8(a)(3) of the act. Section 8(a)(3) reads in particular:

> It shall be an unfair labor practice for an employer... by discrimination in regard to hire or tenure of employment... to encourage or discourage membership in any labor organization.

The company appealed the NLRB decision to a circuit court of appeals. The company argued that it had the absolute, unfettered right to close out a part or all of its business regardless of antiunion motivation. The appeals court agreed and reversed the NLRB decision.

The case was appealed to the Supreme Court. The Supreme Court said that "as far as the Labor Act is concerned, an employer has the absolute right to terminate his entire business for any reason he pleases." But, the Court said, an employer does not have "the ability to close part of a business no matter what the reason." Since Darlington was found to be part of a larger entity, Deering-Milliken, it could not be shut down for antiunion reasons, as long as that was the company's motivation and the closing of Darlington could be shown to be an effort to "chill unionism" in any of the remaining plants of the same employer.[6]

Darlington was ordered to compensate some 500 workers laid off when it closed for the time they lost through the illegal closing. Fifteen years after the Supreme Court decision, and 25 years after the plant's closing, the NLRB was still conducting hearings to ascertain how much money was owed to the dismissed workers by the Milliken interests.

Finally, in November 1980, the Milliken company, the Textile Workers Union (by 1980 a part of the Amalgamated Clothing and Textile Workers Union of America), and the NLRB agreed to end the long litigation by settlement. Under the terms of the settlement Milliken paid $5 million to workers who had lost their jobs in 1956, or, if need be, to the survivors (i.e., the heirs) of those workers.

---

[6] Dennis A. Arnsdorf, "The Darlington Manufacturing Organizing Campaign," *Industrial Labor Relations Forum,* 10:1, March 1974, pp. 1–14.

An Employer Lockout   May an employer lock out its employees when a collective bargaining agreement has expired and the employer's purpose is to put economic pressure on the union to settle a contract on terms favorable to the employer? For many years the NLRB said no. An employer could engage in certain types of "defensive" lockouts, but it could not use the lockout as a weapon in support of its bargaining position, a so-called offensive lockout.

In 1965 the Supreme Court reviewed the NLRB's position on the lockout in a case involving American Shipbuilding Company. American Shipbuilding operated four shipyards on the Great Lakes. The company's work is concentrated in the winter months. Since 1952 the company had bargained with eight unions. Each contract negotiation had been accompanied by a strike. In the summer of 1961 the talks for a new agreement reached an impasse. The union officials assured the company that there would be no strike, but there had been a wildcat strike in February 1961 and the company feared a strike as the work season approached. On August 11 the company locked out employees at two of its plants and began to shut down the other two. Negotiations were resumed, and on October 27 a settlement of the terms of a 2-year agreement was reached. The employees were recalled on October 28.

The union filed an unfair labor practice charge. When the case reached the five-member board, it reaffirmed its earlier policies. The company was not free to lock out, the board said, for economic reasons, especially when there were reasonable grounds to believe a strike was threatened or imminent. A lockout for offensive purposes, said the board, infringes on employee rights to collective bargaining and is discrimination against employees for exercise of their section 7 rights, including the right to strike.

The Supreme Court disagreed. It said that for a violation of section 8(a)(3) to be found, there must be discrimination based on union activity and resulting discouragement of union activity. Use of a lockout without evidence of antiunion motivation and effect does not violate the law. When the employer's intention is merely to obtain a favorable settlement in a collective bargaining dispute, there is no violation of law, the Court said.

Thus, it was established that an employer could use a lockout to bring pressure on the union in contract negotiations. But could a company replace the locked-out employees in order to operate during the lockout? In 1972 the NLRB ruled that a company could, in fact, lock out employees and then resume operations on a reduced scale with temporary employees not covered by the expired contract, of whom some were transferred from some of the employer's other operations and others were secured from an independent contractor (*Ottawa Silicia Co.*, 1972).

Finally, could a company hire *permanent* replacements for employees it had locked out in a bargaining dispute? The board held that a company's lockout became illegal when, during the lockout, the employer unilaterally decided to hire permanent replacements without first consulting the union. This unilateral act was a violation of section 8(a)(3), the board said. Furthermore, the permanent replacement of all bargaining-unit employees who were locked out was a violation of section 8(a)(5), since "it completely destroyed the bargaining unit" and constituted an unlawful withdrawal of recognition of a duly designated union. The board noted in passing an absence of evidence that the union had engaged in an in-plant strike or other concerted improper conduct that might justify the employer's hiring of permanent replacements (*Johns-Manville Products Corp.*, 1976).

Refusal to Bargain   Section 8(a)(5) of the NLRA makes it an unfair labor practice for an employer to refuse to bargain collectively with duly designated representatives of its employees. But what does bargaining collectively entail? Section 8(d) provides that:

> To bargain collectively is the performance of the mutual obligation of the employer and the representative of the employees to meet at reasonable times and confer in good faith with respect to wages, hours, and other terms and conditions of employment, or the negotiation of an agreement...and the execution of a written contract...but such obligation does not compel either party to agree to a proposal or require the making of a concession.

What, then, does the duty to bargain *not* entail? It does not require that agreement be reached on any particular terms. The union and the employer are thereby given very wide latitude to develop their bargaining positions. It does not require the making of a collective bargaining contract unless the parties have reached agreement on important matters. Finally, it does not require either party to make concessions in order to achieve an agreement.[7]

The law's language is broad, and the NLRB and the courts have given it interpretations that have made the duty to bargain a specially arcane and abstruse area of labor relations law. These interpretations have centered on two aspects of the statute's language: the topics of bargaining and the meaning of good faith.

Subjects of Bargaining   The board observed that the statute refers to "wages, hours, and other terms and conditions of employment." Starting from this language, the board, with approval by the courts, has established a three-way classification of bargaining topics. These are:

- Illegal
- Mandatory
- Nonmandatory

An illegal subject is one on which the parties are prohibited from making an agreement. Such a topic is the closed shop, which is prohibited by the labor law. A mandatory subject is one that the parties must bargain about if either wishes to. Mandatory subjects are those found by the board to be included in

---

[7] Howard F. Gospel, "Trade Unions and the Legal Obligation to Bargain: An American, Swedish and British Comparison," *British Journal of Industrial Relations*, 21:3, Nov. 1983, pp. 343–357.

the general rules of "wages, hours, and other terms and conditions of employment." A proposed pay raise and a pension plan are examples of mandatory subjects of bargaining. The board has also held that in negotiations a union or an employer may refuse to execute a contract if an agreement is not reached on a mandatory subject of bargaining. This is referred to as "bringing negotiations to an impasse." When an impasse occurs over a mandatory issue of bargaining, the union may strike or the employer may lock out in support of its bargaining position.

Other issues, which are legal but not mandatory, are called "permissible" issues. A union or an employer may request negotiations over a permissible subject of bargaining but may not carry negotiations to an impasse over such an issue. If a union strikes or an employer locks out over failure to agree on a permissible issue, the strike or lockout is an unfair labor practice.

The Supreme Court upheld the NLRB's distinction between mandatory and nonmandatory subjects of bargaining in 1957. The Worcester Division of Borg-Warner Corporation produced fuel pumps and hydraulic pumps. The United Automobile Workers were certified to represent the bargaining unit. During the negotiation of the first contract, the company insisted on the inclusion of two particular clauses in any agreement and refused to sign an agreement unless both clauses were included. One clause was a negotiation clause that attempted to exclude the national union as a party to the agreement. The second clause required the union to conduct a prestrike secret ballot of all the employees on whether to accept the company's last offer or to go on strike. This was to prevent the union's leadership from calling a strike that the employees did not want.

The union and the employer either agreed on other matters or continued to bargain about them, but the employer refused to execute an agreement without these two clauses, and the union would not agree to them. When the contract expired, the union struck. After a month's strike, the local union gave in, on orders of the national union, and signed the contract with the two clauses in it.

The union then filed charges with the NLRB alleging a violation of section 8(a)(5) of the NLRA. The case ultimately reached the Supreme Court. The Court found that the two clauses were outside the scope of bargaining as defined in section 8(d) of the act (which is quoted above) and that the employer's insistence on them to the point of impasse against the opposition of the union amounted to a refusal to bargain. Hence, insisting on a permissible subject to an impasse in negotiations was a violation of the law. The effect of the Court's decision was to legitimize the legal distinction between mandatory and permissible subjects of bargaining.

There has been considerable controversy about this decision. In a dissent to the Court's decision, Justice Harlan stated that he could not grasp a bargaining concept that enabled one side to propose a particular point, but not to insist upon it: "The right to bargain becomes illusory if one is not free to press a proposal in good faith to the point of insistence." Archibald Cox and

John Dunlop have suggested that Congress intended to apply the duty-to-bargain obligation only to instances involving the formation of a new union-management relation.[8] This view the Court dismissed, so that the mandatory-nonmandatory classification now applies to all negotiations.

What the Court did in *Borg-Warner* was to establish a requirement that the parties bargain over prescribed subject matter independent of the duty to bargain in good faith.[9] Many commentators have been disturbed by the impact of this requirement on collective bargaining. "Armed with the innocuous-appearing power to classify subjects of bargaining and to monitor the bargaining with respect to the classification, the board has acquired extensive powers to affect the agenda and the outcome of negotiations.[10] A further result is that employers and unions [since section 8(b)(3) of the act makes it an unfair labor practice for unions to refuse to bargain collectively with employers] engage in subterfuges. An employer who seeks language about permissible subjects in bargaining may withhold agreement on a wage change as well, since an impasse can be legally created about a wage change.

Heath Larry has commented that the NLRB might have avoided the difficult decisions in the area of the duty to bargain altogether. The categories that the board has developed are "really dancing on the head of a pin."[11] Douglas V. Brown has pointed out that a large proportion of unfair labor practice charges filed involve section 8(a)(5); he proposes reducing the volume of NLRB cases by eliminating section 8(a)(5) from the act.[12] Harry Wellington proposes simply broadening the interpretation of section 8(d) to permit the parties to bargain in good faith about all topics.[13]

Two cases may help the reader to understand the board's application of the classification of bargaining subjects.

• In the construction industry, employees' pensions are provided by multiemployer funds to which individual contractors contribute a specific sum of money for each hour worked by employees. In many instances employers do not pay the required pension contributions, threatening the pension protection that employees have. Construction unions try to mend this problem by negotiating with contractors about pension contributions.

The NLRB held that the provision of performance bonds to guarantee pension payments is a nonmandatory subject of bargaining and found the

---

[8] Archibald Cox and John T. Dunlop, "Regulation of Collective Bargaining by the NLRB," *Harvard Law Review*, 63, 1950, pp. 389–432.

[9] Stanley M. Jacks, "National Labor Policy and the Duty to Bargain Collectively," *Industrial Management Review*, 32, Spring 1967, p. 47.

[10] Guy Farmer, *Management Rights and Union Bargaining Power* (New York: Industrial Relations Counselors, 1965), p. 13.

[11] R. Heath Larry, "Collective Bargaining—A Management Viewpoint," remarks to the Chairman's Task Force on the NLRB, Reston, Va., July 12, 1976 (mimeographed).

[12] Douglas V. Brown, "Legalism and Industrial Relations in the United States," *Proceedings* of the Industrial Relations Research Association, 1970, pp. 2–11.

[13] Harry Wellington, *Labor and the Legal Process* (New Haven, Conn.: Yale University Press, 1968), p. 81.

union guilty of an unfair labor practice in insisting during negotiations that employers post higher performance bonds (*Lathers Local 42 v. Lathing Constructor's Association of Southern California*, 1976).

• In many enterprises employees have lunch in a canteen provided by the employer. In one instance an employer unilaterally increased the price of sandwiches and other items sold from vending machines. The NLRB found that the employer had committed an unfair labor practice by not bargaining with the union over this action (*Ladish Co.*, 1976). In May 1979, in a similar case involving Ford Motor Company, the Supreme Court upheld the NLRB's interposition of the law.

Critics of the NLRB point to such decisions and ask what we are to think of a labor law that denies employees the right to strike for bonds to protect their pensions but permits them to strike over the price of a sandwich offered for sale in a lunchroom.

The Good-Faith Obligation The other part of the duty to bargain involves the good-faith requirement. An employer or a union will be found to have violated section 8(a)(5) if its conduct in bargaining, viewed in its entirety, indicates that it did not negotiate with a good-faith intention to reach agreement. Thus, the legality of the employer's conduct depends primarily on the NLRB's findings with respect to its intent or motivation—rather than on findings with respect to specific actions.

Two aspects of the good-faith obligation are of special importance. One is that an employer has the duty to supply to the union on request any information that is "relevant and necessary" to allow the union to bargain intelligently and effectively. When an employer refuses a union demand, citing inability to meet the costs involved, the company must provide financial information to support its claim. For this reason, in order to limit the information given the union, it has become uncommon for employers to offer a narrowly financial objection to a union proposal.

In a recent case the NLRB substantially extended the duty of an employer to supply information to a union. The International Union of Electrical Workers had requested from Westinghouse Electric Company statistical information concerning the employer's employment practices. In particular, the union sought a breakdown of the company's work force by race, sex, and Spanish surname. The union argued that this information was necessary to permit it to fulfill its obligation under the law to represent fairly all employees of the company. The company disagreed. It argued that matters having to do with its treatment of its female, nonwhite, and Spanish-surname employees were covered by law other than the National Labor Relations Act, and the company refused to furnish the data to the union. The NLRB decided the case in favor of the union. The company was required to furnish the data which the union had requested and also to inform the union of any complaints and charges filed against the company pursuant to various state and federal fair employment practice laws. In this decision, the board seemed to find, implicitly, that the unions have a duty of fair representation of minorities and women under the National Labor Relations Act that includes their obligations under fair employment practice laws (*Westinghouse Electric Corporation*, 1979).

A breach of the duty to bargain in good faith occurs if either side insists adamantly on an initial position as the only basis for an agreement. Thus, were an employer to offer a package increase at the outset of negotiations and refuse to budge from it in later negotiations, an unfair labor practice would probably be found. This finding would occur despite the act's admonition that the duty to bargain does not require the making of a concession. The failure to change an initial position would be inferred to be evidence of a desire not to reach an agreement and therefore a failure to bargain in good faith.

Surface Bargaining Employers are sometimes accused of conducting "surface bargaining." That is, they go through the motions of bargaining, including meeting and holding discussions with the unions, but without any intention to reach agreement. In consequence, labor negotiations may go on interminably without a collective bargaining agreement being reached. Surface bargaining has been held to be an unfair labor practice virtually from the first interpretations of the NLRA, but it is a difficult violation to prove and as difficult to remedy when it is proved.

Some observers maintain that the level of surface bargaining is increasing and point to the growing number of refusal-to-bargain charges filed against employers and the substantial proportion of these charges found by the NLRB to have merit.[14] Not all refusal-to-bargain violations involve surface bargaining, however.

Two examples of alleged surface bargaining may help the reader to understand the sometimes elusive line between legality and illegality in this area of law.

• For 20 years the successive agreement between a company and a union had included a union security clause (see Chapter 5), and for 10 years a dues checkoff. Then in 1978 negotiations the company adamantly refused to continue either clause. The union complained to the NLRB. Was the company refusing to bargain in good faith?

Yes, said the NLRB. No, said the Seventh Circuit Court of Appeals. "Throughout bargaining," said the court, the employer "constantly asserted the same reason for wanting to eliminate union security and checkoff...so that employees would have a free choice concerning union membership."[15] And the company was prepared to reach agreement on all other issues. Hence, there was no violation of the employer's duty to bargain.

---

[14] Benjamin M. Shieber, "Honesty in Bargaining," *AFL-CIO Federationist*, 82:4, April 1975, p. 19. Also, Alan Kistler and Charles McDonald, "The Continuing Challenge of Organizing," *AFL-CIO Federationist*, 83:11, Nov. 1976, pp. 9–13.

[15] *Atlas Metal Parts Company Inc. v. NLRB*, CA 7, No. 80-2498, Sept. 22, 1981.

- For 11 months a company and a union bargained about a contract. During the negotiations the company insisted on *unilateral* control over discharge, discipline, layoff, recall, subcontracting, and assignment of unit work to supervisors.

The NLRB and the Second Circuit Court of Appeals found that the company was engaged in illegal surface bargaining with no intention of entering a collective bargaining agreement.[16]

The board has adopted a standard remedy, which orders a violator to cease and desist bad-faith bargaining and to take appropriate affirmative action. The affirmative actions include bargaining on the request of the other party, posting notices in the work premises containing the violator's pledge to cease the refusal to bargain, and requiring the violator to notify the regional director within 20 days from the date of the order on the steps taken to comply with the order.

When an employer flagrantly uses the bargaining process to frustrate any agreement, the NLRB seeks to reduce the injury to the union by allowing union access to the company bulletin board and by requiring the employer to submit to the union an updated list of employees and their addresses. The board also orders the employer to reimburse the board and the union for all reasonable expenses incurred in the preparation, presentation, and conduct of the case.

This remedy is the strongest the board has in response to charges of failure to bargain in good faith. Also, any strike caused by a section 8(a)(5) violation is judged an unfair labor practice strike, and employees participating in the strike must be reinstated upon request, even if the employer has hired permanent replacements for them.

The Supreme Court has held that the board does not have power to compel an employer to agree to a specific proposal as a remedy for a violation. In the case in point, the board found an employer's refusal to agree to a dues checkoff clause was not done in good faith, but solely to frustrate the making of a collective bargaining agreement. To remedy the bad-faith bargaining, the board ordered the employer to agree to the checkoff clause. The court of appeals upheld the board's order. In reversing the board and the court of appeals, the Supreme Court reasoned that the board's remedial powers are limited by the congressional expression that the obligation to bargain in good faith "does not compel either party to agree to a proposal or require the making of a concession," and held that the board is "without power to compel a company or a union to agree to any substantive contractual provision of a collective bargaining agreement."[17]

---

[16] *NLRB V. A-1 King Size Sandwiches, Inc.*, CA 11, No. 83-3193, May 21, 1984.
[17] *H. K. Porter Co. v. NLRB*, 397 U.S. 99 (1970).

The NLRB, reviewing this decision by the Court, has taken the position that any stronger remedies to be provided for violations of the duty to bargain must be provided by Congress.[18]

UNFAIR LABOR PRACTICES BY UNIONS

Types

Section 8(b) of the National Labor Relations Act proscribes certain activities by labor organizations. Specifically, unions are prohibited by the act from:

• Coercing or restraining employees in their choice of a bargaining representative [section 8(b)(1)(A)]
• Coercing or restraining employers in their choice of a bargaining representative in collective bargaining [section 8(b)(1)(B)]
• Causing an employer to discriminate against employees illegally [section 8(b)(2)]
• Refusing to bargain in good faith with an employer [section 8(b)(3)]
• Engaging in secondary boycotts or jurisdictional strikes [section 8(b)(4)]
• Charging excessive or discriminatory initiation fees [section 8(b)(5)]
• Engaging in featherbedding [section 8(b)(6)]
• Engaging in organizational or recognition picketing [section 8(b)(7)]

Finally, the law prohibits both unions and employers from entering into so-called hot-cargo agreements.

Restraint and Coercion of Employees

Union conduct that is reasonably calculated to restrain or coerce employees violates section 8(b)(1)(A), regardless of whether or not it is successful. A union may violate the law by the conduct of its officers or agents, of pickets on a picket line participated in or ratified by union representatives, or of strikers who engage in coercion in the presence of union representatives who do not repudiate their conduct. Unlawful coercion may take the form of physical assaults, threats of violence, and threats to affect an employee's job status through the employer.

The law does recognize the right of unions to establish and enforce rules of membership and to control their internal affairs. In enforcing its rules a union may, in fact, coerce employees to a degree. But this right is limited to union rules and discipline that affect the rights of employees as union members and that are not enforced by action affecting an employee's employment. A union cannot enforce rules that conflict with public policy. For example, a union cannot enforce a rule that limits a member's right to file an unfair labor practice charge. Finally, a union may not enforce its regulations

---

[18] Elliot Bredhoff, ''The Scope of 'Good-Faith Bargaining' and Adequacy of Remedies,'' *Proceedings* of the Industrial Relations Research Association, Dec. 1973, pp. 109–118.

in an unreasonable manner, such as levying fines that the NLRB finds to be excessive.

The union, which is a statutory bargaining representative, i.e., an exclusive bargaining agent, also has a duty of fair representation to all the employees it represents and may exercise a wide range of reasonable discretion in carrying out its representative function. However, it violates the law if, while acting as an employee's statutory bargaining representative, it takes or withholds action in connection with the worker's employment because of his or her union activities or for any irrelevant or arbitrary reason, such as the employee's race or sex. A union violates the law when it follows certain practices, for example:

• Refuses to process a grievance for an employee because of the employee's criticism of union officers
• Maintains a seniority system with an employer under which seniority is based on the employee's prior representation by the union elsewhere
• Refuses to process a grievance because of the employee's race

How is the law applied in fact? Some examples may be helpful.

• A union refused to refer a person to a job opportunity because he was not a member of the local union or because it assumed he had worked for a nonunion employer in violation of the union's rules. The board found the union guilty of an unfair labor practice and ordered the union to pay the individual $26,966.34 in lost wages and to pay $2060.85 to his pension account (*Plumbers Local 13*, 1976).
• A union refused to represent a laid-off worker in a job assignment dispute. The union took this action by direction of a vote of the union's membership. The NLRB found that the election was a procedure that lacked fairness in determining what the union's duty of fair representation entailed. The unfairness arose, the board said, because the issue of the grievant's proper seniority for layoff purposes was determined by a vote of other employees, who would gain individually if they voted against the grievant. The union should not, said the board, delegate its obligations to a vote of the union's membership (*Teamsters Local 315*, 1975).
• During a strike the union organized a picket line of between 200 and 300 members. The workers massed in front of the driveway to the plant's parking lot. Cars carrying nonstriking employees were turned away. The board held such picketing to be unlawful (*Sunset Line and Twine Co.*, 1948).
• A union refused to process the grievance of an employee in the bargaining unit who was not a member of the union unless the employee paid the union the costs it incurred in processing the grievance. The union made no similar claim on its members, saying that their payment of dues covered the costs of the grievance processing. The union justified its action by saying that it was attempting to protect its members' dues from being eroded by expen-

ditures on behalf of nonmembers. The board found that the union had violated the law in two ways:

1 By charging only nonmembers for grievance representation, it had discriminated against nonmembers.

2 Because grievance representation is due employees as a matter of right, and the union was trying to charge nonmembers for it (*H. O. Canfield*, 1976).

Causing Employers to Discriminate

Unions sometimes violate the law concerning the coercion of employees through the employer instead of directly. This may take the form of pressuring an employer to take action against an employee. Alternatively, a union may agree with an employer in a collective bargaining agreement to an action that violates the law.

A Teamsters local union negotiated a clause in their labor contract by which union stewards received "superseniority." The superseniority involved not only protection against layoffs, but also preference in selecting the routes the stewards would drive. The board found this award of superseniority to union officers was not justified by the need to provide continuity in union representation. Instead, it awarded benefits to union officials denied to other employees and thereby resulted in an inherent encouragement of unionism, which is prohibited by the law. A circuit court of appeals upheld the board (*NLRB v. Milk Drivers and Dairy Employees Local 338, International Brotherhood of Teamsters*, 1976).

In another case, the business agent of a construction union caused the contractor building a paper mill to discharge seven employees for reasons that were personal to the business agent. The agent had complete authority over work performed by union members at the project, the NLRB said in reviewing the matter. The agent appointed all overseers for the contractor and selected workers to be laid off when conditions made it necessary. The agent at one time threw a baseball bat at a union member. At another time he took pistol shots at union members who were attempting to secure signatures on a petition for a new election of union officers. The board found that the union, through its official, the business agent, had committed unfair labor practices (*Fruin-Conlon Corp. v. Laborers Local 282*, 1976).

Many cases come before the NLRB which involve attempts by unions to have employers continue to deduct union dues from the paychecks of persons who are no longer union members. In one such instance, the union insisted that the employer continue to deduct dues from the employees' pay despite the fact that the employees had resigned from the union. However, the employees had not followed the provision of the collective bargaining agreement between the union and the company, which provided that dues checkoff authorizations could be revoked only during a particular 10- to 20-

day period. The board held that this action by the union was *not* in violation of the law (*Frito-Lay*, 1979).

In a superficially similar case, the board reached the opposite conclusion. The union had caused the employer to continue to deduct union dues from the wages of employees who had resigned from the union but had not canceled their outstanding checkoff authorizations. The board held that in light of the language of the authorizations, which said in part "in consideration of the benefits received and to be received by me as a result of my membership in the Union," effective resignation from the union also revoked the checkoff authorization. Thus, by insisting that the employer continue to deduct the dues of these former union members, the union was in violation of the law (*Campbell Industries*, 1979).

Union's Refusal to Bargain

A union, no less than an employer, has a duty to bargain in good faith. A union may breach its duty by any of the following:

- Insisting on the inclusion of illegal provisions in a contract, such as a closed shop or a discriminatory hiring hall
- Refusing to negotiate on a proposal for a written contract
- Striking against an employer who has bargained, and continues to bargain, on a multiemployer basis in order to compel it to bargain separately
- Refusing to meet with the attorney designated by the employer as its representative in negotiations
- Terminating an existing contract and striking for a new one without notifying the employer, the Federal Mediation and Conciliation Service, and the state mediation service, if any
- Conditioning the execution of an agreement on inclusion of a nonmandatory provision, such as a performance bond
- Refusing to process a grievance because of the race, sex, or union activities of an employee for whom the union is the statutory bargaining representative

Periodically the board finds that unions have violated their duty to bargain in good faith. For example:

An employer operated a chain of retail food stores, some of which were combined with drugstores. A local of the Retail Clerks union represented the employees of the company in the food stores, while an independent union was certified by the board to represent the company's employees in the drugstores.

The employer remodeled five of the combined food stores/drugstores and, among other things, eliminated or modified partitions between the two types of operations and installed common checkout counters. The Retail Clerks union thereupon demanded that the employer apply its collective bargaining agreement with the union to the drugstore employees. The employer refused. The union filed a grievance and demanded arbitration. The employer filed an unfair labor practice charge with the board, alleging that the union violated section 8(b)(3) of the act by insisting on recognition, including the demand for arbitration.

The board found that the remodeling did not result in an enlargement of the food store unit by including the drugstore employees in it. The board cited several findings in reaching this result, including separate supervision of food and drug employees, lack of employee interchange, separate administrative chains of command, different merchandising procedures, a separate bargaining history, and the fact that the independent union was certified to represent the drugstore employees.

Hence, the board found, insistence by the retail clerks in bargaining for an inappropriate unit was a breach of the union's duty to bargain in good faith (*Retail Clerks Local 588*, 1976).

Prohibited Strikes and Boycotts

Section 8(b)(4) prohibits a labor organization from engaging in strikes or boycotts or taking other specified actions to accomplish certain purposes or "objects," as they are called in the act. The words "induce and encourage" are considered by the U.S. Supreme Court to be broad enough to include every form of influence or persuasion. For example, it has been held by the NLRB that a work stoppage on a picketed construction project was "induced" by a union through its business agents, who, when they learned about the picketing, told the job stewards that they (the business agents) would not work behind the picket line. It was considered that this advice not only induced the stewards to leave the job, but caused them to pass the information on to their fellow employees. Such conduct informed the other employees that they were expected not to work behind the picket line, in the board's opinion.

This section of the law also prohibits unions from engaging in prohibited actions to compel an employer or self-employed person to join a labor union. It prohibits a union from compelling an employer to enter into a "hot-cargo" agreement, which is prohibited by section 8(e) of the act. "Hot cargo" is a shipment intended for an employer with whom the union has a dispute. Union members may refuse to handle hot cargo. Examples of violations of this section are:

• In an attempt to compel a beer distributor to join a union, the union prevents the distributor from obtaining beer at a brewery by inducing the brewery's employees to refuse to fill the distributor's orders.

• In an attempt to secure for its members certain stevedoring work required at an employer's unloading operation, the union pickets to force the employer either to join an employer association with which the union has a contract or to hire a stevedoring firm that is a member of the association.

• A union pickets an employer (one not in the construction industry), or threatens to picket it, to compel that employer to enter into an agreement whereby it will do business only with persons who have an agreement with a union.

Section 8(b)(5)(B) contains the act's secondary boycott provision. A secondary boycott occurs if a union has a dispute with company A and in furtherance of that dispute causes the employees of company B to stop handling the products of company A or otherwise forces company B to stop doing business with company A. The dispute is with company A, called the "primary" employer; the union's action is against company B, called the "secondary" employer, hence the term "secondary boycott." In many cases the secondary employer is a customer or supplier of the primary employer with which the union has the dispute. In general, the act prohibits both the secondary boycott and the threat of it.[19] Examples of prohibited secondary boycotts are:

• Picketing an employer to force it to stop doing business with another employer who has refused to recognize the union
• Asking the employees of a plumbing contractor not to work on connecting air-conditioning equipment manufactured by a nonunion employer the union is attempting to organize
• Urging employees of a building contractor not to install doors that were made by a manufacturer that is nonunion or that employs members of a rival union
• Telling an employer that its plant will be picketed if it continues to do business with an employer that the union has designated as "unfair"

The law also provides two major exceptions to the prohibitions just described. First, any "publicity, other than picketing," and "any primary strike or primary picketing" are exempted. Second, under specified conditions, truthful publicity, other than picketing, stating that a product produced by an employer with which a union has a primary dispute is distributed by another employer is permitted. This provision of the law permits consumer boycotts, which involve publicity urging consumers not to purchase a particular product from a neutral company. Thus, the Amalgamated Clothing and Textile Workers pursued for several years a consumer boycott against J. P. Stevens & Company. The consumer boycott consisted of urging potential customers at retail stores not to buy J. P. Stevens products. The union could lawfully picket retail stores for this purpose, but could not lawfully urge po-

---

[19] Ralph M. Dereshinsky, *NLRB and Secondary Boycotts* (Philadelphia: Industrial Research Unit, Wharton School, University of Pennsylvania, 1972). Also, Paul A. Brinker and Benjamin T. Taylor, "Secondary Boycott Analysis by Industry," *Labor Law Journal*, 24:10, Oct. 1973, pp. 671–683.

tential customers to boycott the stores entirely simply because those stores handled J. P. Stevens products.

WHY HAVE UNFAIR LABOR PRACTICE CHARGES INCREASED?

During the early 1980s there was considerable concern over a rapid increase in the NLRB's case load. From 28,993 cases in 1966 the load rose to a peak of 57,381 in 1980. Virtually all this growth was in unfair labor practice charges, which rose from 55 percent of all cases filed in 1966 to 82 percent of those filed in 1983.

Table 6-1 shows that the number of alleged unfair labor practices by employers increased rapidly (from 4472 in 1950 to 28,995 in 1983) and that the proportion of the charges found to have merit by the NLRB or the courts slowly increased to more than one-third.

What did such a substantial case load signify? Several alternative explanations were offered. First, it was said that the climate of labor relations in the United States had worsened and that more violations of the law were occurring. The rising case load was said to reflect these developments.

The unions believe that increasing illegality by employers has been reducing union representation. Figure 6-1 compares the percentage of union representation in our labor force from 1967 to 1983 with the number of unfair labor practice complaints against employers. It will be seen from a study of the chart that for many years union representation fell as unfair labor practice complaints rose.

Second, some agreed that employees, unions, and employers were making greater use of the NLRB's processes than before. Much of this alleged greater use was said to be to protect legal rights that people did not previously recognize, or was a device to harass another party, without regard to

TABLE 6-1   UNFAIR LABOR PRACTICES BY EMPLOYERS

	Charges against employers	Fraction found meritorious, %
1950	4,472	N/A
1955	4,362	N/A
1960	7,723	29.1
1965	10,931	35.5
1970	13,601	34.2
1975	20,311	30.2
1980	31,281	35.7
1983	28,995	34.1

Source: Paul Weiler, "Promises to Keep," *Harvard Law Review,* 96:8, June 1983, p. 1780. Also, 48th Annual Report of NLRB.

FIGURE 6-1   Unfair labor practice complaints against employers and union representation as a percentage of the labor force, 1968–1982. Sources: *Unfair labor practice complaints (right axis): NLRB Annual Reports, 1968–1981. (About 75 percent of all charges are settled without litigation.) Union membership as a percentage of the labor force (left axis): Bureau of National Affairs, Directory of U.S. Labor Organizations, 1984–1985, p. 2. Also Bureau of Labor Statistics, Employment and Earnings, 31:1, January 1984, p. 117.* NOTE: 1981 union membership figures estimated by author.

the merits of the charge. For example, it is not uncommon for a union and an employer involved in an economic strike to file charges with the NLRB against each other, only to withdraw them when the strike is settled.

Third, it was charged that the internal processes of the board itself tend to generate cases. The board, like other federal regulatory agencies, finds its budget determined primarily by the volume of its case load. There is a tendency, therefore, to accept an increasing case load and to make little or no effort to reduce it. This is in significant contrast to the efforts made by the board to obtain settlement or withdrawal of cases once they have been filed. Also, of course, the board's jurisdiction had been enlarged to include especially nonprofit hospitals and private colleges and universities. This also contributed to a substantial case load.

Whatever the reasons for the increasing case load in the seventies, it reversed direction in the 1980s. By 1986 NLRB cases had dropped from 57,381 in 1980 to 42,300.

Just as there were several explanations offered for the increasing case load in the 1970s, there are several advanced regarding its decline in the 1980s. It is said that the NLRB's processes became so slow and its membership appointed by President Reagan so ill-disposed to the unions, that the unions ceased to believe they could win unfair labor practice complaints and so ceased filing. Others suggest that the falling case load is an overdue adjustment to the decline of unions in American industry. It is even possible that the falling number of unfair labor practice complaints represents an improvement in American labor relations, a matter to which we shall return in Chapter 8 when we discuss labor-management cooperation.

CHAPTER SUMMARY

American labor law is very much concerned with the procedures used in labor relations. The NLRB closely regulates activities of unions and employers with respect to each other and to employees, and there is a substantial body of decisions on unfair labor practices. Significant matters that are regularly dealt with include prohibiting employers from (1) interfering with employee rights to join or not to join labor organizations (by threats of job loss or plant closings if employees vote for a union, by interrogation of employees and solicitation to discourage union activity, and by unlawful surveillance of union organizers and employees) and (2) discriminating against employees through plant closings, employer lockouts, and refusals to bargain that are motivated by antiunion bias.

It is considered an unfair labor practice for an employer to refuse to bargain collectively with representatives of its employees. However, the language of the law is open to interpretation, and this has made the "duty to bargain" an especially abstruse and difficult area of labor relations law. Interpretations of the duty to bargain have centered on two aspects of the statute: subjects of bargaining and the meaning of "good faith." Bargaining topics have been classified as illegal topics, mandatory topics, and nonmandatory, or permissible, topics. There has been considerable controversy over the legal distinction between mandatory and permissible subjects of bargaining, and the distinction sometimes leads to bargaining subterfuges. A large proportion of the unfair labor practice charges involves this section of the NLRA.

The NLRB also proscribes certain activities on the part of labor unions. These include (1) restraint and coercion of employees (for example, by physical assaults or threats of violence), (2) coercion or inducing of employers to discriminate against employees, (3) refusal to bargain in good faith, for example, by including illegal provisions in a contract, terminating a contract, or striking against an employer who is willing to bargain, and (4) engagement in strikes or boycotts (especially secondary boycotts) to accomplish certain objectives.

The NLRB's case load increased substantially in the 1970s. Most growth occurred in the number of unfair labor practice charges filed. Such growth may indicate that more violations occurred. Alternatively, it may mean that there was a greater use of the NLRB to protect rights or as a means of harassment.

Then in the 1980s the NLRB's case load declined. Some explain that the unions quit filing cases because of lack of confidence in the board. Others say that the climate of labor relations is improving, so that fewer violations are occurring. No conclusive explanation can be given at this time.

QUESTIONS FOR THOUGHT AND DISCUSSION

1 Should an employer be free to close a plant to avoid unionization? Under what circumstances may it do so now? Should the law be modified? How?

2 Several proposals have been made to remove the duty to bargain from the labor laws. What are the advantages of such a proposal? What are its disadvantages? Do you favor the proposal? Why or why not?

3 What is surface bargaining? Do you think it is a serious problem? What, if anything, should be done about it?

4 When is a strike an unfair labor practice? Should unions have an unfettered right to strike?

5 Why does the NLRB have such a rapidly growing case load? Does the case load present a problem, in your view? What should be done about it?

6 In regard to decisions about unfair labor practices, where would you say the NLRB exercises the most discretionary, or interpretative, power?

7 What are the three types of bargaining topics? Do you think the legal distinction between mandatory and permissible subjects of bargaining makes sense? Why or why not?

8 In what ways does the NLRB's power to classify subjects of bargaining give the board power over the outcome of negotiations?

9 What do you think are the more general underlying problems in labor relations that lead both employers and unions to commit unfair labor practices?

10 The Supreme Court has said that the NLRB can reverse its previous decisions or precedents since there is a responsibility to adapt the NLRA to changing patterns of industrial life. What are the pros and cons of this position?

11 Why did the number of unfair labor practice complaints increase rapidly in the 1970s? Why have they declined in the 1980s?

SELECTED READING

Dereshinsky, Ralph M., and Alan D. Berkowitz, *The NLRB and Secondary Boycotts*, rev. ed. (Philadelphia: The University of Pennsylvania, The Wharton School, Industrial Research University, 1981).

Flanagan, Robert, *Labor Relations and the Litigation Explosion* (Washington, D.C.: The Brookings Institution, 1987).

Getman, Julius C., *Labor Relations: Law, Practice and Policy* (Mineola, N.Y.: The Foundation Press, 1978).

National Labor Relations Board, *A Layman's Guide to Basic Law under the NLRA* (Washington, D.C.: U.S. Government Printing Office, 1971).

Taylor, Benjamin J., and Fred Whitney, *Labor Relations Law*, 3d ed. (Englewood Cliffs, N.J.: Prentice-Hall, 1979).

D

MANAGEMENT AND EMPLOYEES

The employment relationship confers authority on the employer. The employer may discipline or discharge workers; the employer may decide what to pay workers and what benefits to provide. In the absence of a union, the only limitations on the employer's authority are those imposed by law or by the marketplace. In the United States, the limits imposed by law are relatively few (as compared with other industrialized countries). The limits imposed by the marketplace vary with the availability of workers and are often few because many people are unemployed and seeking work.

Many American employers value highly the freedom of action which they are allowed as a result of limited government regulation and slack labor markets. But companies behave in many different ways in the use of this freedom. Some establish policies that provide high wages, good benefits, and a generally good working environment for their employees. Others do the opposite. It is to a degree a matter of management choice. Management has the power and exercises it.

The advent of a union changes this. Thereafter, management faces another institution with its own power base—the union.

CHAPTER 7

NONUNION AND UNION

In the United States labor organizations have not organized most employees. Instead, the substantial majority of people continue to work for companies that set labor relations policies unilaterally. This is a surprising fact. In the 1930s and 1940s unions made rapid headway in organizing the employees of private firms. Since that time, there has been stagnation in union growth. There are undoubtedly many reasons why this has occurred, but among them has been the development of sophisticated policies with respect to labor relations by many nonunionized firms. In the first section of this chapter we study the nature of those policies.

TWO EXTREMES OF NONUNIONIZED EMPLOYERS

There are many different types of nonunion employers. Some are very small companies; some are very large. They operate in many different industries and regions of the country. They follow many different kinds of labor policies. Often the only characteristic they seem to have in common is that their employees are not represented by labor organizations. For this reason it is perhaps not appropriate to lump them together into one category; referring to them all as nounionized employers may seem to imply that their most important characteristic is the one they have in common. But this is too negative and too narrow a view. The labor policies of many of these firms are much more positive than is suggested simply by referring to them as *non*unionized. For some of these firms, remaining nonunion is less an objective of their labor relations policies than it is a result of the policies they pursue. But there are also other firms that do not provide good employment standards and whose major labor relations objective is simply to avoid unionization at any cost and by virtually any means.

It is useful to examine the labor relations policies of nonunionized firms at these two extremes, even though most firms would fall somewhere in between. At one extreme we may place the low-standards nonunionized employer. At the other extreme we may place the better-standards nonunionized employer. What labor relations policies characterize the former? The latter? We shall see that it is a fairly simple task to describe the low-standards employer, but that the operations of the employers with higher standards are complicated and require considerable study.

The Low-Standards Employer

The low-standards employer is a firm that survives primarily because of low labor costs. Generally, labor costs are kept down by paying low wage rates, providing few fringe benefits or none, and spending as little as possible on amenities at the workplace. In the garment trades, the operations run by such employers have been known as "sweat shops," a term that has been extended to include all low-standards employers.

Low-standards employers are often poorly managed firms. They not only pay low wages but also make inefficient use of labor. Thus, low labor costs are necessary to keep them in business, by permitting them to compete against more efficient firms. Low-standards employers rarely seek to train employees, to provide for their participation in their jobs in a constructive fashion, or to provide competent supervision. They employ extremely authoritarian management techniques and use discharge as a device to discipline the work force. Ordinarily, they experience high levels of labor turnover. Their personnel practices are haphazard, resulting in a crazy-quilt pattern of wage rates, job assignments, and work loads. They ordinarily give no thought to grievance procedures or communications mechanisms.[1]

The Better-Standards Employer

The better-standards nonunionized employer may be described as a firm that pays wages and fringe benefits comparable to or better than those paid by similarly situated unionized firms (i.e., firms in the same industry and geographic area). Such a firm ordinarily remains competitive in its product market by virtue of efficient management, advanced technology, resource control, an effective sales force, or other such advantages. Better-standards firms

---

[1] The labor relations practices of low-standards employers are described in a number of studies of the high-turnover, low-wage sector of the labor market, the so-called secondary labor market. See, for example, Peter B. Doeringer and Michael J. Piore, *Internal Labor Markets and Manpower Analysis* (Lexington, Mass.: D. C. Heath, 1971), especially chap. 8.

generally conduct employee relations with great care. Hiring, training, disciplining, and discharging are administered in accordance with carefully prepared policies. Employee attitudes are monitored often, two-way communication is encouraged, and grievances are attended to. Managerial direction, although often authoritarian, is applied with a paternalistic concern for the welfare of employees.[2]

Employees are urged to meet with supervisors and are sometimes permitted to take problems to the chief executive officer of the company. Employee committees of an ad hoc nature are encouraged. In the past, standing employee committees were established for communications with management on issues of concern to workers. More recently, however, the National Labor Relations Board has tended to view virtually all employee committees as unions, requiring an existence substantially independent from management and conferring certain separate duties and privileges established by law. Nonindependent committees have been systematically struck down by the NLRB or the courts.[3] In consequence, nonunionized employers have become far more reluctant, or even unable, to establish employee committees.

Better-standards employers are generally as firmly opposed to the unionization of their employees as are low-standards employers. However, better-standards employers usually respond to union organizing attempts in a more sophisticated fashion and generally do not employ overtly illegal methods in opposition to unionization. Instead, reliance is placed on persuasion of employees, generous wage and benefit policies, and legal action that delays an organization campaign. Some employers do not resist unionization itself, but insist upon freedom to operate an "open shop," involving both union and nonunion employees. But the considerable legal restrictions that apply to unionization and to collective bargaining narrowly circumscribe this alternative.

HOW THE BETTER-STANDARDS EMPLOYER OPERATES

The Psychological Contract

The absence of a union means that employees will not have a collective bargaining agreement with their employer. Nonetheless, a contract of one sort or another may exist between the individual employee and the employer. In some industries there is a document, legally binding to a degree, setting forth the agreement between an employee and the firm for which he or she works. The procedure is especially common in radio and television broadcasting. Under the terms of the contract a broadcast station ordinarily agrees to a term of employment (e.g., 2 years) at a specified salary, and the em-

---

[2] For an extensive review of the labor policies of large nonunion firms, see Fred K. Foulkes, *Effective Personnel Policies: A Study of Large Nonunion Employers* (Englewood Cliffs, N.J.: Prentice-Hall, 1980).

[3] Harry Sangerman, "Employee Committees: Can They Survive under the Taft-Hartley Act," *Labor Law Journal*, 24:10, Oct. 1973, pp. 684–691.

ployee agrees to accept whatever assignments are given and not to work for another station for some set period (e.g., during the term of the contract).

Most industries do not have a written contract between each employee and the employer, however. Instead, there exists what may be termed a "psychological contract."[4] This contract is in the form of an understanding between the employee and the employer about the respective rights and obligations of each. It includes more than the wage rate and fringe benefit payments the employee and the firm agree upon. It also involves the expectations of both sides about the employee's performance, the working conditions provided by the employer, and other factors. Because the contract is not in written form, it is not legally enforceable, but it is nonetheless real and significant. If one party believes the other has violated the agreement substantially (psychologists employ the term "cognitive dissonance" to describe this sort of dissatisfaction), difficulties may be expected to arise.[5]

Better-standards employers recognize the importance of the psychological contract and devote care to its content and administration. They attempt to see that the employee's expectations of the job are consistent with their own as employers. They identify possible problem areas. And they hold the employer to his or her understanding with the company and themselves to their commitments to the employee. Thus, while there are not formal, legally binding obligations placed on the employer by a psychological contract, as there are by a collective bargaining agreement, nonetheless better-standards employers are not free to simply do whatever they want in dealing with employees. In fact, self-imposed restraints of the type accepted by an employer under the psychological contract are often as well respected as (or in some cases better than) those imposed from outside with the force of law.

A Supportive Climate

Better-standards employers recognize that employees may perform better and have greater job satisfaction in a workplace climate that is supportive. In consequence, personnel procedures and supervisors' behavior may be established in order to provide support for employees, as well as impose discipline. To a substantial degree, the procedures and behavior of an employer establish the tone of the employee-employer relationship and have less to do

---

[4] M. H. Dunahee and L. A. Wrangler, "The Psychological Contract," *Personnel Journal*, 53:7, July 1974, pp. 518–526. See also John J. Beach and William A. Murray, "The Career Contract," *Management Review*, 68:10, Oct. 1979, pp. 20–28; and Daniel Yankelovich, "The New Psychological Contract at Work," in Clark Kerr and Jerome Rosow, eds., *Work in America: The Decade Ahead* (New York: Van Nostrand Reinhold, 1979).

[5] J. S. Adams and W. B. Rosenbaum, "The Relationship of Worker Productivity to Cognitive Dissonance about Wage Inequities," *Journal of Applied Psychology*, 46, 1962, pp. 161–164. Incidentally, a psychological contract between the individual employee and the firm might be said to exist even when a collective bargaining agreement is in force. In this case the psychological contract might be said to include the provisions of the formal agreement and whatever additional understandings exist between the employee and employer.

with *what* is done than with *how* it is done. Thus, a supportive climate need not imply a weak management or low productivity. Instead, profit-conscious managers may believe that a supportive climate is most efficient at the workplace.[6]

A supportive managerial climate may be contrasted to one that generates defensive, often antagonistic, behavior in employees. The supportive climate exists when the employer adopts such attitudes as problem orientation and provisional views and when he or she permits a degree of equality and spontaneity in the working relationship. A problem orientation means that the employer shows concern for resolving difficulties that arise in the course of the job, rather than requiring the blind carrying out of orders. An employee is thereby made to feel part of a team, to whose mission he or she is expected to contribute. Provisional views set forth by the supervisor often truthfully reflect uncertainty about how a problem should be handled, instead of the supervisor insisting that absolute certainty exists. Provisional views permit the supervisor to learn how to deal with a problem in cooperation with employees and thereby may elicit a more productive result. Finally, a degree of equality in the manager-employee relationship permits better communication, facilitates an employee's constructive involvement in his or her job, and may increase harmony at the workplace.

Better-standards employers have long recognized the value of these aspects of a supportive climate. For example, in 1925 Thomas J. Watson, Sr., the first president of IBM, put the point as follows: "We want manufacturing men to feel that they are executives in the company. The farther we keep away from the 'boss' proposition..., the more successful we are going to be."[7] What Watson and other employers of like mind have sought is a work environment in which supervisors are supportive of employees and employees are encouraged to be contributors to the accomplishment of the task. This need not imply a lack of direction or authority from management, but the practice of supportive management has often made a positive contribution toward running an efficient company and in some instances has seemed to present a barrier to union activity.[8]

Applied Behavioral Science

The twentieth century has seen considerable development of formal methods of surveying the attitudes and behavior of groups of people. To a large degree this work has been done by psychologists studying the activities of peo-

---

[6] Jack Gibbs, "Defensive Communication," *Journal of Communication*, 11:3, Sept. 1961, pp. 141–148.

[7] Thomas J. Watson, Sr., quoted by William Rogers, *THINK: A Biography of Watson and IBM* (New York: Stein and Day, 1969), p. 89.

[8] Michael Beer, D. Quinn Mills, et al., *Managing Human Assets* (New York: Macmillan, The Free Press, 1984).

ple within organizations, especially work organizations, such as business firms or governmental agencies. Various designations have been given to the academic disciplines involved, including "industrial psychology," "organizational psychology," "administrative sciences," and "organizational development." What they all have in common is the attempt to apply behavioral science techniques to the workplace. Since World War II there has been a great outpouring of analysis and suggestions by academic researchers as to how managers should manage, especially with respect to the relationships between supervisory style, the work environment, and worker satisfaction and productivity.[9]

The impact of this research and effort on the management of the average, or representative, firm in the United States probably has not been very great.[10] But some firms have been exceptions, in that they have made considerable use of the methods developed by the social scientists, if not of the managerial prescriptions offered by them. These firms, which include many of the large nonunionized companies, have developed ongoing programs of research into the attitudes and behavior of their employees, undertaken by staffs specially hired for this purpose. These monitoring programs, carried out by questionnaires and interviews, have permitted the companies to be much more aware of the full range of employee contents and discontents and of the changes that are taking place. The usefulness of these programs has persuaded many companies to expand their communication programs. When these surveys by behavioral science researchers are contrasted with the massive industrial spying that many large firms employed in the 1920s and 1930s as a method of monitoring employee discontent, one can see to what a large degree managerial practices have improved.[11]

Often survey results suggest changes in particular management practices. Sometimes these changes are made and sometimes they are not. But in either case application of behavioral research techniques does tend to generate a greater commitment to good communication, flexibility, and creativity in the managerial response to employee concerns.

THE NONUNION SECTOR IN AN OTHERWISE UNION FIRM

In the past several years many industrial firms which were once largely unionized have developed a substantial nonunion sector. Several major companies which in the early 1950s had 80 percent or more of their production and maintenance employees unionized now have less than 50 percent unionized.

---

[9] See, for example, Edgar H. Schein, *Organizational Psychology*, 2d ed. (Englewood Cliffs, N.J.: Prentice-Hall, 1970).

[10] Mason Haire, "Coming of Age in the Social Sciences," second Douglas M. McGregor Lecture, MIT, Cambridge, Mass., March 1967 (pamphlet published by MIT).

[11] Sanford M. Jacoby, "Worker Attitude Testing at Sears, Roebuck and Company, 1938–1960," Institute of Industrial Relations, University of California at Los Angeles, Working Paper No. 112, June 1986.

Researchers Thomas A. Kochan and Anil Verma studied the nonunion sector in a large industrial company. They concluded:

- The development and expansion of the nonunion part of the firm is "an articulation of managements' long-term philosophical opposition to unions";
- The nonunion strategy is driven by philosophical opposition to unions and by differences in labor costs which are lower in the nonunion plants;
- The nonunion strategy is carried out by opening new plants in low-labor-cost regions, keeping their size small and using an "alternative human resource management system";
- The alternative system is based on
  Wages and benefits based on the local labor market not industry averages or union levels,
  Relatively few job classifications, or all-salary programs,
  Emphasis on flexibility in assigning people to tasks,
  Extension of management communications to employees via small groups.[12]

Response to Union Organization Attempts

All nonunionized companies are conscious of the possibility of union organization of their employees, and most wish to avoid it. Less sophisticated managements respond to a union organizing attempt by trying to repress it. Union activists are fired, union organizers are expelled, and the employer does whatever else seems expedient to prevent unionization. Often in this process employers violate the labor laws of the United States and find themselves with substantial legal problems.[13] In addition, the employers have probably offended or alienated many of their employees by their action and have therefore created a poor industrial relations climate at the workplace.

The better-standards nonunionized employers do not ordinarily behave in this fashion. Instead, they pay careful attention to how they may most effectively defeat a union organizing campaign without violating the law or offending employees. Seminars are offered periodically by such organizations as the American Management Association and the National Association of Manufacturers which explain to managers how to oppose an organizing campaign. Also, newsletters and books that explain how to respond to union drives have been prepared by management-oriented writers. For example, Herbert Rothenberg and Steven Silverman list four major labor relations standards that help an employer avoid unionization:

1 The employee has the right to know the conditions under which he works.

2 The employee has a right to reasonable job security, including seniority standards.

---

[12] Anil Verma and Thomas A. Kochan, "The Growth and Nature of the Nonunion Sector within a Firm," in Thomas A. Kochan, ed., *Challenges and Choices Facing American Labor* (Cambridge, Mass.: MIT Press, 1985), pp. 89–121.

[13] For a list compiled by the AFL-CIO of employers' actions that may be taken to avoid unionization, see *American Federationist*, 85:2, Feb. 1978.

3 The employee should have readily available a practical grievance mechanism.

4 The employee should receive a reasonable level of compensation, not the cheapest possible.[14]

Using enlightened personnel policies, often borrowed from unionized firms, many companies have been able to remain largely or completely nonunion. According to one study, firms using enlightened policies to avoid unions were able to reduce the probability that the companies' new facilities would be unionized from 15 percent to less than 1 percent.[15] There is also statistical evidence that in the period 1977 to 1983 there was a substantial shift among large American companies from an objective of trying to get the best bargain with a union to one of trying to keep unions out.[16]

Three important lessons may be learned from this review of employer policy toward unionization attempts.

1 *Ordinarily, opposition to unionization is taken, without question, to be the proper course for management.* There is little or no discussion about whether to accept unionization or not, or even if some type of unionization might be appropriate. Instead, nonunion employers in the United States tend to look upon unionization as an unwarranted interference with management and seek to learn how best to avoid unionization.

2 *Management uses the threat of unionization to encourage itself, and especially its more authoritarian elements, to improve working conditions and personnel practices, with the argument that better practices will prevent unionization.* [17] Often nonunion management borrows its policies directly from unionized firms and may even improve on them. Some nonunion firms thus tend to become more unionlike than many unionized firms.

3 *The influence of the unions in improving conditions in nonunionized firms can be seen clearly in the process by which nonunionized firms imitate the policies of unionized firms.* Because of this behavior, the impact of unions on industrial relations in the United States goes far beyond the firms that are organized by unions. That is, the secondary impact of unions is substantially broader than their primary impact.

---

[14] Herbert I. Rothenberg and Steven B. Silverman, *Labor Unions, How to Avert Them, Beat Them, Out-Negotiate Them, Live with Them, Unload Them* (Elkins Park, Pa.: Management Relations, Inc., 1973), pp. 163–170.

[15] Thomas A. Kochan, Robert B. McKersie, and John Chalykoff, "The Effects of Corporate Strategy and Workplace Innovations on Union Representation," *Industrial and Labor Relations Review*, 39:4, July 1986, pp. 487ff. See also David Wessel, "Fighting Off Unions," *The Wall Street Journal*, May 12, 1985, pp. 1 and 22.

[16] Peter Cappelli and John Chalykoff, as cited in Bureau of National Affairs, *Daily Labor Report* No. 4, Jan. 7, 1986, pp. A4 and A5.

[17] Marvin S. Myers, *Managing Without Unions* (Reading, Mass.: Addison-Wesley, 1976). Myers maintains that if management provides conditions that result in employees having a joint-stake concern with the goals of the company, the reasons people join unions will be eliminated.

It is also important that the reader avoid certain unwarranted assumptions about unionization, including the following:

1 *A company that follows enlightened personnel policies can always remain nonunionized.* This is not so. Plants or companies in some industries and geographic areas are likely to be organized no matter what policies the employer follows. This is because strong unions that will always mount an organizing campaign exist and because union identification among employees, even new employees, is high. For example, in the late 1960s various petroleum and chemical companies began a major expansion of the number and size of their plants in the Gulf Coast region of the United States (involving the states of Texas, Louisiana, and Mississippi). The companies sought, by the application of carefully developed labor relations policies, to keep the new facilities nonunionized. Nevertheless, within about 2 years virtually all the plants were organized by unions, with the exception of those of the DuPont Company, which has operated nonunion for many years in the otherwise highly unionized chemical industry.

2 *A company that follows poor personnel policies will always be unionized at some point.* This is not so, either. In some industries and geographic areas, companies can continue to operate much as they did in the 1930s without serious risk of unionization. This is because some firms are so small, or the unions in the area are so weak, and the employees have so little union consciousness, that organization is unlikely. This situation exists in many service industries in much of the United States (including, for example, laundries, retail shops, and restaurants).

3 *Companies that profess to have good labor relations policies actually have them.* Often companies know what they should do and have policies that commit them to good practices. Yet the press of business activities, the desire to make profits and to control costs, and other factors cause labor relations policies to be ignored.

MANAGING LABOR RELATIONS

Corporate Organization in Industrial Relations

Unionized companies must manage their labor relations. Managers of various responsibilities are involved in industrial relations. Line managers direct the work force. Staff managers have specialized responsibilities for personnel and labor relations functions, such as compensation, hiring, affirmative action, and collective bargaining, to name but a few. General managers have overall responsibility for setting policies and coordinating line and staff personnel, and for the results.

General managers in different companies structure the line and staff relationships very differently. In some companies corporate staff is kept small, providing primarily advice and overall policy direction. Organization of large corporations by semiautonomous divisions under central controls is now pervasive in American business.[18] Line managers in the divisions have industrial relations and personnel staff reporting to them. In other companies, staff at the divisional or plant level have a dual reporting responsibility—partly to plant or divisional line management and partly to corporate staff. Much of what appears in the literature on personnel as an appeal for more "power" for the personnel function is an argument for reporting by plant and division staff directly to corporate staff, rather than to plant or division top managers.

Companies also organize the various personnel and labor relations functions differently. Some companies combine all functions. Others separate labor relations from personnel. General Motors, for example, has corporate vice presidents for both labor relations and personnel. General Electric, however, includes all such functions under a single corporate vice president for employee relations. Nor is the industrial relations–personnel function always at the level of corporate vice president. Some companies have only directors of personnel or of labor relations. The labels "personnel," "labor relations," "employee relations," and "industrial relations," when used in corporate organization by different firms, do not always have the same meaning. The detailed list of personnel and labor relations functions may be distributed differently in different companies between personnel and labor relations, for example.

According to a 1977 survey of major manufacturing companies, 39 percent of personnel services and 47 percent of industrial relations services were performed at the corporate, rather than divisional or plant, level of management.[19]

These statistics suggest that specialists in personnel and labor relations have in the last several decades[20] established themselves particularly strongly at the corporate level in American firms where they have substantial access to senior management. But these achievements for the staff specialists have not resolved problems that occur in the interaction of line and staff managers throughout American corporations.

In corporations, staff executives in labor relations have tended to spend their careers in the function. By 1979, according to the National Industrial Conference Board, "fully four out of five top labor relations executives have spent their whole corporate life in the industrial relations or personnel function."[21] The large number of employee relations staff and the longevity of managers in this specialty suggest that a high degree of professionalism has been achieved by management.

---

[18] Richard F. Vancil, *Decentralization: Managerial Ambiguity by Design* (Homewood, Ill.: Dow Jones–Irwin, 1979), p. 3.

[19] Ibid., p. 244.

[20] Gerald E. Kohler and Alton C. Johnson, *The Development of Personnel Administration* (Madison, Wis.: Graduate School of Business, University of Wisconsin, 1971), Monograph No. 3.

[21] Audrey Freedman, *Managing Labor Relations* (New York: The Conference Board, 1979), Report No. 765, p. 29.

Labor Relations Policies of Individual Companies

There is a range of labor relations policies followed by American corporations that can be described as a spectrum (see Figure 7-1). At one end are companies that adamantly oppose unionization with whatever weapons are at hand. The Kohler Company, a plumbing fixture manufacturer in Wisconsin, typified this policy for many years. The company engaged the United Auto Workers in a lengthy and often violent contest, ending in the early 1970s in a renewal collective bargaining agreement between the company and the union. Another example is the J. P. Stevens Textile Company, which for many years resisted organization by the United Textile Workers of America (now merged into the Amalgamated Clothing and Textile Workers International Union). In 1980, J. P. Stevens and the Amalgamated Clothing and Textile Workers agreed to end decades of struggle over union organizing by concluding a collective bargaining agreement covering those plants which the union had organized and any other which might vote to be represented by the union in the next 2½ years. In return for this concession by the company, the union agreed to give up a national boycott of Stevens products and to cease efforts to have members of the Stevens board of directors resign because of the management's labor policy. The agreement, although important, did not end the contest between the union and the company entirely, however. The union represents only about one-third of Stevens' plants, and the company has indicated that it will continue to oppose unionization in its other facilities.[22]

Other companies do not resist unionization to the last breath but do take a hard line in attempting to remain as free of union interference as possible. Until 1973 a prime exponent of this policy of strong opposition to unions was the General Electric Company. As described by the company, GE's approach emphasized complete and timely communication with all employees, unionized and nonunionized, and treating all employees as individuals first, not as members of a union or other group.[23] In effect, the company attempted to establish compensation and other industrial relations policies for its employees, both union and nonunion, with as little regard for the unions as possible.

In the middle of the spectrum in Figure 7-1 is the policy of neutrality. Many companies leave their individual divisions and plants to work out labor relations matters largely without central corporate direction, unless the financial performance of the division or plant draws attention to failures due in part to poor labor relations. Other companies actively cooperate with labor unions on many matters. An example is the United States Steel Company. In

---

[22] "Agreement Between J. P. Stevens & Co. and the ACTWU," Bureau of National Affairs, *Daily Labor Report* No. 204, Oct. 20, 1980, pp. D1–D3.

[23] See "Our Employee Relations Philosophy and Union Bargaining Approach," Supplement to General Electric Company's *Relations Reviews*, 1969; and Herbert R. Northrup, *Boulwarism* (Ann Arbor, Mich.: Bureau of Industrial Relations, University of Michigan, 1964).

Adamant opposition to unions	Strong opposition	Neutrality	Cooperation	Close cooperation

FIGURE 7-1   The spectrum of labor relations policies of American companies.

the late 1930s, USS became the first major steel company to recognize the United Steelworkers (at that time the Steel Workers Organizing Committee) and for several years was the *only* major steel company to recognize the union. In the ensuing years there have been some difficult strikes against the company, but in general, relations have been good. In 1973 the union and the company achieved a major advance by developing a method of negotiating new contracts without a threat of strike.

Finally, a few American companies have become overly cooperative with unions and have failed to control costs adequately. In the end, these companies have either gone out of business or been acquired by other concerns. An example often cited is the Studebaker Corporation, an automobile manufacturer that went out of business partly as a result of overly expensive labor relations policies.

Organization of Employers

In most European countries business concerns have formed central, nationwide associations of employers. These associations represent the interests of employers in discussions with the government and with the central federation (or federations) of labor unions. In the United States there is no such central employer association. This is surprising because there exists a single major labor union federation, the AFL-CIO, with which a business association might be expected to have dealings.

American employers have established several smaller and sometimes overlapping associations, however, that have a limited amount of labor relations responsibility. Among the largest of these are the United States Chamber of Commerce and the National Association of Manufacturers (NAM). Other groups of a more ad hoc nature exist, including the Business Roundtable. The Roundtable, formed in 1972, is composed of the chief executive officers of 168 of our largest corporations.[24] Each of these associations has much broader responsibilities than labor relations, and none is really a counterpart to the AFL-CIO. In 1976 the Chamber of Commerce and the NAM agreed to merge, with the support of the Roundtable. The merger plan collapsed, however. In part the explanation of the failure of American employers to create a national association is to be found in the wide range of labor policies followed by American companies. Rather than pool their ef

[24] "Business' Most Powerful Lobby in Washington," *Business Week*, Dec. 20, 1976, pp. 60–63.

forts into a single direction, American companies have preferred to pursue independent courses.

There have been three major efforts in the history of this country to persuade American management to voluntarily accept unionization and form a centralized policy-making body, somewhat akin to European models. First, the National Civic Federation in 1900 under Marcus Hanna, a major Republican-party figure, urged such a course. In 1920 President Wilson sought, through the Industrial Conference and the leadership of Herbert Hoover, to perpetuate the development of collective bargaining, which had begun in World War I. Finally, in 1934–1935, under section 7A of the National Industrial Recovery Act (NIRA), the federal government proclaimed the right of workers to form unions and urged management to voluntarily accept them. All three efforts failed. The result was that American unions developed in a hostile environment and that government intervention ultimately occurred. American business still finds itself without central coordination in dealing with government and labor in labor relations matters.

THE DECISION TO JOIN A UNION

Most employees do not actively participate in determining the conditions under which they work. Instead, they accept whatever rules and benefits are established for them. They may grumble at things they don't like and may even quit if they are dissatisfied enough, but they are essentially passive in the relationship. Why is this? In part it is simply apathy. In part it is because an employee does not feel that he or she alone can affect the conditions of the job. In part it is because the employee lacks a method, or a vehicle, for getting his or her message across.

In many instances, both in the United States and abroad, employees form or join organizations that represent them as a group. Employees may call these organizations by many names: associations, benevolent societies, unions, brotherhoods, and so on. Generally, we call such organizations by the generic term "union." In the United States employee organizations are given certain rights and responsibilities by law, again under the general term "union."

There is no single reason why employees join unions. There are several reasons, each of which may be operative at any one time, although some have been of special significance at certain periods of our history. Here are the major ones.

To Obtain an Instrument in Opposition to Management

Employees often join unions in order to have a method of collectively resisting actions of management. When employers cut wages or pay low wages, when employers arbitrarily discipline or dismiss employees, when working conditions are unsafe or too unpleasant, or when managers interfere in employees' personal lives, employees may resist by joining unions. Through the union employees may petition management for changes, and, if unsuccessful, they may resort to a concerted work stoppage—a strike.

Often an employee's initial interest in unionization is a result of dissatisfaction with some aspects of his or her employment. Perhaps the employee believes that wages are too low, or that too much overtime work is being required by management. But dissatisfaction alone will not result in the formation of a union unless the employees are willing to work together as a group. Many employees in this country have reservations about collective action against their employers and so resist joining unions even though they may experience dissatisfaction about aspects of their work life. But where employees accept the concept of collective action, they must take yet a further step, conceptually, in order to be prepared to join a union. They must believe that the union is a device that can yield advantages for them.

Research by behavioral scientists in recent decades has stressed the role of unions as instruments for obtaining the objectives of workers. According to this view, employees differ as individuals, having different objectives with respect to their jobs.[25] Some objectives are common to large numbers of employees, such as dissatisfaction with low pay levels and a desire for wage increases. Other objectives are specific to certain employees, such as a desire to improve working conditions in a particular part of a plant. But for employees to unionize, they must see the union as a potential method of achieving better pay and/or improving working conditions in their particular areas of the plant.

The manner in which employees view unions as an instrumentality has been explored by many survey questionnaires. One study involved interviewing employees who voted in NLRB-conducted union representative elections. Voters were interviewed twice: once before voting and once after. Some 31 elections were surveyed, and 1239 employees were interviewed. Data were collected as to the attitudes of the employees and how they had voted in the election. Statistical analysis of the data revealed that employees who were dissatisfied with wage levels, the behavior of company supervisors, the type of work they were doing, fringe benefits, and their opportunities for promotion were most likely to vote in favor of union representation.[26]

Another study involved 200 randomly selected members of a public employees' union who were asked about their reasons for joining the union. The researchers made a distinction between extrinsic and intrinsic reasons for joining a union. Extrinsic reasons involve obtaining wage and benefit increases, job security, and protection against unfair action by management. Intrinsic reasons include gaining greater influence over day-to-day decisions

---

[25] Victor H. Vroom, *Work and Motivation* (New York: Wiley, 1964).

[26] Jeanne M. Brett, "Why Employees Join Unions," *Organizational Dynamics*, 8:4, Spring 1980, pp. 47–59.

made about the individual's job, both in terms of its quality and in terms of its relation to the organization as a whole and to the persons served by the organization (for example, the clients of a government agency providing social and rehabilitative services).

The researchers found that even though the union members surveyed were professional employees, the extrinsic motives for union membership took precedence. Thus, they concluded that this group of white-collar employees joined a union for reasons quite similar to those found in the major studies of the reasons for which blue-collar workers joined unions: in order to obtain an instrument (the union) by which to better their pay and working conditions.[27]

Union leaders are aware that many workers view unions primarily as instruments by which to attempt to achieve their own personal goals, whether intrinsic or extrinsic. But union leaders are often somewhat hesitant about endorsing this view of unions too completely. Unions cannot always deliver improvements in pay and other aspects of employment. Sometimes conditions do not permit improvements. And employees who have become union members only for short-term benefits may not prove loyal in difficult times.

Union leaders have a somewhat disparaging term for the concept of a union that sees itself only as an instrument for obtaining better conditions for each individual member. They describe such a concept as one of "vending-machine unionism." In the same way that an employee who deposits several coins in a cigarette machine expects to receive a package of cigarettes in return, a union member who pays dues may expect to receive an improvement in pay or working conditions. But a union is not as simple a device as a vending machine, nor is it necessarily as reliable in the short term. There has always been a strain of thought in American unionism that objected to the instrumentalist view, where the objectives of the union were too closely set to the employee's own job satisfaction. "The only way people will see a union as important to their lives," wrote one unionist, "is if they see the union...as an agency that could not only affect wages and working conditions, but also their environment, their children's education and health care, and their prospects for racial justice."[28]

To Participate in Union Activities

Unions are self-help organizations. Employees may join them to obtain certain health or insurance benefits, to participate in educational programs, or to learn about their own business and occupation. They may also join to engage in social or community activities. Through these activities unions constitute a

[27] Kenneth S. Warner et al., "Motives for Unionization among State Social Service Employees," *Public Personnel Management*, 7:3 May–June 1978, pp. 181–191. See also E. Wight Bakke, "Why Workers Join Unions," *Personnel Journal*, 22, 1945, pp. 2–11; and William F. Whyte, "Who Goes Union and Why?" *Personnel Journal*, 23, 1944, pp. 215–230.

[28] Frank Kashner, "A Rank and File Strike," *Radical America*, 12:6, November–December 1978, p. 60.

form of employee self-government that has nothing to do with relations to the employer.

In some skilled trades and professions, unions are the primary organization through which the occupation is regulated, and relationships with employers are a secondary function of the union. In the past, people applying for jobs sometimes had to join a union first in order to be referred to an employer. An arrangement between a union and employers that requires union membership in order for a person to be hired is now illegal in the United States (since 1947), but in some occupations arrangements that have virtually the same effect continue.

To Exercise Leadership

Certain individual employees join unions as an outlet for their own ambitions. They may aspire to leadership and find that the union offers a convenient vehicle. They may hope to get ahead by obtaining an office in the union. Also, employers often notice employees who are leaders in the union, and it is not uncommon to have union officials hired directly into managerial ranks as supervisors or superintendents.

Because of Social Pressure

Many employees join unions simply because other employees urge them to do so. They may be made to feel that they are traitors or malingerers if they do not join. Or they may simply become the object of a friendly but persistent campaign to get them to join the union. Such social pressures are hard to resist, whether their subject be hair styles, personal behavior, or union membership. Many people belong to unions probably for no other reason than an inability to resist social pressure.

Compulsory Unionism

There is no law in the United States that requires an employee to join a union. But in most states the law permits an employer to agree with a union that after a certain period (generally 30 days except in the construction industry, where the period is 7 days) an employee must join the union or be fired. Joining the union ordinarily entails a ceremony and membership pledge and paying dues or assessments. We do not know how many employees are union members solely because of agreements that compel union membership.

WHY EMPLOYEES FAIL TO JOIN UNIONS

Most American employees are not members of labor unions. There are several reasons for this.

Antiunion Attitudes

Many employees believe that unions are either inappropriate or unnecessary. They are suspicious of union leaders and of what they, as members, might be asked to do. Also, many employees hope to be promoted to better jobs and believe membership in a union would restrict their opportunities.

Social Pressures

Employees working in a nonunionized place may be under considerable social pressure not to join a union. They may be made to feel disloyal if they do so. Employees who do not want a union, often aided and abetted by management (although some forms of management involvement are illegal), are likely to exert considerable pressure on other employees not to join a union.

Job Satisfaction

Some employees are generally satisfied with their jobs and have no substantial grievances against management. They may believe that management would consider formation of a union a hostile act by employees, and they see no reason to take such action.

Fear of Reprisal

Some employees do not join unions simply because they are afraid of reprisals by management. Although reprisals for union-related activity are illegal in the United States, the employee may fear that they will occur nonetheless. Fear of being fired because of union activity certainly remains a factor in keeping workers from joining unions, although we do not know how many people are intimidated in this way.

Cost

Unions cost money. An employee who joins a union must pay an initiation fee (generally less than $100, but considerably higher in certain trades) and pay dues on a periodic basis. Dues average about 1 or 2 hours' pay per month, or about 1 or 2 percent of before-tax pay. Whether or not the amount seems large, many workers prefer not to pay it and do not join unions for this reason.

Union Hostility or Indifference

Some people do not join unions because the unions won't accept them. There are many possible reasons why this might occur. Some unions have excluded people on grounds of race, ethnic background, or sex. It is now illegal for unions to refuse membership to anyone on these grounds (as it is illegal for employers to refuse to hire on these grounds), but unfortunately such instances do still occur. Also, some skilled craft unions refuse to accept people who do not have the skills required of a member.

Unions may also simply fail to assist in the unionization of groups of workers. The union may decide that the workers involved are too few or are located at too remote a place to be serviced at a reasonable cost to the union. The union may also decide that there are too few job opportunities for the already-existing union membership or that the workers involved will not make good union members. Finally, a union contacted by a group of employees might decide that the employees seeking membership actually belong to the jurisdiction of a different union and might therefore refuse to accept their application for membership.

Conscientious Objection

Some employees have religious or moral scruples against joining organizations, including unions. For this reason, some employees refuse to become members of labor unions.

WHAT DOES IT MEAN TO HAVE A UNION?

To a Company

The existence of a union has many implications for a company. Probably the most obvious is that the employer must deal with employees as a group and not simply as individuals. In many instances, this may not be as major a difference as it seems, however, because many companies are so large that they already have personnel policies designed to treat employees as members of a group. But what is different is that the company must deal with the union, which represents the workers. And dealing with representatives of a group of people is not at all like dealing with them as individuals.

Managers often complain about this. They distinguish between the union and the employees and then comment upon how reasonable the employees are and how irresponsible and difficult their union representatives are. Yet the union is ordinarily another manifestation of the employees' needs and desires. In part, the employees are able to be reasonable with management because they know the union is there to be more difficult in their behalf.

A company that deals with a union must be very careful in its policies, for the union is always observing what it does and looking for inconsistencies. When a company is inconsistent, treating one employee differently from another in the same situation, then the union will try to get the better treatment for both, and this may be costly and inefficient from the company's viewpoint.

In a union-management relationship the day-to-day activities of both are measured against a contract. The contract is an agreement between the union and the company that sets forth the rights and obligations of each. Actions that management takes with respect to an employee or a group of employees may be judged in light of the contract and found to be permissible or not. The contract is a more rigid form of control on managerial discretion than ordinarily exists in a nonunion situation.

When management is said by the union to have violated provisions of the agreement, it may even have to defend itself before a third and neutral party, an arbitrator, who will decide if there has been a violation. In the United States companies without a union do not ordinarily have their actions subject to review by neutral persons. In other countries, however, there are often laws about labor-management relations at the plant and courts that handle disputes between workers and management, even where a union does not exist. This is one of the reasons that companies in the United States prefer so strongly not to have a union representing their employees. In the absence of a union, American managers have much more discretion in their actions than is the case abroad because there is less law about management-employee relations in the United States.

Finally, when a union exists it is ordinarily more than just a group of employees who band together to deal with an employer. Instead, a union is a human institution separate and independent from the company. The union has its own internal political life; its own objectives, officers, and activities; and its own financial status. It may also be affiliated with other unions in a national body. Whatever the formal organizational characteristics, however, the union is for workers a separate source of involvement and loyalty, apart from the company and often in conflict with it. In this sense, managers often resent unions for reducing the loyalty of company employees.

Each reader may have his or her own view as to whether these results of the existence of a union are for the better or worse. Some think unions are an inappropriate interference with the lives of managers and workers. Others believe unions are a necessary device to protect and assist workers in dealings with management. Whatever a person's view, however, it is obvious that having a union in a company will tend to make a considerable difference in the company's relations with its employees. Whether this difference leads to a good or a bad situation depends on factors we will examine below.

To Employees

Employees who are represented by unions find in the union an advocate in their dealings with management. A union is primarily a service organization that attempts to assist and defend the people it represents. Employees who feel they are not being treated fairly by management may take their questions or complaints to the union, which should investigate their problem and report back to them. In nonunion companies employees are often afraid to press their problems with managers. They may fear for their jobs if they are too persistent in asserting their rights or if they appear to managers to be malcontents. Even though well-managed nonunion firms encourage employees to bring complaints to their supervisors, the inherent suspicion that employees have of their supervisors may make such a procedure of limited value.

Unfortunately, unions do not always treat employees fairly either. Sometimes union officials are too busy to handle problems for certain employees. Sometimes union officials give in to the human temptation to serve union members better than other employees, although they have a legal obligation to represent all employees in a bargaining unit equally. Generally, however, union officials attempt to represent employees equally and well and do provide an independent channel for employees to use in dealing with management.

One way to look at the role of a union in representing employees is in terms of power relationships. An individual employee dealing directly with management is plainly at a great disadvantage if power plays a role in settling his or her problem or complaint. A union, however, exercises power of its own, arising from the collective weight of the employees as a group. Therefore, when an employee encounters management through the instrumentality of a union, the power balance is much more even.

The existence of a union confronts an employee with the decision of whether to participate in the activities of the union or not.[29] In some instances the employee is free to pay dues or not, as he or she decides. In other instances, the employee must pay dues by virtue of a provision in the collective bargaining agreement. But whether an employee pays dues voluntarily or involuntarily, he or she is not obliged to participate in union activities. Unions have meetings, elect officers, and have social occasions. Sometimes unions conduct strikes or participate in boycotts. The individual must determine whether or not to take part in these activities. Usually a union acts by majority vote of the members who attend meetings. An employee must decide whether to go to the meetings and whether to be bound in his or her own actions by the majority rule. Ordinarily, the decisions involved are not difficult, but crises and conflicts arise in which such decisions can be very hard to make.

An employee who actively takes part in the union will also be drawn into the internal life of a broader movement, involving other local unions and the national union. This involvement may make demands on the employee's time and energy outside the workplace. Again, some people welcome such involvements, while others do not.

Finally, the existence of a union presents both management and employees with the possibility that a conflict may develop that cannot be resolved, so that a work stoppage occurs. One major reason why managements object to unions is the fear that if a union exists, it is certain to call a strike at some

---

[29] Michael G. Kolchin and Thomas Hychak, "Participation in Union Activities," *Journal of Labor Research*, 5:3, Summer 1984, pp. 259–261.

time or other. Many employees also fear loss of their pay during strikes. But a union does not guarantee that strikes will occur. Most companies and unions reach agreements without work stoppages. Nor does the absence of a union ensure that if a dispute develops, a strike won't occur.

WHAT PROCESSES ARE ASSOCIATED WITH UNION-MANAGEMENT RELATIONS?

In the United States the existence of a union means that management and the union must do certain things together. Broadly speaking, they must negotiate a contract with each other at periodic intervals; they must administer the contract while it is in effect; and they must cooperate, or compete, with each other in a variety of other activities.

Negotiation of an agreement is a process that we refer to as collective bargaining, and about which we will have much to say in later chapters. Briefly speaking, it means that management and labor each select a team of representatives who will meet with each other to work out the provisions of a contract. If an impasse develops, a strike or lockout may occur.

Contract administration involves the implementation and application of the contract. When disputes develop over the meaning of the contract, management and labor must have some method of resolving the disputes. Ordinarily, they find a way to work the problem out. When this is not possible, there may be a work stoppage, or, much more commonly, some neutral person is asked to decide the issue and both sides agree to accept the decision.

Finally, management and the union both exist in a broader community, in which they are concerned about government, living conditions, social services, and similar matters. They may choose to cooperate with each other on such issues or to be in conflict. Often unions and management try to cooperate at the local level but are in disagreement at the state or national levels. Regardless of what is actually done, however, it is important to realize that the relationship of management and unions is not confined exclusively to the workplace, but inevitably overflows into the wider society of which both are members.

Nonunion companies and employees do not engage in these processes. There is no collective bargaining, no contract, and no contract administration. Because employees do not have their own organization, they are not involved in issues as a group, though individual employees, like individual managers, may be personally involved in politics or social activities.

CHAPTER SUMMARY

In the United States, most employees are not unionized and many employers do not deal with unions. There are many different types of nonunion employers with a wide range of employment standards. At one extreme are the low-standards employers, who keep costs down by paying low wages, providing few benefits, and spending little on workplace amenities. At the other end of the spectrum are better-standards employers, whose labor relations policies are as good as, if not better than, those in unionized companies.

The better-standards nonunionized firms pay wages and benefits comparable to, or better than, those paid by unionized firms and conduct their employee relations with great care. Although they generally oppose unionization, they do so by legal means and by generous wage and benefit plans. Sound employment policies are their best defense against a union. In better-standards nonunionized firms, a kind of psychological contract exists between employee and employer about the rights and obligations of each, rather than a written contract. Personnel procedures and supervisory attitudes attempt to provide support for employees and promote team spirit and loyalty. Some firms consciously use behavioral science knowledge and techniques with their employees, and many have developed practical grievance, or complaint, procedures.

The various personnel and labor relations functions are organized very differently in different companies. Some companies combine all functions, other clearly separate labor relations from personnel, and still others delegate labor and personnel functions in individualized ways. Specialists in personnel and labor relations have, in the last few decades, established their importance at the corporate level, and a high degree of professionalization is beginning to characterize staff functions in labor relations.

American companies follow a wide range of labor relations policies, from adamant opposition to unions to close supervision. The diversity in part results from the fact that there have been no comprehensive nationwide business associations to represent the interest of employers in discussions with government and the AFL-CIO.

There is no single reason why employees join unions. Some of the major reasons are to have a means of effectively resisting unfair or unpleasant working conditions, to get better pay, to be able to participate in benefits and activities sponsored by unions, and, sometimes, to respond to social or union pressure. Employees choose not to join unions, in general, because they are satisfied with their jobs or because they believe unions are unnecessary. They also do not join unions when there are social pressures not to join, when they fear reprisals from management, when unions are not open or available to them, and, sometimes, simply because unions cost money.

When a company has to deal with union representatives rather than directly with its employees as individuals, it needs to be much more careful and consistent in its actions and in how it develops policies. Its actions will be scrutinized and subject to review, its discretion limited by a contract. This is an important reason companies prefer not to have unions. Furthermore, a union is more than just a group of employees. It is a separate institution with its own objectives and claims to the loyalty and involvement of workers.

Employees who are represented by a union have a much more substantial power base in their dealings with management, whether they are union members or not. But the employee is faced with the decision of the extent to which he or she will become involved in the union and support its goals and activities. Both employees and employers fear that if a union comes into a company, strikes will occur. However, strikes are not an inevitable outcome of unionization.

Where a union exists, management and the union must negotiate a contract through collective bargaining and then administer the contract and resolve disputes that develop over its meaning. They may also cooperate or oppose each other on more general social issues involving the local community or the government.

QUESTIONS FOR THOUGHT AND DISCUSSION

1 What is included in the psychological contract between the employer and the employee? What is excluded?
2 Do employees want to join unions only if the employer is doing something wrong? Why or why not? Why might employees in better-standards companies join unions?
3 What are the advantages to a company of remaining nonunionized? What are the advantages of unionization? Can you quantify the advantages? The disadvantages?
4 How do companies manage their labor relations? Should managers who deal with unions be separated from those who do not? Why or why not?
5 Should personnel functions in management be separate from labor relations functions? Why or why not? If you had a company, how would you structure the personnel and labor relations functions?
6 How has the existence of unions improved employment conditions for nonunionized employees? Do you think employers would provide high standards of employment even if there were no threat of unionization? Why?
7 Why do some employees join unions? Why do other employees decline to join unions?
8 What are the most important ways that a union affects employees? In what ways does it affect a company?
9 What type of labor-management relationship is best? Why? What circumstances affect your choice?
10 What are factors that contribute to a cooperative labor-management relationship? Which do you think is most important and why—the attitudes of union officials and management, the methods they use for handling disputes, the economic climate?
11 Should union leaders limit themselves to "instrumental objectives" if this is what union members want or should they be concerned with broader social issues, such as the environment, discrimination, and even corporate ethics?

SELECTED READING

Bakke, E. Wight, *Mutual Survival: The Goals of Unions and Management*, 2d ed. (Hamden, Conn.: Archon, 1966).

Beer, Michael, and D. Quinn Mills et al., *Managing Human Assets* (New York: Macmillan, The Free Press, 1984).

Bilik, Al, "Corrupt, Crusty or Neither? The Poll-ish View of American Unions," *Labor Law Journal*, 30:6, June 1979, pp. 323–333.

Foulkes, Fred K., *Effective Personnel Policies: A Study of Large Nonunion Employers* (Englewood Cliffs, N.J.: Prentice-Hall, 1980).

Myers, Marvin S., *Managing without Unions* (Reading, Mass.: Addison-Wesley, 1976).

Purcell, Theodore V., *Blue-Collar Man: Patterns of Dual Allegiance in Industry* (Cambridge, Mass.: Harvard University Press, 1960).

Rothenberg, Herbert I., and Steven B. Silverman, *Labor Unions, How to Avert Them, Beat Them, Out-Negotiate Them, Live with Them, Unload Them* (Elkins Park, Pa.: Management Relations, Inc., 1973).

E

THE COLLECTIVE BARGAINING PROCESS

At the heart of labor-management relations in the United States is the process of collective bargaining. The term "collective bargaining" is used to distinguish the effort of a union on behalf of a group of employees from the bargaining of an individual employee for himself or herself. Through a union, the employees try to develop a counterweight to the power of the corporation. Through collective bargaining, a contract is created between management and the union which sets forth the rights and obligations of each.

Collective bargaining is sometimes a test of the power of the union against that of management. The relative strength of each side is called bargaining power. But collective bargaining is not only a test of strength—it is also a process of problem solving that involves the concerns of workers and of employers at the workplace.

CHAPTER 8

THE NEGOTIATIONS PROCESS

WHAT IS COLLECTIVE BARGAINING?

Collective bargaining is a process by which management and unions establish terms and conditions of employment. The process is described as "collective" because workers are involved in it as a group and are represented by individuals chosen for that purpose. The process is "bargaining" because it involves give-and-take and, ordinarily, the making of a contract. The contract that results is called a collective bargaining agreement, and it regulates the relationship between the employer and the employees involved.

The bargaining process has been caricatured in a variety of ways: (1) as a poker game combining deception, bluff, luck, and ability, (2) as a debating society with long-winded speeches to impress one's colleagues and possibly have some effect on the opposition, (3) as power politics or pure brute strength in forcing terms of settlement on the weaker party, and, finally, (4) as a rational process in which appeal to facts and to logic reconciles conflicting interests in the light of common interests. All these elements are involved in some degree and combination in the bargaining process.[1] While "mature" collective bargaining no doubt implies enlargement of the rational process, there can be no such thing as complete escape from the other elements.

In the industrial relations system of the United States, collective bargaining has three major functions:

1 *It is a formal procedure* to establish, revise, and administer many of the rules of the workplace.

2 *It is an informal process* by which labor and management deal with each other about many matters of joint concern.

[1] John T. Dunlop and James J. Healy, *Collective Bargaining* (Homewood, Ill.: Irwin, 1953), pp. 53–68.

3 *It is a method* for the settlement of disputes during the lifetime of agreements and on their expiration or reopening.[2]

These are basic processes that every industrial society and economy must somehow carry out. However, not all companies and workers are involved in the collective bargaining process in our country. Many workers are not represented by unions. In these instances the employer unilaterally determines the matters that otherwise are the subject of collective bargaining. But all employers and all employees in our society are much affected by collective bargaining, since the rules and standards established through collective bargaining have an important impact on the nonunionized sector of our economy.

Collective bargaining means many different things. A prominent neutral in the disputes between labor and management described it as follows:

> The term "collective bargaining" sometimes means an amicable exploration of joint problems resulting in friendly agreement; sometimes it means a difficult, suspicious, unfriendly relationship out of which a meeting of minds occurs only after pressure, threats of economic conflict, or strikes or lockouts.[3]

The Setting of Negotiations

Collective bargaining is a broader term than negotiations. But negotiations are at its core. We will spend much of this chapter on negotiations. But first a word about what can and cannot be done in negotiations.

Negotiations usually occur between groups of individuals, one group representing the employer and another group representing the employees. The two groups meet at a chosen place, usually a conference room at some neutral site (i.e., neither the company's offices nor the union's meeting hall), such as a hotel. The two sides are called the "parties" to the negotiations. Each party designates a chairperson.

In some situations the parties begin negotiations on an ad hoc basis. One side usually opens the proceedings by identifying itself and asking the other side to do the same.

The first session of negotiations is normally devoted to presentation of the union's proposals, usually called "demands." The following session is devoted to the presentation of management's counterproposals. The parties thereafter schedule sessions and their agendas as they desire.

A negotiation has not only a physical setting, but one in time. Rarely do the parties enter a negotiation free of the encumbrances of their past relations with each other. In some instances the burden of the past is stifling. Some years ago George P. Shultz investigated industrial relations in the Massachusetts shoe manufacturing industry. The industry was declining, yet the

---

[2] John T. Dunlop, "The Social Utility of Collective Bargaining," in Lloyd Ulman, ed., *Challenges to Collective Bargaining* (Englewood Cliffs, N.J.: Prentice-Hall, 1967), p. 169.

[3] Saul Wallen, quoted in Byron Yaffe, ed., *The Saul Wallen Papers: A Neutral's Contribution to Industrial Peace* (Ithaca, N.Y.: Cornell University Press, 1974), p. 41.

companies and the unions were seemingly unable to come to grips with the problem successfully, although all knew it to be serious. Shultz concluded that the critics of the industry's behavior were

> wrong in placing the blame on the individual businessman, worker, or union leader. An individual may do a capable or even an outstanding job and yet fail to move ahead. Why? Because the local environment which no one person can control binds him to an inflexible pattern of action.... Individuals often struggle in an awkward institutional setting, created by the problems of years past. They are limited to an inflexible pattern of action in the making of today's decisions, and the limits cannot be waved or wished away.[4]

Distributive versus Integrative Bargaining

Collective bargaining is often thought of as a struggle between management and labor in which labor seeks to obtain concessions from management. Management is thought of as possessing economic advantages (such as profits) that labor seeks to wrest from it in the form of wage and benefit increases. Management is also thought of as possessing rights or prerogatives that labor seeks to limit or infringe on by increasing the rights of the workers. In both cases, collective bargaining is thought of as a dispute over the division of authority and of economic gains. This type of bargaining may be described as *distributive,* since it involves the distribution of financial and noneconomic privileges that are thought to be fixed in total amount.

But this is not all that is involved in negotiations. In fact, when one thinks of negotiating outside of the labor relations process, as, for example, between two business people over a possible sale, then bargaining is conceived as a process that results in a gain for both the buyer and the seller. Bargaining occurs over the terms of the transaction, and if the terms are sufficiently unattractive to either side, the transaction need not be made. Collective bargaining also involves this aspect of bargaining. Conflict is minimal, and both sides stand to gain from the bargain that is struck. This type of bargaining may be described as *integrative* bargaining. As defined by its proponents, integrative bargaining

> refers to the system of activities which is instrumental to the attainment of objectives which are not in fundamental conflict with those of the other party and which therefore can be integrated to some degree.... Integrative bargaining and distributive bargaining are both joint decision-making processes. However, these processes are quite dissimilar and yet are rational responses to different situations. Integrative potential exists when the nature of a problem permits solutions which benefit both parties, or at least when the gains of one party do not represent equal sacrifices by the other.[5]

---

[4] George P. Shultz, "Decision-Making: A Case Study in Industrial Relations," *Harvard Business Review,* 30:3, May–June 1952, pp. 105 and 113. George Shultz was later to be Secretary of Labor and then Secretary of the Treasury and Secretary of State of the United States.

[5] Richard E. Walton and Robert B. McKersie, *A Behavioral Theory of Labor Negotiations* (New York: McGraw-Hill, 1965), p. 5.

Many people think of integrative bargaining as involving the cooperation of labor and management in solving problems. In contrast, labor-management conflict is viewed as distributive bargaining. This is probably a confusion of ends and means, however. It is possible for labor and management to approach the resolution of distributive issues with cooperation, not conflict. In fact, it happens often, even though one party is making concessions to the other. Distributive issues need not involve conflict. Alternatively, labor and management are occasionally in conflict over issues that are integrative in nature, and the solution to which, after the conflict is resolved, benefits both parties. We may say, therefore, that there are both types of issues, integrative and distributive, and both types of bargaining, cooperative and conflict-ridden. We may also adopt Walton and McKersie's terminology and describe cooperative bargaining over integrative issues as *integrative bargaining* and conflict-ridden bargaining over distributive issues as *distributive bargaining*. But it should not be forgotten that cooperative bargaining over distributive issues also occurs, as does conflict-ridden bargaining over integrative issues. But we have no special terms for those two situations.

Walton and McKersie differentiate between different strategies and tactics in bargaining, calling them either distributive or integrative. By distributive tactics they mean those generating conflict between labor and management. By integrative tactics they mean those leading to cooperation between labor and management. Other persons make somewhat similar distinctions. Union and management officials often try to distinguish between ordinary negotiations over an agreement (in which they assume an adversarial stance) and quality of work life or other employee participation efforts (in which they try to be cooperative with one another). Yet another distinction is made between the period of negotiations prior to a contract in which labor and management battle with one another, and the period after the contract is concluded in which they cooperate to make it work.

Yet human relations are not so easily compartmentalized. In practice, labor and management negotiations *blend* the various types of tactics to fit the circumstances they confront. For this reason, the separation of negotiation tactics and strategies into integrative and distributive categories is *not* done in the next section.

THE QUALITY OF A LABOR-MANAGEMENT RELATIONSHIP

There are many types of labor-management relationships. The public hears or reads primarily about strikes or threatened strikes in the news media and often presumes that all labor-management relations are antagonistic and strike-prone. The violent language of union leaders and management officials in the context of a dispute is especially attractive as a news item, and the average citizen hearing this language must think poorly of the people using it. Labor-management relations often appear, therefore, as a particularly difficult and unpleasant area.

One of the most glaring examples recently of the continuation of highly publicized labor-management conflict involves Eastern Airlines. In 1986 Eastern, a highly unionized carrier, was purchased by Texas Air Corporation, which operates nonunion Continental Airlines. Continental had been unionized when Texas Air acquired it in the early 1980s, but after a strike which failed, bankruptcy proceedings, and the company's hiring of permanent replacements for strikers, Continental emerged from bankruptcy as a nonunion airline.

Apparently fearing that Texas Air would try to eliminate them, Eastern's unions began a bitter fight against Texas Air and its chairman, Frank Lorenzo. Smarting from adverse publicity, Texas Air filed a lawsuit on May 6, 1988, against two of Eastern's unions, charging them with an illegal "smear campaign" intended to ruin Eastern's business reputation.

In a response, the president of one of the unions commented that Texas Air's lawsuit was like "Al Capone suing Elliot Ness"; that is, like the 1920s era Chicago gangster Capone suing the federal agent Elliot Ness, who sought to convict Capone of various crimes.[6]

But labor-management relations are not all, or even mostly, of this type. Most relations between union and management take place in a reasonably quiet and responsible atmosphere, which is marked at times by disagreements but rarely by open strife. The people involved in labor-management relations generally are there because they believe in the importance of what they do. A survey of several hundred national and local union leaders in 1983 and 1985 found that 53 percent described their relationship with management as cooperative, and 71 percent said management accepts the union.[7] The noisy publicity seekers, the violent and abusive persons in whom the press delights, are a minority.

It is useful to examine a spectrum of labor-management relationships that describes their quality. It is possible for a particular company and union to be assigned to one category, but over time to move to another. The spectrum, therefore, may be interpreted statically (i.e., assigning different companies and unions to a certain category at the same time) or dynamically (i.e., assigning the same company and union to different categories at different periods of time).

Figure 8-1 shows a spectrum of the quality of labor-management relations. At one extreme is a situation in which the union and the employer are in open conflict. Each challenges the other's actions and motivations, cooperation is nonexistent, and work stoppages are frequent and bitter. Next is

---

[6] "Eastern," Bureau of National Affairs, *Daily Labor Report* No. 89, May 9, 1988, p. A-12. See also Jack Barbash, "Collective Bargaining and the Theory of Conflict," *British Journal of Industrial Relations*, 18:1, March 1980, pp. 82–90.

[7] Brian P. Heshizer, "Labor's Perspective on Labor," *Personnel*, June 1986, pp. 58ff.

Open conflict	Armed truce	Working harmony	Labor-management cooperation

FIGURE 8-1   Types of labor-management relations. *(Source: Adapted from Frederick M. Harbison and John R. Coleman, Goals and Strategy in Collective Bargaining, Harper, New York, 1951. See also Benjamin M. Selekman, "Varieties of Labor Relations," Harvard Business Review, 27:2, March 1949, p. 125.)*

shown a situation of armed truce. The two sides view each other as antagonists and are prepared for open conflict (which sometimes occurs), but nonetheless each tries to limit their rivalry so that undue damage is not done to either. Next is placed a situation of working harmony, in which each side respects the other and conflict is limited because of a willingness to engage in give-and-take to settle disagreements. Finally, at the other extreme, is indicated labor-management cooperation. In this situation each side not only respects the other but looks to the other to help resolve common problems. Conflict is strictly limited, so that the overall quality of the cooperative relationship is not undermined.

Because cooperation between labor and management is less well known to the public than its opposite, we cite a few recent examples.

In 1985 General Motors Corporation decided to establish a new subsidiary company, called the Saturn Corporation, to develop, produce, and sell a new automobile. The company began by seeking a much more cooperative relationship with the United Automobile Workers union than is usual for General Motors itself. Saturn and the UAW worked out an agreement calling for very close cooperation in most aspects of the business. For example, the national contract between GM and the UAW (which is discussed in Chapter 18) does not apply to Saturn and the UAW. Saturn's own agreement with the UAW begins with a statement of philosophy: "We believe that all people want to be involved in decisions that affect them. . . ." The contract goes on to call for minimizing "differentiation among people," so that there are no time clocks for workers, no special parking places, entrances, identification, or dining rooms for management, and all are in the same pay and benefits system (though rates of pay differ)—i.e., all employees are salaried.

Each employee is a member of a team or work unit. There are a strategic advisory committee to top management and an operations committee, both composed of management and union officials. Decision making is to be by "consensus," the contract says—rather than by management only. "Consensus" is defined to mean joint problem solving, and, says the contract, "voting, trading, compromise are *not* part of this process."

This agreement is highly innovative and is an indication of an effort to create a much more cooperative climate of labor relations in America. The agreement is also controversial. Some traditionally management-oriented observers say it involves the union far too much in what traditionally should be management decision making. Union-oriented observers insist the agreement "is part of a nationwide corporate anti-union offensive."[8]

It was an employer's group, not unionists, who went to the NLRB to try to block the Saturn agreement, charging that it constituted illegal support by the company for the union. The NLRB's general counsel, however, refused to file a complaint under the law.[9]

With the support of the United States Department of Labor many unions and companies have established cooperation committees. In the steel industry in 1987 seven companies and the Steelworkers union established participation teams by which workers and management, with union involvement, can attempt to improve productivity and working conditions.[10] A survey conducted by the Federal Mediation and Conciliation Service found unions and management generally satisfied with these committees.[11]

Another form of union-management cooperation which has been gaining popularity in recent years involves the use of joint labor-management committees to work on problems of mutual interest. Generally such committees are organized to deal with a specific subject area. The two most frequently mentioned by management are safety and job evaluation. The problems of alcohol and drug abuse also receive attention from joint committees in some companies, involving a cooperative program by which a system is established for early identification of these problems, for referral of the employee for proper treatment, and for a concerned follow-up. Other areas of joint committee effort include quality of working life, labor relations training for supervisors and stewards, profit sharing, and starting up new facilities.[12]

These examples show that labor-management cooperation does occur and that it takes many forms, covering a wide range of situations.

There is, however, resistance to labor-management cooperation. Some people point to the difference in interests that exists—labor's interest being to raise pay levels and managers' interest being to improve profits—and insist that both sides are better served by contest and conflict.[13] Even the NLRB sometimes acts as though the nation's labor laws are opposed to labor-management cooperation. Speaking in 1987, NLRB member Wilford

---

[8] Andrew Remes, "The Saturn Contract," *Economic Notes*, 54:4–5, April–May 1986, pp. 12–13.

[9] John Hoerr, "The NLRB Strikes a Blow for Worker Participation," *Business Week*, June 16, 1986, p. 36.

[10] Aaron Bernstein and Matt Rothman, "Steelmakers Want to Make Teamwork an Institution," *Business Week*, May 11, 1987, p. 84.

[11] Bureau of National Affairs, *Daily Labor Report* No. 107, June 5, 1987, pp. A8–A9.

[12] Joseph A. Loftus and Beatrice Walfish, eds., *Breakthroughs in Union-Management Cooperation* (Scarsdale, N.Y.: Work in America Institute, 1977); and National Center for Productivity and Quality of Working Life, *Directory of Labor-Management Committees* (Washington D.C.: Superintendent of Documents, U.S. Government Printing Office, 1978).

[13] See Barbara Reisman and Lance Compa, "The Case for Adversarial Unions," *Harvard Business Review*, 63:3, May–June 1985, pp. 22–24ff.

Johansen said the law assumes an adversarial role between labor and management.[14]

Yet there would seem to be no logically compelling reason to conclude that because interests differ between labor and management—as the law recognizes—the relationship must be adversarial and conflictual. Differing interests can also be accommodated by cooperation. It is possible for different parties to cooperate to increase the advantage to both. That is what labor-management cooperation is about.

Employee ownership of the stock of a corporation is often espoused as a means of increasing labor-management cooperation. By 1987 there were about 9 million workers covered by employee ownership plans, which are encouraged by American tax laws. Some half million are believed to be in firms more than 50 percent owned by employees.[15] At one employee-owned firm a study showed local union leaders alternatively cooperating and contesting with managers over a four-year period. Strikes have even occurred at plants owned by the workers. This is because even with worker ownership, managers remain and sometimes get into disagreements with employees and unions.[16]

Finally, union officers are sometimes placed on a corporation's board of directors. This is frequent in Germany, but unusual in America. Most American union leaders and top managers seem to believe that for a union leader to serve on a company's board involves too much of a conflict of interest. Labor-management cooperation in America doesn't go that far.[17]

We may characterize cooperation and perhaps working harmony as types of "good" labor relations. What do we mean in detail by the term "good labor relations"? Good labor relations include:

1 *A substantial degree* of industrial peace (that is, the virtual absence of work stoppages).

2 *Acceptance by each side* of the needs of the other as an ongoing institution (that is, the company isn't trying to destroy the union, nor is the union trying to cause the company to lose profits).

3 *Both the company* and the union believe the relationship is equitable (that is, not only is it peaceful, but fair).

4 *The net effect* of the good relationship is not detrimental to consumers or

[14] Wilford Johansen, talk given on Mar. 25, 1987, reported in Bureau of National Affairs, *Daily Labor Report* No. 63, April 3, 1987, pp. A9–A10.

[15] Joseph Raphael Blasi, "The Sociology of Worker Dimensions and Participation," Proceedings of the Industrial Relations Research Association, Dec. 28–30, 1984, pp. 360–369. See also "Employee Stock Ownership Plans," *Employee Relations Law Journal*, 11:1, Summer 1985, pp. 89–105; and Robert D. Hershey, Jr., "Including Labor in the Division of Capital," *The New York Times*, Sunday, April 24, 1988, p. E5..

[16] Tove H. Hammer and Robert N. Stern, "A Yo-Yo Model of Cooperation," *Industrial and Labor Relations Review*, 39:3, April 1986, pp. 337–349.

[17] Charles S. Loughran, "Union Officials as Corporate Directors," *Directors and Boards*, 10:1, Fall 1985, pp. 24ff. Also see Robert Kuttner, "Blue-Collar Boardrooms," *The New Republic*, 3:674, June 17, 1985, pp. 18–23.

to the public (that is, the relationship is not at the expense of other people or institutions).

In contrast, poor labor relations involve a situation in which there are frequent work stoppages, one or both sides are out to destroy the other, the relationship is not believed to be fair by one or both sides, and the net effect on customers and the public is detrimental.

LABOR-MANAGEMENT COOPERATION

Cooperative Relationships

Collective bargaining involves the entire relationship between management and labor. It may be cooperative or adversarial. Figure 8-2 summarizes some of the factors facilitating the development of a cooperative and working re-

FIGURE 8-2 Factors affecting the development of a cooperative relationship between management and labor. *(Source: Adapted from James W. Driscoll, "Problem-Solving Between Union and Management," unpublished paper, MIT, 1979. See also Michael Schuster, "Models of Cooperation and Charge in Union Settings," Industrial Relations, 34:3, Fall 1985, pp. 382–394.)*

lationship between management and labor. The external environment is critically important. Further, the necessary atmosphere cannot develop where the parties are grossly unequal in power or where either side does not accept the fundamental legitimacy of the other. A survey of management and labor negotiators indicated that labor representatives felt that they had more bargaining power than management, but that they accord more respect and acknowledge greater legitimacy to the management side. Management representatives acknowledge less legitimacy to the union and are more sensitive to criticism from the union.[18] Finally, the development of a group of representatives of the company and the union who trust each other, and may resort to outside neutrals and experts on certain matters, makes it possible to approach what could otherwise be divisive issues in a problem-solving way, so that each side has accomplishments and the relationships between the participants are strengthened.

Finally, as Figure 8-2 indicates, there is feedback from the successful accomplishment of difficult tasks to the union and the company which encourages them to deal with each other further in a cooperative fashion. Successful resolution of problems in a cooperative manner helps to create a climate in which future problems can be successfully addressed in a joint fashion. The key to cooperative industrial relations is not the total elimination of conflict, which is an unattainable ideal, but the reduction of the area of conflict to the minimum and the identification of the greatest possible area of common purpose.[19]

There is a sense in which a labor-management relationship can be compared to a marriage. As in a marriage, the two parties are bound to each other indefinitely. They are not like two unrelated individuals who meet once or twice to conclude a transaction or a contract and then are separated. Instead, labor and management must reach an agreement and then live with each other daily according to its terms. And, as in a marriage, what matters most is whether the two parties are trying to make it work or are trying to pick it to pieces. If they are trying to make it work, we may expect a good relationship. If the opposite, then the marriage will be likely to end in divorce and the labor-management relationship in continual, disruptive conflict.

One of the more peculiar developments in labor relations in recent years has involved the degree to which the quality of a labor-management relationship is affected by the efforts of management to keep as much of its operations nonunion as possible. By 1979 a majority of the larger corporations in the United States which dealt with unions (in at least some of their facilities) also had a program to keep unions out of their unorganized plants. But, surprisingly, the corporations centralized responsibility both for keeping good relations with the unions and for keeping the unions out of the companies'

---

[18] L. N. Tracey and Richard B. Peterson, "Differences in Reactions of Union and Management Negotiators to the Problem-Solving Process," *Industrial Relations Journal*, 8:4, Winter 1977–1978, pp. 43–53.

[19] Trevor Owen, *The Manager and Industrial Relations* (Oxford: Pergamon Press, 1979), p. 16.

nonunion plants in the same corporate officer: the vice president for labor relations (or personnel, or human resources, depending on the title used in each company).[20] Despite periodic complaints from the unions that a company cannot have good relations with the unions and at the same time actively try to keep the unions away, with only a few exceptions corporations have been able to keep working relationships with the unions and yet oppose the further organization of their employees by unions.

In 1947 a public-spirited nonprofit organization, the National Planning Association, decided to study not the causes of labor-management conflict, but the causes of industrial peace. They commissioned a set of studies of particular companies and unions to be made by a group of professional researchers. The studies were first published in 1949 and served as the raw material for a group of critical evaluations of the causes of labor peace.[21] The studies concluded that the environmental conditions conducive to industrial peace were more widespread in the economy than was industrial peace itself, so that there was much room for improvement. The authors stressed as important factors the development of positive attitudes by management and labor toward each other and the use of problem-solving, nonlegalistic procedures in dealing with each other.[22]

Quality of Working Life and Employee Participation

Modern-day labor-management cooperation has its origins not in the negotiations process, but in committees formed for particular purposes which operate during the term of a contract. Often, but not always, referred to as "quality of working life programs," these committees vary considerably in their functions among plants and companies. In the auto industry, committees were usually separated both from the contract and from the objective of productivity enhancement. Elsewhere committees deal directly with productivity.

Michael Maccoby has assisted in the development of quality of working life (QWL) programs in several industries. He has defined quality of working life as "a means to move from the bureaucratic-industrial model of scientific management with its fragmentation of jobs and hierarchical control, to a flexible, broadly skilled participative team. This is a more effective way of man-

[20] Audrey Freedman, *Managing Labor Relations* (New York: The Conference Board, 1979), Report No. 765, p. 12.

[21] National Planning Association, *The Causes of Industrial Peace under Collective Bargaining*, C. S. Goldin and V. D. Parker, eds. (New York: Harper, 1949).

[22] Herbert Northrup and H. A. Young have since criticized the original study as being strongly influenced by the favorable economic climate of the time and for having given platitudes as research results. Northrup and Young suggest that several of the companies involved in the study purchased peaceful labor relations at the cost of inefficient practices and unduly generous compensation (Herbert R. Northrup and H. A. Young, "The Causes of Industrial Peace Revisited," *Industrial and Labor Relations Review*, 22:1, Oct. 1968, pp. 31–47).

aging market-drive technoservice work while protecting the rights and dignity of employees."

The term "quality of working life" has been attributed to Professor Louis Davis of the University of California at Los Angeles, who introduced the term in 1972. QWL was used in separate collective bargaining agreements between Chrysler, Ford, and General Motors and the United Automobile Workers (UAW) in 1973, and the term "employee involvement" (a somewhat similar concept) first appeared in a 1979 agreement between Ford and the UAW.

Five major components may be found in these programs:[23]

1 Work redesign   job enlargement, job enrichment, job rotation, modular work group, autonomous work team

2 Pay restructuring   salaried work force, pay for knowledge, unit productivity sharing

3 Time rescheduling   flexible work hours, compressed work week, job sharing

4 Performance development   positive reinforcement, problem-solving quality circles, middle-range planning, physical redesign

5 Administrative review   information sharing, procedural change, training

Although it has its modern beginning in the 1960s, QWL has its deep roots in American life. According to one authority, "Labor Management Cooperation to improve quality of products, worklife and the effectiveness of companies can be traced to the early 19th century."[24]

Another study of labor-management cooperation in the 1920s stresses the importance of economic difficulties for companies and workers in getting companies to work with unions.[25] The economic difficulties of the 1920s stimulated cooperation; the greater difficulties of the 1930s stimulated conflict; the intermediate problems of the late 1960s, 1970s, and 1980s have again stimulated cooperation.

How do QWL programs contribute to a cooperative labor-management relationship? Because of diversity in the programs, an example may be helpful. An automotive parts manufacturer with a history of acrimonious labor relations established a joint labor-management committee at the recommendation of the Federal Mediation and Conciliation Service (see Chapter 11). The company had been through three changes in management in 8 years and was threatened with

[23] Michael Maccoby. "Helping Labor and a Firm Set Up a Quality-of-Work-Life Program," *Monthly Labor Review*, 107:3, March 1984, pp. 28–32, esp. p. 29; and Walter J. Gershenfeld, "Employee Participation in Firm Decisions," in M. M. Kleiner, et al., eds., *Human Resources and the Performance of the Firm* (Madison, Wis.: Industrial Relation Research Association, 1987), p. 125.

[24] Henry P. Guzda, "Industrial Democracy: Made in the USA," *Monthly Labor Review*, 107:5, May 1984, pp. 26–33, esp. p. 26.

[25] Sanford M. Jacoby, "Union-Management Cooperation in the United States: Lessons from the 1920s," *Industrial and Labor Relations Review*, 37:1, Oct. 1983, pp. 18–33.

closing when its major customers announced a 10 percent reduction in the amount they were willing to pay for the company's products.

The committee meets each month for a frank discussion of problems at the plant, including quality control, cleanliness, safety, and productivity. The company shares all pertinent information about the financial status of the company with union representatives on the committee. The program has helped keep the company operating and has improved labor-management relations.[26]

Improved relations are not all that many QWL programs envisage. In fact, Maccoby's definition cited above goes beyond attitudes and relationships to changes in the nature of jobs and increased participation for employees in what have been until now management responsibilities. The distinction between these two aspects of what is now called QWL was noticed early in the modern effort. Writing in 1965, Raymond Miles made a distinction between human relations and human resources as practiced by management. The former has as its key objective to make members of the organization "feel a useful and important part of the overall effort." The human resources concept, in contrast, is that "many decisions may actually be made more efficiently" at other than managerial levels.[27]

In the human resources model, employees participate in management via committees which consider business problems and opportunities. In the general discussion of worker participation in management, three types are distinguished. In America, employees usually participate via teamwork in labor-management committees and sometimes through broader responsibilities in their own jobs. In Europe, participation is often through work councils which are established as required by law. Finally, participation may occur indirectly via union or employee representatives who are members of a company's board of directors. In some European countries worker representation on supervisory boards is required by law. In the United States there is no such legal requirement and union membership on boards is uncommon.[28]

Managers often resist allowing employees greater participation in responsibilities in an enterprise, fearing loss of management power or that employees lack the necessary expertise or loyalty. And unions also have reasons for resisting participation, since it may be a device to get workers to work harder for equal or less pay and may seem to cut the union out of the management-worker relationship. Management resistance and union suspicion make participation proceed slowly.

The little careful research that exists about the reaction of union members to such cooperative efforts as QWL programs shows lukewarm support. One

---

[26] "Auto Supplier," Bureau of National Affairs, *Daily Labor Report* No. 203, Oct. 19, 1984, pp. A-2, A-3.

[27] Raymond E. Miles, "Human Relations or Human Resources?" *Harvard Business Review*, 43:4, July–Aug., 1965, pp. 148–155, esp. pp. 149, 151.

[28] Alan Gladstone and Rose Marie Greve, "Workers Participation in Management: A Framework for Discussion," *Labor and Society*, 9:3, July–Sept. 1984, pp. 217–234. See also William Foote Whyte, "Worker Participation: International and Historical Perspective," *Journal of Applied Behavioral Science*, 19:3, Aug. 1983, pp. 395–407.

study published in 1988 of national data collected 11 years earlier showed that wages and benefits and internal communications between a union and its members were far more important than QWL issues (such as interest in the job) in causing members to be satisfied with their unions.[29]

In Chapter 6 it was mentioned that the courts and the NLRB in the past few years have been enlarging the range of management decisions about which there is no obligation to bargain with a union. In particular, matters relating to the basic strategy of a company, including what businesses to be in, plant closures, and transference of work, need not be discussed with a union. Despite the direction of legal decisions, however, some companies are choosing to include the unions in discussions of exactly this kind in order to gain union and employee support for the company's efforts. Perhaps surprisingly, considering the efforts of some unions to compel companies to bargain about such matters via litigation, other unions will not participate when offered an opportunity. In these situations union leaders apparently fear that participation in management deliberations will coerce them into silence or overwhelm them with detail.[30]

Union resistance to labor-management cooperation also stems from management's increased resistance (since the 1940s) to union organizing.

AFL-CIO secretary-treasurer Thomas Donahue made the point clear in a speech in 1983:

> Opposition by employers is responsible for the current difficult labor-management climate in this country and continuing inability of the labor movement to embrace wholeheartedly some writers' views of "labor-management cooperation."
>
> It is very hard to think about cooperating with the bear while you are wrestling with him.
>
> The fact is that the employers of this nation want to have labor-management cooperation only after we have wrestled with them and pinned their shoulders to the mat. At about that point when the referee counts to two, and just before he tolls the final verdict, they start preaching "cooperation" to us and to all journalists and economists who will listen.[31]

Yet many of the academics and neutrals in labor-management relations who urge union and management to cooperate to improve workers' jobs and enhance job security via more productive enterprises also urge management

[29] Jack Fiorito, Daniel G. Gallagher, and Cynthia V. Fukami, "Satisfaction with Union Representation," *Industrial and Labor Relations Review*, 41:2, Jan. 1988, p. 294. See also Thomas A. Kochan, Harry L. Katz, and Nancy R. Mowen, "Worker Participation and American Unions," in Thomas A. Kochan, ed., *Challenges and Choices Facing American Labor* (Cambridge, Mass.: MIT Press, 1985), pp. 271–306.

[30] Robert B. McKersie, "Union Involvement in Entrepreneurial Decisions of Businesses," in Thomas A. Kochan, ed., *Challenges and Choices Facing American Labor* (Cambridge, Mass.: MIT Press, 1985), pp. 149–166. See also Henry H. Perritt, Jr., "Aspects of Labor Law that Affect Labor Management Cooperation in the Railroad and Airline Industries," prepared for the U.S. Department of Labor, Villanova School of Law, Feb. 19, 1988.

[31] Thomas R. Donahue, "American Unions Continue Struggle as Worker's Voice," *Trowell* (International Union of Bricklayers and Allied Craftsmen), Winter 1983, pp. 23–25.

to recognize the legitimacy of unions.[32] And unions, on their hand, are urged to be selective in their view of worker participation.

> Rather than adopting a uniform position for or against worker participation... union leaders need to think... about the conditions that must exist for worker participation to be in the interest of their members...[33]

CONSTRUCTIVE BARGAINING

Planning Strategy

Labor-management negotiations have become far more complex in recent years. The image of union bargainers banging a table demanding increased wages, and company negotiators refusing with icy faces, is generally out of date. In recent years negotiators have come to the table accompanied by experts in benefit plans and in drafting legally binding language. Even more recently unions have brought investment bankers and consultants able to analyze the company's business situation in great detail.[34] This increasing complexity requires both sides to prepare more carefully for bargaining.

Good negotiators, whether for management or labor, prepare mentally for negotiations.[35] First, they organize the points they want to present in a natural order. Second, they prepare all major alternatives with the reasons for accepting one and rejecting the others. Third, they relate all the points they intend to make to the interests, needs, and wants of the *other* side in the negotiations. These are basic methods of preparing to attempt to persuade others, whether in collective bargaining, sales, or other types of human interactions.[36]

Experienced negotiators are able to go several steps beyond these.

Understanding the Other Group[37]

A negotiator should not expect himself to deal with another organization without having first developed a thorough working knowledge of that organization. He should find answers to the following questions: What is the formal leadership structure of the other organization? Who are its executives or officers? What are

---

[32] Wayne Horvitz, quoted in Bureau of National Affairs, *Daily Labor Report* No. 237, Dec. 8, 1983, pp. A-10, A-11.

[33] Thomas A. Kochan, Harry C. Katz, and Nancy R. Mowen, *Workers Participation and American Unions* (Kalamazoo, Mich.: W. E. Upjohn Institute, 1984).

[34] Elizabeth Kaplan, "Labor Borrows the Tools of Capital from Wall Street," *Dun's Business Review*, Oct. 1985, pp. 60–62.

[35] George E. Constantino, Jr., "The Negotiator in Collective Bargaining," *Personnel Journal*, 54:8, Aug. 1975, pp. 445–447.

[36] Lee H. Hill and Charles R. Hook, Jr., *Management at the Bargaining Table* (New York: McGraw-Hill, 1945), p. 243. This book, now over 4 decades old, remains one of the best available on how to conduct negotiations.

[37] See D. Q. Mills, "Managing Human Relationships among Organizations," *Organizational Dynamics*, 3:4, Spring 1975, pp. 35–50.

their personal backgrounds, their work histories, and their outside affiliations? Is there a struggle for leadership internally, or is there internal stability? What are the informal lines of communication and influence in the organization? What are the objectives—and the history of success or failure—of the organization? How will the other organization approach our own group? Will they expect cooperation or a confrontation? What do they regard as our strengths and weaknesses? Are they anxious for action or patient? How will they react to frustration—and to success? Are they able to deliver on commitments they might make or not?

There are various sources of such information. Most unions publish their constitutions or bylaws, and they often hold meetings, which in many instances the public is free to attend. Recently a representative of a major company involved in labor negotiations in the coal industry decided he needed to know more about the changing leadership and procedures of the United Mine Workers. So he attended their 1973 convention. He was, as a result, in a far better position to understand the union's behavior in the 1974 coal negotiations than other management representatives. And he used his knowledge to help settle the strike.

Organizing Objectives

It is most important to analyze priorities thoroughly. And the best way to do it is to combine various options and hypothetically choose among them. This permits the negotiator's own organization to establish priorities in a systematic way. The results are often surprising to negotiators who thought, incorrectly, that they understood their organization's priorities.

A further advantage of this process to a company is to reveal how difficult it will be to mobilize internally all the related elements of the company that must deal with the problem at hand. Challenges from another organization rarely fit neatly into the corporation's internal structure, so considerable effort is required by a corporation in assigning responsibility for a response. The process of organizing objectives helps to resolve these issues.

Thinking Procedurally

Next, it is necessary to think about how these issues are to be addressed. Which should come first? Should ultimate priorities be revealed at the outset? Is there a logical step-by-step process to be followed, or would it be best to do everything at once? Initially, should the negotiator appear to be well prepared for meetings or simply to be in attendance?

It is often difficult for people who have certain objectives to think not about the objectives themselves but how to attain them. Yet it is critical to structure a particular approach, and it must be done, to a substantial degree, in advance.

Walton and McKersie also distinguish two other subsystems of the general process of negotiations in addition to integrative and distributive bargaining. One of these processes is referred to as *attitudinal structuring*. This refers to the activities and efforts of a management team or union officials to influence the attitudes of the other. Attitudinal structuring is an attempt to change someone else's opinion about something or someone. It is directed at the basic relationships between the people involved in bargaining.

The final subprocess of negotiations is identified as *intraorganizational bargaining*. Because both companies and unions are ordinarily large organizations, there is a necessity on both sides to work out a consensus internally. In a sense, in collective bargaining it always takes three agreements to reach one: There must be an agreement within the union on the final contract. There must be an agreement within the company on the final contract. And there must be an agreement between the union and the company on the contract. Often negotiators say that the internal negotiations are as complex and difficult as those with the other side.

Formal Proposals

Should formal, written proposals be exchanged by the union and the employer in negotiations? Many observers of collective bargaining think that formal proposals assist in bringing negotiations to a constructive conclusion. They suggest that written proposals should be exchanged well in advance of the actual expiration of a collective bargaining agreement. The advantages of this procedure are several. First, the preparation of formal, written proposals requires each side to be specific about what it desires and also to be comprehensive. It will be difficult to alter a proposal or introduce a new one later in negotiations. Second, the advance presentation of written proposals allows each side considerable convenience in analyzing, understanding, and preparing a reply. In this way written proposals may help to avoid the misunderstandings that can develop in verbal communications.

However, there are certain drawbacks to written proposals, especially in the course of negotiations (i.e., after presentation of initial positions):

1 *Written proposals force each side into fixed positions from which they may be reluctant to move, fearing loss of face with their constituents.* To the extent that written proposals tend to lock negotiators into certain positions, they interfere with the give-and-take necessary to successful bargaining.

2 *Written proposals also provide the opportunity for each side to characterize the other's position.* For example, in the 1976 negotiations between Ford Motor Company and the UAW, the company gave the union its first formal, written offer on September 1. The union leadership took the written offer and described it to the press in the following terms: "This is the most regressive offer in all my years of bargaining," said Leonard Woodcock, president of the UAW. "It is entirely unresponsive to any of our problems." On the other side, Ford spokespeople characterized the union's demands as expensive and unreasonable. Such public denunciations have become a common part of auto industry bargaining. In fact, it is not clear what purpose the initial written offers of both sides serve except to be the focus of denunciation by the other side. In the auto industry, as negotiations become more serious, formal, comprehensive proposals are abandoned in favor of a more flexible negotiations posture.

3 *The existence of written demands and responses makes it likely that the final settlement will be compared with initial positions and a judgment made as to which side won and which lost.* This win-lose mentality, given credence by written position statements, can interfere with a problem-solving approach to negotiations.

Factual Studies

Writing in 1964, William E. Simkin, former director of the Federal Mediation and Conciliation Service, put great stress on factual studies by labor and management as a procedure that offered great hope for improving the likelihood of peaceful resolution of labor disputes.[38] Factual studies involve a joint effort by labor and management, at a time well before actual negotiations, to ascertain the facts about a particular problem. This procedure, which emphasizes the review of a particular item, or items, of concern to the parties in a noncrisis atmosphere, is also referred to as "continuous negotiations."

The advantages of factual studies lie in two areas. First, the likelihood is that the parties will be better able to agree on a solution to a problem if both accept the same set of facts about it. To a surprising degree, disputes between labor and management arise because of basic inadequacies of factual information about certain situations. Both sides believe they know the facts, but in reality they do not.

A classic case of a dispute in which the facts were not clear occurred in the 1959 negotiations in the steel industry. Many years before, the companies had proposed inclusion in the collective bargaining agreement of language regarding the establishment and change of local working conditions (this was section IIB of the agreement between United States Steel Corporation and the Steelworkers). Some people in U.S. Steel's management had opposed the company's decision to propose this language. By 1959 there had been a change in U.S. Steel's management, and the company's new negotiators wanted to take this language out of the agreement. The other steel companies were not sure that the matter was very important but went along with U.S. Steel. The union decided to oppose the companies' proposal to delete IIB from the agreement. No one really knew its significance. The result was a strike of 116 days in 1959. The companies were unsuccessful in getting the clause removed, and it remains in the steel agreements to this day.

Certain matters have proved especially susceptible to the factual studies approach. These are matters that are unusually complex. Among them are adjustment to technological change and provisions of pension and health and welfare plans. For the joint study approach to work, certain conditions are needed. Among them are:

---

[38] William E. Simkin, "The Trend to Maturity in Industrial Relations," *Industrial Relations*, 3:1, Feb. 1964, pp. 1–4.

1 A joint will to solve the problems
2 Complete flexibility in discussion for both sides
3 Competent and sophisticated staffs on both sides

The great hopes for the factual studies approach that Simkin voiced in 1964 have receded somewhat in recent years. But joint study remains one of the most constructive procedures available to participants in collective bargaining.

Good Procedures

A list of suggested good bargaining procedures was developed in 1975 by the Joint Labor Management Committee of the Retail Food Industry. After reviewing bargaining procedures in American industry, the committee emphasized that the lack of agreement on basic procedures for bargaining was causing strife in the industry. In the interest of improving bargaining, the committee suggested the following procedures of general applicability:

1 *Contract proposals should be exchanged well in advance of contract expiration.* All proposals should be in writing and easily understood. If either side does not understand the proposals, the parties should meet promptly to clarify all the demands in detail. There must be ample time for joint or separate research and costing and for both parties to secure necessary clearances prior to negotiation.

2 *"Eleventh-hour" bargaining should be avoided.* Experience in other industries has demonstrated that this style of bargaining is counterproductive, frequently causes strikes, and almost never ensures a fair settlement for either labor or management.

3 *The use of the Federal Mediation and Conciliation Service* and appropriate state, local, and private mediation agencies and individuals is a cornerstone of rational collective bargaining.

4 *Negotiations should be conducted at the table, not in the press.* "Negotiating in the press" is damaging to achieving rational results in collective bargaining and leads inevitably to emotional confrontations caused by coverage that is too often inaccurate. If necessary, there should be joint agreement on a news blackout or joint releases to the press.

5 *The strike issues should be fully understood by both parties prior to strike or lockout action.* Contrary to popular belief, the parties often discover after the strike has started that the issues were not fully understood on both sides. The committee recommends that in the event one party or the other believes that the communication needed to clarify strike issues is blocked or broken down, a third party, a mediator, for example, if one is not already in the picture, be asked to clarify the issues for the parties before strike or lockout action is taken by either side.

6 *All possible alternatives should be considered before a strike occurs.*

A further point, not mentioned by the committee but raised in many other discussions of collective bargaining, is the advantage of a problem-solving approach to negotiations (what Walton and McKersie called "integrative bar-

TABLE 8-1   PROBLEM SOLVING VERSUS CONFLICTUAL NEGOTIATIONS

Problem solving	Conflictual negotiations
• Flexibility among alternatives	• Two opposing sides exchanging demands
• Openness in communication	• Secrecy about one's own reaction to the other side's proposal
• Exchange of relevant facts	• Concealment of critical information
• Trust and cooperation	• Threat of work stoppages

gaining"). A contrast can be drawn between the behavioral scientist's paradigm of problem solving by small groups and the often conflict-ridden character of collective bargaining negotiations (see Table 8-1).

Collective bargaining involves several stages, and different approaches to negotiation sometimes characterize them. Thus, in the stage of identifying problems, there is considerable use of the problem-solving approach. In the stage of developing alternative possibilities for agreement, there is some use of the problem-solving approach. But in making decisions about what the contract shall entail, collective bargaining negotiations are often very conflictual.[39] It is at the stage of decision making that collective bargaining is, as one manager described it, "a kind of fist-fight."

Wherever possible, a problem-centered approach should be used—a "let's sit down and talk it over" attitude.[40] When discussion centers on *problems* to be solved, rather than on *demands* or on *rights,* the chances are much better that solutions compatible with the needs of both parties will be found.

HOW NEGOTIATIONS ARE CONDUCTED

The Physical Setting

Labor-management negotiations usually take place in a room with two tables facing each other, with labor seated behind one table, management behind the other. This is the customary format for negotiations, but not the only one available. Many times negotiators give no thought to the physical format, but it can be of psychological importance. For example, the table-facing-table arrangement implies an adversary relationship, in that it appears set up for a contest between opposing teams.

An arrangement more congenial to cooperative problem solving would have the participants from labor and management seated around the same table, or even in a circular arrangement. In such a format, the distinction between the two sides is not so clearly drawn. Also, conversations can take place between

[39] James W. Driscoll, "A Behavioral-Science View of the Future of Collective Bargaining in the United States," Working Paper, Sloan School of Management, MIT, March 3, 1979. See also Ian E. Morley and Geoffrey M. Stephenson, *The Social Psychology of Bargaining* (London: George Allen and Unwin, 1977).

[40] F. H. Harbison and Robert Dubin, *Patterns of Union-Management Relations* (Chicago: Science Research Associates, 1947), p. 152.

various individuals, so that the role of the spokespersons for the two sides is minimized.

The physical format of a negotiation can be manipulated to the disadvantage of one side by the other. In one instance, the company negotiators arranged the room. There was a single table; chairs for the management people were placed on one side of the table, and chairs for the union people were placed on the other side. When the union representatives entered the room, they were pleased by the apparent equality of treatment they had been given and the informality of the arrangements. However, when the two sides were seated, the union people discovered that the company negotiators had placed low chairs on the union's side of the table, so that the union representatives were looking across the table and up at the management people. The union representatives felt uncomfortable and distinctly at a disadvantage.

What Is Happening at the Bargaining Table

There is a way in which all negotiations appear very similar to an outside observer. A group of people, the negotiators, are seen to be engaged in a lively discussion. They are very involved in what they are doing. But is something significant occurring or not?

Often something important is happening. The two sides are engaged in give-and-take, or they are exploring alternatives for resolving a difficult problem.

But in some instances not much is happening at all. The negotiators in the bargaining room are only ratifying the results of struggles which have occurred elsewhere. Sometimes the really difficult problem was to get all the people on the *same side*—management's side or labor's—into agreement on what position to take. Reaching agreement with the other side was relatively easy. Sometimes, the two sides are rigidly tied to conflicting positions, and a strike is occurring which will determine which side, if either, prevails.

For a negotiator it is important to know whether the negotiations process itself is the center of the action or merely a sideshow.

Rituals in Negotiations

Labor negotiations sometimes seem to assume the ritualized character of religious or marriage rites. Negotiations are accompanied by the observance of certain set forms and procedures. Like rituals in other areas of human conduct, those involved in collective bargaining have a purpose. They have evolved for two primary reasons. The first is that observance of rituals imposes a certain order and predictability on what would otherwise be a very uncertain process. Second, rituals help the sides to come to an agreement, in part by limiting the hazards involved for both sides. This latter point is often misunderstood. Because certain things are rituals in negotiations, outside observers often believe them to be archaic and unnecessary appendages to the bargaining process. This is ordinarily not so.[41]

Major rituals involved in collective bargaining are the following:

• The first offer of management is usually a low offer. The first demands of the union are high. Both sides recognize that the offers are not intended to be acceptable, but both sides nevertheless make them. Why?

The initial presentation of somewhat unrealistic offers allows each side to feel out the other without the danger of being unable to retreat from an initial position. High and low offers allow room for later bargaining.

• Normally, no agreement is reached in collective bargaining before the expiration date of the existing collective bargaining agreement. There is almost always, therefore, some eleventh-hour bargaining agreement. Why don't the parties just wrap it up early when they can, rather than waiting until the last minute?

The ritual of the last-minute settlement tends to protect the negotiators on each side from charges by their own constituents that they sold out. In bargaining, neither side gets all it hoped for. When the settlement and the concessions involved in achieving it occur at the last moment, then concessions appear necessary in order to avoid the costs of a strike or lockout. But when concessions are made in advance, the negotiators may be accused of having given in on certain issues without good reason.

In many instances, negotiators are criticized for eleventh-hour bargaining. It is said that this ritual involves the threat of unwarranted work stoppages because the parties too often simply run out of time and don't reach agreement on all issues before a strike deadline passes. This is a significant criticism of the ritual of settling at the last minute.

• A degree of acrimony, name-calling, and other verbal abuse is a ritual in certain negotiations. This is a particularly unpleasant ritual and one that is very difficult to justify or explain to outside observers. This book does not countenance this, but the reader may still see that the practice has certain functions in some instances.

Overt controversy is intended to demonstrate to the constituents of both sides that their advocates are loyal and prepared to do battle for their constituents' interests. It also reminds participants that the bargaining process is a serious matter, undertaken on behalf of others and not for the comfort of the negotiators. Finally, it tends to cause more timid souls to leave the bargaining before the truly serious and stress-producing issues are confronted.

Tactics in Negotiations

Labor negotiations involve two general types of tactics. One type includes those tactics intended to gain an advantage for the person or side who employs them.

---

[41] John T. Dunlop, "The Negotiations Alternative to Markets and Regulations," unpublished manuscript, 1977.

Tactics of the other type are intended to help persuade the other side to accept a point of view. Both are used in negotiations, often interchangeably. Bargaining has much in common with the methods of salespeople in this regard. Many books and articles about bargaining tactics stress methods developed in selling products. Some observers believe that tactics of persuasion are morally defensible, while tactics of advantage are not. This judgment is perhaps best left to the reader. It is made a judgment of even greater complexity by the question of whether the objective to which the tactics are applied is a moral one, and if so, whether this should affect the tactics employed.

Collective bargaining negotiations assume to a degree the aspect of a very complex human game. The stakes for which the game is played are high. The best players of the game are very sophisticated. At the center of the game is the psychology of the situation and of the other players. Such a contest between people is often a very complicated process and one of infinite variety. It is virtually impossible to summarize. A mere list of tactics, of potential moves and countermoves, would far exceed the space allotted to this book. Indeed, the bargaining aspect of labor relations is something that attracts certain people, who find it exciting and psychologically interesting. Below we list and briefly describe some of the tactics employed in collective bargaining. This list is not at all exhaustive, nor is it intended as an endorsement of all the items listed.

Tactics used to gain an advantage:
- Bogey tactics
- "This is all I've got to concede"—holding something back
- Bluffing—insisting that you have, or don't have, something, when the opposite is true
- Prevarication
- Decoys: suggesting for negotiation matters of no real importance
- Contrived emotional outbursts: acting very pleased or very upset about something
- Deliberate errors
- Good-guy-bad-guy: causing one negotiator on a team to pose as friendly and well disposed to the other side while another negotiator on the team is actively hostile.

As described by one student of negotiations tactics, good-guy-bad-guy works in negotiations as follows. One person takes a tough stand, making demands and acting in a rough manner. "Next to him is friendly old Smiley who says little during the discussion. After a while the bad guy shuts up and the good guy takes over. When he makes his demands, they seem reasonable by comparison. Why not? It seems a pleasure dealing with such a nice man after being worked over by that mean one. You can't help feeling that things could have been worse."[42]

[42] Chester Karass, *Give and Take: The Complete Guide to Negotiating Strategies and Tactics* (New York: Crowell, 1974), p. 79. See also Roger Fisher and William Ury, *Getting to Yes* (Boston: Houghton Mifflin Company, 1981).

Bad guys come in nonhuman form sometimes. The bad guy is "company policy" or "union policy," which won't permit something to be done. About the good-guy–bad-guy tactic, the observer quoted above has said, "It works better than it should."

Tactics used to persuade:
• Anticipate objections to a proposal and answer them before they are voiced.
• Agree, then refute—"Yes, but...."
• Stress similarities of position, not differences.
• Offer a problem, not a solution. Wait until the other side recognizes that there is a problem before trying to persuade them to accept a proposed solution.
• Present your own favorite viewpoint last, not first. If someone else announces it before you, let that person have the credit.

Bruce Henderson has described the tactics used by business negotiators in the following way:

> The negotiator's skill lies in being as arbitrary as necessary to obtain the best possible compromise without actually destroying the basis for voluntary mutual cooperation or self-restraint. There are some common-sense rules for success in such an endeavor:
>
> 1 Be sure that your rival is fully aware of what he can gain if he cooperates and what it will cost him if he does not.
>
> 2 Avoid any action which will arouse your competitor's emotions, since it is essential that he behave in a logical, reasonable fashion.
>
> 3 Convince your opponent that you are emotionally dedicated to your position and are completely convinced that it is reasonable.
>
> It is worth emphasizing that your competitor is under the maximum handicap if he acts in a completely rational, objective, and logical fashion. For then he will cooperate as long as he thinks he can benefit. In fact, if he is completely logical, he will not forgo the profit of cooperation as long as there is *any* net benefit.[43]

Negotiations are fraught with opportunity for conflict. If one negotiator criticizes another, it is easy for the second to reply in kind. But this need not be done. A smart negotiator can keep the talks on a problem-solving track by turning aside antagonistic remarks. Recently some of the newer interpersonal-relations approaches have been turned to this topic. Transactional analysis (TA) figures importantly in a recent study, in which the authors describe the interchanges between negotiators (see Table 8-2).[44]

Unsound Attitudes

Negotiations make some people uneasy. Rather than admitting they are uneasy, being patient, and trying to work things out, these people often adopt

[43] Bruce Henderson, *On Corporate Strategy* (Cambridge, Mass.: Abt Books, 1979), p. 28.
[44] Frank L. Acuff and Maurice F. Villere, "Games Negotiators Play," *Business Horizons*, 19:1, Feb. 1976, p. 76.

TABLE 8-2 SOME INTERCHANGES BETWEEN NEGOTIATORS

A comment causing controversy	A response continuing controversy	A response ending controversy
	"What's the use of arguing with you? You're going to get your way anyway."	"Any suggestions for getting us back on the track?"
"I know you're not prepared only because you've had a lot of other problems at the office."	"I've got so many other things on my mind that I'm no good to anybody today."	"Based on the information I brought with me, let's see in what areas we can move forward."
"Your demands are unrealistic!"	"You're the one who's unrealistic."	"Why?"

Source: Frank L. Acuff and Maurice F. Villere, "Games Negotiators Play," *Business Horizons,* 19:1, February 1976, p. 76.

unsound attitudes. These attitudes often result in damage to their own side of the bargaining table and sometimes in damage to the bargaining process as a whole. Some of these attitudes are expressed as follows:

- "Give them what they want."
- "Better make a trade."
- "Frankly, I'm bewildered."

These attitudes have in common a fatalism about the bargaining process that represents withdrawal from the attempt to get any useful result from it. They are a signal of very serious danger for the side whose negotiator(s) professes them and sometimes for the collective bargaining process generally.

In the late 1960s economic and other conditions were such that collective bargaining in the construction industry was very much in favor of the unions. Employer associations took strike after strike over matters they thought were important, only to lose ingloriously. Attempts to get the intervention of outside parties were a failure for a prolonged period (although in the early 1970s both government and the broader business community intervened to stabilize bargaining in construction for a few years). By 1969 and 1970 many employers had simply given up. In their view nothing could be achieved in bargaining. The unions were too strong. A great bitterness crept into the relations between management and labor in the industry.

Attitudes of the type listed above became common. And by the early 1970s a substantial movement to operate construction firms nonunion, without the necessity for collective bargaining, was under way. Many factors caused these changing conditions in construction, but the attitudes generated by years of one-sided bargaining were an important element.

On the other side, some negotiators adopt positions of unreasonable confidence. Some examples are:

- "We're right and we won't budge."

- "We don't have to worry."
- "Stick it to them."

These attitudes reflect a stubbornness and a singlemindedness more appropriate to a military conflict than to collective bargaining. Sometimes it is necessary to be very firm, as all good negotiators know. But rigidity and vindictiveness are danger signals.

Ethical Issues in Negotiations

Negotiations potentially raise a number of ethical issues for those involved. Three of the most important are:

- To what degree, if any, is a negotiator justified in misleading the other party about his or her position, or objectives, or the facts of a matter being discussed?
- Is the outcome fair to both parties? If one side has greater power or skill in negotiations, how far should it press its advantage?
- Are the interests, welfare, and concern of others affected by a negotiation, but not party to it, adequately considered and provided for by the parties to the negotiation? For example, is the public adequately considered in negotiations involving public employees? Or, are customers adequately considered in negotiations by a union and a company?[45]

These issues are inherent in most labor-management negotiations. Sometimes they are considered, and sometimes not. As collective bargaining matures, perhaps unions and managements will increasingly try to resolve such questions in an ethical manner.

The Outcome of Negotiations

No general summary of the outcome of negotiations can be given. All situations are different. It is possible, however, to list the major factors that affect the outcome of negotiations.[46]

Economic Conditions General business conditions in the economy, favorable or unfavorable trends in a particular industry, and the financial condition of particular companies influence both company and union positions in negotiations. Recession and unemployment considerably dampen a union's willingness to strike. But it is important to remember that economic conditions do not necessarily determine, in any absolute or a priori sense, the outcome of negotiations. Bargaining behavior and circumstances of bar-

---

[45] David A. Lax and James K. Sebenius, "Three Ethical Issues in Negotiation," *Negotiation Journal*, 2:4, Oct. 1986, pp. 363–370.
[46] E. Robert Livernash, "Note on Collective Bargaining in the United States" (Boston: Intercollegiate Case Clearing House, 1-676-171).

gaining have been shown in empirical tests to have as much effect on bargaining outcomes as do economic variables.[47]

Company Policies   Especially with respect to the noneconomic clauses in contracts, the extent to which companies have developed policies and taken firm positions with respect to achieving them has drastically influenced the outcome of negotiations. While collective bargaining always limits management rights and prerogatives, the character and degree of limitation vary widely from contract to contract.

Union Policies   Unions have varied considerably in both their militancy and their objectives. The Die Sinkers Conference, a small, strong craft union, has had little concern for pensions, health and welfare plans, and other such "frills." The union wants money in the pay envelope and an 8-year apprentice program. The UAW, in contrast, has been strongly interested in "social breakthroughs." Socially oriented, innovative demands and achievements have characterized the UAW over the years.

Union Politics   While union politics are in some way related to union policies, the political variations among unions deserve separate mention. A union torn by internal factionalism, such as presently exists in the United Mine Workers, presents a difficult problem for management. Some such unions are virtually leaderless and have great difficulty conducting and concluding negotiations. Unions also vary in the degree of "democracy" they exhibit. Political stability is frequently associated with "responsible" behavior.

Union-Management Relations   Benjamin M. Selekman has identified nine types of union-management relations, and his list included conflict, containment-aggression, accommodation, and cooperation.[48] Over the years more and more relationships can appropriately be described as characterized by a significant degree of accommodation. Some negotiating situations have developed sufficient mutual confidence so that neither party seriously considers the possibility of a strike. The United Steelworkers and the basic steel industry have achieved a high degree of accommodation with respect to very difficult issues.

The Conduct of Negotiations   The preparation for negotiations, the art of communicating during negotiations, the timing of proposals, the degree of management initiative, and other elements which might be listed as part of the "technique" of negotiation influence the outcome. Experienced negotiators rarely get boxed into an untenable position or stumble into a strike.

---

[47] Richard B. Peterson and Lane Tracy, "Testing a Behavioral Model of Labor Negotiations," *Industrial Relations*, 16:1, Feb. 1977, pp. 35–50.
[48] Benjamin M. Selekman et al., *Problems in Labor Relations* (New York: McGraw-Hill, 1964), pp. 1–11.

Other Variables Pattern-setting negotiations are normally more tense than pattern-following situations. Union rivalries play their part. Public pronouncements by participants may commit one or both parties to a rigid position. Government policies and official statements may give aid or comfort to one or the other party in major disputes.

MODELS OF BARGAINING

Collective bargaining is such a complex, human, and indeterminate process that it may be surprising to learn that some theorists have attempted to develop formal models of the bargaining process. Certain aspects of collective bargaining seem to invite a rigorously logical treatment. First, economists have long since developed models to analyze and explain the process of price determination in a situation of bilateral monopoly and oligopoly. These models take strategic calculations into explicit account. Bargaining between a union and employer over wage rates has many characteristics of the bilateral monopoly situation and so has invited the extension of those theories to collective bargaining.

Second, the transactions between labor and management are often financial in nature (such as wage and fringe benefits increases) and are therefore subject to quantification. Since the outcome of the process is quantifiable, it seems that some quantitative treatment of the factors producing the result is also appropriate. Furthermore, the expression in a formal, logical manner (i.e., a model) of ideas about what factors affect bargaining and in what ways is a useful procedure for clarifying thought.

Bargaining Power

Much discussion of labor relations is and has been couched in the terminology of "bargaining power." In testimony before the Senate Education and Labor Committee in 1935, William Green, then president of the AFL, used this common phraseology: "The economic conditions which exist today can be corrected only when the bargaining power of the employees is made equal to that of the employers." And to the House Committee on Labor in that same year Green said, "The fundamental necessity [is] for establishment of equality of bargaining power between employer and employee."[49]

The idea of bargaining power as a fundamental determinant of the results of collective bargaining was thus blessed by organized labor. What the unions were seeking, Green was arguing, was not special treatment from Congress, but a mere equalization of bargaining power between workers and employers. In the Wagner Act, Congress accepted this notion and embodied it in the preamble to the act: "The inequality of bargaining power between

---

[49] Quoted in Marion Sadler, "Who Speaks for the People in Collective Bargaining?" *Columbia Journal of World Business*, 4, March–April 1968, pp. 21–26.

employees...and employers...substantially burdens and affects the flow of commerce,'' reads section 1 of the National Labor Relations Act.

Thereafter, with bargaining power thus given legislative sanction as an important concept in American labor relations (it has no exact counterpart elsewhere), employers began to argue that the balance of power had shifted in labor's favor. By the mid-1950s employer complaints about the growth of union power in mass-production industries became frequent. And in the 1960s complaints about union bargaining power in the construction, maritime, and retail food industries increased.

It is not surprising that scholars should have attempted to base models of bargaining on the formulation of a theory of bargaining power. The initial problem was to formulate a careful definition of bargaining power. As used colloquially, the concept is somewhat slippery. Unfortunately, when formulated carefully, the concept tended to become a tautology. A settlement favorable to the company was said to result from the company's bargaining power. But how was the company's bargaining power to be measured? If bargaining power was measured by the degree to which the settlement was favorable to management, then the definition was circular, i.e., bargaining power was bargaining power because it was bargaining power.

To attempt to escape this circularity, scholars developed a definition of bargaining power that stressed the concept of ability to compel the other party to do something:

> Power is defined as the capacity of one subject to carry through its will against the will of another subject.[50]

Alternatively,

> Bargaining power can be defined as the capacity to effect an agreement on one's own terms; operationally, one's bargaining power is another's inducement to agree. If X and Y are in a contest over the terms of their cooperation, X's bargaining power is represented by Y's inducement to agree...while Y's bargaining power is X's inducement to agree.[51]

These two definitions have a superficial similarity but may, in fact, be substantially different. The first definition envisages a substantial element of coercion of one side by the other—''carry through its will against the will of another subject.'' The second definition envisages the result of circumstances broadly affecting both parties. When one party is compelled to seek an agreement by circumstances, the other party is said to have bargaining power. For example, if a company is in difficult financial straits and cannot afford a work stoppage, the union is said to have bargaining power as a consequence of this circumstance.

In recent years attention has been devoted to identifying and measuring

---

[50] Jan Pen, ''A General Theory of Bargaining,'' *American Economic Review*, 42, 1952, pp. 24–42.
[51] Neil W. Chamberlain, *A General Theory of Economic Process* (New York: Harper & Row, 1955), pp. 80–82.

components of bargaining power. The Illini City studies by Milton Derber and others attempted to evaluate the relative impact of environmental and volitional forces on various aspects of bargaining and its outcomes.[52] Other researchers have tried to identify separate categories of bargaining power: legal, political, social, and economic.[53]

Formal Models

Not all theorizing about bargaining employs the concept of bargaining power. Another line of theoretical development attempts to structure the bargaining process in terms of offers and counteroffers.

The analysis begins with a situation in which each party demands an outcome highly favorable to itself. This may be seen in Figure 8-3. In the diagram the two axes (labeled U_1 and U_2, respectively) represent the total amount of "utility" gained by each side. Utility is a concept that is intended to be a quantification of all the benefits, both pecuniary (i.e., directly quantifiable) and nonpecuniary. It is not directly observable or measurable, as a wage rate or the cost of a wage and fringe benefit package would be. In Figure 8-3, party number 2 starts at demand position 2, which has a high utility to party number 2 and a low utility to party number 1. At position 2, party number 2 gets U_{22} utility for itself; party number 1 gets only U_{12} for itself. Party number 1, however, begins by insisting upon point 1, which is more favorable to it than to party number 2. The curve that connects points 1 and 2 may be described as a "utility frontier" and includes the set of points that yields the *highest available* utility to one side that can be obtained, given a *certain amount* of utility for the other side. All points inside the curve are less efficient than those on the curve—outside the curve points are not available because of financial or other constraints.

Then suppose each bargainer deliberates between accepting the other's offer and holding out for his or her own, in the hope that the other will accept it. From the first bargainer's point of view, for example, immediate capitulation would bring about the utility U_{12}, while stubbornness would bring either the greater utility U_{11} if the other surrendered or zero utility if the other proved equally adamant. What is the maximum subjective probability of conflict (C_1) that the first bargainer can rationally stand in holding out for his or her own demand? The answer is, that value of C_1 that will make it a matter of indifference to the bargainer, as a matter of expected utilities, whether he

[52] Milton Derber, W. E. Chalmers, and Milton Edelman, *Plant Union Management Relations* (Urbana: University of Illinois Press, 1965).

[53] D. J. Armstrong, D. Bowers, and B. Burkitt, "The Measurement of Trade Union Bargaining Power," *British Journal of Industrial Relations*. 15:1, March 1977, pp. 91–100; Christine Edwards, "Measuring Union Power," *British Journal of Industrial Relations*, 16:1, March 1978, pp. 1–15; Hervey A. Juris and Peter Feuille, *Police Unionism: Power and Impact* (Lexington, Mass.: D. C. Heath, 1973).

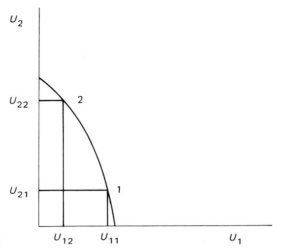

FIGURE 8-3

or she capitulates or holds out indefinitely—that is, the value of C_1 that satisfies the equation $U_{12} = (1 - C_1)U_{11}$. Hence the desired value of C_1 and the corresponding value of C_2 for the second bargainer are:

$$C_1 = \frac{U_{11}-U_{12}}{U_{11}} \qquad C_2 = \frac{U_{22}-U_{21}}{U_{22}}$$

Now specify (and this is the critical part of the theory)[54] that the first bargainer will make at least some concession, and the second will not, if $C_1 < C_2$ (that is, if the first cannot stand as great a probability of conflict as the second); or the second bargainer will be the one to make a concession if $C_1 > C_2$; or they will both make simultaneous concessions if $C_1 = C_2 > 0$. Typically, however, neither makes a complete concession to the other's current demand, but rather concedes only enough to make it the other bargainer's turn to concede, at least a little, whether unilaterally or simultaneously with a corresponding further concession by the first bargainer. In other words, the first bargainer makes a concession when $C_1 \leq C_2$, or when (with reference to the above two equations):

$$U_{11}U_{21} \leq U_{22}U_{22}$$

Hence each concession by the first bargainer raises the utility product that he or she proposes ($U_{11}U_{22}$), and similarly, each concession by the second raises

[54] This model was developed by Zeuthen and is reprinted and discussed in Oran R. Young, ed., *Bargaining: Formal Theories of Negotiations* (Urbana: University of Illinois Press, 1975).

$U_{22}U_{12}$. Accordingly, these utility products are maximized and equated to one another when an agreement is finally reached, with $U_{11} - U_{22} = U_{21}$ at a single point on the utility frontier, and with $C_1 = C_2 = 0$.

This model has been termed a "split-the-difference" model, in that it suggests that, by bargaining, the final position reached between two negotiators is somewhere between the initial positions of the sides. In recent years, researchers have begun to use such models to test the results of actual negotiations to see how well the empirical results can be explained by the theories. In one recent study the researchers concluded that the management and the union did not follow bargaining curves that were symmetrical, so that a split-the-difference model was not altogether appropriate as a measure of the union's wins or losses.[55]

Such models of bargaining are useful in providing insights and conceptual stimulation. They are, however, subject to very significant limitations in their current form. None of these models produces good predictions or satisfactory explanations concerning bargaining in actual situations. Different models result in different and often contradictory results even when applied to idealized situations, and the resultant lack of agreement among theorists of bargaining is increasing, not decreasing. Also, these models all omit various interesting phenomena that are commonly thought of as important features of bargaining. Among these are the multiplicity of issues and their possible incomparability. This circumstance the utility theorists simply assume away by the invention of "utility" itself, which is said to encompass all aspects of a possible bargain into a single, quantitative measure. The fact that negotiations take place drawn out over time and in an atmosphere of considerable uncertainty about what each side can really afford or tolerate also has no place in these analyses. They give no hint, for example, why strikes ever occur.[56]

Recently attempts have been made to develop formal models of the bargaining process that draw their inspiration from the behavioral sciences, rather than from economics. A recent study of this nature presented a conceptual model derived largely from the Walton and McKersie formulation. The model treated the four elements of bargaining as identified by Walton and McKersie as goals in the bargaining process for each side. A questionnaire was sent to negotiators in selected private-sector collective bargaining negotiations that occurred in 1973. The negotiators were asked how well they had achieved their economic goals (distributive bargaining) and their problem-solving goals (integrative bargaining). Negotiators were also asked how successful they had been at improving the working relationship between the

[55] Gary A. Hall and William R. Schriver, "Bluffing in the Bargaining Process: An Empirical Test," *Proceedings* of the Industrial Relations Research Association, Dec. 1977, pp. 286–293.

[56] A positive analytical literature pursuing these themes has begun to appear. For a clear if somewhat technical introduction to its methods, see John Sutton, "Non-Cooperative Bargaining Theory: An Introduction," *Review of Economic Studies*, Oct. 1986, pp. 709–724. See also Oran R. Young, "The Analysis of Bargaining: Problems and Prospects," in Young, ed., *Theories of Negotiations*, p. 391.

FIGURE 8-4

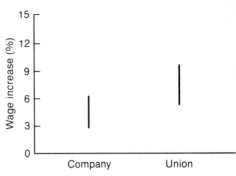

FIGURE 8-5

two sides (attitudinal structuring) and how successful they had been in getting their constituents to agree to their own decisions during the negotiations (intraorganizational bargaining). The researchers concluded that bargaining behavior and conditions had as much effect on bargaining success as did the economic (distributive) variables.[57]

The basic insights that appear in behavioral models of negotiations can be summarized as follows. In the beginning each side to a negotiation faces a given set of economic facts and circumstances. These are similar, but involve differences, for management and labor. As a result of different contexts and different interests, the two sides will differ on the meaning of the current situation and how to deal with it. Thus, a threshold step in the behavioral analysis of a negotiation involves the parties' different perceptions of the situation and expectations as to the outcome of negotiations.

For example, considering a possible wage settlement only, the company and the union's positions may be characterized as having upper and lower limits. In Figure 8-4 the company expects a wage increase in the range of 3 to 6 percent, with the upper figure as high as it is willing to go. The union, in contrast, expects from 9 to 12 percent, with the lower figure its minimum. The result is that with no region of overlap, the most likely outcome of bargaining is a strike.

However, in Figure 8-5 the initial situation is different. The company is prepared to settle between 3 and 6 percent, and the union between 5 and 9 percent. Here an agreement is possible without the parties reevaluating the circumstances and changing their positions. Effective negotiators will discover that an area of agreement exists. If the management negotiator is more skilled than the union counterpart, the agreement will be closer to 5 percent than to 6 percent. If the union negotiator is more skilled, the agreement will be closer to 6 percent. If one or both negotiators are unskilled, there may be

[57] R. B. Peterson and L. N. Tracy, "A Behavioral Model of Problem-Solving in Labor Negotiations," *British Journal of Industrial Relations,* 14:2, July 1976, pp. 159–173; and Peterson and Tracy, "Testing a Behavioral Theory Model," loc cit.

no agreement at all, as one or both sides may fail to discover the range of possible agreement.

Returning to Figure 8-4, if an agreement is not possible, a strike or lockout is likely to occur. The strike has a function, in that it imposes costs on the two parties that force them to change their positions. Ideally and most often, the parties reevaluate their positions and the union lowers its expected increase while the company raises its offer until overlap occurs and an agreement results.

COMPETITIVENESS AND COOPERATION

Beginning in the 1970s many U.S. companies came under intense economic pressure. In many instances the pressure was from foreign competitors. In others it was a result of deregulation which removed government protection and permitted other firms to compete. In still other cases pressure came from domestic nonunion companies which grew up to challenge existing unionized firms. While there were these several sources of increased competition, it was foreign competition, especially from Japanese firms, which received the most publicity. In part foreign competition was made visible to all by the imbalance in U.S. trade. Our country simply bought far more from foreigners than we sold to them.

When firms lost sales to competitors often they had to lay off workers, shut down plants, or otherwise retrench. Many people lost their jobs; others feared that they might lose theirs. A question arose about why U.S. firms seemed unable to compete successfully with those from abroad. Many reasons were offered, including what Americans viewed as unfair support from foreign governments for their own companies. But another critical element was said to be the low productivity and poor quality of American work. And for these problems American labor relations were held partly to blame.

The adversarial, conflict-ridden state of American labor-management relations in many industries was contrasted with more highly productive and quality-conscious work abroad which seemed to emerge out of cooperative labor-management relations. American management and labor were too busy blaming each other for declining competitiveness, it was said, to get together to improve the situation.

Hence, one part of the solution to the problems of the U.S. trade deficit, and to the underlying problem of competitiveness, was sought in increased labor-management cooperation. In April 1988, the Secretary of Labor of the United States, Ann McLaughlin, called for labor-management to improve American competitiveness and productivity.

She criticized what she called "some astoundingly slow thinking on the part of American management about new initiatives in labor-management cooperation." She added that the United States "can no longer afford the dubious battle of adversarial relations." She cited a recent Gallup Poll in which a majority of the executives surveyed singled out workers as the primary cause of quality problems and called the prevailing attitude disclosed in the survey a "ridiculous" one.

"Workers are not part of the problem. They're the source of the solution," McLaughlin said. "Nobody knows more about a job, and how to improve it, than the person who's doing it....Those firms that have established cooperative relationships have made dramatic productivity gains, because everyone involved has a stake in the success of the enterprise," the labor secretary explained.

McLaughlin cited another survey in which only 9 percent of American workers felt they would benefit from their companies' increased productivity compared to 93 percent of Janapese workers interviewed in a similar survey. "Productivity growth depends on a shared interest between management and labor," she concluded.[58]

Despite the labor secretary's apparent pessimism, there were grounds to believe that U.S. competitiveness was already rapidly increasing in 1988. The value of the dollar had declined so much that the volume of U.S. exports was rising quickly. There seemed a greater recognition among management, unions, and workers of the need to increase productivity, cut costs, and improve quality. Although competitiveness was a significant issue in American politics, its demise as an issue, as the trade balance improved, could already be glimpsed in the future. What then of the increased cooperation between labor and management that economic adversity had helped foster? Would it disappear as competitiveness improved? Possibly not. Managers, union leaders, and workers have learned a hard lesson about the consequences of letting productivity and quality slide. Cooperation to remain competitive may become a long-lasting feature of labor relations in many U.S. companies.

CHAPTER SUMMARY

Collective bargaining is the process by which management and unions negotiate the terms and conditions of employment and produce a contract. The major functions of collective bargaining are to establish the rules of the workplace, especially the amount of compensation for employees, and to settle disputes. The negotiation process can be approached to varying degrees as a poker game, a contest of power and wills, or a rational process for reconciling conflicting interests in order to support common goals.

Two types of collective bargaining have been identified. In distributive bargaining a struggle occurs between labor and management for a limited amount of economic and noneconomic advantage (whether profits, rights, or authority) which one party possesses and the other tries to obtain. Integrative bargaining, on the other hand, involves finding solutions to

---

[58] "Labor-Management Cooperation Stressed," Bureau of National Affairs, *Daily Labor Report*, No. 70 (April 12, 1988), p. 12.

problems which benefit both parties or benefit one but not at the expense of the other. In practice, labor-management relations involve both types of bargaining.

There are many types of labor-management relationships, ranging from open conflict to close cooperation. In a cooperative relationship, each side respects the other and they work together to resolve common problems. Labor relations are most likely to be peaceful and equitable when a company is profitable and its market strong so that employees can be paid well and when the corporate owners and the national union are responsible and socially sensitive. A good relationship cannot develop where the parties are grossly unequal in power or where either side does not accept the needs and legitimacy of the other.

Good negotiators use methods which are positive and constructive rather than destructive. These methods include (1) the systematic establishment of priorities and the relating of all points to the interests, needs, and wants of the other side in the negotiation; (2) the detailed understanding of the other group—personally, historically, and organizationally; (3) the presentation of formal written proposals; (4) the mutual conducting of studies to establish the facts; and (5) the use of a problem-solving approach.

Negotiations are conducted in somewhat ritualized ways. The employer and union representatives usually meet at a neutral place, such as a hotel. In the first session the union presents its demands; in the second session management presents its counterproposals. Usually little thought is given to the physical setting, but it can be of importance in influencing the psychological climate. Major rituals in collective bargaining include a low first offer by management and high demands by labor to set the stage for bargaining; "eleventh hour" bargaining, or not reaching an agreement until the expiration of the existing contract is imminent; and acrimony and name calling, which remind the involved parties that the situation is a serious matter. Two types of general tactics are used—tactics intended to gain an advantage for the side that uses them and tactics intended to persuade the other side to accept a point of view.

Negotiations are such a complex and indeterminate process that theorists have attempted to develop formal models of the factors that affect bargaining and the ways they do so. Bargaining power has been suggested as an important determinant in negotiations, and scholars have tried to formulate theories, models, and precise definitions for it. One definition emphasizes coercion of one party by the other. Another definition stresses the circumstances affecting both parties which give one an advantage over the other. Mathematical and other formal models of collective bargaining give clarification, insight, and stimulation, but none provides good predictions or satisfactory explanations of actual bargaining. An aspect of the situation which is important but not easy to take into account in mathematical models is the past history of the relationship of the negotiators and their established attitudes and expectations.

QUESTIONS FOR THOUGHT AND DISCUSSION

1 What are the major functions of collective bargaining in our industrial relations system? How well does it perform these functions?
2 What is distributive bargaining? Integrative bargaining? How are they different?
3 What is quality of working life (QWL)? What are the best methods for achieving employee participation?
4 What role do rituals play in negotiations? Do you think rituals are necessary? Why or why not? Do you think they contribute to good collective bargaining?
5 What model of collective bargaining is most useful to you? Why?
6 What is bargaining power? How has the concept been used to understand the results of collective bargaining? Do you think a precise definition of bargaining power is possible or useful? What do you personally think it consists of?
7 Do you think the attitudes and bargaining behaviors of the participants in collective bargaining negotiations are more or less important in the final outcome than economic conditions and factors? Why?
8 In what ways would jointly conducted factual studies of labor problems improve negotiations? In what situations would they be unlikely to help very much?
9 What is intraorganizational bargaining? How does it affect collective negotiations?
10 How do labor-management relations affect competitiveness? Would greater cooperation solve the competitiveness problem?

SELECTED READING

Gold, Charlotte, *Labor-Management Committees: Confrontation, Cooptation, or Cooperation* (Ithaca, N.Y.: Industrial and Labor Relations Press, Cornell University, 1986).

Peterson, Richard B., and Lane Tracy, *Models of the Bargaining Process: With Special Reference to Collective Bargaining* (Baltimore, Johns Hopkins University Press, 1977).

United States, Department of Labor, Bureau of Labor-Management Relations and Cooperation Programs, *U.S. Labor Law and the Future of Labor-Management Cooperation* (Washington, D.C.: U.S. Government Printing Office, 1986), BLMR No. 104.

United States, Department of Labor, Bureau of Labor Statistics, *Labor-Management Cooperation: Recent Efforts and Results* (Washington, D.C., U.S. Government Printing Office, 1982), BLS Bulletin No. 2153.

Walton, Richard E., and Robert B. McKersie, *A Behavioral Theory of Labor Negotiations* (New York: McGraw-Hill, 1965).

Young, Oran R., ed., *Bargaining: Formal Theories of Negotiations* (Urbana, Ill.: University of Illinois Press, 1975).

9

UNION ORGANIZATION FOR BARGAINING

Both union and management must organize themselves to conduct negotiations. In this chapter we shall examine how unions decide what demands to make on employers for changes in a labor agreement, how unions select their negotiating team, and the role of union officers in these processes. We shall also examine how unions decide whether or not to strike an employer and the factors on which this decision depends. Finally, we shall review the process of ratification of a proposed agreement by the rank-and-file membership of a union. Then we will review in Chapter 10 how management prepares for negotiations and what its objectives are.

THE UNION CHOOSES A NEGOTIATING TEAM

Whether a local union negotiates an entire collective bargaining agreement or only a local supplement to a national agreement with its employer, it still must do certain things to prepare for negotiations. At the outset, it must select a committee to represent it in negotiations. How does a local make this choice? Who are the persons ordinarily chosen to represent it, and why?

The local itself ordinarily selects its bargaining committee at a meeting of the membership. Sometimes the committee is made up of the officers of the local union. More often, some officers serve on the committee, but they are supplemented by rank-and-file members elected specifically for this purpose.

Factors in Choosing a Negotiating Committee

What are the factors that influence the selection of a bargaining committee? First, the choice of bargaining representatives is of political significance in the local union. If an officer fails to be included on the bargaining committee, it may be a signal that he or she is on the way to defeat at the next election or to retirement. A major reason for this is that a position on the bargaining committee gives a potential candidate for office in the local union a good position from which to initiate a political campaign.

Thus, *the choice of a bargaining committee is part of the ongoing political process within a local union.*

It should be noted that employers often resent this intrusion of union politics into collective bargaining. Employers generally believe the political factor to be extraneous and disruptive. They do not like being asked to deal with certain union representatives in preference to others for political reasons or being asked to concede certain issues in order to facilitate the political career of a particular union officer or candidate for office. Yet a union is inherently a political body in which the leadership is chosen by election and, because bargaining is a primary function of the union, internal politics cannot be excluded from negotiations. In some instances, the internal political situation in a union is very stable, so that the incumbent officers have no challengers and the impact of political considerations on collective bargaining is minimized. This situation is unusual, however.

Second, a bargaining committee is usually selected to represent in some way the range of interests among members of the local. An industrial union, for example, needs to include on its committee representatives of both the numerous production workers and the less numerous skilled tradespeople. Sometimes one person is considered sufficiently knowledgeable and trustworthy to be acceptable to all groups. Generally this is not the case. When it is not, it is important that different interest groups, including minority groups, be represented on the negotiating team.

Thus, *the choice of a negotiating committee ordinarily involves making provisions for the representation of the more important interest groups of the local.*

Third, a negotiating committee requires persons with expertise in negotiations and the writing of contracts. These persons may be long-service union officials or union negotiators, or they may be representatives of the national union. Increasingly, professional expertise is provided by lawyers who are chosen by the local union and advise the negotiators on the legal technicalities of the negotiations. In some instances, union lawyers serve as chief negotiators for the union. As collective bargaining agreements have become more complex, and as federal regulation of the terms of contracts has been expanded, the need of union committees for technical and legal expertise has risen.

Thus, *the choice of a negotiating committee requires obtaining expertise in negotiating techniques and legal matters.*

Not all negotiating committees are chosen on the basis of these three principles. But when committees are not so chosen, the collective bargaining process is generally undesirably affected.

Functions of a Negotiating Committee

We may understand these principles of the selection of a negotiating committee better if we ask, "What is the principal function of a union negotiating committee?" A first impression would be that its function is to convey to management the demands of the workers. But any of a number of other devices would serve this purpose, including a mass meeting with management or a letter listing demands. Rather, *the function of a bargaining committee is to work out an agreement.* This is not just a communication task, but one of creativity and compromise.

The real task of a committee is to develop and obtain solutions to the problems raised by the union's membership. After an agreement is reached, the negotiating committee must present it to the workers and sell its provisions so that it will be accepted. Yet this requires explaining to the members not only what was obtained in the negotiations, but what was *not* obtained, and the reasons why these things were not obtained. Often this is the most difficult task the committee faces, far more difficult than the negotiations with the employer.

Why is this so? Why is it so often difficult for union negotiators to sell a proposed agreement to the members? The major reason is that the workers have not been party to the discussions in the negotiations that convince the union's committee members that some demands were impractical, others too costly, and that still others should be traded off against gains elsewhere. The union committee members have probably spent many hours becoming convinced of these things, but the average worker has not. The worker knows only that in the union's list of demands were many that are not included in the proposed contract, and he or she looks to the negotiating committee for an explanation of their omission. It is very important that *it is not the employer who explains to the rank-and-file workers why they obtained some advances and not others in the agreement; it is the union negotiators' job.*

It is almost impossible to stress too strongly the importance of the responsibility of a union negotiating committee to sell the agreement it has reached to the membership. If it does not do so, the proposed agreement may be rejected by the membership, so that negotiations must resume. Employers, fearing rejection of an agreement, often insist on a commitment from the union negotiators to recommend approval of the proposed agreement to the union membership. This is a way of insisting that the union negotiators meet their responsibility to sell the agreement. When union negotiators avoid this responsibility, the negotiations process becomes one of union negotiators running back and forth between the workers and the employers' negotiating committee. In the meantime, confusion reigns and if a strike is in progress, it is prolonged.

Thus, there are three functions of a union negotiating committee:

1 To present the union's demands to the employer
2 To negotiate a tentative contract

3 To explain the proposed settlement, both what was gained and what was not, to the rank and file and obtain their approval of its terms

FORMULATING DEMANDS

Unions have several methods of formulating demands. Generally, however, all methods begin with mass meetings of the rank and file at which lists of desired contract modifications are made up. Any worker can make his or her suggestion, and it will be included on these lists. In some instances, suggestions made in such meetings are allowed to become very impractical, with different persons arguing with each other to see to what extremes demands can be carried. For example, one worker may propose a 10 percent wage increase, another 15 percent, another 25 percent, and so on. The process may end only when its absurdity has become clear to all.

"Wish" Lists

In some instances, these suggestion lists (sometimes referred to as "wish" lists) compiled at mass meetings are taken directly into negotiations with the employer. When this happens, there are several consequences. First, considerable time may be spent by the two sides in narrowing down the list to one from which negotiations can reasonably commence. Second, there is the danger that the two sides may fall into adamant disagreement on one or more extreme demands presented by the union. This is very likely to occur if the employers' representatives insist on characterizing the unions' demands. "This is the most insane thing I ever saw," a management representative might say of a particularly unreasonable union demand. But the union bargainers, in order to save face after such a challenge, may feel obligated to defend that very demand. The result is an impasse that need not have occurred. Third, by taking extreme demands into the negotiations process the union committee may have raised unreasonable expectations in the rank and file. This may result in an unwillingness by the membership to accept the agreement that results from the give-and-take of negotiations.

Winnowing the List

These dangers have persuaded most union representatives to find some method of winnowing the demands put forward by the rank and file into a more restrained package for negotiations with the employer. There are many means by which this may be done. In some cases of local bargaining the negotiating committee treats the list compiled by the membership as a document from which to select a limited number of points as higher-priority items for presentation to management. The more limited list is then presented to the rank and file for approval at another meeting, and items that were omitted are identified and their omission explained. In cases in which negotiations occurred at a regional or national level, involving many locals, a bargaining council ordinarily receives lists of demands from each local and from these lists prepares a more limited package for submission to management.

Finally, in some cases, the officers or staff of a union (either local or national) will prepare a list of demands in the course of the administration of an existing contract and present these demands to the membership for amendment and approval. Demands prepared in this way are usually more comprehensive (less oriented to exclusively economic items) and more realistic in terms of economic items than those gathered at a rank-and-file meeting.

There is always a political risk for a union leader or committee in attempting to limit or rationalize a list of demands. Dissident members of the union or politically ambitious rank-and-filers may charge that the leadership—not the employer—is denying benefits to the workers. Because of this risk, a politically expedient path for union leaders is to collect demands from the rank and file, give them to the employer, and let the employer take the onus for failure to grant them.

Since there is a political risk involved in winnowing demands, it is to the credit of union leaders that they often modify irresponsible lists of demands in an effort to make the bargaining process with management proceed more effectively.

Keeping Demands Separate

A final characteristic of the union's process of compiling demands should be noted. There is, generally, at no point in the process an attempt to cost out the package of demands as a whole. Rather, each issue is considered on its own merits, without regard to the group of demands as a whole. A demand would ordinarily be modified as too extreme only because of its own characteristics, not because it, combined with many other demands, made too large a total cost. Employers, in contrast, often start their preparation from a definite position on what total cost they can afford and are less concerned with its distribution among items. It is, therefore, a characteristic of most negotiations that the union wants to discuss individual items, and the employer, the total cost of a package of items.

Why do unions pay so little attention to total package cost? There are three major reasons. First, unions often lack the financial information and skill to develop cost estimates. Second, workers and unions are not concerned with costs, but rather with benefits, each on an individual basis. Analysis of working conditions and benefits as cost items is foreign to their way of thinking. Third, unions perceive cost control as a managerial function. Consequently, the unions are prepared to leave the problems of estimating costs and their impact on the business to management. They are confident that if a particular demand or package of demands is really too expensive, the employer will not agree to it.

Applying Pressure to Management

Unions know that often managers will resist their demands. Hence, they must consider whether or not to use pressure to try to persuade managers to agree. The most common pressure tactic is the strike, which is discussed below. Another is the boycott, by which the union tries to persuade customers not to buy the products or services of the firm with which it has a dispute. And in recent years the unions have developed new tactics, sometimes referred to as "corporate campaigns," including:

• Pressuring a company's bank and creditors, especially with the help of religious and community groups
• Challenging company applications for industrial revenue bonds, zoning variances, and the like
• Embarrassing directors and officers by picketing their homes, mounting unusually strong personal attacks, opposing management in proxy battles, and communicating directly with stockholders
• Suing the company or individual officers for breach of fiduciary duty, fraud, or racketeering
• Extending boycotts to nontraditional areas: health and life insurance, bank accounts, stock purchases[1]

THE DECISION TO STRIKE

No decision that a union leader or negotiating committee makes is of greater importance than the decision to call a strike. While it is not unusual for union leaders to threaten to strike in support of their bargaining position and to imply that they have no hesitation about calling a strike, this bravado generally conceals serious forebodings. No responsible union leader ever embarks on a strike in a cavalier fashion, because the inherent dangers are too great.

Dangers of a Strike

A strike has its own dynamics. It may be called simply to support a bargaining demand, but it can readily get out of hand. Violence may develop on picket lines. The local police and the courts may become involved in the dispute. The union may incur substantial legal costs protecting itself. In addition, the union leadership will be confronted with the problems of assisting

---

[1] Aaron Bernstein and Michael A. Pollock, "The Unions Are Learning to Hit Where It Hurts," *Business Week*, Mar. 17, 1986, pp. 112 and 114. See also Charles R. Perry, *Union Corporate Campaigns* (Philadelphia: Wharton School, University of Pennsylvania, 1987).

the members of the union who are out of work. If the strike is a long one, union strike benefits may be exhausted and assistance will have to be sought from the public welfare program or unemployment insurance (where legally permitted). A long strike will cause hardship in varying degrees for the strikers, and as difficulties increase, pressure from the families and dependents of the strikers for a return to work will increase. The intelligent union leader knows that while it may be easy to whip up enthusiasm for a strike at the outset, a long strike will see the erosion of that enthusiasm and the union will be increasingly blamed for the hardship involved.

Why Strikes Occur

It has been pointed out that often a strike costs the strikers more in lost wages and benefits than they gain in the new contract when the strike ends. Since this is the case in many instances, why do strikes occur at all? Wouldn't it be more rational for the union to settle for less and avoid a strike (and may not the same be said of management)? We must leave a full discussion of the role of the strike in collective bargaining for Chapter 11, but we can give a partial answer here to this question. In most cases, a strike is provoked by a clash of wills. The costs incurred in the struggle seem of less significance than the humiliation that would be the consequence of a concession. In other instances, unions often embark on strikes without realizing their ultimate consequences. In the initial enthusiasm, union members and their leaders often believe that a work stoppage will quickly bring the company to acceptance of their terms for a settlement. It is only later that it becomes clear that the company has more staying power against the strike than the union had thought. In these cases, if the union had correctly foreseen the cost of the strike, it might have made concessions to avoid it.

Still, most experienced union leaders do calculate the probable length, cost, and outcome of a strike in advance. They recognize that there is little point in leading the rank and file into a strike which the union is unlikely to win. Their own position may be undermined in the process. They estimate the results of the strike by weighing a series of factors, just as their management counterparts do.

Factors Affecting the Results of a Strike

The union leader must assess four major factors in evaluating the potential success of a strike.

1 *What is the capacity of the company to operate without the union members?* In some instances highly automated facilities, such as telephone switching stations, power plants, and oil refineries, can be operated for long periods by supervisory personnel only. In other instances, a plant can operate without certain groups of workers if they are the only ones on strike, such as maintenance workers or janitorial personnel. In yet other instances, plants can be operated with the use of temporary employees, so-called strikebreakers. Whatever the specific method by which the facility continues to operate, a long and perhaps ineffective strike is the likely result.

2 *What will the strike cost the union, and how long can strikers be assisted by the union or the public?* Even though a union may ordinarily provide benefits to its members who are on strike, existing funds cannot support a strike indefinitely. The larger the strike fund, the longer will be the period of support, and the more likely it will be that other local or national union groups will contribute to support the strikers. In some states, welfare assistance may be available to strikers who fall into very severe financial circumstances, and in a few states unemployment insurance may be available to support strikers after a waiting period. The greater the degree of support that can be obtained from private and public sources for the strikers, the more likely a strike is to be effective. Finally, in some industries (especially construction) it is often possible for a union to find jobs for strikers with employers who are not being struck, either in the same or in an adjacent geographic area. In extreme cases, local construction unions are sometimes on strike and every member is still fully employed. The ability of a union to conduct a successful strike in such a circumstance is clearly unlimited.

3 *What will be the role and attitude of public officials toward the strike?* In some areas of the United States, when there is a strike, public officials will order plants shut down to avoid picket-line violence, thereby preventing employers from operating during a strike. Such action is, of course, of great value to a striking union. In other areas of the country, however, local public officials will take the opposite attitude and fully protect employers in their attempts to operate their plants with supervisory or temporary personnel. Such action is, clearly, detrimental to the capacity of a union to conduct a successful strike.

4 *What will be the attitude of the local community?* In many instances a strike can fail simply because the local community is persuaded that the work stoppage is inappropriate. Strikers may be denied assistance from public authorities, denied credit by local merchants, or otherwise discriminated against. Conversely, when the community supports the strike, it may give considerable assistance to the strikers and apply pressure to the employer to reach a settlement. Community attitudes therefore may also affect the success or failure of a strike.

Because of the importance of community support to strikers, the AFL-CIO is considering the establishment of a permanent strike support center. The goal of the center, according to Steelworkers president (and AFL-CIO vice president) Lynn R. Williams, is to "prevent the avoidable strikes and win the winnable strikes." Among the key things which need to be done to support striking workers is to provide health-care coverage for them. The center would also urge member unions to allow time to explore tactics to be used in a strike. During the 1986 strike of the Steelworkers against a major steel company, the AFL-CIO set up a Steelworkers support committee to bring the dispute to the public's attention and to provide moral support for the workers. The proposed strike support center would provide such help for all striking workers—not only on an ad hoc basis.[2]

Experienced union leaders will weigh these four factors before risking a strike, and when conditions are unfavorable, the leaders will avoid work stoppages if possible. Unfortunately, it is not unusual for union leaders (or their management counterparts) to be mistaken in their judgment of the status of these factors and their implication as to whether or not a strike should be called. In consequence, strikes occur that might have been avoided.

CONDUCTING A STRIKE

Once a strike has been called, there are many things which a local union must do. Generally, however, these things may be grouped under two broad categories. First, *the union must conduct the strike against the employer.* Persons must be chosen to picket the gates of the employer's plant, and these picketers must be given instructions and assignments. Pickets signs must be prepared. Union officials must be placed in charge of the picket lines to see that legal requirements are observed. Spokespersons must be identified to handle relations with the news media.

Second, *the union must organize assistance for strikers.* When employees go on strike, their paychecks stop. Often health insurance also stops. Some form of financial assistance is necessary for strikers, and the longer the strike, the greater will be the need. There are several sources of assistance for strikers. Many unions maintain *strike benefit funds,* especially at the national level. A portion of the dues which a member pays to a union goes into a fund to provide financial support to members when they are on strike. Some funds accumulate large sums of money, but when the amount is measured against wages lost in a strike, it often is not really very much. Therefore, strike benefits from the national union are ordinarily made available to locals only under the following conditions: that the strike is approved by the national union as being for a legitimate purpose and that the strikers are shown to have need of the financial assistance. Generally, where strike benefit funds are paid, they average some 20 to 30 percent of the regular earnings of the strikers when they are on the job.

A second source of strike assistance is from *public sources.* In some states strikers are eligible to receive unemployment insurance benefits from the government, and in some states strikers may receive food stamps or general relief payments. But eligibility for benefits and amounts of assistance depend on the laws of each state. Therefore, in putting together a strike assistance program, union officials must contact public agencies, determine eligibility

---

[2] "Panel Proposes a Permanent Strike Support Center," *AFL-CIO News,* Feb. 28, 1987, p. 3.

rules, and then inform the union members who are on strike as to how to apply for benefits.

Finally, assistance for strikers may be available from private agencies, or even from shopkeepers. To obtain such assistance, union officials must meet with the representatives of private charitable agencies in order to notify them of the strike and explain its purpose and the hardship it may cause. If assistance is available, then a method by which the strikers can receive assistance must be set up. Sometimes merchants will extend credit to strikers during the strike. Sometimes local health facilities, such as hospitals or clinics, will also extend credit. Also, other unions or church groups may take up collections for distribution to the strikers and families most in need of aid.

RATIFYING THE AGREEMENT

Many, but not all, unions require formal ratification of a new contract by vote of the membership.[3] Until majority approval of those voting in a ratification election is received, the proposed contract is not final. Union negotiators whose agreement is subject to ratification by the membership are in a position of negotiating without final authority. They may reach an agreement with management on the terms of a new contract and may actually sign the document, but their agreement is not final. It is contingent on a favorable vote of the bargaining unit. Some unions that delegate authority to their negotiators to make a binding agreement nevertheless also have a ratification vote, a procedure that makes the negotiators' authority somewhat irrelevant.

How Ratification Operates

Ratification votes are required in a high proportion of contract negotiations, although they are not required by law. The Taft-Hartley Act did, however, impose on unions a legal duty to represent all members of the bargaining unit fairly, both in negotiations and in the administration of the agreement. Many unions have seized on the ratification vote as a method of demonstrating membership support for the actions of the bargaining committee and as an indication that the union has represented its members fairly.

Ratification elections are held in a wide variety of circumstances. When a local union negotiates an agreement with the employer, the ratification vote may take the form of a ballot in the union hall held after a meeting in which the negotiating committee has explained the terms of the proposed contract. These are relatively simple procedures.[4] In other cases, a ratification vote may be required for a nationwide agreement covering hundreds of thousands of workers. Normally, the vote will be scheduled a week or 10 days in advance, polling places estab-

[3] Clyde Summers, "Ratification of Agreements," in John T. Dunlop and N. W. Chamberlain, eds., *Frontiers of Collective Bargaining* (New York: Harper & Row, 1957), pp. 75–102.

[4] Robert E. Beck, "An Analysis of the Voting on Ratification of a Union Contract Settlement," unpublished master's degree thesis, MIT, 1967.

lished, and a campaign waged for and against the proposed contract. Just counting the votes may take days following the election, and meanwhile speculation about the fate of the contract proposal is rife.

In some industries a ratification vote is required, but not from the membership itself. Instead, a committee selected by the local unions must ratify the agreement. In steel, for example, the national union's wage policy committee must ratify the agreement, but this form of ratification by delegates is unusual.

What factors cause workers to vote for ratification of a contract and what factors cause them to oppose it? Two researchers studied plant-level data relevant to the 1982 and 1984 auto industry agreements with the UAW. As described by the researchers, "the results strongly suggest that the more vulnerable workers are to layoff, the more likely they are to vote for ratification of proposed agreements. The results also show, however, that workers tend to vote against ratification in plants in which, other things equal, the labor relations climate is poor. In addition, comparisons across contracts indicate how voting patterns associated with various plant and worker characteristics change when contract proposals shift toward greater job security and away from increases."

Another study, also of the 1982 automobile negotiations, found that workers in plants with large layoffs will vote in favor of a wage concession *only* if they believe that a concession will save their jobs. Surprisingly, workers in plants with growing or stable employment are actually more likely to vote yes. Finally, the yes vote is smallest in plants with the most adversarial labor relations.[5]

Impact of Ratification Procedures on Collective Bargaining

The ratification procedure introduces some subtle considerations into the negotiations process for both union and management. For the union committee members, it means that their duty to explain and sell the agreement to the membership is given a rigid form. They are forced to take one of three possible positions about the merits of the agreement. First, they may support the agreement by recommending its approval and campaigning for it. Second, they may oppose the agreement and recommend its defeat. Ordinarily, a committee would not recommend rejection of an agreement unless the employer had asked them to submit an agreement with which they were not in accord. Employers do sometimes ask this, however, because they may believe the rank and file will accept the proposed contract although the union negotiating committee will not. In most cases, but not all, proposals submitted at the employer's request without a recommendation for approval by the union committee are defeated. There is one other instance in which a union committee may recommend against ratification. This occurs when the union committee has negotiated the

[5] Peter Cappelli and W. P. Sterling, "Union Bargaining Decisions and Contracts Ratifications: The 1982 and 1984 Auto Agreements," *Industrial and Labor Relations Review*, 41:2, Jan. 1988, p. 195; and Bruce E. Kaufman and Jorge Martinez-Vazquez, "Voting for Wage Concessions: The Case of the 1982 GM-UAW Negotiations," *Industrial and Labor Relations Review*, 41:2, Jan. 1988, p. 183.

agreement but then is unwilling to support it. From the employer's viewpoint, this is tantamount to a betrayal. Nonetheless, it does happen. Third, the union committee may assume a position of neutrality on the question of a favorable ratification vote. Again, for this position to be taken after an agreement was reached in supposedly good faith with the employer would seem dishonest. *The behavior of union representatives with respect to the ratification process can either destroy good collective bargaining relations with the employer or strengthen them.*

When a ratification vote is required, both union and management conduct negotiations with a view toward the ratification process. If management anticipates an unfavorable ratification vote, perhaps on the basis of past behavior by the union, it will attempt to withhold its best offer until after a tentative agreement has been reached and rejected by the membership. If the union suspects management of this strategy, a negative ratification vote is a virtual certainty. When this happens, the ratification procedure may be said to have become merely another hurdle the parties must pass in a *pro forma* way on the path to negotiating a final settlement.

Apparently, the ratification process generally does not follow so predictable a sequence. There does not always exist the temptation for workers to refuse to ratify the first settlement brought to them in hopes of getting more in renewed negotiations ("another bite at the apple," as this process is described by negotiators). Most proposed contracts are ratified on the first ballot by the rank and file. The Federal Mediation and Conciliation Service (FMCS) keeps statistics on ratification votes in many negotiations. These statistics show that ordinarily only about 10 percent of votes result in a rejection of the proposed agreement. But there has been a definite cycle in the behavior of ratification votes over time. The percentage of contract rejections reached a peak in the late 1960s and declined thereafter. The reasons for this peak are unclear, but they may have had to do with the generally unsettled environment of the late 1960s and with the especially low unemployment rates of the period.[6] Low unemployment raised workers' expectations for salary increases and allowed them considerable ease of locating new jobs during work stoppages.

HOW BARGAINING STRUCTURE AFFECTS ORGANIZATION FOR BARGAINING

Superficially, all unions may appear to bargain in the same way. Initially, the local selects a bargaining committee and establishes a procedure to review the proposed terms of a new contract. Then the bargaining committee sits down to negotiate with the employer. Thus, it would appear that bargaining is essentially a process conducted by local unions and employers, who decide what the terms of employment will be. This is what actually occurs in some

---

[6] William E. Simkin, "Refusals to Ratify Contracts," *Industrial and Labor Relations Review*, 21:4, July 1968. See also Donald R. Burke and Lester Rubin, "Is Contract Rejection a Major Collective Bargaining Problem?" *Industrial and Labor Relations Review*, 26:3, Jan. 1973.

situations in which a local union is independent (that is, not part of a national union) or has considerable autonomy. But bargaining by independent or autonomous locals is not the most common situation, so that the view of collective bargaining as depending most on the locals is, as we have said, superficial. In many instances, *the local union is controlled, influenced, or constrained in important ways by the national union with which it is affiliated.* There are four basic structures of collective bargaining on the union side:

1 *Bargaining by the national union* with a limited role for the local unions
2 *Bargaining by locals,* but with national union coordination or control, so-called pattern bargaining
3 *Bargaining by councils of locals* under national union supervision
4 *Independent or autonomous bargaining* by locals (discussed above)

National Negotiations

The national union becomes most intimately involved in negotiations when it is itself party to major aspects of the agreement with an employer (or employers), as, for example, in the steel and automobile industries. In these industries, the national union itself negotiates the economic package (i.e., wages and fringe benefits) with the employers. In industries in which national negotiations do not occur, the role of the national union is reduced and that of the local correspondingly enhanced. Yet even in this situation, the national union may be deeply involved in the bargaining process at the local level. The national union may provide assistance in negotiations at the request of the local union, or it may require the local to submit its proposed agreement to the national union for approval. This latter procedure is especially common when some form of pattern bargaining exists. The national will then insist upon coordinating the activities of the local unions in negotiation in order to obtain the best agreements possible and to prevent undue concessions to the employers. When individual plants of a multiplant corporation are involved, the employer will be doing the same thing, of course.

Pattern Bargaining

Pattern bargaining involving local unions in a single company or industry is an important and widespread form of collective bargaining in our country. It is important to know when and where it exists because the individual collective bargaining agreements may give no hint of it. Each agreement may be signed by a local union and the individual plant or company, and may not make reference to the national union, to other plants of the company, or to other employers. It may therefore appear to an uninformed observer to be the result of autonomous or unconstrained bargaining by local parties. This mistaken view of collective bargaining in many industries is often conveyed by discussions of bargaining that stress the organization and behavior of the local union, as if it operated as an independent body. This is usually not the case at all. As we discuss the ways that local unions organize themselves for bargaining, this word of caution needs to be remembered.

Council Bargaining

When several local unions negotiate through a council structure, there is no need for each local to pick a negotiating committee or to establish a contract review procedure. Each local's officers participate in a selection process through which a bargaining team for the council is assembled. In some instances all the locals involved are represented on the bargaining team; in others, only a few locals are represented. There is a major distinction to be made, however, between the case in which several locals of the same national union negotiate through a council and the case in which several locals of different national unions negotiate together. In the first case, the national union will exert great influence on the council and its activities, even to the extent, sometimes, of appointing the chief officers of the council. In the second case, however, the nationals involved exert less influence and the council structure itself is inherently less stable. Each local involved is likely to demand a voice on the negotiating team, and failing to receive it, may resign from the council. As a practical matter, the larger locals, or those made up of skilled tradespeople, will seek to dominate the council and probably will succeed to a substantial degree. The council of locals from various national unions is, therefore, probably the most fragile of the four structures listed above. In some instances, however, it has endured and operated for many years, especially in shipbuilding and construction in some cities (Detroit, Cleveland, New Orleans, and Dallas among them).

In general, union organization for bargaining is affected by bargaining structure. *The relative authority and responsibility of the local union and the national union are very much a matter of how agreements are actually reached, not of the protocol of who signs specific agreements.* Organization for bargaining on the union side is a very complex picture in which a generalization can be made only at the risk of oversimplification. Still, brevity requires generalization, so that in the pages that follow we describe matters as they affect the greatest number of workers and their employers.

BARGAINING AND THE UNION LEADERSHIP

Unions do much more than simply negotiate collective bargaining agreements. The bargaining process must, therefore, be integrated in some manner into a union's overall functioning. How is this to be done, and by whom?

Primarily, the task of integrating bargaining with other aspects of the union's activities is the responsibility of the union's full-time officers. These officers are elected by the membership for specific terms, as was described in Chapter 3. Union leaders always have a dual responsibility:

1 Responsibility to the desire of the rank-and-file workers who are members of the union

2 Responsibility to the needs of the union as an ongoing organization

In the area of collective bargaining, these two roles of union officers may come into conflict. For this reason it cannot simply be said that the function of union officers in bargaining is to try to get their members what they want. They must also think ahead to the long-term health of the union itself.

Representing Desires of the Membership

An example may help to clarify how the conflict between an officer's duties to the rank and file and to the union itself may arise. Suppose that in a local union there are many young workers and few older workers. In anticipation of upcoming negotiations with the employer, the young workers decide to demand a reduction in pension benefits in order to bring about increased wage levels. "After all," the young workers may say, "we are not likely to be here years from now to collect our pension benefits, so let us take the money now." Since there is a majority of young workers in the bargaining unit, they are in a position to insist that the union negotiators follow their preferences. Yet union officers will see that if the young workers obtain their desires, then the older workers will be embittered, and there will exist the threat of a deep split in the local. With the passage of time such a split could make the local ineffective or even destroy it. Their obligation to the union as a whole, as distinct from any particular majority of its rank and file, requires them to oppose this initiative by the young workers.

Another example involves a situation that is not so obvious, but one that occurs frequently. Suppose the majority of the members of a local union decides to seek a very large wage increase. The union officials, or national union representatives, may be certain that the increase will bankrupt the employer within a year or so. When the employer explains this to the union membership, they profess not to care; after all, they can always get work elsewhere, they say, and in the meantime they will live well. Since this is what the workers want, should the union officials support them? The answer most union leaders would probably give is no, even though they might be voted out of their positions at the next election if they refused. Instead, the union officials have an obligation to attempt to preserve the local union as an institution. This obligation is canceled, many union leaders would say, only if the company cannot support the minimum standards of employment that the national union recognizes in the industry and/or area involved.

Ignoring Desires of the Membership

Some union leaders err at the opposite extreme in negotiations. They pay little or no attention to the views of the union membership, imposing their own views on what should be included in the labor agreement. Employers, who sometimes unfortunately allow themselves to become very isolated from the views of their employees, charge union leaders with ignoring the desires of the membership more often than is justified. Still, it does occur.

In the end, whether a union leader is a demagogue, a tyrant, or simply a responsible union official is largely a matter of judgment. The answer depends on what are believed to be the legitimate interests of the union membership. Legitimate interests may be characterized as honest self-interest, as opposed to greed. One's own individual opinion on what constitutes the appropriate self-interest of union members will determine one's opinion of the fairness of leaders in defending that self-interest.

Unfortunately, in our society there are not many disinterested, knowledgeable third parties to make these judgments (although many people who are *not* qualified by neutrality or knowledge do offer their views). Most union officials must make judgments about their own behavior and follow their own conscience. *In the United States our system of largely free, unregulated collective bargaining means that we as a nation must live with the results of these individuals' decisions on how they should act in positions of responsibility.* This is, of course, just as true of the judgments and behavior of business people as of labor leaders.

Duties of a Responsible Union Leader

What may be said about the duties of a leader who attempts to be responsible in the bargaining process? What should such a person bring to the negotiating process that rank-and-file members of a union negotiating committee are unlikely to offer?

There are three major contributions that responsible union officials can make. They should provide:

1 A concern for the future against the needs of the present

2 A concern for broader interests than those of the bargaining unit directly involved, including the interests of other local unions, of the national union, and perhaps of the industry as a whole

3 A concern for the health of collective bargaining as a process against the short-term interests of either union or management

CHAPTER SUMMARY

The organization for bargaining in a local union involves various stages and considerations. The initial choice of a bargaining committee is very much part of the internal politics of the union and involves balancing the interests of different groups. The choice also has implications for political careers within the union. The function of the bargaining committee is to bring about an agreement between the company and the union and thus involves expertise in negotiating and the ability to justify the agreement to union members. Many unions have characteristic ways of formulating demands. Sometimes a "wish list" is compiled at a mass meeting, then presented to an employer. More frequently, demands are presented in a carefully pared-down form. In most negotiations the union wants to discuss its demands as separate items, whereas the employer first considers the cost of the total package.

To strike or not to strike is a serious decision for a union. A strike is dangerous because there may be unforeseeable consequences such as violence, substantial legal costs, hardship, and loss of morale for union members. Several factors affect the outcome of a strike and are not always correctly weighed by union and management leaders. These include the cost to the union and the availability of assistance, as well as the support or opposition of public officials and the local community.

Many unions require formal ratification of a new contract by vote of the membership. The union negotiator is thus in a position of negotiating without final authority and must explain and sell the agreement to the membership. Once an agreement has been reached in good faith with an employer, it is important that the negotiator sincerely support the agreement, but this does not always happen. Ratification is an unpredictable process. There may be problems of membership division over a contract.

At its simplest, bargaining is a process conducted between local unions and employers to decide the terms of employment. However, in many instances, local unions are very much controlled or constrained by the national union with which they are affiliated. Different bargaining structures or arrangements give the national union and other local unions varying degrees of influence. Pattern bargaining, and bargaining by a local union with behind-the-scenes national union control, are important and widespread forms of bargaining.

Union leaders have responsibility both to the rank-and-file members of the union and to the needs of the union as an ongoing organization. Sometimes these responsibilities conflict. The union membership is often impatient and may tend to give priority to short-term benefits over the long-term health of the union or of the collective bargaining process itself.

QUESTIONS FOR THOUGHT AND DISCUSSION

1 What strategy should a union follow in negotiations? Should it ask for a lot or only what it expects to get? Why?

2 "A good labor leader never gets into a position in which it is necessary to have a strike." Do you agree or disagree with this statement? Why?

3 "If union leaders do not get the members to ratify a proposed agreement, they can always go back to the company for a better deal." Is this statement right or wrong? Why?

4 What is a union official's proper role in labor negotiations? Should the official sim-

ply represent the wishes of union members? Does the official have a leadership function? Does the official have any responsibility to the employer?

5 In your own words, what does it mean that choice of a bargaining committee and the process of bargaining are very much part of the political process of a union?

6 Why, in formulating demands, do unions pay so little attention to working out the total package cost? Would it be in the union's interest to do so?

7 Is having a strike evidence that union leadership has failed in bargaining? Why or why not?

8 Why do workers vote to ratify a proposed contract settlement? To oppose it?

9 Should strikers receive public assistance: unemployment insurance payments, food stamps, relief? Why or why not?

10 What are the various forms of bargaining structure? How does the bargaining structure affect the local union's organization for bargaining? Why is the form of the bargaining structure not always apparent to outside observers?

SELECTED READING

Estey, Martin, *The Unions: Structure, Development and Management,* 3d ed. (New York: Harcourt Brace Jovanovich, 1981).

Sayles, Leonard R., and George Strauss, *The Local Union: Its Place in the Industrial Plant* (New York: Harper, 1953).

10

MANAGEMENT PREPARATIONS FOR NEGOTIATIONS

WHAT DOES MANAGEMENT WANT?

A common view is that management has no other purpose than to maximize profits. As a corollary of this view, many believe that in collective bargaining management simply seeks to obtain the least expensive settlement. In fact, the objectives of management are usually more complicated than these commonly held views suggest.

Fletcher L. Byron, chairman of the board of Koppers Company, Inc., once responded to those who described business as nothing more than profit maximization in the following way:

> I do not believe that my mission is solely to make a profit. Any fool can do that—for a while.
>
> I don't even believe that we should seek to maximize profits....Companies whose profits are out of line with market conditions...are only inviting us to come in and compete...with them.
>
> ...Profits are to a corporation what breathing is to a human being. We cannot live without breathing, and a corporation cannot live without profits. But breathing is not the sole purpose of life...and profits are not the sole purpose of...business management.[1]

Business people pay attention to profits, but their motivations are more complex than profit maximization. Other general objectives (sometimes related to

[1] Fletcher L. Byron, "Let's Close the Gap," a speech before the American Assembly of Collegiate Schools of Business, Apr. 24, 1975 (mimeographed).

profit maximization but sometimes diverging from it) include the survival of the firm for the long term, development of the capacities of the firm's management and its employees, and community service. Not all business representatives express these various objectives in the same way, nor do all firms give equal weight to each. As a result, a lively controversy is continually waged over the motivations of business. But enough firms have objectives other than profit making to require us to take note of this at the outset of the chapter.

In collective bargaining, firms have the following primary objectives:

Not to Be Put at a Disadvantage Vis-à-vis Their Competitors   A firm does not want to have higher labor costs than its competitors. This goal is generally consistent with profit maximization, but it is not the same thing as seeking the cheapest possible collective bargaining agreement.

Firms would often like to pay lower wages than their competitors, if possible. But obtaining such an advantage over competition is not as significant as *not being put at a disadvantage*. The former would assist the firm's profitability, but being put at a disadvantage would threaten its very existence. The two are not of equal importance.

A company may also have a different objective: simply to preserve management prerogatives against the union. The director of corporate industrial relations of a large paper company listed the five worst things, in his view, a company could agree to with a union: joint union-management administration of pension and health-care plans, cost-of-living allowances, increased paid time off (holidays, vacations, etc.), specific work assignments to individual unions, and union representation on corporate boards of directors.[2] (Each of these topics is considered later in this book.) This executive's list includes items which other managers think should be negotiated with a union.

To Keep Shareholders Happy   When we speak of the objectives of a firm, we blur the distinction between the managers and the owners. In some circumstances, shareholders are not concerned with the details of labor negotiations. But sometimes—for example, in industries in which labor costs are quite a substantial part of overall costs—shareholders will be sensitive. A high wage settlement might cause the return on invested capital to fall. The stock market will recognize this and put a cash value on the shares which is low relative to other otherwise similar investments.

When shareholders have cause to be unhappy with the labor bargain managers drive, the managers may lose their jobs. Managers who want to keep their jobs simply have to cut costs. In this way investors, or the capital market, may impose a severe constraint on managerial behavior.

---

[2] Charles S. Loughran, "Five of the Worst Agreements You Can Make with a Union," *Wall Street Journal*, Dec. 10, 1984, p. 26. See also Loughran, *Negotiating a Labor Contract: A Management Handbook* (Washington, D.C.: BNA Books, 1984).

To Pursue Its Chosen Labor Policy   A firm may wish to be seen as a good employer with satisfied employees quite apart from any measures to improve profits directly. It might wish to follow this policy regardless of whether it is unionized or not. (We saw in Chapter 7 that several major nonunion firms are, in fact, better-standards employers.) But a firm cannot gain the good regard of its employees simply by attempting to obtain low-cost agreements. In fact, a firm may not gain employee regard even by paying high wages and providing good fringes and working conditions. These items may be provided and the labor relations climate still be very unsatisfactory. In order to obtain good employee morale, the company must pay attention to personal relationships as well as to compensation levels.

The General Electric Company has had special problems in this area. GE believes itself to be a fair, even generous, employer. Yet in the late 1940s it experienced bitter strikes. Though the strikes were settled and the pay increases employees received were substantial, the company nevertheless received a black eye with many of its unionized employees. For several years thereafter, GE tried to circumvent the unions to convince its employees directly that the company was a good employer. This policy was referred to as "Boulwarism" after its architect, Lemuel Boulware, a vice president of GE.[3] These efforts had mixed results at best. In the late 1960s, after the loss of litigation arising out of the company's policy and after changes in top management, the company abandoned Boulwarism. Relationships with the unions and employees since then have apparently improved.

As union membership has declined in recent years, the labor relations function in American businesses has also changed. In many companies labor relations policies have become less centralized at the corporate level and instead have been decentralized to various operating units. Labor relations staff have become more focused on complex, technical aspects of labor relations, and there has been less innovation from the labor relations staff in many companies.[4]

Generally, firms are not very successful in establishing objectives for their labor relations. In a survey of large companies the hardest questions for the executives to answer were these: "What are labor relations executives trying to foster?" "What outcome is sought?" "Is there any specific objective for the company?" "How is a labor relations vice president evaluated?" Companies gave indistinct responses, such as "We are trying to keep things under control" and "We want no surprises in our labor relations." And most companies reported that they evaluated their labor relations executives only informally, without using financial measures such as the contribution of the labor

[3] Lemuel R. Boulware, *Statesmanship in Industrial Relations* (New York: National Association of Manufacturers, 1964).

[4] E. Tatum Christiansen, "Challenges in the Management of Diversified Companies: The Changing Face of Corporate Labor Relations," *Human Resources Management*, 26:3–4, Fall–Winter 1987–1988, pp. 242–259.

relations function to profitability. Observing this somewhat cavalier attitude, one observer commented, "it need not be over zealously claimed that industrial relations constitute a strategic variable" of the firm.[5]

WHO NEGOTIATES FOR MANAGEMENT?

Collective bargaining for American companies is generally conducted by labor relations specialists with the advice and assistance of operating managers. But collective bargaining may involve issues of major importance to a corporation. As a result, in some instances, top corporate executives get involved in collective bargaining. Ordinarily, however, top corporate officers remain at a distance from negotiations and receive only periodic reports on their progress; the negotiations are delegated to lower levels of management. What factors determine the roles of various levels of management in collective bargaining?

In larger companies labor relations are generally delegated to staff specialists. Among the functions of these specialists is to conduct collective bargaining negotiations. Some large corporations try to push the labor relations function as far down the line as possible. In some firms each plant manager is in charge of labor relations. The plant manager either conducts negotiations or assigns the task to members of his or her staff. Corporate headquarters may monitor labor relations in the plants directly or simply as part of the factors contributing to the overall profitability (or loss) from the plant.

Most multiplant companies are not able to delegate the labor relations function so completely, however. They fear that the union, or unions, that represent their employees will keep track of developments at each plant and use breakthroughs achieved in one plant as the basis for gains in other plants. To prevent this "whipsawing," most large corporations have a central labor relations staff oversee negotiations at all plants.

Small firms, and small plants that are in large firms, often lack industrial relations specialists. Studies have been made to determine if the lack of such specialists on the management side causes labor relations to be less effective in smaller plants. These studies have shown that the lack of specialists is partly offset by the advantages of intimate contact between management and the employees in small plants. Also, small plants are more likely than large plants to have a cohesive work force. Because of these two factors, labor relations in small plants are often better than those in large firms.[6] In part because few major executives make labor relations one of their responsibilities,

---

[5] David Lewin, "Industrial Relations as a Strategic Variable," in M. M. Kleiner, et al., eds., *Human Resources and the Performance of the Firm*, op. cit., p. 36. See also Audrey Freedman, *Managing Labor Relations* (New York: The Conference Board, 1979), Report No. 765, pp. 71–72. See also Tatum Christiansen, "Strategy, Structure and Labor Relations Performance," *Human Resources Management*, 22:1–2, Spring–Summer 1983, pp. 155–168.

[6] See, for example, Sherrill Cleland, *The Influence of Plant Size on Industrial Relations* (Princeton, N.J.: Princeton University Industrial Relations Section, 1955).

larger companies, mostly multiplant, in assembly manufacturing (autos, furniture, food, home appliances, electronics, textiles, metal fabricating) have far higher strike rates than smaller, single-plant companies.[7]

Certain aspects of collective bargaining seem to require top management's oversight and involvement, even in large companies. Among these factors are:

1 *The cost impact* A collective bargaining settlement can be very expensive for a firm, and once the agreement is reached, it is too late for top management to moderate a very big settlement. Chief executives often retain the right to review and approve or disapprove the terms of a proposed settlement with the union.

2 *Internal conflicts* In the course of negotiations, disputes may arise between labor relations staff and the company's production managers, a condition that might require settlement by top management.

3 *The standards of the corporation* The visions and values of a company may become involved in negotiations so that top management may wish to influence the discussions.

4 *Attitudes of personnel* The responsibility of the corporation to maintain its human organization, including the attitudes of management and employees, is involved.[8]

While it is rare for top management to actually sit at the bargaining table, the items just cited sometimes compel their ad hoc intervention.

PREPARING FOR NEGOTIATIONS

Employers must prepare for collective bargaining negotiations just as unions do. Unfortunately, many employers seem to do little more than send a negotiating team with no advance preparation to the table to find out what the union wants. Not surprisingly, negotiations that are begun in this manner often seem to get off on the wrong foot. Management preparation for bargaining should be careful and well thought out. This section describes the process of careful preparation by management. It cannot be said that management always conducts its preparations in this manner. But managements who do prepare carefully have a better time of it in negotiations.

So does the union. This may seem surprising, since a union may be better able to take advantage of an ill-prepared employer than one well prepared for negotiations. But collective bargaining is not simply a contest. It is also a problem-solving activity. Unions often challenge management on issues that trouble employees, counting on management to be able to supply facts about the matter and even to come up with some solution to the problem. An ill-prepared management cannot do these things. The union becomes frustrated,

[7] C. Frederick Eisele, "Organization Size, Technology and Frequency of Strikes," *Industrial and Labor Relations Review*, 27:4, July 1974, pp. 560–571.

[8] See Peter F. Drucker, *Management: Tasks, Responsibilities, Practices* (New York: Harper & Row, 1974), pp. 611–612.

and bargaining degenerates into acrimonious disputes. To avoid such a result is usually in the interests of both parties. For this reason, good management preparation for negotiations is vital both to the company and to the union.

Basic Preparations

There are three steps basic to each employer's preparations for negotiations:

1 *The company must pick the best-suited negotiating and backup teams possible.* It must be especially careful to select people temperamentally suited for negotiations. Labor negotiations can be lengthy, tiring, and stressful situations.

An ideal negotiating team is made up of knowledgeable people who are also temperamentally suited to negotiations. However, because such ideal individuals are not always available, a negotiations team requires a balance of the two types.

2 *A company should, if possible, commit what some writers have called "the extravagance of over-preparations."*[9] It should research and prepare its own positions exhaustively. It should also plan carefully for the eventuality of a strike.

3 *The company should plan the course that it wishes negotiations to follow, and, as much as possible, stick to that course.* Decisions made in the heat of a negotiations session that basically alter the company's negotiating strategy are apt to be erroneous. Consistency in following a planned course is the better approach, although care should be taken not to be unduly rigid should conditions change materially.

The company should plan in advance the issues it wishes to discuss and the sequence of dealing with those issues. It is very important that the company not simply wait to hear the union's demands before preparing its own position. Instead, the company should be prepared to take the initiative in its own list of prepared changes in the contract.

Items to Prepare

The following items are illustrative of those prepared for negotiators by many companies:

1 *A summary* of the previous collective bargaining negotiations with the union.

2 *A book* containing the existing collective bargaining agreement broken up into its separate clauses. A discussion of experience with each clause, pro and con, and changes to be proposed by the company are included. When it is possible to anticipate union demands for changes, these are also identified.

3 *The internal data* of the firm with respect to its labor costs, identified by clause of the contract.

[9] Herbert I. Rothenberg and Steven B. Silverman, *Labor Unions, How To: Avoid Them, Beat Them, Out-Negotiate Them, Live with Them, Unload Them* (Elkins Park, Pa.: Management Relations, 1973), p. 288.

4 *Data* regarding the labor costs of other firms, both competitors, wherever they are located, and noncompetitors in the same geographic area.[10]

5 *Information* about the union, its leadership, history, finances, and any other special circumstances bearing on the union's role in the negotiation.

6 *A list* of the union's expected demands and their impact on the company.

7 *A list* of resource people in the company who are most likely to know, or be able to ascertain quickly, the impact of proposed contract changes on the company's operations and costs.

In recent years management and labor have been applying computer technology to preparations for bargaining. Contract clauses from agreements involving various companies and unions and economic information have been stored in computers and comparisons made of clauses and economic data. These computer outputs are then used as background material by the negotiators.[11]

Sources of Economic Information

The importance of various types of economic data will vary widely from company to company, from union to union, and from industry to industry, but the basic package of necessary information includes wages and fringe benefit levels; economic conditions, both nationally and in a particular industry or company; changes in the cost of living; family budgets for a reasonable standard of living, and increases in productivity and profits.

While the economic facts may not point to specific answers in bargaining, they usually can help narrow the difference, reduce the area of controversy, and indicate the general range of a reasonable settlement. But relying on such material too heavily may lead to an economic debate which strays far from the merits of the negotiations. Negotiations should not be conducted on the basis of who can put together the most impressive-looking or greatest quantity of data.

- Economic information need not be formal or exhaustive to be useful. Its value does not depend on quantity or the use of technical language.
- All data have limitations. They should not be accepted without question—and this applies both to material presented by management and to material selected for the union's own information. Being aware of the limitations includes knowing who is covered and who isn't, how old the material is, whether it's representative or specially selected, what is left out, and the like.
- Selection and interpretation are important. Some types of information

---

[10] Bruce Morse, *How to Negotiate the Labor Agreement* (Detroit: Trends Publishing, 1974).

[11] Abraham J. Siegel, ed., *The Impact of Computers on Collective Bargaining* (Cambridge, Mass.: MIT Press, 1970); and M. J. Fox and K. R. Meisinger, "More Effective Bargaining Through Use of Computers," *Journal of Collective Negotiations in the Public Sector*, 3:1, Winter 1974, pp. 77–90.

TABLE 10-1 BLS PUBLICATIONS

Consumer Price Index—Monthly report of the Bureau of Labor Statistics (BLS) which provides data on changes in the cost of living over the past year.

Urban Family Budgets—Annual report of BLS which provides data on changes in the economic position of an urban family.

Employment and Earnings—Monthly report with information on average hourly earnings for manufacturing in each state and most larger cities.

Area Wage Survey—Reports published separately for some 88 cities each year on wages paid certain clerical, maintenance, and laborer-type occupations.

Industry Wage Survey—Periodic detailed wage and fringe benefit data for specific industries. Information is provided on jobs common to that industry.

Union Wage Scales—Quarterly report on union building trade scales in 100 large cities and annual report on construction, printing, local transit, and local trucking.

Current Wage Developments—Monthly report on recent collective bargaining settlements with a short summary of wage and benefit changes.

The above publications can be obtained by writing the Superintendent of Documents, U.S. Government Printing Office, Washington, D.C. 20402. Press releases are available from the Bureau of Labor Statistics, U.S. Department of Labor, Washington, D.C. 20210.

are pertinent or useful; others are not; much depends on the light in which it is put. It is not enough merely to put some facts on the table; the most appropriate ones must be chosen and they must be put in perspective.

• Inaccurate or weak data can easily be turned against the user. Similarly, unfavorable data cannot be ignored if the negotiator is to be able to respond.[12]

• Many of the most useful publications about price and wage developments are issued by the U.S. Department of Labor's Bureau of Labor Statistics (BLS). Table 10-1 lists seven major BLS publications and indicates how they may be obtained.

Scheduling Preparations for Negotiations

As we saw in the preceding pages, preparing for negotiations is a major matter. Preparations involve many topics and many people. In order to coordinate and accomplish all these activities within the time available, a schedule must be worked out. Table 10-2 describes such a schedule of committee meetings as worked out by one large company. The preparations for negotiations began some 11 months before the expiration date of the agreement. In some industries, corporate preparations consume even longer periods.

The labor relations vice president coordinates the full activities of this com-

[12] The collection of data is important to both managements and unions. A good description of the use and limitations of economic data in negotiations is found in "Collective Bargaining—Lining Up the Facts," AFL-CIO *American Federationist*, 79:3, March 1972.

TABLE 10-2 A SCHEDULE OF COMPANY PREPARATIONS FOR NEGOTIATIONS
(Agreement Expires May 31)

	June	July	Aug.	Sept.	Oct.	Nov.	Dec.	Jan.	Feb.	Mar.	Apr.	May
Management Policy Committee (president, financial vice president, administrative vice president, labor relations vice president) meets quarterly and sets up other committees	O			O			O			O		
Labor Relations Policy Committee (general counsel, labor relations vice president, and others)	O				O		O		O	O		
Benefits Committee (personnel director and others)		O	O	O		O		O	O	O		
Wages Committee			O		O		O		O			
Health and Safety Committee			O		O		O		O			
Equal Employment Opportunity Committee				O		O		O				
Meetings with plant managers			O				O					
Meetings with safety engineers				O			O					
Strike Reaction Committee						O			O	O	O	
Negotiations take place										O	O	O

pany in preparation for negotiations. The meetings of the various committees and meetings with the plant managers and safety engineers are scheduled so that the vice president may devote full attention to one meeting at a time. In this way, all the meetings will not be jammed into the last few weeks before the contract expires. As shown in Table 10-2, negotiations begin in March and the agreement expires at the end of May. A 2-month period for formal negotiations prior to the expiration of an agreement is not unduly lengthy, but it could be too brief if there are many complicated issues to be resolved.

Figure 10-1 describes the activities of a labor relations policy committee in preparing for negotiations. It is this committee which, under the oversight of the management policy committee, is responsible for developing the bargaining strategy of the company. It accomplishes this by relying on the reports of

FIGURE 10-1   Activities of the policy committee. *(Adapted from Ronald L. Miller, "Preparation for Negotiations," Personnel Journal, 57:1, January 1978, p. 38.)*

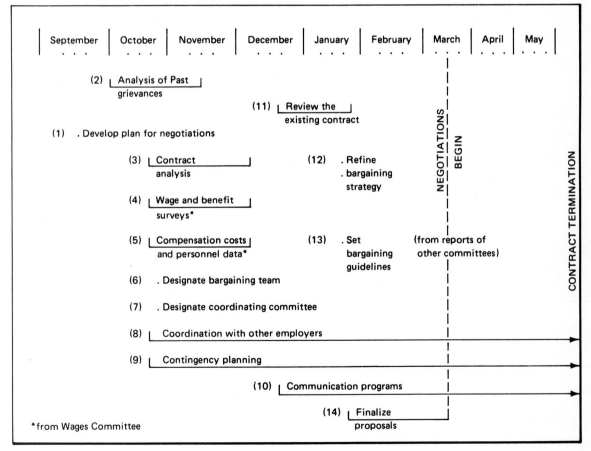

the various other committees regarding their specialized areas and by combining the reports into an overall picture of the upcoming negotiations.

In some companies, with only a few agreements to negotiate and a duration of agreements of 3 years or so, the schedule is simple and straightforward. In other companies, with many agreements to negotiate, there may be many such schedules in progress simultaneously. And when agreements are of only 1 year's duration, there is virtually no pause between preparations for one negotiation and preparations for the next. The lives of labor relations executives and union leaders can therefore be very hectic.

A special problem for management is in the area of communication to managerial personnel affected by labor negotiations but not directly involved in them. Plant managers, superintendents, and foremen fall into this category. A part of the schedule for preparations for negotiations presented in Table 10-2 involves meetings with plant managers and safety engineers, and perhaps supervisors and foremen as well. These consultations are a recognition of these managers' knowledge of first-line relations and of the fact that changes in the collective bargaining agreement may have important effects on them. But company negotiators are rarely able to go much beyond infrequent meetings with supervisory personnel. To involve these people directly in the negotiations is ordinarily too costly in terms of lost production. A partial compromise between full involvement in negotiations and no involvement is obtained by giving supervisors more input to the negotiators on certain issues than on others, especially those issues dealing with work standards and the handling of grievances.

MULTIEMPLOYER BARGAINING

In many sectors of the economy employers do not negotiate with unions on a single-employer basis. Instead, companies form associations that bargain with the union (or unions). This pattern of bargaining is characteristic of construction, coal mining, the maritime trades, longshoring, trucking, clothing manufacture, and printing. Employer association bargaining characterizes many more industries in Europe, and American-based multinational firms often participate in association bargaining in Europe. At first there was some doubt as to whether American firms that did not (and often would not) engage in association bargaining in the United States would agree to do so in Europe. But apparently many of these American companies have adjusted to association bargaining in Europe.[13]

Association bargaining has its own special problems of preparation for negotiations, which differ from those encountered by the single company. This section explores some of the special problems of association bargaining.

---

[13] Solomon Barkin, *Worker Militancy* (New York: Praeger, 1975), pp. 386–387.

Resolving Internal Disputes

The most characteristic problem of association bargaining arises in the potential for conflict between members of the association. The need to gain strength vis-à-vis the union causes the separate firms to join together in an association for bargaining. But many other circumstances tend to divide the companies and prevent their taking a common stand. In the first place, the firms are normally competitors. They often mistrust each other and do not want negotiations with the unions to end in a contract that benefits any other firm more.

In the second place, the firms have different characteristics and different problems, which sometimes cause them to pursue conflicting goals in bargaining. Some firms are large, some small. Some firms may be very profitable, some almost insolvent. Some firms utilize the newest technology, some the oldest. Some firms have a history of cordial relations with the unions, some a history of bitter disputes. Some firms have the loyalty of their employees, some do not. The union, which is usually aware of these differences among the firms, may exploit them for its own purposes.

In the third place, in some industries there is a tradition of treachery among the employers. In the supermarket industry, for example, such behavior is perhaps best exemplified by one large supermarket chain's withdrawal from a major metropolitan area shortly *after* it agreed to an unexpectedly high and pattern-setting wage settlement for that area. Its withdrawal, of course, left its competitors to pay the higher compensation.[14]

At the outset of preparations for negotiations the association must attempt to resolve internal disputes, reach a common position to present to the union, and agree on a joint course of action should a strike occur. Figure 10-2 presents a simplified model of multiemployer bargaining and illustrates the processes we have described. The diagram shows that the union has access

[14] James W. Driscoll, "Joint Labor-Management Committee of the Retail Food Industry," report to the U.S. Department of Labor, Apr. 18, 1978, p. 15.

FIGURE 10-2 Multiemployer bargaining. *(Adapted from Thomas A. Kochan, Resolving Internal Management Conflicts for Labor Negotiations, International Personnel Management Association, Chicago, 1973, p. 9.)*

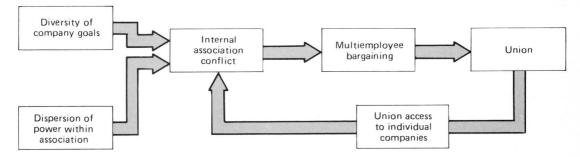

to the individual companies that make up the association. It is very common for disputes between the association and the union to be resolved by individual companies' splitting from the association (either in return for favorable treatment from the union or simply in pursuit of a company's own special interests) until the association collapses. To meet this threat, employer associations often adopt bylaws that legally bind each company to the association's position in bargaining and provide a method by which the association decides on its bargaining stand. A company that fails to support the association as required by the bylaws may subject itself to a financial penalty.

Selecting Bargaining Representatives

Who should represent an association in bargaining with a union? Some associations have only a few member firms, so that the bargaining team can be made up of a representative from each one. This greatly simplifies matters. But most associations have so many member firms that if each were separately represented on the bargaining team, it would be unreasonably large. If only a few firms are to be represented directly in negotiations with the union, how are they to be selected, and how are they to be held accountable to the association as a whole for their actions?

Many associations have established a dues structure to pay for a permanent staff for the association. The staff director (or a person designated by the director) generally participates in collective bargaining negotiations as the representative of all firms in the association. But many business people or firms that belong to associations have reservations about allowing an association staff director very much authority in dealings with the unions. After all, they might say, the director isn't a business person and doesn't really know what is important to business people. Furthermore, the director is someone business people hire, not, like themselves, an officer of a firm. The association director is not the type of person, it might be said, who should be trusted with labor negotiations.

In reply, supporters of a strong role for the association director in the bargaining process point out that reliance on him or her in negotiations offers certain benefits to the association:

1 *The opportunity to have a full-time professional with the knowledge and skill necessary to the job of representing the companies.* Since unions are generally represented by full-time people, this is important. Business people who handle labor negotiations simultaneously with their business duties cannot be expected to perform well for the association.

2 *A greater likelihood that the association will be able to demonstrate continuity and consistency in its policies with respect to the unions.* When the leadership of the association is changed each year, as is common in employer associations that draw their chief officers from the ranks of member companies, the association's policies seem to shift with each new officer. This puts the association at a decided disadvantage vis-à-vis the union.

Thus, there is uncertainty as to which type of representation (professional or business person) is more effective for an employer association in bargaining. A compromise position for the association is to form a labor policy committee of business people. The negotiating team is then made up of members selected from the labor policy committee (and perhaps some business people chosen on an ad hoc basis) and the association executive. The labor policy committee itself meets before, during, and after negotiations and so provides business people with an ongoing view of the labor relations development. This helps add continuity to the association's activities.

Wage Uniformity

An important aspect of the activities of an employers' association is to attempt to apply uniform policies and standard conditions of work to the employees of a number of competing business enterprises. The purpose of uniform policies and conditions is to keep the companies from competing with each other on the basis of wages and working conditions. Instead, competition takes place on the basis of productivity, product quality, sales ability, and other similar factors. The unions, and many employers, fear that competition based on differences in wages and working conditions is destructive of the welfare of employees and perhaps of the better-standards firms as well. In the apparel manufacturing industry, for example, the unions have faced "sweatshop" conditions on a large scale at times in the past but have attempted to eliminate them by organizing employers under a standard contract.

But the matter of establishing standard conditions is complex. In many discussions of multiemployer bargaining, there has been a tendency to regard wage uniformity among firms as the simplest objective to achieve. But even wage uniformity is not a clear-cut concept with a single set of economic consequences. In fact, there are at least seven different basic types of wage uniformity practiced in various industries:

1 Uniformity of rate of pay per *unit of output* (i.e., piece-rate uniformity)
2 Uniformity of rate of pay per *unit of skill and effort* required
3 Uniformity of rate of pay per *hour* of labor of a particular type (i.e., occupational hourly wage uniformity)
4 Uniformity of pay-rate ranges for various occupations
5 Uniformity of minimum rates of pay
6 Uniformity of changes in rates of pay
7 Uniformity of total labor cost per unit of output[15]

The choice among these alternatives (which cannot, except in the most unusual circumstances, be simultaneously pursued) depends in large part on the objectives that the firms in the industry wish to pursue. Type 2 uniformity results in an equitable (with respect to skill and effort expended) distri-

---

[15] Thomas Kennedy, *The Significance of Wage Uniformity* (Philadelphia: The University of Pennsylvania Press, Industry-Wide Collective Bargaining Series, 1949).

bution of earnings among workers of different companies, but other types do not yield this result. Type 7 results in heavy subsidization (by lower wages) of inefficient firms, while Type 3 results in bankruptcies and elimination of the less efficient firms.

Even this brief discussion reveals the complicated and significant choices that associations must make in determining the policies with which they approach labor negotiations. It is dangerous, therefore, to speak of multiemployer bargaining as if a unity of purpose and result existed. There are distinct differences in association bargaining with respect to labor policies pursued.

Legal Status

Multiemployer bargaining has a peculiar status under the National Labor Relations Act (as amended). The NLRB does not ordinarily certify a bargaining unit made up of union representatives and members of a multiemployer group; it is created by labor and management without NLRB involvement. The basic ingredient supporting the appropriateness of the unit is the mutual consent of the parties. This relationship is founded on the unequivocal manifestation by the employer and the union members of the group that all intend to be bound by the results of the prospective negotiations. The formation of this dual unit must be completely voluntary. The NLRB will not sanction the creation of a multiparty unit over the objection of either party, union or employer.[16]

Under present law, once the group is formed and bargaining commences, neither the union nor employer members are permitted to withdraw without the consent of all parties, except under unusual circumstances. This is true even though the decision to bargain jointly in a multiparty fashion is purely voluntary, and in fact must be based on the uncoerced agreement of all parties to enter this bargaining relationship.[17]

The only escape under the "unusual conditions" exemption occurs in those situations in which an employer or the union is faced with dire economic circumstances, circumstances in which the existence of an employer as a viable business entity has ceased or is about to cease. In this respect, the NLRB has held that an employer may withdraw from a multiemployer association after negotiations with the union have begun when the employer is subject to extreme economic difficulties that result in an arrangement under the bankruptcy laws,[18] or when there is an imminent adverse economic condition that will require the employer to close its plant.[19]

---

[16] *Kroger, Inc.*, 148 NLRB No. 69, 1964.

[17] *Hi-Way Billboard*, 500 F.2d 181, 5th Cir., 1974.

[18] *U.S. Lingerie Corp.*, 170 NLRB 750, 1968.

[19] William J. Curtin, "Legal Aspects of Multi-Employer Bargaining," address to the Associated General Contractors of America, Chicago, Jan. 16, 1975 (mimeographed).

A federal court of appeals has held that an employer may withdraw on its own initiative from association bargaining, even without union acquiescence, whenever an impasse occurs in bargaining.[20]

COSTING AN AGREEMENT

An employer must try to keep track of the impact that negotiated changes in wages and benefits will have on its labor costs. Increases in wage rates are rather easily translated into additional costs. For example, if the average hourly wage in the employee unit involved in negotiations is $6, and the employer decides to agree to an increase of $0.60 per hour, effective immediately, then the impact on labor cost is calculated as follows:

$$\$0.60 \times 2000 \times 1000 = \$1,200,000$$

where $0.60 is the amount of the wage increase per hour, 2000 is the number of work hours per year for the average employee, and 1000 is the number of employees in the unit.

A change in the timing of the wage increase may affect this calculation substantially. Suppose the $0.60 wage increase does not take effect until 6 months after the start of the new agreement. Then the company's additional cost in the first year (i.e., the first 12 months) of the new agreement will be:

$$\$0.60 \times \tfrac{1}{2} \times 2000 \times 1000 = \$600,000$$

Put differently, the company's additional costs are:

First month	None
Second month	None
Third month	None
Fourth month	None
Fifth month	None
Sixth month	None
Seventh month	$0.60/hour worked
. . . .	
Twelfth month	$0.60/hour worked

or $0.60 per hour increase for 6 out of 12 months, or one-half of the year.

The shorter the period of time an increase is in effect in the first year, the less it costs the company. But this is true only at the outset. If the company looks beyond the first year of the agreement, then the $0.60 increase must be paid indefinitely.

[20] *NLRB v. Beck Engraving Co.*, 1975.

This is an important matter in bargaining. A company may sometimes have the option of choosing among different proposals—for example, (1) a $0.60 per hour increase immediately or (2) an $0.80 per hour increase effective 6 months after the start of the agreement.

The first proposal would cost the company $1,200,000 in the first year of the agreement, as we saw above. The second proposal would be costed as follows:

$$\$0.80 \times \tfrac{1}{2} \times 2000 \times 1000 = \$800,000$$

Thus, the $0.80 per hour increase is actually less expensive to the company in the first year of the agreement than the $0.60 per hour increase because of the timing involved.

But note that this calculation is valid only for the first year of the agreement. In the second year the calculations are:

$$\$0.60 \times 2000 \times 1000 = \$1,200,000$$

versus

$$\$0.80 \times 2000 \times 1000 = \$1,600,000$$

In order to get a reduced cost in the first year, the company, if it adopted proposal (2), would get increased costs in all subsequent years.

Wage increases also have an indirect impact on costs. Suppose a company figures its labor costs as follows:

$$\$6 \times 2000 \times 1000 = \$12,000,000$$

where $6 per hour is the average wage rate, 2000 hours the average work year, and 1000 the number of employees. But the company also has costs from certain benefits provided employees. For example, suppose the company grants each employee 2 weeks' paid vacation, at a cost calculated as follows:

$$\$6 \times 2 \times 40 \times 1000 = \$480,000$$

where $6 per hour is the average hourly wage, 2 is the number of weeks of paid vacation, 40 is the number of hours ordinarily worked per week, and 1000 is the number of employees.

A wage increase raises the cost of the paid vacation also. Thus, the wage rate paid to persons on vacation rises from $6 to $6.60 per hour in our example. The additional cost to the company of this increase is:

$$\$0.60 \times 2 \times 40 \times 1000 = \$48,000$$

This increase is termed a "roll-up" and is an example of the impact on the costs of certain fringe benefits of a wage increase.

The additional costs of providing increased pension, health-care, life insurance, and dental benefits must be calculated on the basis of sophisticated computations, which take into consideration the expected usage of such benefits. Life insurance companies, pension actuaries, and similar experts are available to help the company estimate additional costs in these areas.

There are certain problems with cost calculations as most firms perform them. The most important limitation is that firms usually base cost estimates on past experience, rather than on estimates about future conditions. This is partly because data are usually available about past experience, while the future is a matter of conjecture. The result is that cost calculations are past-oriented rather than future-oriented. Firms assume that the amount of labor used (in our example, 2000 hours per year $\times$ 1000 employees equals 2,000,000 hours worked per year) and the mix of wage rates at which labor was compensated in the past (in our example, yielding an average wage of $6 per hour) will suffice as guides to the future. But the firms may expect that this will not be the case. For example, if the firm believes its number of employees will decline from 1000 to 800 next year, then a wage increase of $0.60 per hour will cost the firm $960,000 ($0.60 $\times$ 2000 $\times$ 800) instead of $1,200,000.

Also, the analytical techniques used by companies ordinarily stop short of considering the full impact of cost changes on the company. The techniques described above estimate the cost of compensation increases, not the effect of the increases on the firm's profits. Insufficient attention is paid to relationships between the firm's labor costs, volume of production, product mix, and capital investments, and these techniques do not take into account the firm's ability to minimize, by modifying previously formulated corporate plans, the financial consequences of increases in compensation.[21]

CHAPTER SUMMARY

In collective bargaining, management has many objectives, including profit maximization and cost control. In many corporations, there is a balance between concern with the quality of relations with employees and concern with the pursuit of economic well-being. A primary management objective is not to be put at a disadvantage vis-à-vis competitors. However, specific bargaining objectives may be quite diverse from firm to firm and for the same firm in different situations.

Most large corporations have a specialized labor relations staff to oversee collective bargaining for all of the plants of a company advised and assisted by the operating managers. In smaller firms, plant managers may conduct negotiations and sit down at the bargaining table. In some instances, top corporate executives are involved. Chief executives retain the right to review

---

[21] M. H. Granof, *How to Cost Your Labor Contract* (Washington, D.C.: Bureau of National Affairs, 1973), pp. 127–128. See also W. D. Hersel and Gordon S. Skinner, *Costing Union Demands* (Chicago: International Personnel Management Association, 1976).

and approve or disapprove proposed settlements. Top managers will intervene in internal management controversies and in confrontations in which the company's reputation as an employer is at stake.

Employers must prepare for collective bargaining negotiations just as unions do. The better planned and more detailed the preparation, the better the negotiations will go for all parties involved. An effective company prepares by carefully selecting team members who are knowledgeable and temperamentally well suited to negotiation; by planning exactly what it wants to discuss and how; by having internal data on the existing contract with itemized labor costs; and by having data on the labor costs of other firms in the geographic area. Much background material and economic information can now be stored in computers for ease of access and analysis. Preparations for negotiations also need careful scheduling. In some industries, preparations begin a year or more before a contract runs out, so that all issues can be considered and consultations scheduled with plant managers and relevant personnel.

Firms are not usually very successful in establishing objectives for their labor relations or in creating measurements for how well they are doing. Rather than treating labor relations as a strategic variable which can help a company be successful, most simply hope to avoid trouble.

In many sectors of the economy, employers do not negotiate with unions individually. Instead, companies form associations that bargain with the unions. Association bargaining has its own special problems in preparing for negotiations. One of the most notable of these special problems is the potential for conflict between members of the association. Management objectives and tactics in negotiations are complex matters over which companies disagree. Furthermore, the firms are normally competitors and often distrust each other. Having a method for settling internal disputes is critical to the success of multiemployer bargaining. Some associations adopt bylaws which are legally binding. The selection of representatives also presents problems. One solution is to hire a permanent staff for the association to participate in negotiations. Multiemployer bargaining also has a unique legal status under the NLRB.

QUESTIONS FOR THOUGHT AND DISCUSSION

1 What are management's objectives in collective bargaining? Which are most important? Why?
2 What is Boulwarism? Is it a good policy for a company to follow? Why or why not?
3 What steps in management preparation for negotiations are most important? Why?
4 What are the major ways in which multiemployer association bargaining is different from single-employer bargaining? Do the differences work to the advantage of the employers or to their disadvantage? Why?
5 Do smaller companies which lack industrial relations specialists have poorer labor relations or less effective collective bargaining negotiations than larger, multiplant companies which have such specialists? What are the pros and cons of having a specialized labor relations staff?

6 Is industrial relations a strategic variable for a firm? Why or why not? Should it be?

7 What are some of the problems with establishing uniform wages and working conditions for the employees of competing firms by organizing employers under a standard contract? Do you think this plan is beneficial to employees or can it be used to their disadvantage?

8 What are the arguments for and against having a professional staff represent multi-employer associations in collective bargaining negotiations? What is a compromise position that has been tried? Can you think of any other methods of forming a negotiating team or staff for employer associations?

SELECTED READING

Irving, John S., ed., *When Management Negotiates* (Washington, D.C.: National Association of Manufacturers, 1987).

Morse, Bruce, *How to Negotiate the Labor Agreement* (Detroit: Trends Publishing, 1974).

Northrup, Herbert, *Boulwarism* (Ann Arbor: University of Michigan, Bureau of Industrial Relations, 1964).

Ryder, Meyer S., Charles M. Rhemus, and Sanford Cohen, *Management Preparation for Collective Bargaining* (Homewood, Ill.: Dow Jones–Irwin, 1966), p. 53.

Siegel, Abraham J., ed., *The Impact of Computers on Collective Bargaining* (Cambridge, Mass: MIT Press, 1970).

Windmuller, John P., and Alan Gladstone, eds., *Employer's Associations and Industrial Relations: A Comparative Study* (New York: Oxford University Press, 1984).

CHAPTER 11

STRIKES AND DISPUTE SETTLEMENT

WHAT IS A WORK STOPPAGE?

Strikes and Lockouts

Strikes occur when employees as a group refuse to work until changes are made in compensation or conditions of work. The strike is a pressure tactic; it is also a method of notifying other people that a dispute exists between the employer and the workers. Other means of advertising a dispute exist, such as informational picketing and circulation of published material; other means of bringing economic pressure are also sometimes available, as, for example, a product boycott. But the strike, and the threat of a strike, constitute the principal device by which unions in our society apply economic pressure in labor disputes.

The employer has a form of action available that is somewhat analogous to a strike. It is called a "lockout." In a lockout the employer closes the plant or other facility in which a labor dispute exists. The employees are unable to work and do not get paid. As a result, the lockout brings pressure to bear on the employees to settle the dispute.

Strikes and lockouts are forms of economic warfare. As such, they often bring severe losses to those engaged in them and inconvenience to third parties. In some instances, strikes and lockouts disrupt the provision of products or services that affect the health and safety of the public. Because of the sometimes serious consequences of work stoppages, many people have long sought ways to lessen their frequency and ameliorate their impact. Sometimes it is proposed to simply make work stoppages illegal. Sometimes new methods of settling disputes without recourse to work stoppages are proposed. In any case, strikes and lockouts are probably the most visible evidence of labor disputes. They occasion much discussion by the public, and in some instances much frustration and anger.

The Right to Strike

Is there a "right to strike"? "Right to strike" is a phrase heard often in discussions of labor relations. Some people assert that there is a natural right of human beings to refuse to work in conditions and circumstances they do not like. It is a right of Americans, they assert, to refuse to work if they do not want to, and, in fact, the Thirteenth Amendment to the U.S. Constitution does prohibit "involuntary servitude" except as a punishment for crime. Employers may not, therefore, compel unwilling employees to labor for them. Employees may refuse to work, or quit, if they desire.

However, the constitutional prohibition against involuntary servitude establishes an individual right, and therefore is not necessarily applicable to a strike situation. A strike has two characteristics that distinguish it from a simple application of the right to be free of involuntary servitude. First, a strike is a collective action, not an action of an individual. The strike draws its force from its collective character. It is a device used to halt or disrupt the employer's business, not a device simply to free people from an undesired employment. Second, the purpose of the strike is to obtain concessions from the employer. It is an economic weapon. The Thirteenth Amendment apparently did not intend to establish the right of employees to band together to bring pressure to bear on an employer. There is thus no constitutional right to strike. Whether or not there is a natural-law right to strike is best left to philosophers.

There being no constitutionally protected right of employees to strike, efforts have been made in the courts and in Congress both to establish a right to strike and to restrict it. The National Labor Relations Act includes in section 7, "Rights of Employees," the language

> Employees shall have the right...to engage in...concerted activities for the purpose of collective bargaining or other mutual aid or protection.

This language has been held by the courts to establish a statutory right to strike. And section 13 of the act is even more explicit:

> Nothing in this Act, except as specifically provided for herein, shall be construed so as either to interfere with or impede or diminish in any way the right to strike....

However, what Congress bestows it can also take away. Other provisions of the same law prohibit strikes for certain purposes. And some classes of employees are excluded from the protection of the act. Federal government employees and employees of states and local governments are not covered by the NLRA.

The Congress has prohibited strikes by federal employees, and most states prohibit strikes by their own employees and those of municipalities.

IS THE UNITED STATES STRIKE-PRONE?

How frequent are strikes in our country? Is the economy seriously disrupted by them? Do we face a crisis that must be resolved, or are strikes occurring at a rate that we can endure? Most governments keep statistics about strikes, so that we may examine these questions on the basis of some useful data.

The United States is a large country with many firms and employees. It is natural to expect, therefore, that it would have a larger number of strikes than smaller countries, and indeed it does. But is strike activity in the United States more pronounced than abroad when allowance is made for the size of our economy?

Apparently the answer is yes but not a lot. Figure 11-1 shows the number of days of work lost in strikes for each 1000 workers employed for Western European nations and the United States. It can be seen that the United States ranks after Italy, Canada, and Australia in days of work lost because of strikes. Evidently, the United States is only a moderately strike-prone nation.

Do these statistics mean that the United States economy is more disrupted by strikes than those of other countries such as Japan and Germany? Probably only to a small degree. Strikes are not all alike. In the United States strikes tend to occur at predictable intervals, marking the expiration date of multiple-year agreements. Strikes are sometimes lengthy, resulting in a great amount of time lost, but their impact on the economy is very much offset by their predictability. The exception occurs when unionized workers conduct strikes without the authorization of the union. Such a strike is called a "wildcat" strike. In American manufacturing, of 39,475 strikes recorded between 1960 and 1977, 21.5 percent were walkouts during the term of a contract and ordinarily in violation of the contract's no-strike clause and without union authorization.[1] These strikes are largely unpredictable to management, and in consequence can be very costly. When business firms know that their suppliers have a contract expiring and a strike may occur, they are often able to find alternative sources of supply. France, for example, has a much lower proportion of time lost from strikes than the United States does. But strikes often occur in France at unpredictable intervals and are therefore much more costly to business, and sometimes to the economy, than strikes in the United States. The British have both a lot of time lost because of strikes and a great deal of unpredictability as to when they will occur. The result is, in some ways, the most economically damaging situation of all. In Germany, the Netherlands, and Switzerland, however, strikes are predictable in timing and occur less frequently than in the United States.[2]

---

[1] Dennis M. Byrne and Randall H. King, "Wildcat Strikes in U.S. Manufacturing, 1960–1977," *Journal of Labor Research*, 7:4, Fall 1986, pp. 395–401.

[2] Everett M. Kassalow, "Industrial Conflict and Consensus in the U.S. and Western Europe," in Benjamin Martin and Everett Kassalow, eds., *Labor Relations in Advanced Industrial Societies: Issues and Problems* (Washington, D.C.: Carnegie Endowment, 1980), pp. 45–60.

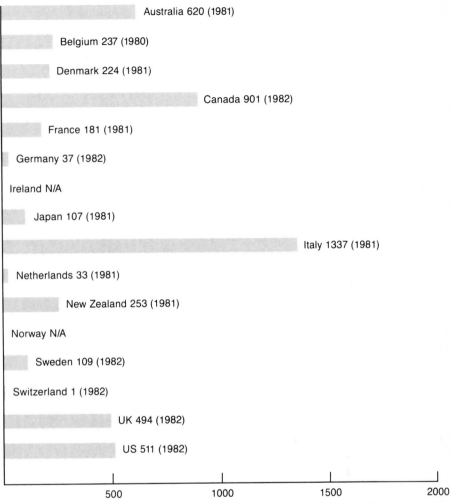

FIGURE 11-1   Average number of days lost in strikes per 1000 workers employed 1968–1982 (the most recent data available). *(Source: Bureau of Labor Statistics, Handbook of Labor Statistics, Bulletin 2175, December 1983, pp. 444–447.)*

Have strikes become more or less frequent in the American economy? Government statistics on strikes begin in 1939 and show that 1946 was the worst year in terms of strikes in our recent history. The record of time lost in recent years has been moderate and generally better than the record of the late 1940s.[3] In the 1980s the frequency and duration of strikes declined substantially as many companies got into financial difficulties and workers feared losing their jobs. In 1987, for example, the American economy lost

---

[3] Douglas A. Hibbs, "On the Political Economy of Long-Run Trends in Strike Activity," *British Journal of Political Science,* vol. 8, 1978, pp. 153–175.

0.02 percent of estimated total working time as a result of work stoppages. It is unlikely that even that much production was really lost, since a great deal of output lost in strikes is later made up by overtime operations after the work stoppage ends. These statistics do not suggest an economy unduly disrupted by strike activity.

STRIKE ACTIVITY BY INDUSTRY

Some industries are much more likely to experience strike activity than others. A study made in the 1950s compared the propensity to strike in various industries on an international basis. Certain industries were high in virtually all countries, especially mining, shipping, longshoring, lumbering, and textiles. The lowest industries in terms of strikes were clothing, public utilities, hotel and restaurant facilities, trade agriculture, and railways. The authors related a high incidence of strikes to the physical isolation of workers and the workplace in industries such as mining, shipping, and lumber and to the difficult nature of the work combined with the uncertainty of employment in those industries.[4]

WHY DO STRIKES OCCUR?

Causes of Strikes

Strikes occur for several reasons. We ordinarily think of strikes being caused by a dispute between an employer and a union over wage rates or benefits or working conditions. But strikes also occur because of disputes over bargaining structure or over the personalities involved in negotiations. Strikes that actually occur for these reasons are usually advertised as strikes about wages or conditions of work. Consequently, government statistics about the causes of strikes show disputes over wages and working conditions as being by far the major cause of work stoppages. Often, however, particularly long and bitter strikes do not arise from a single matter, such as wages, but from a more complex dispute over who should bargain with whom.

One study of strike activity found that 15 percent of scheduled negotiations (i.e., those occurring at the expiration of a collective bargaining agreement) ended in strikes. A key factor causing strikes was found to be the variability, but not the level, of profits. That is, often managers in currently profitable companies feared that profits were going to turn down and so

---

[4] Clark Kerr and Abraham Siegel, "The Interindustry Propensity to Strike," in A. Kornhauser et al., *Industrial Conflict* (New York: McGraw-Hill, 1954), chap. 14. A recent study has questioned the findings of Kerr and Siegel: see P. K. Edwards, "A Critique of the Kerr-Siegel Hypothesis of Strikes and the Isolated Mass: A Study of the Falsification of Sociological Knowledge," *The Sociological Review*, 25:3, August 1977, pp. 551–574. For a later confirmation of Kerr-Siegel see Bruce E. Kaufman, "The Determinants of Strikes over Time and Industries," *Journal of Labor Research*, 4:2, Spring 1983, pp. 159–176.

were reluctant to grant pay increases which union leaders and members felt would be paid out of existing profit levels.[5]

Another careful statistical study of strike activity in the United States between 1971 and 1980 identified the following as influencing strikes:

- Men are more likely to strike than women.
- Companies with substantial sales fluctuations are more likely to experience strikes than others.
- Strikes are less likely in right-to-work states.
- Strikes are more likely in larger bargaining units.
- Strikes are more likely when pay has lagged behind inflation.

But during this period the level of the local unemployment rate and the rate of inflation had little effect on strike likelihood.[6]

Strikes are staged by nonunion workers as well as by unions, but we usually hear much less about such nonunion strikes. This is partly because work stoppages in a nonunion situation tend to be more confused and less clearcut than when a union is involved. Also, almost certainly, the frequency of nonunion work stoppages is considerably less than that of strikes called by unions. Yet it is not uncommon to hear about work stoppages in nonunion plants. Managers in such plants sometimes talk of "blackmail"—the workers' stopping work and threatening to go to a union if the company doesn't give in to their demands. Such incidents very rarely receive the publicity that accompanies strikes by unions, however, and as a result they are not ordinarily included in government statistics about work stoppages.

The Functions of a Strike

Strikes are emotional occurrences, and perhaps it is to be expected that observers would be of two minds about them. On the one hand, strikes are often viewed as evidence of a breakdown in the bargaining process. Implicit in this view is the suggestion that if bargaining were conducted better, strikes would not result. There is considerable merit to this view, as we shall see in later sections of this chapter.

On the other hand, careful observers of collective bargaining also recognize that the strike is an integral part of the bargaining process. The strike has functions to perform that contribute to the resolution of disputes. In this view, a certain frequency of strikes is to be expected as a normal part of col-

[5] Joseph S. Tracey, "An Investigation into the Determinants of U.S. Strike Activity," *The American Economic Review*, 76:3, June 1986, pp. 423–436. See also Cynthia L. Gramm, "New Measures of the Propensity to Strike during Contract Negotiations, 1971–1980," *Industrial and Labor Relations Review*, 40:3, April 1987, pp. 406–421. Ms. Gramm found that strikes occurred in 13.25 percent of all negotiations.

[6] Cynthia L. Gramm, "The Determinants of Strike Incidence and Severity," *Industrial and Labor Relations Review*, 39:3, April 1986, pp. 361–375. See also Woodruff Imberman, "Who Strikes and Why," *Harvard Business Review*, 61:6, November–December 1983), pp. 18ff.

lective bargaining. William Serrin, chief labor reporter for *The New York Times,* put it this way:

> A strike does not necessarily mean negotiations have broken down, only that an impasse still exists or that it simply is not time to settle.[7]

Put in the most extreme form, strikes and the threat of strikes are said to be necessary to make the collective bargaining process work.

What are the positive functions of a strike? How does a strike make collective bargaining work? John Dunlop has listed four functions of the strike:[8]

1 *A strike helps to persuade each side to modify its position in a negotiation.* The pressure of the strike is an independent force compelling both sides toward agreement. This is the most significant and general function of a strike.

2 *A strike may contribute to changing the relationships between bargainers and their constituents.* For example, a management negotiator may want to offer a higher wage increase to the union than his supervisors will permit. But a strike may cause them to urge the negotiator to make the higher offer and so settle the dispute.

3 *A strike may be necessary to change the budget allotments of a government agency.* This is often the function of a strike in the public sector. In negotiations the union may demand increases in compensation greater than those budgeted by the government agency. In the absence of a strike or threat of a strike, the impasse between the agency and the union could continue indefinitely. A strike, however, often generates enough response from public officials, or even the voters, that a rearrangement of budget priorities may occur, allowing a settlement of the dispute.

4 *A strike may be necessary to change bargaining structure.* For example, in 1971 the Bell Telephone System had some 130 contracts expiring over a period of four months. The Communication Worker Unions and the Bell System wanted to get closer to national bargaining. As the local agreements began to expire at the end of April, the CWA extended them on a day-to-day basis. On May 23 the CWA rejected the company's offer for a pattern-setting local agreement. The CWA asked for a strike vote, and received authorization from the employees to call a strike. On June 15, CWA President Bierre set the strike date for July 14. By July 14 virtually all CWA contracts with the Bell System had expired. The strike began on July 14, and was settled one week later. The new agreement established the same expiration dates for almost all contracts, and in 1974 the CWA and the Bell System participated for the first time in what were truly national negotiations.

Theoreticians of the bargaining process make considerable reference to the work stoppage. In describing bargaining power, much emphasis is placed on the strike or work stoppage as the means by which the parties are brought to agreement. This process is shown in Figure 11-2.[9]

---

[7] William Serrin, "Byzantine Strategy in the Transit Talks," *The New York Times,* Mar. 29, 1980.

[8] Adapted from John T. Dunlop, "The Function of the Strike," in John T. Dunlop and N. W. Chamberlain, eds., *Frontiers of Collective Bargaining* (New York: Harper, 1967), p. 120.

[9] John Hicks, *The Theory of Wages,* 2d ed. (New York: St. Martin's, 1966), pp. 146–147. A similar diagram appears in Richard E. Walton and Robert B. McKersie, *A Behavioral Theory of Labor Negotiations* (New York: McGraw-Hill, 1965), p. 56, associated with work done by E. Robert Livernash.

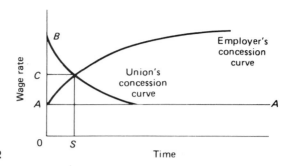

FIGURE 11-2

The diagram is subject to varying interpretations. The essential features are the definition of an employer's concession curve, which begins at *A*, the existing wage rate, and rises over time; and a union's concession curve, which begins at *B*, some desired wage rate well above the current scale, and falls in time toward *A*. The intersection point of the two curves defines a wage rate *C* and a time *S* at which a settlement takes place. But what does the time axis measure? Presumably, it is the duration of a work stoppage, since without a work stoppage, the simple passage of time might not make either party alter its initial position (i.e., the employer's curve would be a straight horizontal line at *A* and the union's curve, a straight horizontal line at *B*). A stalemate would be pictured. In fact, of course, this sometimes happens when a work stoppage is prohibited by law. In the federal government, for example, strikes are illegal and disputes between the employer (a federal agency) and the unions may continue almost indefinitely without either side altering its position.

The diagram may also be used to show other patterns of bargaining. For example, a strike sometimes causes the union's concession curve to *rise*, not fall. That is, as a strike proceeds, the union leadership insists on a higher wage increase than it had before, in order to get the workers back to work and then compensate them for time lost in the strike. Figure 11-3 illustrates this situation. (The union's concession curve should really be given a differ-

FIGURE 11-3

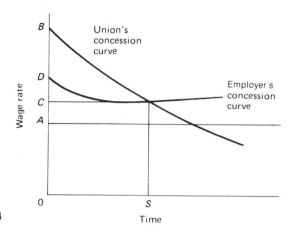

FIGURE 11-4

ent name in this situation.) Alternatively, a strike may induce management to lessen its offer because the company's offer before the strike was high, in hopes of avoiding the costs of a strike (Figure 11-4, point *D*). After the strike was under way, the company could no longer afford its earlier offer. Figure 11-4 describes this situation.

The circumstances of Figures 11-3 and 11-4 can be combined. If a strike causes the union to raise its settlement objective and the company to lower its offers, the result can be a stalemate. Figure 11-5 illustrates this situation. Surprisingly, this situation often occurs in the period immediately following the start of a strike. If it persists, either the company goes out of business or it replaces the union workers, and the union loses the strike.

Ordinarily, however, the progress of a strike tends to cause both sides to make concessions to get an agreement and end the work stoppage. Figure 11-6 illustrates what is probably the most common sequence of events in a work stoppage: the advent of the strike tends initially to deepen the dispute by widening the positions of the parties, but thereafter the gap is closed as the strike wears on.

FIGURE 11-5

FIGURE 11-6

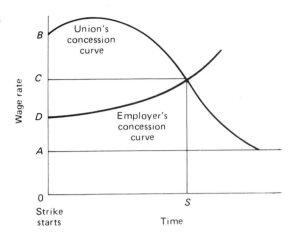

COPING WITH STRIKES

Union Preparations

In preparing for a strike a union must consider three major items:

1 Being sure that the strike is effective
2 Organizing picket lines to keep the strike effective
3 Providing financial support for strikers

The first item is the most important. If a strike is to be effective, it must involve most of the persons in the bargaining unit. The purpose of the strike is to halt the employer's business activity and so bring pressure on the company to settle the dispute that has prompted the strike. The union's attempt to halt the employer's business is often answered by the employer's attempts to keep the business going, as we shall see in the next section.

If the union cannot get employees to quit working, the strike will be ineffective. Some strikes are ineffective. The union's call for a strike is answered with apathy by the employees, many of whom continue working. This is about the worst setback a union can receive. It undermines the union's bargaining position in a strike and calls into question the degree to which the union has the confidence of employees in *any* matter. As a result, an ineffective strike is often followed by a petition to decertify the union as bargaining representative for the employees.

Since the stakes are very high, unions are usually careful to call strikes only when union leadership knows the employees will actually cease work. The union leadership will build up strike talk over a period. It will keep employees informed of developments in negotiations and will prepare the employees for a strike call. The leadership will look for a "strike issue"—some matter of importance to the employees, which can generate the emotional concern necessary to sustain a strike.

A good strike issue depends on the workers' concerns of the moment.[10] Sometimes a wage increase is of great significance to the workers. At other times job security, or even work rules, can be of great concern to employees. In the 1959 steel negotiations, for example, a dispute between the union and the Basic Steel Negotiating Committee of the companies over the size of a wage increase seemed of little interest to the employees. The union could not expect much employee support for a nationwide strike over an increase of a few cents per hour. Inflation was low, job security was reasonable, and workers were not militant about these issues. But when the companies proposed a revision of work rules and at one sweep seemed to threaten the wage levels, working conditions, and job assignments of many steel workers, the union knew it had found a strike issue. The result was a strike of more than 100 days, which ended with no change in the work rules section (section 2B) of the contract.

In order to establish a moral basis for the strike, unions often take a strike vote prior to actually calling a work stoppage. If a majority rejects the motion for a strike, the leadership probably will not call it. However, if a majority votes for a strike, then the union leadership may claim a mandate to call the strike. Also, the majority's authorization of the strike is a strong argument to use in getting somewhat apathetic employees to join the strike.

Once the strike is under way, the union must organize picketing and other strike activity. Picketing is very much regulated by national law and often by local municipal ordinances dealing with public order. The union must organize picketing in conformance with legal requirements or be prepared to confront the consequences of illegal behavior.

The union must also seek to provide financial support for employees who are on strike while their paychecks are cut off. Many national unions maintain funds for the support of strikers. But the level of benefits provided, rules for eligibility, and ability to pay benefits differ from union to union.

Employer Preparations

Operation during a Strike   Employers are aware that the effect of a strike depends critically on the strikers' ability to halt the employer's operations. This focuses the employer's strike preparations on the question of whether or not to attempt to continue to operate the facility during the strike. If the facility can be operated, the strike will have little ability to force the employer into concessions in the bargaining process.

There are three ways to operate facilities in the course of a strike. The first, simplest, and least hazardous method is to take advantage of an ineffective strike. If many employees do not join the strike, it is possible that they will be

---

[10] Woodruff Imberman, "Who Strikes—and Why?" *Harvard Business Review*, 61:6, November–December 1983, pp. 18–28.

able to operate the plant. But a union that conducts its affairs well is not likely to call a strike that is ineffective in getting employees to walk out.

The second method of operating during a strike is to use supervisory personnel to run equipment. In industries that involve much mechanization or automation and consequently a small work force, operation with supervisors is a real possibility. In the telephone industry, for example, most normal operations of the company can be continued by supervisors during a strike. But maintenance, which requires skilled people, and new installations, which are labor-intensive, ordinarily cannot be kept up by supervisors. In the oil industry, refineries can be operated without striking employees, but maintenance becomes a problem. In industries like automotive assembly, electronics assembly, and textile manufacturing, it is virtually impossible to think of operation with supervisors alone. Furthermore, *full* operation by supervisors is ordinarily a short-term expedient at best. This is because lack of maintenance brings operations to a halt or because physical exhaustion overtakes the supervisors themselves. *Partial* operations, however, may be continued in some industries virtually indefinitely.

The third procedure by which struck plants can be operated is by the hiring of replacements for the strikers. In the United States the hiring of replacements on either a temporary or a permanent basis by the employer is legal when employees are engaged in an "economic" strike, i.e., one that is part of a collective bargaining dispute. If the employer has caused the strike by an unfair labor practice, the hiring of replacements is not permitted. Because replacements may legally be hired for economic strikers, it is sometimes said that economic strikers are literally gambling with their jobs.[11]

A company that replaces strikers risks creating great bitterness among its employees who are on strike and risks emotional outbursts that may be violent. Historically, unions have bitterly resented replacements for strikers—calling them "strikebreakers," "scabs," and similar names. The operation of plants by replacements will often invite violence and will usually require police protection of the plants and the replacements. For this reason, many companies do not consider the use of replacements during strikes. Others do, however.[12]

The major strikes that unions have lost in the United States in recent years share the characteristic that the employer has been able to obtain replacements and operate indefinitely in the face of the strike. This is true, for example, of the Florida East Coast Railway strike, which after several years found the railway operating nonunion with replacements. A Los Angeles paper replaced striking reporters, and *The Washington Post* replaced striking pressmen; strikes against those newspapers were defeated. Phelps-Dodge

---

[11] Burr E. Anderson, "Permanent Replacement of Strikers...," *The John Marshall Law Review,* 18:2, Winter 1985, pp. 321–340.

[12] Charles R. Perry and Andrew M. Kramer, *Operating during Strikes* (Philadelphia: Wharton School Industrial Research Unit, University of Pennsylvania, 1982).

Corporation hired replacements and defeated a strike at its copper mining facilities in Arizona.[13]

A Checklist of Management Preparations   In preparing for a strike, management has many things about which to be concerned. A brief list of items that must be considered is given below. The list demonstrates how serious an event a strike is for a company and why it must not be entered into without careful forethought.

- What will be the reaction of nonstriking employees to picket lines?
- How large is the company's inventory? Can customer orders be filled out of inventory for any sustained time?
- Can distribution to customers be maintained through picket lines?
- Will the company lose customers permanently if they are not currently supplied?

If the company decides to try to operate during a strike, it has other significant questions to answer:[14]

- Will salaried personnel volunteer to work during the strike? How will they be paid? At what rates—their own, or those of the workers they replace? How will overtime be compensated?
- Can contractors be brought in? Can power be maintained from the plant's own power plant? Can sabotage by workers who are still in the plant at the start of the strike be avoided? Will the local utility company provide repair services during the strike?
- Can the plant's output be picked up by truck? Will railways provide assistance? Can customers be assured of delivery?
- How will garbage and refuse be picked up? How will food services be provided? Will supervisors and replacements have to live in the plant? Where will they be bedded? Fed?
- How will the strike be monitored? Will supervisors be willing to photograph picket-line activity? Can a strike "log" be kept? Should separate gates be set up for outside contractors?

EMERGENCY STRIKES

We have seen that the strike has a function to perform in making collective bargaining work. Nonetheless, strikes cause inconvenience for those involved and often for the public as well. Strikes sometimes involve disruptions of the public peace. And since strikes are essentially a resort to eco-

---

[13] Robert Roper, "Copper Strikers Refuse to Give Up," *Labor Notes* (Detroit, Michigan), Nov. 20, 1984, pp. 3 and 14.

[14] Leonard C. Scott, "Running a Struck Plant: Some Dos and Don'ts," *S. A. M. Advanced Management Journal*, 38:4, October 1973, pp. 58–61. See also Lee T. Paterson and John Liebert, *Management Strike Handbook* (Chicago: International Personnel Management Association, 1978).

nomic compulsion as a method of resolving disputes, they may seem somewhat barbaric as measured against more peaceful means of settlement.

Much attention has been devoted to developing methods of avoiding strikes. Perhaps the most direct method that can be conceived is simply to prohibit them legally. And, in fact, strikes have often been the subject of legal prohibitions. In the United States today, it is illegal for private employees to conduct strikes for many purposes and it is illegal for most public employees to conduct strikes for any reason (see Chapter 20).

Certain categories of strikes in private industry that are believed to imperil the national health and safety are covered by emergency dispute procedures. The objective of these procedures is to delay strikes and achieve settlement of outstanding issues. The methods used seek to be orderly and uniform in application. They are intended to involve a minimum of direct compulsion and are designed so as not to impose greater hardships on one party than on the other. Maximum scope is left for settlement of the dispute by direct action.[15]

Authority to deal with the labor disputes that create national emergencies rests with the President of the United States, primarily by virtue of the Labor-Management Relations Act, 1947, as amended, and the Railway Labor Act, as amended. The policy permeating both laws is one of encouraging free collective bargaining with a minimum of government intervention. Both rely heavily on mediation and conciliation as the primary government role, and both encourage, rather than impose, voluntary arbitration of collective bargaining disputes.

Both acts contain provisions for dealing with disputes of national dimensions that do not respond to mediation. In both, the status quo, or cooling-off, period—imposed by injunction in the LMRA and by statutory mandate enforceable by injunction in the RLA—is of limited duration. After the cooling-off period expires, the parties are free to use strikes or lockouts. The common terminal provision, either by language of the law or by custom, is the referral of the matter to the Congress by the President.

There is sometimes a controversy about whether or not a national emergency actually exists. In the coal strike of 1977–1978, President Carter announced such an emergency, but researchers since have criticized his finding.[16]

It is the duty of the Federal Mediation and Conciliation Service to assist parties to labor disputes subject to the LMRA to settle such disputes through conciliation and mediation. The statute requires a party desiring termination or modification of a collective bargaining contract to serve written notice on the other party 60 days prior to the proposed termination, modification, or expiration date. It also requires a 30-day notice to the Federal Mediation and Conciliation Service and any available state mediating agency. FMCS may offer its services in any dispute on its own motion.

---

[15] John L. Blackman, Jr., *Presidential Seizure in Labor Disputes* (Cambridge, Mass.: Harvard University Press, 1967).

[16] John A. Ackerman, "The Impact of the Coal Strike of 1977–78," *Industrial and Labor Relations Review*, 32:2, January 1979, pp. 189–195.

The emergency provisions of the Labor-Management Relations Act come into play whenever, in the opinion of the President,

a threatened or actual strike or lockout affecting an entire industry or a substantial part thereof engaged in trade, commerce, transportation, transmission, or communication among the several States or with foreign nations, or engaged in the production of goods for commerce, will, if permitted to occur or to continue, imperil the national health or safety.

Under these provisions, the President may appoint a board of inquiry to investigate the issues involved in the dispute, to ascertain the facts with respect to the causes and circumstances of the dispute, and to report to him within such time as he prescribes. The statute expressly prohibits the board from making any recommendations.

Upon receiving a report from the board, the President may direct the attorney general to petition a U.S. district court having jurisdiction over the parties to enjoin such strike or lockout. If the court finds the threatened or actual strike or lockout meets the criteria of a national emergency, it may issue the injunction.

When an injunction has been issued, the parties are under a legal obligation to make every effort to adjust and settle their differences, with the assistance of the Federal Mediation and Conciliation Service. At the end of a 60-day period, unless the dispute has been settled by that time, the board of inquiry reports to the President on the current positions of the parties, efforts made for settlement, and what the employer's last offer of settlement was.

The NLRB, within the succeeding 15 days, may take a secret ballot of the employees of each employer involved in the dispute on the question of whether they wish to accept the final offer of settlement made by their employer; the NLRB then certifies the results to the attorney general within 5 days.

Upon certification of the results of the ballot, or upon a settlement's being reached, whichever happens sooner, the injunction must be discharged. The President must then present a comprehensive report to the Congress. The parties are thereafter free to resume any strike or lockout.

The procedures exclude from coverage matters subject to the Railway Act, as well as employees of states or political subdivisions thereof. The provisions of the Railway Labor Act dealing with dispute settlement are somewhat different.

It will be noticed that these procedures do not unconditionally prohibit a strike, nor do they provide any specific method of ending the dispute (e.g., compulsory arbitration). They are, therefore, incomplete procedures. Why is this?

"The simplest way to cope with strikes threatening public injury is to ban them," Theodore Kheel testified to a Senate subcommittee. "But that removes the incentive for labor as well as management to adjust their differences." Therefore, Kheel argued, if strikes are to be banned, some form of compulsory arbitration to settle the dispute must be provided. But Senator Robert A. Taft, author of the Taft-Hartley Act and its emergency disputes provisions, was adamantly opposed to compulsory arbitration. He feared it was a step in the direction of government control of wages and prices. So he left the process open-ended after the 80-day cooling-off period. The President was left to do whatever he believed necessary to end the dispute. In an extreme situation, the President can ask Congress to pass a law ending the dispute by setting forth terms of settlement.

> Of course we would like assurance in advance that such strikes will not take place. But it is naive to believe that procedures prescribed in advance that ban strikes and necessarily invoke compulsory arbitration will give us the security we would like to have. We have security in the knowledge that Congress can act to protect us if that becomes necessary.[17]

Kheel referred to this policy as the "policy of ad hoc." It is a policy American Presidents have always followed.

Ad hoc reaction has the advantage that it is unpredictable by the parties and can be suited to the occasion. It therefore permits the President generally to achieve what George Shultz has described as "the great importance of having private parties *be* responsible, *feel* responsible and *take responsibility*" for the settlement of the dispute.[18]

Taft-Hartley's emergency dispute provisions have been invoked only 32 times since the law was passed. In four instances, the disputes were settled before an injunction was issued. Fifteen of the remaining 27 disputes were settled within the 80-day cooling-off period, and 13 were settled afterward. Of those settled after the expiration of the cooling-off period, 5 of the 13 were settled without a strike, while 8 were settled after strikes of varying duration. In only one case was Congress called upon to legislate, and that dispute, the West Coast longshore controversy, was settled before the law was signed.

SETTLING DISPUTES

Mediation

What Is Mediation? Mediation is a process by which a neutral party attempts to help disputing parties reach a settlement of the issues that divide them. Mediation ordinarily does *not* involve the neutral party's acting as a judge, i.e., deciding the resolution of the dispute (a process referred to as "arbitration"). Instead, mediation is a process of persuading the parties to reach an agreement. Mediation of labor disputes has been described as involving "the continuum of possible functions of an impartial person in the

---

[17] Theodore W. Kheel, Jr., "Statement on Emergency Disputes Legislation," Senate Subcommittee on Labor, Mar. 14, 1972, text in Bureau of National Affairs, *Daily Labor Report* No. 51, Mar. 14, 1972.

[18] George P. Shultz, "Strikes: The Private Stake and the Public Interest," Selected Papers No. 8, Chicago Graduate School of Business, 1963.

collective bargaining relationship, beginning with the common idioms of conciliation and going across the scale to, but not including, arbitration."[19]

The continuum spoken of is surprisingly wide. In the past, Americans distinguished various points along the continuum with different terms, as the quotation above implies. "Conciliation" was the least complex process. It involved the attempt to persuade disputing parties to meet and discuss their problems. Often in labor disputes one or the other of the parties refused to acknowledge the other. Conciliation's purpose was, in effect, reconciliation of disputing parties, and its effectiveness resulted from the likelihood that if the parties could be persuaded to meet, they might find a resolution of their dispute. Certainly, they were not likely to settle the dispute if they did not meet. The advent of the National Labor Relations Act, which imposed a legal duty to bargain on management and later (in 1947) on labor also, has largely vitiated the role of conciliation per se.

Mediation has always been a more active process than conciliation. A list of the functions of mediators prepared by William E. Simkin, a former director of the Federal Mediation and Conciliation Service, distinguishes among three categories: procedural suggestions, communication facilitation, and more affirmative actions. Procedural functions include scheduling, conducting, and controlling meetings; establishing and/or extending deadlines; keeping records; and fending off other outside intervention if it is believed likely to be counterproductive. Communication functions include keeping channels open and "gatekeeping." Gatekeeping refers to times when one side would be willing to make a concession on an issue but is afraid that it would be construed as weakness. It may tell the mediator, however, who can suggest that plan to the other side to test for a reaction. Affirmative action functions include ordering priorities; deflating extreme stands or preventing their occurrence; offering creative, substantive suggestions; and making recommendations on individual issues or packages.[20]

Successful mediation depends to a very substantial degree on the skills of the mediator. A mediator who is not acceptable to the parties is useless. But an acceptable mediator who does not know how to assist the parties in reaching an agreement is also useless.[21]

Mediation Agencies   Any person who is acceptable to the parties to a dispute may serve as a mediator. Priests, public officials, college professors, prominent citizens, and other such persons have served as mediators in labor disputes. But the volume of collective bargaining disputes is so large in our country, and the role of mediation so potentially helpful, that various states and the federal government have established public mediation agencies. The most important of these agencies is the Federal Mediation and Conciliation

---

[19] William E. Simkin, *Mediation and the Dynamics of Collective Bargaining*, 2d ed. (Washington, D.C.: Bureau of National Affairs, 1986), p. 27.

[20] Ibid., p. 77.

[21] Deborah M. Kolb, *The Mediators* (Cambridge, Mass.: MIT Press, 1983).

Service (FMCS). FMCS was created by Title II of the Taft-Hartley Act in 1947 and was built upon the conciliation service then existing in the Department of Labor.

FMCS mediators and those employed by the various state mediation agencies are professional mediators drawn generally from the ranks of experienced labor and management representatives.[22] Both labor and management in the United States currently accept, indeed favor, the government's assistance in the resolution of labor disputes through the activity of the various mediation agencies.

An interesting innovation in the work of FMCS is the relations by objectives (RBO) program. The program had its inception in the application of behavioral science techniques to labor-management relations. As described by *Business Week*, the application of one RBO program was as follows:

> Until recently, labor-management relations at Georgia-Pacific Corp.'s pulp and paper mill at Woodland, Me., were about as unpleasant as possible. Long-simmering disputes had damaged morale in the 700-person work force. Disgruntled workers filed grievances over minor annoyances and frequently went on wildcat walkouts. When the plant's five unions struck for three weeks last spring, a portion of nearby U.S. Route 1 had to be closed to protect motorists from strike-related violence.
>
> Though all is still not sweetness and light at Woodland, the situation has greatly improved in the past few months, largely through third-party help by the Federal Mediation and Conciliation Service. But it was not the traditional FMCS role as a mediator in bargaining disputes that brought about the change.
>
> The FMCS's involvement is part of an experimental program, called "Relations by Objective" (RBO), in which the agency provides the expertise for prodding labor and management toward fundamental changes in their basic relationship. The program is aimed at helping employers and unions, hampered by rigid adversary procedures, to root out conflicts and establish new means of dealing with them. Under the supervision of federal mediators, union and management analyze their problems, decide what they would like to see in an ideal relationship, and discuss how to implement these goals....
>
> No one claims that RBO is a panacea for all labor problems at Georgia-Pacific, but both sides say it has improved relations considerably. "When we have a problem, we can just sit down and discuss it," says Yardley [a management representative]. "Eighty percent of the time we get a solution right away. Before, there would have been a grievance filed, and it probably would have gone to arbitration."
>
> Will Sawyer, Woodland's director of industrial relations, is also enthusiastic about the results. "We had an old problem over a modification of work hours for auto mechanics. Under the program, we reached agreement in one meeting. We've had a substantial reduction in the number of grievances, and the grievances that are filed seem to be more meritorious."[23]

---

[22] William E. Simkin, "Code of Professional Conduct for Labor Mediators," *Labor Law Journal*, 15:10, October 1964, pp. 626–637.

[23] "U.S. Mediators Try a New Role," *Business Week*, Apr. 21, 1975, p. 108. See also FMCS, *Report*, 1975, pp. 44–45. Another report on the Georgia-Pacific program appeared in the *AFL-CIO News*, 20:14, Apr. 5, 1975, p. 1.

Arbitration

What Is Arbitration?   Arbitration is a process by which an answer is provided for issues in dispute. Whereas the focus in mediation is on bringing the parties to some agreement, the focus in arbitration is on what the agreement should be. Arbitration, therefore, is like seeking a decision from a judge in a court proceeding. It is a quasi-legal procedure. Sometimes the parties accept an arbitration award as settling their dispute; sometimes they do not.

There are many forms of arbitration. The old meaning of the term in labor relations (in the nineteenth and early twentieth centuries) was analogous to the procedure that we now call collective bargaining. When a dispute arose between an employer and unionized workers, a panel of union representatives and management representatives was assembled to "arbitrate" (i.e., to settle) the dispute. The panel was to make a decision about the dispute that was binding on both sides. In recent times, we have used the term "arbitration" primarily to refer to the decision made by a *neutral* party (but not a court) about a dispute. But some remnants of the old usage continue in cases when panels of labor and management meet to resolve disputes without a neutral.

Recently arbitration has been combined with mediation in a process called "Med-Arb." The process operates by selecting a person as arbitrator of a dispute, but having him or her first attempt to mediate a settlement between the parties. The authority to arbitrate the dispute (that is, to decide it) adds weight to a mediator's recommendations. Mediation is attempted because it is preferred to arbitration because a mediated settlement is one both parties are likely to accept in good faith and attempt to make work, since they made the settlement. An arbitration decision may be binding but is likely to please only one or neither side.[24]

The Council of Industrial Relations   The CIR is a national bipartite tribunal of the International Brotherhood of Electrical Workers and the National Electrical Contractors Association.[25] The CIR renders final and binding decisions in both contract and grievance disputes, and it applies to virtually all agreements (95 percent) in the electrical branch of the industry. To date in its 50-year history the CIR has made more than 2500 decisions, with most rendered since 1947.[26]

---

[24] Jerome H. Ross, "The Med-Arb Process in Labor Agreement Negotiations," Society for Professionals in Dispute Resolution, Occasional Paper No. 21-1, Feb. 1982, Washington, D.C.

[25] Donald J. White, "The Council on Industrial Relations," Industrial Relations Research Association, *Proceedings*, 1971, pp. 16–24, is the primary source for this material on the CIR.

[26] Apart from numerous articles appearing in the monthly *IBEW Journal* and the NECA's monthly *Qualified Contractor*, the following sources contain information on the council: James J. Healy, ed., *Creative Collective Bargaining* (Englewood Cliffs, N.J.: Prentice-Hall, 1965), pp. 89–95; *Congressional Record-Appendix*, May 24, 1962, p. A3876 (remarks of Senator Wayne Morse and article by John D. Pomfret of *The New York Times*); J. Shaughnessy, "Some Aspects of Collective Bargaining in the Electrical Contracting Industry," unpublished dissertation, Catholic University

The council clause, which is incorporated in local union agreements, specifies essentially that "there shall be no stoppage of work either by strike or lockout because of any proposed changes in this agreement or disputes over matters relating to this agreement." It establishes a local labor-management committee consisting of three employers and three union representatives, with all matters to be determined by majority vote. Should that committee fail to adjust the dispute, the clause provides that "such shall then be referred to the Council of Industrial Relations for the Electrical Contracting Industry. Its decision shall be final and binding on both parties hereto." The clause is "evergreen"; that is, it continues to bind the parties without a time limitation unless it is removed by agreement of the local union and its employing contractors. It may not be exercised unilaterally.

The council mechanism is supplemented by an informal arrangement between the NECA and the IBEW, under which in the instance of an unresolved dispute the chairperson or secretary of the local committee is to notify the appropriate IBEW vice president and the regional director of the NECA so that their representatives may assist the local committee in reaching an agreement. This procedure has resolved disputes in an unknown but significant number of cases. Those not resolved have gone to the CIR. The CIR meets quarterly in Washington, D.C., and operates with panels of 12 members, 6 appointed by the international president of the IBEW and 6 by the president of the NECA; the two presidents serve as co-chairpersons of the council. All decisions are by unanimous vote. The CIR has never utilized outside neutrals. With the exception of one case, CIR decisions have been respected and there have been no strikes or lockouts.

The CIR is tailored to fit the characteristics of the industrial relations system in the electrical contracting industry. It has sought to minimize work stoppages and to promote high-quality performance using productive, modern methods. As IBEW President Tracy put it in 1939, "We are on record as willing to cooperate. We know that the interests of neither electrical workers nor electrical contractors can permanently be advanced without the method of rational compromise." This task was performed in an industry expanding secularly, but nevertheless an industry with so few barriers to entry that it is populated by very small employers. Because of low capital requirements, nonunion competition constitutes an ever-present challenge. The fashioning and evolution of the CIR have been a joint effort by national leaders to generate a philosophy and structure of bargaining that would best serve the perceived long-run interests of the respective organizations and their members.

of America, June 1949; Mulcaire, *The International Brotherhood of Electrical Workers, Studies in the Social Sciences,* vol. V (Washington, D.C.: Catholic University of America, 1923), pp. 146–156; M. H. Hedges, *A Strikeless Industry* (New York: John Day, 1930); *The Council on Industrial Relations for the Electrical Contracting Industry,* 9th ed., published by the council, Washington, D.C., January 1968; Derek Bok and John Dunlop, *Labor in the American Community* (New York: Simon and Schuster, 1970), p. 242.

Types of Arbitration by Neutrals In arbitration by a neutral, each side of a dispute presents its position on disputed matters to the arbitrator and the arbitrator decides on what the disposition of each issue should be. Arbitration may be final, or it may be advisory. Final arbitration means the dispute is to be settled on the basis of the arbitrator's decision. Advisory arbitration envisages that the parties will negotiate a settlement using the arbitration decision (the "award") as a guide, but not necessarily holding to it.

Arbitration may be binding or nonbinding. An award is binding if the parties are committed to its acceptance. An award is nonbinding if they may choose to accept it or not. In grievance arbitration (described in detail in Chapter 12), approximately 95 percent of all arbitrators' decisions are binding on the parties (estimate from the American Arbitration Association).

Arbitration may be voluntary or compulsory. It is voluntary if the parties have agreed to utilize the process, and it is compulsory if a government agency requires them to accept arbitration.

These categories allow considerable variations in the form of arbitration employed to settle disputes. Thus, there may be voluntary binding arbitration or voluntary nonbinding arbitration. Similarly, there may be compulsory binding arbitration or compulsory nonbinding arbitration. (Incidentally, nonbinding arbitration is very much like mediation, except that an arbitrator's advice will ordinarily concern the way the parties *should* dispose of the issues, whereas a mediator's recommendations will concern the way he or she thinks the parties can *agree* to dispose of the issues.)

In the United States today, voluntary binding arbitration (involving neutrals) is the primary method of resolution of grievances arising over the terms of collective bargaining disputes.

Grievances are referred to as disputes over *rights,* since they arise from rights of employees or employers that are created by the collective bargaining agreement. Disputes over the terms of new contracts, i.e., in collective bargaining negotiations, are referred to as disputes over *interests,* since they involve the conflicting interests of the two parties. Grievance arbitration is therefore called "rights arbitration" and is, as we have said, very common in the United States. Arbitration of disputes over the terms of collective bargaining agreements is referred to as "interest arbitration." It has been very uncommon in the United States. For the most part, neither unions nor employers in the private sector have been willing to submit such important issues as general wage changes, the establishment of fringe benefits, and working conditions and work rules to neutrals for disposition. They have preferred to rely on collective bargaining and associated economic pressure (i.e., strikes and lockouts) to reach settlement of such issues.[27] Changing circumstances in recent years have generated increasing discussion of interest arbitration, but with one or two exceptions (especially in the steel industry, see Chapter

[27] Raymond A. Smardon, "Arbitration Is No Bargain," *Nation's Business,* October 1974. pp. 80–83.

18), there has been no substantial movement toward interest arbitration in the private sector.[28] In the public sector, however, there has been a greater resort to interest arbitration (see Chapter 20).

ALTERNATIVES TO STRIKES

The Decline of the Strike

The strike has important functions to perform in collective bargaining, but it may be an increasingly uncomfortable tool for unions to use. In 1972 George Meany expressed the view that in the 1970s strikes had become more "painful" than in the 1930s and had "more far-reaching effects." In earlier years, when workers were earning 60 to 70 cents an hour, Meany said, it did not take much in the way of financial aid to keep a family going during a strike, nor did it take long for a family to recover once a strike was settled.

> Things are different today. Simply because collective bargaining has raised living standards and improved and stabilized the financial situation of workers, workers have a great deal more to lose. They have mortgage payments and car payments and college-tuition payments to make—things that did not burden them years ago.

Not only have strikes become more serious for workers, he said, but they are also having a greater impact on industry:

> I have never been enchanted with strikes. They are not fun—they are grim. There are casualties in every strike—economic, human, social casualties. And I'd like to avoid any of these consequences.
>
> Any responsible labor leader considers, as I do, that a strike is never more than the lesser of two evils, adopted by workers as a last resort to protest some grievance that, to them, is worse than not working at all.[29]

The erosion of the strike as a means of settling disputes has also been suggested by John Dunlop, who in 1967 listed the following factors as contributing to the decline of the strike:

1 *Increased ability* of companies to operate during strikes because of automation and increased proportion of professional and supervisory employees.

2 *Unfavorable customer response* (such as beginning to buy from foreign sources).

3 *Increased complexity* of issues, which prevents eleventh-hour pressure settlements. The need for consensus on some issues also prevents use of coercion.[30]

Figure 11-7 shows the decline in days lost due to strikes in American industry from 1947 to 1987.

---

[28] "Arbitration Instead of Strikes," *Industry Week*, 183:2, Oct. 14, 1974, pp. 30–35.
[29] *The New York Times*, May 21, 1972.
[30] Adapted from John T. Dunlop, "The Function of the Strike," in John T. Dunlop and N. W. Chamberlain, eds., *Frontiers of Collective Bargaining* (New York: Harper, 1967), pp. 111–116.

FIGURE 11-7   Days idle due to strikes as a percent of total time worked in the total economy of the United States, 1947–1987. *(Source: Bureau of Labor Statistics, Monthly Labor Review, 107:12, December 1987, p. 94.)*

The increasing dissatisfaction of management and labor with work stoppages has long stimulated a search for new techniques of dispute settlement.[31]

Interest arbitration is potentially a major alternative to the strike as a means of resolving impasses in contract negotiations. A broad-interest arbitration is often used for that purpose. In Germany, the inclusion of clauses in collective bargaining agreements which call for arbitration where there is a breakdown of negotiations has been hailed as a major reason for the apparent success of West Germany's system of industrial relations.[32] And in the United States there have been some important experiments with interest arbitration, especially in the glass, paper, and steel industries.[33] Also, arbitration of contract disputes has had considerable use in public employment, as is described in Chapter 20.

CHAPTER SUMMARY

Strikes and lockouts are forms of economic warfare and often bring severe losses to those engaged in them and inconvenience to third parties. Owing to the sometimes serious consequences of work stoppages, it has been proposed that strikes be made illegal. In response, a "right to strike" has been claimed, and the courts and Congress have established the right to strike as well as restrictions on its use. In general, employees of private firms may le-

---

[31] David L. Cole, *The Quest for Industrial Peace* (New York: McGraw-Hill, 1963); and Howard J. Anderson, ed., *New Techniques in Labor Dispute Resolution: A Report of the 23rd Conference of the Association of Labor Mediation Agencies* (Washington, D.C.: Bureau of National Affairs, 1976). See also Peter J. Brennan, ed., *Exploring Alternatives to the Strike*, Reprint No. 2910, Monthly Labor Review, September 1973 (Washington, D.C.: U.S. Department of Labor, 1974).

[32] "West Germany: The Importance of Arbitration," *European Industrial Relations Review*, 55, July 1978, pp. 21–22.

[33] Charles A. Myers, "Voluntary Arbitration of Disputes over New Labor Contracts," *Sloan Management Review*, Fall 1976, pp. 73–79.

gally strike, though not for illegal objectives. Public employees generally have no legal right to strike. Disputes over wages and working conditions are by far the major causes of work stoppages.

Two opposing attitudes toward strikes exist. In one view, strikes are regarded as evidence of a breakdown in the bargaining process. In the other view, strikes are seen as an integral part of the bargaining process with certain functions to perform in bringing the parties to a settlement. In the latter view, therefore, a certain frequency of strikes is to be expected.

Since the stakes are very high, unions are careful to call strikes only when union leadership knows the employees will actually cease work. Once the strike is under way, the union must organize picketing and also try to provide financial support for employees while their paychecks are cut off. The major strikes that unions have lost in the United States have occurred when the employer has been able to obtain replacements and operate indefinitely in the face of the strike. Thus, employers attempt to continue operations of their facilities through the use of employees who do not join the strike, supervisors, or replacements. Because a strike is a serious event for a firm, a number of questions must be given careful forethought, including the question of whether the company will lose customers if there is an interruption in the filling of orders.

The United States has been a strike-prone nation compared to others, but the frequency of strikes in America has declined dramatically in the 1980s.

Certain categories of strikes in private industry are believed to imperil the national health and safety and are controlled by emergency dispute procedures established by the Taft-Hartley Act in 1947. The fundamental process is one of delaying the strike while attempts are made to resolve the underlying disputes. But the strike is not outlawed per se. The primary governmental role is one of mediation and conciliation and is of an ad hoc nature.

Mediation and arbitration are the two primary means of settling disputes. Mediation is the process by which a neutral party assists disputing groups in settling the issues that divide them. The mediator does not act as a judge, but instead persuades the parties to reach an agreement. Successful mediation depends to a very high degree on the skills of the mediator. Among other functions, the mediator handles the procedures and scheduling of meetings and is an important communications link between the disputing parties. Because of the large volume of collective bargaining disputes, the various states and the federal government have set up public mediation agencies. The most important of these is the Federal Mediation and Conciliation Service. A new program, Relations by Objectives, uses behavioral science techniques to prod labor and management toward fundamental changes in their basic relationship.

Arbitration is a quasi-legal process for settling a dispute. Arbitration of contract disputes, "rights" arbitration, may be advisory or final, binding or nonbinding, voluntary or compulsory. It may or may not involve a neutral party in making the decision. The Council of Industrial Relations of the Electrical Construction Industry is a major example of an arbitration body which does not involve a neutral. The council must reach a unanimous decision on the dispute, and its decisions are final and binding. Arbitration over the terms of collective bargaining agreements, or interest arbitration, is very uncommon.

The increasing dissatisfaction of management and labor with work stoppages has stimulated a search for new methods of dispute settlement. Interest arbitration is a potential major alternative to the strike when collective bargaining negotiations fail.

QUESTIONS FOR THOUGHT AND DISCUSSION

1 Are there too many strikes in the United States? Why or why not? Should efforts be made to reduce the number of strikes? If so, what kinds of efforts would be useful?

2 Strike activity in the United States has declined dramatically in the 1980s. Why? Is this good, or not so? For whom?

3 What functions does a strike perform? Could these functions be performed differently? How?

4 What are the most important factors in a union's preparation for a strike? A company's? Why?

5 Should strikes be illegal? Would a prohibition of strikes be effective? Why or why not?

6 What are the most important functions of a mediator? What skills does an effective mediator need to have?

7 How are labor disputes that create national emergencies handled? Why are the procedures "incomplete," noncompulsory, and ad hoc? What actions can the President take to settle the dispute if the situation becomes extreme?

8 What are the differences between arbitration and mediation? What types of arbitration are these?

9 What are the changes in the labor force that have made strikes and work stoppages unattractive as a method of persuasion in disputes? Do you think striking will ever become obsolete? Why or why not?

10 What are arguments for and against the hiring of replacements for striking employees?

SELECTED READING

Baer, Walter E., *Strikes* (New York: ANACOM, 1975).

Blackman, John L., Jr. *Presidential Seizure in Labor Disputes* (Cambridge, Mass.: Harvard University Press, 1967).

Dunlop, John T., *Dispute Resolution* (Dover, Mass.: Auburn House, 1984).

Feuille, Peter, *Final Offer Arbitration* (Chicago: International Personnel Management Association, 1975).

Folberg, Jay, and Alison Taylor, *Mediation: a Comprehensive Guide to Conflict Resolution* (San Francisco, Jossey-Bass, 1984).

Kolb, Deborah M., *The Mediators* (Cambridge, Mass.: MIT Press, 1983).

Levin, Edward, and Daniel V. DeSantis, *Mediation: An Annotated Bibliography* (Ithaca, N.Y.: New York State School of Industrial and Labor Relations, Cornell, 1978).

Loewenberg, J. Joseph, et al., *Compulsory Arbitration: An International Comparison* (Lexington, Mass.: Lexington Books, 1976).

Simkin, William E., *Mediation and the Dynamics of Collective Bargaining*, 2d ed. (Washington, D.C.: Bureau of National Affairs, 1986).

Wheeler, Hoyt N., *Industrial Conflict: An Integrative Theory* (Charleston: University of South Carolina Press, 1986).

12

GRIEVANCES AND ARBITRATION

ADMINISTERING THE COLLECTIVE BARGAINING AGREEMENT

Labor relations involve more than negotiating a labor agreement. In fact, in the view of most management and union officials, the real test of effective labor relations begins after the agreement is signed. The acid test is found in the day-to-day administration of the agreement. From the point of view of the union, it must obtain in practice the employee rights that management has granted on paper. That is, the union must seek to enforce the agreement. From the viewpoint of management, the major concern is to establish its right to manage the business and to keep operations running.

The language of a collective bargaining agreement is generally broad. But the implementation of the agreement involves its application to myriad small details that arise in the day-to-day operation of the enterprise. It has been said that management usually gives away more in the administration of an agreement than in the negotiation of the agreement. Similarly, unions may feel that they sometimes lose in application what they thought they had gained at the bargaining table. Hence, the administration of a collective bargaining agreement is a matter of substantial concern to both management and labor.

HANDLING GRIEVANCES

What Is a Grievance?

A grievance is an alleged violation of the rights of workers on the job. It may occur in one of several forms:

- As a violation of the collective bargaining agreement
- As a violation of federal or state law
- As a violation of past practice
- As a violation of company rules
- As a violation of management's responsibility

A grievance is to be distinguished from a complaint in that a complaint by workers that does not involve one or more of the violations listed above is not a *bona fide* grievance.

Grievances ordinarily arise under the provisions of a collective bargaining agreement. For example, if the contract provides that the workday shall be from 8 a.m. to 5 p.m. and a worker is ordered to report for work at 7 a.m., he or she may file a grievance, alleging a violation of the contract. Whether or not a violation actually exists may be a complicated matter to determine. In the example given, it may be that the company has the right to schedule work at hours other than 8 to 5, but may be required to pay a premium wage scale (e.g., time and a half) for the hour worked from 7 a.m. to 8 a.m.

A violation of federal or state law may serve as the basis for a grievance, since, while a collective bargaining agreement is binding on both parties, it cannot be in violation of the law. A union may therefore pursue a violation of law through the grievance procedure. This is not very common, however, since other places, especially government regulatory agencies, exist as alternatives in which to file charges alleging violations of law.

Violation of past practice by the company may also serve as a basis for grievances. Past practice is a shadowy area for grievances, since to substantiate a grievance the union must show that the practice has existed for a considerable time and has been accepted by both parties.

Violations of company rules by the company ordinarily arise with respect to matters not treated by the collective bargaining agreement. Suppose, for example, that company rules provide for dismissal of a worker after three garnishments (i.e., seizure of his or her paycheck to pay debts), but the worker is discharged after only two such incidents. The worker might protest the company's misapplication of its own rules.[1]

Finally, grievances may arise out of the failure of the company to meet its managerial responsibilities, even if the collective bargaining agreement is silent on the specific matter involved. For example, a union may protest an unsanitary, unhealthy, or poorly lighted workplace, alleging that management has a general responsibility to provide a workplace free of such hazards.

The No-Strike Pledge

Under most collective bargaining agreements grievances are not simply left up to the parties to settle. Too often management and labor are not able to

---

[1] *AFL-CIO Manual for Shop Stewards* (Washington, D.C.: AFL-CIO).

agree on whether a violation by the company has occurred, or they are subsequently not able to decide what should be done about it. When there is no agreement, the parties would ordinarily be left to strike or implement a lockout in support of their position. This does in fact happen in some situations in the United States, and it is the ordinary procedure in Great Britain. But this procedure has certain major disadvantages. Primarily, it threatens to escalate minor grievances into major confrontations, involving work stoppages that affect many people. Because of this danger, it has seemed reasonable in the United States to try to find a method of resolving grievances without resort by either party to economic force. The result has been a procedure that utilizes neutrals to decide disputes that the parties cannot resolve themselves. This procedure is called grievance arbitration.

However, grievance arbitration alone does not prevent strikes or lockouts. After all, the union or company might decide to resort to economic force to settle the dispute before it ever reaches arbitration. Alternatively, either side might refuse to accept the arbitrator's award and resort to economic force to prevent its implementation. Furthermore, management has often been very reluctant to permit a neutral to make decisions affecting its conduct of the business. For management to agree to binding arbitration, there needed to be some *quid pro quo* from the union.

The procedure that has evolved to resolve these various problems is for management to accept binding arbitration of grievances in return for a no-strike pledge by the union. A typical no-strike pledge in a collective bargaining agreement reads as follows:

> It is hereby agreed by the Union and the Company that since this Agreement provides for the orderly and amicable adjustment and settlement of any and all disputes, differences and grievances, there should be no resort to strikes (which includes stoppages or slowdown of work) by the employees nor any lockout by the Company of any employee or group of employees, during the term of this agreement. [The term of a collective bargaining agreement is most often 3 years in the United States. The average term is less, however, because many agreements are 1 or 2 years in duration, but few are more than 3 years. The average term of agreement is, therefore, about 2.5 years.]

This language is legally binding and may be enforced in the courts. It requires the union not to strike over a grievance and requires both management and the union to accept neutral arbitration of unresolved grievances as binding and therefore legally enforceable upon both. The obligations of a union under the no-strike pledge in an agreement are the issue in the case of the "phantom strike," discussed in the Arbitration Exercises at the end of the text.

Probably 90 percent of all collective bargaining agreements in the United States have a no-strike pledge in them, but a large minority of these pledges are conditional in one form or another. In some instances a strike is permitted after the conclusion of the grievance procedure when binding arbitration by a neutral is not provided by the collective bargaining agreement. For example, in the General Motors–UAW agreement, the union is permitted to file grievances over production standards established by the company, but these grievances do not become the subject of arbitration. Instead, the union may strike over unadjusted work standards disputes after a certain number have accumulated. In contrast, in the pulp and paper industry somewhat similar disputes (which involve the wage rates established by the company for newly created jobs) are not submitted to arbitration, but the union rarely strikes about these matters. The accumulated grievances over new job rates are included by the parties in their negotiations at the termination of the existing collective bargaining agreement. In agreements in other industries the union is permitted to strike when the company refuses to honor an arbitration award or refuses to submit a dispute to arbitration.

In some industries, arbitration is not used at all to resolve grievances. For example, under the National Master Freight Agreement between the Teamsters and Trucking Employees, Inc., all grievances must be heard by a joint labor-management committee. A majority vote of the committee members is required to resolve any grievance. The committee comprises an equal number of union and employer representatives (usually three of each).

The Grievance Procedure

Virtually all collective bargaining agreements include some form of grievance procedure. The purposes of the procedure are:

- To settle disputes arising during the life of the agreement
- To establish an orderly method for handling disputes
- To provide for the union's role in processing the grievance of a single employee
- To allow either side to appeal the results of grievance negotiation step by step until a final and binding decision is reached

A complete grievance procedure in American industry would be as shown in Table 12-1.[2] A five-step procedure is somewhat unusual, however. Table 12-2 indicates that the most frequent number of steps in a grievance procedure is three, with arbitration following. A typical three-step procedure is shown in Figure 12-1.

A further aspect of the formal grievance procedure is that the grievance is set out in written form. The written grievance spells out who the grievant is, when the incident leading to the grievance occurred (it may, of course, be ongoing), and where the incident happened. The grievance also indicates why the complaint is considered a grievance and what the

---

[2] Adapted from *AFL-CIO Manual for Shop Stewards.*

TABLE 12-1 A COMPLETE GRIEVANCE PROCEDURE

	Union representative	Company representative	Time limit for management decision	Time limit for union approval
Step 1	Worker and union steward	Supervisor	3 days	3 days
Step 2	Union chief and shop steward	Department or plant superintendent	5 days	5 days
Step 3	Grievance committee chairperson	Personnel director	5 days	5 days
Step 4	Grievance committee chairperson and national union representative	Top	10 days	10 days
Step 5	Arbitration by a neutral			

grievant thinks should be done about the matter. A typical grievance form appears below.

Employee's Name _____ Identification No. _____
Job Title _____ Department _____ Shift _____
Supervisor _____
Nature of the Grievance _____
_____
Adjustment Desired _____
_____
Date _____
Signature of Employee _____
Signature of Union Official _____
(Copies to be distributed to management, steward, grievant)

There are many instances in which the filing of grievances is not limited to the initiative of individual employees. More than a third of the collective bargaining agreements with grievance provisions permit the union to file grievances on its own behalf. In general, these grievances deal with management practices or changes that affect a large number of employees or with rights

TABLE 12-2 STEPS IN GRIEVANCE PROCEDURES
(Frequency Expressed as Percentage of Contracts Containing Grievance Provisions)

	Number of steps					
	1	2	3	4	5	Total
Overall frequency	7	21	46	22	4	100
Manufacturing	3	13	50	29	5	100
Nonmanufacturing	13	34	40	10	3	100

Source: Bureau of National Affairs, *Basic Patterns in Union Contracts: Grievance and Arbitration,* Washington D.C., 1983.

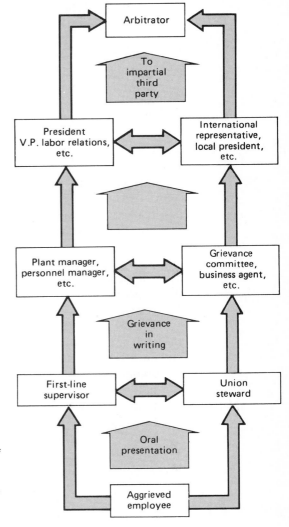

FIGURE 12-1 Typical grievance procedure. *(From Robert W. Eckles et al., Essentials of Management for First-Line Supervision, Wiley, New York, 1974, p. 529.)*

specifically granted to the union under the agreement. Management may file grievances in 28 percent of agreements. Industries in which management is especially likely to be able to file grievances are furniture and electrical machinery manufacturing and the maritime industry.[3]

An example of the specific grievance procedure employed by a major corporation and a union is instructive.

The grievance procedure used by General Motors and the UAW has four basic steps. These steps are outlined in several paragraphs of the national

[3] Bureau of National Affairs, *Basic Patterns in Union Contracts: Grievance and Arbitration* (Washington, D.C., 1983). See also Thomas F. Gideon, "A Comparison of Alternate Grievance Procedures," *Employee Relations Law Journal*, 5:2, Autumn 1979, pp. 222–233.

agreement. The first step is a meeting between the employee and his or her supervisor, since an employee's closest contact with management is through the supervisor. Any time during the discussion, the employee may ask for the services of the union committee member.

A grievance not settled at the first step is then taken to the "step and a half." Here, the employee's union committee member and another member of the shop committee meet with the employee's supervisor and the general supervisor.

Grievances unsettled at this point progress to the second step, a meeting between the shop committee and the labor relations department. These meetings are usually held weekly, with any grievances that are at the second step being discussed.

An appeal of an unsettled grievance to the third step must be approved by the regional director of the union. The regional director decides whether to appeal the grievance after reading both the union's and management's "Statement of Unadjusted Grievance." A meeting would probably involve such personnel as the regional director of the union, the chairperson of the shop committee, the personnel director, and the director of labor relations.

Many unions have a policy that up to this third step in the grievance procedure the grievance "belongs" to the employee. This means that the union will process a grievance through the second (or, in some instances, the third) step of the grievance procedure at the grievant's request. But when the grievance is not settled and reaches the third step of the procedure, then it becomes the union's grievance. This means that the union will now exercise its judgment as to whether or not the grievance has merit, and whether additional time and financial resources of the union should be spent in carrying it forward. Many local unions submit the question of whether to take a grievance to arbitration to a formal vote of the membership.

When a union decides not to carry a grievance forward, the person or persons who brought the grievance are sometimes disappointed. In some instances they try to carry the matter further themselves. This raises the question of their right to do so. In one case, the grievant, an employee of Pabst Brewing Co. in Peoria, Illinois, was discharged. The grievance filed on his behalf by the union was denied by the company. The union then decided not to carry the matter to arbitration. The grievant hired his own attorney, and the question whether the discharged employee had the right to carry the matter to arbitration after the union's decision not to do so was presented to an arbitrator. The arbitrator ruled that the employee did not have such a right. The right to arbitrate under a collective bargaining agreement, the arbitrator ruled, is "not ordinarily incident to the employer-employee relationship.... It is the union which has the right to take grievances to arbitration, not the individual employee."[4]

---

[4] Pabst Brewing Co. and Frank Genusa, Arbitrator John Day Larkin, Oct. 6, 1979, reported in Bureau of National Affairs, *Daily Labor Report* No. 237, Dec. 7, 1979, p. Al.

The final step in the GM-UAW grievance procedure is the appeal to an impartial umpire. Each party presents its case in writing, including a statement of facts and position, to the umpire. A hearing is then usually held for each case. The decision of the umpire is binding on all parties.

One type of grievance, called a "policy" grievance, has been used extensively in the last few years. This type of grievance is one that a union committee member files on behalf of the union.

A formal grievance procedure has several functions:

1 *It provides a mechanism* to adjust employees' complaints or to clarify disputes over the rights and obligations of the employer.

2 *It brings the matter* in a formal, prearranged way to the attention of union officials and management.

3 *It defines and narrows the nature* of the complaint.

4 *It provides a structure* of meetings between union and management at various levels that may result in settlement of the grievance.

From the viewpoint of the American industrial relations system as a whole, the formal grievance process has two major advantages. First, it makes sure that workers can get a hearing for their complaints and that problems are not simply allowed to fester. Second, it identifies and defines specific complaints, thereby permitting isolation of different matters from each other and lessening the likelihood that the accumulation of minor dissatisfactions may lead to major industrial relations problems. In the absence of a formal grievance procedure, there is a tendency for management to disregard employee complaints and for unions to seize upon minor items as the occasion for major disputes (i.e., as "the straw that broke the camel's back"). This sort of occurrence is common in Great Britain and France, for example.

The existence of binding arbitration as the last step in a grievance procedure has an important impact on the process as a whole. As described by a British observer of labor relations: "The instance of an arbitrator as a last recourse during the life of the agreement means that management cannot depend on imposing its views by power and thus is forced to consider its actions before the event as well as to justify them afterwards. This is a vital factor [and is precisely what] has all too often been missing in Britain."[5] An American analyst of grievance procedures emphasized the importance of arbitration in providing credibility to the entire grievance process by noting that "workers are, perhaps, as interested in an assurance of justice *before* the act as in justice through the grievance procedure after the act."[6]

---

[5] A. W. J. Thomson and V. V. Murray, *Grievance Procedures* (Lexington, Mass.: D. C. Heath, 1976), p. 169.

[6] James W. Kuhn, "The Grievance Procedure," in John T. Dunlop and N. W. Chamberlain, eds., *Frontiers of Collective Bargaining* (New York: Harper, 1967), p. 257.

Unfortunately, the mere existence of formal grievance machinery does not ensure that it will work. Sometimes grievances pile up and the formal machinery cannot deal with them all. Delays and frustration result. Sometimes the procedure is at fault, but other times management may be guilty of intentionally delaying the procedure, or the union may be guilty of misusing it by filing so many grievances that the system collapses. In a study of grievance procedures, Harold W. Davey noted, "It is critically important...to remember...that *persons are more important than procedures.*" Whether grievance procedures really work depends on "the talent and tenacity of personnel (both management and union) involved in the pre-arbitration stages."[7]

Attempting to improve the effectiveness of grievance procedures, some managements and unions have begun to utilize mediation prior to the final resort to arbitration. The mediation process is informal—unlike arbitration, which generally involves attorneys, transcripts of proceedings, written opinions, and arbitrators themselves. As such, mediation is less time-consuming and less expensive.[8] But it is not necessarily final, since the mediator makes no decision, and even after mediation there may be an arbitration proceeding.

Research has demonstrated that the structure of a grievance procedure affects the rates and levels of settling grievances and the time it takes to do so.[9] An experiment in the bituminous coal industry, in which the grievance procedure has often been ineffective in preventing strikes over grievances, found that when grievances were mediated prior to arbitration, strikes were substantially reduced.[10] Also, a study of grievance processes in four major industries found that grievance procedures varied in volume of use and effectiveness among industries. Grievance rates per 100 employees were twice as high in basic steel plants as in retail stores and public schools. Perhaps surprisingly, the same study showed that the fairness of the settlement of the grievance when rated by employees on a scale of 1 (low) to 10 (high) was in the 4 to 6 range in each of the four industries. It seems disappointing that the grievance system, now in use some 50 years in American workplaces and credited by outside observers with promoting industrial peace and fair treatment of employees, should get no better endorsement from employees than the midrange of an evaluation scale.[11]

---

[7] Harold W. Davey, "What's Right and What's Wrong with Grievance Arbitration," *The Arbitration Journal*, 28:4, December 1973, p. 217.

[8] "Grievance Mediation," Bureau of National Affairs, *Daily Labor Report* No. 93, May 15, 1987, pp. C1ff. See also Leonard Bierman and Stuart A. Youngblood, "Resolving Unjust Discharge Cases: A Mediatory Approach," *The Arbitration Journal*, 40:1, March 1985, pp. 45–60.

[9] Joseph Lowenberg, "Structure of Grievance Procedures," *Labor Law Journal*, 35, January 1984, pp. 44–51.

[10] Jeanne M. Brett and Stephen B. Goldberg, "Grievance Mediation in the Coal Industry: A Field Experiment," *Industrial and Labor Relations Review*, 37:1, October 1983, pp. 49–69.

[11] David Lewin, "Empirical Measures of Grievance Procedure Effectiveness," *Labor Law Journal*, August 1984, pp. 491–499.

Sources of Grievances

Employers and union officials have long noted the great variety of experience under grievance procedures.[12] Some companies have few grievances filed; some have many. Within a company, some plants have many grievances, some few. And even within a single plant, some departments have few grievances filed, some many. Why do these differences exist?

What factors influence union and management in decisions about grievances? A study showed that unions rarely consider the financial impact of a grievance on management (i.e., if the grievance is lost by management) in deciding whether or not to file a grievance. The more severe the management disciplinary action, the more likely the union was to grieve. Also union leaders were not less inclined to file a grievance just because management discussed the issue with them before taking action. The frequency with which union leaders file grievances is related to how managers perceive union leaders—the more often grievances are filed, the less favorable are management attitudes.[13]

There have been several studies of grievance procedures, some focusing on the personal characteristics of grievants. A statistical study of the 6-year grievance file of one plant of a major corporation distinguished among four groups of employees. One group was made up of nongrievants, another of repeated grievants, a third group of one- or two-time grievants, and a fourth group of people who filed grievances because of the company's disciplinary action against them. The study indicated that those individuals who filed only a few grievances were regarded as better workers and seemed more knowledgeable of the contract than others. The group of discipline-related grievants was so-called problem employees with a history of personal difficulties, both at work and in other settings. Surprisingly, the multiple grievants were not very different from the nongrievants.[14] This study, and others like it, seem to presume that the rate of grievances filed is a result of characteristics of employees. Is that presumption reasonable?

The most careful and complete study of grievance behavior was made in the plants of five basic steel companies. Within each company at least two departments were studied in considerable depth—one with a relatively high grievance rate (i.e., grievances filed per employee) and one with a relatively

---

[12] Sumner H. Slichter, James J. Healy, and E. Robert Livernash, *The Impact of Collective Bargaining on Management* (Washington, D.C.: Brookings Institution, 1960), p. 698.

[13] Chalmer E. Labig, Jr., and I. B. Helburn, "Union and Management Policy Influences on Grievance Initiation," *Journal of Labor Research*, 7:3, Summer 1986, pp. 270–284. See also Michael J. Duane, Ross E. Azevedo, and Urton Anderson, "Behavior as an Indication of an Opponent's Intentions," *Psychological Reports*, 57, 1985, pp. 507–513. See also Chalmer E. Labig, Jr., and Charles R. Greer, "Grievance Initiation," *Journal of Labor Research*, 9:1, Winter 1988, pp. 7ff.

[14] John Price et al., "Three Studies of Grievances," *Personnel Journal*, 55:1, January 1976, pp. 33–37. See also P. Ash, "The Parties to the Grievance," *Personnel Psychology*, 23, 1970, pp. 13–37; and W. W. Ronan, "Work Group Attitudes and Grievance Activity," *Journal of Applied Psychology*, 55, 1971, pp. 500–502.

low one. "Since the essence is a charge that the agreement has been violated," the authors said, "differences in grievance rates among departments reflected either differences in the number of charges made or differences in the manner in which complaints, problems, and charges were resolved and recorded by the parties. Grievance rates count and reflect only formal charges reduced to writing. The grievance process, however, involves informal and oral activity as well...."[15]

The study identified three types of factors that influence the grievance and resolution process. "However," the authors wrote, "the factors do not operate independently.... If the grievance procedure is to be truly understood... then the environmental, union, and management variables must be seen as interdependent."[16] There are three dimensions of the environment—(1) task organization and work environment, (2) technological change, and (3) socioeconomic conditions—and three dimensions of union and management influences—(1) leadership, (2) organization, and (3) policy. A high-grievance-rate situation involves, in various ways, an unfavorable task environment, aggressive union leadership, and ineffective managerial decision making. Apparently, the frequency of grievances is not simply a function of the characteristics of the employees.

Nonunion versus Union Grievance Handling

Nonunion companies vary a great deal in their methods of handling employee grievances. At one extreme, better-standards nonunion employers often have a well-established grievance procedure, usually terminating with the chief executive officer of the corporation. Often referred to as "the open door," this policy provides that any employee may ultimately carry his or her complaint or observation to the top officer of the corporation. Usually, of course, complaints do not go so far and are adjusted in one way or another at lower levels of the company. Other policies include:

- The "executive detective," in which a senior executive investigates major concerns on a case-by-case basis and recommends action to top management.
- "The ombudsman," in which a senior executive works full time to help conflicting parties negotiate settlements to their disputes.
- "Top management as final appeal," in which the chief executive officer or another senior executive is the final step for appealing management decisions.
- "The management hearing committee," in which an appeal to a group of managers is the final step in a progressive grievance review process modeled after union grievance procedures.[17]

Some nonunion corporations provide for the final resolution of grievances by

---

[15] E. Robert Livernash and David A. Peach, *Grievance and Resolution: A Study in Basic Steel* (Cambridge, Mass.: Harvard University Press, 1974), p. 2.
[16] Ibid., p. 131.
[17] Edmund M. Diaz et al., "A Fair Nonunion Grievance Procedure," *Personnel*, 39:4, April 1987, p. 14.

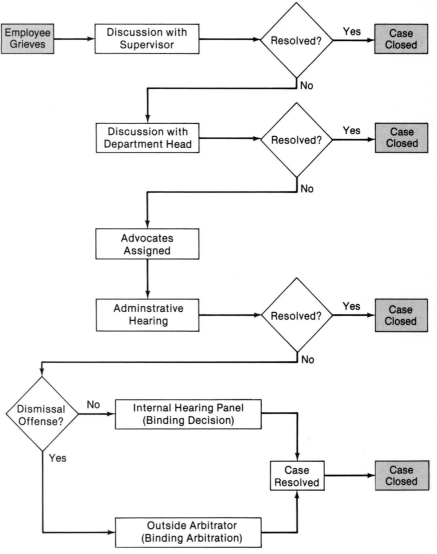

FIGURE 12-2 Grievance process for nonunion employees. *(Source: Edmund M. Diaz, John W. Minton, and David M. Saunders, "A Fair Nonunion Grievance Procedure," Personnel, 39:4, April 1987, p. 14.)*

the decision of a neutral arbitrator, selected by the company and the employee, with the company paying for the process.[18] A complete grievance procedure for nonunion employees ending in binding arbitration by an outside neutral party is diagrammed in Figure 12-2. The procedure is designed to meet three objectives: "(1) a complete say for each side in airing the grievance; (2) a stong connotation of justice, since a professional, neutral third party renders

[18] Robert Coulson, "Fair Treatment," *Arbitration Journal*, 33:3, September 1978, pp. 23–29.

decisions; and (3) benefits for both parties based on the opinion of a 'cool-headed' professional."[19]

This is unusual, however. Ordinarily the procedure terminates with a final decision by a high level of management. A recent study of the advisability of acceptance of arbitration by nonunion companies concluded against it. Either the process will not be used, the author decided, or if it is, and management loses, management will get a "black eye." Better to avoid a neutral altogether, the companies were advised.[20]

In the case of poor-standards nonunion employees, employee grievances may be simply ignored or the employee discharged for raising complaints. Nonunion employees do not have the protection of collective bargaining agreements, by definition, but neither are they completely without bargaining power. In fact, they have available to them such weapons as slowdowns, work stoppages, and similar tactics.[21] Grievance disputes may thus become the occasion of generalized strife between employees and the employer. Because of the lack of a formal grievance procedure and its protection for unorganized employees, a proposal has been made that there be statutory protection against employee dismissal in nonunion situations, with arbitration of grievances over discharge.[22]

A surprising, and ironic, consequence of the formal grievance procedures of union contracts is that, while unionized employees fare better than the employees of low-standards nonunion firms, they sometimes fare less well than the employees of better-standards nonunion firms. This is because supervisors in the union context sometimes seem to concentrate only on the formal rules of the collective bargaining agreement and pay little attention to the human rights of employees. In effect, the procedure sometimes becomes too formal to be fair. When the union and management each recognize this situation, it can apparently be corrected.[23]

Employment at Will

In the absence of a collective bargaining agreement, management in the United States has enjoyed the legal right to discharge employees at will (i.e.,

---

[19] Diaz et al., "A Fair Nonunion Grievance Procedure," p. 25.

[20] Richard L. Epstein, "The Grievance Procedure in the Nonunion Setting: Caveat Employer," *Industrial Relations Law Journal*, 1:1, Summer 1975, pp. 120–127.

[21] Leonard R. Sayles and George Strauss, *The Local Union: Its Place in the Industrial Plant* (New York: Harper, 1953), chap. 6.

[22] Clyde W. Summers, "Individual Protection against Unjust Dismissal: Time for a Statute," *Virginia Law Review*, 62:3, April 1976, pp. 481–532; and Robert Abelow, "From the Editor," *Industrial Relations Law Journal*, 1:4, Spring 1976, p. 521. Clyde W. Summers, "Protecting All Employees against Unjust Dismissal," *Harvard Business Review*, 58:1, January–February 1980, pp. 132–139. See also Jack Stieber and John Blackburn, eds., *Protecting Unorganized Employees from Unjust Discharge* (East Lansing: Michigan State University, 1983).

[23] William H. Warren, "Ombudsman plus Arbitration: A Proposal for Effective Grievance Administration without Public Employee Unions," *Labor Law Journal*, 29:9, September 1978, pp. 562–569.

on its own discretion)—whatever the reason. Recently, however, this situation has begun to change. First, Congress and state legislatures have passed laws protecting employees in many areas. For example,

Employee rights are being expanded at the state and local level by:

- Right-to-know laws requiring companies to divulge information on hazardous substances used in the workplace (25 states)
- Laws protecting corporate and government whistleblowers (21 states) [see below]
- Court decisions eroding employment-at-will doctrine (30 states)
- Laws prohibiting any mandatory retirement age (19 states)
- Laws requiring notice of plant shutdowns and severance pay for affected workers (3 states)

Employee privacy is protected by:

- Limits on data about individuals that government can disclose to employers (10 states, plus Federal Privacy Act of 1974)
- Laws limiting use of polygraph tests for job applicants (20 states); giving employees access to their personnel files (9 states); restricting use of arrest records in hiring process (12 states)

Standards for a safe and healthful workplace are established by:

- Occupational Safety & Health Act of 1970; 24 state laws
- Federal Mine Safety & Health Act of 1977

Basic protection against discrimination in hiring, promotion, and discharge is granted by:

- Civil Rights Acts of 1964
- Age Discrimination in Employment Act of 1967; 1978 amendment disallowing mandatory retirement before age 70
- State and local laws, some of which add protection for marital status and sexual orientation

Sex discrimination in pay is prohibited by:

- Equal Pay Act of 1963
- Some federal court decisions requiring equal pay for comparable work

Funding, vesting, and other standards for pensions and other benefit plans are set by:

- Employee Retirement Income Security Act of 1974; state laws

National minimum wage, 40-hour work week for regular pay, and other working conditions are set by:

- Fair Labor Standards Act of 1938; state wage and hour laws (all states)

Company ability to discharge and discipline employees for union activity is limited by:

- National Labor Relations Act of 1935; Railway Labor Act of 1926[24]

Also, courts have begun to review the doctrine of "right to fire at will" and in some cases have found in favor of employees who challenged it.

A 1959 lawsuit set the precedent for the challenge to employment at will. Interestingly, though a union was involved as the employer in the precedent-setting case, change in the employment-at-will doctrine is most significant to corporations and where employees are *not* represented by a union. An employee had been ordered by his employer to lie (i.e., commit perjury) before an investigative legislative body. The employee refused and was fired. The California Appellate Court ruled that "it would be obnoxious to the interests of the state and contrary to public policy and sound morality to allow an employer to discharge any employee...on the ground that the employee declined to commit perjury."[25]

Since 1959, courts have further limited the employment-at-will doctrine. Several cases have involved complaints that employees who had been promised lifetime jobs were laid off. Several courts have held that even if there were no formal contracts, a promise is binding on the employer if given explicitly or put in a personnel manual.[26] But in what circumstances a company's personnel manual becomes a legally enforceable contract is also now the subject of extensive litigation.[27]

Other cases challenge the reasonableness of management actions. An employee who was fired for dating a fellow employee was permitted by an Oregon court to sue the employer for "outrageous conduct," defined as being "beyond the limits of social toleration."[28] In another instance a nurse was fired from Scottsdale Memorial Hospital 3 months after being promoted to a management position. Three months before the promotion, she, her supervisor, and others joined in a camping and rafting trip. The nurse alleged that she refused to join in the group's staging of a parody of the song "Moon River," which allegedly concluded with members of the group "mooning"

---

[24] John Hoerr et al., "Beyond Unions," *Business Week*, July 8, 1985, p. 73.

[25] *Petermanos v. International Brotherhood of Teamsters* (1959). See Thomas R. Horton, "If Right to Fire Is Abused, Uncle Sam May Step In," *The Wall Street Journal*, June 11, 1984, p. 18.

[26] "Company Offer," Bureau of National Affairs, *Daily Labor Report* No. 115, June 14, 1984, p. A3.

[27] "Courts Split," Bureau of National Affairs, *Daily Labor Report* No. 90, May 9, 1984, pp. A3, A4, A5.

[28] *Patton v. J. C. Penney Co.*, Bureau of National Affairs, *Daily Labor Report* No. 215, Nov. 6, 1985, pp. A1–A2.

the audience. The Arizona Supreme Court found that the nurse, who was an at-will employee, was wrongfully discharged after she refused to engage in conduct that arguably would have violated the state's indecent exposure statute.[29]

Until the legal challenge to employment at will, employees received legally enforceable protection from discharge only via a union contract. Now employee rights are being created by court decision, and nonunion employees are receiving protection previously available only to union-represented employees. While supporting enhanced employee rights, the unions are concerned that the breakdown of the employment-at-will doctrine may make union membership less attractive, since protection from discharge without just cause is becoming available to nonunion employees. In fact, Montana has adopted legislation that limits employers' right to fire to just cause only, effectively giving nonunion employees the same rights as union employees. Yet some observers believe that court protection is less reliable for employees than union representation, and they've come to the conclusion that the employment-at-will doctrine should not be modified by the courts.[30]

Management Initiative

Implicit in the American system of handling grievances in the unionized sector of industry is a very important principle. A grievance arises as a complaint by the union about a specific action by management. That is, the management takes action and the union reacts. Employees and the union have the obligation to obey directives of management, *even when they believe the directives violate the agreement.* The recourse of the employee and the union against an action of management that they believe to be improper is through the grievance procedure. They have no right to unilaterally countermand the management directive. If the company has in fact violated the agreement, the arbitrator has the authority to fashion a remedy that will make the employees whole for the contract violation.

Suppose, for example, that management requires employees to report for work on a Saturday and states its intention to pay them only straight time. The employees and the union, however, believe that the agreement requires double time. Rather than refusing to work until the dispute is resolved, the employees must report to work and file a grievance about the rate of pay. If an arbitrator later upholds the union's interpretation of the agreement, he or she may order the company to pay the workers double time for the day in question. (The employer's right to assign increased work loads to teachers is

---

[29] *Wagenseller v. Scottsdale Memorial Hospital,* Bureau of National Affairs, *Daily Labor Report* No. 134, July 12, 1985, pp. A2–A3.

[30] Susan L. Catler, "The Case against Proposals to Eliminate the Employment-at-Will Rule," *Industrial Relations Law Journal,* 5:4, 1983, pp. 471–522. See also Brian Heshizer, "The Implied Contract Exception to At-Will Employment," *Labor Law Journal,* 35:3, March 1984, pp. 131–141.

the issue in the case of the "overworked teachers" in the Arbitration Exercises at the end of the text.)

Management's willingness to pay a high price in return for strike-free day-to-day stability is too often overlooked. This attitude was aptly summarized some years back by Harry W. Anderson, General Motors vice president for industrial relations at the time:

> The public doesn't understand about these highly publicized settlements: the big thing we're buying is the union's collaboration in making that grievance system work. That day-by-day union performance on dealing with grievances and keeping production going smoothly is a damn-sight more important than the money deal we make with Walter [Reuther].[31]

Thus, management preserves its initiative to run the business, without the union's giving up its rights under the agreement. This principle is of critical importance when contrasted with procedure in Western Europe, where management must often bargain with the union about proposed changes *before* the company can put them into effect. The result is often considerable inefficiency. However, even in the United States, because companies often do not want to risk having to make financial payments after the fact for violations of the agreement, management may check with the union before directing some action that the union may feel is improper. (The authority of the employer not to replace a supervisory person in a plant's toolroom is questioned by the union in the case of "the leaderless toolroom" in the Arbitration Exercises at the end of the text. And management's decision as to whether an employee is permanent or temporary is challenged in "the constant temporary employee.")

Although the practice by which management acts and the union reacts (through the grievance procedure) is still predominant in the United States, it has come under some harsh criticism. The following resolution was adopted by the 1978 convention of the International Union of Electrical Workers:

> *Contractual Provisions which Guarantee That Workers are "Innocent Until Proved Guilty" and Eliminate the Concept that Employees Must "Obey Now and Grieve Later."*
>
> Knowing that collective-bargaining agreements can be violated with relative impunity and that they can continue contractually impermissible practices while the arbitration process drags on for months, many employers are encouraged to routinely violate agreements. Contractual requirements to preserve the *status quo* until the arbitration of the dispute is completed, and elimination of the notorious rule that workers must obey contractually impermissible orders and grieve the violations later, would go far to promote speedier resolution of disputes and eliminate employer incentive to violate the contract, as well as the injustice of leaving workers and their unions with no meaningful remedy. Finally, a contractual requirement that in most cases employers must convince an arbitrator that there is just cause for discipline and discharge, before an employee is disciplined, would prevent many cases of arbitrary and unjust discipline.

[31] Ben Rathbun, "Labor Arbitration: Britain and the U.S.," *Atlantic*, January 1969, p. 24.

GRIEVANCE ARBITRATION

How Arbitration Works

When management and the union are unable to resolve a grievance submitted by the union, the union must make a decision on whether to proceed to the final step of the grievance procedure: arbitration. The union may choose not to go to arbitration for any of several reasons. It may believe the process is too costly, or it may believe that its case is not strong enough to win before a neutral. The union has a legal duty of fair representation to all employees in the bargaining unit, so it cannot legally refuse to carry the grievance forward to arbitration for such reasons as the race of the grievant, an internal union political dispute with the grievant, or the grievant's nonmembership in the union.

If the union decides to carry the dispute to arbitration, it so notifies the company. At this point the union and the company must select an arbitrator. (Sometimes more than one arbitrator is selected. In some cases a panel is also selected, consisting of one employer representative, one union representative, and one neutral.) The parties may select an arbitrator in any of several ways. They may agree upon a person known to both. Many times companies and unions select a permanent arbitrator or a panel of arbitrators to hear their disputes. Alternatively, they may ask some public official or other person to select an arbitrator for them. Most commonly, however, they make a request for an arbitrator to either the American Arbitration Association (AAA) or the Federal Mediation and Conciliation Service (FMCS). The AAA is a nonprofit organization with regional offices in many cities. Both the AAA and FMCS maintain lists of arbitrators, who are selected on the basis of their own application. The AAA and FMCS select only people who can show, through references, some experience with labor-management relations and acceptability to both management and labor as neutrals.

Most arbitrators are lawyers, but not all. Others are trained as economists, psychologists, or priests or ministers. Some arbitrators serve full time in that capacity. Many others teach at universities. There is a professional society of arbitrators, the National Academy of Arbitrators, to which some, but not all, arbitrators belong. In the mid-1950s there were fewer than 25 full-time arbitrators in the country. By 1986 there were more than 300.[32] Both the AAA and FMCS provide rules for the conduct of labor arbitration.[33]

Upon request, either the AAA or FMCS will submit a panel of arbitrators to the parties for their selection. The list usually includes about five names. The parties may choose an arbitrator together, may ask for additional names, or may choose by elimination. The latter process is one in which first one side, then the other, strikes a name. If there is an odd number of names on

---

[32] Richard M. Reilly, American Arbitration Association, Northeast Region, Memorandum, Oct. 28, 1986, p. 1.

[33] See remarks of Mark L. Kahn, President, National Academy of Arbitrators, printed in Bureau of National Affairs, *Daily Labor Report* No. 106, June 1, 1984, pp. D1, D3. See also John Smith Herrick, "Profile of a Labor Arbitrator," *The Arbitration Journal*, 37:2, June 1982, pp. 18–21.

the list, the one remaining after each side has struck the same number of names is chosen as the arbitrator.

What characteristics do union and management representatives prefer in an arbitrator? A recent study reports that the quality most sought after in an arbitrator is previous experience in arbitration. Of course an arbitrator who was known to favor one side or the other, or who had a bad reputation for how he or she conducted a hearing, would not be chosen simply because of experience. Also, arbitrators with certain backgrounds were preferred for certain types of cases. For example, arbitrators who are lawyers were preferred for cases which involved whether or not the issue was in fact subject to arbitration under the contract. For cases involving wage incentives and job evaluation matters, arbitrators with experience in industrial engineering were preferred. Finally, arbitrators who are economists were favored for cases involving the financial interests of the parties.[34] Fifty-four percent of arbitrators are lawyers, and most lawyers who are arbitrators believe that legal training is important for an arbitrator.[35]

The parties notify the AAA or FMCS of their choice, and the arbitrator is then informed by the agency involved. A time and place are established for a hearing. The parties attend the hearing, with or without legal counsel, as they desire. Each side presents its case in turn. Ordinarily, if the union has filed the grievance, it proceeds first. In discharge cases, however, the company usually goes first. Most collective bargaining agreements provide simply that discharge shall be for "just cause." The obligation of establishing just cause is the employer's, and so it proceeds first. Whether or not an employer may discharge an employee for being convicted of a drug-related crime is the issue in the case of "the imprisoned employee" in the Arbitration Exercises at the end of the text.

The arbitrator may ask the spokesperson (often an attorney) for each side to make an opening statement summarizing its case. These statements explain the dispute to the arbitrator and include what provision of the collective bargaining agreement (or what law, or what work practice or responsibility of management) has allegedly been violated and what remedy the union seeks. Then each side calls its witnesses, who are questioned by both sides.[36] A final summation by both sides completes the hearing. The parties sometimes also file formal written statements (so-called briefs, although they are often lengthy) with the arbitrator. The arbitrator thereupon studies the ma-

---

[34] Julius Rezler and Donald Petersen, "Strategies for Arbitrator Selection," Bureau of National Affairs, *Daily Labor Report* No. 123, June 26, 1978, pp. D1–D10.

[35] Jeffrey Small and J. Timothy Sprehe, "Report of American Arbitrator Association Survey of Labor Arbitrators," Bureau of National Affairs, *Daily Labor Report* No. 234, Dec. 5, 1984, pp. E1ff. See also Charlotte Gold, ed., "The Legalization of Arbitration," *Study Time* (New York: American Arbitration Association, 1978); David E. Bloom and Christopher L. Cavanagh, "An Analysis of the Selection of Arbitrators," *The American Economic Review*, 76:3, June 1986), pp. 408–422; and Nels E. Nelson, "The Selection of Arbitrators," *Labor Law Journal*, 37:10, Oct. 1986, pp. 703–711.

[36] Edwin Levin and Donald Grody, *Witnesses in Arbitration* (Washington, D.C.: Bureau of National Affairs, 1987); and Marvin F. Hill, Jr., and Anthony V. Sinicropi, *Evidence in Arbitration*, 2d ed. (Washington, D.C.: Bureau of National Affairs, 1987).

terial and the testimony given and renders a decision. Ordinarily the decision is accompanied by an opinion setting forth the nature of the dispute, the facts of the matter, the positions of the parties, and the arbitrator's analysis of the dispute, as well as the decision (called an award). Arbitration awards are expected to be resolved within 1 or 2 months after the conclusion of the hearing (or the date of submission of final briefs to the arbitrator).

Arbitrators charge a daily fee for their services, plus expenses. In 1985, the FMCS has reported, the cost of an average grievance arbitration was $1,468.20, of which $1,286.76 was the arbitrator's fee (an average fee of $370.27 per day) and $181.44 was for expenses.[37] The parties split the arbitrator's fee and expenses. In 1985, for the American Arbitration Association, the average arbitrator's fee was $317 per day; the average total bill to the parties for an arbitrator was $1200; and the average wait for a hearing was 6½ months.[38] (The AAA also charges a fee for the provision of its administrative services.)

Union and management each incur substantial costs for legal representation, case preparation, and time of representatives spent in an arbitration proceeding. It is not uncommon to hear complaints that the arbitration process is too costly. Perhaps it is, but cost also serves a purpose in reducing the number of cases and thereby helping to prevent backlogs of unresolved cases from developing.

In the railway industry, under the Railway Labor Act (see Chapter 4), the federal government pays for arbitration of grievances. One result has been a somewhat indiscriminate filing of grievances and a backlog of more than 21,000 cases in 1982.[39]

A study of 6500 arbitrations from 1982 to 1984 found that one-third concerned discipline and/or discharge of employees, one-tenth concerned wages, one-twentieth concerned lay-offs, and the remainder involved some 18 other matters. Discipline was by a factor 3 times the most frequent issue of arbitration.[40] (For examples of disciplinary arbitration, see "the mysterious timecards" and "the imprisoned employee" in the Arbitration Exercises at the end of the text.)

Arbitrators differ in the manner in which they conduct hearings. Some arbitrators take an active part, asking questions of witnesses and making statements. Others are virtually silent, preferring to let the parties make (or fail to make) their own cases as best they can. Arbitration is an adversary proceeding, like a trial in court, and a good case may be lost through poor preparation and presentation.[41]

There is a lively controversy among arbitrators as to whether or not an arbi-

[37] FMCS, *Report*, 1979, p. 43. See also John Zalusky, "Arbitration: Updating a Vital Process," *AFL-CIO American Federationist*, 83:11, November 1976, pp. 1–8.

[38] Robert E. Meade, quoted in Bureau of National Affairs, *Daily Labor Report* No. 93, May 14, 1986, p. A11.

[39] Gil Vernon, "Public Funding for the Arbitration of Grievances in the Railroad Industry," *The Arbitration Journal*, 38:3, September 1983, p. 32.

[40] Earl Baderschneider and Charlotte Gold, "Labor Arbitration Case Trends," *Study Time* (a publication of the American Arbitration Association), October 1984, p. 43.

[41] John Smith Herrick, "Labor Arbitration as Viewed by Labor Arbitrators," *The Arbitration Journal*, 38:1, March 1983, pp. 39–48.

trator should attempt to compensate for the poor presentation of one side or the other at an arbitration hearing. Some arbitrators are reluctant to question witnesses and otherwise take an active role because the labor and management representatives may have a reason for how they are presenting the case, and not simply be incompetent. Also, if the arbitrator's initiative in the hearing helps one side and thereby harms the other, the side which is harmed may feel that the arbitrator has not acted in an impartial manner. But other arbitrators feel strongly that the arbitrator must do all in his or her power to see that the hearing results in a correct decision by the arbitrator about the issue presented. Labor and management "should have their issues resolved on the basis of all the facts that I can uncover," said one arbitrator, "rather than upon the skill of advocacy demonstrated by their representatives."[42]

Arbitration is a quasi-legal procedure. Chief Justice William H. Rehnquist of the Supreme Court has described arbitration as being between the instant decisions made by a sports umpire and the lengthy process used by a court.[43] Most arbitration decisions may be enforced in court, but the full range of due process requirements of the courts is not applied to arbitration proceedings. Witnesses, for example, may or may not be sworn, depending on the preference of the parties and on state law. Transcripts of arbitration hearings may or may not be made. If they are made, one or the other party (or both) pays for the transcript. As a result of its quasi-legal status, arbitration may be very formal (i.e., like a courtroom proceeding) or very informal (i.e., like a grievance meeting in a company), depending on the preference of the arbitrator and the parties and on the importance of the issue (very important issues seem to require greater formality).[44] In 1986 employers were represented by attorneys in 77 percent of arbitration cases, and unions in 52 percent. Transcripts were ordered in 22 percent of hearings, and lawyers filed formal briefs in 59 percent of cases.[45]

An arbitrator's function is usually to interpret the collective bargaining agreement between the parties. Agreements often include such language as:

> The arbitrator shall have no authority or power to add to, detract from, or alter in any way the provisions of this agreement or any subsequent amendments thereof.

The restriction of the arbitrator to the application of the agreement has probably increased the stature and use of arbitration. Rather than have the arbitrator apply his or her own standards of what is right in a given situation, the arbitrator is bound to apply his or her judgment to the language of the con-

---

[42] Allan G. Dash, Jr., quoted in *Study Time*, American Arbitration Association, April 1978, p. 4. See also Howard R. Sacks and Lewis S. Kurlantzick, *Missing Witnesses, Missing Testimony and Missing Theories: How Much Initiative by Labor Arbitrators?* (Stoneham, Mass.: Butterworth, 1988).

[43] William H. Rehnquist, "A Jurist's View of Arbitration," *The Arbitration Journal*, 32:1, March 1977, pp. 1–7.

[44] Martin F. Scheinman, *Evidence and Proof in Arbitration* (Ithaca: New York State School of Industrial and Labor Relations, Cornell, 1977); and Marvin J. Hill and Anthony V. Sinicropi, *Evidence in Arbitration* (Washington, D.C.: Bureau of National Affairs, 1981).

[45] Robert Coulson, President, American Arbitration Association, letter, Jan. 20, 1987.

tract to determine what the parties agreed to. Thus, the arbitrator's discretion is not unfettered. This reduces the risk of receiving a bad decision, which both management and labor assume when they go to arbitration.

An arbitrator is often reluctant to ignore the law in making a decision, however. Despite the parties' instructions to rule only on the language of the collective bargaining agreement, arbitrators recognize the fact that legal requirements normally take precedence over private contracts. Still, an arbitrator is not a judge and may be inexpert in interpreting the law. As a result, an alleged conflict in a specific grievance between provisions of a collective bargaining agreement and certain legal requirements presents a difficult problem for an arbitrator.

A description of the arbitration process may become a bit more graphic if we list a few of the mistakes that are made by novices.[46]

• Since precedents are important in court proceedings, it is often assumed that they are important in arbitration. In fact, precedents have a considerably lesser role in arbitration. Arbitrators may choose to be guided by the decisions of other arbitrators, but they may also disregard other decisions. This is because the arbitrator is usually using as his or her standard of judgment the collective bargaining agreement between the parties, and decisions reached under other agreements may not seem relevant. But even decisions reached under the same agreement may not seem precedent-setting to different arbitrators. (It may be hoped that a single arbitrator, encountering a dispute between the same parties a second time, and under the same agreement, will feel bound by his or her earlier decision.) A lively debate on the proper role for precedents in arbitration is under way in the professional associations of arbitrators.[47]

Failing to recognize the limited role of precedents in arbitration, people new to the procedure often compile lengthy lists of alleged precedents for the arbitrator. Sometimes the list is simply that—a list. The arbitrator is not even informed why the parties believe the precedent cited is relevant and what point it makes. Apparently, the arbitrator is expected to figure that out alone.

• Parties sometimes shout loudly, pound the table, and make similar demonstrations of hot feelings in an attempt to convince the arbitrator of their sincerity. This is virtually useless, for arbitrators are aware of the lawyer's adage "When you don't have the facts, pound the table."

• Novices in the arbitration process often forget its function, which is to inform the arbitrator of the facts and seek a favorable judgment. Instead, they use the hearing as a place to continue their argument with the other side. When this occurs, the parties may fail to make their best case. They often neglect to tell the arbitrator what remedy they seek and why. Parties who

---

[46] There are several book-length descriptions of the arbitration process. See, for example, Walter E. Baer, *The Labor Arbitration Guide* (Homewood, Ill.: Dow Jones–Irwin, 1974); and Maurice S. Trotta, *Arbitration of Labor-Management Disputes* (New York: AMACOM, 1974).

[47] Philip Harris, "Precedent in Arbitration," *The Arbitration Journal*, 32:1, March 1977, pp. 26–34; Ken Jennings and Cindy Maria, "The Role of Prior Arbitration Awards in Arbitral Decisions," *Labor Law Journal*, 29:26, February 1978, pp. 95–106.

are experienced in arbitration do not leave such significant matters to the arbitrator's imagination.

Revolution

Labor arbitration has early roots. During the Revolutionary War an ironmonger was assigned to forge and stretch a chain across the Hudson River to prevent the British from using the waterway in a campaign against Washington's army.

He demanded a tuppence more than the going rate as "danger pay" on the grounds that if he was caught he would be doomed. His boss refused the extra stipend and, to settle the dispute quickly, a local citizen of good standing in the community was selected to hear both sides. The worker got his tuppence.[48]

Frequency of Arbitration

We have seen that the vast majority of collective bargaining agreements in the private sector include binding grievance arbitration by neutrals. Similarly, in the public sector grievance arbitration appears in most agreements, though not as pervasively as in private contracts (about 75 percent in the public sector, versus more than 90 percent in the private sector).[49]

There are no statistics that indicate the total number of grievance arbitration cases. Both the AAA and FMCS, however, publish statistics regarding arbitrations conducted under their auspices. (These data include some interest arbitration cases, but the majority is grievance arbitration.) Table 12-3 lists the growth in the number of grievance arbitrations between 1966 and 1987. It will be noted that growth was very rapid until the 1980s. Interpretation of these data is unclear. The growth of arbitration did not mirror any similar growth in unionization of employees. In consequence, the data probably indicate increased use of arbitration by existing parties. Whether or not this reflects greater employee discontent or more employer disregard of the collective bargaining agreement is uncertain. Possibly the AAA and the FMCS are receiving a greater proportion of all arbitrations, so that their increased case load does not reflect growth in arbitration as a whole. In any case, these are speculative matters at the present.[50]

Expedited Arbitration

A formal grievance procedure followed by arbitration can be a time-consuming process. In 1973 FMCS director W. J. Usery noted that the aver-

---

[48] Lawrence Stessin, "Speed Is of the Essence," *The New York Times*, Feb. 17, 1974. p. F2.

[49] Paul D. Staudhar, "Grievance Arbitration in Public Employment," *The Arbitration Journal*, 31:2, June 1976, pp. 116–124.

[50] Joseph Krislov, "The Supply of Arbitrators," *Monthly Labor Review*, 99:10, October 1976, pp. 27–30.

TABLE 12-3 GRIEVANCE ARBITRATION

	AAA labor cases (calendar-year basis)	FMCS arbitrator appointments (fiscal-year basis, July-July)
1966	4,007	—
1967	4,437	—
1968	5,028	—
1969	5,892	—
1970	6,337	5,318
1971	6,658	5,759
1972	7,657	6,263
1973	8,569	6,665
1974	10,261	7,612
1975	13,251	10,278
1976	14,333	10,509
1977	14,661	11,985
1978	16,437	12,527
1979	16,669	13,232
1980	17,062	13,911
1981	17,664	13,219
1982	17,038	12,317
1983	17,516	13,729
1984	17,211	11,156
1985	15,717	10,891
1986	15,978	N/A
1987	17,500*	N/A

*Through November.
Sources: AAA data are from AAA; FMCS data are from 34th Annual Report of FMCS, p. 34.

age time consumed from the first step of the grievance procedure to the arbitrator's award in FMCS arbitration cases was 257 days.

"It has often been said," Usery observed, "that time is money. But in the highly human area of resolving disputes that have a direct impact on the lives of people, time is a far more cherished commodity. For a worker to have to wait nine months and longer to find whether a discharge will stick is cruel to the worker, places a strain on his family and friends, and is costly to management both in dollars and in employee morale."[51] By 1985 the time consumed by the average FMCS arbitration case was approximately 402 days.[52] This was, in the view of most people, too long, and in industries that employed panels of arbitrators (instead of selecting arbitrators on an ad hoc basis from the AAA or FMCS) delays were often even longer.

[51] W. J. Usery, speech to AAA Conference, reported in Bureau of National Affairs, *Daily Labor Report* No. 233, Dec. 4, 1973, p. A13.
[52] FMCS, Automated Information Systems Arbitration Statistics, 1985.

In order to shorten the process, some companies and unions have begun to experiment with a streamlined form of arbitration. Chrysler Corporation, the UAW, and the AAA have cooperated in the attempt. As described by the UAW, "accelerated arbitration" works as follows:

> A Chrysler worker's grievance was recently fully processed and resolved within eight weeks through the use of a new UAW-Chrysler "accelerated arbitration" pilot program, UAW Vice Pres. Douglas A. Fraser reported.
>
> Currently in effect at four Chrysler plants on an experimental basis, the streamlined procedure shortens by at least six months the time needed to resolve such grievances under the normal four-step arbitration procedure.
>
> The pilot program follows a letter of understanding in the 1973 UAW-Chrysler agreement. The new process involves an informal hearing, with no briefs or transcript and no formal rules of evidence.
>
> In the first test of the pilot plan, Charles Alexander, a heavy press operator at the Sterling Stamping plant and member of Local 1264, was suspended for two days after being charged with running too much scrap on a machine he was operating.
>
> Alexander won his case when the Arbitrator—who is selected from a rotating panel from the American Arbitration Association and must render a written decision within 72 hours of a hearing under the expedited procedure—awarded the worker two days' pay after deciding that Alexander had not been given adequate training on the machine he was operating when disciplined.[53]

Other experiments are under way in the steel industry, between General Electric and unions that represent its employees, and in some 500 other companies.[54] The experience in steel has been particularly noteworthy. The system of expedited arbitration was introduced in 1971. In 1977 the companies and the union felt it to have been so successful that they ceased to refer to it as an experimental program. Under the rules of the program written decisions are due from arbitrators within 48 hours of the hearing, and written legal "briefs," transcripts of the testimony at the hearing, and formal rules of evidence are shunned. Lawyers are rarely involved in presentation of the cases. By 1982 there had been some 8773 decisions in 301 plants involving 239 different arbitrators.[55]

Who Wins Arbitration Cases?

Does management prevail in most arbitrators' decisions, or does the union win more often? Many managers, in particular, seem to presume that arbitrators are generally supportive of trade unions and therefore tend to render decisions in favor of the unions.

---

[53] UAW, *Solidarity*, September 1974.

[54] Lawrence Stessin, "Expedited Arbitration: Less Grief over Grievances," *Harvard Business Review*, 55:1, January–February 1977, pp. 128–134.

[55] Winn Newman and Carole W. Wilson, "Promise and Performance of Arbitration from a Union Point of View," Bureau of National Affairs, *Daily Labor Report* No. 106, June 1, 1983, pp. D1, D9.

There are no comprehensive data on which to base a conclusion as to whether management or unions do better in arbitration. However, the American Arbitration Association has reviewed its records to give an answer for 1986. Fifty-one percent of disputes were decided by arbitrators in favor of management, 32 percent were decided in favor of unions, and 17 percent were split.[56]

Persons familiar with arbitration know that these data, and others like them, should be regarded with care. They are very much affected by the attitudes with which management and labor approach arbitration. Some companies take only very strong cases to arbitration; others take almost any dispute at all. Unions differ as well in what they choose to send to arbitration. As a result, a preponderance of victories for management may represent no more than a more careful winnowing of what disputes managers allow to go to an arbitrator. Also, a study of 1869 arbitration cases found little or no connection between arbitrators' backgrounds, education, past occupation, and other characteristics and the proportion of decisions awarded to union or management.[57]

Many managers object strongly to the authority of arbitrators (which has been upheld by the courts) to reinstate employees who have been discharged from employment. These managers feel that arbitrators view the discharge of an employee as analogous to capital punishment for a criminal and are therefore very reluctant to permit discharges to stand. A recent study indicated that when discharged employees are reinstated by an arbitrator, they ordinarily perform as satisfactory employees (in management's view) who make normal progress and have few if any disciplinary problems. Nonetheless, the researcher found, managers continue to view the order to reinstate discharged employees as unacceptable and wrong, despite the evidence of the positive and practical results of arbitrators' decisions to reinstate.

Another study investigated the effect of the gender of grievants on the decisions of arbitrators in 104 discharge cases. The results indicated that, other things equal, women were twice as likely as men to have their grievance sustained; in cases where the grievance was sustained, women were 2.7 times more likely than men to receive a full reinstatement rather than a partial reinstatement; and in cases where suspension was imposed in place of discharge, women received, on average, a suspension 2.1 months shorter than men. These results are consistent with those of studies of the treatment of women in the criminal justice system.[58]

[56] Robert Coulson, letter, Jan. 20, 1987, op. cit.

[57] Herbert G. Heneman III and Marcus H. Sander, "Arbitrators' Background and Behavior," *Journal of Labor Research*, 4:2, Spring 1983, pp. 115–124.

[58] Arthur Anthony Malinowski, "An Empirical Analysis of Discharge Cases and the Work History of Employees Reinstated by Labor Arbitrators," *The Arbitration Journal*, 36:1, March 1981, pp. 31–46; and Brian Bemmels, "The Effect of Grievants' Gender on Arbitrators' Decisions," *Industrial and Labor Relations Review*, 41:2, January 1988, pp. 251ff.

Arbitration and the Law

What is the status of arbitration awards under the law? Can the loser in an arbitration appeal the decision to a court? On what grounds? Questions such as these can be given brief answers, but only if the reader understands that many qualifications must go unstated. In individual situations there may be important exceptions to the general rules set out here.

Generally an arbitration award cannot be appealed in court on its merits. For example, suppose a union loses a decision but thinks the arbitrator made a mistake in interpreting the agreement. Perhaps the issue was discharge, and the union believes the arbitrator was incorrect in his or her interpretation of the "just cause" language of the agreement. If the company were a private corporation covered by the National Labor Relations Act and the union were to appeal to a state court, the court would probably direct the union to a federal court, saying the federal court would have jurisdiction. The federal court would probably refuse to hear the union's appeal, since it is ordinarily the policy of the courts not to review an arbitrator's actions with respect to the merits of the dispute.

There are several reasons for this policy. First, federal judges have little training or experience in labor matters and are often willing to leave them to the expertise of arbitrators. Second, the federal courts' case load is already too large, and accepting appeals from arbitrators' decisions would swamp the system. Third, the Supreme Court has given support to the arbitration process in a series of decisions. In one instance the Court described the grievance procedure in the contract as "a part of the continuous collective bargaining process," and as "the means of solving the unforeseeable by molding a system of *private law*."[59] The federal courts have been understandably reluctant to step into this system of private law.

Judicial deferral to arbitration has become a basic tenet of national labor policy. There are four key Supreme Court decisions concerning the status of arbitration and the law:

- In *Textile Workers Union v. Lincoln Mills*,[60] the Court rejected the common-law rule against enforcement of agreements to arbitrate. Instead, the Court spoke of a federal respect for collective bargaining reflecting from the policy of our national labor laws. In order to facilitate the national policy, the Court ordered the parties to arbitrate a dispute.

- Three years later, citing *Lincoln Mills* as precedent, the Court decided three Steelworkers cases (the so-called Steelworkers' Trilogy), and thereby solidified arbitration's place. In the first of these cases, *United Steelworkers v. American Manufacturing Co.*,[61] the Court wrote:

> The court should be confined to ascertaining whether the party seeking arbitration is making a claim which on its face is governed by the contract. Whether

---

[59] *United Steelworkers of America v. Warrior and Gulf Navigation Co.*, 363 U.S. 574 (1960).
[60] 353 U.S. 448 (1957).
[61] *United Steelworkers of America v. Warrior and Gulf Navigation Co.*, 363 U.S. 564 (1960).

the moving party is right or wrong is a question of contract imterpretation for the arbitrator.

• In the *United Steelworkers v. Warrior and Gulf Navigation Co.*, the Court sought to demonstrate the efficacy of arbitration in the sphere of collective bargaining and that since it is "the substitute for industrial strife," and the elimination of industrial strife is the prime objective of our national labor policy, it must be accorded great respect. Justice William O. Douglas wrote for the majority of the Court:

> The collective bargaining agreement states the rights and duties of the parties. It is more than a contract: it is a generalized code to govern myriad cases which the draftsmen cannot wholly anticipate.... Arbitration is a means of solving the unforeseeable by making a system of private law for all the problems which may arise and to provide for their solution in a way which will generally accord with the variant needs and desires of the parties.... Apart from matters that the parties specifically exclude, all of the questions on which the parties disagree must therefore come within the scope of the grievance and arbitration provisions of the collective bargaining agreement.

• Finally, in *United Steelworkers v. Enterprise Wheel and Car Corp.*,[62] the Court further insulated the arbitrator by fashioning a standard of limited review. Justice Douglas warned the courts that

> The refusal of courts to review the merits of an arbitrator's award is the proper approach to arbitration under collective agreements. The federal policy of settling labor disputes would be undermined if the courts had the final say on the merits of the awards.

The courts will, however, review certain types of appeals from arbitration, which can be broadly described as concerning procedural matters. If an arbitrator's award can be shown to have been obtained by fraud or to be arbitrary and capricious, i.e., not addressed to the issues at hand, a court might set aside the award. Alternatively, if an arbitrator can be shown to have exceeded his or her authority under the agreement, or if the award violates a federal statute, a court might hear an appeal to set aside an award. As a practical matter, appeals on such grounds may result in a review by the court of the merits of an arbitrator's decision.[63] Also, courts will review a contract and decide what is appropriate where two or more arbitrators have issued conflicting rulings.[64]

In sum, the Supreme Court directed the lower courts to bow out of most labor disputes under collective bargaining agreements. Also, when courts were asked if a dispute was arbitrable, they were instructed to make a strong

---

[62] 363 U.S. 593 (1960).

[63] George H. Freedman, "Correcting Arbitrator Error: The Limited Scope of Judicial Review," *The Arbitration Journal*, 33:2, June 1978, pp. 9–16.

[64] "Appeals Court," Bureau of National Affairs, *Daily Labor Report* No. 196, Oct. 7, 1983, pp. A8, A9.

presumption of arbitrability. Finally, the courts were to enforce arbitration awards unless the award was clearly inconsistent with the contract.

Thus, the arbitration process under a collective bargaining agreement seemed insulated from the involvement of federal courts. But in the 1980s this began to change. The Supreme Court directed lower courts to decide disputes between labor and management about whether or not a particular matter was subject to arbitration under the labor agreement. Previously, the courts were expected to let an arbitrator make the decision about arbitrability.[65] Further, the courts seem to be more willing to overturn arbitrators' decisions in grievance cases simply because they disagree. In what may be a significant case, the U.S. Court of Appeals of the Fifth Circuit set aside an arbitrator's decision that a company must reemploy an employee it had fired. The employee had been arrested by police in the company's parking lot in his car, which was filled with marijuana and marijuana smoke. The company discharged the employee. The union grieved. An arbitrator reinstated the employee. A federal district court upheld the arbitrator, but the circuit court of appeals reversed the arbitrator and let the company fire the grievant. The case (*Paperworkers v. Misco*) is now before the Supreme Court. Will the Court reinforce the *Steelworkers* cases which kept federal courts out of arbitration, or will there be a new judicial activism in which courts substitute their judgment for that of arbitrators? We must wait for the decision.

The Taft-Hartley Act (section 301) permits suits in federal court by and against labor organizations. Some individual employees have successfully sued unions to get an arbitration decision overturned. For example, in 1967 Anchor Motor Freight Inc., an Ohio trucking firm, discharged several drivers for allegedly submitting inflated motel receipts for reimbursement by the company. Teamsters Local No. 377 took the matter to a joint grievance committee, but the discharges were sustained. The drivers subsequently obtained their own attorney, who investigated the matter and discovered that a motel clerk had falsified the motel receipts and pocketed the difference. Nevertheless, the drivers were unsuccessful in obtaining a rehearing before the grievance panel.

The drivers then brought an action in federal district court against Anchor, the Teamsters local, and the international union. The drivers alleged that the falsity of the charges could have been discovered with a minimum of investigation, that the Teamsters had made no effort to ascertain the truth of the charges, and that the union had violated its duty of fair representation.

The Supreme Court ultimately heard the case and ruled that when a union had violated its duty of fair representation and had thereby seriously undermined the integrity of the arbitration process, the arbitration decision should not be sustained by the courts.[66]

---

[65] *AT&T Technologies, Inc. v. Communication Workers of America*, U.S. Supreme Court, 84-1913, Apr. 17, 1986.
[66] *Hines v. Anchor Motor Freight, Inc.*, Supreme Court (1976).

Courts may enforce the obligation of a union to honor a no-strike pledge by issuing an order restraining a strike and directing the parties to proceed to arbitration.[67] A court may order a company to honor the arbitration clause of its agreement. In some instances the courts have ordered arbitration when a no-strike clause existed in the agreement but an arbitration process did not. In other cases a court has prohibited a strike when an arbitration clause existed in the agreement but a no-strike clause did not. The courts have, therefore, apparently inferred the existence of an arbitration clause from the existence of a no-strike pledge, and vice versa, in certain specific circumstances. By such actions, the courts have sought to compel labor and management to a peaceful resolution of grievance disputes through arbitration.

This policy of the courts which favors arbitration of disputes between management and labor is referred to as the presumption of arbitrability. It is applied by the courts to the private sector. But it does not exist for the public sector. Whereas in the private sector a matter must be explicitly excluded from arbitration, in the public sector a matter must be specifically set forth in the contract as being arbitrable; otherwise it is not arbitrable unless both parties agree to have it arbitrated at the time it arises.[68]

Finally, federal courts will enforce arbitration awards upon the appeal by one side that the other is refusing to implement the award. Once again, however, such an appeal may open to the courts' review the whole circumstances of the award, perhaps including its merits. Suppose an arbitrator ruled for the union. The company believed the decision incorrect, so it refused to honor it. The union asked a federal court to order the company to implement the award. The company defended its refusal by describing the award as deficient in certain ways. The court might then review the company's objections to the award prior to making a decision about whether to order the award implemented.

Arbitration is thus protected by the courts but is also subject to review in certain cases by them. And the law seems to change at times. For example, strikes by one union in support of another have generally been thought to be illegal in the United States, either as a violation of the no-strike pledge in the collective bargaining agreement or because the strike constitutes an illegal secondary boycott (i.e., a strike directed against one employer for the purpose of bringing pressure to bear on another). Recently, however, the Supreme Court ruled that federal courts may not issue injunctions to stop a union from striking to support another union in certain circumstances, even though the no-strike provision of the collective bargaining agreement covers the matter. However, the Court did say that the strike was an arbitrable matter and that the question of whether the strike violates the no-strike pledge in the agreement should go to an arbitrator. The courts, however, in this in-

---

[67] *Boys Market Inc., v. Retail Clerks Union*, 398 U.S. 235 (1970).

[68] *Liverpool Central School District v. United Liverpool Faculty Association*, New York State Court of Appeals, No. 464, 1977.

stance would not enforce the no-strike pledge with a court order for the union to return to work. This dispute was not, the Supreme Court found, an "arbitrable grievance." (Presumably the Court meant the dispute was not a grievance, since it also ruled that the matter was arbitrable.)[69]

The continuing development of substantive law about employment practices has put pressure on the insulation of arbitration from the courts. Arbitrators are now sometimes asked to base a decision not on a collective bargaining agreement, but on federal law. Should arbitrators do so? In 1967 this matter was discussed at the meetings of the American Academy of Arbitrators. Bernard Meltzer argued that arbitrators should decide only if the agreement had been violated and leave to the courts the decision as to whether the agreement itself contravened statutory law. Robert Howlett took the opposite position. He argued that each contract must be presumed to include all applicable laws and that arbitrators should interpret and apply all applicable laws.[70]

In particular, the Civil Rights Act has raised important issues of the relationship of courts to the arbitration process. Ordinarily under American law if a matter has been given a hearing and a decision has been rendered in one forum (such as arbitration), then the complaining person is not entitled to another hearing and another decision in the same matter. But in a significant decision involving charges of racial discrimination against an employer, the Supreme Court ruled that an employee may press a complaint of racial discrimination both in the grievance and arbitration procedures under collective bargaining and also in the Equal Employment Opportunities Commission and courts under Title VII of the Civil Rights Act.[71]

Would the right of a person to go to court even after arbitration cause arbitration to decline? Many observers in the mid-1970s thought so. But not so, say researchers recently. A survey of attorneys who represent employees, unions, and companies shows that arbitration of discrimination cases has continued.[72]

Arbitration and the NLRB

Sometimes an event occurs at the workplace that is viewed by the union as a contract violation, but that also may involve an unfair labor practice on the part of the employer. How should such a situation be handled? Should the NLRB adjudicate the incident as an unfair labor practice? Alternatively, should the dispute be handled as a grievance that may go to arbitration for

---

[69] *Buffalo Forge Co. v. United Steelworkers of America et al.*, Supreme Court, 75-339 (1976).

[70] For an excellent summary of the Meltzer-Howlett controversy, see Michael I. Sovern, "When Should Arbitrators Follow Federal Law?" in *Arbitration and the Expanding Role of Neutrals* (Washington, D.C.: Bureau of National Affairs, 1970), pp. 29ff.

[71] *Alexander v. Gardner-Denver*, 415 U.S. 36 (1974).

[72] Michele M. Hoyman and Lamont E. Stallworth, "Arbitrating Discrimination Grievances in the Wake of Gardner-Denver," *Monthly Labor Review*, 106:10, October 1983, pp. 3–10.

final resolution? This problem arises in part out of the somewhat contradictory language of two different sections of the National Labor Relations Act. Section 10(A) says that the NLRB's authority to decide unfair labor practice cases "shall not be affected by agreement, law, or otherwise." But section 203(d) reads in part: "Final adjustment by a method agreed upon by the parties is hereby declared to be the desirable method for settlement of a grievance dispute arising over the application or interpretation of an existing collective bargaining agreement."

In 1971 the board made its most ambitious attempt to reconcile these two aspects of the labor law with respect to a certain case. During negotiations an employer had tried without success to bargain for a wage increase for skilled maintenance personnel greater than the increase given to other employees. After the negotiations, the employer unilaterally made the wage increase. The company also reassigned two employees and instituted certain wage-rate changes. The union filed refusal-to-bargain charges. The company argued that it was empowered to make the changes under the existing collective bargaining agreement. It granted that the union had a right to dispute the changes but said the dispute should be settled through the grievance-arbitration procedure provided for in the agreement. In its majority opinion the NLRB agreed with this contention, stating that the situation was "essentially a dispute over the terms and meaning of the contract between the union and the employer." The NLRB went on to argue that arbitration makes available a "quick and fair means for the resolution of this dispute including...a fully effective remedy for any breach of contract which occurred."[73]

This decision of the board has been labeled the "*Collyer* Doctrine," or the "doctrine of deferral to arbitration." The doctrine has been highly controversial.[74]

In 1977 the NLRB modified it in the *General American Transportation* case. The board would henceforth defer to arbitration about disputes over a collective bargaining agreement, but not over disputes over employees' legal rights (those established by the labor laws). In 1984 the board reversed the *General American Transportation* decision and returned to the *Collyer* doctrine (*United Technologies*).[75]

---

[73] *Collyer Insulated Wire Co.*, 192 NLRB 150 (1971).

[74] Paul Hays, *Labor Arbitration: A Dissenting View* (New Haven, Conn.: Yale, 1961); Edward Miller, "Deferral to Arbitration: Temperance or Abstinence?" *Georgia Law Review*, 7, Summer 1973; Peter Nash, "Development of the Collyer Deferral Policy," *Vanderbilt Law Review*, 27, January 1974; Peter Nash, "Comment: The NLRB and Deferral to Arbitration," *Yale Law Journal*, 77, 1968. (Edward Miller was chairperson of the NLRB and Peter Nash was general counsel of the NLRB at the time of the *Collyer* decisions.)

[75] United Technologies Corporation, 268 NLRB No. 83, Jan. 19, 1984. See also Curtis L. Mack and Ira P. Bernstein, "NLRB Deferral to the Arbitration Process," *The Arbitration Journal*, 40:3, September 1985, pp. 33–43; and M. J. Fox, Jr., and Sheldon A. Wolstein, "The Current State of the NLRB's Decisions for Deferral to Arbitration," *Journal of Collective Negotiations in the Public Sector*, 15:2, 1986, pp. 99–105.

Though the *Collyer* doctrine remains controversial, it is one which in its present form constitutes an important legal recognition of the role of the grievance process and arbitration in resolving labor-management disputes.

Wildcat Strikes

A wildcat strike is an unofficial strike, i.e., a strike not sanctioned by the union. Such strikes occasionally occur in the United States in disregard of the arbitration process and in violation of the no-strike pledge in collective bargaining agreements. The union is responsible for abiding by the agreement, and management is often able to obtain federal court enforcement of the obligation to go to arbitration rather than to strike. In such a situation the union is obligated to use its best efforts to end the strike.

A wildcat strike places the union in a difficult position. The union leadership is, after all, supposed to be the workers' champion in dealings with management. But when the workers engage in an unauthorized strike, the union officials, who must try to get them to return to work, risk compromising their own position. The strikers may accuse the union officials of selling out to management. Because of this risk, some union leaders are less than forthright in their efforts to end wildcat strikes. Some managements believe that union leaders actively, but behind the scenes, encourage wildcat strikes.

How can management help avoid wildcat strikes? First, an effective, rapid grievance procedure will usually remove potential trouble spots, so that matters do not fester and become the occasion for a wildcat strike. Second, when wildcat strikes occur, management should enforce the rules against unauthorized work stoppages quickly and comprehensively. Tolerating wildcat strikes usually tends to encourage more of them.

The wildcat strike has been the subject of some of the strongest language uttered by arbitrators. Saul Wallen, for example, returned to the topic of the unofficial strike several times:

> In return for the concessions made to the union in collective bargaining, the employer secures one concession that is basic to his security as well as to the security of the men in his employ. That is a pledge that during the term of the agreement when a dispute arises it will be disposed of by processing through the grievance procedure. Implicit in the pledge to use the grievance procedure to settle such disputes is an understanding that work will be continued without interruption by either strikes or lockouts so that the company may continue to offer its services to the public and the men will continue to earn wages to their mutual benefit.
>
> Whoever on the union's side subverts this commitment by instigation, leading, condoning, or participating in a wildcat strike attacks the fundamental basis of collective bargaining. He defiles that which the union has set out to achieve—a fair agreement to cover the term of employment. He dishonors the pledged word of his union leadership and despoils the efforts of those who preceded him in erecting the structure of industrial relations which has replaced the jungle warfare of an earlier day....

This is the lesson which must be learned from the case at hand—that illegal work stoppages serve all involved ill; that they are antiunion as well as antimanagement in nature; and that they undo that which the long history of collective bargaining as we know it in this country has striven to create....

That is its purpose. The grievance procedure may appear to take longer than it should but its end result is justice through reason.[76]

CHAPTER SUMMARY

A major test of effective labor relations is in the day-to-day administration of the collective bargaining agreement. A grievance is an alleged violation of the rights of workers on the job. Generally, a grievance alleges a violation of rights under a collective bargaining agreement, but it need not be limited to this. A grievance is not just a complaint; it is a more carefully and precisely written statement of a problem. In the past, when grievances were not satisfactorily resolved, unions often went on strike. But a better way of handling such problems has evolved in the United States over the past 40 years. Collective bargaining agreements now set up a formal procedure in which grievances are written down and considered in a series of three to five steps which involve higher-level management and union personnel at each successive step. Grievances which remain unsettled may be submitted to a neutral party for a decision that is legally binding on both parties. The union ordinarily agrees not to strike over grievances, and the company and the union both agree to be bound by the arbitrator's decision. This procedure is the cornerstone of American labor relations. It limits work stoppages and provides a stability to our labor relations which is often absent abroad.

When management and the union cannot resolve a grievance submitted by a union, the union must decide whether to proceed to the final step of the grievance procedure: arbitration. Arbitrators are private judges who are selected by a variety of means. Sometimes companies and unions have a permanent arbitrator or panel of arbitrators to hear their disputes. Most often, an arbitrator is requested from the American Arbitration Association or the Federal Mediation and Conciliation Service. Most arbitrators are lawyers.

Arbitration is an adversary proceeding like a trial in court. In a hearing, the arbitrator listens to testimony. After the hearing the arbitrator studies any written briefs and renders a decision. Arbitration decisions may be enforced in court, although the full range of due process requirements of the courts is not applied to arbitration proceedings. An arbitrator's function is usually to interpret the collective bargaining agreement between the parties, not to apply his or her standards of what is right in a given situation.

A formal grievance procedure followed by arbitration can be time-consuming. In order to shorten the process, some companies and unions have begun to experiment with accelerated, or expedited, arbitration. Under

---

[76] Byron Yaffe, ed., *The Saul Wallen Papers* (Ithaca: New York State School of Labor and Industrial Relations, Cornell, 1974), pp. 52–54.

one such program, decisions were due from arbitrators within 48 hours of a hearing.

The courts have sought to compel labor and management to a peaceful resolution of grievances through arbitration. The Supreme Court has given support to the arbitration process in a series of decisions, and judicial deferral to arbitration has become a basic tenet of national labor policy. However, the Civil Rights Act and other areas involving statutory violations have raised questions about the independence of arbitration from the courts and NLRB.

Arbitration sometimes competes as a forum for dispute settlement with the NLRB, although the NLRB has deferred to arbitration as a preferred means of dispute settlement. The Collyer Doctrine, or the doctrine of deferral to arbitration, is a controversial policy which constitutes an important legal recognition of the role of the grievance process, and arbitration, in resolving labor-management disputes.

QUESTIONS FOR THOUGHT AND DISCUSSION

1 How does a grievance differ from a complaint, or gripe? Should a union process all complaints as grievances? Why or why not? What standards should a union use in deciding whether to process a grievance?

2 Should management have the right to file grievances? What types of grievances?

3 Should the law require nonunion companies to submit employee grievances to arbitration? Why or why not?

4 Is arbitration a good way to settle grievances? Why or why not? Is there a better way? If so, what is it?

5 Should an arbitrator help one side make its case if it is inexpertly represented? Why or why not?

6 The success of the arbitration procedure depends on the willingness of unions and employers to let persons from outside their own ranks make decisions about matters which both unions and employers feel very strongly about and in which they have significant financial interest. Unions and companies in other countries are often unwilling to give the power of decision through arbitration to an outsider. Why do you think American firms and unions accept this system?

7 What is the relationship of the courts and the NLRB to the arbitration process? When is arbitration subject to review by the courts? Do you think arbitration should exclude alleged violations of the statutes?

8 Should an arbitrator ever base a decision on federal law rather than on a collective bargaining agreement?

9 Why do you think there are so many steps in the grievance procedure? Should the process be shorter?

10 What explanations exist for differences in grievance rates between companies, plants, and even departments? Does the number of grievances filed result from the characteristics of employees or from other factors?

11 How can management or the union help prevent wildcat strikes?

12 What is the presumption of arbitrability? How is it applied in the public and the private sectors?

SELECTED READING

Bureau of National Affairs, *Grievance Guide*, 6th ed. (Washington D.C., 1982).

Elkouri, Frank, and Edna Elkouri, *How Arbitration Works*, 4th ed. (Washington, D.C.: Bureau of National Affairs, 1985).

Gould, William B., *Strikes, Dispute Procedures, and Arbitration: Essays on Labor Law* (Westport, Conn.: Greenwood Press, 1985).

Hays, Paul, *Labor Arbitration: A Dissenting View* (New Haven, Conn.: Yale University Press, 1966).

Landis, Brook I., *Value Judgments in Arbitration: A Case Study of Saul Wallen* (Ithaca: New York State School of Industrial and Labor Relations, Cornell, 1977).

Livernash, E. Robert, and David A. Peach, *Grievance and Resolution: A Study in Basic Steel* (Cambridge, Mass.: Harvard University Press, 1974).

Repas, Bob, *Contract Administration: A Guide for Stewards and Local Officers* (Washington, D.C.: Bureau of National Affairs, 1984).

Shils, Edward B., et al., *Industrial Peacemaker: George W. Taylor's Contributions to Collective Bargaining* (Philadelphia: The University of Pennsylvania Press, 1979).

Yaffe, Byron, ed., *The Saul Wallen Papers* (Ithaca: New York State School of Labor and Industrial Relations, Cornell, 1974).

Zack, Arnold, and Richard I. Block, *The Labor Agreement in Negotiation and Arbitration* (Washington D.C.: Bureau of National Affairs, 1983).

F

SUBJECTS OF COLLECTIVE BARGAINING

The bargaining power of companies and unions is used for specific objectives. Among the most common objectives are those involving the setting of particular wage rates, benefits, and working conditions. But bargaining power is not all there is to establishing wages and conditions of work. The actions of management and labor must also reflect the environment in which they are to be carried out. Wages must be adjusted so that employees may keep up or improve their standard of living. But wages must also be balanced so that a company may sell its products at a fair profit. Working conditions must be adjusted to meet changing circumstances in production and also to meet the changing expectations of employees about what a job ought to involve.

CHAPTER 13

THEORIES ABOUT WAGES

Probably no subject is more central to labor-management relations than is compensation. The amount of compensation, its forms, and the processes by which it is determined are vital issues to both employers and employees. At a superficial level, the matter may not appear to be very complicated. Presumably, the employer wants compensation to be low, the employee wants it to be high. But this observation provides very little basis on which to understand the problems that questions of compensation entail.

Ordinarily we think of pay as wages or salaries, and these are, in fact, the most important forms of compensation. But they are not the only forms. Employees also receive benefits, such as pensions and health insurance, as compensation for performing their jobs. And employees often get paid when they are *not* working, in the form of paid holidays, vacations, and sick leave, for example. Performing a job entitles an employee to a set of benefits in addition to a wage or salary.

There was a time when an employee received little from a job except an hourly wage. But as different forms of pay and benefits have developed, the content of compensation packages has become much more complex. This development has introduced confusion into our terminology and therefore requires great care in the use of words. Table 13-1 sets out the major terms relating to compensation practices. Briefly, pay and benefits make up compensation. Pay, in turn, is composed of wages, salaries, and/or incentive earnings. "Earnings" is sometimes used as a synonym for pay. Benefits include three different general types and many more specific forms, which will be discussed later.

There is great variation in the amount of pay and the form and quantity of

TABLE 13-1 TERMS RELATING TO COMPENSATION

Compensation:	The total value of what an employee receives from an employer for performing a job
Wage rate:	A rate of pay per hour
Pay (or earnings):	The amount of money an employee receives
Salary:	A weekly, biweekly, monthly, or annual rate of pay
Incentive earnings:	Pay based on the amount of work an employee performs
Benefits:	**1** Payments to an employee that are not directly related to an hour's work or to quantity of work performed (e.g., paid holidays, paid vacations)
	2 Services provided to employees (e.g., health care, pensions)
	3 Payments made on behalf of employees to purchase services or benefits (e.g., health insurance, life insurance)

benefits attached to different jobs. Some jobs are high-paying jobs; some are low-paying. Some jobs carry many benefits; others carry few or none. Some high-paying jobs also have high benefit levels; other high-paying jobs have few or no benefits. And the same is true for low-paying jobs. In the American economy the range from high to low and the composition of compensation packages are very wide; new approaches are appearing constantly.

Some difficult issues in compensation involve how low, or how high, it is to be set. Even if a company were free to set compensation with total disregard of the wishes of its employees, it would still have to establish compensation at a level in accord with its other personnel needs and policies. It would have to set compensation at a level at which workers would accept jobs. To the extent that the company required skilled workers, it would have to set compensation at a level that would induce workers already possessing the skills to accept its jobs or induce workers without skills to acquire them. Conversely, if employees had so strong a union that they could set wages without regard to the employer's wishes, they would still have to be careful not to set so high a wage that costs rose until no one purchased the product of their employer, and their jobs were lost. In effect, because neither firms nor employees exist independently, they must have due regard for setting compensation at levels that neither cause the firm to have no workers nor cause the workers to have no jobs. *The market*, composed of other firms and employees, *sets these limits.* But within these limits, or even, for a short while, outside them,[1] there is much range for disagreement.

[1] A firm may set compensation below the market level, or a union may set it above the market level, in the short run because it takes market forces time to operate. Thus, a firm paying its employees below the market level may experience an increasing number of vacancies before it takes corrective action, and a union setting rates above market levels may see unemployment rise for a while until it reacts to the unwillingness of consumers to purchase the high-priced products the union's members produce.

How is the setting of compensation levels to be explained? What causes some wage rates to be different from other wage rates? What factors cause one person to earn more than another person? These are questions about which people have long speculated, and extensive studies have been conducted in an attempt to answer them.

Elsewhere in this book, space is devoted to theories about various labor relations phenomena. There are theories about such things as the formation and the development of American business, the development of American labor unions, negotiations and the results of negotiations. In addition, there are theories about grievances, strikes, and dispute resolution. Theories are, after all, simply the explanations which various people have given of phenomena. Theories sometimes have a special importance, however. In some instances theories, because they are widely held, have strongly affected certain events (i.e., the theories become actors in the process, not merely distant explanations). In other instances theories are so widely held that people believe they know how certain things occur and will not hear of any other explanation. Sometimes people even intentionally ignore facts that do not fit their theories.

Theories often affect what is actually done in wage setting. Because some people believe that wage rates should always increase in step with consumer prices, formulas have been established which cause such increases. Because other people believe that wages should increase only step by step with productivity, the government has sometimes announced the rate of productivity increase as a guideline for wage increases without reference to price changes (as was done in 1962). In addition, because some people believe wages are set by supply and demand, they think unions really don't accomplish anything for their members. In contrast, because other people think wages are set by bargaining, they dismiss any discussion of economic factors in negotiations or elsewhere.

Theories also sometimes cause people to become blind to certain types of influences. A union leader may say, for example, that wage setting is a bargaining process, not an economic process. "I don't care what the company can afford to pay; I have to get a big increase in pay for my members or I won't get reelected." Or a business person may say, "The marketplace will set the right wages for my employees, so I don't have to have any policy about what I pay them." And government officials may say, "The whole wage-setting process depends on the economic situation, so there is no influence we can have on it. We might as well leave it alone. It doesn't matter what the structure of bargaining is, or how companies and unions negotiate, or with whom." Other government officials may say, "Wages are set by a political process, just like prices. The big, strong organizations get big increases. It doesn't matter about the economic situation. We ought to attack the organizations, not their behavior." Is there merit in any of these views?

FACTORS INCLUDED IN A WAGE THEORY

Theories of compensation were easier to understand when wages made up virtually all of compensation. But this is no longer the case. It is necessary now to inquire what a theory is trying to explain. A wage rate is a relatively simple concept, and comparisons can easily be made among wage rates. Benefits (such as pensions and holidays) complicate measurement and comparison a great deal. A theory which dealt with wages and benefits in all their variety would be a very cumbersome thing. So theorists use a simplification which reduces fringe benefits to their estimated monetary value, as if they were an addition to the wage rate, and compares these package values. For some purposes this is a valid procedure, but for others it is not. For example, a wage rate (i.e., dollars per hour) has the advantage of being the same amount for both the employer and the employees. But a pension plan is not the same amount. Consider two pension plans that promise the same benefits but cost different employers different amounts. If each pension is valued by its cost to the employer, then one group of employees is estimated to get a higher pension, although both groups of employees get the same dollar benefit when they retire. Yet if the pension plan is given a value based on its benefit level, then it appears that the cost of the plan is the same for both companies when, in fact, one company pays more for the pension than the other. Many benefits have this characteristic when they are valued, reflecting the fact that benefits separate costs from advantages to the employees. In contrast, when a wage rate is valued, cost for employers and benefits for employees are identical. To a very large degree, benefits exist because labor and management know that benefits cannot be measured as simply as a wage rate. (That is, an employer may offer a particular benefit because the union gives that benefit a higher value than the company estimates its costs to be.)

But in order to simplify, theorists ignore these complexities and instead they arbitrarily use the estimated cost to the employer. In studying the theories, the student must do the same. But it is important to keep in mind the limitations of such precise and quantitative analyses. Let us, however, assume for the purposes of this chapter that wages and fringe benefits can be usefully combined into a single measure of the compensation package. Also, let us, for convenience, follow the terminology of economic analysis (although technically incorrect) and call that package a "wage."

Differences in Compensation

The American economy involves a very large number of different rates of compensation. Some people make a great deal more money from their occupations than others. Since earnings are the major factor by which living standards are established, the inequality in earnings is reflected to a large degree in inequality in living standards. This inequality is a social as well as an economic phenomenon and occasions considerable comment.[2] Some people think the amount of compensation should be essentially alike for all jobs. Others believe differences in compensation are necessary to provide work incentives and to reflect different economic situations. Just how does compensation differ among working Americans? How much does it differ? How has it changed over the years?

Compensation differs in the United States in several ways. The most important differentials are:

- Geography
- Occupation
- Industry and plant size
- Demography
- Union representation

It is very difficult, if not impossible, to separate these influences from each other. For example, suppose we compare wages in different sections of the country. Wages of the average worker in the South tend to be below those of the average worker in the North. But what is the reason for this? Is this a result of lower living costs in the South? Is it a result of a different industrial mix (with less high-wage heavy manufacturing in the South than in the North)? Does it result from a different mix of occupations (with fewer high-paid professional and skilled workers in the South)? Is it because the Southern labor force includes a higher proportion of minority workers (who have received less pay than white workers)? Or, finally, is it a result of a higher level of union organization in the North than in the South?

Alternatively, one could compare wages among industries. The steel industry pays considerably higher wages on average than does the textile industry. Why? Some may say because steel is naturally a higher-wage industry because of the economics of the marketplace. Others point out that the steel industry is concentrated in the high-wage North, rather than the South. Still others note that the steel industry has a higher proportion of skilled workers in its labor force than the textile industry, and skilled workers ordinarily earn higher pay. Finally, some might argue that steel has very few women workers, while textiles employ very many women (who often earn less pay than men).

In discussions about why one group of workers receives more than others, it becomes clear that cause and effect can become very confused. Elaborate studies are necessary to unravel the factors which establish differentials, and there continue to be disputes about the methods and findings of these stud-

---

[2] See Lester C. Thurow, *Generating Inequality* (New York: Basic Books, 1975); and *The Zero Sum Society* (New York: Basic Books, 1980).

ies. That differentials exist is incontrovertible, however, and there is evidence that they change over time.

Geographic Differences

In the United States, wage and total compensation levels tend to be highest in the West, intermediate in the North and East, and lowest in the South. In part, these regional differentials reflect the distribution of occupations and industries and the different composition of the labor force in various regions. But more significant are the regional differences which exist within industries and within occupations. For example, in industries such as retail food, paper, and furniture, companies operating on a national scale tend to pay less in Southern markets than elsewhere. (Some industries, however, have the same wage structure in North and South, especially where a uniform national collective bargaining agreement exists.)

Studies have been made to try to identify the reasons for the North-South regional differentials. It is tempting to give the reasons used above, i.e., that the South has few major manufacturing industries and a low-wage occupational and population mix. But why should wages vary between North and South in the same occupation and in the same industry, as they often do? There was much interest in this topic at the end of World War II. Richard Lester, summarizing two studies, concluded, "The average North-South wage differential varies widely and irrationally from industry to industry."[3] By the term "irrationally" Lester apparently meant that the existence and size of the differentials could not be explained by the expected economic differences between industries and geographic regions. More recent studies, using the considerable data which have accumulated since the late 1940s, suggest that much of the North-South differential is a result of a less educated work force and the greater proportion of blacks in the South.[4]

Another major aspect of geographic diversity in wages involves urban, suburban, and rural areas.[5] Generally, urban areas pay higher wages than suburban areas, and both pay more than rural areas. This tends to be true in all geographic regions.[6] In recent years, however, the movement of industry to suburban locations has reduced the suburban-urban differential.

[3] Richard A. Lester, "Diversity in North-South Wage Differentials," *Southern Economic Journal*, 12, January 1946, p. 242; and "Southern Wage Differentials," *Southern Economic Journal*, 13, April 1947, pp. 386–394.

[4] Gerald Scully, "Interstate Wage Differentials: A Cross-Section Analysis," *American Economic Review*, 59:5, December 1969, pp. 757–773; L. E. Galloway, "The North-South Wage Differential," *Review of Economics and Statistics*, 45:3, August 1963, pp. 264–272; George D. Stamas, "The Puzzling Lag in Southern Earnings," *Monthly Labor Review* 104:6, June 1981, pp. 27–36.

[5] Victor R. Fuchs, "Hourly Earnings Differentials by Region and Size of City," *Monthly Labor Review*, 90:1, January 1967, pp. 22–26.

[6] Davis S. Thomsen, "Biographic Differentials in Salaries within the U.S.," *Personnel Journal*, 53:9, September 1974, pp. 670–674.

Among metropolitan areas, pay levels tend to be higher in the larger areas. One study shows that larger establishment (plant) size and greater levels of unionization also are correlated with higher earnings levels.[7] Living costs are higher in the Northeast and West than elsewhere in the country. Do geographic wage differences reflect this? No, says a recent study, unless industry differences are accounted for.[8]

Occupational Differences

People in different occupations earn different amounts. Table 13-2 shows the median annual earnings in the United States in 1985 by broad occupational group. It can be seen that the executives, managers, and administrators earned, on average, almost twice as much as service workers. Within each occupational group are even wider differentials among the detailed jobs which make up a broad grouping.

Industrial Differences

Average earnings differ substantially among industries. Table 13-3 shows the percentage divergence from the average of all private-sector industries for major sectors of the economy in 1947 and in 1986. The range is wide. In construction and mining, average hourly earnings exceeded the average in the total private economy by 42 percent in 1986. In retail trade, 1986 hourly earnings were only 69 percent of those in the total private economy. Construction average hourly earnings in 1986 were more than double those in retail trade

[7] S. E. Baldwin and R. S. Daski, "Occupational Pay Differences among Metropolitan Areas," *Monthly Labor Review*, 99:5, May 1976, pp. 29–35.
[8] John E. Buckley, "Do Area Wages Reflect Area Living Costs?" *Monthly Labor Review*, 102:11, November 1979, pp. 24–29.

TABLE 13-2   MEDIAN INCOME BY OCCUPATIONAL GROUP, 1985

	Men	**Women**
Executive, administrators, and managerial	$33,530	$20,565
Professional specialty	32,812	21,781
Technical and related support	26,266	18,177
Sales	26,445	12,682
Administrative support, including clerical	22,997	15,157
Machine operators, assemblers, and inspectors	20,786	12,232
Handlers, equipment cleaners, helpers, and laborers	15,755	12,704
Service workers	16,824	10,204
Total (Average)	24,195	15,624

Source: U.S. Bureau of the Census, *Current Population Reports*, series P-60, No. 154, 1986.

TABLE 13-3 AVERAGE HOURLY EARNINGS IN MAJOR SECTORS OF THE ECONOMY AS A PERCENT-
AGE OF ALL PRIVATE-INDUSTRY AVERAGE HOURLY EARNINGS, 1947 AND 1986

	1947	1986
Total private economy	100	100
	($1.23)	($8.76)
Construction	139	142
Transportation and public utilities	(N/A)	133
Mining	135	142
Manufacturing	108	111
Wholesale trade	107	107
Finance, insurance, and real estate	98	95
Services	(N/A)	93
Retail trade	73	69

*N/A—not available.
Source: U.S. Department of Labor, *Employment and Training Report of the President* (Washington, D.C.:
U.S. Government Printing Office, 1976). Also, *Employment and Earnings,* 34:1, January 1987, p. 225.

in 1986. In 1947 these sectors of the economy had much the same ranking,
though the range of difference was smaller.

More detailed data on specific industries can also be obtained. Among
manufacturing industries, for example, in 1986 motor vehicles and equipment, primary metals (especially steel manufacturing), and petroleum refining had the highest average hourly earnings. The apparel, leather, and textiles industries had the lowest earnings. Again, the highest-level industry
had earnings more than double those in the lowest-level industry.

Studies of the factors underlying earnings differences among manufacturing industries normally identify as causal factors such items as size of firm,
market structure, profitability of firm, and level of productivity per
employee.[9] Plant size is another important factor in wage differences. Several
studies have shown that, for various reasons, larger plants tend to pay
higher wage rates.[10]

Demographic Differences

Groups in our population do not make the same average earnings. In 1982
black workers had 23 percent less income, on average, than white workers.
Female workers in 1985 made 35 percent less on average than male
workers.[11] Younger workers made 38 percent less on average than older

[9] Frank C. Ripley, *The Structure of Wages in United States Manufacturing Industries, 1948 to 1964*
(New York: American Iron and Steel Institute, 1970); and Mark Lutz, "Quit Rates and the Quality of the Industrial Wage Structure," *Industrial Relations,* 16:1, February 1977, pp. 61–70.

[10] Richard A. Lester, "Pay Differences by Size of Establishment," *Industrial Relations,* 6:3,
October 1967, pp. 57–67; and Stanley H. Masters, "Wages and Plant Size: An Interindustry Analysis," *Review of Economics and Statistics,* 5:3, August 1969, pp. 341–345.

[11] U.S. Bureau of the Census, *Current Population Reports,* series p-60, No. 154, 1986.

workers.[12] Handicapped workers make less on average than non-handicapped workers. These are comparisons of averages, and in each instance there are exceptions. But the basic patterns in our society are unmistakable.

What causes pay differences on a demographic basis? To a large degree, differences in average pay among demographic groups reflect the different occupations, industries, and geographic areas in which people work.[13] But some of the difference is also explained by sex and race discrimination. Even within the same occupation, industry, and area, or even the same company or plant, women and blacks have often been paid lower than men and whites.[14] Some statistical studies have attempted to isolate the impact of this type of discrimination in establishing pay levels by standardizing average income statistics for region, industry, and occupation. These studies indicate that this sort of discrimination continues to exist in the United States, despite the fact that it is now illegal.[15] A study of earnings data suggests that the wage gap between whites and blacks has been narrowing and that between women and men decreased from 39 percent in 1978 to a 35 percent pay difference in 1983.[16]

Discrimination also operates by closing educational and occupational opportunities to women and blacks. Persons confined to lower educational and occupational levels receive lower earnings.[17] Discrimination as a legal problem was treated in Chapter 2.

Differences Resulting from Union Representation

Do unions cause workers who are represented by unions to earn more than other workers? Many people would say yes. But the evidence is not quite clear. In some instances, unions probably are responsible for wages being above what they would be in the absence of the unions. But in other instances, they are not. So the answer to the question of the impact of unions on wages tends to be "It depends."

---

[12] Earl F. Mellor, "Investigating Earning Differences," *Monthly Labor Review*, 107:6, June 1984, p. 19. See also Stanley H. Masters, *Black-White Income Differentials* (New York: Academic Press, 1975). Richard B. Freeman, "Changes in the Labor Market for Black Americans, 1948–1972," *Brookings Papers on Economic Activity*, 1, 1973, pp. 67–120.

[13] J. G. Hawerth, "Earnings, Productivity and Changes in Employment and Discrimination during the 1960s," *American Economic Review*, 65, March 1975, pp. 158–168.

[14] R. S. Goldfarb and J. R. Hosek, "Explaining Male-Female Wage Differentials for the Same Job," *Journal of Human Resources*, 11:1, Winter 1976, pp. 98–108.

[15] James V. Koch and J. F. Chizmas, Jr., *The Economics of Affirmative Action* (Lexington, Mass.: Lexington Books, 1976); and Carol L. Jusenius, "The Influence of Work Experience, Skill Requirements, and Occupational Segregation on Women's Earnings," *Journal of Economics and Business*, 29:2, Winter 1977, pp. 107–115.

[16] E. Mellor, op. cit., p. 26.

[17] M. A. Ferber and H. Lowry, "Sex Differentials in Earnings: A Reappraisal," *Industrial and Labor Relations Review*, 29:3, April 1976, pp. 377–387.

If a comparison is made of the pay rates of unionized employees versus nonunionized employees in the United States, unionized employees on average receive substantially higher pay. On average for 1986, union workers received an average weekly wage 37 percent higher than non-union employees (this includes all industries). The differentials were highest in percentage terms for union versus nonunion women and union versus nonunion black workers.[18] Figure 13-1 compares the median weekly earnings of union and nonunion workers by industry. A survey taken by the federal government in May 1973 showed that union workers' hourly earnings exceeded those for nonunion workers by as much as 44 percent for workers making transportation equipment and as little as 4 percent for salespersons.[19]

There has been considerable statistical investigation of this topic. Many studies have sought to determine if the existence of a union causes wages to be higher, where other factors are the same. In a pioneering study, H. G. Lewis estimated the proportionate wage advantage of union members over workers in the nonunion sector to be 15 percent in 1955–1958 but essentially

[18] U.S. Department of Labor, Bureau of Labor Statistics data, reported in *AFL-CIO News* 32:9, Feb. 28, 1987, p.1.
[19] P. M. Ryscavage, "Measuring Union-Nonunion Earnings Differentials in the U.S.," *Monthly Labor Review*, 97:12, December 1974, pp. 3–9. See also Paul L. Scheible, "Changes in Employee Compensation, 1966–72," *Monthly Labor Review*, 98:3, March 1975, pp. 10–16.

FIGURE 13-1   1986 median weekly earnings: union and nonunion compared. (*Source: Bureau of Labor Statistics, Household Data, 1986.*)

zero in the late 1940s and 38 percent in the early 1930s.[20] Subsequent studies, using better data sources, have come to a consistent general result: unions do tend to cause wages to be higher for the persons they represent.[21] But the studies vary widely in the amount by which the unions improve wages. Two recent studies of white males found a union advantage of 11 and 24 percent respectively.[22] These studies are consistent with Lewis's finding that the wage effect of unions varies over time and across industries.[23]

For example, a study of the impact of unionization on the compensation of white-collar employees found that overall union scales tend to exceed non-union pay by 3.5 to 4.0 percent and that these figures rise to 7.1 percent when fringe benefits are included in the comparison.[24]

Another study found that the relative wage advantage for union over non-union workers was 13.8 percent for plant-level agreements, 50.2 percent for craft-locality, agreements of a type common in the construction industry, and 19.6 percent for national agreements. And yet another study of construction found a 51.1 percent advantage for union workers.[25]

In another interesting statistical investigation, O. Ashenfelter estimated that unions increase the wages of black males covered by union agreements by 21 percent above what they would otherwise be. Ashenfelter also found that unions increased the wages of white males by 10 percent.[26] There have also been investigations of the impact of unions on wages in particular occupational groups and industries. For example, a study of 25,000 schoolteachers in 455 independent Oklahoma school districts in 1974–1975 came to the following conclusions:

[20] H. G. Lewis, *Unionism and Relative Wages in the United States: An Empirical Inquiry* (Chicago: University of Chicago Press, 1963). See also H. G. Lewis, "Union Relative Wage Effects: A Survey of Macro Estimates," *Journal of Labor Economics* 1:1, 1983, pp. 1–16.

[21] John Pencavel, "A Reconsideration of the Effects of Unionism on Relative Wages and Employment in the United States: 1920–1980," *Journal of Labor Economics*, 2, 1984, pp. 193–204.

[22] Harry C. Bentiam, "Union-Nonunion Wage Differential Revisited," *Journal of Labor Research*, 8:4, Fall 1987, p. 381; and Ronald L. Oaxaca and Michael R. Ransom, "Searching for the Effect of Unionism," *Journal of Labor Research*, 9:2, Spring 1988, p. 144. See also L. W. Weiss, "Concentration and Labor Earnings," *American Economic Review*, 56, March 1966, pp. 96–117; F. P. Stafford, "Concentration and Labor Earnings: Comment," *American Economic Review*, 58, March 1968, pp. 174–181; and A. Throop, "The Union–Non-Union Wage Differential," *American Economic Review*, 56, March 1966, pp. 79–99.

[23] P. M. Ryscavage, loc. cit.

[24] Joseph R. Antos, "Union Effects on White Collar Compensation," *Industrial and Labor Relations Review*, 36:3, April 1983, pp. 461–479.

[25] Janet C. Hunt, B. F. Kiker, and C. Glyn Williams, "The Effect of Type of Union on Member-Nonmember Wage Differentials," *Journal of Labor Research*, 8:1, Winter 1987, pp. 59–68 (esp. p. 64); and Jeffrey M. Perloff and Robin C. Sickles, "Union Wage, Hours and Earnings Differentials in the Construction Industry," *Journal of Labor Economics*, 5:2, 1987, pp. 174ff.

[26] O. Ashenfelter, "Racial Discrimination and Trade Unionism," *Journal of Political Economy*, 80, May-June 1972, pp. 435–464.

(1) The existence of union activity significantly increases teachers' earnings, and (2) This increase is accomplished by inflating the value of educational attainment and years of service [in establishing pay scales].[27]

But is it unionism that creates a wage advantage for workers, or is it the collective bargaining process? For the private sector in the American economy, this question is not very important. In virtually all instances employees who are in a union also bargain collectively with their employer. Unionism and bargaining are so intimately coupled that a researcher cannot estimate their separate effects on wage levels.

In the public sector, however, unions exist where law does not permit, or even forbids, collective bargaining. By comparing wages for unionized employees who bargain collectively with wages for unionized employees who don't bargain collectively—and standardizing for other factors that might create a difference in wages—researchers can identify the separate influences of unionism and collective bargaining. When this analysis was done, it turned out that unionism alone did not create a wage differential with nonunion employees. The differential was created in favor of those people who had the collective bargaining process working for them. *Collective bargaining, not unionism alone, creates a wage advantage.*[28]

Why don't union employees receive a larger differential over nonunion employees? There are probably several reasons. First, some nonunion employers make it a policy to pay their employees just above the union rates, in order, in part, to discourage unionization. The activities of the union therefore affect both union and nonunion employees almost equally, although by different processes. Second, unions cannot simply ignore economic factors. When nonunion employers pay below the union scale and unionized employers compete with them, the union must often moderate its wage demands so as not to cause the unionized employers to become noncompetitive. In the construction industry, for example, the unions are often confronted in negotiations with demands from the employers that wage increases be kept low to avoid having additional construction projects awarded by owners to nonunion contractors. In recent years, construction unions have often agreed to specially low wage increases to meet nonunion competition. Third, some companies can afford to pay more than others. But unions are not always able to discriminate among such companies, that is, to get higher wages from some than from others. Suppose, for example, that a union tries to keep many firms unionized and must do so by having all the firms pay the same wage rate. In such a case, the union is probably keeping the wages paid by the company with the higher ability to pay below what they might be in the absence of the union.

[27] Alexander B. Holmes, ''Effects of Union Activity on Teachers' Earnings,'' *Industrial Relations*, 15:3, October 1976, pp. 328–332.

[28] David Lewin, ''Wages and Unionism in the Public Sector: The Case of Police,'' *The Review of Economics and Statistics*, 63:1, February 1981, pp. 53–59.

These three reasons suggest why unions are not able to raise the wages of the people they represent any more than the statistical studies indicate. But there are people who believe unions don't really have even the effect the studies show. Instead, they believe, unions in general tend to organize the firms with a high ability to pay, i.e., firms which would tend to be high-wage firms even if they were nonunion. In the view of these observers, unions have little or no impact on wages.[29]

It is unfortunate that after many years of investigation and the completion of a large number of careful studies there should be so little agreement among economists on many basic questions on the impact of labor unions on wages. The survey of the research literature given above demonstrates the continuing controversy about this matter. A recent review of the economic evidence (relying on a much larger sample of the literature than can be cited in a textbook such as this) comes to the following conclusion: "The preponderance of evidence indicates that union effects on a wide variety of economic variables...represent real (not illusory) impacts." Thus, the review concludes, "The operating assumption that trade unions have important real effects is strongly supported by the...evidence."[30]

OLDER THEORIES OF WAGES

There are many theories of wages, and each has had a period of popularity. Newer conceptions, fitting changing circumstances, have displaced older theories in popularity. Each theory has a kernel of truth. This kernel of truth has caused old theories to persist and to remain with us even today in the minds of some people.

In part the persistence of old theories reflects the function of any theory. A theory is not a once-and-for-all explanation. Instead, it is a simplification of reality which serves a useful purpose. The questions people ask about wages change over time, and the theories which are popular change according to the use to which they are put. But the questions which are most popular at any given time are not the only ones asked, just the most popular. When other questions are asked, the older theories are sometimes brought out to answer them, for the newer theories may be silent on the matter.

Among the older theories, somewhat discredited by researchers today but still alive in the thoughts and behavior of many people, are the following:

The Wages Fund

The wages fund doctrine starts from the observation that all goods and services are the product of labor. Thus, labor produces everything, but it does

---

[29] George E. Johnson, "Economic Analysis of Trade Unions," *Proceedings* of the American Economic Association, *American Economic Review*, 65:2, May 1975, pp. 23–28.

[30] Richard B. Freeman and James L. Medoff, "The Impact of Collective Bargaining: Illusion or Reality?" in Robert McKersie, D. Quinn Mills, and Jack Stieber, eds., *Industrial Relations in the United States: A Critical Assessment* (Madison, Wis.: Industrial Relations Research Association, 1982).

not receive all that it produces. Instead, much of production goes into rents, profits, interest, and the support of nonworking persons. The problem for theory, therefore, is to explain how these "deductions" occur and what their magnitude can be expected to be. What is left of output after the deductions is called the "wages fund" and goes to the workers. The distribution of the wages fund among workers results in wage rates. If there are many workers, the wage rate goes down. If there are few workers, the wage rate goes up.[31]

This theory, which is not held in much regard by economists today, is nonetheless much subscribed to by workers and union officials. At the end of the First World War, the wages fund doctrine provided much of the impetus for limiting immigration of workers to the United States. The present-day opposition of the unions to a greater volume of immigration arises in large part from the fear that a larger number of workers will depress wage rates. (Incidentally, more sophisticated economic theories might also call for immigration restrictions, but on other grounds.)

The Subsistence Theory

The subsistence theory of wages is the result of the application of a theory of population growth to the question of wage levels. Over a period of 300 years (beginning in the 1500s) there developed in Europe a theory of population to which the name of Thomas Malthus, an English clergyman writing in the early 1800s, was ultimately attached. The theory held, in brief, that human populations tend to increase much more rapidly than it is possible to increase the food supply. In Malthus's words:

> The main peculiarity which distinguishes man from other animals in the means of his support is the power which he possesses of very greatly increasing these means. But this power is obviously limited by the scarcity of land and by the decreasing proportions of produce which must necessarily be obtained from the continual additions of capital applied to land already in cultivation.[32]

In consequence, Malthus said, the human population would exert constant pressure on available food supplies.

The pressure of population on food supplies could be expressed as a falling level of wages. The wage level would decline as population expanded until the subsistence level was reached. Wages could not long remain below the subsistence level because people could not survive. As population growth drove wages down, Malthus thought, wars, disease, and other phe-

---

[31] Adam Smith (*The Wealth of Nations*) held such a theory of wages. See Joseph A. Schumpeter, *History of Economic Analysis* (New York: Oxford University Press, 1954), pp. 662–663.

[32] Thomas Malthus, "A Summary View of the Principle of Population" (first published in 1824), in *On Population: Three Essays* (New York: New American Library, 1960), p. 15.

nomena would periodically reduce the population suddenly, so that wages could rise above subsistence and the cycle could begin anew.

The Iron Law of Wages

Malthus's doctrine permitted wages to fluctuate around the subsistence level. But a German theorist, Ferdinand Lassalle, converted the Malthusian theory into one in which wages were kept at a level of bare subsistence. Relying upon population pressure and the exploitation of workers by landowners and employers, he held that wages would not rise substantially above subsistence level. This bleak doctrine Lassalle named "the iron law of wages."[33]

Marginal Productivity Theory

The unrelieved pessimism of the iron law gave way in the latter part of the nineteenth century to a far more optimistic and complicated theory. In part, this occurred because wages, in fact, did not show evidence of falling toward bare subsistence levels. Instead, production outran population, and in many areas of the world, wages rose despite a rapidly increasing population. Malthusian theories fell into disrepute, only to be resurrected in our own day as the pressure of population on food supply again appears to be approaching dangerous levels in the underdeveloped nations of the world.

Marginal productivity theory abandoned the effort to explain all wage rates at once and instead concentrated on individual rates. The theorists ap-

[33] Schumpeter, op. cit., p. 650.

FIGURE 13-2   Total output.

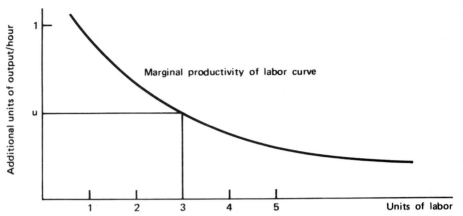

FIGURE 13-3   Marginal productivity of labor.

plied the law of decreasing returns, which holds that as successive units of labor are applied to land (or to capital), more output is produced each hour, but at a decreasing rate. Figure 13-2 shows this relationship. The *additional* output obtained by adding units of labor can also be calculated and plotted (Figure 13-3). Thus, the first unit of labor produces 1 unit of output (see Figure 13-2). The second unit of labor produces just a bit less than 1 unit of output (point *o* in Figure 13-3). The third unit added produces a little less additional output than did the second, etc. This relationship is called the "marginal productivity of labor."

The essence of marginal productivity theory is the proposition that if the units of labor which are used are specified, then the wage rate is determined to be the amount of output the marginal unit of labor produces. Thus, if 3 units of labor are used, the wage rate is the amount of additional output produced by the third unit of labor. In Figure 13-3 we may read that amount from the point in the curve at 3 units of labor; this output is labeled *u* on the vertical axis. Furthermore, according to marginal productivity theory, *all* units of labor receive what the marginal unit produces. And since the 3 units together produce more than three times what the third unit produces, a surplus is left from total production for rents, profits, and other purposes.[34]

CONTEMPORARY WAGE THEORIES

Broadly, wage theories may be classified as emphasizing either market (i.e., supply and demand) or bargaining. The market analysis conceives of transactions involving individuals (not large groups) and of simple behavioral pat-

[34] The best statement of the marginal productivity theory of wages is in John R. Hicks, *Theory of Wages* (London: Macmillan, 1932). A second edition was published by St. Martin's Press, New York, in 1964. For a recent critical analysis of the theory, see Robert H. Frank, "Are Workers Paid Their Marginal Products?" *American Economic Review*, 74:4, September 1984, pp. 549–571.

terns. Employers are presumed to try to buy labor at the lowest price and workers to look for the highest wage, with little regard by the employer for the characteristics of workers and their unions or by workers for characteristics of employers and their corporations. In fact, in most circumstances, the matter is more complicated. The theories which attempt to include this complexity in the analysis, by paying greater attention to the characteristics of employers and workers, may be characterized as bargaining theories (or "institutional" theories, because they consider the importance of labor market institutions, such as unions and corporations). But the bargaining theories also incorporate supply-demand analysis.[35] They simply give it less significance in the total picture. And even among bargaining theories, some stress economic factors more than others.

Supply and Demand

What Is Supply-Demand Analysis? The difficulty with marginal productivity theory is that it is only half of a theory of wages. It describes what the wage rate will be if the number of units of labor is specified, but doesn't tell us how to determine the number of units of labor which will be used. It is, therefore, incomplete. Alfred Marshall, an English economist, described the problem by saying that wages (and product prices also) are determined by a supply and demand process which is like a pair of scissors, in that both blades are needed to make a cut. The marginal productivity theory of wages was only one blade of the scissors, the demand side.[36] Where was a theorist to find the other blade?

The supply side consisted of the willingness of workers to offer labor at various wage rates. Presumably, as wage rates rose, the amount of labor offered would increase. Thus, a diagram could be drawn which showed a supply of labor curve (see Figure 13-4).

A labor market may now be said to exist. On one side are potential employers, who will hire labor and will be prepared to hire more labor the lower the wage rate. On the other side of the market are workers, who are prepared to sell labor. It may be expected that more people will be willing to work, and many already working will be prepared to work longer hours, as the wage rate rises. At some point, a bargain will be struck in the labor market and a transaction will occur. The bargain will set a certain wage rate and a quantity of labor which is hired by employers and sold by workers.

This market process may be put into diagrammatic form. Figure 13-5 shows the value of output in a standard monetary unit, i.e, dollars per hour. This simplifying procedure is reflective of a modern economy in which em-

---

[35] Thomas A. Kochan and Richard N. Block, "An Interindustry Analysis of Bargaining Outcomes: Preliminary Evidence," *Quarterly Journal of Economics*, 91:3, August 1977, pp. 431–452; F. R. Warren-Boulton, "Vertical Control by Labor Unions," *The American Economic Review*, 67:3, June 1977, pp. 309–322.

[36] Alfred Marshall, *Principles of Economics*, 8th ed. (London: Macmillan, 1961), p. 569.

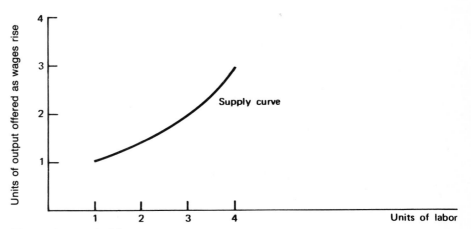

FIGURE 13-4   The supply curve for labor.

ployers sell output for money and pay workers in money. The marginal productivity curve is shown as a demand curve for labor.

The demand and supply curves intersect at a single point, marked e in Figure 13-5. At that point, the quantity of labor demanded by employers (point q) is equal to the quantity of labor workers are willing to provide (point q also). At the intersection of the curves e, the market "clears," and a wage rate w and employment level q are determined. The point e may be called an "equilibrium point." This process is what is meant by such commonly used phrases as "supply and demand set our wage rates," and "the market will set wages."

Suppose the market is not allowed to operate. Instead, the government sets a wage rate by administrative action at point $\bar{w}$ in Figure 13-6. What will

FIGURE 13-5   The labor market.

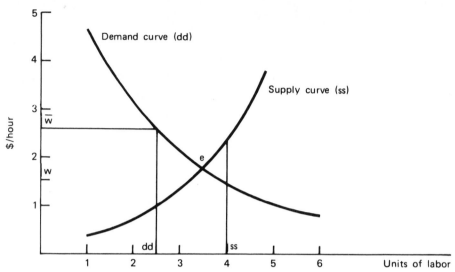

FIGURE 13-6 Unemployment in the labor market.

happen? At a wage rate equal to $\bar{w}$, employers would want to hire only the number of units of labor market *dd*. But workers would offer a number of units of labor equal to *ss*. There would be more persons looking for work than employers would want, and the difference would be called unemployment.

The supply and demand curves are not fixed, but instead move their position (and alter their shape) as conditions which affect them change. For example, suppose a corporation makes blue jeans, but jeans suddenly lose popularity with consumers. Then the demand curve for labor to produce jeans will shift down to the left in our diagram. This means that at any wage rate, the company will hire fewer workers than it would have hired before. Since the supply curve of workers is unchanged and the market clears, the wage rate and the number of people hired will both fall. Suppose the wage rate remains at its old level, however, perhaps as a result of a provision of a collective bargaining agreement. Then the number of workers the company employs would decline more than if the wage rate also fell.

The effect of a change in the wage rate on the level of employment can be measured on either the demand or the supply curve. Consider the demand curve. For any point on the curve, make the following calculation: If the wage rate is reduced a little bit, how much will the quantity of labor demanded increase? Figure 13-7 provides an illustration of this calculation. Now divide the change in the wage rate by the level of the wage rate (at point *y* on the vertical axis in Figure 13-7), then divide the change in the quantity of labor demanded by the previous number of units of labor (at point *x* on the horizontal axis in Figure 13-7). Both these numbers are ratios

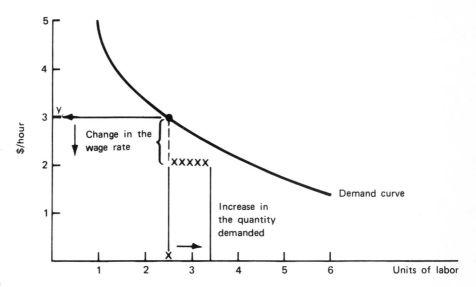

FIGURE 13-7

(or can be converted to percentages). Finally, create a ratio of the two ratios, that is, divide the percentage change in the level of employment (i.e., units of labor) by the percentage change in the wage rate. This ratio is the wage elasticity of employment demand or, for short, the "elasticity of demand."

An elasticity of demand which is greater than unity means that if wages are decreased, demand for labor will rise by *more* than a proportionate amount. (For example, if wages are reduced by 1.0 percent, employment will rise by 1.5 percent.)

An elasticity of demand which is equal to unity means that if wages are decreased, demand will rise by the *same* proportionate amount. (For example, if wages are reduced by 1.0 percent, employment will rise by 0.5 percent.)

An elasticity of demand which is less than unity means that if wages are decreased, demand for labor will rise by less than 1 proportionate amount. (For example, if wages are reduced by 1.0 percent, employment will rise by 0.5 percent.)

The Usefulness of Supply-Demand Analysis Supply-demand analysis is more complicated than the wages fund, subsistence, or even marginal productivity theory. But it is also more useful. In fact, many people in the United States think in terms of supply and demand and utilize it in determining their approach to many labor relations issues. When there is unemployment, business people often urge that wages be reduced in order to reduce unemployment. Unions, on the other hand, want wages to remain at existing levels, and so suggest that the government generate more spending.

This additional expenditure will cause the demand curve for labor to shift to the right and result in more people being hired (see Figures 13-8 and 13-9).

Supply-demand analysis is also called "partial equilibrium analysis." This term means that only one market (e.g., for a single occupation) is being studied at a time. What is happening in other markets will certainly affect the one being studied, but those effects are ignored in order to simplify the analysis. Like other simplifications, this one has disadvantages. In some situations the failure to take account of developments elsewhere causes the analysis of a single market to be incorrect. For example, a union may decide that if it agrees to an employer proposal to lower the wage rate, then workers will receive more employment. This conclusion is supported by supply-demand analysis. But what if, simultaneously, the product these workers produce is losing its popularity with consumers? Then the demand curve for the workers' services will be falling and may cancel out any potential employment gained from a lower wage rate. This situation also points out that the demand for labor is a "derived" demand. It comes solely from the demand of consumers for the product of labor. There is *no* demand for labor if there is no demand for the goods or services that labor produces. Therefore, to understand particular labor markets, one must also understand particular product markets.

There are other theories about wages in addition to those we have reviewed. Many economists have written about the subject, and each has a somewhat different approach. It is necessary, therefore, to be highly selective in reviewing theoretical work. The choice of only a few theorists for mention is not intended to disparage the work of others, nor to suggest to stu-

FIGURE 13-8   Reducing unemployment by lowering wages. A reduction in wages from w_1 to w_2 stimulates hiring to rise from q_1 to q_2 and causes unemployment to decline from UE_1 to UE_2.

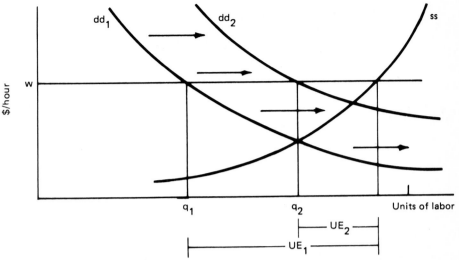

FIGURE 13-9 Reducing unemployment by increasing demand. An increase in spending by consumers causes the demand curve to shift from dd_1 to dd_2 and the number of employees hired to rise from q_1 to q_2, thus causing unemployment to decline from UE_1 to UE_2.

dents that there is not more to learn. In this section we will review the major types of current wage theories, in part by selecting the work of certain theorists for comparison and contrast.

Human Capital Theory

Previously in this chapter we reviewed differences in pay rates by occupation. These pay differentials reflect, in part, the degree to which people have made an investment in learning skills or a profession. An explanation of occupational pay differentials has developed around this insight, which is called "human capital theory." This theory stresses the financial costs of education to a person. These costs are of two types. First, there are the direct expenses of education, such as tuition, books, and living expenses. Second, there are the costs which come from not working while attending school or training courses. The earnings which people do not get because they are in school or in training are called "forgone earnings," or "opportunity costs," and are the hidden costs of education. (If a person is in an apprenticeship program, forgone earnings are the difference between the wages an apprentice receives and the wages which could be earned in some other occupation.)

Human capital theory holds that a person bears the cost of education (and/or training) because he or she expects higher earnings in the future. In other words, education or skills training is like an investment of capital in a business, which pays dividends later. Because education is an investment in a person, it is human, not business, capital. The educated person expects to earn more in the future than the uneducated person. The pay differences between occupations are said to represent the return on the human capital invested. The higher the level of education (and consequently, the greater its cost), the higher the pay is predicted to be.[37] The exact amount of the return on human capital invested changes over time. Currently, the financial return on investment in education appears to be declining.[38] And human capital theory as an explanation of the differences in pay among occupations has been subjected to criticism. Too many other factors which affect pay levels are left out by human capital theory, say its critics.[39] Finally, the few direct statistical tests that have been made of human capital theory do not support it. James Medoff and Katherine Abraham, for example, showed that in several large companies, the higher rates of pay went not to the best performers (which human capital theory predicts), but instead to the older employees.[40]

Medoff and Abraham explain this phenomenon by arguing that unions reflect their members' preferences in causing companies to pay older employees more than their contribution to production, and younger employees less than their contribution. Human capital theorists instead suggest that there is an implicit contract between each individual employee and his or her employer, reflecting the individual's own preference with respect to his or her earnings over the person's career with the firm.[41] In this theory, the date at which an employee receives pay has no direct connection with the time he or she does the work for which he or she is paid.

Efficiency Wage Theory

Another body of new theories (sometimes taken to include the preceding) goes under the name of efficiency wage theory.[42] It focuses on situations in which profit-maximizing firms want to pay employees more than it would cost to hire replacements. If firms were uninterested in hiring cheaper workers, unemployed job seekers could bring no downward pressure on wages by offering to work for less. Interest in these theories derives from the macroeconomic question of why there seems to be involuntary unemployment.

The two most interesting versions of this approach turn on the firm having information about its workers that is in some serious way incomplete. In one of these, workers vary in their innate productivity. For simplicity, sup-

---

[37] Gary Becker, *Human Capital* (New York: Columbia University Press, 1964).

[38] Richard B. Freeman, *The Overeducated American* (New York: Academic Press, 1976).

[39] Michael J. Piore, "The Importance of Human Capital Theory to Labor Economics—A Dissenting View," Industrial Relations Research Association, *Proceedings* of the Twenty-Sixth Annual Meeting, Dec. 28–29, 1973, pp. 251–258.

[40] James L. Medoff and Katherine G. Abraham, "Experience, Performance and Earnings," *Quarterly Journal of Economics*, 95:4, December 1980, pp. 703–736.

[41] C. Azariadis, "Implicit Contracts and Underemployment Equilibria," *Journal of Political Economy*, 83, December 1979, pp. 1183–1202; and Bengt Holmstrum, "Contractual Models of the Labor Market," *American Economic Review*, 71, May 1981, pp. 308–313.

[42] For an introduction to the literature, see Janet Yellin, "Efficiency Wage Models of Unemployment," *American Economic Association Papers and Proceedings*, May 1984, pp. 200–205.

pose there are two productivity levels—high and low. Firms want to hire the highly productive and to pay them according to that productivity. But suppose that status can only be measured with any accuracy after some time on the job. Suppose high-productivity workers can always work for themselves and pay themselves more than low-productivity employees are worth to the firm. Then the only way the firm could tempt them to apply for a job would be to offer a wage higher than that it would pay a low-productivity worker. Over a range, raising the wage above the low-productivity level would increase the numbers of desirable workers in the applicant pool. Under some circumstances the firm's average productivity might rise more than proportionately to the wage.

Alternatively, suppose, the firm knows from the start everything about the workers' skills. (Suppose, to be extreme, they are all alike.) But suppose that it is difficult to monitor what they actually do—in particular, that it is difficult, though not impossible, to monitor whether or not they sometimes shirk. If there is some disutility to work—effort is unpleasant—and if the firm's job pays no better than the one an employee would get if he or she were fired and had to find another, then the temptation to shirk would be strong. The employee might well not get caught. Even if the employee does, the next job he or she will get will be just as good. Only if the job pays distinctly better than alternative employments will there be some real cost to getting caught. But if there is such a cost, employees would be motivated to shirk less. Paying more than the market-clearing wage would increase the efficiency of the labor employed. Both these theories have been formulated mathematically.[43] The point they make is that there are circumstances under which wages would settle above market-clearing levels. How common those circumstances are turns on particular details of jobs. In many jobs one person would be from the start more or less as productive as the next. In many jobs it is quite easy to monitor how hard people are working. Yet in many, neither of these is true. The jury is still out on how helpful these theories are in understanding the structure of wages. The only thing that is clear from the data is that there is something to explain.[44]

These controversies among theorists need concern us no longer, other than to recognize that the processes by which pay is established are complex and sophisticated. Theorists are attempting to reflect these changes in their models. In addition to supply and demand, wage determination involves unions, collective bargaining, the education and skill of individual employees, and the preferences of people for the time sequence in which they receive pay.

---

[43] The basic ideas are elaborated in Andrew Weiss, "Job Queues and Layoffs in Labor Markets with Flexible Wages," *Journal of Political Economy*, June 1980, pp. 526–538; and Carl Shapiro and Joseph E. Stiglitz, "Equilibrium Unemployment as a Worker Discipline Device," *American Economic Review*, June 1984, pp. 433–444.

[44] See Krueger and Summers, "Efficiency Wages and the Inter-Industry Wage Structure," forthcoming in *Econometrica*; and Dickens and Katz, "Industry and Occupational Wage Patterns and Theories of Wage Determination," forthcoming in the *Quarterly Journal of Economics*.

Institutional Theories

Institutional Theories Which Stress Economic Factors The major fact from which all bargaining theories start is the existence of unions. Because unions exist, the establishment of wages is different from what it would otherwise be. (Presumably, the large corporation also has an important impact on wage determination, but this has never been of great interest to theorists.) What difference does a union make to wage determination? How does a union behave? How is the union to be incorporated into the body of wage theory?

A corporation may be said to exist in order to maximize profits. That is a great oversimplification, since corporations have other purposes as well, but it is a powerful analytical tool. Because it can be assumed that a corporation wishes to maximize profits, important aspects of its behavior can be predicted. (This is, of course, the essence of the theory of the firm in economic analysis.) If an objective could be isolated for unions analogous to profit maximization for a firm, then the analysis of wage determination could be improved.

In 1944, John T. Dunlop undertook to develop such a theory of wages. "What do unions seek to maximize?" he asked. Unions do not simply seek to maximize wages. If they did, they would create too much unemployment. Unions recognize this relationship clearly. Craft union leaders will often say "it does no good to have the highest-wage nonworking people around." Alternatively, unions do not maximize employment, for that would require very low wage rates. Instead, the two objectives—high wages and high employment—are balanced (or "traded off") against each other. To reflect this balancing, Dunlop proposed to treat the unions as maximizing the product of employment times wages, that is, the total amount the company pays in wages, its "wage bill." (Mathematically, this occurs at the point on the demand curve where the elasticity is equal to unity.)

Using the rule that unions attempt to maximize the wage bill, Dunlop developed the conditions under which that would occur. Also, he analyzed the impact of product market characteristics on wage determination. For example, if a union dealt with a company that had a monopoly on the product it sold, the union could probably get a higher wage bill than if the union dealt with many competing firms selling the same product. But even this result might be altered under certain conditions in the product market. Dunlop's analysis demonstrated how complex wage determination can be, involving as it does the interaction of product market and labor market factors. He pointed out that wages are related to various combinations of labor and product market structures which are numerous "almost without limit."[45] It is this complexity of situations, of course, which nourishes collective bargaining in

---

[45] John T. Dunlop, *Wage Discrimination under Trade Unions* (New York: Macmillan, 1944), p. 82.

the United States and which results in the maze of different wage patterns that exist in our economy.

Institutional Theories Which Stress Noneconomic Factors   Dunlop was soon challenged with respect to his emphasis on the economic motivation of unions. Arthur Ross, writing in 1948, objected that a union was less of an economic institution than a political one. A union does not sell labor, Ross argued. It participates in the establishment of the price of labor, but the sale is made between the worker and the employer. Nor is the union mechanically concerned with the quantity of labor sold, i.e., with the number of workers employed in the branch of the economy in which it is interested. Instead, it is vitally interested in the size of its own membership, but this is not the same thing as the number of workers employed, except in the case where an industry is 100 percent unionized.

What a union is really interested in, said Ross, is its own survival and wellbeing.[46] In developing a wage policy, the union would take its own interests into account first of all. In some instances this would result in behavior which tended to maximize the wage bill (as Dunlop had argued). But in other instances, the union would not be interested in the wage bill at all. For example, if a union were challenged by another union for representation rights at a plant, it might negotiate not a big wage agreement but a moderate one, to gain the company's assistance in warding off the challenge. Or it might seek a big increase in wages to get the support of the employees. The point, Ross argued, was that the decision was based on political considerations, not on the automatic pursuit of the maximum wage bill. It would "satisfice," not maximize.

These two contrasting views of union behavior—the union as an economic maximizer versus the union as a political satisficer, referred to as the Dunlop-Ross debate—continue to absorb theoreticians. One recent study concluded that when union members are most worried about the risks of being laid off, they behave as Dunlop-type economic maximizers; when union members are most concerned with the risk of a strike, they will behave as Ross-type satisficers.[47]

Ross also introduced a concept which he labeled "orbits of coercive comparison." In many instances, he argued, a union is in such an intimate relationship with another union or with certain employers that it virtually has to follow a wage pattern which has been established. For example, the local unions of the United Automobile Workers which represent employees of Ford Motor Company are not free to negotiate independently of what occurs at General Motors. If the Ford locals took a lower settlement, the workers at

---

[46] Arthur M. Ross, *Trade Union Wage Policy* (Berkeley: University of California Press, 1948).

[47] Bruce E. Kaufman and Jorge Martinez-Vazquez, "The Ross-Dunlop Debate," *Journal of Labor Research*, 8:3, Summer 1987, pp. 291–304. See also Jeff Borland, "The Ross-Dunlop Debate Revisited," *Journal of Labor Research*, 7:3, Summer 1986, pp. 293–305.

Ford would complain. If the local unions at Ford tried to get a larger settlement, the company would resist very strongly, since it would not want its competitive position vis-à-vis General Motors weakened. The Ford locals are, therefore, in an orbit of comparison which is so strong as to be "coercive." Ross viewed these orbits as essentially political factors affecting union wage policy.

Resolving the Conflict Between Theories

For a while there ensued a lively debate in academic journals between the partisans of the economic and political theories of union wage behavior. In 1957 Dunlop again addressed the issue and attempted to go beyond the controversy with Ross. Wages and employment seemed to be related, he said, in a vastly more complex manner than could be "fruitfully portrayed in a Marshallian demand curve."[48] Instead of trying to explain the setting of a single wage rate (as his and Ross's work had done), Dunlop argued that wage theory needed to approach wage determination through the concept of the wage structure, i.e., the manner in which existing wage rates affect the establishment of other wage rates. "Instead of reducing wage setting to the problem of a single rate, the task...is...the problem of the setting and variation in the whole structure...of rates."[49] To help in this process, Dunlop proposed two concepts: a "job cluster" and a "wage contour." A job cluster is a group of jobs so closely interrelated (by technology, administrative organization, or custom) that they have one key wage rate. A wage contour involves a group of firms so closely interrelated (by product similarities, similar labor sources, or custom) that they have common wage characteristics. (The concept has a certain similarity to Ross's orbits of coercive comparison.) Wage contours have industrial, occupational, and geographic dimensions. For example, the basic steel industry constitutes a wage contour expressed in the basic steel collective bargaining agreement and having the following dimensions: industrial—basic steel; occupational—those jobs involved in making steel; geographic—nationwide. Much of the process of determination of wage rates, said Dunlop, depends upon the job cluster and wage contour into which a particular situation falls.

Dunlop apparently hoped that following the publication of "The Task of Contemporary Wage Theory," economists would begin to study and describe job clusters and wage contours as they actually exist in the economy. There has been some research of this nature.[50] Primarily, however, theorists

---

[48] John Dunlop, "The Task of Contemporary Wage Theory," in J. T. Dunlop, ed., *The Theory of Wage Determination* (London: Macmillan, 1975), p. 11.
[49] Dunlop, "The Task of Contemporary Wage Theory," p. 15.
[50] Otto Eckstein and Thomas A. Wilson, "The Determination of Money Wages in the American Economy," *Quarterly Journal of Economics*, 25:3, August 1962, pp. 379–414; Otto Eckstein, "Money Wage Determination Revisited," *Review of Economic Studies*, 35, April 1968, pp. 133–143; Michael L. Wachter, "The Wage Process," *Brookings Papers on Economic Activity*, 2, 1974,

2 How do you think wage rates, or levels of compensation, should be determined?

3 What social consequences have different wage theories had? How have people used wage theories to justify certain kinds of social policies or actions?

4 What is the difference between market-oriented and institution-oriented wage theories?

5 Do unions help those they represent to earn more than nonunion employees? Support your answer.

6 What is meant when it is said that the market sets the wage rate?

7 Why do wage levels vary in different occupations and industries? What factors are most important? Is it fair that people get different rates of pay? Why or why not?

8 What theory of wages seems most useful to you? Why?

9 What factors are most important in wage setting today? Why?

10 Do employers and employees think about wages in the same way? Does it matter if they have different theories? Why?

SELECTED READING

Dunlop, John T., *Wage Determination under Trade Unions* (New York: Macmillan, 1944).

Flanagan, Robert J., and Daniel J. B. Mitchell, "Wage Determination and Public Policy," in Thomas A. Kochan et al., eds., *Industrial Relations Research in the 1970's* (Madison, Wis.: Industrial Relations Research Association, 1982), pp. 45-94.

Hicks, John R., *A Theory of Wages*, 2d ed. (New York: St. Martin's Press, 1964).

Kerr, Clark, *Labor Markets and Wage Determination: The Balkanization of Labor Markets and Other Essays* (Berkeley: University of California Press, 1977).

Ross, Arthur M., *Trade Union Wage Policy* (Berkeley: University of California Press, 1948).

CHAPTER 14

WAGE SETTING IN PRACTICE

ESTABLISHING PAY RATES

The theories examined in Chapter 13 attempted to explain the causes of wage differentials in primarily economic terms. In practice, however, wage setting is an administrative process which strongly reflects pervasive social mores and which is influenced by an economic context. There are many different methods by which the form and amount of compensation are established. They are summarized and categorized for ease of presentation in Table 14-1. At the top, different procedures are listed on the basis of which actor makes the final decision on the rate of compensation. There are four actors identified: the employer, the employee, the union, and the government. At the bottom, different criteria are listed by which compensation may be established. Any actor may use any criterion, although, in fact, certain actors place great reliance on some criteria and little reliance on others.

Each of the four actors may act unilaterally, i.e., without reference at the point of decision to the others. Thus, the employer may set a rate of pay for a job and offer it to present or prospective employees on a take-it-or-leave-it basis. And a union may also set a rate of pay and offer it to employers on a take-it-or-leave-it basis. (Today in the United States this would be a very unusual procedure. However, 75 years ago, it was common in some industries. The union simply held a meeting and by vote adopted a wage rate. The union members then informed the employers of their decision and refused to work at less than the adopted rate.[1]) An employee may decide that he or she

TABLE 14-1 METHODS OF ESTABLISHING COMPENSATION

Actors

Employer unilaterally
Employee unilaterally
Union unilaterally
Government unilaterally
Employer-employee jointly
Employer-union jointly

Criteria

Reaction
Surveys
Formulas
Job evaluation plans
Pay by performance

Note: Unilateral action does not necessarily imply action by a single individual without influence or approval by others. The actors listed, except the individual employee and some employers who are sole proprietorships, are actually not individual persons but organizations (such as a corporation, a union, or a government agency), so that unilateral action by the organization may entail internal procedures between elements of the organization that involve many persons in a joint decision. A corporation, for example, may "unilaterally" set wage rates by what is in effect a bargaining procedure between the personnel department and the operations department.

is entitled to a certain rate of pay and announce that he or she will leave if the company refuses to pay it. However, in most cases only employees with special skills or knowledge are able to do this successfully. Last, a governmental body may establish rates of pay and by law prevent employers from hiring, or workers from taking jobs, except at that rate of pay.

The four actors may also set compensation in conjunction with each other. Theoretically, compensation could be determined in different cases by any two, any three, or all four acting together. In practice in the United States, compensation is usually set by joint action only between employers and individual employees or between employers and unions. Only these two forms of joint action are shown in Table 14-1. Joint determination of compensation between unions and employers is referred to as collective bargaining, of course.

There are also several criteria by which compensation is established. Table 14-1 lists five criteria but does not define them. Briefly, they may be described as follows:

[1] See, for example, Royal Montgomery, *Industrial Relations in the Chicago Building Trades* (Chicago: University of Chicago Press, 1927); and William Haber, *Industrial Relations in the Building Industry* (Cambridge, Mass.: Harvard University Press, 1930).

- *Reaction.* Rates are set according to the apparent needs of the moment, without any formal process.
- *Surveys.* Rates are set by reference to surveys taken to determine rates of pay and benefits for employees in specific occupations, by industry type and geographic area. Discretion is retained by the actor(s) setting the rates as to the specific level at which rates are set.
- *Formulas.* Rates are set by reference to some outside factor(s) in a way that permits no discretion concerning the specific level at which rates are set.
- *Job evaluation.* Rates are set by reference to a list of occupations in which each occupation is given a rating based on certain numerical factors with respect to other occupations, and pay scales are made to reflect the measured differences among occupations.
- *Pay by performance.* Rates are set by reference to the amount of work each individual employee (or group of employees) performs.

These criteria by which compensation is determined are extremely important to labor-management relations. They are also quite complicated. At this point we will examine the first four criteria in greater detail and review simplified examples of each. Pay by performance is also discussed in this chapter.

Reactive Criteria

Perhaps the setting of rates of compensation by simple reaction should not be dignified by calling it a criterion; certainly it is not a systematic procedure. Yet it is probably the criterion most used by employers, especially employers acting unilaterally. In such a process, pay rates are established and adjusted in a series of ad hoc steps. For example, suppose that the secretary who works for a manager is offered a job at higher pay in another company. In order to retain the person's services, the manager raises the rate of pay. No attempt is made to survey other rates in or outside the company, nor are conditions such as cost of living considered. The increase is simply offered and accepted, and a new rate of compensation is established.

Alternatively, suppose a small machine shop in a large corporation had many job orders in the past but now has very few. To stretch its budget, the manager meets individually with each employee and proposes that either the person's wage rate be reduced or the person be laid off. Several employees agree to having their wage rate reduced, again without reference to factors other than the manager's interpretation of how the employee should react to a shrinking budget.

To take a final illustration, suppose that the same manager of the machine tool shop has the opposite problem 6 months later, i.e., too many orders to fill. The manager offers the most skilled employees a bonus for each order they complete. In each of these cases, the requirements of production affect compensation in an ad hoc way.

These illustrations are not meant to imply that the process of setting compensation on such an expedient basis is necessarily wrong, but it does cause problems in the course of time. Especially in large organizations, after a while such a process results in people who are doing the same work receiving very different rates of pay. For instance, our first example concerned an increase in a secretary's pay because of another job offer. But other secretaries did not get such an offer and received no increase in pay. Should all secretaries doing the same job, i.e., working for managers of a certain level, receive the same pay, or should those who get offers to work elsewhere get more pay? How much more?

The wage and salary policies of corporations exist to answer such questions, and they do so by application of one or another of the remaining four criteria used in establishing compensation.

Compensation Surveys

Employers, governmental agencies, and unions participate in systematic wage and salary surveys, often unilaterally and sometimes jointly. The most careful surveys proceed by definition of an occupation, which usually involves the comparison of job descriptions, and by the collection of pay-rate and benefit data from all major employers in the appropriate geographic area who have that job category. A survey that is not done carefully can be very misleading. For example, it may mix unrelated job categories by failing to define carefully the categories of jobs being surveyed; or it may omit major employers. Another mistake is collecting pay-rate data for different companies at different times, instead of having all data cover the same time period. Still another danger is to fail to have all benefits carefully reported.

Despite these pitfalls, wage and salary surveys are very popular with employers. Many major companies belong to survey groups with other employers in major metropolitan areas. The companies exchange information about compensation. The data are used by companies in determining adjustments to make for their own employees or in collective bargaining with labor unions representing their employees.[2]

The federal government also conducts surveys of wages by occupation and area and publishes them periodically.[3] Labor unions have not, until recently, participated to any marked degree in compensation surveys. Instead, unions have tended to rely on informal surveys of rates reported by other unions when queried by letter or phone. Recently, however, some national unions have begun to keep computerized records of rates of pay and benefits negotiated by the union with various employers.

The use of survey data by the various actors in determining wages differs.

[2] See J. D. Dunn and Frank M. Rachel, *Wage and Salary Administration: Total Compensation Systems* (New York: McGraw-Hill, 1971).

[3] See various occupational wage surveys published by the Bureau of Labor Statistics, U.S. Department of Labor.

In collective bargaining situations both management and unions use survey data to prepare positions and to answer the claims of the other side. When employers unilaterally set compensation, surveys are used to provide a data base for the application of policy. A large employer may use survey results to tell it when to raise its rates of pay. Unions seeking to represent clerical workers often charge that the cooperation among employers to compile survey data and the use of these data by companies in the ways just described constitute a form of monopolylike collusion against the interests of workers. Whatever the merits of such charges, the use of survey data by firms in establishing pay rates is quite extensive.

Governmental agencies survey rates of pay by private employers in certain occupational categories as a method of establishing pay levels for the government's own employees in those categories. The federal government uses such a procedure—called a wage board procedure—to establish rates of pay for most of its blue-collar workers.[4] Many municipal governments utilize pay surveys to establish compensation for municipal employees as well. It is often the policy of governmental agencies to pay the exact amount determined by the survey. This procedure virtually converts the survey process of determining compensation into a formula process. It also places great importance on the survey technique, since the survey results no longer serve as a guide to policy, which can be supplemented by other information, but serve to implement the policy as well. A survey is often too unreliable for such use.

For example, suppose that the purpose of a survey is to establish the rate of pay that a city will have for its maintenance machinists. Suppose also that a major private employer of machinists will not cooperate in the survey and that the union representing the city's machinists believes the private employer pays higher than other employers in the area. The determination of the rate of pay for the city's machinists by survey alone may not yield an accurate result, since the survey is incomplete, and will probably cause a dispute over pay between the city and its employees.

Formulas Based on Wages

The essence of a formula approach to determining compensation is that it removes discretion from the determination of compensation. Formulas provide that compensation will be set at a level, or adjusted at a rate, determined by some outside measure. The most popular pay formulas tie the pay of a particular group of employees either to the pay scales of other employees or to the cost of living.

Formulas based on wages are less common than those based on prices, but are important nonetheless. Among the most significant wage-based formulas now existing are:

[4] See Chapter 21.

- The wage formula from the national agreement between the International Union of Elevator Constructors and the elevator construction contractors. The formula essentially provides that each local of the national union (except in New York City) shall annually meet with its employer association to review the wage increases obtained by other construction trades (some 16 or so) in the locality during the year. A complicated process results in the selection of a few trades and the averaging of their increases. The elevator constructors' local receives an increase equal to the average increase of the trades selected.
- The wage formulas, referred to as "me-too" clauses, that appear fairly frequently in various craft union collective bargaining agreements. As an example of the use of a me-too clause, suppose one union negotiates a certain pay increase for its members. If 1 month later, a second union negotiates a *larger* increase for *its* members, the members of the first union automatically get the higher increase also. Such clauses have been common at various times in collective bargaining agreements in the construction and maritime industries.
- The highest-rate formulas obtained by some municipal employees. These formulas (either city ordinances or provisions of collective bargaining agreements) provide that certain categories of municipal employees will receive the highest rate of pay established in a group of other cities, which are named in the provision. For example, San Francisco is reported to have had a municipal ordinance requiring that firefighters and police receive a rate of pay at least equal to the highest in any of the six largest cities of California.
- Crews of railway trains are paid on a formula which has a dual basis. The formula dates from the early 1900s and is referred to as dual because both *mileage,* the distance traveled by the crew, and the *length of time* the crew is on duty are used to determine pay.[5]

Formulas Based on Prices

Protecting Purchasing Power   The most common formula for the determination of wages is one that provides that wage rates shall be adjusted upward in step with the cost of living. The logic of such a provision is to see that workers are able to maintain their standard of living. When the prices of food, clothing, housing, medical services, and other items consumed by employees rise, then unless their earnings also rise, they cannot continue to consume at the same rate as before. To measure purchasing power, wages must be adjusted for changes in the cost of living. Thus, we may refer to a wage rate—for example, $5 per hour—as a "money" wage rate. Now, suppose an employee earned $5 per hour in 1970 and also $5 per hour in 1985. Was he or she as well off in terms of purchasing power in 1985 as in 1970? Not at all. Between 1970 and 1985 prices paid by consumers rose 167 percent, according to the U.S. Bureau of Labor Statistics. Now, if the employee in our

[5] Henry H. Perritt, Jr., "Development of a Railroad Labor Cost Function," *Transportation Research Forum,* 1979, pp. 416–423.

example wished to have the same purchasing power in 1985 as $5 per hour gave in 1970, what rate of pay would be required in 1985? The answer, of course, is 167 percent more than $5 per hour, or $13.35 per hour.

Alternatively, if the employee received $13.35 per hour in 1985, it would not buy in 1985 what $13.35 would buy in 1970. How much would be needed in 1970 to buy what $13.35 would buy in 1985? Prices were 167 percent lower, so that the amount needed in 1970 would be $13.35/2.18 = $5.00 This measure, the wage rate divided by the price index of a particular year, we refer to as a measure of "real," not "money" wages.

- *Real wages* are wages adjusted for changes in the cost of living, also called wages in "constant-dollar" terms.
- *Money wages* are wages expressed in the currency of today.

Escalator Clauses   In order to protect the purchasing power of employees from price inflation, many collective bargaining agreements include a provision that wage rates shall be periodically adjusted in an amount determined by the rate of increase in consumer prices. Such a clause is called a cost-of-living escalator clause and is referred to as an escalator or a COLA (cost-of-living adjustment) clause. The essential element of an escalator is some measure of changes in living costs. Most escalator clauses use the national Consumer Price Index (CPI) prepared by the federal government's Bureau of Labor Statistics, but some agreements use the index for a particular city. The automobile industry escalators, which cover workers in both Canada and the United States, use an average of the Canadian and American indexes.

Escalator clauses differ considerably in the specifics of the formula that is used to relate wage changes to the price index. Adjustments may be made every 3 months (quarterly), every 6 months (semiannually), or each year. The two most common methods are:

- The contract provides a 1-cent increase in wages for each 0.4 (or 0.3) point change in the price index. Thus, if the price index rises from 150.3 to 150.9 from January through March, a quarterly increase of 1.5 cents (if 0.4) or 2 cents (if 0.3) is made.
- The contract provides an increase in wages equal to the percentage increase in the price index. Thus, if the price index rises from 150.3 to 150.9 from January through March, a quarterly increase of 0.399 percent is made in the wage rate (as a practical matter, the increase would probably be leveled off to 0.4 percent). So, if the wage rate were $5.60, an increase of $0.02 would be made.

The first method, which ties a cents-per-hour wage increase to points in the price index, is more common. These formulas usually result in less than a percent-for-percent change. Thus, using the formula of a 1-cent increase in wages for each 0.4 point increase in the price index, a movement of 1 percent in the index (given a base of 150.3) would be 1.5 points. This would yield a wage increase of 3.75 cents per hour ($0.0375). At a wage rate of $3.75, this is a 1 percent increase. At any wage rate above $3.75, however, $0.0375 is less than a 1 percent increase. If the wage rate were $5.60, for example, the increase of $0.0375 would mean an increase of only 0.67 percent.

In the United States today most escalator clauses yield an increase in wages that in percentage terms is less than the increase in the price index. On the average, escalators cause wages to rise about one-half the percentage increase in the cost of living.

Some escalator clauses provide a limitation on the size of cost-of-living adjustments in wages. These limits are called "caps." For example, a contract might provide that wages were to be increased 1 cent for every increase of 0.3 points in the price index, up to a limit of $0.12 increase in any given year. An increase of 3.6 points in the price index would yield a $0.12 increase in wages; but no further increase in wages would occur, even if the price index continued to rise, until the year was over.

Increases in wages that are the result of an escalator may be "folded" into the wage-rate base or kept separate from it. Suppose that the wage rate is $5.60 per hour and the escalator provides a 1-cent increase for each 0.3 point increase in the price index. Then an increase of 0.6 points yields a wage increase of $0.02. If the COLA increase is folded in, the new wage rate is $5.62 per hour. If it is not folded in, then the wage rate remains $5.60 per hour *plus* $0.02 per hour; i.e., the worker is paid *as if* the wage rate were $5.62 per hour. Why does this matter? Folding in is important because of pay premiums. Overtime, for example, is usually paid at time and a half the regular hourly rate of pay. If the COLA increase is folded in, the worker gets overtime pay figured on a higher base rate than if the COLA increase is kept separate.

Such items as the specific terms of an escalator clause, its frequency, whether or not it has a cap, and whether or not (or when) a COLA increase is folded in to base rates are subjects of collective bargaining between management and labor. In some agreements management and labor even set up an escalator, and then the union "borrows" some portion of the escalator to devote to other purposes, such as buying health insurance, so that the workers do not get the full escalator in their paychecks. Bargaining over escalators is, therefore, very complex, and the arrangements that are worked out are as varied as the imagination of people can make them.

History and Economic Significance of Escalators During the 1920s escalators appeared in certain major agreements, but thereafter virtually disappeared until an escalator was included in the 1948 contract between General Motors and the United Automobile Workers. These clauses became more popular in the 1950s; in 1960 about half of all agreements covering 1000 or more workers involved an escalator clause. By 1970 this proportion had dropped to 25 percent. But under the impact of price inflation in the 1970s, the escalator regained popularity and at one point covered 60 percent or so of workers covered by major agreements (or about 15 to 20 percent of all workers in the private sector in the United States).[6] In the 1980s inflation slowed, and the proportion of contracts with escalators declined rapidly, to about 35 percent of major contracts.

Since 1948 a debate has continued, at varying levels of intensity, as to the economic impact of cost-of-living clauses. Are they inflationary or not? Those who argue that they are not inflationary say that in the absence of an escalator, workers would obtain even larger wage increases. This is partly because the escalator represents acceptance of the government's figures for the amount by which the cost of living has increased. These official figures could, of course, be distrusted as underestimates. Proponents of the clauses sometimes argue that they are not inflationary because by definition, in their view, no wage increase is inflationary if it merely follows, and does not exceed, a prior price increase.

Those who believe escalators are inflationary base their opinion on two grounds. First, it may be argued that because they are a formula, escalators eliminate discretion in adjusting to unusual circumstances. For example, in 1980 the automobile industry was in deep recession in the United States. Tens of thousands of workers were on indefinite layoff, and the companies were choked by excessive inventories. Consumer prices were continuing to increase rapidly, however (at an 18 percent annual rate), so that the cost-of-living escalator in the automobile agreements continued to cause a rapid rise in wages and costs, despite the depressed sales and employment conditions in the industry. It is doubtful that any other means of wage setting would have resulted in large wage increases in the automobile industry at that time. Second, escalators force wage increases to follow rapidly behind increases in the cost of living (often with a lag of only a few months), so that what in some cases could be temporary price increases become part of an irreversible upward movement of wages and prices. This, it may be argued, was part of the process by which the energy price inflation of 1979 was translated into the rapid *general* wage and price inflation in 1980.[7]

Job Evaluation Plans

Job evaluation is a systematic method of appraising the worth of each job with respect to every other job in an organization. Wage rates are then established for various jobs in a manner that reflects their relative worth. A job evaluation system first develops careful descriptions of each job. In most

---

[6] Victor J. Sheifer, "Cost-of-Living Adjustment," *Monthly Labor Review*, 102:6, June 1979, pp. 14–17.

[7] For an analysis of the impact of cost-of-living escalators on inflation, see H. M. Douty, "Study of the Relationship between Cost-of-Living Escalation Clauses and Inflation," a paper prepared for the Council on Wage and Price Stability, executive office of the President of the United States, Aug. 20, 1975; also, Marcelle V. Arak, "Indexation of Wages and Retirement Income in the United States," *Federal Reserve Bank of New York Quarterly Review*, 3:3, Autumn 1978, pp. 16–23. See also Wallace E. Hendricks and Lawrence M. Kahn, "Cost-of-Living Clauses in Union Contracts," *Industrial and Labor Relations Review*, 36:3, April 1983, pp. 447–460.

plans jobs are then rated according to a system that assigns points for various characteristics of the job. In production jobs the factors are usually divided into four major categories: skill, effort, responsibility, and job conditions. A typical job evaluation plan (such as that of National Electrical Manufacturers Association, NEMA) has eleven major factors grouped in the four categories mentioned above.

Skill

1 Education
2 Experience
3 Initiative and ingenuity

Effort

4 Physical demand
5 Mental-visual demand

Responsibility

6 For equipment or process
7 For material or product
8 For safety of others
9 For work of others

Job Conditions

10 Working conditions
11 Hazards

There is a set maximum number of points that may be assigned to each factor. For example, education is given 14 points and experience 22 in the NEMA plan. When a job is studied, it is given a rating on each factor. A job in which education plays a major part could receive as many as 14 points. A job in which experience is critical could receive as many as 22 points in that category. The maximum points assigned to each factor add up to 100 total points for all 11 factors, although no job gets this many points.

The particular factors on which jobs are rated differ among companies and among the types of occupations considered. Clerical jobs in the NEMA plan, for example, are rated on 6 factors, not 11. The six factors are education, experience, complexity of duties, monetary responsibility, contacts with other people, and working conditions. Even supervisory jobs are rated, with additional factors, such as type and extent of supervision, included in the evaluation.[8]

---

[8] Ernest J. McCormick, *Job Analysis: Methods and Applications* (New York: AMACOM, 1979). For a union viewpoint, see John Zalusky, "Job Evaluation: An Uneven World," *AFL-CIO Federationist*, 85:4, April 1981, pp. 11–20.

The actual implementation of a job evaluation plan is a complex process[9] and can be only briefly summarized here. Once jobs are rated according to the factors, they are ranked by total points awarded. The jobs are then placed in a distribution, and wage rates (or ranges of rates) are assigned to each job. The advantages of such a system are that

- A centralized, uniform system for setting pay rates for each job in relation to every other job is used.
- A frame of reference is established for settling disputes over the rate of pay on individual jobs.
- Procedures exist for reviewing new or changed jobs and setting rates of pay for them.

There are several disadvantages to job evaluation plans. Among the disadvantages are the following:

- There is a certain inflexibility in the structure of wages and jobs.
- The possibility exists that if employees don't understand or accept the factor-rating system, it will generate disputes.

An example may help to make clear the potential inflexibility of a job evaluation system. In the aftermath of World War II a very complex job evaluation system was established for the basic steel industry. The system now includes 33 job classes, which in 1976 ranged in pay scales from $4.625 per hour for job classes 1 and 2 to $7.942 per hour for job class 33 (the rates are the standard hourly wage rate for nonincentive jobs). During the 1960s maintenance crafts jobs (such as carpenter, pipefitter, and bricklayer) were slotted in job classes 13 to 15, near the middle of the wage range. But as wage rates for these occupations rose rapidly in the construction industry, the steel companies ran into trouble. The steel industry's maintenance people were leaving for higher-paying jobs outside steel, and the steel companies were not able to hire competent maintenance employees at the existing rate of pay. Yet how would the steel companies raise the pay of the maintenance crafts? There had been no change in the education, experience, skill, hardship, or other aspects of the job on which the job evaluation rested.

To resolve the problem, the steel companies and the Steelworkers union in their 1968 negotiations simply agreed to pay maintenance tradespeople at a pay grade two levels above that to which they were entitled by the job evaluation plan. A painter, for example, who was slotted by the value of his or her job into job class 13 was henceforth to be paid at the rate that applied to job class 15.

This example also demonstrates the distinction between an *internal* and an *external* wage structure. The job evaluation plan placed trades occupations correctly within the internal wage structure, i.e., the group of jobs that exist

---

[9] See Charles A. Myers and Paul Pigors, *Personnel Administration: A Point of View and a Method,* 7th ed. (New York: McGraw-Hill, 1973), chap. 20.

in the steel industry. But the placement of the trades occupations in the external wage structure, that is, among the jobs outside steel, was different. When the two structures got sufficiently out of line with each other, the steel industry had to adjust its own internal system.[10]

FACTORS AFFECTING WAGE DETERMINATION

While wage determination involves very complicated procedures, the major factors that affect it are few. The complexities and great difficulties of wage determination arise in the application of these factors to specific cases. There are four principal factors involved in wage setting: comparability among wage rates, changes in the cost of living, ability of employers to pay, and productivity of employees (see Table 14-2). We have already discussed the impact of changes in the cost of living on wages in the preceding section, and productivity is discussed in Chapter 18, so we may limit our attention in this section to the two remaining factors: comparability and ability to pay.

Comparability among Wage Rates

Probably the largest number of wage decisions are based simply on the comparison of wage rates. This judgment includes both the setting of individual rates and the setting of groups of rates. For example, if a company hires a new person into a secretarial job, it will probably determine that secretary's rate of pay by looking at what it is already paying secretaries. Similarly, if a union that represents unskilled laborers is negotiating with an employer who hires both skilled craftspeople and laborers, the negotiations will surely start from the proposition that the laborers' rate of pay is to be below that for the skilled trades. In some instances, pay setting is made very simple by comparisons. In many cities firefighters and police receive pay "parity," that is, they receive the same rate of pay. If the police get a raise, the firefighters ask for the same raise.

Many other groups of employees have established certain differentials with other groups of workers as a matter of historic practice. For example,

---

[10] See Peter B. Doeringer and Michael J. Piore, *Internal Labor Markets and Manpower Analysis* (Lexington, Mass.: Heath-Lexington Books, 1971), for a discussion of internal and external labor markets.

TABLE 14-2 FACTORS AFFECTING WAGE DETERMINATION

- Comparability among wage rates
- Ability of an employer to pay
- Productivity
- Changes in cost of living

licensed mechanics may traditionally receive 50 cents per hour more than un-licensed mechanics. When the increase is determined for licensed mechanics, the unlicensed mechanics get the same amount. Differentials may also be of a percentage nature. For example, in a certain city carpenters traditionally re-ceive 5 percent more than cement masons. Thus, if the rate of pay of carpen-ters is to be determined, and the rate of pay of cement masons is known, wage setting requires an increase for the carpenters that again places that trade's rate 5 percent above that of the cement masons.

The wage rates that exist at any specific time may be referred to as a struc-ture of rates. The determination of one rate by reference to others in the structure is the essence of wage determination by comparability of rates. The wage structure as a factor in determining wages draws its importance from circumstances that affect both employees and employers.

Preference of Workers   The attitudes of workers toward the wages re-ceived for their labor depend, in large degree, on their perception of the wages others receive. This phenomenon is referred to in economic literature as the existence of interdependent utility (or welfare) functions among indi-viduals. A definition has been offered by Piore:

> The interdependence hypothesis is that the individual's utility is a function not of the level of absolute income, but of the level of income *relative* to that of other in-dividuals with whom he has social contact. (Social contact . . . includes not only di-rect contact, but exposure to superior goods through entertainment and advertis-ing media.)[11]

The effect of the interdependence of utility functions is to establish behav-ioral relations among groups and individuals in the labor market with respect to wage rates. When a group of workers perceives itself at a disadvantage with respect to the wages of other groups, several directions of activity are possible. The first is to accept being behind, although it is undesired. It can-not be doubted that even strong preferences of workers are sometimes al-tered and wage differentials accepted, although this process is often likely to be difficult. A second response is for individuals to desert the work in ques-tion for better-paying work. This certainly happens, but in most cases it is not a feasible alternative for the group as a whole. The third alternative is to attempt to have wage relationships readjusted to what are believed to be ap-propriate levels. This latter response is very marked in its affect on wage de-termination. It should also be noted that the workers' perception of a disad-vantage may be that of being either behind other relevant rates or insufficiently ahead of them. The perception of a disadvantage of either sort is very largely a matter of group or individual psychology and is much af-fected by general social mores and attitudes (e.g., a largely competitive social

---

[11] Michael J. Piore, "Interdependent and Irreversible Utility Functions and Wage Behavior," manuscript, Feb. 9, 1978, p. 9.

atmosphere may generate strong tendencies for those with high wages to attempt to remain well ahead; a less competitive society may show less behavior of this nature).

Whatever the institutional process by which wages are determined, the concern of workers for the interrelationships of wage rates exerts considerable influence. Whether employers establish wage rates in conjunction with individual workers or through negotiations with a union representing the work force collectively, workers find means of expressing their interest in the comparison of their own wages with those of others. Perhaps this process of wage comparisons is least visible in the situation in which an employer establishes a job rate unilaterally and workers are not directly consulted. Adjustments in wage rates in this situation conform primarily to the employer's perception of a need for a change in wage rates, often as the result of an inability to hire workers of the characteristics desired (in skill, age, or education). Yet even here, employers often resort to area wage surveys in conjunction with other employers as the primary information on which to base a decision to adjust wage levels. By this procedure employers reflect the concerns of employees for the comparison of wages.

Normally, particular groups of employees are not concerned with the comparison of all wage rates, nor even of their wages with the average level of wages in general. Rather, custom, existing practices, overt agreement, or the force of economic conditions directs attention to a specific rate or group of rates other than those of the workers involved. The dimensions of wage comparisons may include geographic, occupational, industrial, and demographic factors.

Interestingly, the element in union wage strategy that involves the comparison of wage rates is often referred to by researchers as a noneconomic (or political) element. Wage comparisons may be referred to as noneconomic only in order to limit the label "economic" to the circumstances of employment, unemployment, productivity, and profitability of the firm. In a broader sense, wage comparisons are only another economic factor in wage determination, for the roots of comparison lie in the attitudes of individuals toward their appropriate position in the distribution of society's goods and status—a matter very much economic in character, as well as sociological or political.

Attitudes of Employers Business enterprises are no less concerned with relative wages than are the workers they employ, although many of the concerns of business are of different origin. Wage rates constitute an important part of employee compensation, which is in turn one of two elements that determine unit labor costs (the other is productivity). Unit labor costs affect pricing and the competitive position of a firm and thereby its profitability. Other things being equal, a firm paying lower wage rates than its competitors is in a position to achieve lower prices, and higher sales and profits; or, in contrast, firms paying higher wage rates are at a potential disadvantage. In a tight labor market, a firm paying lower wages than its competitors may be unable to attract labor. There are, therefore, varying pressures for dispersion or uniformity in the wage structure in different economic circumstances. In addition, relative wages affect the competitive positions of substitutes in the product market, so that the fortunes of whole industries are dependent to some degree on relative wages. It is not uncommon, therefore, to find employers essentially unconcerned with the rate of increase in money wages as long as the relative wages of competitors in the same industry and of firms producing substitute products are not altered to their disadvantage.

Employers' concern with relative wages often goes beyond comparison with the rates that their competitors pay. For example, in many production processes substitutions may be made among various grades and skill levels of workers in response to alterations in wage differentials, so that the hiring policies of the firm may be affected by changes in relative wages. Also, substitutions of machinery and materials for labor often result from increasing relative wages (as well as from increasing wages by comparison to machinery and materials cost). Finally, changes in relative wages across international boundaries may affect the competitiveness of various products in international markets. In consequence, employers must be deeply concerned with the structure of wages, as well as with the money level of wages or rate of increase.

Problems in Comparing Wage Rates   The principle that wage rates for one group of employees should be adjusted to the rates of a comparable group has an alluring simplicity. Unfortunately, the apparent simplicity vanishes when an attempt is made to give meaning to the concept of comparable wage rates in a particular situation.[12] Some of the more important difficulties are:

• The content of jobs that have the same title may differ considerably among different employers. The range of duties covered by the same job titles is far less standard than it is thought to be. As a result, when the wages paid by different employers to people with the same job title are compared, the comparison may not be valid. For example, a maintenance engineer in one plant may be an apprentice, nonlicensed electrician, while in another plant the title "maintenance engineer" may refer to a licensed electrician, or at another plant to a person with an electrical engineering degree. It would be an error to compare the rates of the maintenance engineers in the three plants as if the jobs or the people performing them were in reality identical.

• While the content of a group of jobs may be the same, the methods of wage payment may differ so much that the determination of the rates to be compared may be difficult. For example, in one factory, machinists may be paid exclusively on an hourly rate. In another factory, however, the machinist may receive hourly pay, incentive pay, and even a bonus each Christmas if the company

[12] John T. Dunlop and James J. Healy, *Collective Bargaining*, rev. ed. (Homewood, Ill.: Irwin, 1955), pp. 86–90.

makes a profit that year. When a comparison of pay is made between the two groups, which types of pay should be included and which excluded?

• Employees with the same jobs may have different degrees of regularity of employment, so that even if wage rates are identical, annual earnings are not. Maintenance mechanics ordinarily make less per hour than construction mechanics, but they often make more money in the course of a year. This is because maintenance employees often work a full 2000-hour work year, while construction workers average only 1200 to 1400 hours. Which comparison is better—the comparison of hourly wage rates or that of annual earnings?

Nor are these the only issues involved in the application of wage comparisons. Other significant influences are the geographic area in which comparisons are appropriate, which industries can be fairly compared, and which employers should be compared. An example of each may be helpful:

• *Geographic comparisons.* The Post Office has a nationwide wage structure in which employees in a particular job get the same pay, wherever the employees are located. Because the cost of living is believed to be highest in metropolitian areas and in certain regions of the country, such as the Northeast, this uniform pay policy occasions considerable dissatisfaction. Employees in high-cost locations believe that their wages should be compared with other employees in the same region and not with other employees in the Postal Service who live in different regions.

• *Industrial comparisons.* In the 1930s, when commercial airlines were developing, a dispute arose between airline pilots and the companies about the appropriate rate of pay for pilots. Some companies allegedly took the position that pilots for passenger airlines were much like bus drivers and should be paid accordingly. In the end, pilots and the airlines, with government involvement, worked out a procedure for determining the pay of pilots that paid no attention to comparability with bus drivers.

• *Employer comparisons.* In the retail food industry, some supermarket chains are unionized and some are not. When compensation standards in the unionized firms are discussed between the companies and the unions, it is ordinarily the position of the companies that the unions should consider the rates of pay of nonunionized firms. The unionized firms argue that they cannot afford to pay very much above what nonunionized firms pay, because if the unionized firm pays much higher it will not be able to compete successfully. On the other hand, the unions often reply that they are not concerned with the rates that nonunionized firms pay and that the appropriate place to look for comparisons among wage rates is with other unionized firms.

Ability of an Employer to Pay

When employees want a pay increase, or when a union demands one, an employer may reply that it cannot afford to pay the increase. A company might say that it will have no profits at all if it must pay a wage increase, or a hospital or an agency of government might say that although it doesn't make profits, it still must meet its costs, and a pay increase would cause it to run deficits (i.e., cause its expenditures to exceed its revenues).

Ordinarily an employer doesn't tell the whole story if it simply says it cannot pay a wage increase. It may be able to pay for some level of wage increase, but not others. The employer should say, "I cannot pay an increase of more than _____ ." Also, it may be that there should be a condition attached to the employer's position, such as "The company cannot pay a wage increase without raising prices" or "The hospital cannot pay a wage increase without getting increased payments from Blue Cross–Blue Shield" or "The city cannot afford a pay increase without raising taxes."

In fact, the ability of an employer to pay additional wages often depends on its ability to raise its revenues or cut its costs in order to make more money available for employee compensation. This is often misunderstood. Employees and unions often believe that companies can pay wage increases out of their profits without having to increase prices. Sometimes this is the case. But in most instances compensation of employees is so large a part of the firm's costs (averaging 50 to 60 percent for most firms) and profits are so small a proportion (averaging, before taxes, about 6 to 7 percent of sales) that a substantial wage increase would totally eliminate profits. For example, a compensation increase of 10 percent will cost a firm 6 percent of its total costs (if it spent 60 percent of its costs on employee compensation) and almost fully eliminate a 6 percent rate of profits on sales. The firm would have no profits to distribute to its stockholders as dividends or to its managers as bonuses or to use for expansion.

As a consequence, firms ordinarily must make some adjustments in their business practices to be able to pay for compensation increases. Sometimes these adjustments take the form of price increases; sometimes, cost reductions; sometimes, reductions in the work force. In most cases firms do not discuss these matters in detail with their employees or with the unions that represent their employees. Instead, the firms prefer to keep these methods of adjustment as much a matter of managerial prerogative as possible. Sometimes, however, when price increases are threatened by a company as a result of union wage demands, the union will challenge the company's assertion that a price increase is required. Similar situations arise in negotiations between unions and governmental agencies. A union may challenge a mayor's or governor's position that a tax increase will be needed to pay for increased employee compensation. The union may claim that cutting executives' salaries and other alleged "frills" would allow the compensation increases to be paid without higher taxes.

Sometimes the ability of a company to pay is not considered in wage setting. When wages are set by a process involving association bargaining on the employer's side, the ability or inability of any particular firm to meet the increased compensation levels is not of any particular significance to the wage increase that is determined. Some firms are very profitable and could pay more. Other firms are in difficult straits, and some even go bankrupt because they cannot pay the new rates. But the advantage of having all firms paying the same rates of compensation, especially when they compete for business with each other, takes precedence for the union over dealing with firms individually.

However, the ability of a firm to pay may sneak in the back door, so to speak, of association bargaining. Although an employer association may represent many member firms, its committee for bargaining with a union will be much smaller. The particular firms on that committee may influence bargaining a great deal. If one firm represented on the committee is near bankruptcy, it may exercise great weight in trying to get a low settlement, and vice versa if a firm is doing very well.

In the public sector, disputes between governmental agencies and unions are often sent to arbitrators for settlement. This happens because the strike is not available as a tool to bring about dispute settlement. In the private sector, strikes are more common and resort to arbitration to settle contract terms is less common. Whenever an arbitrator has a case concerning increased compensation in which unions are involved, he or she must decide how to deal with an inability-to-pay claim. In the past, arbitrators in public-sector compensation disputes have tended to disregard the claims of public managers that they were unable to pay the compensation increases demanded by unions. The arbitrators left the public agencies to find the additional funds wherever they could.[13] Recently, however, the financial difficulties of many cities have caused arbitrators to be more careful in evaluating the merits of inability-to-pay claims by public agencies. Increased recognition of inability-to-pay claims by arbitrators has resulted in increased sophistication in the evidence submitted to back such claims. Table 14-3 lists evidence offered by public officials in attempting to justify inability-to-pay arguments.

The problem of determining the ability of a firm in the private sector to pay compensation increases is as complex as the analogous problem in the public sector. Among the major difficulties encountered in the private sector are such issues as:

- What is the pay period over which one is concerned with ability to pay? A firm may be able to pay a large increase for a short period but not for a longer one.
- What is the effect of the proposed compensation changes on costs of the firm? The answer will depend on changes the company may make in its methods of production and on the volume of production as well.
- What rate of return on its investment is the company entitled to? This issue may also be phrased another way: How much profit should the company receive?

---

[13] In some situations the ordinances of a municipality or a collective bargaining agreement explicitly denies the arbitrator the right to exceed city budget limitations, but such instances are unusual.

TABLE 14-3   FACTORS DETERMINING THE FINANCIAL STATUS OF A COMMUNITY

- Budget priorities
- Budget limitations
- Previous budget
- Budget amount as property tax levy
- Comparative equalized tax rates among communities
- Pending litigation with significant possible financial liability for the community
- Median family income
- Actual budget approved by city council or taxpayers
- Loss or gain in revenues
- Level of debt service (i.e., interest costs of community's debt)
- Reduction in services that might be required if budget is exceeded

Source: Charles C. Mulcahy, "Ability to Pay: The Public Employee Dilemma," *The Arbitration Journal*, 31:2, June 1976, pp. 90–96.

- To what degree can the company raise prices to cover additional costs? The character of the company's product market will largely determine the answer to this question. If the market is very competitive, the company may have little opportunity to raise its prices. If the market is much less competitive, price increases may be rather easy to make.

Two-Tier Pay Plans   When many American companies got into financial difficulties in the late 1970s and early 1980s due to recession at home and competition from foreign companies, they and some unions inaugurated a new pay system. Called a "two-tier" system, it provided substantially lower pay scales for newly hired employees than for those already on the payroll, even in the same jobs. And the new, low rates were not intended to be temporary—that is, a probationary or introductory rate—but to be permanent.

By 1985, 9 percent of new labor contracts had two-tier pay plans.[14] Some observers saw the plans as a great advantage for management.[15] But employees thought the plans unfair, and soon morale problems developed. Unions began to try to negotiate the lower rates out of the contracts. By 1987 two-tier plans were on the decline.[16]

Lump Sum Payments   In the 1980s because of the difficult economic situation of many firms, a new form of wage payment developed. Companies were reluctant to raise pay rates because the new rates had to be paid in the future, whatever the sales and profitability of the firms. So companies began

[14] Bureau of National Affairs, *Daily Labor Report* No. 15, Jan. 17, 1986, p. B1.

[15] Irwin Ross, "Employers Win Big in the Move to Two-Tier Contracts," *Fortune*, Apr. 29, 1985, pp. 82–92. See also Sanford M. Jacoby and Daniel J. B. Mitchell, "Management Attitudes toward Two-Tier Pay Plans," *Journal of Labor Research*, 7:3, Summer 1986, pp. 221ff.

[16] Agis Salpukas, "The Two-Tier Wage System is Found to Be a Two-Edged Sword by Industry," *The New York Times*, July 21, 1987, pp. 1 and D22. See also John T. Dunlop, "Industrial Relations: Old and New," *The Worklife Report*, 1988, pp. 1–3.

to propose lump sum payments to workers—akin to bonuses—instead of wage-rate increases. By 1986 and 1987 more than one-third of employees covered by union contracts got lump sum bonuses, a remarkably high percentage for a wage method which had hardly existed in collective bargaining agreements only a few years before.[17]

Paying for Knowledge   An even more dramatic innovation in pay systems involves paying employees only partially by the job they do, but also paying according to their skill levels and knowledge. Broadly skilled employees can be more valuable for companies because they can do many different things. In organizations where employees are expected to use their own discretion and work under little supervision and in cooperation with others, skill-based pay appears to have important advantages.[18]

Tying Executive Pay to that of Workers   Finally, in what may be the most unusual development of all, Chrysler agreed in 1988 with the United Auto Workers that executives of the company would not receive bonuses unless workers receive profit sharing plan payments. For the first time, what executives receive was tied to workers' pay.[19]

CHAPTER SUMMARY

The many different methods by which compensation is established can be divided into two general groups. One group is classified according to what actor or organization makes the decision about pay level. There are four actors identified: the employer, the employee, the union, and the government. Each actor may act unilaterally or in conjunction with another. In practice, compensation is usually set by joint action between employers and individual employees or between employers and unions.

The other group of methods is classified according to what process is used to set the pay level. Five processes by which compensation is established are reactive processes, surveys, formulas, job evaluation plans, and pay-by-performance plans. In the reactive process, rates are set according to the apparent needs of the moment without any formalities. The method is expedient and unsystematic. A valued employee may receive an offer of a job at higher pay elsewhere. The employer responds by raising the rate of pay for this particular person.

Employers, governmental agencies, and unions participate in systematic wage and salary surveys, and wage rates are set by reference to these sur-

---

[17] "Lump-Sum Bonuses," Bureau of National Affairs, *Daily Labor Report* No. 59, Mar. 30, 1987, pp. B1 and B2. See also "Lump-Sum Pay," *AFL-CIO News*, May 2, 1987, p. 6.

[18] Nina Gupta, G. Douglas Jenkins, Jr., and William P. Curington, "Paying for Knowledge," *National Productivity Review*, 5:2, Spring 1986, pp. 107–123. Also, "Skill-Based Pay," Bureau of National Affairs, *Daily Labor Review* No. 230, Dec. 1, 1986), pp. A12–A15.

[19] Bureau of National Affairs, *Daily Labor Report* No. 88, May 6, 1988, p. A8.

veys. Wage and salary surveys are very popular with employers. Despite their many problems the use of survey data by firms in establishing pay rates is quite extensive. However, the survey results are used only as a guide to policy and are supplemented by other information and considerations.

The essence of the formula approach to determining compensation is that it removes discretion from the determination of compensation. Rates are set by reference to some outside factor with no discretion regarding the specific level. The most common formula for the determination of wages is one that provides that wage rates shall be adjusted upward in step with the cost of living. Many collective bargaining agreements include a provision that wage rates shall be periodically adjusted in an amount determined by the rate of increase in consumer prices. This cost-of-living clause is referred to as an escalator or a COLA (cost-of-living adjustment) clause. There has been continuous debate for over 30 years as to whether or not cost-of-living clauses have an inflationary impact on the economy.

Job evaluation is a systematic method of appraising the worth of each job in an organization. Wage rates are then established for various jobs in a way that reflects their relative worth. Jobs are rated according to a system that assigns points for various characteristics of the job. Once jobs are rated according to the chosen factors, they are ranked by total points awarded. Wage rates are then assigned to individual jobs.

Pay by performance involves the provision of high pay to employees whose performance the employer considers best. There are four major factors which affect wage determination: comparability among wage rates, the ability of an employer to pay increased compensation, productivity of the workers involved, and changes in the cost of living. Comparability and ability to pay are discussed in this chapter. Comparability is the single most important factor in most pay decisions. Probably the largest number of wage decisions are based simply on the comparison of wage rates. The wage rates that exist at any specific time are referred to as a structure of rates. The determination of one rate by reference to others in the structure is the essence of this form of wage determination. Comparability as a standard for pay setting has roots in both the attitudes of individual workers and the economic and social behavior of firms. The principle that wage rates for one group should be adjusted to the rates of a comparable group seems invitingly simple, but there are important difficulties with making such comparisons.

The ability of an employer to pay increased compensation is also a very important factor in setting wage rates. Employees and unions often believe that companies can pay wage increases out of their profits without having to increase prices. In most instances this is not so. The ability of an employer to pay additional wages frequently depends on its ability to raise its revenues or cut its costs. Firms ordinarily have to make adjustments in their business practices to be able to pay for compensation increases. The ability or inability of firms to pay wage increases adds complexity to employer association bargaining. In the public sector, the ability of municipal or state governmental bodies to provide pay increases to their employees is becoming a major issue.

Two-tier, lump sum, skill-based pay , and executive bonuses tied to workers' profit sharing are innovations in compensation which try to accommodate employer needs for cost control and better performance with employee needs for higher earnings.

QUESTIONS FOR THOUGHT AND DISCUSSION

1 What factors affect a company's decision on the method of establishing pay? Which are the most important factors?
2 How does a cost-of-living escalator work? Are escalator clauses a good idea for management? For labor? Why or why not?
3 What are some of the issues that enter into collective bargaining over escalator clauses?
4 What is a job evaluation plan? How is it related to compensation? What are the major advantages of such plans? The major disadvantages?
5 Why are wage comparisons important in setting wage rates? What are the hazards in making wage comparisons?
6 How do social, cultural, and class values enter into job evaluations?
7 What is the difference between real wages and money wages? When is it important to make this distinction? How is it used?
8 Are cost-of-living escalators inflationary? On what do you base your opinion?
9 What are some of the problems with relying on wage surveys to set wage rates?
10 The attitude of workers toward their wages depends on their perception of the wages others receive. When a group of workers perceives a disadvantage with respect to the wages of another group, what actions are usually taken? Discuss the above phenomenon and the problems involved in comparing wage rates with regard to (1) the current debates over equal pay for comparable work and (2) the increasing movement of women into the work force and the feminist demand for wages for housework.
11 What are the advantages and disadvantages of lump sum pay, two-tier pay, skill-based pay, and tying executive bonuses to workers' profit sharing? To workers? To managers?

SELECTED READING

Doeringer, Peter B., and Michael J. Piore, *Internal Labor Markets and Manpower Analysis* (Lexington, Mass.: Heath-Lexington Books, 1971).

Dunn, J. D., and Frank M. Rachel, *Wage and Salary Administration: Total Compensation Systems* (New York: McGraw-Hill, 1971).

Myers, Charles A., and Paul Pigors, *Personnel Administration: A Point of View and a Method*, 8th ed. (New York: McGraw-Hill, 1977).

CHAPTER 15

BENEFITS

DEVELOPMENTS IN BENEFITS

The most important development in employee compensation in recent years has been the proliferation of benefits (also called "compensation supplements"). Before World War II virtually all compensation was in the form of pay for time worked. In 1929 supplements to pay for time worked in private industry were only 1.4 percent of total compensation. By the advent of World War II, supplements were still only 3.4 percent of total compensation.[1] But during the war supplements were allowed more favorable treatment under the wage-price controls system, and benefits began to spread. By 1982 after 3½ decades of steady growth, benefits constituted 36.7 percent of total compensation for larger firms.[2]

Benefits now exist in an almost bewildering variety. Some are provided by the federal government, and the employer, and often the employee personally, are required to pay a tax to the government to support the benefits. These are so-called required or legally mandated benefits. Their most important components are Social Security, workers' compensation (an accident insurance program), and unemployment insurance. Other benefits are provided "voluntarily" by employers, either by unilateral action or as a result of collective bargaining. Among the more important benefits of a voluntary nature are premium pay for overtime and shifts, paid vacations, paid holidays,

---

[1] Alvin Bauman, "Measuring Employee Compensation in U.S. Industry," *Monthly Labor Review*, 93:10, October 1970, pp. 17–23.
[2] United States Chamber of Commerce, *Employee Benefits* (Washington, D.C., 1983).

paid sick leave, health insurance, pensions, severance pay, and supplemental unemployment benefits (SUB).

In 1986, the Bureau of Labor Statistics (U.S. Department of Labor) surveyed benefits provided to 21 million employees (both union and nonunion of medium and large firms) in the private sector. The survey shows both the percentage of employees covered by various benefits and whether the employer paid the full cost of the benefit (a noncontributory plan), or whether the employee paid part of the cost (a contributory plan). The data are given in Table 15-1. Note that most benefits are provided on a noncontributory, or fully paid (by the employer), basis. Note also the wide variation in the degree to which various benefits are provided. For example, virtually all employees receive some paid vacation, but only 10 percent receive a paid lunch period. Note finally the variation between benefits received by different occupational groups. For example, 93 percent of professional and administrative and technical and clerical employees receive paid sick leave, compared with only 45 percent of production workers.

There are groups, however, who have little or no benefit coverage. For ex-

TABLE 15-1 PERCENT OF FULL-TIME EMPLOYEES PARTICIPATING IN EMPLOYEE BENEFIT PLANS, PRIVATE INDUSTRY, UNITED STATES,* 1986

Employee benefit program	All employees (%)	Professional and administrative employees (%)	Technical and clerical employees (%)	Production employees (%)
Paid				
Holidays	99	99	100	98
Vacations	100	99	100	100
Rest time	72	58	69	82
Sick leave	70	93	93	45
Personal leave	25	33	35	15
Lunch time	10	3	4	17
Accident and sickness insurance	49	28	35	69
Noncontributory†	41	22	28	59
Long-term disability insurance	48	68	60	30
Noncontributory†	38	52	47	24
Health insurance	95	96	94	96
Noncontributory†	54	52	45	61
Pension plan	89	92	92	87
Noncontributory†	76	78	78	74
Life insurance	96	97	96	95
Noncontributory†	87	87	86	86

*Excluding Alaska and Hawaii.
†Provided at no cost to employee.
Source: Bureau of Labor Statistics, U.S. Department of Labor, *Employee Benefits in Medium and Large Firms, 1986*, Bulletin No. 2281, June 1987, p. 4.

ample, in 1979, only 15 percent of more than 14 million part-time workers in private industry had health-care insurance. For part-time workers in agriculture, only 3 percent had coverage (97 percent did not).[3] Some of these workers may be covered by the health insurance plans of other family members; some may have purchased health insurance on their own; but many apparently have no coverage at all.

Developments in benefits continue at a rapid rate. New benefits are added. Old benefits are modified, and their functions are enlarged. New concepts emerge. Keeping up with developments in the benefits area is the subject of several periodic publications, issued by the Chamber of Commerce of the United States,[4] the Bureau of National Affairs,[5] the Conference Board,[6] the U.S. Civil Service Commission,[7] and others.[8] The complexity of benefits, eligibility requirements, and other special provisions of benefit plans defies summarization.

By the 1970s benefits had become a major part of American compensation practices. Collective bargaining was increasingly involved in issues relating to benefits. Special procedures had been established in many instances to negotiate benefits. Specialized technical staffs, particularly for pensions and health insurance, had been created in many companies and unions. And the costs of benefits continued to rise at a more rapid rate than other elements of compensation, even during the inflationary period of the early 1970s. It has become impossible to understand American collective bargaining without a considerable knowledge of benefits.

PENSION PLANS

Pensions are a method of providing income, usually in the form of a monthly check, to persons after they cease working for a living (i.e., retire). In the United States we have developed a complex system of providing pensions that combines both private and public sources of funds. Our system is coming under increased stress as the proportion of our population that is at or beyond retirement age increases, partly because of increasing life expectancy. In response to this stress, the pension system has been, and now is, undergoing considerable review and change.[9]

---

[3] "Labor Department Study," reprinted in Bureau of National Affairs, *Daily Labor Report* No. 176, Sept. 11, 1981, p. D4.

[4] Chamber of Commerce of the United States, *Employee Benefits*, Washington D.C.

[5] Bureau of National Affairs, *Basic Patterns in Union Contracts*, Washington, D.C.

[6] The Conference Board, *Profile of Employee Benefits*, New York.

[7] U.S. Civil Service Commission, *Comparisons of Major Employee Benefit Programs*, Washington, D.C.

[8] Employee Benefit Research Institute, *Fundamentals of Employee Benefit Programs*, Washington, D.C.

[9] William Graebner, *A History of Retirement* (New Haven, Conn.: Yale University Press, 1980).

Types of Pensions

Private pension plans are set up by business concerns for the purpose of providing benefits to their employees.[10] An employee earns credits by length of service with an employer and receives a pension the amount of which is determined in large part by the credits the employee has accumulated. Private plans differ greatly in their characteristics. Some plans are paid for partly by the employer and partly by the employees. Plans with employee contributions are known as contributory plans. Plans in which the employer pays the full cost of the pension plan are called noncontributory plans. Plans may be provided by a single employer, and are so designated, or by an association of employers (a multiemployer plan). Plans may be cost-based or benefit-based. In a cost-based plan, the employer (and perhaps the employees) contributes a certain amount of money (e.g., 80 cents per hour worked) and benefits are purchased from an insurance company or are provided by the plan in whatever amount the contributions will support. In a benefit-based plan, the company agrees to provide a specific level of benefits and then proceeds to obtain that coverage as it desires. Sometimes the company buys a benefit plan from an insurance company. In other cases the company sets up a fund from which benefits are to be provided. In still other instances, the company does not fund the plan at all, but merely pays out benefits as they come due from its income. When a company does not set up a fund to cover future benefit payments, it is said to have an unfunded pension liability, a matter to which we will return later.

Calculating the costs of a pension plan or the impact on costs of a change in benefits is a very complicated matter. First, since benefit payments are not made to retirees in a lump sum, but as a stream of monthly checks, the problem is to assess the volume of the flow, not the total cost of the pension plan. Second, pension benefits are contingent liabilities to a pension plan or a firm. That is, whether or not the plan will have to pay benefits depends on the life span of its employees. People in some occupations have a long life expectancy, causing probable benefit payments to be high. In other occupations, employees have a shorter life expectancy and pension costs are correspondingly lower. Also, the costs of a pension plan depend on the age distribution of a company's work force. An identical pension plan provided by two employers will usually be more expensive for the employer whose employees have the higher average age. A firm with a high rate of turnover among its employees will also tend to have a less expensive pension plan because its employees will not, on the average, accumulate many credits toward their pensions because they will not have been with the company long. Calculations that consider the impact of employee life expectancy at retirement, current age, and turnover on pension costs are called actuarial computations and are usually performed by specialists. The result of the mix of types of

[10] Dan M. McGill, *Fundamentals of Private Pensions* (Homewood, Ill.: Irwin, 1975).

pension plans, characteristics of employees, and different methods of actuarial computations is a very complicated private pension system.

The system is not very old in the United States. In 1940 only some 3.8 million employees were covered by private pension plans (about 13.6 percent of total private nonagricultural employment); other workers had no private pension coverage. In 1978 some 50 million workers were covered (about 50 percent of total private nonagricultural employment). In a 1987 study of medium and large firms nearly 89 percent of all surveyed workers were covered by some retirement pension plan.[11] The pension movement received its big impetus at the end of World War II. In 1946 the United Mine Workers and the federal government (then in control of the bituminous coal mines) negotiated a pension plan. In 1949 the National Labor Relations Board[12] ruled in a case involving Inland Steel Company that the company was required by the National Labor Relations Act to bargain about pensions with the Steelworkers union. In 1949 private pension plans were adopted in both the steel and automobile industries.[13] During the middle to late 1950s pension plans appeared in such industries as construction and trucking. In these industries pensions were provided on a multiemployer basis.

Public pension plans cover employees of federal, state, and local governments. Plans may be provided by the states or municipalities, and federal employees are covered by plans made available by the federal government. Ordinarily these plans are not funded. They have developed rapidly in recent years and in the 1970s became the subject of heated collective bargaining between public employee unions and various levels of government. The eligibility requirements and benefits provided under these plans are as varied as those under private pension plans.

Social Security is a federal program that provides monthly financial payments to eligible persons. Eligibility depends primarily on age (benefits ordinarily begin at age 65, but may in some instances start earlier) and on the so-called coverage of the program. Coverage refers to persons who are employers or employees in jobs covered by the Social Security Act. Covered employment is primarily in the private sector. The Social Security system is financed largely by taxes paid by covered employers and employees. An employee gains eligibility by working for the requisite length of time in covered employment and by paying taxes during that employment.

The Social Security system was instituted by Congress in 1935, to take effect in 1937. There was a court challenge to the constitutionality of the tax on employers and employees that was to finance the retirement pensions, but the Supreme Court upheld the law in 1937.[14] The law has been revised sev-

---

[11] Bureau of Labor Statistics, *Monthly Labor Review*, 106:7, July 1983, p. 2.
[12] *NLRB v. Inland Steel Co.* (77 NLRB 1, 21 LRRM 1316).
[13] George Ruben, "Major Collective Bargaining Developments—A Quarter-Century Review," *Current Wage Developments*, 26:2, February 1974, pp. 42–54.
[14] *Helvering v. Davis*, 301 U.S. 619 (1937); and *Steward Machine Co. v. Davis*, 301 U.S. 548 (1937).

eral times since the 1930s and has been expanded to cover more employers and employees, to provide more benefits, and to collect more taxes to pay for the benefits. By 1975 more than 9 of every 10 people age 65 or older were eligible to receive Social Security benefits, and about 95 percent of those who had reached age 65 were receiving benefits.

The benefits paid by the Social Security system are subject to certain provisions that, in the view of many people, affect the adequacy of the system. Among the more important of these provisions are (1) persons receiving Social Security benefits do not get as much income in benefit payments as they earned prior to retirement (the ratio of Social Security benefits to previous annual earnings is called a replacement ratio) and (2) if a person who receives Social Security earns income by working, the payment received from Social Security is reduced by half the amount earned (with a certain amount of earnings excluded from the benefit reduction).

Many American retirees receive benefits from both Social Security and a private retirement plan. In the 1950s the pension agreements negotiated by unions with private employers ordinarily tied benefits to Social Security benefits, the company picking up the difference between Social Security and a specified level of benefits. This is referred to as an approach involving a Social Security offset. In the 1960s the offset provision was eliminated from many of the private plans, so that today the typical collectively bargained pension plan provides benefits over and above any Social Security benefits received. However, because of the increasing cost of private pension plans, many employers are again proposing to include a Social Security offset in their pension programs. Labor unions have been generally opposed to this proposal.

Issues Involving Pensions

An adequate level of benefits is not easy to define. Initially, pensions were conceived of as providing a minimum income to protect elderly persons from poverty. Yet even within the concept of pensions as providing a minimum "floor," there was room for disagreement about adequacy. Wilbur J. Cohen, formerly Secretary of Health, Education, and Welfare and knowledgeable about the Social Security system, once referred to the concept of Social Security as providing a minimum floor as follows:

> Some people think of the floor as a bare, rough-hewn, cabin floor; others as a solid oak floor, polished and waxed. I like to think of it as a floor with a kind of Bigelow carpet on it not only to keep my feet warm, but giving me some esthetic pleasure, also.

In recent years, pensions have been increasingly designed to provide more than a minimal level of income. Among the standards offered for evaluating the adequacy of benefit levels are the following:

• A benefit level that would meet the observed needs and living styles of the aged

- A benefit level that would provide a retired person with a standard of living similar to the one he or she had while working
- A benefit level that would provide sufficient income to allow a retired person to enjoy a living standard roughly equivalent to that currently enjoyed by the working population

These standards may be used to evaluate the level of benefits provided under Social Security or under private pension programs, or their combined effect. As a practical matter, another standard that has considerable importance may be set forward:

- The level of benefits desired by a group of people as evidenced by their willingness to purchase or bargain for them

Presumably, groups of employees and employers may differ in the importance they attach to pension benefits. If Social Security provides a floor, then private pension plans may provide a substantial amount of additional coverage or very little, depending on the preferences of employees and employers as revealed in the bargaining process.[15]

Coverage of people under pension plans in the United States is very uneven. Some people draw pension benefits from several sources and have very adequate pensions. Others receive no benefits at all—not even Social Security. While the number of people who are covered by no plan at all is small, there are nevertheless such cases. This is because the pension system in the United States, both private and public, is related to job experience. A person earns eligibility for pension benefits through employment. People who have very unstable work histories, or none at all, or who have been self-employed and made no provision for Social Security or retirement, may receive no benefits at all. The American system of pensions, and of other social services as well, is very much more related to each individual's work experience than is generally the case abroad.[16]

Private pension plans confront their own special problems of coverage. In general, if a firm or group of firms has considerable turnover of employees, it may wish to establish a pension plan that rewards only those who stay with the company or in the industry. If benefits are divided among many short-term and long-term employees, it may be possible to give only low benefits at an acceptable cost. But if benefits are provided only to long-term employees, the level may be higher at an acceptable cost. Unions and companies frequently make decisions about coverage and eligibility on this basis.[17]

Vesting of pension benefits is a related issue. Employees often change jobs, or even leave the labor force entirely, for various reasons. When an em-

[15] Derek C. Bok, "Emerging Issues in Social Legislation: Social Security," *Harvard Law Review*, 80, 1968, pp. 717–764.

[16] Gaston V. Rimlinger, "American Social Security in European Perspective," in William Bowen, ed., *The American System of Social Insurance* (New York: McGraw-Hill, 1968), pp. 213–240.

[17] James H. Schulz et al., "Private Pensions Fall Far Short," *Monthly Labor Review*, 102:2, February 1979, pp. 28–32.

ployee leaves a company prior to retirement, should he or she lose all rights to a pension benefit? If not, how long should a person be employed by a particular employer, or under a particular multiemployer plan, before becoming eligible for some benefits? A pension plan is "vested" when the employee will receive a benefit upon retirement regardless of future employment with the company.

Funding (i.e., setting money aside to pay future benefits) of pension plans protects the employee should the company go bankrupt or otherwise be unable to pay a pension when it becomes due. In the 1960s Studebaker Corporation ceased to operate in the United States and terminated many employees, all of whom lost their pension benefits, despite collective bargaining agreements that had supposedly established pension rights. Funding of the pension program would have prevented this. But funding is also expensive and may limit the level of benefits that are to be provided.

Early retirement is increasingly common in the United States; but what impact does early retirement have on pension benefits or eligibility? Many pension plans now provide for reduced benefits if an employee retires at age 62. Other plans permit an employee to retire after 20 years of service, regardless of age, and receive full benefits.

Do pension plans keep workers from leaving? Studies show that workers covered by pensions are less likely to change jobs than are those not covered, but this is largely due to higher pay in jobs that provide pensions.[18]

Costs of Providing Private Pensions

The cost to employers of providing pensions has been rising rapidly and now has reached very substantial proportions. Most companies set aside money (i.e., provide funding) for only a part of their potential liability for pension costs. There remain unfunded pension liabilities created by the accrued pension benefits of persons who work, or have worked, for the company.

The amount of unfunded pension liability can be very large. Several large American corporations report unfunded pension liabilities that exceed the corporations' entire net worth. Where this occurs, potential pension costs can adversely affect a company's ability to raise capital by borrowing or issuing stock. In recent years companies with a weakening financial position have had to bargain with unions over special devices to reduce the unfunded pension liabilities of the companies.

Management of Assets of Private Pension Plans

The assets of pension funds are very substantial. Private funds now have more than a trillion dollars in assets and have become a major factor in the

---

[18] Alan Gustman and Thomas Steinmeier, "Pensions, Wages and Job Mobility," National Bureau of Economic Research, Paper No. 2426, 1988.

market for stocks, bonds, real estate, and other investments. Ordinarily, these funds are managed by corporate executives or by professional investment managers chosen by corporate executives. In recent years the unions have objected to how the funds are invested, finding that many pension plans negotiated by unions but managed by business executives have their funds invested in nonunion companies.

Multiemployer pension plans sometimes have both union and nonunion trustees. Sometimes these trustees manage the plan's investments rather than hire professional investment managers. Sometimes union and management trustees are alleged to have used the funds unwisely or even illegally, perhaps for personal benefit. A major controversy of this nature has developed with respect to some of the larger pension funds of the International Brotherhood of Teamsters.

ERISA

In 1964 the Congress of the United States began hearings into the performance of private pension plans. Abuses of the system were uncovered, and Congress began drafting a pension reform bill. Finally, in 1974, Congress passed a law regulating private pension plans. The act is entitled Employees' Retirement Income Security Act (ERISA) and is one of the most complex pieces of federal legislation ever written. The law contains 75,000 words, covering several hundred pages, plus a 100-page explanatory report by the congressional conference committee (including members of both the House of Representatives and the Senate) that finally cleared the bill for passage.[19]

ERISA imposes standards on private pension plans that cover many of the topics discussed above. A summary of the act is provided in Table 15-2. The term "fiduciary standards" means the standards of financial behavior to which trustees of the funds are now held by law. The "prudent man" rule means, in brief, that a trustee must behave as a court would expect a fictional rational person to behave. Failure to do so causes the trustee to be liable personally for financial losses by the fund. Lawyers have already begun to debate what a "prudent man" serving as trustee of a pension fund would do.[20] And employers, faced with the new financial and legal complexities introduced into pension plans by ERISA, have terminated some plans and begun reviewing others.[21]

---

[19] Noel A. Levin, *ERISA and Labor-Management Benefit Funds*, 2d ed. (New York: Practising Law Institute, 1975).

[20] Mary Green Miner, *Pension Plans and the Impact of ERISA* (Washington, D.C.: Bureau of National Affairs, 1977), Personnel Policy Forum Survey No. 119, and "Fiduciary Standards and the Prudent Man Rule under ERISA," *Harvard Law Review*, 88:5, March 1975, pp. 960–979.

[21] Robert D. Paul, "Can Private Pension Plans Deliver?" *Harvard Business Review*, 52:5, September–October 1974, pp. 22–37.

TABLE 15-2 HIGHLIGHTS OF THE PENSION REFORM LAW

Participation	Prohibits plans from requiring an age of eligibility greater than 25 or a period of service longer than 1 year, whichever is later.
Vesting	Prohibits plan vesting provision from being less liberal than one of the three following minimum standards: **1** 100 percent vesting after 10 years of service. **2** 25 percent vesting after 5 years of service, increasing yearly until 100 percent after 15 years **3** 50 percent vesting as soon as the sum of age and years of service (after 5 years) totals 45, reaching 100 percent 5 years later
Funding	Requires plan to fund current year's benefit accruals and amortize any unfunded costs over 30 years (40 years for existing multiemployer plans)
Fiduciary standards	Establishes the "prudent man" rule as the basic standard of conduct, outlaws various transactions between parties-in-interest, and prohibits investment of more than 10 percent of fund assets in employer securities or real estate
Reporting and disclosure	Requires the plan to provide participants with a comprehensive booklet describing pension plan provisions and to report annually to the secretary of labor on numerous operating and financial details of the plan
Plan termination insurance	Creates a federal insurance organization to protect beneficiaries against loss of vested pension on plan termination where assets are inadequate. Protects benefits up to $750 per month. Initial annual premium for this coverage is $1 per participant (50¢ for multiemployer plan participants) and began on date of enactment for both single- and multiemployer plans
Portability	Encourages some voluntary portability by allowing a worker, if the employer agrees to it, to transfer his or her pension rights tax free from one employer pension fund to another by establishing a tax-free individual retirement account
Joint and survivorship option	Requires a married worker, unless the worker specifically requests the plan's normal retirement benefit, to receive a pension payable for his or her lifetime and continuing in 50 percent of that amount to the spouse if the spouse survives the employee (the worker's normal retirement benefit may be actuarially reduced to pay for the cost of this provision)

*Old plans are those established prior to Sept. 2, 1974. New plans are those established on or subsequent to Sept. 2, 1974.

†Effective dates on some provisions have been delayed by regulations.

Source: Lawrence T. Smedley, "Pensions a Year Later," *AFL-CIO American Federationist,* 82:10, October 1975, p. 19.

HEALTH INSURANCE

As with pensions, the surge in the growth of health insurance plans came after World War II. Significant growth occurred in a variety of benefits provided by health insurance. The most frequent protection provided to employees is so-called regular medical coverage, which covers a range of medical services short of the more serious procedures. Hospitalization and surgery are covered separately. Insurance against death and dismemberment and temporary disability is also often provided. Major medical insurance, which protects the employee against the financial burdens of a prolonged illness, is infrequent, but such plans are beginning to appear.[22]

The extent of coverage of employees of nonunionized firms by health plans is largely unknown in any comprehensive fashion. Many of the better-standards nonunion firms provide extensive medical coverage, comparable to that provided under collective bargaining agreements. Low-standards firms do not provide such coverage. The firm may have a nurse on the premises, or a doctor on retainer to the firm, for the care of employees, but little else is provided in the way of health care.

The health insurance plans provided by American industry exist in an unusual context. The United States alone of major industrialized nations provides no comprehensive national medical care program.[23] As a result, the health-care insurance that many members of our population receive is provided by their employers. The loss of a job can place the employee and his or her dependents in grave financial difficulties should they experience illness while not covered by health insurance. While insurance can be purchased from health insurance companies, it is expensive and many people do not buy it. Major recessions, with their accompanying loss of jobs by millions of workers, may cause people to lose their health insurance when they lose their jobs. During recent business downturns Congress provided, through the unemployment insurance system, funds to assist unemployed workers in obtaining health coverage.

A current major problem is the rapidly rising cost of health care. For several years health costs have risen faster, sometimes much faster, than prices in general. Because many companies have experienced rapid cost increases, health-care costs are now a major factor in collective bargaining. Management and labor, with government assistance,[24] are constantly searching for less expensive methods of obtaining health care. In some cases rising health-care costs have stimulated an offensive by management and labor to control costs.

Among the ways unions are helping management to cut health-care costs are:

---

[22] Bruce Spencer, *Group Benefits in a Changing Society* (Chicago: Charles D. Spencer and Associates, 1982).

[23] Bert Seidman, "Health Security: The Complete Rx," *AFL-CIO American Federationist,* 82:10, October 1975, p. 10.

[24] In 1976, for example, the President's Council on Wage and Price Stability conducted a series of hearings in major cities across the nation to explore methods of reducing medical care costs with business and labor. The results were published under the title "Labor-Management Innovations Controlling Costs of Employee Health Care Benefits," *Federal Register,* 41:182, Sept. 17, 1976, pp. 40298–40326.

Second opinions Requiring employees to seek them before surgery.

Audits Encouraging workers, often with financial rewards, to check their hospital and doctor's bills for accuracy.

Pretesting Encouraging medical tests prior to hospital admission of workers.

Precertification Setting up a review board to determine on a case-by-case basis whether hospitalization is necessary—and for how long.

Outpatient surgery Providing incentives for doctors to perform some simple operations in their offices or clinics rather than in the hospital.

Treatment review Monitoring present and past treatments to ensure that they are both appropriate and needed.

Insurance checks Cross-checking policies to stop payments of the same bill by different insurance companies.[25]

Collective bargaining over medical care is unusually complicated. The union and the company must not only determine the money to be spent, but must also negotiate for the delivery of the health-care services. The cost and quality of the services obtained may be as important as raising the money to pay for them. There are various ways by which health care may be obtained. The three major methods[26] are:

- Commercial insurance company plans
- Provider-sponsored plans
- Prepaid group-practice plans

(Providers of health care are institutions such as hospitals or clinics.) Most insurance is purchased by unions and employers from insurance companies or service corporations (like Blue Cross–Blue Shield), which are financial intermediaries between the employer and the union and the providers of health services. There have been experiments with the other methods listed above, however. Several decades ago the United Mine Workers established a union-management health and welfare fund committee on the national level which negotiates at the community level with health-care providers. And in California the Kaiser Corporation has experimented since the 1950s with a prepaid plan. Under such a plan a group of physicians is paid to care for employees on an ongoing basis—not on a fee-for-services-performed basis. The concept is that the health of the employees will be maintained by regular visits to the doctors, checkups, and preventive medicine, and thus larger bills for care after a disease has struck the employee will be avoided. The financial experience under the Kaiser Plan, and some others, was so favorable that Congress in 1974 passed a law to foster the development of Health Maintenance Organizations (HMOs), i.e., prepaid group health plans such as California's Kaiser-Permanente Medical Care Program. Recent experience

---

[25] Adapted from "Chopping Health Care Costs," *Business Week*, Mar. 31, 1986, p. 78.
[26] Robert W. Hetherington et al., *Health Insurance Plans* (New York: Wiley, 1975).

with the HMOs has been less favorable financially, and business and labor are continuing to search for new methods of providing health care. In order to facilitate exchanges of information about health care (and other matters), labor-management health, welfare, and pension trust funds have established an organization, the National Foundation of Health, Welfare, and Pension Plans, which meets periodically and assists trustees in the management of these plans.

In 1988 Congressional proposals surfaced to require employers to offer health insurance to workers. Some states adopted such laws. Mandating employer health plans was emerging as an alternative to a governmental system of national health insurance.

SUPPLEMENTAL UNEMPLOYMENT BENEFITS

What source of income exists for workers who are laid off from their jobs? Until the 1930s, people without jobs either went on general relief (so-called welfare), lived with relatives, or simply existed as best they could. In 1932 the state of Wisconsin adopted a state program of unemployment insurance. Under such a program, laid-off workers could register with the state and receive income payments. In 1935 the federal government included in the Social Security Act a provision allowing states to establish unemployment insurance systems and providing the tax base to finance such a program. This act was the foundation of our current unemployment insurance system. The system is best described as a state-federal system, for there are numerous differences between the states in the administration of the program, but there are also some standards that are required by the federal government.

The states have considerable latitude in establishing the eligibility requirements and levels of benefits provided for workers who are unemployed. In many states the eligibility requirements and benefits provided have seemed inadequate to unions, causing supplemental unemployment benefit funds (SUBs) to be established in some industries.

In 1955 the United Auto Workers demanded a guaranteed annual wage from the automobile companies. The union's purpose was to protect the earnings of workers from layoffs. Ford Motor Company countered with a proposal for a SUB plan. The union accepted the plan, and it quickly spread to the other auto companies. Since 1955 the UAW has extended the plan to many of its agreements with auto supply companies, and the steel industry has picked up the plan. But the idea has not spread widely. By 1970 only 2.5 million workers were covered by SUB plans. In 1972 the Sheet Metal Workers International Association, which is primarily a construction union, advanced a SUB plan as part of a proposed package of employee benefits and obligations entitled the SASMI (Stabilization Agreement in the Sheet Metal Industry) plan. Many employees in the sheet metal industry opposed the SUB feature of the plan very strongly, arguing that employers should not pay people for not working (i.e., not pay people who had been laid off). The SASMI plan occasioned several lengthy strikes in the industry and various legal challenges, but by 1976 the plan was incorporated in many local Sheet Metal Workers agreements. Elsewhere in the economy, however, SUB gave no indication of spreading rapidly.

SUB plans differ in many details, but basically involve the establishment of a fund from which laid-off employees may draw benefits. The unions and employers negotiate the amount to be paid to the fund. Benefits are usually set to provide the difference between what the employee receives as unemployment insurance and some proportion of his or her ordinary take-home pay. For example, the auto agreements have provided 52 weeks of benefits making up (with unemployment insurance) 95 percent of take-home pay. In some cases, as in the steel industry (beginning in 1969), SUB plans are incorporated as part of a broader program to provide earnings protection to employees.

In the late 1970s and early 1980s there occurred substantial layoffs which threatened to, and sometimes did, exhaust the SUB plans. In response the unions began to negotiate new types of job security plans which tried to avoid layoffs, not simply provide income security for those who lost work. Under the 1984 agreements in the auto industry the companies committed funds to develop jobs for union members in nonautomobile areas. The companies also set aside funds for retraining workers who lost their jobs. Under the 1987 agreements, companies undertook to guarantee current job levels in key plants except in the event of an industrywide sales slump, to close no plants, and to replace half the workers lost through attrition (i.e., retirement, resignation, or ill health).[27]

OVERTIME AND PREMIUM PAY

Establishment of the hours of work has been a major trade union interest. For many years unions sought to reduce the length of the workday and work week. In 1870 the average workday was 11 hours long and the work week 6 days long. By 1890 the workday had declined to an average of 10 hours. And today the average workday hovers between 7 and 8 hours. In the twentieth century the 6-day week has given way to a standard 5-day week. Instead of working 66 hours per week, as in 1860,[28] the modern employee averages 35 to 40 hours per week.[29] Since 1948, however, average weekly hours have ceased to decline.[30]

---

[27] Jacob M. Schlesinger and Joseph B. White, "Ford and UAW Agree," *Wall Street Journal*, Sept. 18, 1987, pp. 7 and 9; and Wendy Zellner and Aaron Bernstein, "The UAW," *Business Week*, Sept. 14, 1987, pp. 125–129.

[28] *Statistical History of the United States* (Stamford, Conn.: Fairfield, 1957).

[29] Archibald A. Evans, *Hours of Work in Industrialized Countries* (Geneva: International Labor Office, 1975).

[30] John D. Owens, "Workweeks and Leisure," *Monthly Labor Review*, 99:8, August 1976, pp. 3–8.

For 85 percent of American employees, the standard work week is 40 hours.[31] In Europe, however, significant reductions in the standard length of the working day have occurred. Under an agreement between management and labor in the metal working industries in Germany, the basic work week was reduced from 40 hours in 1984 to 37 hours in 1987. This agreement has received attention from unions and employers in other countries, including the United States, and might prove to be pattern-setting.[32]

In order to discourage employers from working employees beyond the established normal workday and work week, unions have sought to negotiate premium pay arrangements for work outside the normal working hours. Thus, collective bargaining agreements ordinarily provide that work beyond 8 hours in a day, or 40 hours in a week, or on Saturdays, Sundays, or other holidays should be paid at a premium.[33] Federal law requires most private companies to pay time and a half after 40 hours in a week, and requires some companies to pay time and a half after 8 hours in a day. The overtime premiums now in effect in American industry usually provide time-and-a-half pay for work beyond 8 hours a day and 40 hours a week, and double time for work on Sundays and other holidays. But in some industries (especially construction) all overtime is often required to be paid at double time, and in some cases the rate for working on a holiday is triple time.

This discussion implies that negotiation about overtime premiums is an uncomplicated matter. In fact, this may not be so. The basic steel industry agreement, for example, devotes six full pages of text to the matter of the normal hours of work and the overtime premium. The agreement deals with the following issues:

- Normal hours of work
- Scheduling
- Posting of schedules
- Starting time
- Conditions under which overtime rates apply
- Overtime computation
- Holiday liability

The federal government has passed legislation that deals with overtime. Federal law (the Fair Labor Standards Act) requires that employers covered by the law must pay their employees time and a half for all hours worked beyond 40 hours a week. Overtime premium pay is not required for hours worked beyond 8 hours in a day. The overtime requirements extend to most

---

[31] Bureau of Labor Statistics, "Employee Benefits, 1981," in Bureau of National Affairs, *Daily Labor Report* No. 186, Sept. 24, 1982. p. E-11.

[32] "Global Drive Launched to Cut Workweek," *AFL-CIO News*, July 4, 1987, p. 4. Also see "Reduced Workweek," Bureau of National Affairs, *Daily Labor Report* No. 87, May 7, 1987, pp. C1–C3.

[33] A 1976 study casts doubt on the degree to which overtime premiums actually induce employers to schedule less overtime. See Bevars D. Mabry, "The Sources of Overtime," *Industrial Relations*, 15:2, May 1976, pp. 248–251.

employers in the private sector, but there are numerous exceptions. For example, boat salespeople, cotton-ginning and sugar-processing employees, and hotel and restaurant employees are largely exempt from the overtime provisions. The major exception is made for certain broad classes of employees, however—professional, executive, and administrative personnel are exempt from the overtime requirement. Federal regulations provide the basis for determining whether particular employees are exempt or nonexempt. The provisions of collective bargaining agreements with respect to overtime supplement the federally mandated overtime provisions.

PAID TIME OFF

Employees are often paid wages or salary for time that they do not work. The principal arrangements of this nature involve paid holidays and paid vacations. Major collective bargaining agreements in the United States now provide about 10 or 11 paid holidays each year. Employees not covered by such agreements usually receive fewer holidays. Paid vacations may involve from 1 to 4 weeks, depending on the length of service that an employee has accumulated in a company. In 1982 hours paid by employers exceeded hours worked by 7 percent.[34]

The result of continuing increases in paid time off is to provide employees with an increasing amount of leisure time for which they receive compensation. There has been some speculation that employees prefer increased leisure in the form of holidays and vacations to a shorter work week. Since the late 1940s, the evidence is of a general stability in daily and weekly hours worked, but considerable growth in paid time off.

EMERGING ISSUES IN BENEFITS

A number of new benefits are being discussed in collective bargaining, and experimental applications are in progress. These benefits grew rapidly in the 1970s, but at a slower rate in the early 1980s due to recession and other economic difficulties. Improvement in the economy in the mid-1980s promised a resumption in the benefit growth.

- *Alternative working schedule.* Several different schemes are receiving wide attention. One consists of flexible working hours—a system in which the employee is obligated to put in a certain number of hours (e.g., 8 hours a day), but may do so on any schedule he or she desires during the day. According to one researcher, "flexitime" began in Germany in 1967. This researcher estimates that by 1977, 13 percent of U.S. organizations were using flexitime and that 6 percent of the U.S. work force was on the flexitime

---

[34] Kent Kunze, "New BLS Survey Measures Ratio of Hours Worked to Hours Paid," *Monthly Labor Review*, 107:6, June 1984, pp. 3–7.

arrangement.[35] A second scheme involves staggered work hours—a system in which employees work on a changeable schedule. A third scheme involves a shorter, or compact, work week—a system in which employees work four 10-hour days or some similar schedule. And in the late 1980s proposals for a 6-hour workday for working mothers began to be made. Only if this is done, it is argued, can families remain together. The unions remain, of course, interested in reductions in both the number of days and number of hours worked in a week.[36] Some collective bargaining agreements provide for 35-hour weeks and/or 4.5 days of work per week.

• *Prepaid legal services.* Some unions are now negotiating for the establishment of legal services funds. In an increasingly complex and legalistic society, workers, like other citizens, feel the need of legal assistance. However, employees may not know how to obtain qualified legal assistance or how to get it at reasonable cost. To answer this problem, unions, consumer cooperatives, student groups, and similar organizations had established about 3500 legal service plans by 1978. Legal service plans may have "open" or "closed" legal panels. An open panel allows the plan's members a choice of attorneys; a closed plan allows a choice limited to a group of previously selected attorneys.[37] Because of opposition to legal services plans from some bar association groups, the sponsors of the plans sought to prevent states and municipalities from regulating the plans.[38] In 1974 Congress, in the ERISA legislation, provided that only the federal government can regulate benefits established by collective bargaining agreements, including legal services plans.[39]

• *Profit sharing plans.* Under some benefit plans, employees share in the profits of a firm. When the company does well, employees get a bonus; when the company loses money, employees receive only their regularly established pay. Profit sharing plans have existed for many years. In the most recent decade, they have grown rapidly. Large companies, such as those in the auto industry, have established profit sharing plans for unionized workers. Motivations for establishing the plans include giving employees a "share of the action" and giving employees a stake in the company's success. According to one study, by 1978 fifteen million U.S. workers were covered by profit sharing plans.[40] By the late 1980s, the number is undoubtedly much larger.

---

[35] Stanley D. Nollen, "Does Flexitime Improve Productivity?" *Harvard Business Review*, 57:5, September–October 1979, pp. 12ff. See also Donald J. Petersen, "Flexitime in the United States," *Personnel*, 57:1, January–February 1980, pp. 21–31.

[36] Harriet G. Weinstein, *A Comparison of Three Alternative Work Schedules* (Philadelphia: University of Pennsylvania, 1976). Also David M. Maklan, *The Four-Day Workweek* (New York: Praeger, 1977).

[37] Sandy DeMent, "A New Bargaining Focus on Legal Services," *AFL-CIO American Federationist*, 85:5, May 1978, pp. 7–10. Also Guvenc G. Alpander, "Prepaid Legal Services," *Industrial and Labor Relations Review*, 31:2, January 1978, pp. 172–182.

[38] Theodore J. St. Antoine, "Growth Patterns in Legal Services," *AFL-CIO American Federationist*, 83:2, February 1976, pp. 19–21.

[39] "Federal Bill Preempts Prepaid Regulations," *Trends in Legal Services*, 1:3, August 1974, p. 1.

[40] "Profit-Sharing Plans Grow Strongly," *The New York Times*, May 12, 1983, p. 27.

• *Employee stock ownership plans (ESOPs).* Under an ESOP, an employee has an account that is credited with contributions made to the plan by the company in proportion to the employee's level of compensation. When an employee dies, retires, or leaves the company, the ESOP account is translated into the stock of the company. ESOPs are receiving support for several reasons. First, the employees become owners of the company, as stockholders, and many employers believe this will help employees to be more productive members of the company. Second, employees receive additional compensation in the form of the ESOP contributions, which are not taxed until the ESOP accounts are converted into stock. Third, certain tax benefits allow an employer to raise capital by the establishment of an ESOP.[41]

• *Benefits "cafeteria style."* Under the 1978 federal tax legislation (sections 125 and 135) companies were for the first time authorized to offer flexible, or "cafeteria-style" benefits.[42] Under these plans employers provide minimal (core) coverage in life and health insurance, vacations, and pensions. The employee then selects additional benefits to suit his or her own needs, using credits (up to some specified total cost) based on salary, service, and perhaps age.

Among the choices available to employees are such benefits as birthdays off, travel, day care for children, discounts on company products, free lunches, automobile insurance, legal assistance, parking, and savings plans.[43] Despite the seeming attraction of such plans, they have not spread widely. In 1986 only 2 percent of American employees were eligible for flexible benefit plans. About 5 percent were eligible for reimbursement accounts which pay expenses not covered by a company's regular benefits package.[44]

ESOPs have received increasing use in recent years. Favorable tax treatment, the effort of management and unions to cooperate in the workplace, and economic adversity for many companies have created an environment in which ESOPs have proliferated. In some instances, employees have bought their company via ESOP, and taken pay cuts as they tried to rescue their jobs at a failing company. ESOPs are not restricted to unionized employees, however. About 30 percent of companies with ESOPs have unions, and only 10 to 15 percent of the total ESOP work force is unionized.[45]

These new concepts have been spreading quickly in American industry. The development of benefits has ordinarily followed a certain pattern. The unions have pressed for the adoption of new benefits along the following steps:

[41] Wallace F. Forbes and Donald P. Portland, "Pros and Cons of Employee Stock Ownership Plans," *Business Horizons*, 19:3, June 1976, pp. 5–12.

[42] Davis S. Thomsen, "Introducing Cafeteria Compensation," *Personnel Journal*, 56:3, March 1977, pp. 124–131.

[43] Michael Waldholz, "'Cafeteria' Benefits Plans," *The Wall Street Journal*, May 9, 1983, p. 58.

[44] U.S. Department of Labor, Bureau of Labor Statistics, *Employee Benefits in Medium and Large Firms*, Bulletin No. 2281 (Washington, D.C.: U.S. Government Printing Office, 1987).

[45] "Hopes and Fears Are Mixed," Bureau of National Affairs, *Daily Labor Report* No. 75, Apr. 18, 1984, pp. C1, C3.

1 *Winning recognition* of the employers' obligation to furnish the benefit by securing it in the contract, if only in very small measure

2 *Liberalizing the benefits* negotiated in successive contracts

3 *Working to eliminate* qualifications and restrictions placed on eligibility to receive the benefit[46]

New benefits sometimes spread quickly. Others spread very slowly, if at all. The rate of adoption of benefit innovations is partly dependent on the economic climate and the capacity of employers to accept new costs.

CHAPTER SUMMARY

An almost bewildering variety of benefits has become a major part of American compensation practices of recent years. Benefits constituted almost 37 percent of total compensation by 1982 and continue to develop rapidly. Some benefits are provided by the federal government, and the employers pay a tax to the government to support the benefits. These so-called legally mandated benefits include Social Security, worker's compensation, and unemployment insurance. Other benefits, which are provided by employers to various degrees, include premium pay for overtime and shifts; paid vacations, holidays, and sick leave; health insurance pensions; severance pay; and some unemployment benefits.

The pension system was not substantially developed before 1940. In 1949, an NLRB decision required employers to bargain with unions about pensions. Pension plans developed rapidly thereafter. There are now many private pension plans provided by business concerns for their employees. Private plans have very different characteristics. There are contributory and noncontributory, single-employer and multiemployer, cost-based and benefit-based plans. Calculation of the cost of a pension plan or the impact on cost of a change in benefits is very complex. The government-provided Social Security system, which was instituted in 1935, interacts in various ways with private pension plans. The Social Security offset in private pension plans is a controversial issue.

There are many other important issues involving pensions which are of importance in collective bargaining. These issues include the standards which should be used to evaluate the adequacy of benefit levels, the question of who is covered and who is not covered by a plan, the problem of early retirement, and certain financial aspects of pension plans, such as vesting, funding, and unfunded liabilities. The assets of pension funds have been very substantial and are a major factor in the investment market. Controversies have developed around who manages these investments and how the funds are invested and for whose benefit. In 1974, Congress instituted the Employees' Retirement Income Security Act

---

[46] Donna Allen, *Fringe Benefits: Wages or Social Obligations?* (Ithaca, N.Y.: Cornell University Press, 1964).

(ERISA) in order to regulate private pension plans. ERISA imposes standards on private pension plans including the financial behavior to which trustees of the funds are now held by law.

The United States has no comprehensive national medical insurance program, and as a result the health insurance of much of the population is provided by employers. The rising costs of employer health insurance plans, which have grown steadily in amount and type of coverage since World War II, are a major issue in collective bargaining. The union and the company not only must determine the money to be spent, but also must negotiate for the delivery of health-care services. Most insurance is purchased from insurance companies or service corporations like Blue Cross–Blue Shield. There have been other experiments, however, with prepared group health-care plans administered by Health Maintenance Organizations.

The current unemployment insurance system is a state-federal system. In many states, the level of benefits provided workers has seemed inadequate and unions have pressed to establish supplemental unemployment benefit funds (SUBs) in some industries. SUB plans basically involve the establishment of a fund from which laid-off employees can draw benefits. The United Auto Workers was instrumental in the development of these plans as a means of protecting workers from layoffs.

Establishment of the hours of work has been a major trade union interest. Unions helped establish the 40-hour work week and have sought to negotiate premium pay arrangements for overtime work. Paid time off, i.e., paid vacations and holidays, has also been part of major collective bargaining agreements. A number of recent benefits which are in an experimental stage include prepaid legal services, employee stock ownership plans, and alternative work schedules, or "flexitime."

Recent proposals for improving benefits include requiring all employers to provide health insurance to workers and establishing a 6-hour workday for employed mothers.

QUESTIONS FOR THOUGHT AND DISCUSSION

1 Why do you think benefits have become such a major and growing part of American compensation practices?

2 What advantages do employers gain, if any, from providing benefit plans for employees?

3 Do you think the proliferation of a variety of benefits as a significant part of employee compensation is beneficial to employees, employers, and society in general? Discuss the advantages and disadvantages to each.

4 What are some of the problems associated with the U.S. pension system? In what ways could the entire system be improved?

5 What standards should be used to determine an adequate level of benefits in a pension program?

6 Should a retired employee's income from other sources (e.g., Social Security or working) be evaluated in determining the level of his or her pension?

7 Will employees in the future want a shorter work week or a shorter workday? Will employees prefer more holidays or longer vacations? How can a company predict these choices?

8 Should the government take a larger role in providing health care than it now does? Is the present private system involving employers and unions adequate?

9 Should there be a 6-hour workday for employed mothers? Why or why not?

SELECTED READING

Bowen, William, ed., *The American System of Social Insurance* (New York: McGraw-Hill, 1968).

Greenough, William C., and F. P. King, *Pension Plans and Public Policy* (New York: Columbia University Press, 1976).

Hetherington, Robert W., et al., *Health Insurance Plans* (New York: Wiley, 1975).

Levin, Noel Arnold, *ERISA and Labor-Management Benefit Funds*, 2d ed. (New York: Practising Law Institute, 1975).

Levitan, Sar A., *Shorter Hours, Shorter Weeks: Spreading the Work to Reduce Unemployment* (Baltimore: John Hopkins Press, 1977).

Sibson, Robert E., *Compensation* (New York: AMACOM, 1974).

CHAPTER 16

RIGHTS OF MANAGEMENT, UNIONS, AND EMPLOYEES

MANAGEMENT'S RIGHT TO MANAGE

The Advent of a Union

The advent of a union has certain implications for management. Before its employees organize, management has the unilateral authority to make decisions about the conduct of the business. After unionization, it finds its authority limited in many ways. While management largely preserves the right to take action, it nevertheless may find its decisions questioned and in some instances reversed. It is not surprising that management sometimes seeks to retain or recapture as much of its once unhindered authority as possible.

In the absence of a union, management holds virtually unlimited authority. It may exercise its authority with care or be arbitrary. How does it work? Suppose the company decides to discharge an employee. Other employees may think the penalty is too harsh, but management retains the full authority. Or suppose the company decides to grant a wage increase. The boss tells the employees that they get a small increase. The employees say thank you but mumble behind the boss's back, "The stingy so-and-so." But management has sole authority.

When a union comes in, however, there is a change. There is countervailing power. The employees can take collective action. They can close the plant down. The transition period is very difficult for management. The union may abuse its power. The company resents it. But the union and the company cannot conduct a power struggle every day, and so some basis for uninterrupted production must be found. This basis is usually a collective bargaining agreement.

There is an evolution in the power relationship between a company and a union. At the beginning the company has unfettered authority. Then the union appears. There is a period of transition marked by power struggles over many types of issues. An agreement is reached, which becomes the basis of the relationship. But what are to be the respective rules for the management and the union? What rights does each have?

Management Rights in the Collective Bargaining Agreement

In order to retain as much authority as possible in the direction of the workplace, management has sought to include certain provisions in collective bargaining agreements. Some provisions spell out the functions of management. Others limit the scope of the agreement to certain items. The former are described as "management rights" clauses. The latter are called "savings" clauses.

A typical management rights clause reads as follows:

The Company retains the exclusive right and responsibility to manage the business and plants and to direct the working forces subject to the provisions of this Agreement, including the right to hire, suspend, or discharge for proper cause or transfer and the right to relieve employees from duty because of lack of work or for other legitimate reasons.

The intent of this language is to retain for the company the authority to do anything not explicitly limited by the language of the agreement. Suppose the contract were silent about promotions, and management were to decide to establish a test for promotions. If the union objected, management would argue that the management rights clause gave it the authority to establish the test. In practice, however, a management rights clause is not as useful as it might seem. The effect of the clause is limited in several ways. Arbitrators will often rule that a long-standing practice is part of the agreement, even if not spelled out, so that management may not change it with impunity. Also, an agreement that includes a no-strike pledge by the union is presumed to cover all disputes between the parties. An arbitrator might be unwilling to invest unilateral authority in the hands of management while holding the union to a no-strike pledge. Last, the company has a legal duty to bargain about many matters and may be required to do so, regardless of the employer rights clause in the agreement.

Management rights statements now appear in about 76 percent of agreements. Management specifically retains the right to frame company rules in 28 percent of all contracts. The decision to close the plant, to relocate, or to build new facilities is reserved to management in 11 percent of all agreements. The right to institute technological changes is reserved to management in 17 percent of contracts.[1]

---

[1] Bureau of National Affairs, *Basic Patterns in Union Contracts* (Washington, D.C.: Bureau of National Affairs, 1983), p. 63.

Rights reserved for management are not found only in the management rights and savings clauses of agreements; managerial authority is delineated throughout collective bargaining agreements. For this reason, many managers believe that enumerating so-called management rights in a particular clause of the agreement actually limits those rights rather than allowing them to remain broad and unstated. To meet this criticism, some agreements provide that management rights listed in the agreements are not necessarily all-inclusive (i.e., others also exist).

Where there are rights, there are also obligations. Above, the reserved rights of the employer were described. And it has been noted that these rights are modified in many ways by the collective bargaining agreement. In later pages many of the specific limitations imposed on management by the language of a collective bargaining agreement will be mentioned. But it is also useful to point out here that with reserved rights go certain implied obligations of management. These obligations need not be spelled out in a contract with a labor union to be found binding on management. For example, among these implied obligations is the maintenance of a safe and healthy workplace.

LIMITATIONS ON MANAGEMENT RIGHTS

Subcontracting

Many things done in a plant or other facility by the employees of a company could, in fact, be done on a specialized basis by other firms. When management makes a contract with another firm to do things that might be done by its own employees, the process is called "subcontracting" (or contracting out). There are many types of subcontracting. A company might decide not to employ janitors or cleaning personnel and hire a custodial service contractor. A firm that has construction operations to be done at a plant site might choose not to do them with its own maintenance crews and could contract out the work to a construction firm. Or a company might develop a new part for one of its products but, instead of producing the part itself, might contract with another company to supply the part. Each of these examples involves an action by management that may create a labor relations dispute over subcontracting.

Managements usually argue that they should be free to operate their businesses on as low-cost a basis as possible. Subcontracting is often a method of obtaining goods or services more cheaply than the company could produce them itself. In consequence, there should not, they argue, be restrictions on subcontracting.

The unions reply that subcontracting often deprives union members of their jobs. When a company decides to subcontract janitorial service or maintenance, it may lay off its existing custodial or maintenance staff. The union argues that it cannot be indifferent to a matter that may have such an important impact on the employees it represents. Therefore, it often insists on being involved in the decision-making process about subcontracting.

There are, of course, legal questions involved. Must management bargain with the union over a subcontracting decision? The National Labor Relations Act says that management has a duty to bargain with respect to "rates of pay, wages, hours of employment, or other conditions of employment" [section 9(a)]. Is subcontracting such a matter?

In 1964 the Supreme Court decided that subcontracting was a matter about which management has a legal obligation to bargain. The court case arose from a dispute between Fibreboard Paper Products Corporation and the United Steelworkers of America. The company had a plant in Emeryville, California. Since 1937 the union had represented maintenance employees at the plant. In September 1958 the union and the company entered the latest of a series of collective bargaining agreements, which was to expire on July 31, 1959. The union sought to set a time and place for negotiations prior to the end of July, but the company delayed. On July 27, 1959, the parties met and the company informed the union that it had determined that substantial savings could be effected by contracting out the work. The company gave the union a letter which read, in part, "In these new circumstances, we are sure you will realize that negotiation of a new contract would be pointless." This was because the company intended to discharge all its maintenance personnel, who would be replaced by employees of the maintenance contractor, Fluor Maintenance, Inc. Thereafter, on July 31 the company terminated the employment of its maintenance personnel, and Fluor employees took over. The Steelworkers union conducted an unsuccessful strike against the company and filed unfair labor practice charges with the NLRB. After several years of litigation, the case reached the Supreme Court.

The Court held that the company was obligated to bargain with the union before making the decision to subcontract work that would otherwise have been performed by employees represented by the union. The company was obligated to rehire for existing maintenance jobs the employees it had laid off and to pay 36 employees a total of $330,931.95 in back pay.[2]

The Court's decisions have had an impact of course. The decisions do not say that a company must not subcontract, but rather that it must bargain with the union about subcontracting. The rationale is to allow a union an opportunity to make such adjustments as might be necessary to retain the jobs affected by the subcontracting, if the union wishes. As a practical matter, the obligation to bargain also left employers with less initiative in the matter and has probably contributed to less subcontracting than would otherwise have occurred. By 1983, 50 percent of union contracts imposed some limitation on subcontracting (an increase from 28 percent in 1965). Only in 2 percent of the contracts, however, was subcontracting of bargaining-unit work strictly pro-

---

[2] *Fibreboard Paper Products Corp. v. NLRB*, 397 U.S. 203 (1964). The financial payment was reported in Bureau of National Affairs, *Daily Labor Report* No. 248, Dec. 24, 1969.

hibited. In most of the clauses, advance consultation about subcontracting is all that is required. In 23 percent of the contracts, subcontracting is prohibited if layoffs exist or would result from subcontracting.[3]

There is great variety in the arrangements which unions and employers make with respect to subcontracting. The General Motors Corporation and the United Auto Workers have agreed that employees with seniority in the company (that is, those not on probation) should not be laid off as a "direct and immediate result of work being performed by any outside contractor" on the company's premises. When management does decide to subcontract work, it further agrees to notify the union in advance.

Other agreements sometimes go much further than this. Teamsters Local No. 959 in Alaska and the Associated General Contractors of Alaska agreed to an arrangement on subcontracting which provided that the employers could not subcontract any work which the Teamsters might do (that is, work that was in the Teamsters' work jurisdiction, see Chapter 3) unless:

- The subcontractor's employees were members of the union.
- The subcontractor agreed to the same terms and conditions of employment binding between the union and the general contractors.

This was, of course, a very favorable contractual provision for the union. Unfortunately for the union, the Federal Trade Commission decided that the provision was in violation of the federal antitrust laws, and the union and the contractors were forced to remove the provision from the agreement. According to the FTC, the purpose of the provision was not to protect the jobs of Teamsters from being lost as a result of subcontracting (the clear purpose of the GM-UAW arrangement) but rather to cause potential subcontractors to recognize the union as representative of their employees in order to get business (so-called top-down organizing) or, alternatively, to exclude nonunionized firms from doing business with the contractors party to the agreement with the Teamsters. This latter purpose was in violation of the law, the FTC decided.[4]

Work Transfer

In January 1982, Milwaukee Spring Company asked United Auto Workers Local 547 to forgo a scheduled wage increase and to make other concessions to reduce the company's labor costs at a plant in Milwaukee. The union refused. Two months later, the company announced its intention to transfer assembly operations to a nonunion plant and to lay off 32 workers in Milwaukee. In the subsequent litigation, the union and the company agreed that the company's motive was economic in nature and was not based on antiunion opinions. Had the latter been the case, the company's action

---

[3] Bureau of National Affairs, *Basic Patterns*, p. 64.
[4] Bureau of National Affairs, *Daily Labor Report* No. 138, July 18, 1978, pp. A1 and A2.

would have been illegal under the *Darlington* case law (see Chapter 6). But, the motivation was economic. Was the company's action legal? The Auto Workers thought that it was not and filed an unfair labor practice complaint.

In October 1982, the NLRB agreed with the union. The company's purpose, it found, was to avoid the wage provisions of the contract. Consequently the company was prohibited from implementing its decision to relocate assembly operations without the union's consent during the term of the contract. This was because the labor laws prohibit an employer from making a unilateral change in wages or working conditions during the term of a collective bargaining agreement.

In the 15 months following the October 1982 decision, the terms of several NLRB members expired and President Reagan replaced them with more conservative appointees. In January 1984, the NLRB again reviewed the *Milwaukee Spring* case. This time, the board found no violation of the law. "We have searched the contract in vain for a provision requiring bargaining unit work to remain in Milwaukee," the board said. The transfer of work did not disturb wages and conditions in Milwaukee (i.e., those employees who were not laid off received the wages and conditions called for by the agreement), and so there were no unilateral changes by management in working conditions and wages. The company had a duty to bargain with the union about the effects on employees of the proposed transfer, but if the company and union could not agree, the company could transfer the work unilaterally, so long as the contract did not specifically prohibit it.[5] The law had thus made a complete circle. Prior to October 1982, an employer could transfer work for economic reasons but had to bargain with the union over its consequences. After October 1982, an employer could not transfer work. Finally, after January 1984, an employer could again transfer work.

In April of 1984, the NLRB further widened employers' authority to transfer work. Otis Elevator Company had decided to consolidate research and development operations and closed a facility. The employees involved were transferred. The company did not bargain with the union about the move. The union complained to the NLRB. In 1981, the NLRB found against the company. Later, the courts returned the case to the board. The board reviewed the case in light of the Supreme Court's 1981 ruling in *First National Maintenance v. NLRB* that there was no duty to bargain for an employer if the decision to move or close a facility or operations involved the basic scope and nature of the enterprise, such as consolidating or subcontracting work or installing labor-saving machinery. Hence, the NLRB said in 1984, reversing its

[5] "NLRB Okays Employers Authority," Bureau of National Affairs, *Daily Labor Report* No. 16, Jan. 25, 1984, pp. AA1–AA2; Joann S. Lublin, "NLRB Rules," *The Wall Street Journal*, Jan. 25, 1984. See also "BLS Study of Contract Provisions on Plant Closure and Relocation," Bureau of National Affairs, *Daily Labor Report* No. 166, Aug. 27, 1981, pp. E1—E14.

1981 position, that Otis Elevator could consolidate its facilities and transfer employees without bargaining with the union.[6]

It is apparent from the recitation of cases that the law in this area is in continual flux and that it may change at any moment as cases make their way through the NLRB and the courts. Nonetheless, a summary is useful to try to identify where American law now stands on the important question of managerial prerogatives with respect to the transfer of work from a unionized facility.

Until 1964, unless an employer gave up in bargaining its right to close a plant or transfer work from a facility, the employer could transfer work or close a plant at will, so long as it was not motivated by the purpose of denying its employees union representation (*Darlington*). Then, in 1964, the Supreme Court held that a company had a duty to bargain about subcontracting work. The duty extended to both the decision and its impact on employees (*Fibreboard*). In 1981, the Supreme Court said that if a company's decision to close a facility, transfer work, or subcontract was based on the basic scope of its business, it need not bargain with the union (*First National Maintenance*). And in 1984 the NLRB said a company that wished to transfer work solely to avoid the costs of a union contract could do so as long as it had first bargained with the union, even though the company and the union failed to reach agreement (*Milwaukee Spring*, 1984). In summary, litigation in the 20 years since the *Fibreboard* decision first broadened, then narrowed the unions' gains under *Fibreboard*, and in the end, the law is very close to where it stood before *Fibreboard*—namely, that a company can transfer or subcontract work without the union's agreement at any time unless the company has restricted its rights by explicit provisions in the collective bargaining agreement.

Work Standards

The aspect of union behavior that generally appears least defensible to management and the public involves rules about the performance of work. In the United States the term "featherbedding" has developed to describe rules that require payment to employees for work not done or work not needed. There are many variations of featherbedding. Sometimes unions object to the introduction of new technology. The union attempts to preserve existing jobs by prohibiting the use of new technology. In other cases unions seek to establish rules about crew size. Rules of this kind specify the number of workers on a particular type of paper machine, the size of the crew in the cockpit of an airplane, the number of workers in a gang of structural steel erectors, or the size of a longshore gang unloading a ship. Changing technology sometimes makes these crew restrictions very expensive.

[6] Ben A. Franklin, "Labor Board," *The New York Times*, Apr. 11, 1984, p. A20. Also, "Otis Elevator," Bureau of National Affairs, *Daily Labor Report* No. 70, Apr. 11, 1984, pp. A11, A12.

A third type of restriction that is often especially galling to management involves the jurisdictional lines of different crafts or craft unions. Jurisdictional lines separate the work assignments that are allegedly the property of one trade from the assignments allegedly the property of another trade. For example, an electrician may install a wire box, but only a carpenter is allowed to cut through the wall to create the opening for the box. When the work of one trade is incidental, as, for example, when a carpenter must be assigned to only a few minutes' work so that the electrician can proceed (or vice versa), the employer may incur great expense. Yet collective bargaining agreements sometimes obligate employers to respect trade jurisdictions to such a degree.

Surprisingly, management is often involved in the establishment of uneconomic work practices. "Make-work rules do not usually begin as attempts by unions to force employers to hire an excessive number of workers."[7] Instead, the employer at one time imposes a rule or agrees with the union on a rule that seems to make perfect sense under the conditions then prevailing. In the course of time, however, changes in technology or working conditions diminish the appropriateness of the rule. As time passes, the gap becomes wider, and the more out of date the rule becomes, the more expensive it is to the employer. But, as the rule becomes outdated, the number of employees dependent on it grows. Hence, management more desperately seeks a change, and the union more vigorously rejects it.[8]

Successorship

If a company acquires a facility from another company, what is the status of the union and the labor agreement at the acquired facility? Is the successor firm obligated to honor the labor agreement? This question has an important bearing on management on both sides of the transaction. A labor agreement may severely restrict what an existing or successor management can do to make a facility more efficient or profitable. If a facility is currently unprofitable, partly because of aspects of the labor agreement and of labor relations in general, the sale price of the facility would be improved if the successor firm were not bound to the labor agreement. If the successor were potentially free of the labor agreement, the value of the facility to both buyer and seller could be much enhanced. A new management's hands would not be tied by the labor agreement, and therefore it might be able to eliminate inefficient practices. Further, management believes it should be able to buy, or sell, a facility without buying or selling a labor agreement with it.

The unions, however, object to a process by which an employer may un-

---

[7] Sumner Slichter, James Healy, and E. Robert Livernash, *The Impact of Collective Bargaining Management* (Washington, D.C.: Brookings, 1960), p. 317.

[8] See John T. Dunlop and Derek Bok, *Labor and the American Community* (New York: Simon and Schuster, 1970), pp. 271–274, for a discussion of the firemen's dispute over work rules in the United States in this century.

load a labor agreement simply by selling the facility. There is no protection for workers in such a circumstance. Wage rates, fringe benefits, and working conditions would all be adversely affected for the workers involved.

In the absence of litigation, the companies and the unions involved may either work out their dispute or apply economic force to each other. That is, the successor employer may agree to recognize the union and the existing collective bargaining agreements or may attempt to bargain changes in the agreement. It might also choose to ignore the agreement, forcing the union to conduct a strike to enforce the agreement, if it is able to do so.

Alternatively, either side may choose to litigate the matters in dispute. Not surprisingly, there has been substantial litigation about the obligations and rights of successor employers. The law with respect to successorship has been set forth in three major decisions of the Supreme Court. The result seems to be that a successor employer has little legal responsibility to the employees of the acquired facility and can, in fact, conduct the acquisition in such a way that it has no responsibility. This is the case even if the acquired company and the union have a successorship clause in their agreement. A successorship clause provides that any change in management or in the identity of the parties to the contract will not invalidate it, but rather that the new management must assume the contractual obligations of its predecessor. (In 1983 about 34 percent of agreements had such a clause.)[9] This clause cannot ordinarily be enforced against the successor employer, however. The clause may be enforced against the selling corporation, but often that corporation is bankrupt or otherwise unsuitable for a legal proceeding. In some cases a union might seek to enjoin the sale of the facility if the company's obligations under the successorship clause are not being met.

The three successorship cases decided by the Court are as follows:

• When John Wiley, a publisher, acquired Livingstone, the employees of the acquired company were taken into John Wiley in total. The Supreme Court then required Wiley to go to arbitration of certain disputes under the terms of the labor agreement between Livingstone and the union (*John Wiley v. Livingstone*, 1964).[10]

• While Burns International Security Service did not retain all employees of a predecessor company, there was, the Court found, a substantial continuity of employment (*Burns International*, 1972).[11] There was no obligation for Burns to abide by the terms of the existing agreement, but Burns did have a duty to bargain with the union.[12]

[9] Bureau of National Affairs, *Basic Patterns*, p. 5.

[10] *John Wiley and Sons, Inc. v. Livingstone*, 376 U.S. 543 (1964).

[11] *NLRB v. Burns International Security Service, Inc.*, 406 U.S. 272 (1972).

[12] See also Charles G. Bakaly, Jr., and I. S. Bryan, "Survival of the Bargaining Agreement: The Effect of *Burns*," *Vanderbilt Law Review*, 27:1, January 1974, pp. 117–132; also Harvard Law Review Editors, "The Bargaining Obligations of Successor Employers," *Harvard Law Review*, 88:4, February 1975, pp. 759–778; also Jules I. Crystal, "Successor and Assigns Clauses," *Labor Law Journal*, 33:9, September 1982, pp. 591–595.

• Howard Johnson acquired back a franchise, that of Grissom, Inc., to operate a motel and restaurant in Detroit. Grissom had a contract with the local union and a successorship clause. However, the purchase agreement between Johnson and Grissom released Johnson from all obligations under the labor agreement. Johnson dismissed Grissom's employees, 55 in number, and hired 45 persons, 9 of whom were former employees of Grissom. The court held that Johnson had no obligations under the agreement, and no duty to bargain, since there was no substantial continuity of employment (*Howard Johnson Co.*, 1974).[13]

A noteworthy aspect of the Court's decision in *Howard Johnson* was its comments about inefficient work practices.[14] The Court seemed explicitly to recognize the cost burden placed on management by the working rules of a collective bargaining agreement and seemed to countenance Howard Johnson's management's desire to acquire a company unburdened by those obligations.

The National Labor Relations Board has moved quickly to disabuse employers of the notion that they may unload a union by selling the facility when there is no economic motivation. In January 1974 Macomb Block and Supply, Inc., purchased William Moors, Inc., and hired none of Moors' employees. The Teamsters union, which represented Moors' employees, filed an unfair labor practice complaint. The NLRB found that Macomb's refusal to hire Moors' employees was because of their union affiliation, not for economic reasons, and ordered Macomb to hire the former employees of Moors.[15] An economic motivation for the successor employer not to hire employees of the predecessor firm (apparently including the motivation to be rid of a labor agreement) is protected by the *Howard Johnson* decision, but an antiunion motivation is prohibited by the National Labor Relations Act. What effect this legal distinction has in practice, if any, is difficult to surmise. The net effect of *Howard Johnson* in opening to management the opportunity to unload expensive labor agreements and unions in the name of greater economic efficiency seems substantial.[16]

THE RIGHTS OF THE UNION

Union Security Provisions in Collective Bargaining Agreements

Background Unions in the United States have ordinarily insisted that some understanding regarding the status of the union be included in collec-

---

[13] *Howard Johnson Co. v. Detroit Local Joint Executive Board, Hotel and Restaurant Employees International Union*, 73 U.S. 632 (1974). See Michigan Law Review Editors, "The Impact of Howard Johnson...," *Michigan Law Review*, 74:3, January 1976, pp. 555–585.

[14] James Severson and Michael Willcoxon, "Successorship under *Howard Johnson*: Short-Order Justice for Employees," *California Law Review*, 64:3, May 1976, pp. 795–844.

[15] *Macomb Block and Supply, Inc., v. Teamsters Local 247*, NLRB, May 12, 1976.

[16] In June 1976, Senator Harrison Williams filed a union-backed bill in Congress to overturn the *Howard Johnson* and *Burns* decisions by requiring a successor employer to be bound by an existing collective bargaining agreement.

tive bargaining agreements. Prior to the 1930s, this understanding often took the form of a so-called closed shop. An employer who recognized a closed-shop arrangement agreed to employ only union members. Sometimes this meant that the company would inform the union when it needed additional employees and the union would refer its members. In other cases, the company would hire as it wished, but anyone it hired had to be or become a member of a union in order to stay employed. The closed shop not only attempted to keep nonunion employees out, but excluded members of other unions as well. The closed shop was very common in the railways, in construction, in printing, and in the maritime trades. It protected the status of the union, both from employers who might wish to destroy it, and from other, or rival, unions. Its nemesis was the so-called open shop, in which there was no union control.

Campaigns by employers to destroy the unions have been a periodic occurrence in American history. The contest for control between management and the unions has often centered around the issue of union security. In no industry has the contest been more lengthy, costly, and involved than in construction.

> The unions had an early start in organization (in the late 1800s) and before the building-trades employers were aware, the closed shop ... was already established in the larger building centers. In other industries, particularly in manufacturing, the employers were able to curb the closed-shop movement.[17]

After 1900, open-shop manufacturers were threatened by the advance of the building trades unions. The unions first attempted to exclude nonmembers from working at particular crafts and later from building construction generally. Finally, they attempted to unionize the manufacturers of products used in building by refusing to install products manufactured by nonunion workers. Open-shop manufacturers found it necessary, or convenient, to reply by helping to "correct" conditions in the building trades as a means of protecting the nonunion status of their own establishments. In 1900, for example, in Chicago the employers locked out the unions, insisting that the Building Trades Council, the craft unions' coordinating group, disband. The unions resisted, unsuccessfully. Contractors who tried to operate with unions were denied materials by the lumber and other building supply dealers and were denied credit by the banks. The unions surrendered after a 7-month battle. The Building Trades Council disbanded, and open-shop clauses appeared in the agreements.[18] But 2 years later, the council had reassembled and the closed shop was reappearing.

This struggle over union security in the construction industry, together with the role of manufacturing firms in the struggle, is one of the oldest themes of American labor relations. There is not much written about it, but it

---

[17] William Haber, *Industrial Relations in the Building Industry* (Cambridge, Mass.: Harvard University Press, 1930), p. 238.
[18] Ibid., pp. 376–379.

is an important factor in many disputes, including political problems, that on the surface appear to be about other matters. The most recent visible manifestation of this dispute began in the late 1960s. Manufacturers, describing themselves as owners, formed a national organization to influence labor relations in the building industry (the Construction Users Anti-Inflationary Roundtable). The users sought both to influence the behavior of the unions and to facilitate the growth of open-shop construction.

Construction is not the only industry in the United States in which long struggles have occurred about union security. In the 1930s the advent of the industrial unions occasioned a new and very bitter round of disputes. Union security provisions were an especially significant factor in many labor disputes arising during World War II, for example. Since the government was attempting to prevent work stoppages in order to maximize war production, it was drawn into these disputes. Employers insisted, without success, that noneconomic issues (especially union security) should not be the concern of government agencies. However, the government recognized the maintenance-of-membership formula (see definition below) as a basis for union security arrangements during the war.

After the Second World War, changes in the National Labor Relations Act affected the legality of certain types of union security arrangements. The introduction of law and the courts into the struggle over union security has modified its form without substantially resolving the disputes. In some industries and areas today, union security is not a serious issue. In others it is. This has always been the case and continues to be so in the United States.

This long-continuing concern for union security is peculiar to the United States. It stems in part from the opposition of employers to unions and the methods they have used to thwart unions. The yellow-dog contract, the blacklist, and similar methods seemed to require a union to securely establish its own position.[19] In addition, the threats of bids by rival unions and the resistance of the American Federation of Labor to dual unionism (which is common in continental Europe) reinforced the interest in union security.

Types of Union Security In 1947 Congress wrote into the Taft-Hartley Act statutory provisions about union security. In so doing, Congress made union security provisions a matter of litigation before the NLRB and in the courts. Litigation has resulted in a complex series of definitions and classifications about union security provisions. We now have, therefore, a much more precise set of terms to describe different forms of union security. Whether the whole matter is not rendered even more complex as a result is open to question. Certainly union security and the law about union security continue to be a very divisive issue in American labor relations.

---

[19] Paul E. Sultan, "The Union Security Issue," in Sumner Slichter et al., eds. *Public Policy and Collective Bargaining* (Madison, Wis.: Industrial Relations Research Association, 1962), pp. 88–120.

Under section 2(11) of the Railway Labor Act (1926), which covers railways and airlines, Congress provided that unions and employers may enter into a union-shop agreement requiring all employees within the unit to join the union within 60 days after commencing their employment. Under the Wagner Act (1935) a somewhat different approach was taken to union security in the rest of private industry. The act read simply:

> Nothing in this Act..., or in any statute of the United States, shall preclude an employer from making an agreement with a labor organization...to require as a condition of employment membership therein....

This provision of the National Labor Relations Act was construed to permit virtually any form of union security, including the closed shop. But in 1947, in the Taft-Hartley Act, Congress amended the law to permit employers to agree to require union membership as a condition of employment only on or after the thirtieth day following the beginning of such employment. With this provision, the closed shop was outlawed and the 30-day union shop permitted. Court decisions since that time have generally permitted other forms of union security arrangements with a "lesser" significance than the union shop. The phrase "required as a condition of employment" means that the employer may legally be required by the union to discharge an employee who does not conform to the union security provision; hence the description of the union shop as "compulsory unionism."

• *Closed shop* Membership in a union is required as a condition of employment. The closed shop is generally illegal in the United States.
• *Union shop* Becoming and remaining a union member is required as a condition of employment after the thirtieth day of employment (or later). The union shop is generally legal in the United States, except in certain states, as we shall see below.
• *Agency shop* All employees who do not join the union pay a fee in lieu of dues to the union for its services as a bargaining agent.
• *Maintenance-of-membership shop* All employees who choose to become union members must remain so as a condition of employment.

The term "union membership" is used in each of these definitions. But what does it mean? Ordinarily a union has a constitution and bylaws. It also has a method of application for membership and an initiation ceremony, and members are bound to its internal procedures. These internal procedures usually include disciplinary proceedings for violations of the union's constitution and bylaws. Does the legal phrase "membership in a labor organization" envisage all this?

Apparently it does not. The Taft-Hartley Act [section 8(a)3] includes this language:

> No employer shall justify any discrimination against an employee for non-membership in a labor organization (A) if he has reasonable grounds for believing that such membership was not available to the employee on the same terms and

conditions generally applicable to other members, or (B)...was denied or terminated for reasons other than the failure of the employee to tender the periodic dues and the initiation fees uniformly required as a condition of acquiring or retaining membership.

Thus, union membership is defined essentially as paying dues and initiation fees as uniformly levied by the union on all members. An employer cannot be required to discharge an employee because the employee refuses to obey a union bylaw or because the employee is expelled from the union, as long as the employee continues to be willing to pay dues.[20]

The closed shop is often defined as meaning that the employer agreed to hire only union members. It is now illegal. Does this mean an employer cannot agree to hire from a union hiring hall? The courts have ruled that a hiring-hall arrangement is legal, even if the employer agrees it will hire *only* from the union's hiring hall, as long as the union does not refuse to refer people who are not union members. The union may, however, give priority to people who have worked at the trade the longest and may refuse to refer those lacking skills. In consequence, union halls usually refer almost entirely union members, and some observers have concluded that the hiring hall is a closed shop in disguise. Hiring-hall arrangements are especially common in construction, longshoring, and the maritime trades.[21]

Furthermore, an exception was provided in the 1959 amendments to the Taft-Hartley Act, permitting a 7-day, not a 30-day, union shop in construction. In consequence, a union may require an employer in the construction industry, pursuant to a clause in the collective bargaining agreement, to discharge an employee who refuses to become a member of a union after 7 days on the job.

A final form of union security arrangement that is often combined with any of the above arrangements, or may exist independently, is the dues checkoff (see Chapter 7). Under a checkoff arrangement, the employer deducts union dues from the employees' paychecks and forwards the money directly to the union. This requires an individually signed authorization from each employee permitting the deduction, or checkoff. The union is relieved, by this procedure, of the expensive and time-consuming task of collecting dues from each member. Employers, however, end up bearing the administrative cost, which they sometimes allege to be substantial.

Unions in industries involving casual work, in which employees move among firms, rarely use a checkoff. The workers carry union books, which are stamped each time they go to the union hall and pay their dues. The books show that the workers are in good standing with the union. Checkoffs are only beginning to appear in such industries. Not long ago in construc-

---

[20] Glenn A. Zipp, "Rights and Responsibilities of Parties to a Union-Security Agreement," *Labor Law Journal*, 33:4, April 1982, pp. 202–217.

[21] U.S. Department of Labor, Labor Management Services Administration, *Exclusive Union Work Referred Systems in the Building Trades* (Washington, D.C., 1970).

tion, the Laborers' Union negotiated agreements including a $0.10-per-hour-worked dues checkoff. All members of the union authorize the employer to deduct $0.10 per hour of work from their paychecks to be forwarded to the union.

Union security provisions were found in 99.5 percent of all agreements in 1983 if checkoff and hiring-hall provisions are included in the total. The union shop is the most common form of union security provision. A modified union shop appears in some agreements. It provides that employees who were not members of the union before or on the effective date of the collective bargaining agreement are excluded from the 30-day union membership requirement, but that all new employees are covered. In some instances, special groups of employees, such as students, temporary workers, and religious objectors (i.e., persons who object to belonging to any organization other than a religious sect), are excluded. The agency shop appears in 12 percent of agreements; the maintenance-of-membership shop in 4 percent.[22]

Originally, the Taft-Hartley Act required a vote by employees to authorize a union-shop clause in a collective bargaining agreement. Experience in the early 1950s with this election procedure was that union-shop clauses were ratified overwhelmingly. In consequence, the election requirement was abandoned. However, section 9(e)1 of the act authorizes petitions for elections to withdraw the union's right to a union security clause. Occasionally the NLRB conducts such elections, which sometimes result in the removal of the union security provision from the agreement.[23]

Right-to-Work Laws

Scope and Extent   One of the most unusual provisions of our labor laws is section 14(b) of the Taft-Hartley Act:

Nothing in this Act shall be construed as authorizing the execution or application of agreements requiring membership in a labor organization as a condition of employment in any State or Territory in which such execution or application is prohibited by State or Territorial law.

This provision is peculiar because it invites states to explicitly override the provision of the federal statute that legalizes union security clauses in collective bargaining agreements. This provision has spawned a group of state laws that have been generally called "right-to-work" laws.

A right-to-work law provides that it shall be illegal for management and unions to agree to clauses in their contracts that make membership in a labor organization a condition of employment. Twenty-one states now have such

---

[22] Bureau of National Affairs, *Basic Patterns*, pp. 85–86.
[23] See, for example, *Retail Clerks Local 1001 v. Lyons Apparel, Seattle, Washington* (NLRB election proceeding, July 1, 1975).

laws: Alabama, Arizona, Arkansas, Florida, Georgia, Idaho, Iowa, Kansas, Louisiana, Mississippi, Nebraska, Nevada, North Carolina, North Dakota, South Carolina, South Dakota, Tennessee, Texas, Utah, Virginia, and Wyoming. In 1976 Louisiana passed a right-to-work law, the first state to do so since Wyoming in 1963. In 1986 Idaho passed a law, increasing the number of states from 20 to 21. Meanwhile, the unions sought, without success, to amend the law in Arkansas to make it less restrictive. And in Missouri, an employer-supported initiative to enact a right-to-work law failed on November 7, 1978, when voters defeated the proposed statute 60 percent to 40 percent.

The right-to-work laws in each state are alike in prohibiting the union shop but are dissimilar in their provisions on what other, if any, forms of union security are permitted. The agency shop, for example, is apparently legal in 10 of the states with right-to-work laws.

The scope and available remedies at law vary widely from state to state. Some consist solely of a general statement disallowing denial or abridgement of the right to work contingent upon union membership.

> In addition, some laws prohibit (1) "combinations" or "conspiracies" to deprive persons of employment because of nonmembership...(2) strikes or picketing for the purposes of inducing an illegal agreement...(3) denial of employment to any person because of membership or nonmembership...(4) conspiracy to cause the discharge or denial of employment to an individual by inducing other persons to refuse to work with him because he is a nonmember.[24]

Many of the right-to-work states provide no penalties for violation of these laws; others merely have misdemeanor violations, generally providing approximately $100 fines and from 10 days to 12 months in jail.[25] Some states allow only injunctive relief (i.e., relief by court order).

Right to Work: Pro and Con Those who support right-to-work laws argue that union membership should not be required as a condition of employment. They assert that if a union provides services, then people will join. If it does not provide services, people will not join. This is consistent, they say, with our freely competitive economy. They believe the union shop is unfair because it may compel workers against their will to join unions in order to have a job; hence the name of the state statutes: "right-to-work" laws. Further, compulsory unionism is said to provide too much power to union leaders without placing checks on their performance, because the unions do not have to maintain the workers' support in order to receive dues. Also, unions may use dues for political purposes to which workers object, and workers should not, therefore, be compelled to contribute to unions.

Opponents of right-to-work laws advance several reasons for their oppo-

[24] Labor Law Group, *Labor Relations and Social Problems* (Washington, D.C.,: Bureau of National Affairs, 1973), p. 51.

[25] Bruce S. Warshal, "Right to Work; Pro and Con," *Labor Law Journal*, 17:3, March 1966, pp. 135–136.

sition. First, they object to the name "right to work" for these state laws. The laws do not provide a right to work, they point out. Instead, what the laws do is weaken unions. Second, the states with right-to-work laws are generally Southern and Midwestern states with low wage levels. These states have the right-to-work laws in order to keep wages low, it is argued.

> The "right-to-work" law does indeed strike at the very heart of the institution of collective bargaining, and thereby seeks to eliminate or weaken one of the most viable tools for uplifting poor and minority workers from the bottom of the economic ladder.... "Right-to-work" laws become but another means to perpetuate the "cycle of poverty" and the informal system of racism in the United States.[26]

Third, the unions argue that right-to-work laws permit some employees to get a "free ride" at the expense of those who support the union. The union has a legal obligation to bargain on behalf of all employees (members and nonmembers) and to represent all fairly in handling grievances and other matters. A union shop assumes that all employees pay their fair share of the cost of these services by the union. A right-to-work law permits some employees to evade paying their fair share. Fourth, the unions point out that right-to-work laws are supported by a national organization, the National Right to Work Committee, which is heavily financed by employers. The fact that employers actively support the right-to-work laws proves, the unions say, that the real purpose of the laws is to hinder the unions, not to protect the rights of individual employees.

A summary of the arguments for and against right-to-work laws is given in Figure 16-1.

Impact of Right-to-Work Laws   Right-to-work laws have been a major source of controversy between labor and management. In consequence, one might expect to find that right-to-work laws have had an important impact on union strength wherever the laws exist. However, the studies that have been done are largely inconclusive concerning the impact of the laws. There have been few major studies done since the late 1950s, and what has been done (including those of the late 1950s) has been largely contradictory and inconclusive.

Data on union membership clearly show a difference in union strength between states with and without right-to-work laws. States without such laws tend to have larger and more effective labor movements. However, it is not clear whether these differences are because of right-to-work legislation or come from other factors. It can be argued that states with a weak labor movement have right-to-work laws because the unions are weak—rather than that the unions are weak because of the right-to-work law. The weakness of the unions in right-to-work states may be because of a limited industrial base, historical factors, and other such matters.

In 1971 Neil and Catherine Palomba did a study of the "causes" of right-

[26] *AFL-CIO Federationist,* 83:8, August 1976, p. 20.

PRO

Union security agreements interfere with an individual's exercise of a precious liberty —that of working.

Union security agreements also burden an individual in liberties of

- association
- speech
- religion

Voluntary union membership promotes responsible union leadership.

If an employee does not want to be represented by a union, he or she has no moral obligation to pay for it.

Since federal labor law prohibits an employer from discrimination on the basis of union membership, discrimination on the basis of nonmembership should also be prohibited.

CON

Free riders who benefit from union representation but do not share the costs of union membership have an unfair advantage.

Union security arrangements are merely an application of the democratic principle that the majority should rule, because a majority of the workers presumably voted for union representation.

Union security arrangements ensure that the union's status as the bargaining representative is not undermined through employer discrimination against union members.

Union security agreements promote

- industrial stability and labor peace
- responsible labor leadership
- the strength of unions to the benefit of employees as a whole because a secure union is felt to be a responsible union

---

FIGURE 16-1 Pro and con on right-to-work laws. *(Source: Thomas R. Haggard, Compulsory Unionism: The NLRB and the Courts, Industrial Research Unit, Wharton School, The University of Pennsylvania, Philadelphia, Pa., 1977.)*

to-work legislation. Their findings concluded that the passage of an RTW law was contingent on the debtor/creditor status of the state (debtor states pass such laws) tempered by the degree of unionization prior to passage (only debtors with low degrees of prior unionization pass such laws).[27] However,

[27] Neil A. Palomba and Catherine A. Palomba, "Right-to-Work Laws: A Suggested Economic Rationale," *Journal of Law and Economics*, 14, October 1971, pp. 475–483.

in 1974 Moore, Newman, and Thomas published a study partly repudiating the Palombas' findings. Their results indicated that not just prior unionization, but "the blue-collar composition of the work force, the level of agricultural employment, the South geographic region, the degree of urbanization, and the state's population density are important in distinguishing between non-RTW and RTW states."[28] Neither study directly addressed the question of the legislation's effect on union growth, but both indirectly argue that the differences between RTW and non-RTW states may come from factors other than the existence of the law per se.

In a study of union-shop votes in the steel and auto industries, James Kuhn concluded:

> The evidence clearly suggests that the loss of the union shop to unions now enjoying it would, in itself, bring about a drop in membership. The union shop has brought in an average of one new member for every six voluntary members. Under the modified union shop in steel and autos during the early 50's . . . around 5% of the workers dropped or stayed out when they could. Were there no forced membership, as in most steel and auto plants, to initiate workers into the union, the percentage would no doubt be higher.[29]

One of the largest studies conducted on the subject concluded that (1) the laws had little effect on labor relations in RTW states, except perhaps Iowa and Mississippi; (2) the laws have not "busted" any unions; (3) few members have resigned from unions; (4) there is very little effective enforcement of the laws; and (5) in the building construction industry, the laws are generally violated.[30]

The most careful study of the impact of a right-to-work law in any single state was that done by Frederic Meyers on the Texas statute. In his study, Meyers looked at organization patterns in a number of industries. He wrote:

> My considered conclusion, based on 10 years of close observation of labor relations in Texas, is that the right-to-work statute, taken by itself and apart from the whole body of state labor legislation (especially the law against secondary boycott) has had a minimal direct effect. In the traditional areas of the closed shop, the law has been generally disregarded, and the practices that have continued are illegal under federal as well as state legislation. In the industries in which initial hiring is in the hands of the employer, the forms of the law have been observed, and union membership has not been a formal condition of continued employment, yet, organization of the unorganized has proceeded at a remarkably rapid rate since 1947 even though the statute may have changed the general attitude toward unionism in some marginal cases and thus impeded the maximum growth of the labor movement.[31]

---

[28] William J. Moore et al., "Determinants of the Passage of Right-to-Work Laws: An Alternative Interpretation," *Journal of Law Economics*, 17, April 1974, p. 210.

[29] James W. Kuhn, "Right-to-Work Laws—Symbols or Substance?" *Industrial and Labor Relations Review*, 14, July 1961, p. 592.

[30] "Right-to-Work Laws," *Fortune*, 56:8, September 1957, pp. 235–236.

[31] Frederic Meyers, *Right-to-Work in Practice*, A Report to the Fund for the Republic, Inc., New York, 1959, pp. 4–5. See also Meyers, "Effects of State Right-to-Work Laws: A Study of the Texas Act," *Industrial and Labor Relations Review*, 9:11, October 1955, pp. 77–84.

While Meyers found no direct effect of the right-to-work law on union membership, he did note certain applications of the law to limit union strength. He found that Texas courts have used the right-to-work statute not only to protect nonunion employees from discharge but also to deny the power to remedy discrimination against union employees. Furthermore, he argued that the law had hurt the quality of labor-management relations by forcing unions to take a lot of small, adamant stands in order to mitigate the constant threat of lost membership and had significantly reduced the amount of cooperation between the unions and management.

Several statistical analyses of the impact of right-to-work laws have been made recently. Reynolds, Edwards, and Cebula found that the apparent effect of right-to-work laws in reducing wages simply reflects the lower cost of living in the Southern states.[32] Thomas M. Carroll argued that while right-to-work laws when newly passed do not cause union membership to fall abruptly, the laws do contribute over time to weak unionism in right-to-work states.[33] In contrast, Henry S. Farber found that right-to-work laws do not decrease unionism, but merely express or mirror the preexisting taste of workers against unions.[34] Consistent with Farber's findings, the study of two other researchers shows that right-to-work laws seem to have no impact on the frequency of unfair labor practice charges against employers.[35]

THE RIGHTS OF EMPLOYEES

Seniority

Types of Seniority   One of the most fundamental issues in labor relations is how advantages and disadvantages are to be divided among employees. When an opportunity for promotion arises, who is to receive it? When layoffs are necessary, what employees are to lose their jobs? Unions cannot insulate employees against the ill fortune of a company, nor can they obtain for all workers the same opportunities for advancement. But unions are vitally interested in the basis for the decision as to which employees gain benefits and which endure losses. Left to themselves, employers ordinarily utilize a series of standards by which to allocate benefits or losses. Among these standards are length of service with the company, job performance, and perhaps personal loyalty to the company or supervisor. Unions, however, usually advance length of service (i.e., seniority) as the most important, and often the

---

[32] M. D. Reynolds, M. Edwards, and R. J. Cebula, "Right to Work Laws and Cost of Living Differences," *American Journal of Economics and Sociology*, 45:2, April 1986, pp. 247–254.

[33] Thomas M. Carroll, "Right to Work Laws Do Matter," *Southern Economic Journal*, 50:2, October 1983, pp. 494–509.

[34] Henry S. Farber, "Right-to-Work Laws and the Extent of Unionization," *Journal of Labor Economics*, 2:3, 1984, p. 319.

[35] Ralph D. Elliot and James R. Huffman, "The Impact of Right-to-Work Laws on Employer Unfair Labor Practice Charges," *Journal of Labor Research*, 5:2, Spring 1984, pp. 165–176.

only, criterion for making distinctions among employees. Why seniority has such prominence among many groups of workers is an important question. It is partly because seniority seems to conform to a basic sense of fair dealing. Also, seniority is an objective standard. Seniority can be measured in a way that less simple criteria, such as ability, performance, or loyalty, cannot.

Ben Fischer, formerly of the United Steelworkers of America, has described the reasons for which workers and unions strongly support seniority:

Workers place so much store in seniority because it is the only viable and equitable known method for resolving employee competition. Here are some of the reasons:

1 Length of service does reflect experience, and experience is an asset to those who must manage or direct the work process as well as to the worker seeking advancement.

2 Seniority systems provide employees with reasonable opportunities to plan their careers based on some judgment of personal preference and projected potentials. Thus, an employee can plan to achieve jobs or types of work which appear to suit him, taking into account the relative seniority of others who are potential competitors.

3 A proper seniority system should also permit persons who are victims of job, process, or operation abandonment to choose a new career with consideration given for past service and for the advantage of his general work experience.

4 As a worker grows older, there is a tendency for his immediate economic needs to increase; seniority tends to dovetail with this general condition. As a worker grows still older, his needs tend to peak, but in many establishments his last years of employment determine the amount of his pension. A higher base during his preretirement years often generates higher pensions and even determines the level of surviving spouse benefits.

5 As a worker advances, because his standard of living tends to increase, the impact of pay reduction or layoff creates economic hardship. The alternative for the older worker—planning his life around the minimum plant rate—would be unrealistic indeed.

6 The older worker tends to lose mobility. Many factors discourage older workers from moving. They cannot learn new ways so easily. Work and social habits become fixed. If changing jobs means changing residence, then the departure from a well-established place in a community or neighborhood becomes more difficult as a worker (and his family) age. Thus, his dependence on his place of employment tends to grow.

7 In balance, management does better with a stable work force. Retraining entails significant cost for management. Most training is not some formal process, but usually comprises exposure to the job, the nearby jobs, the specific work process, the safety hazards, and countless work practices. Seniority systems that are well conceived tend to give reasonable weight to stability factors.[36]

How is seniority defined and measured? Ordinarily each employee has a seniority date, usually the date of hire by the company. A list, in order of

[36] Ben Fischer, "Seniority Is Healthy," Industrial Relations Research Association Spring Meetings, 1976, pp. 497–503.

oldest to most recent seniority date, is maintained by the company. But the district in which seniority is exercised may vary. Sometimes seniority is defined as length of service with the company, but in other cases seniority is measured as time in the particular plant or department in which the employee works. Some companies keep two seniority lists, with companywide seniority applying to some situations and plant or department seniority applying to others. Generally, employees' seniority dates with the company are the dates that they were hired. Sometimes the ranking of employees hired on the same day depends on the hour at which each employee was hired.

Certain questions arise about seniority measurement. Do absences from work reduce total service time or not? The general answer has been that certain types of absences may reduce seniority status, but not all types. Absence for compulsory military service, for example, counts toward seniority by law. Layoffs sometimes count for seniority and sometimes do not. Full-time duty for the union sometimes counts and sometimes does not. The differences depend on the provisions of the collective bargaining agreement.

"Superseniority" means the assignment of artificial and superior seniority dates to certain employees. This concept apparently originated in the 1930s and came as much from management initiative as from that of the unions.[37] Confronted by growing union demands for seniority systems, many companies were anxious to exempt key employees from the impact of possible layoffs based on seniority. They argued that a group of key employees was necessary in time of layoff, regardless of their length of service with the company. The result was a list of persons excluded from the seniority list. In effect, these persons received superseniority for layoff purposes.

But the unions also had a group that they wanted to protect from layoff— union officers, especially stewards. The unions argued that these persons were essential to the unions' functioning during layoffs. In collective bargaining, these persons were sometimes given superseniority.

But the question has arisen, "To what should superseniority apply?" A contract negotiated between a union and a limousine service provided that union-designated stewards "shall be granted superseniority for all purposes," including layoff and recall, overtime or weekend work, vacation periods, assignment to higher pay classifications, and the opportunity to bid for more favorable shift assignments. A complaint was filed with the NLRB about this contractual provision. A policy of the NLRB set forth in its decision in the Dairylea case in 1976 holds that superseniority should not be extended beyond layoff and recall rights, because to extend it further would illegally imply that the employer will grant better benefits to union members than to persons who are not union members. The NLRB found that the agreement between the limousine service and the union did go beyond the permissible limits. The NLRB therefore limited the coverage of the superseniority provision to layoff and recall. But on appeal, a U.S. court of appeals overruled the

---

[37] Slichter, Healy, and Livernash, *Collective Bargaining*, p. 128.

NLRB to the extent that it permitted superseniority to apply to selection of working shifts as well as to layoff and recall. The court justified its decision by stating that superseniority for choice of working shifts would assure a steward greater accessibility to his or her coworkers and thus assist the steward in performing in a way that would be to the benefit of all employees (not just union members).[38]

Implicit in this rationale is that superseniority is not likely to be permissible when it fails to facilitate the representation of employees. American Can Company and a United Steelworkers local had included in their bargaining agreement a provision that in the event of layoffs employees with the longest continuous service would be the last to be laid off and the first to be recalled. However, the agreement also contained a provision that superseniority would "apply to a total of not more than ten local union officers and grievance committeemen who, notwithstanding their positions on the seniority roster, shall have preferential seniority in case of layoff or recall."

When the company laid off employees with greater seniority to retain two union officials who were not stewards (one was on the safety committee; the other was sergeant at arms at union meetings), the employees sued. The NLRB found the application of the clause to be illegal, and the Tenth Circuit Court of Appeals affirmed the board's decision.

According to the court, superseniority clauses are discriminatory and to a degree adversely affect employees' rights. It says that "these clauses encourage service in union offices by rewarding such service with privileges," and adds that "[p]erhaps such clauses encourage employees to be active in the union." To avoid committing an unfair labor practice, "the union bears an initial burden of demonstrating that officers awarded superseniority have duties which relate directly to the effective and efficient functioning of the bargaining unit."[39]

Seniority applies to matters other than layoffs, as mentioned above. A brief list of applications of seniority demonstrates its importance in American labor relations:

- Layoffs
- Recalls
- Transfers
- Job assignments
- Work assignments
- Shift preferences
- Selection of days off
- Overtime assignments
- Vacation privileges
- Parking privileges

[38] *Connecticut Limousine Service v. Teamsters*, 1979.
[39] "Superseniority," Bureau of National Affairs, *Daily Labor Report* No. 177, Sept. 14, 1981, pp. A7, A8.

In each of these areas, some employees are granted advantages that others do not have. This may be described as the application of *competitive status seniority*. That is, these issues involve seniority as a method of choosing who among the employees will receive benefits.

Seniority is often not the only criterion employed, however. Employers often refuse to promote on the basis of seniority alone; they want to make promotions based upon the work record (especially dependability) and ability of employees. As a result, many collective bargaining agreements provide that with respect to promotions, seniority will prevail when ability is the same. Disputes between management and labor on whether ability is or is not the same between two employees are common. A distinction is sometimes made between sufficient ability and relative ability. A union may argue that a senior employee has a right to a promotion because he or she has sufficient ability to do the job. Management, however, may prefer to promote a less senior employee who has relatively greater ability. The union usually defends the senior employee's right to the promotion. Such disputes are commonly resolved by grievance arbitration.

Seniority is also a basis for the receipt of benefits by employees when competition between employees is not involved. The types of benefits that depend on seniority include:

- Vacations (employees with longer service often receive more vacation)
- Pensions
- Severance pay
- Holidays
- Sick leave
- Life and health insurance
- Supplemental unemployment benefits
- Wage increases
- Automatic promotions
- Bonuses

These applications of seniority (i.e., so-called benefits seniority) do not involve choices between employees. Each employee receives greater benefits as his or her length of service, i.e., seniority, grows.

James Medoff and Katharine Abraham studied seniority and layoffs in both union and nonunion work groups. They found that over 80 percent of private-sector employees, excluding those in construction or agriculture (both of which industries make little use of seniority), enjoy substantial protection against losing their jobs—almost as if a law existed providing some job protection with seniority. As it would be with a law, the practice applies to union and nonunion workers both, although seniority is given more weight in union than nonunion situations when promotions are involved.[40]

---

[40] Katherine G. Abraham and James L. Medoff, "Length of Service and Layoffs in Union and Nonunion Work Groups," *Industrial and Labor Relations Review*, 38:1 October 1984, p. 96; and Abraham and Medoff, "Length of Service and Promotions in Union and Nonunion Work Groups," *Industrial and Labor Relations Review*, 38:3, April 1985, pp. 408–420.

Another study found that unions, specifically, tended to raise the likelihood of layoffs for younger workers, and to lower them for older workers.[41] Finally, Abraham and Medoff also conducted a survey of pay practices, seniority, and employee performance in American industry which seems to show a close connection between seniority and pay level. According to the two researchers, there are large earnings advantages associated with length of company service, and these advantages cannot be explained in terms of the better productivity of the more highly paid employees.[42] D. Quinn Mills also found that employees are often advanced to higher-paying jobs not because of their superior skill, ability, or performance, as the human capital model may imply, but because of their greater length of service.[43]

Layoffs   Layoffs involve one of the most important applications of competitive status seniority. American firms are quick to cut costs by layoffs when business declines. Examples abound, including the well-known 1979–1980 massive layoffs in the automobile industry.

Firms in Japan and Western Europe are often far more reluctant to place the burden of unemployment on their employees. This reluctance stems partly from a fear of union retaliation if layoffs occur. Large nonunion firms in the United States are also reluctant to lay off employees for fear of unionization. James Medoff concluded as the result of a statistical investigation that "adjustment [to business downturns] through layoffs is substantially greater in unionized firms than in comparable nonunionized firms."[44] Thus, most unionized firms in the United States do not hesitate to make layoffs. In the past, American unions have obtained management acceptance of seniority as the basis for layoffs. And in return, management has obtained union acceptance of layoffs when business downturns occur.

This is not to say that American unions are insensitive to layoffs. Unions often try to avoid substantial layoffs. For example, the Communication Workers of America proposed a four-step program to avoid layoffs to Bell Telephone in 1975. "CWA demands, the contracts notwithstanding...," wrote CWA President Watts to AT&T's vice president for labor relations:

1 Advancement of vacations
2 Removal of all temporary and occasional employees
3 No overtime scheduling except for emergencies
4 No subcontracting[45]

---

[41] Francine D. Blau and Lawrence M. Kahn, "Unionism, Seniority, and Turnover," *Industrial Relations*, 22:3 Fall 1983, pp. 362–373.

[42] James L. Medoff and Katharine G. Abraham, "The Role of Seniority at U.S. Work Places: A Report of Some New Evidence," Working Paper No. 1175–80, Sloan School of Management, MIT. November 1980.

[43] D. Quinn Mills, "Seniority versus Ability in Promotion Decisions," *Industrial and Labor Relations Review*, 38:3, April 1985, pp. 421–425.

[44] James L. Medoff, "Layoffs and Alternatives in U.S. Manufacturing," *American Economic Review*, 69:3, June 1979, p. 380.

[45] Bureau of National Affairs, *Daily Labor Report* No. 42, Mar. 3, 1975, p. A1.

Other unions have attempted to negotiate short work weeks and other work-sharing arrangements to prevent layoffs.

Recently, there has been renewed interest in alternatives to layoffs as a means of adjusting to business declines. In the recession of 1979, for example, a number of firms chose to place employees on reduced work schedules rather than to lay some employees off.[46] A barrier to greater use of work sharing as an alternative to layoffs has been that workers on a part-time schedule caused by a lack of work are not eligible for unemployment benefits (provided by the state governments with federal assistance), whereas workers on full layoff are ordinarily eligible for public unemployment benefits. In California, an experimental provision of the state's unemployment compensation law has in the past few years permitted unemployment benefits to be paid to workers on a work-sharing arrangement, where both the company and the union involved agree. A study of the California law found that union members and leaders who experienced work sharing under the law preferred it to layoffs.[47] Arrangements like that in California may, in the future, result in less reliance on layoffs in response to business declines, and therefore to lessened importance of seniority as a device to allocate among workers the difficult burden of joblessness. Table 16-1 lists 12 alternatives to layoffs.

How does seniority work in a layoff? A layoff system involves the interaction of three considerations:

1 *The criteria* to be used in selecting the employees to be laid off
2 *The unit* to be chosen for layoff purposes
3 *The right* of an employee to bump another in lieu of layoff[48]

These considerations are all interrelated.

A union's desire to increase the security of the senior employees has usually led it to request the widest possible unit. A wide unit permits the senior workers affected by a layoff to move anywhere in the plant to a job they are capable of performing. As an alternative, unions have often sought liberal bumping rights if the units were narrow. Companies, on the other hand, have usually preferred the narrower unit because it decreases costly bumping and also decreases movement by senior workers to jobs for which their qualifications are dubious.

If a union gains plantwide seniority and extensive bumping privileges, it sometimes arouses the resentment of employees who are victims of constant displacement. This is particularly true when the senior worker is manifestly

[46] Nancy J. McNeff et al., "Alternatives to Employee Layoffs: Work Sharing and Prelayoff Consultation," *Personnel,* 55:1, January–February 1978, pp. 60–64. Also Barney Olmstead, "Changing Times: The Use of Reduced Work Time Options in the United States," *International Labor Review,* 122:4, July–August 1983, pp. 479–492.

[47] "Union Leaders, Members Voice Approval," *World of Work Report,* 6:10, October 1981, pp. 73, 75, 76.

[48] Slichter, Healy, and Livernash, *Collective Bargaining,* p. 157. See also Daniel B. Cornfield, "Seniority, Human Capital, and Layoffs: A Case Study," *Industrial Relations,* 21:3, Fall 1982, pp. 352–364.

TABLE 16-1 ALTERNATIVES TO LAYOFFS

• Temporary layoffs	• Lending of employees
• Early retirement	• Retraining
• Vacations	• Volunteer reductions
• Shorter work weeks	• Sabbaticals
• Work sharing	• Demotion (bumping down)
• Transfers	• Out-placements

ill-equipped to do the job in question. In some extreme situations, even the senior bumper finds his or her security to be short-lived. Sometimes within a matter of hours or days the senior worker, too, is bumped by a still more senior employee newly affected by the layoff.

Selection of the seniority unit and the degree of bumping privileges usually depend on the characteristics of the enterprise and the bargaining unit. If there is great homogeneity in the work force, the unit is likely to be broad; if the unit is narrow, the right to transfer in lieu of layoff will be greater. On the other hand, the more varied the skills required in an enterprise, the narrower the unit is likely to be and the more restricted will be the bumping rights.

The use of a broad, plantwide layoff system need not be disruptive per se if there are strict limitations on bumping and if it is insisted that workers have qualifications for the jobs to which they are transferred. Some companies join the union in preferring the wide unit if these safeguards exist. Although the seniority unit for layoff purposes is the department or the division, the worker with the least seniority who is laid off from such a unit is then free to apply to the industrial relations department for placement on a plantwide basis if he or she has a certain length of service. Supervisors, however, occasionally protest the turnover resulting from plantwide seniority. Because the pattern of movement becomes fixed—with customary seasonal variations—employees tend to become trained in advance by normal replacement arrangements; consequently, the cost of plantwide movement at the time of layoff is minimal and, in the company's judgment, is more than offset by the gain in employee morale.

Adherence to very narrow units has given rise to serious and obvious inequities. If the unit is as narrow as a job, occupation, or even a department, a worker with considerable length of service may be laid off from the plant, while junior employees are retained on jobs that the laid-off worker is capable of doing.

Slichter, Healy, and Livernash[49] cited the following case history, which dramatizes the evils of a broad seniority unit with relatively unrestricted bargaining rights. The history describes the procedure followed until 1955 in a large automobile company.

---

[49] Slichter, Healy, and Livernash, *Collective Bargaining*, p. 159.

Under the layoff procedure in effect, a worker, if displaced either by the elimination of his job or by the transfer of another worker, could displace any worker with less or no seniority in the bargaining unit. There were no limits on bumping rights except that a man first had to be displaced, which was apparently not too difficult to arrange. A man could bump another employee with as little as one day's less seniority. Bumping rights were not confined to occupational groups but could be exercised plantwide on as many as 950 different jobs. The way the company identified the various jobs (by letter code based on the job rate) made it almost impossible to determine by payroll records what an employee's actual experience had been. Sometimes very different jobs bore the same code, while very similar jobs carried different codes.

A man who exercised his bumping rights was allowed ten days "break-in or qualifying time" to demonstrate his ability to do the job. Until qualification was proved, the transferee was paid ten cents per hour below the day rate and was not made part of the incentive group. Also the worker originally on the job remained on it to train his replacement until the latter was qualified. The replacement could disqualify himself any time within the ten-day period and proceed to bump still another employee junior to him. To exert bumping rights an employee did not have to have any apparent qualifications or knowledge of the job in question. An inexperienced man could displace an experienced worker. For example, an elevator operator could bump an experienced assembler. While a foreman could disqualify a man, this right was not used frequently.

Still another feature of this chaotic layoff procedure was a thirty-day period allowed employees to exert their bumping rights. Stated differently, they could spend up to thirty days shopping around from the one job to another. Movements were so frequent and numerous that the company had to hire three employees just to trace the bumpers. It was estimated that under this seniority system it cost the company more than $1500 to lay off eight people.

The above procedures led to complex strategies and connivances known as "scientific bumping." To manipulate the system to maximum advantage, workers would "buy" bumping rights for ten dollars and make deals with foremen. An integral part of the process was reciprocal relations with other employees. Men often walked around the plant for several days searching for desirable jobs held by workers with less seniority. In some instances deals were made with foremen so that a worker could be displaced and thus be eligible to bump, hopefully to a better job. Another strategem was known as "hand-on-shoulder bumping." Assume five men, each with a different seniority standing. The most junior of the group would bump onto a job. He would then be bumped by the next senior man bumped onto the job. Then the remaining members of the group would repeat the process on another job and on successive jobs.

In the last two quarters of 1953 the company spent $1.5 million carrying two men on jobs at a time when it was trying to effect a sizeable layoff.

However, just as plantwide seniority does not necessarily mean indiscriminate bumping rights, so too the narrowest seniority unit (job or occupational seniority) does not mean an almost complete absence of these rights; other features of the total layoff procedure are important. For example, one plant of a large electrical manufacturing company has had what is known as "code seniority." In effect, the unit is the occupational classification, and the person with the least seniority in that classification will be the first laid off. However, when notified of an impending layoff, an employee may assert seniority bumping rights within three days in lieu of accepting layoff. The employee may bump into an occupation in which he or she had previously worked and has acquired seniority; by definition this means the employee must have worked in the other occupational code at least 30 days. Experience has shown that employees are anxious to acquire seniority in a number of different codes, thereby increasing their bumping rights at the time of layoff. Even under this narrow-unit approach, therefore, bumping is encouraged.[50]

General Implications of Seniority   The use of seniority as a standard for layoffs, recall, training opportunities, and promotions has certain substantial implications for the way the labor market functions in this country.

1 *Perhaps most important, seniority reduced mobility among industrial workers.* The longer a worker is on a particular job, the greater are the rights he or she accumulates from increasing seniority. If the worker left the job, those rights would be lost. The worker would have to start accumulating seniority at some other company or plant. Not surprisingly, the loss of job protection (which seniority provides) is a barrier to people moving from job to job.

More than 20 years ago, Clark Kerr pointed to the effects of the seniority system in industrial plants:

> The craft worker moves horizontally in the craft area, and the industrial worker vertically in the seniority area. Inter-occupational movement is reduced for the former and employer-to-employer movement for the latter....Job rights protect but they also confine. Reduction of insecurity also brings reduction of independence....The more secure are the "in," the greater the penalty for being an "out."[51]

It is Kerr's conclusion that seniority rules probably reduce workers' freedom and retard their efficiency more than the craft rules "which are the customary target of criticism."

2 *Seniority does provide greater security in the workplace for long-service employees.* By doing so, seniority undoubtedly contributes to a gain in morale among employees. Probably, the extensive use of seniority tends to reduce labor relations strife by eliminating much potential managerial favoritism in the treatment of employees.

3 *The effect of seniority provisions on young workers is probably substantial.* Some ambitious and able young workers probably avoid or leave jobs in certain companies because they feel their chances to move ahead are limited by the seniority advantages of older workers. The lack of rigid seniority provisions is probably an advantage to nonunion employers in providing oppor-

---

[50] Ibid., p. 161.
[51] Clark Kerr, "The Balkanization of Labor Markets," in E. Wight Bakke et al., *Labor Mobility and Economic Opportunity* (New York: Wiley, 1955).

tunities for rapid advancement to young people and thereby assists the company in attracting and retaining good personnel.

4 *Seniority may have a direct effect on reducing efficiency in industry.* When seniority becomes the sole criterion for job assignments, then the flexibility needed for efficient operation can be as much affected as by rigidity in craft lines.

5 *Competitive status seniority inevitably creates serious internal problems for the union.*[52] While seniority rules are designed to regulate and systematize competition among workers for job rights, this fact does not relieve the union from pressure. The formulation of the rules themselves requires the compromise of a great variety of competitive interests among union members. Even in the use of benefit seniority there are competitive interests that cause difficulty for the union. For example, during negotiations a union was confronted by a sharp division between junior and senior employees over the question of whether the vacation liberalization to be sought should be the addition of a fourth week for those with more than 25 years' service or the reduction of the qualification for a third week from 15 years' to 10 years' service.[53]

Other Rights of Employees—An Old View versus a New View

When collective bargaining first developed and the principal law applying to employee-employer relations was the National Labor Relations Act, there was one view of the rights of employees with respect to the corporation and the union. But as George Hildebrand has pointed out, this view has been largely replaced in recent years with the passage of many statutes by Congress which bestow rights on individuals, independent of the collective bargaining agreement.[54]

In the older view, which still has some applicability, the union and the company were the source of the rights of employees through their joint action in negotiating a collective bargaining contract. The employees in the bargaining unit were a sort of third-party beneficiary of the agreement. But the agreement belonged to the union and the employer who could jointly take whatever actions seemed appropriate under it, including modifying its terms. Should a modification of the terms of the agreement, or some decision of the union and the company as to how it was to be administered, have an adverse impact on an employee or group of employees, that was merely incidental.

But since the passage of the Civil Rights Act of 1964, and also since the

---

[52] Leonard R. Sayles, "Seniority: An Internal Union Problem," *Harvard Business Review*, 30:1, January–February 1952.

[53] Slichter, Healy, and Livernash, *Collective Bargaining*, p. 140.

[54] George H. Hildebrand, "The Prospects for Collective Bargaining in the Manufacturing Sector, 1978–1985," in Hervey A. Juris and Myron Roomkin, eds., *The Shrinking Perimeter: Unionism and Labor Relations in the Manufacturing Sector* (Lexington, Mass.: Lexington Books, 1980), pp. 105–106.

impact of the Landrum-Griffin Act on how the internal affairs of unions are conducted, there has emerged a body of law which creates new rights for employees independent of the collective bargaining agreement. Both management and labor have had to "adapt" to these changes. Under this new body of law, employees are able to initiate complaints against either management or the union or both.

For example, Wayne Martin, a member of a local union, witnessed a fellow employee drinking an alcoholic beverage on the job, and was present when the employee was caught by a supervisor. At an arbitration hearing Martin testified against the employee. Meanwhile, the union had threatened to fine him if he did so. Martin filed a complaint with the NLRB, but the board dismissed the complaint. The Sixth Circuit Court of Appeals disagreed and found that the union had violated the law by attempting to coerce Martin.[55]

Under Title VII of the Civil Rights Act of 1964 a nationwide local of construction pipefitters was found guilty of maintaining an exclusively white male membership, and was ordered to alter its practices.[56] Incidents like this are significant, but should not necessarily be thought of as proving that unions generally discriminate. Instead, two recent studies indicate that unions have helped increase minority and female employment in our society,[57] and that black members of local unions participate as much as do white members.[58]

In a potentially very significant case, now on appeal to the Supreme Court, the ability of unions to use certain fees paid to them by nonmembers is being challenged. Specifically, 20 nonunion employees of telephone companies have been required to pay an agency fee to a union which represents them but to which they do not belong. They filed suit objecting to the union's using the funds for any purposes (such as political activity or organizing new members) other than collective bargaining or grievance handling. The courts (up to the Supreme Court) have agreed with them. Should the union lose in the Supreme Court, where the case now is being heard, its ability to conduct a wide range of activities will have been limited.[59]

A Changing Work Force

Law is not the sole source of the new rights of employees. Another important force has been the changes that have occurred in the characteristics of the

---

[55] *NLRB v. International Union of Electric Workers, Local 745*, Sixth Circuit Court of Appeals, No. 84-5031, Apr. 10, 1985.

[56] *Equal Employment Opportunity Commission v. Pipe Fitters Local 798*, United States District Court of Northern Oklahoma, No. 84-C-730-C, Sept. 5, 1986.

[57] Jonathan S. Leonard, "The Effects of Unions on the Employment of Blacks, Hispanics and Women," *Industrial and Labor Relations Review*, 39:1, October 1985, pp. 115–136.

[58] Michele M. Hoyman and Lamont Stallworth, "Participation in Local Unions: A Comparison of Black and White Members," *Industrial and Labor Relations Review*, 40:3, April 1987, pp. 323–342.

[59] *Beck v. Communications Workers of America*, Fourth Circuit Court of Appeals, Nos. 83-1955 and 83-1956, Sept. 12, 1986.

work force, its needs and attitudes. To a substantial degree, employers and unions have developed policies and negotiated collective bargaining agreements to fit the needs and circumstances of what may be called the "traditional" worker. In the past, the traditional worker was a married male who was employed but whose wife was not. The male was, therefore, not only the worker but also the sole support of the family.

While the traditional worker continues to receive considerable attention from unions and management, he has long been a minority of the work force and is rapidly becoming a rarity. In 1960, for example, 30 percent of the American work force could be described as traditional workers. But by 1986, only 12 percent could be so described. The largest group by far in the labor force in 1986 consisted of workers living in multiearner families. Even single people (workers not living in a husband-wife family) outnumbered the traditional worker in 1986. (Single people constituted 21 percent of the labor force in 1986.)

The work force of the 1980s is on average younger and better educated and includes more women and minorities than did the American work force in the past. This work force has different attitudes, different needs, and different aspirations than did the work force of the past. And where the law has not kept up with these changes, the new work force has been seeking changes itself in how employers and unions structure the work environment.

Yet, though the work force is now younger on average than it was years ago, it has once again started to age. This is a consequence of fewer people now entering employment than in the 1960s and 1970s. As the work force ages, the concerns of older workers—including discriminatory dismissals by some companies that believe older workers are less productive and cost more than younger workers—have received more attention.[60]

Some of the major issues that arise in the relationship of the individual employee to the employer are described in the next few pages. Some of these issues have been around for a long while, but others are as new as the new work force.

Employees' Political Activities

On Saturday, May 1, 1976, a young supervisor for a large American corporation went to a political demonstration at Herald Square in Manhattan. While at the demonstration, he apparently responded to police efforts to control the crowd by driving a van into two New York City police officers and then into a third, mounted police officer.

The supervisor was never sent to jail for this incident. However, he was interrogated at length by his employer about the demonstration and, according to him, about his political beliefs. These beliefs were considerably more radical than those commonly espoused by executives of the corporation. He was suspended from his job and later discharged.

[60] See American Association of Retired Persons, *Workers Over 50*, Washington, D.C., 1988.

Did the company have the right to discharge this supervisor for his actions at a political demonstration and for his political beliefs? The company said it did. "Public policy in our free enterprise system has never been defined to require a private employer to pay and support an individual who advocates a position inimical to the best interest of the employer," the company argued.

The supervisor brought suit in the courts of New York for damages from the company deriving from his discharge. As of this writing, he has not been successful in his suit. An employee who has no employment contract and belongs to no union, the company has contended in court, "may be terminated at any time for any reason or for no reason, under American law."[61]

The company's statement is not entirely accurate. There are many reasons for which a company may not discharge an employee under American law, including discrimination based on race, creed, sex, or national origin. These restrictions on employers' behavior arise from federal laws. But the issue in the case of the supervisor is whether or not American law prohibits dismissal for the type of political activities in which he engaged and for the type of political belief which he espoused.

This issue is now being addressed by state courts all over the United States. The New York courts are reviewing the case of the supervisor who attended the May 1, 1976, political demonstration. In Michigan, the state Supreme Court ruled on June 10, 1980, that an employer cannot discharge an employee without just cause unless a job contract (written or oral) specifically provides for termination at the will of the employer.[62] But there are questions which remain to be resolved. For example, will the Michigan decision be adopted in other states? The rights of employees in these circumstances are very much in a state of flux in the 1980s. What is apparent is that the new work force is demanding greater rights and more personal freedom in the workplace than its predecessors did. This is nowhere more evident than in the question of the rights of "whistle-blowers."

Protection for Whistle-Blowers

On August 23, 1977, a chemist working for the city water department of a Florida city found contaminants in the water supply of a neighborhood in the city. He cut off the water and tried to clear up the pollution. His supervisor admonished him for acting on his own and too quickly. Several days later, discovering that the pollution continued, he advised residents of the area not to drink the water until the problem was cleared up. Again he acted on his own. His supervisor discharged him for insubordination.

The chemist took his case to the city's Civil Service Board, which upheld his firing. Then he complained to the U.S. Department of Labor under the

---

[61] Tom Goldstein, "Business and the Law: On Dismissing an Employee," *The New York Times*, Apr. 13, 1979.
[62] *Toussaint v. Blue Cross and Ebling v. Masco* (1980).

provisions of the Safe Drinking Water Act of 1974, which reads, "No employer may discharge any employee...because the employee has... participated...in any action to carry out the purposes of this [act]." The Labor Department found that the chemist had been illegally discharged, but refused to order him reinstated in his job, because, the department said, he had not filed his complaint with the department within the 30 days allowed.[63]

The Florida chemist's difficulty is one which many employees, particularly professional and technical people, have confronted in recent years. Should an employee report to the public, or take action, when he or she finds a problem that may affect the public and which the employer has not or will not take action to alleviate? Should the employee "blow the whistle" on the employer?

Some companies have decided that they should permit employees to do just this. A policy adopted by Cummins Engine Company, for example, states:

> The company is prepared to help any employee resolve a moral dilemma and to ensure that no employee is put at a career disadvantage because of his or her willingness to raise a question about questionable practice or unwillingness to pursue a course of action which is inappropriate or morally dubious.[64]

Furthermore, by 1979 eight federal laws had been passed which included so-called employee protection sections. These sections prohibit adverse actions by employers against employees who assist in carrying out the purpose of the statutes. These eight laws are

- Occupational Health and Safety Act
- Federal Water Pollution Control Act
- Safe Drinking Water Act
- Toxic Substances Control Act
- Resource Conservation and Recovery Act
- Clean Air Amendments
- Federal Mine Safety and Health Act
- Nuclear Regulatory Commission Authorization Act

Employer Records and Employee Privacy

Employers maintain in the course of business many records about their employees. When an employee is interviewed for a job, a file is prepared which contains information about the applicant's age, education, work history, health, and other matters. If the applicant is hired, the company will ordinarily maintain a file on the individual's work history and performance at the

---

[63] Rosemary Chalk and Frank von Hippel, "Blowing the Whistle," *The Boston Globe,* Aug. 12, 1979.

[64] Henry B. Schacht, address to the First National Seminar on Individual Rights in the Corporation, New York City, May 10, 1978, p. 5 (mimeographed). See also David W. Ewing, *Do It My Way or You're Fired!* (New York; John Wiley, 1983).

company. Any disciplinary actions may be documented. Health problems may be recorded. Even financial problems that come to the attention of the company may be noted and filed.

To an increasing degree, employees may be required by their employers to take lie detector tests for any number of reasons, including control of theft from the company. Psychological tests are also now a part of the personnel file of many employees. The questions asked in the course of lie detector tests and psychological interviews may seem to many employees to be very personal in nature and far removed from the requirements of their jobs.

What rights does an individual employee have to restrict the use to which a company puts his or her personnel file? Can the company distribute the contents of such a file to other companies or to interested persons? And may an employee refuse to take lie detector or other tests? And if an employee takes the tests, what use may be made by the company of the information obtained?

In recent years concerns about employee privacy have become much more intense as advances in communications and information technology make the transference of data about employees much easier. By 1979, six states had laws affecting the privacy of personnel records. The law in Michigan, for example, gives employees access to their personnel files and restricts disclosure of negative information in the files about an employee. A federal law to protect employee privacy has been advocated for several years, and hearings have been held in Congress on various aspects of the problem. Meanwhile, there is no federal statute, and self-regulation by private companies continues to increase. There is reason to suspect, unfortunately, that only the larger corporations have been diligent in establishing policies to protect employee privacy and that the problem of invasions of employee privacy continues to grow elsewhere in the economy.[65]

CHAPTER SUMMARY

The advent of a union in a plant and the subsequent negotiations of a collective bargaining agreement present a change in the power structure of the plant. Management previously had unilateral authority to make all decisions, but the union represents a countervailing power. The agreement now establishes the right and responsibilities of the company, the union, and the workers.

In order to retain as much authority as possible, management has sought to have its own rights established by the inclusion of certain provisions in the agreement. A clause which lists management's rights is now common. However, such a clause is not always as useful as it may seem. Along with the rights, there are obligations. For example, management has a legal obligation to bargain with a union about subcontracting. Management is sometimes ob-

---

[65] Bureau of National Affairs, *Daily Labor Report* No. 129, July 3, 1979, pp. A2–A6.

ligated to observe work standards and respect rules about work assignments. There has also been a substantial amount of litigation on the rights and obligations of successor employers who acquire facilities with already-established unions and labor agreements.

The contest for control between management and the unions has often centered around the issues of union security. The concern of American unions for their security arose, in part, from the long opposition of American employers to the existence of unions. In 1947, the Taft-Hartley Act established statutory provisions about union security. The closed shop, in which membership in a union is required as a condition of employment, was outlawed. The union shop was permitted, in which membership is required only after 30 days of employment. The union shop is now the most common form of union security. Other forms are the agency shop, the maintenance-of-membership shop, hiring halls, and the dues checkoff.

Right-to-work laws restrict the opportunity for a union and an employer to agree to a union security clause. These state laws, existing in 21 states, are a constant source of legislative dispute in Congress, and they are a major source of controversy between labor and management. Supporters of right-to-work laws claim that the union shop is unfair because it compels workers to join unions in order to have a job. Opponents say that the laws do not provide the right to work and instead are intended to weaken the unions and keep wages low. Unions complain that the laws allow some employees to get all the benefits of a union's presence without sharing the expense of supporting it.

Seniority is one of the major means by which the rights of employees are protected through a collective bargaining agreement. It is the method by which employees lay claim to extra benefits or decide who is to bear hardship. Benefit seniority involves advantages such as increased vacation or pension benefits, which are gained at no cost to others. Competitive status seniority refers to the method for deciding who is to have advantages when there is competition for them. For example, under a rule of seniority, those persons longest at a plant would obtain promotions and would be last to be laid off in an economic downturn. The application of seniority to layoffs is a particularly important matter. American firms resort to layoffs to cut costs when business declines. When a reduction in the work force occurs, senior people in a plant move to different jobs and "bump" those with less seniority.

Changes in the needs, attitudes, and character of the work force have brought a search for greater rights and more personal freedom and privacy in the workplace. Many statutes have been passed in recent years which create new rights for employees independent of the collective bargaining agreement. Challenges to restrictions on employees' political activities, the right of employees to privacy, discrimination against older workers, and protection for "whistle-blowers" are among the issues that have been addressed recently.

QUESTIONS FOR THOUGHT AND DISCUSSION

1 What are management rights? Does a management rights clause in a collective bargaining agreement help management keep some rights? Why or why not?

2 What is a right-to-work law? Does your state have such a law? Should it? Why or why not?

3 Why do unions favor seniority provisions? Is seniority good for society as a whole? Why or why not?

4 What are the implications of seniority systems for labor market functions? Can you think of any other systems or methods for dividing advantages and disadvantages among employees besides seniority systems, such as a strict meritocracy? Discuss the pros and cons of each alternative you propose.

5 How have changes in the work force affected the rights of employees? Should there be increased protection of employees' political activities, right to dissent from corporate policy, and privacy? Why or why not? Are there any disadvantages to increased employee rights? For whom?

6 If a company acquires a facility from another company, what is the status of the union and the labor agreement at the acquired facility? Review the major Supreme Court cases on the problem of successorship. Do you agree with the decisions? Why or why not?

7 What are the different types of union security arrangements or provisions? Are some more acceptable than others and for whom? What are the pros and cons for the different forms of union security?

8 What effect have right-to-work laws had on labor relations?

9 How do seniority systems work in a layoff? What are some of the problems and complications associated with layoffs and bumping privileges? Under what conditions do seniority privileges in layoffs seem to work effectively?

10 Younger workers are sometimes preferred to older ones. Why do you think this occurs? Should it?

SELECTED READING

Hill, Marvin, Jr., and Anthony V. Sinicropi, *Management Rights: A Legal and Arbitral Analysis* (Washington, D.C.: Bureau of National Affairs, 1986).

James, Edgar N., "Union Democracy and the LMRDA: Autocracy and Insurgency in National Union Elections," *Harvard Civil Rights—Civil Liberties Law Review*, 13:2, Spring 1978, pp. 247–356.

McKelvey, Jean T., ed., *The Duty of Fair Representation* (Ithaca: New York State School of Industrial and Labor Relations, Cornell University, 1977).

Slichter, Sumner, James Healy, and Robert E. Livernash, *The Impact of Collective Bargaining on Management* (Washington, D.C.: Brookings, 1960).

Swift, Robert A., *The NLRB and Management Decision Making* (Philadelphia: Industrial Research Unit, Wharton School, The University of Pennsylvania, 1974).

CHAPTER 17

PRODUCTIVITY AND EMPLOYMENT SECURITY

Long-term declines in American productivity and overall international competitiveness have begun to have a very visible impact on collective bargaining agreements. This has been particularly true in the manufacturing sector, hard hit by foreign competition. But these changes also have effected newly deregulated industries such as banking, transportation, and telecommunications. Here we look at the response of the more highly unionized manufacturing sector. How capable has our industrial relations system been in meeting challenges of increasing productivity while providing a measure of employment security for its work force?

PRODUCTIVITY

What Is Productivity?

Productivity is a measure of efficiency. The efficiency of a car can be judged in terms of miles per gallon of gas, for example. In a similar way, the efficiency of labor can be determined, but we ordinarily refer to this measure not as "efficiency" but as "productivity." A measure of labor productivity would be obtained by measuring the output of a particular product and dividing it by the number of hours worked by the men and women who produced the product. Thus, if a crew of workers using a paper machine produces 10 tons of paper each week and the crew consists of seven people, each of whom works 40 hours per week, then the rate of productivity is approximately 0.035 tons, or 70 pounds, per worker hour.

While this may seem a simple concept, it in fact reflects a very complex situation. In our example, the rate of productivity is given in terms of output per worker hour and is referred to as "labor productivity." But the measure cannot be assigned to any particular worker—it measures the rate of output of the group as a whole. Also, the amount measured depends on the machine. It is not a measure of labor productivity in isolation, but one of labor productivity using the particular paper machine involved. It is not a measure, therefore, of the effort made by workers (which is an input); it is a measure of the results they achieve, and this depends on many factors besides their own effort.

We begin to see that while productivity is not a very complicated concept, it reflects a very complex process. At one time the chairman of the United States National Commission on Productivity made this point by saying that the trouble with analyzing productivity was that

> Virtually everything affects productivity [including] education and mobility of the labor force, technology, capital, economics...the common cold....[1]

So many factors affect productivity that various groups use the concept to measure different things. The result, of course, is considerable confusion.

Managers think of productivity as a measure of how much output they are getting from the labor, materials, and equipment they buy. They know that if they can get productivity to rise, they can generate a wider gap between costs and revenues and so earn a larger surplus, or profit.

Workers and unions tend to think of productivity as a measure of how hard a person works. Often they resist attempts by management to increase productivity because they are suspicious that the purpose is to make them work harder. However, it is also true that the productivity of workers would go up if they worked not harder, but "smarter"—perhaps even using less effort to get their work done.

Economists have yet a different view of productivity. Like business people, they focus on how rapidly productivity improves. They know that increased living standards can result from increasing productivity, because it represents more output to be distributed among consumers. But economists know not to identify any particular factor as the cause of increases (or decreases) in productivity without careful research. Efforts have been made at the level of the national economy to determine what factors are responsible for improving productivity. These studies suggest that the major factors include increased capital investment (i.e., the mechanization of production), increased skill and education of the work force, and better methods of doing things (or "know-how").[2]

---

[1] John T. Dunlop, then chairman, National Commission on Productivity and Work Quality, testimony before the Senate Committee on Government Operations, Dec. 16, 1974 (Washington, D.C.: U.S. Government Printing Office, 1975).

[2] E. F. Denison, *Accounting for U.S. Economic Growth, 1929 to 1969* (Washington, D.C.: Brookings, 1973). This study focuses on explaining economic growth, but evidence regarding labor productivity can be derived from it. See also National Research Council, Panel to Review Productivity Statistics, *Measurement and Interpretation of Productivity* (Washington, D.C.: National Academy of Sciences, 1979).

TABLE 17-1 MANUFACTURING: CHANGES IN OUTPUT, EMPLOYMENT, AND PRODUCTIVITY IN THE UNITED STATES AND ITS MAJOR TRADING PARTNERS (PERCENT CHANGE, 1972–1986)

	Output (%)	Employment (%)	Output per hour (%)
United States	38	0	38
Japan	84	4	83
Germany	22	− 17	52
France	23	− 20	57

Source: U.S. Department of Labor, Bureau of Labor, Bureau of Labor Statistics, Office of Productivity and Technology, July 1988.

How the United States Compares Internationally

The productivity of American companies compared with foreign competitors is of increasing importance to everyone's future economic life in America. The United States has always been a leader in technological innovations, developing and marketing new products and effectively managing the work force. Yet, in the 1970s, the U.S. lost much of its lead, and as the 1980s came to a close, it was not clear that the United States could reassume a position of leadership.

Table 17-1 shows that on average, for the last 15 years, U.S. output per hour (productivity) has risen at a rate substantially below our major trading partners—Japan, Germany, and France. This relatively low increase in productivity is one factor that economists point to in suggesting that the United States may continue to have difficulty maintaining a position of international business competitiveness. However, we should note that toward the end of those 15 years, the situation began to improve. Productivity increases in the United States jumped from an average of 1.8 percent per year during the 1970s to 5 percent annually from 1981 to 1986. Time will tell whether this country will be able to maintain this rate of increase.

Effects of Deregulation, Recession, and International Competition

We look here primarily at the manufacturing sector of the U.S. economy because changes in this sector may lead to widespread changes in other sectors.[3] Figure 17-1 shows the decline in the percentage of manufacturing jobs as a part of the total number of jobs in the U.S. economy. In 1969, for example, almost 29 percent of the jobs in the United States were in manufacturing. By 1986, only 19.1 percent were.[4] Figure 17-2 shows what this means in actual numbers of manufacturing jobs in the United States. Be-

[3] Daniel J. B. Mitchell, "Recent Union Contract Concessions," in *Brookings Papers on Economic Activity*, No. 1, 1982 (Washington, D.C.: Brookings), pp. 165–204.

[4] For a fuller discussion, see Daniel Quinn Mills and Malcolm R. Lovell, "Competitiveness: The Labor Dimension," in Bruce R. Scott and George C. Lodge, eds., *U.S. Competitiveness in the World Economy* (Boston: Harvard Business School Press, 1985), pp. 429–454.

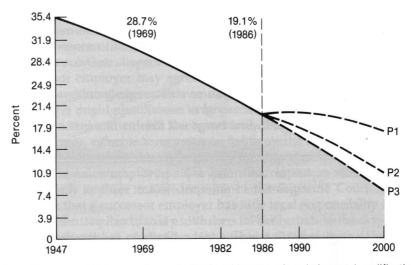

P1 *Competitiveness and high economic growth.* Tracks with some minor, judgmental modifications, the Bureau of Labor Statistics high economic growth rate for manufacturing to the year 2000. Manufacturing as a percentage of employment as forecasted by BLS is possible only with a combination of factors involving greater productivity resulting in part from improved labor-management relations and high general economic growth.

P2 *Competitiveness and low economic growth.* Tracks combination of BLS intermediate and slow growth rate. Manufacturing as a percentage of employment as forecasted by BLS with low-moderate general economic growth is possible only with a combination of factors involving greater productivity resulting in part from improved labor-management relations.

P3 *Noncompetitiveness.* Forecast based on continuation of present trends, although there may be short-term variations; for example, the upturn in the business cycle. The course of the U.S. economy extrapolated from trend since 1947, which is associated with declining competitiveness in the last two decades.

FIGURE 17-1 Projections of Current Trend—Manufacturing Employment in the United States as Percent of Total Employment.

tween 1981 and 1982, nearly 2 million jobs were lost. Few suggest they will be recreated in the manufacturing sector.

Some economists have concluded from these trends that the United States is in a process of decline, or as one pair of authors put it, "deindustrialization."[5] Observers suggest that, if current trends continue, future generations of Americans cannot necessarily look forward to the rising standard of living that previous generations have enjoyed. Others say that these observations are too pessimistic and that the U.S. economy can adapt to these changes.

Plant Closings

As the subtitle of one important work suggests, plant closings, the abandonment of communities as their economic bases disappear, and the toll on in-

[5] Barry Bluestone and Bennett Harrison, *The Deindustrialization of America* (New York: Basic Books, Inc., 1982).

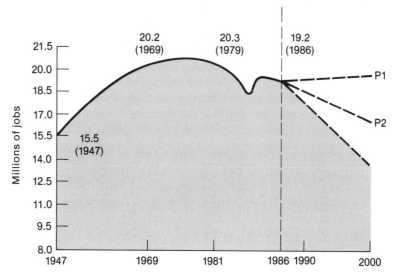

P1 *Competitiveness and high economic growth.* Tracks with some minor, judgmental modifications, the Bureau of Labor Statistics high economic growth rate for manufacturing to the year 2000.

P2 *Competitiveness and low economic growth.* Tracks combination of BLS intermediate and slow growth rate.

P3 *Noncompetitiveness.* Forecast based on continuation of present trends, although there may be short-term variations; for example, the upturn in the business cycle.

FIGURE 17-2 Projections of Current Trend on Manufacturing Employment in the United States (millions of jobs).

dividuals who lose their jobs have had pervasive and serious consequences between 1981 and the present. The number of plant closings increased dramatically during the 1981–1982 recession. This had led to a search for alternatives to closings and the development of programs for those displaced.[6] Some collective bargaining agreements anticipate and provide some measure of protection for workers who lose their jobs due to plant closings.[7] In other cases, income support for qualified workers through state-administered unemployment insurance programs is the major protection afforded workers. Until recently, only two states, Maine and Wisconsin, have had legislation requiring notification to workers whose plants are being shut down. By the end of 1983, plant closing legislation was being considered in 17 states and two cities.[8] The lack of legislation in the United States regarding plant clos-

---

[6] Paul F. Gerhard, "Finding Alternatives to Plant Closings," *Industrial Relations Research Association spring meeting, Proceedings,* May 2–4, 1984, pp. 469–474.

[7] U.S. Bureau of Labor Statistics, *Major Collective Bargaining Agreements: Plant Movement, Interplant Transfer, and Relocation Allowances* (Washington, D.C.: U.S. Government Printing Office, July 1981) (Bulletin No. 1425–20).

[8] Bennett Harrison, "The International Movement for Prenotification of Plant Closures," *Industrial Relations,* 23:3, Fall 1984, pp. 387–409.

ings stood in sharp contrast to the legislative requirements of European countries. There, prenotification is legislated in almost every country; the longest, 12 months, in Germany, is a requirement introduced as part of the 1976 Co-Determination Act.[9] In 1987 the Congress passed a bill requiring advance notice of major layoffs or complete shutdowns, but it has not yet been finally enacted into law.[10]

INCREASING PRODUCTIVITY

Can Productivity Be Increased?

Managers and the general public are, with few exceptions, of the view that increased productivity is to be encouraged. The benefits from increased productivity in terms of increased output and potentially lower costs and prices seem obvious. Workers and unions are less certain. Increased productivity may manifest itself in layoffs, so that workers fear loss of their jobs. Or increased productivity may require greater effort or other changes that the workers do not welcome. For these reasons, it is unusual for the workers directly affected to welcome increasing productivity, unless their concerns are somehow accommodated.

Unions are in the most ambivalent position. On the one hand, unions recognize the potential benefits of increasing productivity in terms of general living standards. They also recognize that increasing productivity may provide a margin out of which employers may pay better wages. On the other hand, the unions often reflect the concerns of workers about their job security or the resistance of workers to the changes in their jobs that accompany increased productivity. The memory of a time when increasing productivity simply meant increasing effort requirements is a strong one. As a consequence of this divided attitude, unions ordinarily attempt to keep the pace of productivity change to a manageable level, while also attempting to obtain for the workers a share of the benefits of increasing productivity.[11]

These differing attitudes toward increasing productivity set the stage for problems between management, unions, and workers. The various ways in which the problems are dealt with are the subject of the next few pages. A special aspect of this topic is the misunderstanding that surrounds it. Managers and the public find it difficult to understand why workers and unions would resist progress of the type that yields increased productivity and often view such resistance as evidence of ignorance and stubbornness. Workers and unions, in contrast, find it difficult to understand why they should be

---

[9] Ibid.

[10] Betty Southard Murphy, "Pros and Cons," *Labor Law Reports* (Washington, D.C.: Commerce Clearing House, Inc.), 18:9 June 1987, pp. 1–3.

[11] Thomas R. Donahue, "Technology: Using It Wisely," *AFL-CIO American Federationist*, 86:9, September 1979, pp. 5–8.

expected to accept with equanimity what they perceive to be a threat to their livelihood, or comfort, or both.

Unilateral Actions by Management

Most factors that contribute to increased productivity are in the domain of management. This is true in both unionized and nonunionized environments. While we often assume that in a nonunion facility management is free to institute methods that will yield high productivity without objection, this is not necessarily so. Nonunionized workers will sometimes act in concert, especially as a result of shared fears or apprehensions, to oppose technological change. Furthermore, nonunionized workers often cooperate surreptitiously to set a slower pace of work or a lower level of production than the company desires.[12] The same sort of thing happens also, perhaps more easily, in the union context. For example, the warehouse director of the Eastern Conference of Teamsters commented that too often it is the case that a new warehouse employee will pick 125 to 135 items from the shelves each hour. But after acquiring regular employee status and the protection of seniority, the same employee will fall back to much lower rates of production.[13]

Employers have traditionally responded to such problems in one of three ways:

1 By tightening discipline
2 By imposing changes in production methods
3 By attempting to persuade workers to assist in raising production levels

There are no statistics to indicate the general success or failure of these efforts. Careful observation of American industry through the statements of its leaders suggests a continuing concern with problems of productivity, however, and some impatience with the apparent failure of efforts to improve efficiency.

To a degree, the persistence of management frustration about the level of productivity in American society reflects failures on the management side. Too often, outdated and inefficient practices are so much an accepted part of an enterprise or institution that management doesn't think they can be altered. So, rather than implementing improvements through discussions with workers and supervisors, management simply complains about bad work habits. If a problem exists that merits criticism, then it also deserves a serious effort by management to improve the situation.

But if management wishes to obtain changes in the behavior of workers, it must be prepared to put its own house in order where a change is warranted. Managers often fail to raise the issue of work productivity because they are

---

[12] In 1931 S. B. Mathewson wrote a classic study of such practices, which is, unfortunately, now out of print: *Restriction of Output among Unorganized Workers* (New York: Viking Press, 1931).

[13] Morand Schmidt, speech to the Teamsters Warehouse Division meeting in Boston, cited in Bureau of National Affairs, *Daily Labor Report* No. 163, Aug. 21, 1975, p. A7.

afraid to reveal the limitations of their own knowledge about what is really going on in the workplace. For example, in 1974 the Bureau of National Affairs conducted a survey of companies regarding their methods of measuring employee performance. While most large companies have methods of evaluating the performance of production workers, only 30 percent had any actual measurements of productivity. And for office employees, while 80 percent of the companies had some form of performance evaluation program, only 11 percent had any productivity measure.[14]

Managers are often afraid to raise the issue of productivity for fear it will open the door for discussion of other aspects of management priorities. Consequently, in many collective bargaining negotiations the work standards of the shop floor are studiously ignored by both management and union officials, neither wishing to demonstrate how little it knows about the actual day-to-day process in the workplace or to initiate a discussion that might get out of hand.

If management is serious about wanting to improve productivity in a facility in a substantial way, it must make a substantial effort. A complete plan for attempting to obtain higher productivity in the workplace would include the following elements:

- A study of the sources of difficulty
- The development of a program to remedy the defects
- An attempt to persuade the workers and union, if any, of the need to improve productivity
- A willingness to alter managerial practices that contribute to lessened productivity
- A willingness to tighten work discipline
- A willingness to reward success by workers in increasing productivity

Unfortunately, many managements are not prepared to take this difficult route. Instead, they look for some simple solution.[15] There are many people who are willing to sell managers some particular scheme to improve productivity without much effort. In 1975 a study listed nine such schemes, any one of which might have its place in a serious program to improve productivity, but none of which was of much value when relied on in place of a more comprehensive effort. The nine "fallacies of management" are given in Table 17-2.

Conflicts over Productivity

Strikes   In recent years strikes over productivity issues have been especially lengthy and bitter. The issues have primarily concerned work rules that

[14] "Employee Performance: Evaluation and Control," *BNA Personnel Policies Forum*, 108, February 1975.

[15] Bruno Stein, "Management Rights and Productivity," *The Arbitration Journal*, 32:4, December 1977, pp. 270–278.

TABLE 17-2 FALLACIES OF MANAGEMENT IN TRYING TO INCREASE PRODUCTIVITY

1 Following the leading companies (i.e., doing just as others do)
2 Decentralizing (i.e., shifting responsibility)
3 Leaving the problem to the personnel department
4 Treating the work force as a fixed asset
5 Issuing platitudes about productivity in the company's own publications
6 Relying exclusively on computer printouts (i.e., statistical information) for evidence about operations
7 Trying to speed up the workers' pace
8 Trying to improve jobs
9 Hiring a consultant

Source: A. A Imberman (president, Imberman and de Forest, management consultants, Chicago), "The Low Road to High Productivity," *Conference Board Record*, 12:1, January 1975, pp. 29–40.

the companies have felt impeded efficient production, sometimes dealing with the introduction of new, labor-saving machinery.

In the spring of 1975 General Dynamics took a 4-month strike by the Marine and Shipbuilding Workers at its Quincy, Massachusetts, shipbuilding division. In July 1975 the Electric Boat Division (builders of submarines for the U.S. Defense Department) of General Dynamics, located at Groton, Connecticut, took a 5-month strike by the 11 craft unions of a metal trades council. Again the issue was work rules. The company described the dispute as due to the unions' resistance to modernization of work rules and the need for job flexibility in the modern economy. The unions, in contrast, described the dispute as resulting from an attempt by the company to disregard traditional job jurisdictions of the various crafts, in an attempt to create assembly-line methods. In effect, the company sought authority under the collective bargaining agreement to assign members of the various trades (including carpenters, grinders, welders, and steamfitters) to work outside their own crafts that was "incidental" to their jobs. The unions professed concern that the company was trying to reduce the number of jobs. Both strikes were settled in similar fashion. The unions and the company agreed to establish joint labor-management committees, but with different functions. At Groton the committees were to review individual job assignments, while at Quincy the committees were to review proposals for changes in production methods with the purpose of increasing productivity.[16] Since then, a number of joint labor-management committees have sprung up in a variety of industries (see Chapter 8). Early indications are that these committees can effectively address a variety of issues.[17]

[16] "Productivity and Efficiency Agreement Implemented at General Dynamics Corporation," Bureau of National Affairs, *Daily Labor Report* No. 51, Mar. 14, 1975, pp. A12–A13.
[17] *Resource Guide to Labor Management Cooperation*, U.S. Department of Labor, Labor-Management Services Administration (Washington, D.C.: U.S. Government Printing Office, September 1982).

In the newspaper industry, as in shipbuilding, most disputes have ended in settlements of one type or another. But in one strike, the union was forced from the company's premises for good. On October 1, 1976, the printing press operators (members of the International Printing and Graphic Communications Union) struck *The Washington Post* when management refused to abandon demands for changes in the work rules. The *Post* objected that existing rules required more workers than were necessary to do the job and allowed excessive earnings for some workers. When the contract expired, the strike began in a wave of sabotage that crippled the *Post*'s 12 printing presses. The *Post* was able to publish during the strike by having its printing done outside Washington and in December 1975 began to replace the strikers with other employees.[18]

Finally, International Harvester Company demanded major changes in work rules from the United Auto Workers as negotiations began in the fall of 1979 for a new 3-year collective bargaining agreement. A 5-month strike resulted, in which both the company and the workers lost considerable income. The company was unable to obtain most of the changes in work practices which it sought.

What is the impact of strikes on productivity? A careful investigation found that shop-floor confrontations between management and labor during the term of collective bargaining agreements (sometimes wildcats, sometimes strkes permitted by the contract) caused a reduction in U.S. manufacturing productivity in the mid-1960s but played little role in the much bigger productivity slowdown that began in the mid-1970s.[19]

Moving the Plant   Many employers are reluctant to take lengthy strikes in an effort, often futile, to obtain changes in working rules. In some industries employers simply prefer to close the least efficient plants and move production elsewhere. This pattern of behavior has been much followed in the rubber industry, for example. Much of the employment in the rubber industry was once concentrated in the Akron, Ohio, area. In 1950, for example, the "big four" rubber companies (Goodyear, Goodrich, General, and Firestone) employed some 51,000 persons in Akron. By 1975 the total had declined to 32,000 and was continuing to fall. A number of factors contributed to the decisions of the companies to shift production to plants in areas other than Akron. Among these factors were the age of the plants, which caused machinery and plant layouts to become increasingly obsolete; lower wage rates elsewhere; inefficient work practices at the plants; and the shift of the market for tires to the South and West in the United States. The low productivity of the Akron plants was a factor that management and labor could possibly

---

[18] See *The Washington Post,* Intercollegiate Case Clearing House 9-677-076 and 9-677-077.

[19] Sean Flaherty, "Strike Activity, Worker Militancy, and Productivity Change in Manufacturing," *Industrial and Labor Relations Review,* 40:4, July 1987, pp. 585ff. See also Sean Flaherty, "Strike Activity and Productivity Change: The U.S. Auto Industry," *Industrial Relations,* 26:2, Spring 1987, pp. 174–184.

have rectified. During the early 1970s repeated efforts were made by management, labor, and community groups to revive Akron's prospects in the rubber industry. One such program, in 1972, was entitled "Make Akron Competitive" ("Hey MAC"). It was hoped that this program would increase productivity in the plants. Unfortunately, these cooperative efforts were largely unsuccessful, and the movement of rubber industry production from Akron has continued, leaving in its wake bitter recriminations from management and labor representatives as to who was responsible. In rubber, the unfortunate legacy of these moves is especially important, since many thousands of unemployed workers remain in the areas production has moved away from.

Why does management move a plant when the process is costly and may cause ill feelings? A short answer is that it may be less expensive to move than to continue production at the old plant. The advantages of moving include:

- Lower wage rates
- A new work force
- A new physical setup
- New equipment
- A new labor agreement or none at all

Many managers believe that when the labor relations in an existing facility have gotten into a very bad state, with much conflict, low productivity, and consequent high costs, there is no real alternative to establishing a new facility somewhere else. They do not believe there is much chance of turning a bad labor situation around. And although there may be a few examples of successful turnarounds of nonproductive plants, and although attempts to do this continue, the evidence as a whole appears to lend support to those who say that it is better to start over elsewhere. The recession of the early 1980s intensified these pressures.

Outsourcing As labor costs have risen in the United States and companies have become increasingly multinational in their approaches, outsourcing, or the shifting of production overseas, has increased. This has posed threats to the employment security of some American workers in several industries.

In some cases, unions have tried to put restriction on the ability of a company to move production abroad. This trend has not been limited to the manufacturing sector; it has also taken place in industries such as the computer industry where some companies have shifted subassembly production work to third world countries where labor costs are substantially lower.

Litigation Employers may also challenge in the NLRB or the courts work practices that inhibit productivity. Ordinarily, an employer who has negotiated in an agreement with a union a clause that restricts productivity cannot simply file suit against the practice. But other parties, both management and union, who are affected may sometimes find a way to challenge the practice in court.

An important example of the use of litigation to loosen work practices occurred in the longshoring industry. Longshoremen, represented by the International Longshoremen's Association (the ILA), have traditionally loaded and unloaded ships' cargo. In recent years, however, more and more cargo has been shipped in containers the size of truck trailers and longshoremen have been left with fewer individual cargo units to load and unload.

Some shipping companies exist that ship only containers. These companies want to have the containers put on and taken off ships by the longshoremen, but not unpacked or repacked by them. In 1958 the ILA protested the use of boxes that were 8 cubic feet in size and began a strike against the New York Shipping Association, Inc. (NYSA). A memorandum of settlement following the strike stated in part that "any employer shall have the right to use any and all types of containers without restriction or stripping by the union."

With further advancements in containerization, work stoppages marked the expiration of ILA-NYSA collective bargaining agreements. During these disputes, longshoremen stripped and restuffed containers shipped by Consolidated Express as the containers crossed the piers. These incidents lasted 2 or 3 weeks and generally containers from Consolidated went through the port without interference. A 57-day strike occurred in 1967, when the ILA demanded that its longshoremen stuff and strip all containers crossing the piers. In 1969 ILA and NYSA negotiated the "Rules on Containers," which provided that longshoremen would unload and reload containers sent to the port from locations within a 50-mile radius. The rules provided that if a container was shipped through the port without having been stuffed or stripped by longshoremen, the offending steamship carrier would pay a penalty of $250 per container.

In 1970 the liquidated damages imposed on the carriers were increased to $1000 for each offense. The enforcement plan was tightened in 1973, when ILA and the shipping association announced that they would penalize companies whose containers weren't handled by ILA. With this, some of the companies that shipped containers (express companies, not shipping companies per se) filed a complaint with the NLRB, charging that the ILA was trying to take work away from the Teamsters, who were the representatives of their employers.

It is interesting that the express companies had no standing under law to complain of the additional cost or inefficiency created by the ILA-NYSA agreement. They could complain only that the purpose of the practice was to obtain work illegally from members of another union. The ILA defended itself by saying that it had traditionally done the work in question. But the

NLRB found against the ILA and thereby invalidated a position that has the effect of reducing productivity.[20]

In 1979, however, the U.S. Court of Appeals for the District of Columbia Circuit reversed the NLRB and upheld the legality of the work rules negotiated by the ILA and the NYSA. The court held that the work rules barring the stripping of containers by nonlongshore personnel within 50 miles of each port were a responsible attempt to deal through collective bargaining with "an extremely thorny industrial issue: technological innovation versus job security." The court concluded that Congress has chosen to allow the parties themselves to deal with labor problems generated by technological change. The broad policy choice of Congress would be "frustrated" if the courts and the NLRB were to "upset reasonable efforts by the parties to achieve some level of accommodation...." The court added that "unwarranted interference" by the NLRB and the courts "could inject a massive dose of uncertainty into the planning functions of both management and labor."[21]

As a general rule practices by nonunion or union labor that restrict productivity are not illegal unless they have some additional purpose that is itself illegal. An attempt to obtain pay for work not done is illegal, for example, but pay for work not needed may be legally required, as long as the services are performed. Because the law does not prohibit nonproductive practices per se, the use of litigation as a method of reducing nonproductive practices is of limited value.

Productivity Bargaining

Beginning in the 1970s much attention has been focused on a procedure referred to as "productivity bargaining." The essence of this concept is that "changes in working practices that raise output per man hour are implemented by employees in return for higher rates of pay."[22] Alternatively, productivity bargaining may be described as the employer's receiving from the union a quid pro quo for a wage increase, in the form of a relaxation or modification of working practice that will result in greater productivity.[23]

Productivity bargaining is not new.[24] Employers in certain fields have long

---

[20] *ILA v. Consolidated Express, Inc., et al.*, 221 NLRB No. 144, Dec. 9, 1975. See Bureau of National Affairs, *Daily Labor Report* No. 237, Dec. 9, 1975, pp. A13–A15.

[21] *ILA and Council of North Atlantic Shipping Associations v. NLRB*, Sept. 25, 1979.

[22] E. H. Phelps Brown in the foreword to Ronald Edwards and R. D. V. Roberts, *Status, Productivity and Pay: A Major Experiment: A Study of the Electric Supply Industry's Agreements, 1961–1971* (London: Macmillan, 1971), p. xii.

[23] Ibid., pp. xiii and xiv. See also C. Laurence Hunter, "Productivity Bargaining Abroad: An Evaluation," in G. G. Somers et al., *Collective Bargaining and Productivity* (Madison, Wis.: Industrial Relations Research Association, 1975), pp. 169–194.

[24] United Kingdom, National Board for Prices and Income, Report No. 23, *Productivity and Pay during the Period of Severe Restraint*, December 1966, and Report No. 36, *Productivity Agreements*, June 1967.

entered negotiations with labor unions with a list of demands that would, if agreed to by labor, increase productivity and thereby reduce the employer's costs. What is new is the degree of attention being devoted to the subject. To say that there is a corresponding increase in the success of productivity bargaining would probably be incorrect.

There has been interest in, and publicity accorded to, productivity bargaining in the United States. The examples of industrial conflict involving the shipbuilding and newspaper industries that were cited in previous pages had their origins in demands by management to alter inefficient working practices. In many other cases companies have practiced productivity bargaining with less dramatic results but with some success. An official of one large American corporation described his company as going after individual items to save money. The approach is very specific. The company persuades or embarrasses the union and, by persistence in negotiations, obtains the removal of costly but inefficient items. An example, cited by the same management official, involved the company's paying for setup time on machines. In the past, certain workers had come in early to get the machines running by starting time, and the company had paid them 15 minutes' time for this. Later the plant went to a continuous, three-shift operation. The machines were now running constantly, and no setup was involved. Yet 12 years after the company went on three shifts, it was still paying setup time. The company's attempt to get this costly practice eliminated constituted, in the company's view, productivity bargaining.

Productivity bargaining is far more complex and difficult than it sounds, however. Not only do the unions or workers who are directly involved often resist the company's initiatives, but additional burdens are placed on management. Companies are required to study their production processes, learn where inefficiencies lie, and determine which improvements would be most beneficial. And even when a good case for change can be made, it too often takes the crises of a threat of layoffs or shutdowns to get unions to agree to necessary improvements in efficiency.[25]

When productivity bargaining does proceed, it has further pitfalls. First, managements often give away too much. Productivity improvements result from capital expenditures, training expenditures, and similar factors as much as from concessions made by labor. If a disproportionate part of the savings gained from productivity improvements is obtained by labor, the company may experience financial difficulties. It is often difficult to identify the sources of productivity improvements and in what proportion they occur. Second, when one group of workers in a plant or industry gets additional money because it relinquished certain conditions, others may demand the same money without giving up anything. And often these other groups are

---

[25] Robert B. McKersie and L. C. Hunter, eds., *Pay, Productivity and Collective Bargaining* (London: Macmillan, 1973). Also, Lincoln Fairley, *Facing Mechanization: The West Coast Longshore Plan* (Los Angeles: University of California Institute of Industrial Relations, 1979).

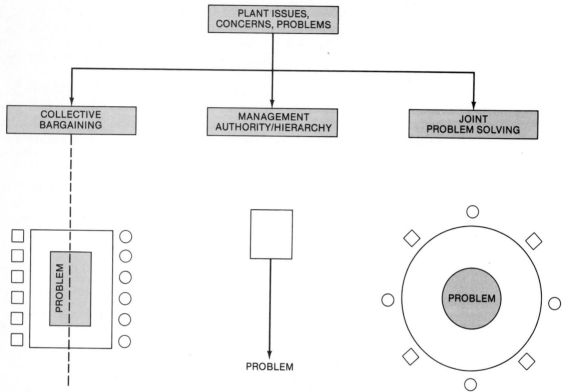

FIGURE 17-3 Three-pronged problem-solving process in unionized organizations. (*From John Belcher, Jr., "The Role of Unions in Productivity Management," Personnel, 65:1, January 1988, p. 57.*)

prepared to strike. Thus, the actual cost to the company of obtaining a concession may be much higher, because of secondary increases, than it had first appeared to be. In fact, workers often bitterly resent seeing other workers receive financial benefits for giving up uneconomic practices. They see this process as one in which the company rewards those who have slowed it up in the past. For these reasons, productivity bargaining is complex and hazardous and more often involves small gains than large breakthroughs.

Instead of relying on the collective bargaining process to improve productivity, many companies and unions in the 1980s have turned to a third approach, one involving joint problem solving (see Figure 17-3). In this approach, a joint labor-management committee meets to try to improve operations.

An example will help to make clear how the joint problem-solving approach works.[26]

[26] John Belcher, Jr., "The Role of Unions in Productivity Management," *Personnel*, 65:1, January 1988, pp. 57-58.

An experience at the Xerox Corporation provides a clear example of the use of labor-management cooperation to improve organizational performance and save jobs. In 1981 Xerox conducted a study that indicated that some of the company's products were not competitive in the international marketplace. Xerox determined that it could save $3.2 million by subcontracting certain component parts that were then being manufactured in-house. The savings, which were considered vital to reestablishing the company's competitive position, would be realized by closing down an entire department and laying off 180 employees.

In an effort to avert this major loss of jobs, the Amalgamated Clothing and Textile Workers Union asked management to establish a joint union-management study team to investigate ways to improve efficiency in the affected department. Although management was initially reluctant because it believed only labor cost reductions could make this department competitive again, it nonetheless agreed to try the cooperative strategy.

The study team, which consisted of six hourly and two management employees, was given six months to develop its recommendations. Team members received specialized training and pursued their task on a full-time basis. They were given the freedom to explore any activities that might result in cost reduction.

An executive labor-management policy committee was formed to support this effort. This group consisted of top union and company executives and had ultimate responsibility for approving the study team's recommendations.

Through a variety of means—soliciting suggestions from employees, conducting informal discussions, and visiting other companies—the study team identified 40 possible improvement projects, nine of which were ultimately selected for in-depth investigation: (1) improved production equipment, (2) changes in work flow, (3) changes in work responsibility, (4) methods for reducing scrap, (5) improved work-order reporting procedures, (6) improved computer usage, (7) stabilization of the employee population, (8) production control and overhead adjustments, and (9) reduced occupancy costs, such as floor space and utilities.

At the end of six months, the study team presented proposals that would result in a total savings of $3.7 million. The proposed changes were significant, including the redesign of the department's physical layout, the expansion of employee responsibilities, reductions in overhead, and the creation of self-managing work groups.

Many of the changes, which the joint policy committee implemented over an eight-month period, flew in the face of traditional union and management prerogatives. Such changes probably could not have been made without the collaborative spirit that grew out of the joint labor-management process.

Concession Bargaining

A widespread response to the difficult economic times of the early 1980s was the growth of concession bargaining. Historically, in good economic times, unions have come away from the bargaining table with higher wages, better benefits, more or better work rules or rights under the contract. A concession bargain is one where the new collective bargaining contract provides less than before: fewer rules and benefits, less money.

Although unions and the employees they represent are not, of course, pleased with a concession contract, some see it as a necessary response to the long-term economic conditions of an industry or the financial weakness of a given plant or company. But concession contracts are ratified by the membership only when a majority is convinced that they will save jobs or the company and/or provide employment security in the long run. Some companies have demanded concessions from employees where they were not clearly needed. In other words, some companies "cried wolf." This made the task of developing labor-management cooperation to deal constructively with the common problems faced by management and labor more difficult.[27]

Which industries have been most affected by these changes? Table 17-3 shows industries where concessions have been agreed to by unions and the sharp decline in employment that helped convince workers of their need.

According to a survey on concession bargaining, unions have most frequently traded off immediate wage increases or benefits for more employment security. This is a change from the historic union position that has been to push relentlessly for job security—guarantees for specific jobs, rather than employment security—guarantees for overall employment levels. Table 17-4 shows that unions are now willing in some instances to trade off specific jobs for employment security on behalf of their members. They are also now more willing than in the past to grant more flexibility in work rules governing the workplace in job assignments, hours of work, seniority, wages, incentive pay and teamwork, in exchange for employment guarantees.[28] What casual factors lay beneath the concession movement? Each industry, company, plant, and union has a unique tale, but there are two underlying influences. First, unions had to make concessions where the companies' labor costs had gotten far ahead of competitors'. This is not to say, however, that in all instances in which labor costs were high, the unions made concessions. In some instances they did not, with varying results. Layoffs occurred; plants were closed; some companies went bankrupt; but other companies recovered due to other influences. Labor costs, it must be remembered, are not the only factor affecting a firm's competitiveness.

Second, employers were less willing to give pay increases to avoid strikes. Fearing that pay raises would cripple the company, many held firm for concessions and got them.[29]

---

[27] For a fuller discussion see D. Quinn Mills, "When Employees Make Concessions," *Harvard Business Review*, 61:3, May–June 1983, pp. 103–113. See also Richard B. Freeman, "In Search of Union Wage Concessions in Standard Data Sets," *Industrial Relations*, 25:2, Spring 1986, pp. 131–158.

[28] "A Work Revolution in U.S. Industry—More Flexible Rules on the Job Are Boosting Productivity," *Business Week*, May 16, 1983, p. 100.

[29] Daniel J. B. Mitchell, "Alternative Explanations of Union Wage Concessions," *California Management Review*, 28:1, Fall 1986, pp. 95–107.

Incentives

Pay systems can be designed to reward employees directly for their individual performances.[30] Many companies utilize such systems. These systems depend on a careful delineation of the elements of a job and on the setting of standards for the level of production expected. Records are kept of each worker's daily output, and the workers' rate of pay depends on the amount of work done, measured against the established standard. A minimum rate of pay protects·those workers who fail to meet the production standards, whether because of material shortages, machinery breakdown, or simply failure to perform. Ordinarily, however, a worker who repeatedly fails to perform well will be dismissed by the company.

Sometimes incentives apply not only to individuals but also to a group.

[30] Mitchell Lokiec, *Productivity and Incentives* (Columbia, S.C.: Bobbin Publications, 1977).

TABLE 17-3 JOB LOSSES IN SELECTED INDUSTRIES RECEIVING WAGE CONCESSIONS

	Cumulative percent change in employment	
Industry	Prerecession peak to recession trough*	Prerecession peak to July 1984
Copper ores	− 50.4	− 51.3
Construction	− 29.8	− 4.6
Metal cans	− 28.8	− 27.1
Primary aluminum	− 37.7	− 24.1
Fabricated structural metal	− 29.5	− 23.5
Farm machinery	− 48.4	− 43.2
Construction machinery	− 59.6	− 44.0
Metal working machinery	− 28.6	− 19.0
Motor vehicles and equipment	− 35.7	− 17.4
Blast furnace and basic steel products	− 43.7	− 41.2
Meat packing plants	− 17.2	− 12.0
Tires and inner tubes	− 27.9	− 20.7
Trucking and trucking terminals	− 17.3	− 4.8
Air transportation	− 5.4	4.7
Food stores	− †	13.5
Ship and boatbuilding	− 20.7	− 10.9
Total private nonfarm	− 4.4	4.9

*Peaks and troughs are specific to the individual industries. The absolute decline in employment totaled about 4 million in the industries listed; private nonfarm employment fell 1.9 million between February 1980 and December 1982.

†There was no trough for this industry.

Source: U.S. Department of Labor, *Supplement to Employment and Earnings*, July 1984, and recent monthly issues of *Employment and Earnings.*

TABLE 17-4 WHAT UNIONS SOUGHT IN RETURN FOR CONCESSIONS*

	Percentage of situations in which company sought concessions
More job security	46
No-layoff policy	17
Guaranteed number of jobs	17
Earnings protection	17
To represent more employees	23
Role in corporate governance	31
Consultation on investment	8
Changes in bargaining structure	8

*Data derived from interviews with 35 companies.
Source: Daniel Quinn Mills, "When Employees Make Concessions," *Harvard Business Review*, 61:3, May–June, 1983, pp. 108–109.

When a group incentive plan exists, each member of the group receives a certain proportion of the pay allocated to the group as a whole.

The most carefully systematized incentive programs are run by industrial engineers (professional employees who establish production standards). Basically, an industrial engineer observes workers performing a task and takes measurements of the time they require to complete it. From these measurements, the engineer develops a standard that the average worker is supposed to be able to meet. In one of the more popular systems, one widely used in textiles and apparel manufacturing, the company pays for units of production; the basic unit is a minute of work. A standard of work volume is, therefore, the 60-unit hour. Most production workers can exceed this and therefore earn more money. An incentive system is said to be "loose" if too many employees exceed the standard by too much. Generally a good system should not permit the expected average production volume for an employee to get above 20 percent beyond the standard, that is, beyond a 72-unit hour.

A company's staff of industrial engineers not only does time studies but also sets pay rates and tells the employees about the rates and about changes in the rates. Sometimes the incentive system is so crucial to the profitable operations of the firm that the industrial engineers even administer the payrolls of the company.

An incentive system must be kept up to date if it is to be effective. Changes in materials, machinery, and know-how cause standards to loosen in time. If standards become too loose, an incentive plan may be said to be "demoralized." In a demoralized plan workers meet their production quotas very quickly and have a great deal of leisure time. While such a situation may be comfortable for the workers, it often leads to bankruptcy for the firm.

On the other hand, the attempts of management to keep an incentive system up to date are a constant source of labor relations troubles. Workers often resent time studies when the studies bring technological improvements and the subsequent imposition of tighter production standards. The result is that, while many companies like the idea of using incentives to pay for workers' performance, they are unwilling to accept the problems that keeping an incentive system current entails. In consequence, incentive systems are less common in American industry than the more simple procedure of an hourly rate of pay.

JOB SECURITY VERSUS EMPLOYMENT SECURITY

Labor and management traditionally held conflicting views over what increased productivity means. Recent contract negotiations in the auto industry suggest, however, that a new, more common view of the problem may be developing.

Some unions have opposed the introduction of new technology or other changes designed to enhance productivity, fearing members' jobs would disappear. But recently negotiated agreements suggest that when both sides can begin to think of employment security (guarantees of employment at a company) rather than job security (security in a specific, detailed job defined by a job description or history), progress can be made toward meeting the concerns of both parties in this controversial area.

In the 1987 agreements between the United Auto Workers and the auto companies, the union achieved its goal of a guaranteed employment level (GEL) at many plants (subject only to a major business downturn) and in return agreed to improve productivity at the plants.

Innovative employment security provisions have been agreed to in the airline industry and in communications. The recasting of the problem from job security to employment security enabled labor and management to search together, not as adversaries but as joint problem solvers, for solutions to one of the major problems affecting the industry.

Is employment security for workers a positive motivator to better performance? The current evidence is yes. The few companies which provide employment security say that it helps workers to lay aside fears of job loss and get on with the job.[31] Is job insecurity a motivator also? The evidence is no. A study of workers in a single plant after a layoff showed that the productivity of those who remained did not rise. If insecurity were a motivator, the survivors of a layoff would be expected to perform better.[32]

CHAPTER SUMMARY

The efficiency of labor is referred to as productivity and can be measured in terms of output per work hour. However, productivity depends on a great many factors besides human effort, and there are important differences in

---

[31] D. Quinn Mills, *The IBM Lesson* (New York: Times Books, 1988). Also see Daniel Forbes, "The No-Layoff Payoff," *Dun's Business Month,* July 1985, pp. 64–66.

[32] Casey Ichniowski, *The Economic Performance of Survivors after Layoffs: A Plant-Level Study* (Cambridge, National Bureau of Economic Research, Working Paper No. 1807, 1986).

conceptions of what productivity measures. Managers tend to think of productivity in terms of employees working harder. Some economists have been interested in understanding what factors could improve productivity. These factors include increased capital investment, increased skill and education of the work force, and better methods of doing jobs.

Managers and the public feel that increased productivity should be encouraged. Unions and workers are more ambivalent. They fear loss of jobs and the demand for greater efforts. Both unionized and nonunionized workers will sometimes act together to oppose technological changes and to set a slower pace of work or a lower level of production than the company desires. Employees, in response, tighten discipline, change production, and try persuasion. Often, both management and the unions lack knowledge of the day-to-day processes in the workplace and are pessimistic about changing inefficient practices that are ingrained in the institution. Improved productivity demands a substantial effort and a comprehensive plan rather than a simple solution. Strikes over productivity issues have been lengthy and bitter. In some industries, employers have chosen to close inefficient plants rather than fight. Employers may use the NLRB or the courts to challenge work practices that inhibit productivity. However, because the law does not prohibit nonproductive practices per se, the use of litigation as a method of reducing nonproductive practices is of limited value.

But there are signs that labor and management are more willing than they have been in the past to seek solutions together over the issues of productivity and its relationship to employment security. Many see a more constructive and problem-solving approach between management and labor that is to the advantage of both.

QUESTIONS FOR THOUGHT AND DISCUSSION

1 What is productivity? Why are there labor-management conflicts over productivity? How can such conflicts be minimized? How can they be resolved when they occur?
2 Should pay be related to performance? What factors affect the success or failure of an incentive system? Why? What are some of the disadvantages of individual incentive systems?
3 Can productivity be increased? How? Do speedups work? What is the difference between efficient production and a speedup?
4 Should productivity be increased? Consider this question from the point of view of management, the unions, and the public in general.
5 Why does management often choose to move a plant rather than fight over issues of productivity? Why are managers sometimes afraid to raise issues of work productivity?
6 Why is productivity bargaining so complex and difficult?
7 What is featherbedding and what are some of its various forms? Can you propose any reasonable methods for preventing the proliferation of such noneconomical work practices as make-work rules, restrictions on the introduction of labor-saving

technology, and unnecessary jurisdictional restrictions on work assignments? Your proposals should carefully consider the needs of both management and the union.

8 What is the difference between job security and employment security? What is necessary for people to have employment security?

SELECTED READING

Bluestone, Barry, and Bennett Harrison, *The Deindustrialization of America: Plant Closings, Community Abandonment, and the Dismantling of Basic Industry* (New York: Basic Books, 1982).

Davis, Louis E., and Albert B. Cherns, eds., *The Quality of Working Life*, 2 vols. (New York: Free Press, 1975).

Garson, G. David, and M. P. Smith, eds., *Organizational Democracy: Participation and Self-Management* (Beverly Hills, Calif.: Sage, 1976).

McKersie, Robert B., and L. C. Hunter, eds., *Pay, Productivity and Collective Bargaining* (New York: St. Martin's Press, 1973).

Mills, D. Quinn, *The IBM Lesson* (New York: Times Books, 1988).

Sheppard, L. Stewart, and Donald C. Carroll, eds. *Working in the Twenty-First Century* (New York: Wiley, 1980).

Somers, Gerald G., et al., *Collective Bargaining and Productivity* (Madison, Wis.: Industrial Relations Research Association, 1975).

G

DIFFERENT PATTERNS OF RELATIONS IN THE PRIVATE SECTOR

The way in which collective bargaining is conducted differs dramatically among industries. Some industries utilize national-level bargaining between large companies and industrywide unions. Other industries rely on plant-by-plant bargaining or on bargaining by localities. At one extreme, General Motors and the United Automobile Workers negotiate one bargain, covering several hundred thousand unionized employees. At the other extreme, the building trades unions and their employers negotiate about 6000 separate bargains, locality by locality, to cover 1.5 million unionized workers.

The degree of centralization and other aspects of bargaining structure and practice affect the relative power of the unions and employers substantially. Also, bargaining structure affects what can actually be accomplished in collective bargaining. In some instances, the parties can act almost without regard to economic, political, and other conditions; in other instances, the parties are virtually forced to act as economic, political, and other conditions dictate.

CHAPTER 18

BARGAINING STRUCTURE: MANUFACTURING, MINING, AND CONSTRUCTION

THE STRUCTURE OF COLLECTIVE BARGAINING

The various forms of bargaining relationships that exist may be referred to as the "structure" of bargaining. There are several different ways to describe the bargaining structure of the American economy, and we shall review several of them here. But this review, or any review, is necessarily largely by example, because the actual structure is far too complex to be represented on paper. There are millions of places of work, hundreds of thousands of separate firms, almost 200,000 collective bargaining agreements, tens of thousands of local unions, and, therefore, far too many bargaining relationships to describe except by summary and example.

Bargaining structure is important because it affects other aspects of the collective bargaining relationship. Economists have suggested that bargaining structure affects bargaining outcomes such as wage inflation, job satisfaction, and the relative wage levels set for different jobs. Decentralized bargaining structures may lead to greater strike activity. Bargaining structure may also affect the balance of power between labor and management by influencing the economic and financial leverage each possesses.[1]

An Overall View of Bargaining Structure

Table 18-1 presents a summary of the bargaining structure of 42 important industries or sectors of the economy in the United States.[2] The classification

---

[1] Wallace E. Hendricks and Lawrence M. Kahn, "The Determinants of Bargaining Structure," *Industrial and Labor Relations Review*, 35:2, January 1982, pp. 181–195.

[2] The size of the list is dictated by convenience. It could be expanded considerably, although without significant additional value in providing examples.

TABLE 18-1 STRUCTURE OF BARGAINING

| Relations among negotiating units | Type of employer negotiating unit | | |
| | Multiemployer A | Individual employer | |
		Companywide B	Company subunit (plant) C
I An industrywide agreement for unionized companies	Bituminous coal Trucking (not local cartage)	Postal Service	
II Strong national pattern	Glass containers Fur Baseball, football Basic steel	Nonferrous metals Meat packing Aluminum Cigarettes Containers, metal Automobiles	Oil refining Cement
III Middle national pattern	Apparel	Shoes Railings Airlines Rubber Textiles	Plumbing manufacture Telephones
IV Weak national pattern	Longshoring Maritime	Electrical machinery Cement	
V Regional pattern	Farm workers	Supermarkets Shipbuilding Lumber Furniture	Paper converting Pulp and paper
VI No pattern (or local pattern)	Hotels Building construction	Local transit Utilities Public education Health Newspapers and printing	Chemicals

Source: Adapted and updated from David H. Greenberg, "The Structure of Collective Bargaining and Some of Its Determinants," *Proceedings* of the Industrial Relations Research Association, 1966, p. 345.

is by type of employer negotiating unit and by relationships between bargaining units. The majority of the industries listed involve privately owned companies, but some sectors operated by governmental agencies are included also. The table does not reflect the type of union negotiating unit or other aspects of bargaining structure, which will be mentioned later.

The table has 18 separate categories, only two of which (IC and IVC) are without an entry. The absence of entry IC indicates that no major industry is characterized as having negotiations with individual companies at the plant level but also having industrywide bargaining. In fact, the two concepts are substantially inconsistent with each other. Thus, we see that industrywide negotiations with a multiemployer bargaining unit take place in such industries as bituminous coal and over-the-road trucking (IA). Alternatively, an industrywide agreement is negotiated by a single company, the U.S. Postal Service, now a private corporation (IB). The agreement is industrywide because the Postal Service has a legal monopoly on transmitting the mail. The table also suggests by the frequency of entries in column B that negotiations by individual employers on a companywide basis are most common in the United States, but that the relations among negotiating units vary across the entire spectrum from a strong national pattern in the settlement to no pattern (or local patterns). Negotiations on a plant basis and negotiations on a multiemployer basis are both less common.

Additional Perspectives on Bargaining Structure

Table 18-1 has certain limitations. It does not indicate whether in the industries identified a single union or several unions exist. Nor does the table indicate whether a single union bargains with one employer or several, or whether a national union or the locals alone are engaged in negotiations. Nor does the table indicate where a single corporation is involved in several industries, rather than only one. Finally, the table fails to describe whether bargaining occurs at a single level or at multiple levels. Each of these items is an additional, important aspect of bargaining structure.

Table 18-2 reclassifies the 42 industries from Table 18-1, indicating the characteristic size of employers and the number of the national unions with which the employers negotiate. Nine categories are given in the table, and at least one industry is identified in each category. The table shows, for example, that in petroleum refining, automobiles, and basic steel and rubber manufacturing, a single national union negotiates with several large companies (IA). In contrast, in interstate (or over-the-road) trucking, a single national union (the Teamsters) negotiates with many small companies (IIA). The table suggests that industries usually do not have a single union, or many unions, but instead, a small group of national unions (column B). Once again, the table demonstrates the wide range of bargaining structures that different industries have.

Bargaining structure may also be described by identifying the industries in which individual national labor unions are engaged in bargaining. Some na-

TABLE 18-2 INDUSTRIES CLASSIFIED BY NUMBER OF NATIONAL UNIONS AND BY CHARACTERISTICS OF EMPLOYERS

Characteristics of employers	Number of national unions representing workers		
	Single national union (primarily) A	Few unions B	Many unions C
I Large companies primarily	Petroleum refining Automobiles Basic steel Rubber Containers, metal	Railways Meat packing Textiles Utilities Cigarettes Telephones Chemicals Electrical machinery Airlines Glass containers Postal Service Aluminum	Supermarkets Nonferrous metals Plumbing manufacture
II Small companies primarily	Trucking Fur Shoes	Longshoring Apparel Furniture Farm workers	Building construction Newspapers and printing
III Both large and small companies	Bituminous coal Baseball, football Paper converting	Cement Lumber Pulp and paper Hotels Public education	Maritime Local transit Health

tional unions deal only with a single industry, others with several. The Teamsters, for example, represent employees in many industries, including interstate trucking, local cartage, retail food, construction, and various manufacturing industries. The Steelworkers negotiate for employees in basic steel, steel fabricating, cans, aluminum, nonferrous metals, and even for small numbers of employees in construction, chemicals, and other industries. The International Brotherhood of Electrical Workers represents employees in construction, utilities, electrical manufacturing, telephones, and broadcasting. Other unions, like the Graphic Arts International Association or the American Federation of Television and Radio Artists, are confined largely to a single industry or a closely related group of industries.

Similarly, individual companies may possess subsidiaries in many different industries and may negotiate in several different industries with different unions. The rise of the conglomerate corporations has made this much more common in recent years, but multi-industry companies are not new; United States Steel, for example, through its various subsidiaries, negotiates agreements in not only basic steel, but also steel fabrication, bituminous coal, cement, and construction. The total complexity of bargaining structure becomes apparent as one examines it from various perspectives.

However, students should not expect to absorb all the material contained in these tables. Rather, they should study the tables as examples of the variety and complexity of the nation's collective bargaining structure. The tables should also be of use as reference points in the discussion of the specific form and development of collective bargaining in various sectors of the economy.

Multilevel Bargaining

Bargaining structure is not only a matter of who bargains with whom. In addition, there may be different methods of bargaining about different issues. Often, bargaining occurs at different levels with respect to different issues. When this occurs, certain major items (including wages and grievance procedures, for example) may be included in the primary contract between the parties, but there may also be negotiated supplemental agreements. These supplemental agreements are ordinarily of two types. First, special agreements may be negotiated by the primary parties (for example, a national union and an automobile company) to deal with certain specific issues, such as pensions, benefit plans, wage incentives, or job evaluation. For instance, General Motors and the United Automobile Workers negotiate a 6-year pension agreement, while the national contract between the parties is only for 3 years. Second, when there are companywide negotiations, plant-level supplements dealing with such matters as working conditions at the individual facilities may also be negotiated. Local union leadership and plant managers at each location negotiate these supplemental agreements, and strikes are common when impasses occur in the negotiations. Plant-level supplements are commonly negotiated in automobiles, basic steel, and similar industries involving multiplant companies and companywide or industrywide negotiations.

The variety of bargaining arrangements is very great and beggars classification or generalization. In the rubber industry, for example, wages and benefits have been negotiated on an alternating schedule, with benefits agreements running longer than wage agreements (as in autos). In a particular multiplant division of the Mead Corporation, seven separate local unions of five different national unions have negotiated jointly for a pension plan for many years. Other aspects of the contracts between the corporation and the union are negotiated separately with the different unions.[3]

---

[3] "Locals Favored...," *The Paperworker* (published by the United Paperworkers International Union), March 1975, p. 3.

In general, such particular arrangements in different industries seem to be increasing, and they add markedly to the complexity of the bargaining process. The existence of such arrangements also makes it very difficult to generalize about the degree to which bargaining is centralized in an industry.[4]

Centralized Bargaining

Centralized, or industrywide, bargaining, as practiced in the basic steel industry, for example, has been the subject of considerable criticism. It is argued that centralized bargaining has two major disadvantages. First, it is said that by giving the labor union a monopoly of the industry's labor force and eliminating competition from other unions or unorganized workers, centralized bargaining allows the union to negotiate a monopoly wage. This wage is alleged to be higher than would otherwise be the case and to come not out of profits but out of the pockets of consumers through price increases.[5] Second, centralized bargaining is alleged to take away the influence of individual employees on negotiations and to destroy democratic participation in trade unions. George Brooks, once a trade union official and later a professor at Cornell University, has been especially forceful in presenting this point of view. He argues that the most important characteristic of collective bargaining structure is the locus of decision making and authority. And, Brooks says, for years there has been a steady tendency in manufacturing toward more centralized bargaining. The result has been a decline of the energy and vitality of local unions. Brooks favors plant-centered unionism, with collective bargaining at the plant level only.[6]

Several studies in the mid-1960s confirmed the tendency Brooks cited toward centralized negotiations. In the agricultural implements industry (involving such companies as International Harvester and John Deere), for example, Arlyn Melcher categorized bargaining structure as follows:

Physical location of negotiations	Contract results		
	Master contract	Master and local supplements	Local supplements
Central	1	2	3
Central and local	4	5	6
Local	7	8	9

---

[4] E. Robert Livernash, "Special and Local Negotiations," in John T. Dunlop and N. W. Chamberlain, eds., *Frontiers of Collective Bargaining* (New York: Harper & Row, 1967), pp. 27–49.

[5] Fritz Machlup, "Monopolistic Wage Determination," *Wage Determination and the Economics of Liberalism* (Washington, D.C.: Chamber of Commerce of the United States, 1974), pp. 49–82.

[6] George W. Brooks, "Unions and the Structure of Collective Bargaining," in Arnold Weber, ed., *The Structure of Collective Bargaining* (Glencoe, Ill.: Free Press, 1960), pp. 123–140.

This classification yields nine different possible combinations of physical location of negotiations and contract results. Melcher found a trend toward the category marked 1, central negotiations and a master contract.[7]

Congress for many years debated amending the Taft-Hartley Act to prohibit industrywide bargaining (the Ball Amendment). At one point, this amendment failed to pass by a single vote in the U.S. Senate. Had it passed, bargaining might have been restricted to the company level by law. The company level is also, as we see in Melcher's description, subject to considerable centralization, however.

Events in the 1970s and 1980s have moderated concern about centralized bargaining. In many industries the emergence of important bargaining about local supplements to industrywide or companywide agreements has caused bargaining to become more like Melcher's category 5 (central and local negotiations for a master agreement and local supplements) instead of the highly centralized category 1. For example, in 1985 the major companies in the basic steel industry ended a 30-year practice of joint national negotiations with the United Steelworkers of America. Major economic problems have also arisen in industries with highly decentralized bargaining, such as supermarkets and construction. Thus, it no longer appears to many managers that they would have more difficult labor relations if the bargaining were centralized.

A National Bargaining Round

Since many large industries in the United States negotiate on a 3-year cycle, it is possible to view the economy as a whole as having a cycle in collective bargaining. This cycle is ordinarily referred to as a bargaining, or wage, "round."

When does one round end and another start? As with any ongoing cycle, the choice of a starting point is discretionary with the observer. In recent years it has been customary to use the negotiation of the national master freight agreement between the Teamsters and the trucking companies as the start of a 3-year round. In this conception, there was a 1976–1978 negotiating round as follows:

Negotiation	Expiration date of agreement
National master freight (trucking)	March 1976
Rubber manufacturing	June 1976
Automobile manufacturing	September 1976
Basic steel manufacturing	July 1977
Bituminous coal mining	December 1977 (settled after a long strike in March 1978)

[7] Arlyn S. Melcher, "Central Negotiations and the Master Contract: An Analysis of Their Implications for Collective Bargaining," *Labor Law Journal*, 16:6, June 1965, p. 353.

Similarly, there was a 1979–1981 wage round as follows:

Negotiation	Expiration date of agreement
National master freight	March 1979
Rubber manufacturing	June 1979
Automobile manufacturing	September 1979
Basic steel manufacturing	July 1980
Bituminous coal mining	March 1981

According to this concept, as each negotiation proceeds it affects those that follow it. Central to the concept of a national bargaining round is the assertion that there is a national pattern in bargaining among otherwise largely unrelated industries.

Yet, in 1984, the regularity of the round was challenged. Under the pressure of an intense recession, the automobile companies negotiated several months prior to the expiration date of the agreement, and they concluded a 2-year agreement, not a 3-year agreement. Hence, in 1984, the auto industry negotiated again—this time they concluded a 3-year agreement. Autos had moved their negotiations from the first year of a round to the last. This altered round, the 1982–1984 round, was as follows:

Negotiation	Expiration date of agreement
National master freight	March 1982
Rubber manufacturing	April 1982
Automobile manufacturing	April 1982 and September 1984
Basic steel manufacturing	July 1983
Bituminous coal mining	September 1984

By 1985–1987 companies and unions were so much engrossed in their own separate problems that the relationship of one negotiation to another was lost. Adverse economic conditions had eroded comparison bargaining. But this is not to say that the practice may not reassert itself.

The concept of a national bargaining round is controversial. There are many difficulties with the concept. First, there are many industries in the United States which negotiate and as the number considered is increased beyond the five listed here, it becomes hard to fit them into the pattern.

Second, it is difficult to show that the bargains reached in different industries are really related in some important way to each other. Several researchers have tried, with generally inconclusive results, to demonstrate statistically that bargaining rounds exist.[8]

---

[8] Daniel J. B. Mitchell, *Unions, Wages and Inflation* (Washington, D.C.: Brookings, 1980). Also, Clinton Bourden, *Pattern Bargaining, Wage Determination, and Inflation: Some Preliminary Observations on the 1976–78 Wage Round* (Boston: Harvard University Graduate School of Business Administration, Working Paper 78-30, September 1979).

Although the concept of a national bargaining round cannot be said to have been shown scientifically to be valid, it is often useful in practice. Over a 3-year cycle, as one industry negotiates and then another, public attention follows first one negotiation and then another. The representatives of labor and management in each industry keep themselves fully aware of developments in the negotiations of those industries which precede their own negotiations. And while no industry follows slavishly the pattern set by another, still there is an influence exerted by each negotiation on those that follow it.

BASIC FEATURES OF MANUFACTURING

Manufacturing enterprises are at the core of an industrial society and are the type of economic activity most often brought up in discussions of labor relations. Manufacturing is the single most important sector of our economy, now involving some 19.2 percent of total employment. For many decades manufacturing has been of roughly similar importance in our economy. During this long period, agricultural employment has fallen substantially as a percentage of the whole and service employment has risen considerably. Yet manufacturing has remained largely stable as a percentage of total economic activity, though it has dropped off slightly in the 1980s (see Table 18-3).

Manufacturing ordinarily involves a factory at a fixed location, in which machinery is installed. Materials are delivered to the factory and products are shipped from it. The work force reports on a fixed schedule for work and is usually closely supervised by managerial personnel. These characteristics of manufacturing employment are not exactly like those in other sectors of the

TABLE 18-3   DISTRIBUTION OF EMPLOYMENT BY SECTOR OF THE ECONOMY, 1986

	Percentage of total employment
Total employment (nonagricultural establishments)	100.0
Private, total	83.3
Mining	0.7
Contract construction	4.9
Manufacturing	19.2
Transportation and public utilities	5.3
Wholesale and retail trade	23.8
Finance, insurance, and real estate	6.3
Services	23.1
Government, total	16.7
Federal	2.9
State and local	13.8

Source: Bureau of Labor Statistics, *Employment and Earnings*, 34:1, January 1987, p. 223.

TABLE 18-4 CHARACTERISTICS OF EMPLOYMENT IN MANUFACTURING

- A fixed place of production
- A relatively stable work force
- A close identification of workers with the company
- A relatively regular working schedule
- A relatively well-defined set of tasks for each worker
- A work force made up of a relatively large proportion of unskilled and semiskilled workers
- A relatively closely supervised work environment
- Repetitive output of a product or a product line, as opposed to custom-designed items

economy, and they should be carefully noted by the reader (see Table 18-4). While other sectors of the economy possess some of these attributes, no other sector combines them all.

Many important features of labor relations in manufacturing derive from the basic characteristics of employment in the manufacturing sector. For example, collective bargaining agreements commonly involve only a single company (although there are exceptions in certain industries). Also, agreements must include provisions relating to working conditions specific to each particular plant, although there may be a more general agreement with a company that covers items common to all its facilities. Great concern is expressed in labor negotiations in manufacturing about the competitive status of employees (including, for example, which employees are to be laid off first and which are to be given first chance at recalls, promotions, or transfers). But there is almost no concern about hiring decisions—these are left to management. These concerns are in dramatic contrast to the concerns of workers and unions in construction, for example. In construction, employers negotiate as a group (in associations) and agreements cover all the work sites in a geographic area. It is very uncommon to negotiate specific standards for a single job site (unless it is a very large project). Also, since projects open and close continually and there is no job security in construction, there is little concern among workers about who is laid off or who is eligible for recall or promotion. However, there is great concern about how companies conduct their hiring. Thus, the characteristics of employment in different sectors of the economy determine what issues are of importance in bargaining and even the manner in which bargaining is conducted.

Manufacturing is not a homogeneous group of activities (although all manufacturing shares the characteristics we have identified in Table 18-4). Manufacturing consists of many different industries, each of which is unique in its own way. Some manufacturing industries are very large, some quite small. Some are located in a single geographic region, others are nationwide. Some involve very profitable firms, some do not. Some industries are expanding rapidly, some are stagnant, and some are declining. Some industries produce a wide range of products, some very few. Some production processes involve a relatively large input of labor, others involve a relatively large input of machinery and/or materials. All these differences in manufacturing industries are reflected in variations in the labor relations of the industries.

In manufacturing, as elsewhere in the economy, labor relations defy simple description or explanation. The most likely suppositions are often incorrect. For example, very large, nationwide, multicompany industries (like autos or steel) often have a simpler bargaining structure than far smaller industries with fewer companies (like some building materials industries). Furthermore, in some industries bargaining occurs at the plant level, so that employees are able to take an active, direct role in negotiations. In other industries negotiations occur through representatives at the national level, and the individual employee, although consulted as part of a group and kept informed, ordinarily has no direct role in the negotiations process. Yet, generally in the United States, wages and conditions of work are better for workers in the latter than the former case. Can one conclude that there is a trade-off between economic gain and personal participation for the individual worker? Probably not. But the question points out the difficulty of generalizing from a group of labor relations systems that vary so greatly.

In the following pages of this chapter we shall review briefly the labor relations structure and experience of the automobile manufacturing industry. It is chosen for its intrinsic interest and because it exemplifies a form of labor-management structure. While the particular arrangements in an industry do reflect a historical adjustment to the conditions of that industry and therefore cannot be said to be random, particular arrangements are not inflexible either.

THE AUTOMOBILE INDUSTRY

The Companies

Three large companies dominate the production of automobiles in the United States: General Motors, Ford, and Chrysler. In total sales, GM is the largest by a considerable margin, but Ford and Chrysler are both giants by the standards of most industries. Each company is not only an automobile company but a broadly diversified enterprise with major revenues from the sale of products other than automobiles. There is also a fourth domestic automobile producer, very much smaller than the other companies, American Motors.[9]

In a development which may have major consequences in the future, Japanese auto companies have begun locating manufacturing plants in the United States. By 1988 Honda, Nissan (Datsun), and Toyota had U.S. plants and Mazda was preparing to open a facility.

The Union

The production employees of the American automobile companies are members of the United Automobile Workers (UAW). Two Japanese companies

---

[9] Lawrence J. White, *The Automobile Industry* (Cambridge, Mass.: Harvard University Press, 1972).

TABLE 18-5 THE UNITED AUTOMOBILE WORKERS (UAW)

Headquarters	Detroit, Mich.
Membership	1,017,000
Local unions (number)	1,403

Source: Bureau of National Affairs, *Directory of U.S. Labor Organizations, 1986–1987* (Washington, D.C., 1986, p. 40).

have UAW representation in their American plants (Toyota and Mazda) and two do not (Honda and Nissan). The union is headquartered in Detroit (see Table 18-5) and has more than 1 million members. The UAW is not confined to employees of the auto companies, however. Many other firms operate as suppliers to the automobile companies, manufacturing and selling parts. The UAW has organized the employees of many of these companies. The UAW also represents the employees of the major companies that manufacture trucks, agricultural implements and machinery, and construction machinery. Further, the UAW represents employees in the manufacture of aircraft and plumbing fixtures and even some public employees in Michigan.

Collective Bargaining

The UAW has a department for each of the automobile companies. The departments are composed of the locals at the plants of each company and a staff that is knowledgeable about the company involved. Each company has a national agreement with the UAW, with local supplements, negotiated at the plant level, to the national agreement. The national agreement establishes the economic package and certain nationally applicable working conditions and dispute procedures. The local supplements deal with conditions of work, grievances, and the like at each facility.

There is no industrywide bargaining in autos, but there are companywide negotiations. The national contracts between the UAW and Ford and General Motors expire on a single date, usually after a 3-year term. The UAW does not seek to bargain simultaneously with all three companies, however. It picks a target company, announces its choice publicly, and seeks to settle an agreement with that company. Once a settlement is reached with the target company, the union will try to obtain an agreement on similar terms with the remaining companies. (The Chrysler settlement is made a year after the Ford and GM contracts.)

The selection of a target company carries with it the identification of the company that will be struck if an agreement is not reached before the expiration date of the contract. Much of the strategy involved in the choice of a target involves the determination of which company the UAW may hope to strike most successfully. But the union must also seek a company that is profitable enough to give a good settlement and one that is not so profitable that the other companies would not meet the terms of the pattern settlement.

TABLE 18-6 THE UAW's TARGET COMPANY IN NATIONAL
AUTOMOBILE NEGOTIATIONS, 1955–1987

1955	Ford
1958	Ford
1961	American
1964	Chrysler
1967	Ford
1970	General Motors
1973	Chrysler
1976	Ford
1979	General Motors
1982	Ford
1984	General Motors
1987	Ford

Table 18-6 lists the UAW's target companies from 1955 to 1987. Ford was selected six times; General Motors, three times; and Chrysler, twice. The company selected as the UAW's target in any given year is in a difficult position. It faces the unpleasant likelihood of being shut down by a strike while its competitors are producing. Yet it has the opportunity to seek a settlement on grounds more favorable to it than to its competitors.

After the national agreement is reached with a company, local negotiations go ahead. Strikes often occur at certain plants. For example, when a parts manufacturing plant is on strike over local issues, the whole company may come to a standstill because of the lack of that part (or parts). From the company's point of view, a general shutdown brought on by a few local strikes is very expensive. This has been occurring more frequently in recent years and has made the companies increasingly dissatisfied with the entire bargaining procedure.

Business Difficulties and Union-Management Cooperation at Chrysler

In 1979 Chrysler ran into serious business difficulties. Foreign automobile manufacturers (particularly Japanese firms) were taking a larger proportion of the American market. And Chrysler products were also losing sales to other U.S. manufacturers. In order to avoid bankruptcy, Chrysler sought and obtained, with UAW support, financial assistance from the banks and a loan guarantee from the federal government. For its part, the UAW accepted lower wages and fringe benefits at Chrysler than at GM and Ford. In effect, Chrysler joined American Motors as an exception to the pattern bargaining in the automobile industry.

In return for its accommodation to the economic difficulties of Chrysler, the UAW obtained significant advances in its relationship to the corporation. First, the national president of the UAW was elected to

Chrysler's board of directors. Second, the UAW obtained a role in determining the investment strategy of the pension funds managed by Chrysler on behalf of its members. Specifically, the union and Chrysler agreed that in the future, part of the company's pension contributions will be used to fund "socially desirable projects," such as housing for low-income persons, rather than to buy common stocks or government securities, as in the past.[10]

Work Standards and Skilled Workers

An important peculiarity of automobile labor relations is that the companies (GM in particular) will not agree to include certain areas of dispute in the coverage of the grievance and arbitration procedures of the national contract. The establishment of production standards (such as the speed of an assembly line) and health and safety standards and the setting of wages on new jobs are excluded under the GM agreement. The union retains its right to strike in disputes over these issues and exercises it in some instances. The highly publicized strikes at the GM assembly plant at Lordstown, Ohio, in the early 1970s were largely a result of work standards disputes not subject to arbitration. In 1976 the company made a special effort to clear up a backlog of grievances at the Lordstown plant. The effort was welcomed by the union and was apparently successful in establishing a better labor relations climate at the plant.

The position of skilled workers in automobile industry negotiations is unique. The UAW is an industrial union, including in its membership unskilled, semiskilled, and skilled workers. Skilled workers are a well-organized numerical minority in the union (making up perhaps 20 percent of the UAW's automobile industry membership). The National Labor Relations Board has effectively prevented skilled workers from leaving the UAW by insisting that such a secession (called "craft severance") can take place only through a companywide election. This procedure has proved too costly for the skilled tradespeople to attempt, but still the skilled trades have formed a separate caucus in the UAW and have sought a degree of independence. In 1966 the UAW's constitution was amended to permit the skilled trades to vote separately on a contract offer. In 1973 the skilled trades rejected the national-level settlement with Ford. The UAW, however, did not permit the skilled trades to strike, nor did it declare the Ford settlement rejected (since the majority of all Ford employees had voted in favor of the contract). But the union did go back to the bargaining table with Ford to seek certain adjustments in the new contract on behalf of the skilled workers. The UAW's experience with the discontent of skilled workers demonstrates that industrial unionism does not resolve the conflict between skilled and other workers but merely makes it internal to a single union.

---

[10] Robert B. Reich, "Bailout," *Yale Journal on Regulation,* 2:26, 1985, pp. 163–224.

Pattern Bargaining beyond the Big Three

After the national settlement is reached with the big three automobile companies, the UAW negotiates with many parts manufacturers and other suppliers of the automobile industry normally seeking to obtain settlements similar to the agreements with the big three. Often, however, smaller companies cannot afford the automobile package, and an agreement less favorable to the union is negotiated. A study of the UAW's bargaining in the period from 1946 to 1957, for example, showed that only 26 percent of the companies (employing 40 percent of the employees in the sample) followed the autos pattern closely. The rest of the companies obtained agreements below the autos pattern.[11]

VARIETIES OF BARGAINING PATTERNS

This discussion of bargaining in the steel and automobile industries illustrates the variety of arrangements that exist in various industries.

Chapter 1 pointed out that although the image most people have of union-management relations is that of one company dealing with one union, in fact most relationships are more complicated. In addition to the one-to-one situation, the major types of union-management relationships are:

- Several companies dealing with a single union
- Several unions dealing with a single company
- Several companies dealing with several unions

Nor does this list exhaust the variety of arrangements. For example, a single company may negotiate with one or more unions on a plant-by-plant basis, or in a single negotiation at the company level, or it may do *both*. If it does both, one level of negotiation may precede the other or they may occur simultaneously.

Whatever form a bargaining relationship takes, it is likely to have some relation to certain other employers and unions. In a sense, all collective bargaining relationships—indeed, all circumstances by which wages and conditions of employment are established—are related to each other because each is part of the economic and social system as a whole. In the overall system, all elements are subject to influence from all other elements. For example, in economics there exists a special area of study in which the interactions of all wages and prices are studied for their impact on each other. (It is called general equilibrium analysis.) There is no such formal name for the study of the interactions of various companies and unions in the collective bargaining process taken as a whole, but we speak of certain interrelationships as involving "patterns" in negotiations.

Just as certain wages and prices are closely related while others are not, certain negotiations are very much interdependent while others are less

[11] Harold M. Levinson, "Pattern Bargaining: A Case Study of the Automobile Workers," *Quarterly Journal of Economics*, 74:2, May 1960, pp. 296–317.

so. When a group of negotiations is very closely related, we may speak of "pattern bargaining." Essentially, pattern bargaining means that a particular union and employer, by arrangement, settle their own negotiations on the basis of a pattern developed elsewhere. Examples of pattern bargaining can be found in virtually all sectors of the American economy. However, there are several distinct types of pattern bargaining:

• *Strong national pattern.* Once the pattern-setting agreement is made, other unions and employers follow the pattern very closely.

• *Middle national pattern.* Once the pattern is established, there may be minor deviations made by particular unions and companies.

• *Weak national pattern.* An initial agreement may or may not become a pattern or may become a pattern for some settlements but not others.

• *Regional pattern.* A pattern-setting settlement is followed, weakly or strongly, by all other units in a particular geographic region.

What settlement becomes the pattern? In many instances, a pattern is established by an initial, or first, settlement, regardless of which firm, plant, or union makes it. In other instances, a particular firm and union set the pattern each time.

In the deep recession of 1981–1982 several companies and unions abandoned pattern bargaining to try to work out contracts specially designed for their own economic situations. As pattern bargaining declined, some observers pronounced it dead. This was probably premature, however, since economic recovery beginning in 1983 restored the patterns to some degree.[12]

Why do employers and unions follow patterns at all? Many don't, of course, but those that do have the following primary reasons. Employers will follow a pattern ordinarily because they do not want to have higher labor costs than their competitors. Although the company might like to pay less, perhaps, than the pattern, the union would probably strike to resist that. The union follows a pattern because it can show its members that they receive as much as other people in their line of work and because it can show the company that its labor costs are comparable with those of its competitors. The union might like to receive more than the pattern allows, but the company is likely to resist this strongly. Thus, a pattern is followed because neither side objects strongly to following it, but each objects strongly to not following it: The union objects to receiving less, and management objects to giving more.

MINING

Basic Features

Mining industries are not a large part of the American economy in terms of employment or revenues, but they have a strategic spot in the economy and have figured largely in American labor relations. The major mining industry

[12] Audrey Freedman and William E. Fulmer, "Last Rites for Pattern Bargaining," *Harvard Business Review*, 60:2, March–April 1982, pp. 30–34ff.

is bituminous coal. Coal production is currently concentrated east of the Mississippi but is growing in the West. The labor relations of the industry are scarred with violence. It is characterized by industrywide bargaining and a single national union.

In 1986 mining employed some 716,000 people in the United States, approximately 0.7 percent of total nonagricultural employment. Coal was much the largest of the mining industries, employing some 165,000 people.

Employment in mining has certain distinguishing characteristics. Perhaps the most important of these is the isolation of the workplace and living quarters of the miners from the places where a majority of the population lives. Living in small communities made up primarily of miners, and at a distance from other citizens, miners have developed a strong sense of their own identity and a sense of separation from the broader society around them. These attributes have helped to create strong loyalties among miners to their unions.

The Companies   Companies in the coal industry are widely diversified in size and type. Independent coal companies, many of them small operations, produce about half of the coal mined. The rest is produced by subsidiaries of noncoal companies, including some known as "captive suppliers" to coal users. Important groups are subsidiaries of oil companies, steel companies, and electric utilities. Both steel and electric companies use coal as fuel and are heavily dependent on independent producers as well as on their own captive mines.

Different economic interests exist among the major ownership groups. First, the steel companies are concerned with the impact of the price of coal on the price of steel. Second, the oil companies are not committed to coal itself and may move their investment out of coal if returns are not adequate. Third, the independent coal operators are tied to coal as their primary business. Thus, some companies are fully committed to coal, while for others it is at least partly a sideline.

The Bituminous Coal Operators Association (BCOA) represents the industry in national collective bargaining. Within the BCOA, attitudes toward labor relations are as diverse as the economic interests of the producers. The independent coal operators tend to view labor primarily as part of the production process. Few of these firms have labor relations professionals. The steel companies' need for cheap coal to help them make steel produced in the United States competitively leads them to press for low wage settlements. They are also influenced by their relationships with the sophisticated and fairly cooperative United Steelworkers, who represented employees in the steel production process. The oil companies consider themselves enlightened in industrial relations. The BCOA's internal governance system gives the few large companies the greatest influence—despite the fact that the BCOA is overwhelmingly composed of small companies.

Despite these divergent interests, there are powerful incentives holding the BCOA together, and the companies prefer a joint negotiation with the miners' union.

The Union   The United Mine Workers of America (UMW) represents employees in the coal industry. An industrial rather than a crafts union, it represents all workers at the mines, both skilled and unskilled. The UMW also includes building and construction workers who are employed by contractors to do construction work at the mines. The UMW's membership is approximately 180,000 active miners and 90,000 retired workers. UMW membership is virtually confined to the coal industry.

The UMW was formed from the merger in 1890 of two early unions. Poor leadership and intense internal strife characterized its early years. Chronic excess production capacity and cutthroat price competition plagued the industry. Collective bargaining contracts were often violated by owners. Illegal wage cuts and strikebreaking were common.

The union grew strong and united under the leadership of John L. Lewis. Lewis was president of the UMW from 1920 to 1959 and was one of the most prominent people in the U.S. labor movement.

During the 1950s employment declined in coal mining. The union sought peaceful contract settlements and constant meetings with coal operators in order to sustain smooth, continuous production. The union also established stiff penalties for wildcat strikes. Union policy endorsed mechanization of coal production and the closing of smaller, inefficient mines even at the cost of increased unemployment. This policy was an effort to protect the industry from cheaper alternative energy sources, and thereby to preserve employment opportunities for miners.

Lewis retired in December 1959. In his 40 years of leadership, he stamped union loyalty deep in the hearts of the miners. He left a legacy of union solidarity and absolute respect for a picket line.

Collective Bargaining   Ordinarily the UMW and the BCOA negotiate a national contract every 3 years. The contract is complex. The 1978 agreement had 30 major articles and covered 101 general job classifications and almost 1000 job titles.

Health insurance and pension benefits for miners were provided by a series of special trusts. The trusts were funded by contributions made by employers for each hour worked and for each ton of coal mined. Operators also made contributions to the trusts for each ton of coal mined by non-UMW workers.

Prior to the 1974 contract negotiations, all health and pension benefits were paid for by a single fund, to which employers paid a royalty on each ton of coal produced. Surface mines produced far more coal per worker day than underground mines, and yet employees of each type of mine drew equally on the benefits. This meant that surface mine operators were paying substantially more to cover each employee's benefits than underground operators. A dispute over this issue almost broke apart the BCOA before 1974.

As part of the 1974 negotiations, the employers developed a plan to restructure the trusts, and the union accepted the plan. The 1950 pension trust would provide pensions for miners who retired prior to 1976. The 1950 benefit trust would provide health benefits to the same group. (About 82,000 miners and surviving spouses were covered under these plans.) The 1950 trusts would be funded by royalty payments as in the past. Pension and health benefits for current miners and their families and for miners who retired after 1976 would be funded by employer contributions made for each hour worked. These were the 1974 pension trust and 1974 benefit trust. Over a period of years, the new funds would replace the old ones, with benefits costs being tied to employee hours worked.[13]

The late 1970s and early 1980s saw substantial unemployment among the UMW's members and the growth of nonunion coal production. After an especially long and bitter strike in 1977–1978, the union and the companies slowly began to improve their relationship[14]—leading to a 40-month agreement signed in September 1984—the first settlement without a strike in many years.

CONSTRUCTION

Construction is not an industry (like autos, for example), but a sector of the economy (like manufacturing or mining). It is not as large a sector as manufacturing, but still it employs some 4 to 5 million people and includes several hundred thousand firms. The sector may be subdivided either by type of construction product or by specialization of firms. The major branches of construction by type of product are residential buildings, nonresidential buildings, highways, dams and other engineering projects, pipelines, electrical transmission lines, and industrial and power plants. If the specialization of contractors is used to categorize firms, the resulting major divisions are general contracting, heavy and highway contracting, and specialty trades contracting (e.g., electrical, plumbing, and masonry contracting).[15]

Construction is a sector of the economy which has many unique features. A physical product is produced, as in manufacturing, but instead of being produced at a plant and shipped to a customer, it is produced at a site selected by the purchaser. Nor is the product standardized. Instead, each facility is designed to order, on a custom basis. The product is not priced and advertised for sale, but instead a unique price is determined for each project. Rather than the customer's buying a completed product, the customer contracts with a particular construction firm to build the project for a fixed price or on a cost-incurred basis.

These characteristics of the product and its pricing have a major effect on the characteristics of employment in construction.[16] Table 18-7 lists several

---

[13] William Miernyk, "Coal," in Gerald G. Somers, ed., *Collective Bargaining: Contemporary American Experience* (Madison, Wis.: Industrial Relation Research Association, 1980), p. 32.

[14] Charles R. Perry, *Collective Bargaining and the Decline of the United Mine Workers* (Philadelphia: Industrial Research Unit, Wharton School, University of Pennsylvania, 1984).

[15] Government statisticians use the classification by constructor specialization in reporting employment and earning data, and by type of product in reporting expenditures and output.

[16] See "Strategic Factors in Industrial Relations in the Construction Industry," *Labour and Society*, 4:4, October 1979, pp. 415–432.

TABLE 18-7 CHARACTERISTICS OF EMPLOYMENT IN CONSTRUCTION

Considerable shifting of employees between work sites
Considerable shifting of employees between employers
Identification by the employee with a craft or occupation, not with an employer
A relatively large portion of skilled workers
Much self-supervision
Very unstable employment opportunities
Dangerous and often difficult work conditions
Intermixing of employees of different employers at a single project site
Construction of nonstandard (i.e., custom-designed) products
Intermixing of members of different unions at a single project site

aspects of construction employment which, taken as a whole, cause the sector to have a unique place in the American economy. Especially important is the assembling of contractors and subcontractors with various specializations to build a particular project. This results in specialization of the work force and intermixing of the employees of different employers.[17]

The Employers

Construction firms range from very large to very small and are very numerous. General contractors take responsibility for an entire project, but subcontract most of the actual construction. Most firms operate in a particular locality or region, but some are national in scope. Those that operate nationally are generally specialized to a particular branch of the industry.

Most firms hire employees in only one or two trades, although general contractors may hire in as many as five or six trades. The average firm in construction has fewer than 10 employees, and of these most are temporary in that they do not work for a single employer for a full year, but move from employer to employer as the availability of work dictates.

In order to deal with the union that represents the workers (or "mechanics") in a trade, the employers ordinarily join together in an association. The association is governed by its bylaws and ordinarily negotiates an agreement with a local union. The associations are not limited to labor relations activities, but also lobby with governmental agencies on behalf of their members, provide legal services, promote construction, and handle public relations and similar functions. Local employer associations are often affiliated with national bodies.[18]

Because of the peculiar economic conditions and characteristics of employment in construction, employers and unions are placed in a much more in-

[17] For a discussion of the management problems caused by subcontracting, see J. A. Grimes, "Personnel Management in the Building Trade," *Personnel Journal*, 47:1, January 1968, pp. 37–47.
[18] Daniel Quinn Mills, "Labor Relations and Collective Bargaining," in Julian E. Lange and Daniel Quinn Mills, eds., *The Construction Industry: Balance Wheel of the Economy* (Lexington, Mass.: Lexington Books, 1979), pp. 59–82.

timate relationship than that usually found in other industries. Contractors and unions must negotiate not only wages and working conditions but also hiring and training practices. A special provision of the National Labor Relations Act [section 8(f)] permits unions and contractors in construction to sign prehire agreements, by which an employer agrees to recognize a union to represent its employees before it hires employees and without an election being held. Also, in an unstable industry, the development and retention of a skilled labor force require that employers and unions agree to practices to preserve the job opportunities of craftspeople. The problem, of course, is to adopt policies that are effective in protecting employment opportunities without either unduly restricting needed expansion of the labor force or promoting uneconomic practices.

Not all crafts, branches of construction, or geographic areas are unionized at all or to the same degree. But all contractors, union or nonunion, are influenced by the labor relations policies of the others. Wages in the union segment influence what nonunion contractors must pay. Frequently, nonunion scales are below union scales, but union workers are often considered better mechanics. Many contractors feel that the wage rate paid employees is less important than the productivity of the workers. Because of higher productivity, union employers can sometimes pay higher wage rates but nonetheless have lower labor costs than nonunion contractors.[19]

The segment of the construction industry that is not governed by collective bargaining agreements has usually been pictured as a fringe around the unionized segment of the industry. However, the segment of the industry outside of collective bargaining has apparently been growing rapidly relative to the whole industry. Furthermore, significant parts of this segment are becoming structured and its industrial relations formalized—not under labor agreements, but under policies adopted by nonunion employer associations.

The industrial relations arrangements of construction now operate in three forms, which are in stiff competition for dominance in the future: (1) the system under collective bargaining agreements, (2) open-shop (i.e., nonunion) arrangements under national or local policies of contractor associations (the "merit shop"), and (3) the sector of individual enterprises pursuing policies apart from either collective bargaining or a formal organization of contractors (the truly "unorganized" sector). In a sense, the merit-shop associations have adopted many of the substantive industrial relations policies and procedures of collective bargaining (such as apprenticeship programs, health and welfare plans, and even, in some few instances, the hiring hall). But decision making is under the control of a local or national employers' association without union involvement or participation.

We do not know what proportion of construction activity or employment is open-shop. There are no reliable statistics on the degree of organization in

---

[19] Steven G. Allen, *Unionized Construction Workers Are More Productive* (Washington, D.C.: Center To Protect Workers' Rights, November 1979).

construction, although superficial surveys are sometimes taken. However, a number of indicators of the importance of the nonunion sector are available.[20] According to the best information within the industry, a relatively larger proportion of contractors than of employees is in the nonunion sector (i.e., the average number of workers employed by nonunion contractors is smaller than the average number employed by union contractors). For example, in the housing industry, a major employer association estimates that more than half of the employers are nonunion and some 70 percent or so of all housing is constructed by nonunion builders. Nonetheless, many large metropolitan areas have a majority of housing done by union builders. Much industrial and power plant construction is unionized, while commercial and office building is more often nonunion. On balance, by 1985 slightly less than one-half of construction employees were represented by unions.

The Unions

The building and construction labor force comprises more than 20 crafts and many more specialties. In the union sector, a group of 18 or 20 national unions represent workers. It is customary to speak of these unions as crafts unions, but most represent more than a single craft or specialty. For example, the United Brotherhood of Carpenters and Joiners of America represents not only carpenters and joiners but also piledrivers, millwrights, soft-floor layers, and dock builders. Outside construction, the union represents workers engaged in maintenance of industrial plants and production workers in sawmilling, lumbering, cabinetmaking, and similar endeavors. Other major construction unions are also agglomerations of specialists around a central, or main, craft. Thus, while construction unions may be generally described as crafts unions, they are more accurately considered to be a form of crafts-industrial unionism.

Collective Bargaining

Structure   The structure of collective bargaining in construction is extraordinarily complex. There is considerable variation by branch of the industry, geographic location, and craft. In consequence, only a very general description can be given. There are some 5000 to 7000 collective bargaining agreements in the industry, most negotiated between local unions and employer associations. The agreements run for 1 to 5 years and average about 18 months. Each year, therefore, 2000 to 3000 agreements are negotiated.[21]

Table 18-8 summarizes bargaining structure in various branches of the industry. The only branch in which all the trades are involved in negotiations

---

[20] Howard G. Foster and Herbert R. Northrup, *Open Shop Construction* (Philadelphia: Industrial Research Unit, Wharton School, The University of Pennsylvania, 1975).

[21] D. Quinn Mills, "Construction," in Gerald Somers, ed., *Collective Bargaining*, pp. 49–98.

TABLE 18-8 BRANCHES OF THE CONSTRUCTION INDUSTRY, PRINCIPAL UNIONS, AND GEOGRAPHIC COVERAGE OF AGREEMENTS

Branch	Principal unions	Geographic coverage of agreements
Highway construction	Carpenters Laborers Operating engineers Cement masons Teamsters	Local
Pipeline construction	Pipefitters Operating engineers Laborers Teamsters	National
Electric transmission lines	Electricians (IBEW)	Local
Industrial and power plant construction	Pipefitters Ironworkers Electricians (IBEW) Boilermakers Millwrights (United Brotherhood of Carpenters) Carpenters Laborers	National and local

Note: For building construction, see Table 18-9.

is building construction, and this branch is described in detail in Table 18-9. In the pipeline industry each of the four trades listed negotiates a national agreement with the Pipeline Contractors Association, and the four unions and the association maintain a policy committee to resolve disputes. In the industrial construction industry, the individual companies and an association (the National Constructors Association) negotiate national agreements with the unions listed, but the companies also apply, in most instances, many terms of the building agreements generally in effect where a project is located.

Table 18-9 lists the major national employer associations in the building construction industry, the principal unions with which they deal, and the usual geographic coverage of agreements. The five or six trades with which the Associated General Contractors negotiate are called the "basic trades." Electricians, pipefitters, and sheet metal workers are members of the "mechanical trades." (Where an association is ordinarily referred to by a set of initials, the initials are given in Tables 18-8 and 18-9.)

Wage Structure Trades negotiate separately, and the relative position of each in wages and benefits is an important aspect of negotiations. The skilled-versus-unskilled differential in construction is as important as in steel or automobiles, but is determined not by a single industrial union and em-

TABLE 18-9 BARGAINING STRUCTURE IN BUILDING CONSTRUCTION: MAJOR EMPLOYER ASSOCIA-
TIONS AND UNIONS

Employer association	Principal unions	Geographic coverage of agreements
Associated General Contractors (AGC)	Carpenters Laborers Operating engineers Teamsters Ironworkers (rod workers)	Local or state
National Association of Homebuilders (NAHB)	Carpenters Laborers Bricklayers	Local or state
Mason Contractors Association of America (MCAA)	Bricklayers	Local
National Electrical Contractors Association (NECA)	Electricians (IBEW)	Local
Elevator Constructors Employers Association	Elevator constructors	National (except New York City)
Mechanical Constructors of America (MCA)	Pipefitters	Local
Sheet Metal and Air Conditioning Contractors National Association (SMACNA)	Sheet metal workers	Local
National Erectors Association	Ironworkers (structural)	Local
International Association of Wall and Ceiling Contractors (IAWCC)	Plasterers	Local
National Insulation Contractors Association (NICA)	Asbestos workers	Local
Painting and Decorating Contractors Association (PDCA)	Painters	Local
National Roofing Contractors Association (NRCA)	Roofers	Local
Plumbing, Heating, and Cooling Contractors National Association (PHCCNA)	Plumbers	Local

ployers, but by decentralized bargaining. There is a tendency for differentials to be resistant to change,[22] but study of a period reveals that significant changes do occur.

Table 18-10 lists the trades in order of national average hourly compensation for 1950 and 1980 (the most recent data available). It can be seen that

[22] George Strauss, *Unions in the Building Trades* (Buffalo, N.Y.: University of Buffalo, June 1958), Series 24, 2.

TABLE 18-10 BUILDING TRADES RANKED BY AVERAGE WAGE AND BENEFITS COMPENSATION PER HOUR 1950* and 1980

1950		1980	
Trade	Hourly rate	Trade	Hourly rate
Bricklayers	$2.83	Electricians	$16.80
Plasterers	2.80	Plumbers and pipefitters	16.28
Painters	2.62	Carpenters	15.28
Plumbers and pipefitters	2.57	Bricklayers	15.26
Electricians	2.54	Plasterers	14.53
Carpenters	2.37	Painters	14.25
Laborers	1.65	Laborers	12.26

Note: All data are building construction rates only.
*In 1950, benefits were not a significant part of compensation.
Source: Bureau of Labor Statistics and Construction Services Division, U.S. Department of Labor. For 1980 data, see *Current Wage Developments*, 32.9, September 1980, p. 44. In the early 1980s the government ceased to collect these data, and no information is available for the period following 1980.

electricians replaced bricklayers as the highest-paid workers, and that plasterers fell back considerably. In general the mechanical trades moved up over the period. This was due in part to the growing importance of industrial and power plant construction, which uses the skills of the mechanical trades in a disproportionately large amount.[23] Laborers remained at the low end of the distribution, but the percentage differential from bottom to top narrowed from 71.5 percent to 33.0 percent. Similarly, the differential between carpenters and laborers (especially important since members of these two trades are numerous and work closely together in building construction) declined from 43.6 percent in 1950 to 25 percent in 1980.

The table identifies three major changes in construction industry wage structure as developed in collective bargaining in the period from 1950 to 1980:

The substantial increase in wage and benefit rates (which also occurred to a degree in other sectors of the economy)

The movement to the top of the rate structure by the mechanical trades

The narrowing of the wage differential between laborers and members of the skilled trades

Collective Bargaining Reform Construction has been under pressure from the federal government to reform its bargaining structure since the mid-1960s. Rapid inflation and frequent work stoppages were exacerbated by decentralized bargaining. Beginning in 1968 several joint labor-management-government committees endeavored to settle strikes, dampen inflation, and bring about a greater role for national unions and employer associations in local bargaining, in

---

[23] See D. Q. Mills, *Industrial Relations and Manpower in Construction* (Cambridge, Mass.: MIT Press, 1972).

order that wider concerns could affect the outcome of local negotiations. The most successful of these efforts was the Construction Industry Stabilization Committee, which operated from 1971 to 1974.[24]

In December 1975, Congress passed a bill mandating certain changes in the labor relations structure of the construction industry. The bill provided for the establishment of a national committee composed of union, management, and neutral members to oversee bargaining in the unionized section of construction. The bill, originally called the Construction Industry Collective Bargaining Bill, passed Congress as Title II of the so-called Situs Picketing bill. President Ford vetoed the bill, and in 1976 the 8-year experiment with a national labor relations committee in construction was ended.[25]

These efforts did not end attempts to reform collective bargaining practices in construction, however. In 1982, a group of large industrial companies, the Business Roundtable, issued a series of reports aimed at altering construction industry practices.[26] And, in 1984, the unions and contractor associations at the national level announced a "Market Recovery Program"—a cooperative effort to attempt to regain work from nonunion contractors.[27]

As the growth of nonunion firms accelerated in construction in the 1970s, many union firms established nonunion subsidiaries. This practice, known as "double-breasting," has been much opposed by the unions. A bill to prohibit double-breasting has been introduced in Congress, and may pass at some point. Aspects of the double-breasting controversy have also been litigated at the NLRB and in the courts. For example, in 1984 a construction local union learned that a company with which it had an agreement was going out of business and turning its work over to a nonunion firm. The union asked for information about the nonunion firm, a subsidiary—it turned out—of the union firm. The company refused to provide information. The union complained to the NLRB, which ordered the company to provide the information, and a circuit court of appeals upheld the NLRB.[28]

The revitalization attempts of the unionized sector of construction take two forms. One involves adjustments in pay levels and working practices to achieve greater cost effectiveness. The other involves the development of closer cooperation between management and labor. As the president of the Bricklayers International Union described this effort,

[24] Clark G. Ross, "The Construction Wage Stabilization Program," *Industrial Relations*, 17:3, October 1978, pp. 308–314. Also see D. Q. Mills, "Explaining Pay Increases in Construction: 1953–1972," *Industrial Relations*, 13:2, May 1974, pp. 196–201.

[25] Donald E. Cullen, *The Bargaining Structure in Construction: Problems and Prospects* (Washington, D.C.: Labor-Management Services Administration, U.S. Department of Labor, 1980).

[26] "Implementation Urged," Bureau of National Affairs, *Daily Labor Report* No. 243, Dec. 17, 1982, pp. A2–A5.

[27] "Union Sector," Bureau of National Affairs, *Daily Labor Report* No. 211, Oct. 31, 1984, pp. C1–C4. See also Jeffrey M. Perloff, "Labor Market Adjustments in the Unionized Contract Construction Industry," *Journal of Labor Research*, 2:2, Fall 1981, pp. 337–353.

[28] *Corson and Gruman Company v. NLRB*, CA 4, No. 86-3816 (1987).

At the national level, construction unions are increasing...their involvement in strategic planning for the industry.[29]

CHAPTER SUMMARY

The various forms of bargaining relationships that exist are referred to as the structure of bargaining. There are several different ways to describe the bargaining structure of the American economy. One classification is by the type of employer negotiating unit (multiemployer, individual employer, etc.) related to the relationships between negotiating units, e.g., whether there is an industrywide agreement or only local agreements. There are a number of other important dimensions which could be added to these two factors. Bargaining structure is not only a matter of who bargains with whom. There are also different methods of bargaining about different issues.

Many large industries in the United States negotiate every 3 years. This cycle is referred to as a bargaining, or wage, round. Negotiations in different industries precede or follow one another. As a negotiation in one industry proceeds, it affects those that follow it, forming a kind of national bargaining pattern. The significance of the effects of one negotiation on others has decreased substantially in the 1980s, however.

The characteristics of employment in different sectors of the economy determine what problems or issues are of importance in collective bargaining and even the manner in which bargaining is conducted. Manufacturing is a very important sector of our economy. Its characteristics of employment are not exactly like those in other sectors of the economy. Manufacturing usually involves a factory at a fixed location in which machinery is installed. The work force is relatively stable and made up of a large proportion of unskilled and semiskilled workers who identify closely with the company. The work force reports for work on a fixed schedule and is usually closely supervised by managerial personnel.

Collective bargaining agreements in manufacturing commonly involve only a single company. A general agreement covers items common to all facilities of the company, but there may be supplemental provisions relating to working conditions specific to each particular plant. There is great concern in labor negotiations about the competitive status of employees but little about hiring decisions. However, there is no single or simple form of labor relations in manufacturing. There are a variety of different practices with respect to bargaining format, issues, and results.

The automobile industry illustrates a different form of labor-management structure. Large companies dominate the production of automobiles in the United States. Most negotiate with the United Auto Workers, and most of

---

[29] John T. Joyce, "Codetermination, Collective Bargaining and Worker Participation in the Construction Industry," in Thomas A. Kochan, ed., *Challenges and Choices Facing American Labor* (Cambridge, Mass.: MIT Press, 1985), p. 267.

the employees of the auto companies are members of the UAW. Several companies have national agreements with the UAW, and local supplements to the national agreements are negotiated at the plant level. The national agreement establishes the economic package and certain nationally applicable working conditions and dispute procedures. The local supplement deals with conditions of work and grievances at a particular plant. There is no industrywide bargaining in autos.

There are a variety of bargaining arrangements that exist in other industries. In addition to one company bargaining with one union, there are several other major types of bargaining relationships. For example, several companies may deal with a single union or vice versa. Other variations include negotiations that occur on the plant level or at the company level.

In negotiations, certain stable kinds of interrelationships are called patterns. When a number of negotiations are very closely related, pattern bargaining is said to occur. A particular union and employer settle their negotiations on the basis of a pattern established elsewhere.

The coal industry has been significant in American labor relations. It has industrywide bargaining and a single national union. The most distinguishing characteristic of employment in mining is that the workplace and living quarters of the miners are isolated from population centers. As a result, the miners have a strong sense of identity and separateness that creates strong loyalties to the unions and distrust of the mining companies.

Companies in the coal industry are widely diversified in size and type. Independent coal companies produce about half the coal mined. The rest is produced by companies which are subsidiaries of the heavy users of coal—the oil, steel, and electric companies. The Bituminous Coal Operators Association (BCOA) represents the industry in collective bargaining and embodies the diversity of economic interests which characterizes the producers. Despite divergent interests, the companies prefer a joint negotiation with the miners' union. The United Mine Workers of America (UMW) represents the workers in the coal industry. It is an industrial union and represents both skilled and unskilled mine workers.

Construction is a sector of the economy which includes several hundred thousand firms. Construction can be divided by type of construction project, e.g., housing, or it can be divided by the specialization of the firms, e.g., highway contracting. Employment in construction has many unique features. The product is custom-built, individually priced, and produced on a site chosen by the purchaser. Each project involves an assemblage of various specializations. Employees shift among work sites and employers and identify with their craft or occupation. Employment is unstable, often dangerous, and nonstandardized. Construction firms vary greatly in size and are very numerous. In order to deal with unions, employers ordinarily join together in an association which negotiates with the union. The building and construction labor force is represented by a group of 18 or 20 national unions which are crafts-industrial in form. The nonunion segment of the construction industry appears to be growing rapidly. Its labor relations are being formalized by the policies of nonunion employer associations. These are called open-shop or merit-shop arrangements.

The structure of collective bargaining in union construction is extraordinarily complex. There is considerable variation by branch of the industry, by geographic location, and by craft. There are between 5000 and 7000 local, national, and state collective bargaining agreements in the industry. Occupations negotiate separately, and the relative position of each in wages and benefits is an important aspect of negotiations.

QUESTIONS FOR THOUGHT AND DISCUSSION

1 Why is the structure of collective bargaining so complicated in the United States? Is this a strength or a weakness of our industrial relations system?

2 Is centralized bargaining better than plant-level bargaining? Better for whom? Why?

3 Should the automobile companies bargain as a group? What would be the results if they did?

4 What is pattern bargaining? How does it work? Give examples. Where does pattern bargaining occur in the auto industry?

5 How does the industrial-versus-craft-union conflict enter into labor relations in the auto industry? Why do you think this occurs?

6 Many major coal companies are owned by larger companies from the steel and oil industries. What difference does this circumstance make to labor relations in the coal industry? Why?

7 Construction has a very decentralized structure of bargaining. What are the advantages of such a structure? What are the disadvantages? Why?

8 In what ways are construction labor relations different from those in various manufacturing industries you have studied? What are the causes of these differences?

9 There are three forms of industrial relations arrangements in the construction industry which are in stiff competition for dominance in the future. What are they? Do you think one form will come to predominate? Why or why not?

10 Should the government act to reduce the number of unions and go to a national bargaining system? Why or why not?

SELECTED READING

Alinsky, Saul, *John L. Lewis* (New York: Putnam, 1949).

Barnard, John, *Walter Reuther and the Rise of the Auto Workers* (Boston: Little Brown, 1983).

Bourden, Clint, and Ray Leavitt, *Union and Open Shop Construction: Compensation, Work Practices and Labor Markets* (Lexington, Mass.: Lexington Books, 1980).

Jensen, Vernon H., *Heritage of Conflict: Labor Relations in the Nonferrous Metals Industry up to 1930* (Ithaca, N.Y.: Cornell University Press, 1950).

Katz, Harry C., *Shifting Gears: Labor Relations in the U.S. Automobile Industry* (Cambridge, Mass.: MIT Press, 1985).

Lipsky, David B. and Clifford B. Donn, *Collective Bargaining in American Industry* (Lexington, Mass.: Lexington Books, D. C. Heath, & Co., 1987).

Mills, Daniel Quinn, *Industrial Relations and Manpower in Construction* (Cambridge, Mass.: MIT Press, 1972).

Northrup, Herbert R., *Open Shop Construction Revisited* (Philadelphia: The Industrial Research Unit, The Wharton School, The University of Pennsylvania, 1985).

Weber, Arnold, ed., *The Structure of Collective Bargaining* (Glencoe, Ill.: Free Press, 1960)

LABOR-MANAGEMENT RELATIONS IN THE PUBLIC SECTOR

There are important differences between labor-management relations in private business and those that exist in the public sector. Among the most apparent differences are those that are created by the application of different laws. The National Labor Relations Act does not apply to employees of federal, state, and local governments. Instead, there are very many different laws passed by the federal government, state governments, and municipalities, each covering employees in their own jurisdictions. A common characteristic of these laws is that they usually deny employees the right to strike.

Despite the absence of a legal right to strike, public employees have joined unions to a larger proportion than have private employees. And public employees, by virtue of their close familiarity with law, generally are very conscious of their rights and obligations. In public employment, therefore, the power balance and the procedures and topics of bargaining are often quite different from those found in the private sector of our economy.

CHAPTER 19

COLLECTIVE BARGAINING AND THE LEGAL CONTEXT IN THE PUBLIC SECTOR

There is considerable diversity of labor relations in the public sector. There is no federal law that applies uniform regulations to labor relations of states and municipalities. Each state has its own laws governing public employee labor relations. In the federal government a statute now governs labor relations; this statute replaces a series of presidential executive orders and provides a framework for union representation and collective bargaining. The situation that exists in the public sector is one of transition, experimentation, and development.

STATE AND LOCAL GOVERNMENT

Growth in State and Local Government Employment and Unionization

In the period since the end of World War II, the number of employees of state and local government has grown from 3.5 million to some 13.8 million and increased from 8.2 percent of nonagricultural employment to 13.8 percent (1986). Today roughly one employed person in seven in the United States is an employee of some state or local governmental agency.

Employees of state and local governments serve in a variety of capacities. Among public employees are police, firefighters, sanitation workers, nurses, health aides, engineers, clerks, prison guards, utility workers, and others. This is a substantial range of occupations, demonstrating the wide variety of matters with which public employee relations are concerned. Slightly more than half of all public employees are involved in education, primarily as teachers. Hospitals and police protection account for the next largest groups, followed by highway maintenance.

Employee Organizations

Some 5 million state and local government employees belong to unions or employee associations—48.8 percent of all full-time workers. This is a larger degree of organization than exists in the private sector and is the result of substantial growth in recent years. About half of organized state and local government employees belong to unions, and about half belong to employee associations.[1]

What is the difference between a union and an employee association? In the past, unions were commonly alleged to be primarily concerned with wages, benefits, work rules, and similar aspects of the employment relationship. Associations, in contrast, were said to have a greater concern for the professional aspects of employment, including the quality of public service and of the people performing it. In recent years, these distinctions have become blurred. Unions that represent public employees have come to have much more concern for professional standards, and employee associations now evidence far greater interest in the economic aspects of employment. So substantial has the change been in the employment associations that many now promote collective bargaining and even engage in strikes, activities previously associated with unions only.

The Bureau of Labor Statistics classifies organizations of public employees as unions or associations on the basis of how the organization describes itself. Some differences do still exist between the two. Most public employee unions are affiliated with the AFL-CIO and take part in the activities of organized labor. Most employee associations do not wish to have this identification with working people from other sectors of the economy. This difference reflects the tendency of public employees in urbanized and industrialized states to belong to unions, whereas public employees from suburban, rural, and less industrialized areas tend to belong to associations. Too much should not be made of the union-versus-association dichotomy, however, for the groups are behaving more and more alike with regard to their employers and the public in general. The issues that divide organized public employees into unions and associations are primarily internal ones and are not reflected in external behavior.

There are many organizations representing state and local government employees. Several are unions and several are associations. The largest organization is formally not a union, but rather an association (the National Ed-

[1] "Almost Half," Bureau of National Affairs, *Daily Labor Report* No. 6, Jan. 12, 1982, p. B1. See United States Bureau of the Census, "Labor-Management Relations in State and Local Governments: 1980," Special Studies No. 102 (Washington, D.C.: U.S. Government Printing Office, 1982).

ucation Association). The larger unions are the American Federation of State, County and Municipal Employees (AFSCME), which represents public employees across a wide spectrum of occupations, including police in some localities, and the American Federation of Teachers, which represents public-school teachers, especially in larger cities and towns.[2] The firefighters' union represents most nonvolunteer firefighters and is affiliated with the AFL-CIO. The International Conference of Police Associations does not have as complete representation of police as the Firefighters does of firefighters. The Police Association affiliated with the AFL-CIO only recently, having been outside the Federation partly because of a jurisdictional dispute that caused opposition from other police employee unions already in the Federation. Another large group of police is represented by the Fraternal Order of Police, not affiliated with the AFL-CIO. The Teamsters also represent some police officers.

Other unions that are not primarily representative of public employees, but nonetheless represent substantial numbers of them in various geographic areas, include the Service Employees, the Laborers, and the UAW.

The Employers

State and local government employees work for a variety of different agencies of government. There are so many agencies, in fact, that the federal government takes a census in order to find out how many agencies of government exist. In recent years the count has been over 78,000 separate units of government, including towns, school districts, water conservation districts, and so on.[3] Some 13,375 of these agencies have bargaining units.[4] These agencies have various degrees of authority under the laws of the state or municipality that created them. In some cases an agency is simply an administrative organ of a state or municipal government, but in others, especially in school districts, the agency may be a quasi-independent branch of government.

This multiplicity of agencies raises the question of who the employer of state and local government workers really is. Is it the immediate agency? Is it the chief executive officer of the municipality, or county, or state (e.g., the mayor of a city or governor of a state)? Or, since in our republican form of government considerable authority rests in the legislature, is the employer the legislative body, whether city council or state legislature? Labor relations in the public sector are very much complicated by this issue, which has no

---

[2] Jack Stieber, *Public Employee Unionism: Structure, Growth, Policy* (Washington, D.C.: Brookings, 1973).

[3] U.S. Bureau of the Census, *Labor-Management Relations* (Washington, D.C.: U.S. Government Printing Office, 1978), Social Studies, No. 88. In 1976, 12,368 governmental units reported having a labor relations policy, and 27,418 written collective bargaining agreements were in effect.

[4] Ibid.

exact parallel in the private sector. It is not uncommon for a union or an association to reach an agreement in collective bargaining with an agency of government, only to have another agency or legislative body refuse to honor it. Many difficult disputes have been created in this manner.[5]

Many cities and states have begun to organize themselves more effectively to handle labor relations.[6] The function of representing the agencies of local or state government in labor relations is delegated to a special entity created for this purpose, often called an Office of Employee Relations or Office of Collective Bargaining. This office coordinates, and indeed conducts, negotiations for the city or state and helps in administering any labor agreements that may exist. Furthermore, it is becoming more common for states and localities to require that any economic settlements with unions or associations be approved by vote of the legislature or city council before becoming binding on the government. In this way the legislative body's power to control public expenditures is preserved. Unfortunately, however, this procedure invites conflict by the legislative bodies with agreements made by public managers.[7]

The labor problems of state and local government officials are receiving greater recognition as their importance increases. In 1973, for example, a survey of urban administrators listed 12 functions of management in American cities and found that although labor relations was ranked eleventh in current involvement by the managers, it was given third place in estimated future importance, with only citizen participation and intergovernment relations listed above it. Such currently significant functions as preparing a budget and designing programs are listed below labor relations. This survey was cited in 1975 by a committee of the federal government established to investigate ways of strengthening public management.[8]

Collective Bargaining

The structure of collective bargaining in state and local government has many similarities to that in the private sector. Unions or employee associations meet with their employers (either the managers of agencies or officials of the municipality or state) to negotiate agreements that are binding on the two parties for a specified term. Ordinarily the union is the exclusive representative of a certain unit of employees and negotiates wages, benefits, and working conditions on their behalf. These features of state and local government

[5] David T. Stanley, *Managing Local Government under Union Pressure* (Washington, D.C.: Brookings, 1972).

[6] Milton Derber, "Management Organization for Collective Bargaining in the Public Sector," in B. Aaron et al., eds., *Public-Sector Bargaining* (Washington, D.C.: Bureau of National Affairs, 1979), pp. 80–117.

[7] John F. Burton, "Local Government Bargaining and Management Structure," *Industrial Relations*, 11:2, May 1972, pp. 123–139.

[8] Executive Office of the President of the United States, *Strengthening Public Management* (Washington, D.C.: U.S. Government Printing Office, 1975), p. 26.

labor relations are much like those of the private sector. But there are important differences.

First, the strike is usually illegal for public employees, a matter to which we will return in the next chapter. Second, labor negotiations involving public employees have a very pronounced political aspect. Union and association leaders often conduct negotiations on three fronts simultaneously: by meeting directly with public managers, by lobbying with the legislative body involved, and by attempting to influence the voters. Public managers often complain that the unions go around them to the legislature and the voters, thereby frustrating true collective bargaining. The unions, on the other hand, charge that public managers often fail to make a commitment for the legislative body, so that the unions must lobby in order to gain their objectives.[9]

Third, many governmental bodies already possess civil service systems that regulate employee relations. These systems were established on a widespread basis in American municipalities and states in the late nineteenth and early twentieth centuries. Their purpose was to restrict political influence and corruption in public employment. They utilized commissions, expert staffs, and regulations to control the processes of hiring, promoting, compensating, and dismissing government employees. Methods of instituting and investigating complaints by employees about allegedly unfair practices were also included.

Collective bargaining has as one of its objectives the establishment of rules and procedures of a similar nature, but collective bargaining uses different methods. To establish rules, it employs a process of negotiation, not enactment by a legislative body or promulgation by a commission; and to enforce rules, it relies on a grievance procedure that generally ends in a decision by a neutral, instead of an investigatory process that ends in a decision by a commission.[10] Thus, civil service and collective bargaining stand as potential rivals.

In recent years the legislatures of several states have tried to sort out the relationship between collective bargaining and civil service systems. In some states the merit system under civil service is simply excluded, by state law, from bargaining between public employers and state and local governments. Also, some states have spelled out where collective bargaining can supersede provisions of civil service codes. For example, California's 1977 law for state employees lists relevant sections of the state's civil service code that can be modified or set aside by collective bargaining. Modifications like those of state laws have lessened the apparent conflict of collective bargaining and civil service procedures, and thereby suggest that both systems may continue to exist in the future.[11]

---

[9] R. Theodore Clark, Jr., "Politics and Public Employee Unionism: Some Recommendations for an Emerging Problem," *University of Cincinnati Law Review*, 44, 1975, pp. 680–689.

[10] Stephen L. Hayford and Richard Pegnetter, "Grievance Adjudication for Public Employees," *The Arbitration Journal*, 35:3, September 1980, pp. 22–29.

[11] B. V. H. Schneider, "Public-Sector Labor Legislation—An Evolutionary Analysis," in B. Aaron et al., eds., *Public-Sector Bargaining*, p. 211.

The Structure of Bargaining

The structure of bargaining in state and municipal governments is surprisingly complex. Some cities and states bargain with many separate unions and associations. Others negotiate with only a few. When there is a multiplicity of bargaining units, it is because employees are organized by occupation or public agency (or department). When there are few units, it is because large, broadly representative groups exist (somewhat analogous to industrial unions in the private sector).

Until recently the number of bargaining units with which a municipality or state dealt was largely a matter of historical accident,[12] but in the past few years some cities and states have passed laws that allow public employee relations agencies to establish new, and fewer, bargaining units and to conduct elections to determine union representation. This process is creating a rationalized and simplified bargaining structure in many areas.

A study examined the establishment of public employee bargaining units in seven jurisdictions—Hawaii, Massachusetts, Michigan, New Jersey, New York City, Minnesota, and Wisconsin. These places were selected because they vary with respect to the laws and procedures they use to regulate and conduct public employee collective bargaining. The experiences in these jurisdictions were compared with each other and with those in the federal government. They covered such topics as unit determination procedures; criteria; treatment of special employees, such as supervisors, confidential employees, and guards; and bargaining unit structure. The study concluded that the use of broad bargaining units tended to improve the operation of collective bargaining arrangements involving large public employers.[13]

How the Difference between Profit and Nonprofit Organizations Affects Collective Bargaining

It is common to group organizations in the United States into three very general classifications:

1 Private, profit-making businesses
2 Private, nonprofit concerns
3 Governmental agencies

Let us cite just a few examples. Private, profit-making businesses include large corporations like General Motors and General Electric, but also the corner grocery or drugstore. For this classification it doesn't matter whether or not the business makes a profit—what matters is whether or not it intends (or hopes) to do so. Private, nonprofit concerns include such organizations as

---

[12] New York City, for example, negotiates with several hundred bargaining units, while Philadelphia has only about five. See Derek C. Bok and John T. Dunlop, *Labor and the American Community* (New York: Simon and Schuster, 1970), p. 324.

[13] Richard S. Rubin, *Public Sector Unit Determination, Administrative Procedures and Case Law* (Washington, D.C.: U.S. Government Printing Office, 1979).

hospitals and schools run by religious or charitable groups (e.g., a Baptist hospital or a Roman Catholic parochial school). Governmental organizations include various agencies of federal, state, and municipal governments, such as public school systems, water departments, and the unemployment insurance office. It is characteristic of governmental organizations that they profess to exist and function for the public good. Often the public good is offered as an excuse for poor financial performance. But it should not be forgotten that private business also professes to serve the public good and that the corporate charters issued to private business originally, and still today to a degree, were for the purpose of allowing a business organization to meet a public need.

These three groups of organizations can be split into two different two-way classifications. Thus, one may speak of the *private* versus the *public* sector, in which classifications 1 and 2 are lumped together and contrasted against 3. For many purposes this is a useful classification—for federal laws apply to labor relations very differently in the private versus the public sector. Alternatively, one might stress the importance of the distinction between *for-profit* organizations and *not-for-profit* organizations, in which classification 1 is contrasted with 2 and 3 together. To evaluate the usefulness of this classification, we must ask how important the role of profit is to the way in which labor relations are handled. Put another way, does the objective of making a profit cause managers in for-profit organizations to behave very differently in labor relations from the way managers in not-for-profit organizations do?

What is profit? Essentially, profit is a surplus—what remains after expenses are subtracted from revenues. Profits are used for two major purposes. They may be reinvested in the enterprise in order to expand its facilities or to make it more efficient. Or profits may be used to provide dividends to stockholders (or, in some cases, to provide bonuses to management and/or workers). When a company has no profits or negative profits (i.e., expenses exceed revenues), it is said to have losses. Generally high profit levels are an indication of success in a business, while losses will result in bankruptcy or a change in management, or both. The purpose of business is often defined as making the largest possible profit. Some companies probably do operate this way. But often companies try to maximize profits only after other objectives are met, including product quality, employee compensation, community citizenship, and so on. This does not mean that businesses are good-hearted organizations that are concerned first about the public and only then about profits. On the contrary, there is much range of dispute with businesses over whether particular policies are appropriate for the public good. But business corporations do not constantly seek higher profits regardless of other considerations. Most business executives do not behave that way, especially in labor relations.

Because business seeks to make as much profit as possible, subject to its other policies, a business is often at odds with its employees or labor unions over how much additional employee compensation is appropriate. Thus, business has a motivation to resist employee demands at some point. But do not-for-profit organizations, both private and governmental, have this motivation?

The answer is almost certainly yes. While not-for-profit organizations may not calculate and report profits, they are nonetheless cost-conscious. The level of costs cannot ordinarily be allowed to exceed budget limits without either a cutback or a change in management. Thus, it is clear that not-for-profit organizations have an incentive not to suffer persistent budget deficits, and this is analogous to a profit-making firm's desire to avoid losses. But does a not-for-profit organization have any incentive to generate budget surpluses? Yes, it does. A mayor may use a surplus to reduce taxes, or to initiate new programs, or to provide salary increases. A public official is probably not as surplus-conscious as a business executive is profit-conscious. Still, the same motivation exists for both.

Some readers will object that public agencies and other nonprofit organizations are notoriously wasteful and persistently overrun their budgets. Furthermore, when tax revenues are high, public employers sometimes appear simply to throw money away on salary increases, additional hiring, and other superfluous activities. This also is true. But private business is not immune to this behavior. Some business corporations continue year after year with substantial losses (for example, certain railways). And in periods of economic boom private business often spends money in ways later shown to have been profligate. Where then is the difference?

The difference between profit-making and not-for-profit organizations is primarily one of degree. Private profit-making business is far more cost-conscious, on the average, than not-for-profit organizations. Profit-making firms are better managed; their control and accounting practices are better developed to accurately reflect expenses and to keep up a continual monitoring of revenues and expenses.[14] The managers of profit-making enterprises usually know more about their organizations, their objectives, and the constraints they face. But this is changing, and the managerial revolution that has improved management in the profit sector in this century is now reaching the not-for-profit sector. As not-for-profit organizations become more cost-conscious, we may expect them to behave increasingly like profit-making enterprises. For labor relations analysis, therefore, the difference between profit-making and not-for-profit organizations is less significant than one might have thought at first glance.

This is not to say that there are not large differences between collective bargaining in the public and private sectors; there are large differences, as is indicated in the next section of this chapter. But the differences tend to stem from causes other than the fact that the public sector is made up of not-for-

---

[14] Joseph L. Bower, "Effective Public Management," *Harvard Business Review*, 55:2, March–April 1977, pp. 131–140.

profit organizations. The factors that cause public-sector labor relations to be different from those in the private sector have to do with the role of politics in the public sector, the division of the employer side into several different decision-making bodies, and the differences in laws governing labor relations in the public and private sectors.

State Regulation of Labor Relations

At present there is wide variability in the manner by which states regulate their own labor relations and those of their municipalities. Approximately 36 states have fairly comprehensive statutes dealing with public employee relations—the others do not. Where comprehensive statutes do not exist, labor relations are governed by ad hoc acts of the state legislature, by common law, or by municipal ordinance. The state laws that now exist are not at all uniform. For example:

• Collective bargaining is permitted in 31 states for public employees. Nine states have so-called meet-and-confer laws. A major addition to the states which permit collective bargaining occurred in 1982 when Ohio passed a public employee bargaining law. The law permits strikes after mediation and fact-finding procedures are exhausted.

• Ten states do not permit collective bargaining for public employees.

• Twenty-two states provide for *broad-scale bargaining*, in that negotiations are over wages, hours, and terms and conditions of employment. The same number of states allow for negotiation or consultation on grievance procedures.

• Eleven states permit some or all public employees to *strike* but usually under limited circumstances; 32 states prohibit strikes altogether, while 7 states are virtually silent on the matter.[15]

Comprehensive labor relations statutes have been passed in a number of states.[16] Statutes of this nature provide:

• The right of employees to join unions or associations[17]

• A method of establishing bargaining units and of determining union representation

---

[15] Based on a study done by the American Federation of State, County and Municipal Employees, March 1985.

[16] A state-by-state listing of the provisions of labor relations laws for public employees can be found in U.S. Department of Labor, Labor Management Services Administration, *Summary of Public Sector Labor Relations Policies*, Washington, 1981. For an up-to-date survey of state and local bargaining arrangements, see Donald S. Wasserman, *American Federation of State, County and Municipal Employees*, Washington, D.C.

[17] In *AFSCME v. Milton Underward* (North Platte, Nebraska), the Eighth Circuit Court of Appeals of the United States held that the right of free association guaranteed by the First and Fourteenth Amendments to the Constitution extends to membership in a labor organization and denies municipalities the privilege of prohibiting membership in unions by their employees.

- Collective bargaining when a union or association is selected by employees in a bargaining unit
  - Issues about which bargaining may take place
  - Prohibition of strikes (or permission for them in limited instances)
  - Procedures for resolving disputes

What causes states to enact laws requiring public-sector agencies to bargain with unions which represent their employees? There has been a debate as to whether already-established unions cause such laws to be enacted (that is, simply making legal what already is occurring) or whether the passage of collective bargaining laws causes unions to grow. Gregory Saltzman has investigated this issue. He found that during the period 1959 to 1978, enactment of the laws caused growth in the number of teachers covered by union contracts, rather than the other way around.[18]

What do public employees bargain about? In contrast to the common practice in private industry, public employee unions do not hesitate to negotiate about policy issues as well as about wages, hours, and conditions of work. Teachers' unions, for example, raise questions of educational policy in collective bargaining. One study found that 46 percent of teacher agreements regulated the curriculum; 59 percent regulated student placement; and 96 percent regulated teacher placement.[19]

Under the pressure of increasing concern about high public expenditures and high tax rates, several state governments have begun to enact laws which substantially restrict the gains unions can win in collective bargaining. Some states have written management rights provisions into their laws. Others have exempted specific topics from bargaining, such as the size of classes in public schools, the work load of public employees, and the staffing of equipment (including, for example, fire trucks). In legislation and by decisions of state administrative agencies (state public employee relations boards) and of state courts, the concept of mandatory and nonmandatory subjects of bargaining has been carried over into public labor relations from the private sector. But in the public sector, the definitions of what are mandatory and what are permissive subjects of bargaining often differ in detail from the definitions used in the private sector.

In some states the public employers have not been content simply to narrow the range of mandatory subjects of bargaining. Instead, they have gone further by arguing not that there should be a narrow range of mandatory subjects, but that there should be no voluntary subjects of bargaining at all. In New Jersey, for example, the state's Supreme Court found that there could be only two categories of issues in bargaining in the public sector:

[18] Gregory M. Saltzman, "Bargaining Laws as a Cause and Consequence of the Growth of Teacher Unionism," *Industrial and Labor Relations Review*, 38:3, April 1985, pp. 335ff.

[19] Steven M. Goldschmidt and Leland E. Stuart, "The Extent and Impact of Educational Policy Bargaining," *Industrial and Labor Relations Review*, 39:3, April 1986, pp. 350ff.

"mandatorily negotiated terms and conditions of employment and non-negotiable matters of governmental policy."[20] Under this doctrine (which is the exception rather than the rule) public employee unions can negotiate only about matters clearly specified in state law; all other matters are left to the sole discretion of public management.

Differences in the law affecting collective bargaining between the public and private sectors are not limited to matters of inclusion or exclusion. Other differences go to fundamental questions of the administration of collective bargaining agreements. For example, in the private sector there is a presumption that a dispute involving the interpretation of an agreement is arbitrable (see Chapter 12). But in the public sector, there is no presumption of arbitrability. Instead, there must be a clear statement in the contract of an intention to arbitrate a matter before the courts will find that the matter is, indeed, subject to arbitration.[21] As a result of this 1977 decision, public-sector grievance arbitration was reduced. More matters went to court. In 1981 the New York courts tried to reverse the trend by using a decision in another case to urge the parties not to delay arbitration by "hair-splitting" tactics.[22]

Should There Be a Federal Statute?

The existing confused and often contradictory patchwork of state laws and local ordinances regarding labor relations has suggested to some observers the value of a federal statute that would apply a uniform set of rules and procedures to all states and localities. Bills that would accomplish this purpose have been introduced in Congress. They are of two general types. One type would simply apply the provisions of the Taft-Hartley Act, which regulates private-sector labor relations, to state and local governments. The other type would involve a comprehensive set of regulations tailored explicitly to state and municipal labor relations.

In 1976 the U.S. Supreme Court ruled that the federal government could not regulate employment practices of the states and of municipalities with respect to their own employees (*National League of Cities v. Usery*). This decision has thrown into doubt the legality of proposed federal statutes dealing with the labor relations of states and municipalities. But several writers are not convinced that the decision in *National League of Cities* completely closed

---

[20] *Ridgefield Park Education Association v. Ridgefield Park Board of Education*, New Jersey Supreme Court (1978).

[21] *Liverpool Central School District v. United Liverpool Faculty Association*, New York State Court of Appeals (1977).

[22] In *The Matter of the Board of Education of the City of New York*, Robert Glaubman, New York State Court of Appeals (1981).

the door on a federal statute. Believing that the decision was a bad one, they call on the Supreme Court to modify it.[23]

Public employee unions (organized as the Coalition of American Public Employees) have been major supporters of a separate federal statute for state and local government employees. They see two major advantages. First, federal legislation would permit in some states gains for unions and collective bargaining that cannot be obtained in the states themselves. Second, standard legislation would greatly reduce the difficulty and cost involved in operating the unions, in contrast to the current confused situation, in which different procedures exist in each state.

States and municipalities largely oppose federal legislation. They argue that the states and localities should be left to work out their own problems, and they question the constitutionality of a federal statute applying to state and municipal employees. They also argue that the highly publicized strikes and other difficulties of state and local labor relations are simply a matter of a transition and that the situation will improve without federal legislation.[24]

It is interesting that the union-supported bill, which has AFL-CIO backing, calls for granting the right to strike to state and local government employees. However, the leadership of some of the major public employee unions (especially Jerry Wurf, general president of AFSCME) recognizes that a bill with this provision cannot pass Congress. Therefore, Wurf argued at the AFL-CIO convention in 1975 for giving up the right to strike for certain public employees in hopes of getting other desirable federal legislation. Martin Ward, president of the United Association of Pipefitters, opposed Wurf's proposal to give up the demand for the right to strike, and it was beaten by the convention.

An alternative to the comprehensive federal statute sought by the unions would be one which establishes only certain minimum standards for each state to meet. Under such a statute, for example, states would be required to permit public employees to form unions and to bargain collectively, to establish orderly procedures to deal with all matters concerning employee representation, to establish an impasse procedure for the settlement of disputes where the strike is prohibited, and to establish an independent state agency to administer the state's statutes. Unions, employees, and public employers would have the right to appeal the agency's decisions to the courts.[25]

---

[23] B. V. H. Schneider, "Public-Sector Labor Legislation," and Benjamin Aaron, "Future of Collective Bargaining in the Public Sector," in B. Aaron et al., eds., *Public-Sector Bargaining*, pp. 222 and 308.

[24] Jay Erstling, "Federal Regulation of Non-Federal Public Employment," *Labor Law Journal*, 24:11, November 1973, pp. 739–754. Also, Thomas R. Colosi and Steven B. Rynecki, eds., *Federal Legislation for Public Sector Collective Bargaining* (Chicago: International Personnel Management Association, 1975).

[25] Benjamin Aaron, "Future of Collective Bargaining," in B. Aaron et al., eds., *Public-Sector Bargaining*, p. 309.

THE FEDERAL GOVERNMENT[26]

In 1985 the federal government employed some 2,902,000 people in civilian occupations[27] (up from 1,892,000 in 1947). These employees ranged from construction mechanics in naval shipyards to aeronautical engineers employed by NASA. While a considerable amount of federal employment is concentrated in the Washington, D.C., metropolitan area, other federal employees are located throughout the nation.

Unionization and collective bargaining among federal employees are not recent. In fact, federal employees were among the first in the nation to organize. Crafts unions of workers in federal printing plants, naval yards, and arsenals were active in obtaining a reduction in the workday from 12 hours to 10 in 1840. By 1868 these unions had achieved, through lobbying and legislation, a reduction in the workday to 8 hours. So effective did the unions become in influencing Congress that in 1902 President Theodore Roosevelt issued an executive order forbidding federal employees from petitioning Congress in their own behalf. This so-called gag rule was affirmed and strengthened by President William Howard Taft in 1909. In turn, Congress, in 1912, in an act written specifically for postal employees (the Lloyd-LaFollette Act), provided the right to federal employees to organize unions and petition Congress.

Presidents continued to refuse to recognize the unions of federal employees. Presidents Herbert Hoover and Franklin Roosevelt made strong statements that collective bargaining as practiced in the private sector could not belong to federal employees. It was not until President John F. Kennedy's administration that actions favoring collective bargaining began.

The largest union of federal employees is the American Federation of Government Employees, which is an AFL-CIO affiliate. A rival union, not affiliated with the AFL-CIO, is the National Association of Government Employees (NAGE), which began in the Quincy, Massachusetts, naval shipyard and remains headquartered in Boston. There is also a National Labor Relations Board Union, which represents employees of the board's various offices.

Among the most important federal labor organizations historically were the unions in the Postal Service. For years their unions bargained with Post Office management over issues of work conditions and work load and lobbied with considerable success in Congress for pay raises. Other federal employees thereafter generally received similar increases, also by congressional action. In 1971 the United States Postal Service was reorganized as an independent agency of the federal government with authority to negotiate its own labor agreements. The unions and the Postal Service negotiated a collective bargaining agreement in 1973, including wage rates and benefits, and the postal employees were cut off from the federal employment system. Ta-

[26] Jon Brock and Richard Martin of the John F. Kennedy School of Government at Harvard University assisted in the preparation of this material.
[27] Including Postal Service employees.

TABLE 19-1 SELECTED UNIONS REPRESENTING EMPLOYEES OF THE U.S. POSTAL SERVICE

	Membership
American Postal Workers Union	255,000
National Association of Postal Supervisors	35,000
National Association of Letter Carriers	275,000
National Association of Rural Letter Carriers	63,000
Laborers International Union (mail handlers)	40,000
National League of Postmasters	N.A.
National Alliance of Postal and Federal Employees	20,000

Source: Bureau of National Affairs, *Directory of U.S. Labor Organizations, 1986–7, and Daily Labor Report,* Oct. 26, 1984, p. A11.

ble 19-1 lists the major postal unions active in 1985. Each of the organizations listed is primarily a postal employee union except the Laborers International Union, which in 1968 absorbed the Mail Handlers Union.

Extent of Unionization in the Federal Government

Unions currently represent about 60 percent of all civilian federal employees (excluding the Postal Service), and about 80 percent of all Postal Service employees. Non-Postal Service employees are grouped into two primary classifications: wage board and general schedule. Wage board employees are generally blue-collar workers, and general schedule employees are primarily white-collar workers. Wage board employees are paid an hourly rate; general schedule employees are salaried. Wage board employees number approximately 500,000 and work primarily at government installations, such as shipyards. General schedule employees number about 1.5 million and include most other federal government workers. (There is also a senior executive service of top managers.) Some 80 percent of wage board employees and 55 percent of general schedule employees are represented by unions which have the authority to be the exclusive representatives of employees in designated units (this is analogous to the situation in the private sector).[28]

Exclusive recognition occurs when a majority of the employees in an "appropriate unit" have elected the union as their representative in a secret-ballot election. The Federal Labor Relations Authority (FLRA) is responsible for making appropriate unit determinations. The authority specifies that the determination that a group of employees constitutes an appropriate unit will be based on specific criteria: community of interest among the employees, promotion of effective dealings with the agency concerned, and promotion of

---

[28] *Analysis of Data and Report on Union Recognition in the Federal Service,* Federal Personnel Manual, Bulletin No. 711–81, Apr. 30, 1980. All figures cited are based on data accumulated by the Office of Personnel Management, U.S. Government.

efficiency of operations in the agency. Once exclusive recognition is conferred on a union, that union becomes the sole representative of the employees for collective bargaining purposes. Consequently, competition among rival unions for exclusive recognition is frequently intense.

Short of exclusive recognition, the union seeks the right to "consultation." The Civil Service Reform Act (CSRA) specifies that if "no labor organization has been accorded exclusive recognition on an agency basis, a labor organization that is the exclusive representative of a substantial number of the employees of the agency" will be granted "national consultation rights." The union's right to consultation requires management to inform the union "of any substantive change in conditions of employment." Additionally, the union must be given time to present its "views and recommendations" on the proposed changes. Management must then consider the union's response before reaching a final decision and provide the union with a written explanation of the action taken. The FLRA establishes criteria and resolves questions involving the right to consultation and exclusive recognition.[29]

The Civil Service Reform Act of 1978

The current framework of labor-management relations in the federal sector is defined by the Civil Service Reform Act of 1978 (CSRA). It represents a codification of 2 decades of evolving federal labor-management policies. During that time, two executive orders, the first by President Kennedy in 1962 and the second by President Nixon in 1969, established the basic parameters of federal policy. Amendments to the Nixon order in 1971 and 1975 further clarified federal labor-management doctrine.

The CSRA retains the spirit and concept of federal labor-management policy embodied by the executive orders while incorporating several new provisions. In addition, the CSRA realized a long-standing goal of organized labor in the federal sector: the creation of a legislated federal labor-management program.

In addition to the change from executive order to statute, the CSRA authorized a structural reorganization of the federal agencies responsible for personnel management and labor relations. As of January 1979, the Civil Service Commission (CSC) was abolished and replaced by three new agencies:[30]

1 The Office of Personnel Management (OPM) assumed the CSC personnel management functions and replaced CSC as the central personnel office for the federal work force. While OPM retains an Office of Labor Relations to

---

[29] Federal Labor Relations Authority, "The Federal Service Labor-Management Relations Statute (Chapter 71 of Title 5 of the U.S. Code and Related Amendments to 5 USC 5596(b)—the Back Pay Act)," FLRA Document 1071, January 1980, pp. 20–22.

[30] "Introducing the Civil Service Reform Act," U.S. Civil Service Commission, Washington, D.C., November 1978, pp. 3–4.

assist federal managers, policy and adjudicatory functions have been assigned to the Federal Labor Relations Authority.

2 The Merit System Protection Board (MSPB) was created as an independent agency designed to safeguard the principles of the merit system and to protect employees against abuses of that system.

3 The Federal Labor Relations Authority (FLRA) replaced the previous Federal Labor Relations Council and assumed most of the labor relations functions in the federal sector. The Labor Department's responsibilities are now limited primarily to cases involving standards of conduct. The FLRA was designed as an independent agency modeled on the National Labor Relations Board.[31]

Establishment of the FLRA realized an important goal of labor: creation of an independent, neutral, full-time authority to oversee labor-management issues in the federal sector. The Kennedy order (EO 10988) vested responsibility for supervision of the overall federal labor-management program in the CSC with limited assistance from the Department of Labor. Although that provision of the executive order appears innocuous, it was not acceptable to organized labor. They contended that even if the labor-management decisions made by the CSC were impartial, CSC's involvement created the impression that management made all the decisions.[32] The CSC was, after all, the central personnel management agency of the federal government.

Subsequent designers of federal policy attempted to correct the image that management controlled labor relations in the federal sector. The Nixon executive order (EO 11491), created the three-person Federal Labor Relations Council to make policy and supervise the federal labor-management program. The members, who decided cases involving unfair labor practices and grievances, included the CSC chairperson, the secretary of labor, and the director of the OMB. Although generally applauding this step as an improvement, labor noted that the CSC and other executive agencies continued to provide staff for the council's activities. In that respect, EO 11491 failed to establish the independence from presidential control and the appearance of complete impartiality now provided by the FLRA. Under the provisions of the CSRA, the three bipartisan members of the FLRA are appointed for staggered 5-year terms and can be removed only by the President and only for cause.

The Scope of Bargaining

A major area of contention between labor and management is in the defining of the appropriate range of negotiable issues. In the federal sector the scope

---

[31] Henry B. Frazier, "Labor-Management Relations in the Federal Government," *Labor Law Journal*, 30:3, March 1979, pp. 133–138.

[32] Murray B. Nesbitt, *Labor Relations in the Federal Government Service* (Washington, D.C.: Bureau of National Affairs, 1976), p. 129.

of bargaining is legally restricted by two factors which do not operate in the private sector. First, no bargaining outcome is permitted to change federal law. Since the legislative branch is entrusted with the sole authority to make laws, representatives of the executive branch are not allowed to change the law through bargaining.

The second limitation on bargaining in the federal sector is the merit system, designed to eliminate political and other inappropriate influences from personnel actions in the federal civil service. This concept requires that hiring, transfers, and promotions in the federal sector be based solely on merit considerations and leaves relatively little room for bargaining over such issues as job rights and access. Merit requirements for personnel actions are administered by statute and by regulations promulgated by the central Office of Personnel Management. The strong congressional endorsement of the merit system is apparent in the CSRA's creation of an independent Merit Systems Protection Board.

As labor has sought the right and opportunity to bargain collectively with management over matters of mutual interest, a fundamental concern of management has been the formal safeguarding of management rights. Management rights are areas in which management has retained, through statute, the exclusive right to make the final decision and which are not, therefore, within the scope of bargaining. In the tradition of the executive orders, the CSRA identifies specific areas as management rights. Bargaining on these areas, including the agency's mission, budget, number of employees, and procedures for internal security, is therefore prohibited. Bargaining is permitted, but not required, in such areas as the technology, means, and methods of performing the agency mission. Bargaining is mandatory for such areas as procedures for resolving grievances.

Establishing Compensation in the Federal Sector

For most federal employees compensation is not established by collective bargaining. How is it done? In the distant past each agency, and Congress, had its own system. Prior to 1968 there were some 60 different wage systems within the federal government. In October of that year the government established a coordinated federal wage system, and the system has been based on the principle of establishing comparability with the private sector. This principle received a strong statement in the Pay Comparability Act of 1962, which declared it a matter of policy that the prevailing wage rates in each occupation be based on comparability with the private salary rates. In 1967 the Federal Employees Salary Act authorized the President to make pay adjustments to close the gap between federal and private pay rates, and in 1969 and 1970 such adjustments were made.

Under the present system the President, rather than Congress, determines the amount of a pay adjustment. Congress must specifically cancel a pay raise by legislation, but it need not act for a pay increase to be granted. In late

1970 the system was established as it operates today. The system has several steps, the major ones being:

1 *The Bureau of Labor Statistics* conducts a national survey of private-sector salaries (the PATC survey).

2 *The President* designates an agent, usually the director of the Office of Management and Budget or the director of the Office of Personnel Administration, to review the PATC survey and make a recommendation.

3 *The Federal Employees Pay Council,* a group of five leaders of the principal federal employees' unions, makes a recommendation to the President's agent.

4 *The Advisory Committee on Federal Pay,* three individuals drawn from the private sector, submit their own recommendations to the President.

5 *The President,* after a year's study of steps 1 through 4, makes an independent decision, based on these recommendations, on what increase shall be given federal employees.[33]

The system we have just described establishes the pay of general schedule workers but is extended in various ways to many military employees also. Wage board employees are governed by an older system of pay surveys in localities in which the federal employees work.

CHAPTER SUMMARY

In recent decades, unionization and collective bargaining have expanded in the public sector. Elaborate procedures for representation elections and for mediation and arbitration have been established to resolve public employee disputes. In the federal government, a statute now governs labor relations, providing a framework for union representation and collective bargaining. But there is no federal law that applies uniform regulations to labor relations of states and municipalities. Towns and states are free to regulate their labor relations with their own employees as they see fit.

The number of employees of state and local government has grown considerably in the last 40 years, and there is a substantial range of occupations. Employee organization has also grown substantially. About half of the organized state and local government employees belong to unions and to employee associations. Combined unions and associations are becoming more alike with regard to their employers and the public in general, and there is little clear difference between the two. Most public employee unions are affiliated with the AFL-CIO and identify with organized labor. Employee associations do not. The largest unions are the American Federation of State, County, and Municipal Employees (AFSCME) and the American Federation

---

[33] Sharon P. Smith, *Equal Pay in the Public Sector: Fact or Fantasy?* (Princeton, N.J.: Industrial Relations Section, Princeton University, 1977).

of Teachers (AFT). The largest public employee association is the National Education Association.

The employers in state and local government are more difficult to identify than private employers. It is possible to identify the employer as the agency head, the mayor, the city council, the state legislature, or the governor. There is often considerable uncertainty as to who has the authority to commit the government to a particular wage settlement in collective bargaining negotiations. Many of the complications and disputes which accompany public employee bargaining arise out of the lack of structure on the employer's side.

Collective bargaining in state and local government has many similarities to that in the private sector, but there are important differences. The strike is usually illegal for public employees. Labor negotiations have a definite political aspect to them, which involves lobbying and influencing voters. Many governmental bodies already possess civil service systems that regulate employee relations by methods other than collective bargaining. An important question is when collective bargaining can supersede provisions of civil service codes.

The structure of bargaining in state and city governments is very complex, involving hundreds of separate unions and associations. There is wider variability in the ways states regulate their labor relations and those of their cities. Currently, 36 states have comprehensive statutes dealing with public employee relations. There has been considerable debate over mandatory and nonmandatory subjects of bargaining and the exemption of specific topics from bargaining. A federal statute that would apply a uniform set of rules and procedures to all states and localities has been proposed to replace the confusing array of state laws that now exists.

Unionization and collective bargaining are extensive in the federal government. Federal employees were among the first workers in the nation to organize. The federal government has a much more complete format structure for dealing with labor relations than exists in state and local government. The current framework of labor-management relations in the federal sector is defined by the Civil Service Reform Act of 1978, which codified decades of evolving federal labor-management policies. The CSRA established a federal labor-management program and authorized the structural reorganization of the federal agencies responsible for personnel management and labor relations.

For most federal employees, compensation is not established by collective bargaining. The Pay Comparability Act of 1962 declared it a matter of policy that the prevailing wage rates in each occupation be based upon comparability with private salary rates. These are generally ascertained by a national survey of private-sector salaries. Congress must act to provide raises for federal employees, and often uses the pay comparability data to establish the amount of increases.

QUESTIONS FOR THOUGHT AND DISCUSSION

1 Should government employees be able to have unions? Why or why not?

2 How do labor relations in the public sector differ from those in the private sector?

3 A federal statute has been proposed that would apply a uniform set of rules and procedures to labor relations in all states and localities. What are the advantages and disadvantages and to whom? Do you think such a statute will be passed and would you favor it? Why or why not?

4 How does the difference between profit and nonprofit organizations affect collective bargaining? What differences would you expect to find and why?

5 What differences are there between the civil service system for handling employee relations and the process of collective bargaining?

6 Does management control labor relations in the federal sector? How has the dominance of management been limited?

7 What did the Civil Service Reform Act of 1978 do? What further advances still need to be made to improve labor relations in the public sector?

8 What has caused the growth of state and local government employment since 1947? What impact has rapid growth had on labor relations? Is the pattern of rapid growth changing now?

9 What are the differences between a union and an employee association? How important are the differences? In the future will unions and employee associations become more alike or less alike?

10 What matters are subject to collective bargaining in the federal government? Should there be a wider scope of bargaining? Why or why not?

SELECTED READING

Aaron, Benjamin, Joyce M. Majita, and James L. Stern, eds., *Public-Sector Bargaining*, 2d ed. (Washington, D.C.: Bureau of National Affairs, 1988).

DeAngelis, Tony, David Lutes, and Gene Daniels, *Public Sector Collective Bargaining*, rev. ed. (Minneapolis: University of Minnesota Industrial Relations Center, 1983).

Freeman, Richard B., "Unionism Comes to the Public Sector," *Journal of Economic Literature*, 24:1, March 1986, pp. 41–86.

Levitan, Sar A., and Alexandra B. Noden, *Working for the Sovereign: Employee Relations in the Federal Government*, Policy Studies in Employment and Welfare, 39 (Baltimore: Johns Hopkins University Press, 1983).

Salerno, Charles A., *Police at the Bargaining Table* (Springfield, Ill.: Charles C Thomas, 1981).

CHAPTER 20

PUBLIC EMPLOYEE IMPASSES AND THEIR RESOLUTION

LEGAL PROHIBITIONS AGAINST PUBLIC EMPLOYEE STRIKES

All federal and most state and local employees are currently legally denied the use of the strike. Not only are the unions or associations prohibited from calling work stoppages, but individual employees are often prohibited from joining or participating in organizations that advocate or assert the right to strike against the government. Thus, in an action amending the Taft-Hartley Act, adopted on August 9, 1955, Congress established that

> No person shall accept or hold office or employment in the Government of the United States who participates in any strike or asserts the right to strike against the Government of the United States.... or is a member of an organization of Governmental employees that asserts the right to strike against the Government of the United States... knowing that such organization asserts such rights.

Yet strikes by public employees are not unusual and have also occurred in the past. Perhaps the most famous such strike occurred in 1919, when the Boston police quit work because of the refusal of the city police commissioner to permit police officers to form a union affiliated with the AFL. On Sunday, September 8, a strike vote was taken among the city's 1544 police officers; 1134 voted to strike, 2 were opposed, and others did not vote. At 5:45 p.m. on Monday, September 9, 1127 police quit work. The result was a night of violence and crime in the city in which 9 people were killed and 23 wounded. The situation was finally brought under control by the militia. The strike collapsed on September 10. Commenting on the strike, Massachusetts Governor Calvin Coolidge (later President of the United States) said, "There is no right to strike against the public safety by anybody, anywhere, anytime." Seventy years later police strikes are generally no more successful at getting a union. A study of 600 nonunion police departments found that strikes have not helped police gain union representation.[1]

In the aftermath of the Boston police strike, public employee unionism was checked and strikes by public employees were halted. Nonetheless, strikes did sometimes occur. During the 1930s work stoppages on public employment projects were not uncommon. One author, writing in 1940, titled a study *One Thousand Strikes of Government Employees*.[2] Since the end of World War II data have been compiled on the frequency of work stoppages by public employees and the number of persons involved. There were relatively few stoppages until the mid-1960s, but the number of stoppages was high in 1969, 1970, and 1975. Throughout the rest of the 1970s and into the 1980s, the number of strikes by public employees remained at a relatively high level (by historical standards). In 1980, for example, there were some 502 strikes by employees of state and local governments.[3] When one considers that virtually all these work stoppages were illegal, interesting questions are raised concerning the effectiveness of legal prohibitions in avoiding stoppages.

On August 3, 1981, approximately 11,500 federally employed air traffic controllers, members of the Professional Air Traffic Controllers Union (PATCO), went on strike. The President of the United States, declaring the strike to be illegal, immediately announced that any striking controller who failed to report back to work within 48 hours would be dismissed. Three days later, approximately 12,000 dismissal notices were mailed, and the secretary of transportation announced, "It's over. Our concern is rebuilding the system." The government proceeded to hire replacements for the strikers. The strikers sued to regain their jobs. On November 14, 1984, the Supreme Court refused to hear an appeal by 34 former air traffic controllers fired after the 1981 walkout. The Court let stand lower court rulings that President Reagan did not exceed his authority by ordering the firings because the controllers—all federal employees—broke the law when they struck and refused to return to work.[4]

So ended the most dramatic and widely publicized strike of public employees in the United States since the Boston police strike of 1919. And the

---

[1] Ray Richard, "Police Strike Boston in 1919," *Boston Globe*, Sept. 16, 1969, p. 22; and Casey Ichniowski, "Police Recognition Strikes," *Journal of Labor Research*, 9:2, Spring 1988, pp. 194ff.

[2] David Ziskind, *One Thousand Strikes of Government Employees* (New York: Columbia, 1940). For current data, see U.S. Bureau of the Census and U.S. Labor-Management Services Administration, *Labor-Management Relations in State and Local Governments: 1978, State and Local Government Special Studies No. 95* (Washington, D.C.: U.S. Government Printing Office, July 1980).

[3] United States Bureau of the Census, *Labor-Management Relations in State and Local Governments: 1980, Special Studies No. 102* (Washington, D.C.: U.S. Government Printing Office).

[4] Bureau of National Affairs, *Daily Labor Report* No. 220, Nov. 14, 1984, p. A8. See also David B. Bowers, "What Would Make 11,500 People Quit Their Jobs?" *Organizational Dynamics*, 3, Winter 1983, pp. 5–19; and Herbert R. Northrup, "The Rise and Demise of PATCO," *Industrial and Labor Relations Review*, 37:2, January 1984, pp. 167–184.

PATCO strike of 1981 ended just as the police strike of 1919 ended: The strike collapsed and the strikers lost their jobs.

Surprisingly, perhaps, the ultimate outcomes of the Boston police strike and the air traffic controllers' strike were similar. Years after the strike the Boston police unionized and today bargain with the city. In the fall of 1986, 5 years after the PATCO strike, air traffic controllers, many of whom were originally hired to replace strikers, began to form a new union. Nine months later, the National Air Traffic Controllers Association (NATCA) supplanted PATCO as bargaining agent via an election held in the spring of 1987. According to reports, controllers were upset over what were said to be insensitive, authoritarian supervisors and the unwillingness of the Federal Aviation Administration to take remedial action. NATCA, however, has pledged not to strike.[5]

Not all public employee work stoppages are strikes, of course. In contrast to the private sector, where strikes are generally legal, unions and associations in the public sector have an interest in avoiding the semblance of a strike. Therefore quasi-strikes, or "job actions," are common, but are only occasionally included in strike statistics. These actions include sickouts, slowdowns, demonstrations, "blue flu" (so called because of its use by police as an excuse for mass sick calls), mass resignations, and other forms of work protest.

When strikes do occur, public authorities are often quick to respond. For example, under the law of New York State (the Taylor Law, after its principal author) public employees are denied the right to strike, and those who take part in illegal walkouts not only are not paid for the time on strike but are required to forfeit an additional day's pay for each day spent on strike. As a result of a brief strike in the spring of 1980 by the employees of New York City's transit system, the employees lost pay equal to double the amount of time they were out on strike. In some instances, it is now said, public agencies count on some savings due to strikes as a way to balance their budgets. Also, union leaders who encourage illegal walkouts are subject to jail terms, and it is not uncommon for leaders of strikes to be sent to jail.

Nonetheless, workers sometimes ignore the prohibition and conduct illegal strikes. What conditions make strike prohibitions effective? The success of a prohibition against strikes is likely to depend on the following factors:

1 *The weight of public opinion* against strikers is a strong weapon to prevent, or to bring to an end, illegal strikes. However, when strikers live in isolated communities and have a strong sense of grievance against outsiders, public opinion in the society as a whole may have no restraining impact.

---

[5] "New Air Controllers' Union Forms," Bureau of National Affairs, *Daily Labor Report* No. 188, Sept. 29, 1986, pp. A3–A4; "Air Controllers Choose Union by More Than 2–1 Margin," Bureau of National Affairs, *Daily Labor Report* No. 112, June 12, 1987, pp. A9–A10. See also Arthur Shostak and David Skocik, *The Air Controllers' Controversy: Lessons from the PATCO Strike* (New York: Human Sciences Press, 1986).

2 *The degree to which* strikers can be replaced by other workers who can effectively perform their jobs is a major determinant of whether an illegal strike can be halted. Small groups of highly skilled employees may be virtually impossible to replace and so may strike successfully despite legal sanctions.

3 *The degree of internal disagreement* within the union is an important factor. If the union is united, the threat of legal compulsion to end a strike may only increase the strikers' determination to persevere, but a disunited group may easily be induced to return to work.

4 *The threat of the arrest* or forced dispersion of strikers by police, whether to free property or to prevent illegal picketing, is sometimes, but not always, effective. Elected public officials are often unwilling to risk violence by ordering police to disperse strikers.

SHOULD PUBLIC EMPLOYEES BE ALLOWED TO STRIKE?

Some commentators believe public employees should be allowed to strike. They cite the following principal arguments in support of a right to strike for public employees:

- A right to strike is necessary to make collective bargaining work; without the threat of a work stoppage the employer has no incentive to bargain.
- All employees should have the right to undertake concerted activities to better their working conditions.
- Strike prohibitions are not necessarily effective.
- Jail terms and fines are unreasonably punitive as a response to a work stoppage.

Those who advocate continuing the prohibitions against public employee strikes offer the following arguments:

- The public is the government, and the government is the sovereign (that is, the lawful authority). A strike, which is force or compulsion, directed against the public is intolerable—no such right can be said to exist.
- Public services are too important to be disrupted by strikes.
- There are ways other than strikes to settle public employee disputes.

Those who oppose public employee strikes insist that a strike against the government is not like a strike against a private employer. George Taylor, co-author of New York State's Taylor Law and one of the nation's foremost labor relations experts, said:

The right to strike has not been accorded to employees in the public sector. The wherewithal to pay wages does not derive from a competitive marketplace, but through taxes levied and budgets enacted by elected government officials. In a representative government the elected officials are responsible for determining the amount of taxes we pay and how the total revenue is to be allocated among claimants so as to maintain a viable society. In some respects, the legislative body may be looked upon as the counterpart of competitive forces or the market in private industry.[6]

Thus, in public-sector employment, there does not exist a product marketplace to determine whether wages and other labor costs are raised too high, or set too low, through competition.[7] In consequence, the use of a strike by public employees to raise compensation or increase other benefits cannot be constrained except by a legislative procedure. Further, in the private sector a strike is directed against the employer—to cause it to lose money—and harm to customers or to the public is incidental. In the public sector the objective of the strike is to do harm to the public, the taxpayer, the citizenry.[8]

Some observers have tried to discover a middle way between the prohibition of strikes by public employees and the legalization of all walkouts. A distinction is made between those work stoppages which potentially endanger the public health and safety (for example, those by police or firefighters) and those by other public employees, which may inconvenience the public but do not threaten its wellbeing (for example, walkouts by municipal office workers or by public works employees). Employees performing so-called nonessential services for government can, it is argued, be permitted to strike legally.[9] In further support of this position, state laws which permit collective bargaining by public employees have been studied to determine how effective such laws are in discouraging illegal strikes. State laws that prohibit bargaining as well as strikes were also studied. These studies indicate that laws permitting bargaining had only a mild tendency to encourage strikes whereas laws prohibiting bargaining were not effective in preventing illegal strikes.[10] Thus, some observers have concluded, since strikes cannot be effectively prohibited, and since many public services are not essential to the public health and safety, large numbers of public employees in the nonessential areas can be permitted the right to strike, although it must be denied to workers performing essential functions.

[6] George W. Taylor, "Using Factfinding and Recommendations in Impasses," *Monthly Labor Review*, 92:7, July 1969, pp. 63–64.

[7] The argument is that if compensation is set too high, the product will not sell, or other workers will seek the jobs at lower pay scales; and if compensation is set too low, workers will leave for other jobs. Thus, the marketplace is argued to establish an appropriate level of compensation among firms and occupations in the private sector. "In the private sector...negotiators are typically limited by such restraints as the entry of nonunion competitors, the impact of foreign goods, substitution of capital for higher-priced labor, the shift of operations to lower cost areas, the contracting out of high-cost operations to other enterprises, slowdown of unprofitable plants and operations," etc. [D. Bok and J. T. Dunlop, *Labor in the American Community* (New York: Simon and Schuster, 1970), pp. 334–335.]

[8] Harry Wellington and Ralph K. Winter, Jr., *The Unions and the Cities* (Washington, D.C.: Brookings, 1971).

[9] John F. Burton, "Can Public Employees Be Given the Right to Strike?" *Labor Law Journal*, 21, August 1970, p. 472.

[10] John F. Burton, Jr., and Charles E. Krider, "The Incidence of Strikes in the Public Employment," in Daniel S. Hammermesh, ed., *Labor in the Public and Nonprofit Sectors* (Princeton, N.J.: Princeton University Press, 1975), pp. 161–170.

The debate about the advisability of a legal right to strike for some or all public employees has been conducted actively in the United States since the mid-1960s. In the 1980s, public employees continue to be generally denied any right to strike (although Hawaii, Minnesota, Pennsylvania, and Ohio permit strikes by nonessential public employees).[11] It would appear that for the foreseeable future the advocates of a complete or partial right to strike for public employees will not be successful in achieving such a right in any appreciable number of political jurisdictions.

RESOLVING LABOR-MANAGEMENT DISPUTES IN THE PUBLIC SECTOR

In the absence of a legal right to strike for public employees, there is a tendency for disputes between management and labor to continue indefinitely without resolution. Without the strike or threat of a strike, neither side is under substantial pressure to settle matters in dispute. In this circumstance, how can disputes be resolved?

There has been considerable experimentation in the public sector with alternative methods of dispute resolution. Most states and the federal government now specify various procedures which management and labor are to use in an effort to resolve disputes without recourse by the unions to illegal strikes. There is not space in this text for a comprehensive description of these various procedures and the experience which has occurred with them. However, several of the more important procedures are described below.

Resolution of Labor-Management Disputes in the Federal Government

A major concern of the Civil Service Reform Act of 1978 (CSRA) involves enlarging and strengthening the procedures for resolution of labor-management disputes. In part this is accomplished by the creation of independent third-party machinery. In addition to directing the federal labor-management program, the Federal Labor Relations Authority makes the final decision in disputes between unions and federal agencies. The authority is further empowered to seek judicial enforcement of its orders.

The CSRA retained the Federal Service Impasse Panel (established by President Nixon), whose mission is to assist in resolving negotiating disputes in which the bargaining parties cannot reach agreement and in which an impasse has been declared. The impasse panel constitutes a separate element of the FLRA and is composed of "a chairman and at least six other members." The function of the panel is "to provide assistance in resolving negotiation impasses between agencies and exclusive representatives." The panel does not become involved until "voluntary arrangements, including the services

---

[11] Richard A. Lester, *Labor Arbitration in State and Local Government* (Princeton, N.J., Industrial Relations Section, Department of Economics, Princeton University, 1984), pp. 209–210.

of the Federal Mediation and Conciliation Service, or any other third-party mediation" have failed. Mediation involves a neutral third party's (frequently assisted by impartial fact-finding) attempting to find a solution agreeable to both parties. Similar to the executive orders, the CSRA specifies that if mediation has failed, either party may request a decision by the panel. Alternatively, the parties may agree to submit to binding arbitration, in which a neutral third party imposes a solution on the bargaining parties. The arbitration procedure, however, must be approved by the impasse panel.

The FLRA is also involved in dispute resolution when an unfair labor practice has been alleged. Similar to the NLRB, the FLRA has a general counsel to investigate and prosecute unfair labor practices. The CSRA identifies specific actions by management or labor that constitute unfair labor practices. Management is not permitted, for example, to "encourage or discourage membership in any labor organization," to "refuse to consult or negotiate in good faith," or to "enforce any rule or regulation which is in conflict with any applicable collective bargaining agreement." A change instituted by the CSRA is that any agency which issues a new regulation that conflicts with a negotiated agreement already in effect is guilty of an unfair labor practice. The union is not permitted to "coerce, discipline, fine, or attempt to coerce a member of the labor organization as punishment or reprisal," to "discriminate against an employee with regard to the terms or conditions of membership in the labor organization," or to "refuse to consult or negotiate in good faith."

A final area of dispute settlement discussed by the CSRA is that of negotiated grievance procedures. In addition to specifying that all negotiated agreements must include a negotiated grievance procedure, the act requires that all negotiated grievance procedures include binding arbitration as the final step. Previously, arbitration had been an optional provision.

The CSRA also expanded the permissible scope of the negotiated grievance procedures. The act specifies that all matters which federal laws allow to be grieved will be included in the scope of the grievance procedures unless specifically excluded. Thus, parties will no longer be negotiating matters into coverage under their grievance procedure—they will be negotiating them out.

A number of areas are specifically excluded by the CSRA from coverage by grievance procedures. Among the areas excluded are grievances involving retirement, suspension for national security reasons, and prohibited political activities. However, many areas which under the executive orders could be resolved only by statutory appeals procedures are now automatically included in the negotiation procedures. Included in these areas are reductions-in-force actions and removals, suspensions, and demotions for performance reasons.

The stipulation in the executive orders that any labor-management dispute must be processed through one channel only is repeated in the CSRA. Thus, the unions must decide whether to seek redress for alleged wrongs through unfair labor practice channels, grievance arbitration, or statutory appeals procedures.

Dispute Resolution at the State and Local Government Level

State and local governments have a greater need for effective disputes resolution machinery than does the federal government. This is because bargaining at the state and local government level ordinarily includes important subjects excluded from federal government bargaining (in particular, compensation). It has been common, therefore, for state and local governments to require that disputes over the terms of collective bargaining agreements be submitted to various procedures designed to resolve such conflicts. The most important such procedures involve mediation by a neutral party, fact-finding, and binding arbitration. Mediation was described in Chapter 11. In a fact-finding procedure, the parties to a dispute submit whatever information they believe relevant to a potential resolution of the dispute. A neutral fact-finder then makes a study of the evidence and prepares a report on the facts. This procedure is often quite useful where there are important disagreements between unions and employers over the truthfulness of the information each is using. In collective bargaining, comparisons with rates of pay and working conditions of groups of employees other than those involved in the immediate negotiations are common, but it is often difficult to determine the exact pay scales and conditions of work of other employee groups. A fact-finding procedure helps to dispel uncertainty over these matters and thereby helps the parties reach agreement.

Fact-finding ordinarily goes beyond fact-finding, however. There is therefore a sense in which the name is a misnomer.[12] Instead of limiting themselves to the determination of matters of fact, most fact-finders proceed, often with statutory authority, to prepare a set of recommendations as a suggested basis of settlement of the dispute by the union and public employer involved. In this way, fact-finding assumes the character of a mediation process. In some states the law explicitly authorizes either management or labor or both to ask the fact-finder to attempt to mediate the dispute to a peaceful resolution.

Neither fact-finding nor mediation necessarily results in a contract between management and labor. Consequently, binding arbitration of a dispute is often resorted to, either as a matter of law (so-called compulsory arbitration) or by agreement between union and management. This sort of arbitration is described in Chapter 11 and is commonly referred to as "interest arbitration."[13]

Interest arbitration of collective bargaining disputes has become a controversial matter.[14] Many municipal employers apparently feel that arbitrators

---

[12] Thomas A. Kochan, "Dynamics of Dispute Resolution in the Public Sector," in B. Aaron et al., eds., *Public-Sector Bargaining* (Washington, D.C.: Bureau of National Affairs, 1979), p. 182.

[13] Charles J. Morris, "The Role of Interest Arbitration in a Collective Bargaining System," *Industrial Relations Law Journal*, 1:3, Fall 1976, pp. 427–531.

[14] Peter Feuille, "Selected Benefits and Costs of Compulsory Arbitration," *Industrial and Labor Relations Review*, 33:1, October 1979, pp. 64–76. See also David E. Bloom, "Collective Bargaining, Compulsory Arbitration and Salary Settlements in the Public Sector: The Case of New Jersey Municipal Police Officers," *Journal of Labor Research*, 2:2, Fall 1981, pp. 369–384.

have been too generous in the awards made to public employee unions in the interest arbitration process.[15] As a result, some states now specify the factors arbitrators must consider in making their awards. Cost-of-living and comparable wage rates, items favored by the unions, are ordinarily specified; but productivity and the ability of the employer to pay, items favored by management, also are now often specified.

Arbitrators as a rule do not, understandably, feel that their awards have been more favorable to the unions than to the public employers. Instead, arbitrators argue that they have had a difficult time fashioning contracts where there is little experience to guide them.[16]

One arbitrator has prepared a list of the most important qualities of an arbitrator:

- A sense of constructive relationships between people and organizations
- A sense of a reasonable bargain
- A sense of the value of facts and how to identify them
- A sense of the criteria which are relevant to a particular case[17]

Whatever the merits of this controversy, the search for substitutes for the strike in settling public-sector disputes has been long and imaginative and is continuing. Many types of arrangements have been developed, and experimentation is continuing.

One basic feature of disputes procedures that seems to be standing the test of time is that the settlement of economic disputes must be somehow related to the legislative and budgetary process.[18] That is, the school committee, city council, or state legislature, as the case may be, must somehow be bound, either by participation in negotiations or by a separate act of approval of a negotiated settlement, to what the public manager and union establish as the terms of a contract.

On other matters there is less clarity. Some participants in public-sector impasse procedures prefer open-ended mediation and fact-finding, which permit the parties to devise methods to resolve disputes on an ad hoc basis. Others prefer clearly delineated procedures ending in binding arbitration or some other method of finally resolving the issues between the parties.[19] At this stage, all that is certain is that the questions of the role of the strike in

---

[15] Thomas A. Kochan et al., *Dispute Resolution under Fact-Finding and Arbitration: An Empirical Evaluation* (New York: American Arbitration Association, 1979). Also, Patricia Compton-Forbes, "Interest Arbitration Hasn't Worked Well in the Public Sector," *Personnel Administration*, 29:2, February 1984, pp. 99–104.

[16] Jean T. McKelvey et al., "Interest Arbitration in the Public Sector," *Arbitration Journal*, 37:4, December 1982, pp. 3–31.

[17] Tim Bornstein, "Interest Arbitration in Public Employment," *Labor Law Journal*, 29:2, February 1978, pp. 77–86.

[18] See *Report of the Governor's Committee on Public Employee Relations*, State of New York, Mar. 31, 1966, p. 33, where this proposition was first set forth.

[19] Joseph R. Grodin, "Political Aspects of Public Sector Interest Arbitration," *California Law Review*, 64:3, May 1976, pp. 678–702. Also, D. S. Chauhan, "The Political and Legal Issues of Binding Arbitration in Government," *Monthly Labor Review*, 102:9, September 1979, pp. 35–41.

public-sector labor relations and of alternatives to the strike involving various methods of dispute settlement remain in a state of transition and flux.

FINAL OFFER ARBITRATION

In the effort to minimize resort to binding arbitration of contract disputes, several variations of binding interest arbitration have been developed. Professor Richard A. Lester studied interest arbitration in nine states and cities and reached the following conclusions:

1 *The systems of interest arbitration analyzed have tended to receive increased acceptance, and performance under them has improved as the parties and the neutrals have had the benefit of experience over an extended period of time....*

2 *Over an extended period in many jurisdictions (for example, Michigan, Wisconsin, New Jersey, and New York City), more and more of the arbitration awards have actually been agreed upon by the negotiating parties.* Essentially, they are collectively bargained contracts....

3 *A public sector arbitration program works more satisfactorily where (a) the parties (management and union) participate extensively in the process and (b) representation of the parties in negotiations and arbitration proceedings is approximately equal in sophistication and advocacy, including the marshaling of supporting material.* Participation includes such items as choice of the form of arbitration, selection of an arbitrator or arbitration panel, influence on the arbitration proceedings, and a role in shaping the award....

4 *Experience has shown that no one form of arbitration or set of procedures is best suited for application in every state; instead, different forms (or combinations of forms) and various procedures have worked well over time in particular states, due partly to the education-adaptation process.* To illustrate, this study shows that the following forms of arbitration have worked effectively in the named states: (a) last-offer-by-package in New Jersey and in Wisconsin; (b) last-offer-issue-by-issue with a tripartite panel in Michigan and combined with fact-finder recommendations serving as a third offer with a single arbitrator in Iowa; and (c) conventional arbitration with a tripartite panel in New York State and with the right to strike as an alternative to arbitration in less-essential employment in Minnesota.[20]

One of the most interesting of these variations is final offer arbitration. Final offer arbitration was designed in theory to prevent frequent recourse to binding interest arbitration for the settlement of bargaining impasses, particularly, but not exclusively, in the public sector.[21] Final offer arbitration is pro-

---

[20] Richard A. Lester, "Lessons from Experience," *The Arbitration Journal,* 41:2, June 1986, pp. 34–37. See also Richard A. Lester, *Labor Arbitration in State and Local Government* (Princeton, N.J.: Industrial Relations Section, Princeton University, 1984).

[21] Use of final offer arbitration in the *private* sector has occurred primarily in the construction industry. In southern Nevada, final offer procedures exist in collective bargaining agreements between various employer associations and Laborers, Bricklayers, Hod Carriers, Teamsters' concrete truck drivers, and Teamsters' lumber industry workers. There is also a final offer procedure in the contract between the Oregon-Columbia chapter of the Associated General Contractors and the Operating Engineers.

posed as a response to the criticisms of conventional arbitration, especially its alleged "chilling," or deterrent, effect on the bargaining process.

The chilling effect argument states that if either party anticipates, for whatever reasons, that it will receive more from the arbitrator than from the negotiated settlement, it will have an incentive to avoid the trade-offs of good-faith bargaining and cling to excessive or unrealistic positions in the anticipation of tilting the arbitration outcome in its favor. In such a case, "The compromising nature of the conventional arbitration award—i.e., the arbitrator gives more than the employer has offered and less than the union has asked for—significantly reduces the costs tied to the uncertainties associated with continued disagreement."[22] Therefore, given its availability, conventional arbitration usage will increase as an alternative to bargaining. The available evidence shows that though conventional arbitration "does not immediately and inevitably destroy collective bargaining, there is evidence that conventional arbitration has often reduced the incentive to bargain."[23]

The purpose of interest arbitration is to resolve disputes, not to create them. Unfortunately, when the parties to collective bargaining are aware that if they do not reach agreement, the dispute will be submitted to an arbitrator for decision, this knowledge may affect their behavior in negotiations. Specifically, union or management negotiators, or both, may decide not to try to reach agreement, but rather to take their chances in arbitration. The existence of an arbitration procedure thereby stimulates disputes by having a sort of "narcotic effect" on bargaining.[24]

Final offer arbitration is a binding mechanism that requires an arbitrator to select, without modification, one of the final offers from the parties in a bargaining impasse. This procedure is intended to increase the parties' incentive to bargain by *retaining* the more equal distribution of costs of disagreement between union and management provided through any binding dispute resolution procedure, but *eliminating* the reduction of disagreement costs that produce the chilling effect of conventional arbitration. Since the arbitrator is not allowed to compromise between the parties' positions, the parties will be induced to develop ever more reasonable positions prior to the arbitrator's decision, in hope of winning the award. These mutual attempts to win neutral approval should result in the parties' being so close together that they will create their own settlement. Thus, "the final offer procedure was purposefully designed to contain the seeds of its own destruction. However, even if the procedure does not self-destruct, i.e., if an award does become necessary—the parties would have narrowed the area of disagreement

---

[22] Peter Feuille, *Final Offer Arbitration* (Chicago: International Personnel Management Association, 1975), p. 12.

[23] Gary Long and Peter Feuille, "Final Offer Arbitration: 'Sudden Death' in Eugene," *Industrial and Labor Relations Review*, 27:2, January 1974, p. 189.

[24] Henry S. Farber and Harry C. Katz, "Interest Arbitration: Outcomes and the Incentive to Bargain," *Industrial and Labor Relations Review*, 33:1, October 1979, pp. 36–54.

enough, that whatever the arbitrator's choice, the award would be reasonable."[25]

A study of New Jersey's final offer arbitration procedure found that union offers have been selected most of the time in final offer arbitration cases. The selection was due to conservative union officers, the researchers reported, resulting in lower average wage increases under the final offer arbitration provisions than under the conventional arbitration provisions of the New Jersey statute.[26]

Though final offer arbitration has been employed since about 1966, substantial use of the procedure did not take place until 1971. Since the early 1970s, there has been experimentation with final offer arbitration in several areas, and there have been a number of careful evaluations of its effectiveness.[27] In general, it appears that final offer arbitration is no more successful than conventional arbitration (in which the arbitrator fashions an award as he or she thinks best) in avoiding bargaining impasses, but that final offer arbitration is more successful in achieving settlements prior to the actual issuance of an arbitrator's award.[28]

The most serious limitation of final offer arbitration arises from its greatest strength. As an incentive to bargain, final offer arbitration offers the motivation of fear. That is:

> The possibility that either party "may lose the entire ballgame" in arbitration acts as a psychological, economic, and political incentive for both parties to reach their own agreement. This one-or-the-other criterion generates just the kind of uncertainty about the location of the arbitration award that is well-calculated to recommend maximum notions of prudence to the parties and, hence, compel them to seek security in agreement.[29]

Unfortunately, however, if the parties do not settle the dispute, but instead avail themselves of a final offer arbitration proceeding, then one side must "win" and the other "lose" in the choice. The resulting collective bargaining agreement is not a document agreed upon by both sides, or even the best document that the judgment of an arbitrator could create. It is the position of one side. The other side can hardly be expected to have much respect or regard for it as a contract. In the judgment of one careful student of final offer arbitration:

---

[25] Feuille, *Final Offer Arbitration*, p. 13. See also Hoyt N. Wheeler, "Compulsory Arbitration: A 'Narcotic Effect'?" *Industrial Relations*, 14:1, February 1975, pp. 117–120.

[26] Orley Ashenfelter and David E. Bloom, "Models of Arbitrator Behavior: Theory and Evidence," *American Economic Review*, 74:1, March 1984, pp. 111–124.

[27] James L. Stern et al., *Final Offer Arbitration: The Effects on Public Safety Employee Bargaining* (Lexington, Mass.: Lexington Books, 1975).

[28] Thomas A. Kochan, "Dynamics of Dispute," p. 173. See also Angelo S. DeNisi and James B. Durkin, "Final Offer Arbitration and the Naive Negotiator," *Industrial and Labor Relations Review*, 35:1, October 1981, pp. 78–87.

[29] Carl M. Stevens, "Is Compulsory Arbitration Compatible with Bargaining?" *Industrial Relations*, 5:2, February 1966, p. 46.

Final offer arbitration...in fact has no greater deterrent effect than conventional interest arbitration, and...final offer arbitration awards are significantly, and almost inevitably, worse than conventional arbitration awards.[30]

Despite its introduction as a procedure intended to avoid having a narcotic effect on bargaining, final offer arbitration has been accused of reducing the incentive of the parties to reach agreement.

In Massachusetts the effort to keep final offer arbitration from stultifying collective bargaining has resulted in the creation of a special mediation procedure. The procedure is unusual in that it is the result of a joint effort by unions and employers to find a better method of resolving disputes than final offer arbitration and because it involves a special panel of union and management representatives in the mediation process.

Massachusetts in 1974 enacted a statute providing for last-best-offer arbitration in disputes over the terms of collective bargaining agreements for police officers and firefighter units of the cities and towns in the state. By 1977, management of the cities and towns became convinced that the arbitration process worked to the advantage of the unions. So public managers began to lobby the legislature of the state to revise or repeal the final offer arbitration law. The effort to alter the law quickly became immersed in a major political controversy. In 1977, partly in order to avoid further statewide political turmoil, representatives of the municipalities and the unions proposed the establishment of a joint committee to attempt to resolve disputes without recourse to binding arbitration. The unions and the employers asked the state legislature to grant the joint committee legal status. The legislature thereupon created a 12-member committee consisting of 6 management representatives, 3 union representatives from the firefighters, 3 from the police, and an impartial chairperson (John T. Dunlop). The committee arrangement permits the coordination of police and fire negotiations in the approximately 400 separate negotiations which occur in Massachusetts for contracts involving police and fire employees. The Joint Labor Management Committee for Police and Fire (as it is formally designated) has been successful in reducing the length of time involved in disputes over the renegotiation of agreements and has reduced the proportion of disputes which go into binding arbitration.[31]

CHAPTER SUMMARY

All federal and most state and local employees are currently legally denied the right to strike. Yet strikes by public employees have occurred in the past and are becoming more frequent. Financial loss and jail sentences have been

---

[30] Peter Feuille, "Final Offer Arbitration and the Chilling Effect," *Industrial Relations*, 14:3, October 1975, p. 311. See also Nels E. Nelson, "Final Offer Arbitration: Some Problems," *Arbitration Journal*, 30:1, March 1975, p. 50–58.

[31] John T. Dunlop, "Massachusetts: Joint Labor-Management Committee for Police and Fire," in Dunlop, *Dispute Resolution* (Dover, Mass.: Auburn House, 1984), pp. 242–247. See also Jonathan Brock, *Bargaining beyond Impasse* (Boston: Auburn House, 1982).

used to enforce the strike prohibition. When in the 1970s strikes by public employees reached an all-time high level, the effectiveness of legal prohibitions against strikes was called into question. The effectiveness of the legal prohibition depends on the degree of public opinion against the strike, the degree of internal disagreement in the union, the extent to which the strikers are replaceable, and the willingness of public officials to risk public censure by using force against strikers.

Whether public employees should be allowed to strike is still an open question. On the one hand, strikes seem necessary because without the threat of a work stoppage the employer has no incentive to bargain. On the other hand, a strike against the government is not like a strike against a private employer. Some public services are too important to be disrupted by strikes. In the private sector, the employer is harmed. In the public sector, the public in general is harmed. One alternative that has been considered is to distinguish work stoppages which potentially endanger the public health and safety and those which do not. Large numbers of public employees in nonessential services could be permitted the right to strike, although it would be denied to others.

Without the legal threat of a strike to force dispute settlement, various methods have been tried to move disputes to a resolution. The Federal Labor Relations Authority (FLRA), which is similar to the NLRB, was created to make final decisions in disputes between unions and federal agencies. The FLRA is also involved in dispute resolution when an unfair labor practice has been alleged. A Federal Service Impasses Panel also acts to resolve negotiating disputes after and only after the services of other third-party mediators have failed. Furthermore, the Civil Service Reform Act of 1978 requires that all negotiated agreements include a negotiated grievance procedure with binding arbitration as the final step. The CSRA also expands the number of matters to be included in the scope of the negotiated grievance procedures.

State and local governments have a greater need for effective dispute settlement machinery than does the federal government. They therefore require the submission of disputes to various types of procedures designed to resolve the conflict. The most important procedures of this type involved mediation by a neutral party, fact-finding, and binding arbitration. Fact-finding involves the submission by disputing parties of whatever information they believe to be relevant to resolution of the disputed issue. The fact-finder then prepares a set of recommendations as a suggested basis of settlement.

Arbitration of collective bargaining disputes has become controversial because many municipal employers feel that arbitrators have been too generous with awards made to public employee unions. Furthermore, the knowledge that a dispute will be submitted to an arbitrator for a decision is alleged to reduce the incentive for good-faith bargaining. One party or the other may anticipate that it will receive more from the arbitrator than from a negotiated settlement and so will cling to unrealistic positions. Final offer arbitration was designed to prevent frequent recourse to binding interest arbitration. It requires the neutral arbitrator to select, without modification or compromise, one of the final offers from the parties in a bargaining impasse. Ideally, it induces the parties to develop very reasonable positions in hope of winning the award. However, final offer arbitration has also been criticized for reducing the incentive of parties to reach a settlement.

QUESTIONS FOR THOUGHT AND DISCUSSION

1 Do you think public employees should have the right to strike? Why or why not?
2 What is the best method for resolving disputes in the public sector? Why?
3 What are the different channels, or ways, in which a federal labor-management dispute may be processed?
4 Why do you think strikes by public employees are becoming more frequent in spite of the legal prohibitions against them?
5 Can you suggest original methods for resolving disputes in the public sector—or avoiding them—without recourse to strikes?
6 What are some of the alternative methods of dispute settlement in the public sector which the CSRA of 1978 has been instrumental in creating or maintaining?
7 How does final offer arbitration work and why was it developed? Is it successful?
8 Should police be treated differently with respect to the right to strike than other public employees? Should firefighters be treated differently?

SELECTED READING

Bent, Alan Edward, and T. Zane Reeves, *Collective Bargaining in the Public Sector: Labor-Management Relations and Public Policy* (Menlo Park, Calif.: Benjamin Cummings, 1978).

Blackburn, Jack, and G. Busman, *Understanding Unions in the Public Sector* (Los Angeles: Institute of Industrial Relations, University of California, 1977).

Lewin, David, Peter Feuille, and Thomas Kochan, *Public Sector Labor Relations: Analysis and Readings* (Glen Ridge, N.J.: Thomas Horton, 1977).

AN ASSESSMENT OF LABOR-MANAGEMENT RELATIONS

Both the use of power by managers and unions and the establishment of rights to replace power as a means for the resolution of disputes in labor-management relations have consequences for the broader society in which we live. Collective bargaining contributes to industrial peace by channeling workers' discontent into peaceful paths through which improvements may be made. But in some instances collective bargaining seems to have established levels of compensation and conditions of work which give American companies very high costs. The result is inflation and the loss of production jobs because consumers are buying cheaper imported goods.

CHAPTER **21**

THE CONSEQUENCES OF COLLECTIVE BARGAINING

Unions are an important part of mid-twentieth-century American life. With unionization has come the expansion of the process of collective bargaining. The functions of unions and of collective bargaining include the representation of employees vis-à-vis management and the economic betterment of the employees. Each union does its best to accomplish these functions. What are the consequences of these efforts? What is the impact of collective bargaining on management? And what is the impact of collective bargaining on our economy?

These are general questions. They are not the same as asking, for example, about the impact of collective bargaining on a particular company or the impact on the economy of collective bargaining in a particular industry. The answers to the general questions may not be the same as the answers to the particular questions. For example, unions may be said to have only limited impact on our economy as a whole, but a particular union may have had considerable impact on a particular company or industry. What is true of a particular situation may or may not have general validity.

IMPACT OF COLLECTIVE BARGAINING ON MANAGEMENT

Collective bargaining affects management in many ways. Some effects are significant; some are not. Collective bargaining causes management to follow a different procedure in its dealings with its employees. Instead of unilateral determinations, management must meet and bargain with the union about what changes are to be made at the workplace. But collective bargaining affects management in more ways than this. Some of the most important impacts that collective bargaining has on management are described below.

1 *Collective bargaining compels management to set long-term corporate strategies regarding employees and employment practices.* The failure to adopt consistent strategies with respect to employment practices opens management to claims from a union for the most favorable treatment in all respects. Management inconsistencies may be pointed out by the union and are often resolved in the union's favor.

For example, a company that asserts the right to discharge employees for failure to perform work satisfactorily but keeps performance records about some employees and not others is likely to be prevented by the union from making any discharges at all for performance reasons. If the company discharges an employee without performance records, the union may argue that the discharge is unmerited, since poor performance cannot be proved. After all, the union may say, the company keeps performance records for some employees, and it could have done the same for this person it now wishes to discharge. An arbitrator may be likely to agree. If the company wishes to discharge a person about whom it has records for poor performance, the union may object that the discharge is discriminatory. After all, the union might argue, records are not kept for all employees. Apparently the company simply prepared documentation because it wanted to get rid of this particular employee. How is the union, or the employee, or the arbitrator to know if the discharged employee's work performance is actually poor, since there are no records for other employees by which to make a comparison? It may be inferred, the union might say, that the company has some unspoken motive for discharging the employee and that poor work performance is a contrived excuse for discharge. An arbitrator is again likely to agree. In order to preserve its capacity to discharge for poor performance when a union is present, a company will probably feel compelled to adopt a consistent policy of maintaining performance records on all employees.[1] (It should be noted that consistency in employee practices is good personnel policy in any company, unionized or not. But the presence of a union tends to give management an extra, and significant, incentive for consistency and carefully thought-out policies.)

Most large American corporations that deal with unions feel that to be successful they must establish an industrial relations policy and a specialized, strong, and effective industrial relations staff. One purpose of such a policy and staff is to retain for management as much discretion and initiative as possible in its dealings with the union. General Motors Corporation offers an example of top management in a very large concern that has a clear perception

---

[1] Thomas R. Knight, "The Impact of Arbitration on the Administration of Disciplinary Policies," *The Arbitration Journal*, 39:1, March 1984, pp. 43–56. See also Randall W. Eberts, "How Unions Affect Management Decisions: Evidence from Public Schools," *Journal of Labor Research*, 4:3, Summer 1983, pp. 239–247.

of the long-run importance of the issues involved in labor relations policies. General Motors saw that the unions threatened the freedom of management to run the company's manufacturing and assembly plants and that this freedom would be gradually rubbed away unless the company was willing, if necessary, to fight to protect it. Top management determined which issues it felt it might control and then made it clear to the union and to its line managers that the company was prepared at any time to take strikes over certain matters that top management regarded as essential to effective operation of the company.[2]

2 *Collective bargaining tends to require management to become aware of the day-to-day problems in the operation of the business.* In the past, prior to the advent of collective bargaining, senior management in many companies tended to concentrate on such matters as financial performance, sales, mergers, and organizations, to the exclusion of matters dealing with employees. Working conditions, safety matters, work rules, make-work practices, and similar matters were left to subordinate management. With the advent of unions, however, senior management was required to see that there were responsible corporate officers assigned to pay attention to these matters, so that they would not become the cause of disputes with the union or the source of growing inefficiency in the company.

3 *Collective bargaining establishes a "common law of the shop," which subjects management actions to scrutiny by third parties.* Management is no longer free to take action or alter rules as it desires. A framework of rules is established by which management must act and which it cannot unilaterally alter. And a grievance procedure is set up to protect workers' rights.

4 *Collective bargaining permits management, in some instances, to get more employee satisfaction for its money.* The union provides a mechanism by which employees can make known their preferences with respect to the form, content, and amount of compensation. Thus, management can expect to see its compensation dollar divided up in a way that makes the most sense to its employees and thereby enhance employee satisfaction. Collective bargaining has been the source of most innovations in compensation practices, including virtually all types of benefits. Nonunion employees have copied many or most of these compensation practices, but it is unlikely that they would have developed to any substantial extent in the absence of collective bargaining.

On balance, unionized employees receive higher levels of benefits and devote a larger proportion of total compensation to benefits than do nonunion employees. A study of data for 1977, the most recent study available, found that unionized employees received benefits costing 24.2 percent of their total compensation, and nonunion employees received benefits costing 13.1 percent of total compensation. Health-care benefits for unionized employees were double those for nonunionized employees, both in dollar terms and as

---

[2] Sumner H. Slichter, James Healy, and E. Robert Livernash, *The Impact of Collective Bargaining on Management* (Washington, D.C.: Brookings, 1960).

a percentage of total compensation. Pension benefits for unionized employees were three times as generous in dollars and as a percentage of total compensation for unionized employees.[3] These data indicate that unions have induced management to devote larger resources to benefits than in the nonunion situation.

Not only does unionism tend to raise the share of compensation devoted to benefits, particularly to pensions, vacation pay, and life, accident, and health insurance, but it also appears that where management negotiates with a union that represents production workers, it tends to extend the union's preference for high benefits to nonunion, nonproduction workers as well.[4] Unions also help their members to be more knowledgeable than nonunion employees about the importance of benefits and more conscious of the level and value of the benefits they receive. It appears that unions are likely to cause firms to establish pension programs, but they do not cause pension benefits to be higher for union employees than for nonunion employees who have pension programs.[5] Conversely, unions do not cause employers to be more likely to provide health insurance for union workers than for nonunion workers, but they do cause the health benefits provided to be better for union workers than for nonunion workers.[6]

5 *Collective bargaining permits management to better meet the needs of its employees without having to feel naively altruistic or disloyal to the principles of cost minimization.* It seems unfortunate that many managers should feel reluctant to meet the needs of employees because of the fear that they will appear naively softhearted or that their own supervisors will look with disfavor on their actions. But, though unfortunate, it is an important factor in the behavior of managers. This is so even if meeting employees' needs can be argued to be long-run good business. As a philosopher has remarked, "It is folly to expect people to see their own best interests."

Collective bargaining provides a mechanism by which managers may sometimes do what they would like to do but cannot, because of constraints upon them. Unions serve as advocates of the employees and are able to employ economic force to back their demands. Many a manager finds it convenient to be, or appear to be, compelled to accede to employee demands. Managers often believe that concessions made to employees are for the good of the company and are glad that collective bargaining offers an occasion to take such action.

[3] John A. Zalusky, quoted in Oscar A. Ornati, "The Impact of Collective Bargaining on Employee Benefits," in R. F. Foulkes, ed., *Employee Benefit Handbook* (Boston: Warren, Gorham, and Lamont, 1982). See also Richard B. Freeman, "The Effect of Trade Unionism on Fringe Benefits" (National Bureau of Economic Research, Working Paper No. 292, October 1978).

[4] Richard B. Freeman, "The Effect of Unionism on Fringe Benefits," *Industrial and Labor Relations Review*, 34:4, July 1981, p. 489.

[5] Duane E. Leigh, "The Effect of Unionism on Workers' Valuation of Future Pension Benefits," *Industrial and Labor Relations Review*, 34:4, July 1981, p. 510.

[6] Louis F. Rossiter and Amy K. Taylor, "Union Effects on the Provision of Health Insurance," *Industrial Relations*, 21:2, Spring 1982, pp. 167–177.

6 *Collective bargaining makes changes more difficult to achieve at the workplace.* By establishing formal rules and causing informal practices to become precedent makers, collective bargaining tends to make production processes more rigid. This is the greatest complaint managers have about collective bargaining and unions. It is a more important matter than unions' raising wage levels. Managers often say, "I don't mind high wages as long as we get the productivity." Or they say, "High wages are all right; what really gripes me is the low productivity."

7 *Collective bargaining reduces the profitability of firms and may alter investment behavior.* Economic studies in the early 1980s concluded that in capital-intensive and highly concentrated (that is, few companies) industries, unionism reduces profitability substantially by bargaining for higher wages and benefits than nonunionized employees would be likely to obtain. In the most competitive industries, unionism appears to have little impact on the profitability of firms.[7] In moderately concentrated industries where nonunion and unionized firms compete against one another, unionized firms appear to earn substantially lower profits than nonunion firms. When firms lose a union election, on average there is a 3.8 percent loss of equity value in the stock market, suggesting, say the authors of the study from which this estimate is taken, that unions have a negative impact on profitability.[8]

Subsequent studies did not dispute the negative impact of unions on profits, but did challenge the association of union impact with concentrated industries. Instead, unions had the greatest impact when a company had a large market share, lots of research and development, and was insulated from foreign competition.[9]

Because of the negative impact of unions on profitability, managers have an incentive to try to avoid unionization. But if unions cannot be avoided, the return to capital can be increased by maintaining inefficient plants in production and by minimizing new investment. While protecting profitability to a degree, this strategy is costly to firms because it decreases growth and innovation.[10]

Recent research underlies these conclusions about union effects on profitability and companies' resultant disincentives to invest. The implications of these findings are that American unions by pursuing higher wages and benefits, and American managers by limiting investment to protect short-term

---

[7] Richard B. Freeman, "Unionism, Price-Cost Margins and the Return to Capital" (Cambridge, Mass.: National Bureau of Economic Research, Working Paper No. 1164, December 1983).

[8] Kim B. Clark, "Unionization and Firm Performance," *American Economic Review*, 74:5, December 1984, pp. 893–919; and Richard S. Ruback and Martin B. Zimmerman, "Unionization and Profitability," *Journal of Political Economy*, 92:6, 1984, pp. 312ff.

[9] Barry T. Hirsch and Robert A. Connolly, "Do Unions Capture Monopoly Profits?" *Industrial and Labor Relations Review*, 41:1, October 1987, pp. 118ff.

[10] Carliss Baldwin, "Productivity and Labor Unions," *Journal of Business*, 56:2, April 1983, pp. 155–185. See also Pankaj Tandon, "Internal Bargaining, Labor Contracts, and a Marshallian Theory of the Firm," *American Economic Review*, 74:3, June 1984, pp. 381–393.

profitability, may have together undermined the leadership position of many American firms and industries in the international marketplace.

IMPACT OF COLLECTIVE BARGAINING ON THE ECONOMY

On Productivity

Unions are widely believed by American management to restrict efficient work practices and thereby to contribute to low productivity. Managers generally believe that they can get greater efficiency out of their plants and can more easily make money-saving changes in production methods in the absence of unions. This is a major reason for the continuing strong opposition of American management to unionization. In Europe and Japan, where employers are often less adverse to unionization of their employees, unions and collective bargaining are far less concerned with on-the-job practices and therefore appear to place fewer restrictions on management's operation of the workplace.

This is a very important matter. Defenders of unions and collective bargaining in this country ordinarily point to two results of collective bargaining as justification for it: the protection afforded individual employees against the arbitrary actions of management and the improved economic benefits that unions often obtain for the people they represent. Rarely do defenders of unions and collective bargaining voice support for union jurisdictional claims and disputes or for certain work rules and restrictions on technological innovation. These are seen as unfortunate but understandable and probably inevitable accompaniments of unionization.[11]

On the other hand, many who oppose unionization do not do so because of opposition to grievance procedures or high wages, but rather because of their belief that unions insist on inefficient production processes.[12] How valid are these beliefs of managers?

There have been only a few careful statistical inquiries into the impact of unions on productivity. Table 21-1 summarizes several of these studies. A broad study of all major manufacturing industries indicated a productivity advantage for unionized firms of 20 to 25 percent. Studies of the wooden household furniture and cement industries indicated productivity advantages for unionized firms of 6 to 15 percent. Finally, two studies of the bituminous coal industry conducted about 10 years apart gave strikingly different results. In 1965, unionized underground mines were 25 to 30 percent more productive than their nonunionized counterparts. By 1975, virtually the opposite was true. Finally, a study of construction concluded that apprentice-

---

[11] Richard P. Maher, "Union Contract Restrictions on Productivity," *Labor Law Journal*, 34:5, May 1983, pp. 303–310.

[12] Barry T. Hirsch and Albert N. Link, "Unions, Productivity, and Productivity Growth," *Journal of Labor Research*, 5:1, Winter 1984, pp. 29–37. See also William E. Fruhan, Jr., "Management, Labor and the Golden Goose," *Harvard Business Review*, 63:5, September–October, 1985, pp. 131–141.

TABLE 21-1 ESTIMATES OF THE IMPACT OF UNIONISM ON PRODUCTIVITY

Setting	Estimated increase or decrease in output per worker due to unionism (%)
All two-digit standard industrial classification (SIC) manufacturing industries	20 to 25
Wooden household furniture	15
Cement	6 to 8
Underground bituminous coal	− 20 to −25

Source: Richard B. Freeman and James L. Medoff, "The Two Faces of Unionism," *The Public Interest,* 57, Fall 1979, p. 80.

ship training and job referral systems enhance productivity in union construction, while jurisdictional disputes and restrictive work rules lower it. On balance, union construction workers were found to be more productive than nonunion workers.[13]

Among these studies, possibly the most complete was that conducted by Kim Clark on the cement industry. Clark was able to standardize his estimates of worker productivity for the size of plants, hours of work, location of plants, capacity of plants, and age and capacity of individual kilns in the plants. When these factors were accounted for, the study indicated that unionized plants were 6 to 8 percent more productive than nonunionized plants (as Table 21-1 indicates). Clark was also able to investigate the factors which caused the unionized plants to be more productive. In general, the higher wages and better working conditions in unionized plants did attract a better-quality work force, but the contribution of this factor to the productivity advantage of the unionized plants was small (in the neighborhood of 1 to 2 percent of the 6 to 8 percent union advantage). The changes in managerial practices brought about by unionization were identified by Clark as of substantial significance and were estimated to be a major contributor to the union productivity advantage.[14]

A study of 31 plants of a large multinational firm for the period 1975 to 1982 found that unionization increased the capital-labor ratio and improved management performance, but it also raised the absenteeism rate. A net positive effect on productivity remained even when these channels of union influence were controlled for, a result that may reflect an improved labor relations climate or improved labor quality associated with unionization.[15]

Finally, in the study of manufacturing industries listed in Table 21-1, re-

[13] Steven G. Allen, "Unionized Construction Workers Are More Productive," *Quarterly Journal of Economics*, 99:2, May 1984, pp. 251–274.

[14] Kim B. Clark, "The Impact of Unionization on Productivity: A Case Study," *Industrial and Labor Relations Review*, 33:4, July 1980, pp. 451–469.

[15] Robert N. Mefford, "The Effect of Unions on Productivity in a Multinational Manufacturing Firm," *Industrial and Labor Relations Review*, 40:1, October 1986, pp. 105ff.

searchers found a productivity advantage for unionized firms but also found that this productivity advantage was reflected in a wage advantage of approximately equal magnitude, so that the labor costs in production of union and nonunion establishments were approximately identical.[16]

In the 1980s Steven G. Allen has studied productivity in union and nonunion construction. On privately owned construction projects union productivity is higher, but on publicly owned projects unions are less productive.[17] These studies are comparisons at points in time.

Over long periods, however, other studies show that unions have had little impact on productivity growth in manufacturing but are associated with slower productivity growth in construction.[18]

Also, it appears that in downturns both unionized and nonunionized companies keep more employees than they really need, so that when sales resume, production increases fast without additional labor and productivity expands rapidly.[19]

A study of grievance activity by unions demonstrated that higher grievance activity is often a result of management efforts to increase productivity, and that increased grievances have a slight negative impact on productivity.[20]

One unusually broad study of the auto industry found that from 1959 to 1976 "worker attitudes negatively influenced productivity growth and unit costs, resulting from the failure of both management and labor to create a satisfactory work environment." Another showed no influence of unions on productivity in the auto parts industry.[21]

All in all, these results are somewhat difficult to reconcile with the strongly held view in management, and also, it would seem, in the general public, that unions do not contribute to increased productivity, but rather tend to reduce productivity. It is possible that unions are able to organize the more productive plants and also, as Clark argued, are able to spur management to greater effort to make unionized plants more productive in order to offset higher labor costs which often accompany unionization.

---

[16] Charles Brown and James L. Medoff, "Trade Unions in the Production Process," *Journal of Political Economy*, 86:3, 1978, pp. 355–378.

[17] Steven G. Allen, "Unionized Construction Workers Are More Productive," *Quarterly Journal of Economics*, 99:2, May 1984, pp. 251–274. Also see Steven G. Allen, "Unionization and Productivity in Office Building and School Construction," *Industrial and Labor Relations Review*, 39:2, January 1986, pp. 187ff.

[18] Steven G. Allen, "Productivity Levels and Productivity Change under Unionism," North Carolina State University, draft, March 1986.

[19] Jun A. Fay and James L. Medoff, "Labor and Output over the Business Cycle," *American Economic Review*, 75:5, September 1985, pp. 638–655.

[20] Casey Ichniowski, "The Effects of Grievance Activity on Productivity," *Industrial and Labor Relations Review*, 40:1, October 1986, pp. 75–89.

[21] J. R. Norsworthy and Craig A. Zabala, "Worker Attitudes, Worker Behavior and Productivity in the U.S. Automobile Industry," *Industrial and Labor Relations Review*, 38:4, July 1985, pp. 544ff; and Robert S. and Roger T. Kaufman, "Union Effects on Productivity," *Journal of Labor Research*, 8:4, Fall 1987, p. 79.

On Wages

Among all major demographic groups in the American labor force, union members earn more than persons not represented by unions. Figure 21-1 shows the union-nonunion differential in usual weekly earnings for 1986 (the most recent data available). These data are not adjusted for industry or geographic area, but in Chapter 13 we saw that unionized workers tend to receive higher pay and benefits than nonunionized workers in the same industries and localities.

What is the effect of unions on the earnings of nonunion workers? It is well recognized that unions, in addition to directly affecting their members' wages, may have an indirect effect on the earnings of nonunion workers also. There are two ways by which this might occur, and they are in some senses opposites of each other. On the one hand, unions may cause employers of nonunion labor to raise wage rates in order to avoid the possibility of unionization. In this way, the union sector of the economy may be said to be a wage-leader, or to set a pattern of wage increases for the nonunion sector to follow. Because the mechanism through which pattern following by nonunion employers is thought to operate is one of defensive action against the

FIGURE 21-1   Usual weekly earnings of employed full-time wage and salary workers by labor organization memberships. 1986. (*From Bureau of Labor Statistics, Employment and Earnings, 34:1, January 1987, p. 221.*)

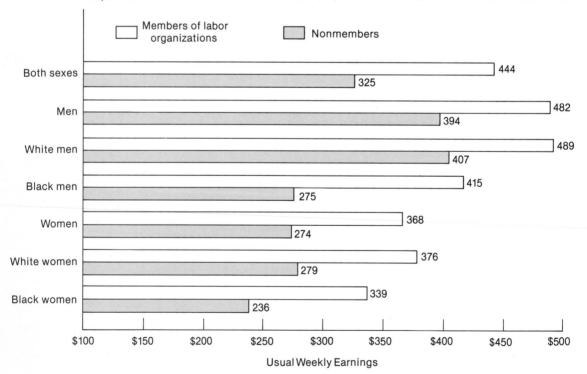

possibility of union organization, this potential effect of unions on the earnings of nonunion workers may be described as a "threat effect."

On the other hand, unions may affect the pay of nonunion workers by limiting the jobs available in the union sector (as a result of high wage levels) and thereby forcing many workers into the nonunion sector. Faced with a large supply of labor, nonunion employers may be able to lower wage rates and yet be able to attract all the labor they need. In effect, the unions' efforts to raise wages in the union sector cause the supply curve of labor to shift outward into the nonunion sector, with a consequent fall in the equilibrium wage rate in the nonunion sector (see Chapter 13). This may be called a "crowding effect."

Which effect is the more important in actual practice? Do unions tend to raise the wages of nonunion employees or to lower them? What would be the wage levels of persons who are currently nonunion employees if unions did not exist? Would the wages paid be higher or lower?

Lawrence M. Kahn has investigated these questions. In a series of statistical studies he has argued that the empirical evidence is that in the long run the crowding effect seems to dominate the threat effect, so that in geographic areas and industries with strong union representation, the wages of nonunion workers tend to be lower, compared with those of the workers represented by unions, than they would otherwise be.

Does this mean that unions do not have very much effect on inflation, because as they raise wages for union members, they simultaneously cause wages for nonunion workers to decline? Not necessarily, Kahn answers, since there may be a different impact in the short run than in the long run. In the short run, it appears that in industries where there are strong unions, union wage gains are passed on to nonunion workers (the threat effect). Thus, Kahn concludes that unions are an inflationary force in the short run and yet tend to force down the pay of nonunion workers and thereby widen the income distribution (and further segment the labor force between high- and low-paid workers) in the long run.[22]

Kahn's work is interesting and important, but it cannot at this stage be accepted as conclusive. For one thing, it does not identify the process by which the short-run dominance of the threat effect is transmitted into the long-run dominance of the crowding effect. For another, his research efforts are necessarily concentrated in particular labor markets, industries, and time periods and can be generalized only with some uncertainty. Broadly, however, his work is consistent with Johnson and Mieszkowski's more theoretical study, which argues that most, if not all, of the gains of union labor are

---

[22] Lawrence M. Kahn, "Unionism and Relative Wages: Direct and Indirect Effects," *Industrial and Labor Relations Review,* 32:4, July 1979, pp. 520–532; "Union Strength and Wage Inflation," *Industrial Relations,* 18:2, Spring 1979, pp. 144–155; "The Effect of Unions on the Earnings of Nonunion Workers," *Industrial and Labor Relations Review,* 31:2, January 1978, pp. 205–216; and "Union Spillover Effects on Organized Labor Markets," *The Journal of Human Resources,* 15:1, 1980, pp. 87–98.

made at the expense of nonunion labor and not at the expense of profits (i.e., that unions raise wages primarily through indirectly lowering the wages of nonunion workers).[23]

On Income Inequality

Even if unions do tend to cause a widening of the differential between union and nonunion wages, this alone is not enough to cause us to conclude that unions on balance increase inequality in incomes in the United States, as Kahn and Johnson and Mieszkowski argue. This is because there are differentials in income among people working in the same establishments as well as differentials among people working in different establishments. What has been the impact of unions on the differentials in pay among people working in the same plant?

Richard Freeman studied this question. He found that unions have the effect of substantially reducing the inequality of pay among workers in the same establishment. In particular, unions reduce pay differentials both among blue-collar workers and between blue-collar and white-collar workers. Thus, in nonunion plants the pay differences tend to be wider than in union plants. This narrowing effect tends to be much larger, Freeman found, than the effect unions have in increasing the wage differential between union and nonunion plants. As a result, Freeman concludes that unions on balance contribute to reducing wage inequality in the United States rather than to increasing it.[24]

On balance, do unions reduce or increase economic wellbeing for our country as a whole, via their impact on wages? It will be remembered that the impact has two elements: raising union wages above nonunion wages, but lessening the pay gap between people in different jobs in unionized establishments. Recent theoretical analyses, which use general equilibrium models to look at all causal interactions, find that unionism has a negligible effect on overall economic efficiency in our economy.[25] This result occurs despite widely divergent adjustments in prices and output in various industries which result from unions' impact on wages.

---

[23] H. G. Johnson and P. Mieszkowski, "The Effects of Unionization on the Distribution of Income: A General Equilibrium Approach," *The Quarterly Journal of Economics*, 84, November 1970, p. 560.

[24] Richard B. Freeman, "Unionism and the Dispersion of Wages," *Industrial and Labor Relations Review*, 34:1, October 1980, pp. 3–23; Gregory M. Duncan and Duane E. Leigh, "Wage Determination in the Union and Nonunion Sectors: A Sample Selectivity Approach," *Industrial and Labor Relations Review*, 34:1, October 1980, pp. 24–34; Richard B. Freeman, "Union Wage Practices and Wage Dispersion within Establishments," *Industrial and Labor Relations Review*, 36:1, October 1982, pp. 3–21; and Barry T. Hirsch, "The Interindustry Structure of Unionism, Earnings and Earnings Dispersion," *Industrial and Labor Relations Review*, 36:1, October 1982, pp. 22–39.

[25] Robert H. DeFina, "Unions, Relative Wages, and Economic Efficiency," *Journal of Labor Economics*, 1:4, 1983, pp. 408–429.

On Inflation and Unemployment

The impact of collective bargaining on management is easier to discern than the impact of collective bargaining on the economy. This is because many factors in the economy affect each other, and causality is difficult to identify. For example, the behavior patterns of unionized and nonunion firms are often so closely related that it is hard to identify which is responsible for specific events. Nonetheless, unions are associated with many of our major economic problems. Unions appear to contribute to inflation and to unemployment by virtue of some of their policies, although they probably do not do so intentionally. Unions in the United States ordinarily profess opposition to inflation, just as they oppose unemployment, but their actions sometimes seem to contribute directly to increased inflation and increased unemployment.

When unions seek wage increases for their members, they contribute to inflationary pressures. They also appear to increase unemployment by making it more expensive for business to hire workers. But each individual union would disclaim responsibility for either result; the union seeks only to protect its members against rising prices or to obtain better living standards for them. But when many unions simultaneously push for higher wages, the pressure is inflationary and may create unemployment as well.

Inflation in our modern economy usually takes the form of a spiral. Prices rise, then wages rise, then prices, then wages; or wages rise, then prices, then wages, then prices. There is much debate on the question of whether wages or prices are to blame for inflation. If wage increases start inflation, then unions appear to bear a special responsibility. If price increases start inflation, then companies appear to bear a special responsibility.

But this is a sterile debate. Unions do not set out as a group to raise wages. Individual unions pursue wage policies in an economic context that they themselves do not control. It is the systematic interaction of wage and price decisions and economic events that generates inflation, not individual unions.

Furthermore, unions do not make wage decisions alone; such decisions are made by unions and employers in the collective bargaining process. It is more appropriate, therefore, to inquire into the impact of collective bargaining on the economy than the impact of unions alone.

Collective bargaining, wage increases, unemployment, and inflation are mixed up in a web of causes and effects. Economists have tried in many ways to untangle the web. No one way is fully satisfactory, but each has kernels of truth. What are the most important of these formulations?[26]

Cost-Push Inflation Unions and big corporations are alleged to be special contributors to cost-push inflation. Unions contribute by seeking wage

---

[26] C. G. Williams, "The Role of Unions in Inflation: A Survey Article," *Relations Industrielles,* 37:3, 1982, pp. 498–527.

increases that are greater than productivity gains at times when there are unemployed people or unused production capacity. Economists would prefer, it appears, that when unused human and mechanical capacity exists in the economy, wages and prices should remain stable and increased consumer or government expenditures should cause increased employment and production, not increased wages and prices. In a perfectly competitive economy, it is said, this is what would occur. But a perfectly competitive economy does not have unions or large corporations. These organizations use their market power to raise wages and prices even when unutilized production resources exist and so create a cost-push inflation.

This is a plausible explanation of inflation and one that has considerable support. Cost-push inflation has now found its way into the economics textbooks. Unfortunately, its logical (or theoretical) foundations are weak. It is, in fact, difficult to demonstrate that a cost-push from collective bargaining is a significant, autonomous contributor to general inflation.[27] Fritz Machlup made this point as follows:

> An inflation of effective demand [i.e., a demand-pull] is a necessary condition not only for a demand-pull inflation of consumer prices, but also for a cost-push inflation. Without an expansion of demands, the cost boost would result in less production and less employment, not in a continuing rise in the level of consumer prices.[28]

Demand-Pull Inflation Demand-pull inflation is said to result from too much money chasing too few goods. Too much money means a volume of expenditures so large that it will more than exhaust total production at existing price levels. When such a volume of expenditures exists, prices rise to cause the volume of expenditures and product (and services) sales to be equal.

The principal contributor to demand-pull inflation is usually said to be the federal government. Either the government spends too much more than it receives, i.e., runs too large a deficit, or the Federal Reserve Board, which controls the nation's money supply, creates too much money (an error of monetary policy). Collective bargaining is not usually alleged to contribute to a demand-pull inflation, but of course it can do so. Wage increases also become purchasing-power increases, and these have the same potential effect on prices as do other types of spending (including government expenditures). Federal authorities might neutralize the additional expenditures through fiscal or monetary policy, but their failure to do so need not be thought to make them the cause of the demand-pull inflation.

---

[27] William G. Bowen, *The Wage-Price Issue* (Princeton, N.J.: Princeton, 1960).
[28] Fritz Machlup, "Another View of Cost-Push and Demand-Pull Inflation," *Review of Economics and Statistics*, 42:2, May 1960, pp. 125–139.

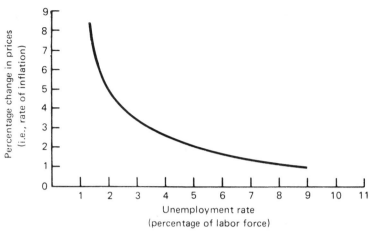

FIGURE 21-2   An idealized Phillips curve.

The Unemployment-Inflation Trade-Off   Yet another description of modern economic problems emphasizes the relationship between unemployment rates and wage increases. This explanation of inflation begins from the observation that often in the economy when unemployment rises, the rate of change in wage rates declines; conversely, when unemployment falls, the rate of change in wage rates accelerates. Thus, wage changes and unemployment appear to be *inversely* related. Furthermore, since wage changes and price changes tend to move together, the relationship between price increases and unemployment appears to be inverse as well. The inverse relationship between price and unemployment is called a Phillips curve, after the economist who popularized the concept. An idealized Phillips curve is shown in Figure 21-2. The shape of the curve implies a *trade-off* between unemployment and inflation. As unemployment rises, a trade-off in the form of less inflation is obtained. As unemployment falls, a trade-off in the form of higher inflation results. Figure 21-2 is said to be idealized because it is not drawn from actual data; it is drawn to show an inverse relationship that may or may not be found in the actual statistics on the economy. In fact, it is difficult or impossible to plot actual data and get the smooth Phillips curve shown in Figure 21-2. (For actual data for the period from 1961 to 1986, see Figures 21-3 and 21-4.)

Regardless of statistical problems in identifying the actual Phillips curve, the idealized, or conceptual, curve has a powerful influence on economic thinking. Underlying the relationship is the view that high unemployment causes wage increases (and therefore price increases) to be moderated. Those

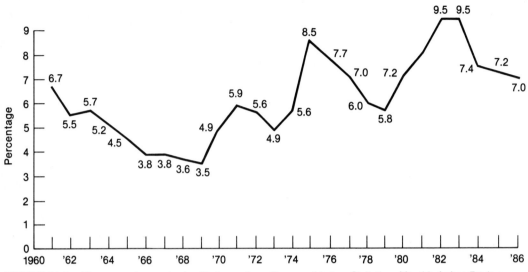

FIGURE 21-3   The unemployment rate. (*Data are from Bureau of Labor Statistics, Monthly Labor Review, 110:10, October 1987, p. 69.*)

FIGURE 21-4   The cost of living. (*Data are from Bureau of Labor Statistics, Monthly Labor Review, 110:10, October 1987, p. 87.*)

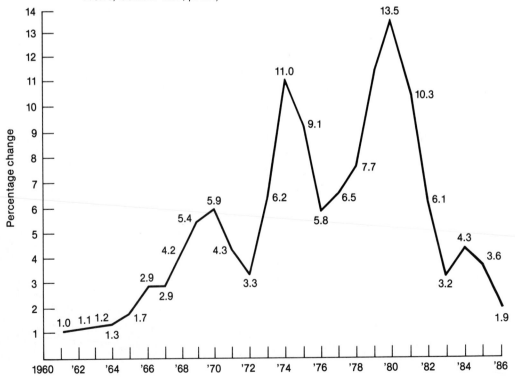

who think in terms of a Phillips curve argue that unions cause economic difficulties by pushing the government to pursue policies of low unemployment and thereby causing wage and price inflation.

The unions do not deny that they favor low unemployment, but they argue that low unemployment need not necessarily mean inflation. They say that intelligent government policies would achieve low unemployment and reasonable price stability simultaneously.

A One-Way Street   There would not be so much inflation in our economy if periods of rising prices were followed by periods of declining prices. This process of inflation and subsequent *de*flation used to occur. In the nineteenth century, periods of inflation and deflation so closely offset each other in the United States that the price level on the average was relatively stable. But after the great depression of the 1930s, general price declines disappeared. Even recessions, like those in 1979 and in 1980, did not cause prices to decline. The rate of increase of prices (i.e, the rate of inflation) did subside, but inflation itself continued.

One factor contributing to the persistence of inflation in our economy today is that collective bargaining has tended to put a floor under wage rates. Decreases in going wage rates have become exceedingly uncommon, even in major recessions. (In isolated instances involving exceptionally unfavorable economic circumstances, decreases in wage rates are sometimes agreed to, whatever the general economic conditions. During the construction industry depression from 1980 to 1982, for example, with some local crafts unions having almost *every member* unemployed, the unions agreed to reduce wage rates in the hope of stimulating some construction activity.) In 1984, for example, with more than 7 percent of the labor force unemployed, wages rose in the United States an average of about 5 percent. Wage increases were partly a result of price increases, as the inflationary spiral continued through the recession. The failure of wage rates to decline, even in periods of substantial recession (the so-called downward rigidity of wages), contributes an upward bias to the general level of wages and prices and therefore to inflation.

Does Collective Bargaining Restrain Inflation?   Against these unfavorable aspects of collective bargaining should be balanced a series of aspects favorable to economic stability. Surprisingly, some of these potential contributions to economic stability are simply the other side of the coin, so to speak, of those unfavorable aspects just listed.

First, collective bargaining in the United States normally entails fixed-term contracts, so that wage rates and benefits are established with a degree of certainty for a period of several months to several years. In inflationary booms, the practice of fixed-term agreements imparts great initial resistance to a wage-price spiral. It is not likely that any other wage-setting mechanism could be so inflexible in the short run,[29] partly because American labor organizations abide by agreements so that the wildcat strikes and payment of wages above negotiated levels—common practices in Western Europe—do not usually occur in this country.

Second, collective bargaining may in some instances prevent noneconomical practices from entering the industrial workplace during business expansions. This is done by directing the attention of managers at each negotiating session to what high sales volume and ready cash availability are doing to loosen production standards in their plants. Management is, as a result, in a better position to control costs than it would be otherwise.

Third, the process of collective bargaining itself and the grievance machinery of unionized plants permit a comparatively orderly approach to the resolution of production and industrial relations problems that commonly develop in a period of business expansion. Through the grievance procedure especially, such problems are often resolved at their origin or, in the case of unresolved grievances, by private voluntary binding arbitration during the term of agreement, thereby greatly reducing the likelihood of work stoppages, strikes, or other disruptions. Such disruptions, whatever their cause, are not only expensive themselves—but may often become the occasion for demands for wage or benefit increases.

The Net Impact of Collective Bargaining on Inflation   But, the reader might object, surely it is possible to conclude more about the net impact of collective bargaining on wage inflation than what has been said above. Probably the most complete exposition of this question has been made by Sumner Slichter. Slichter concluded that unions tend to impart a small inflationary bias to the economy. However, his most interesting analysis related to the more long-term consequences on the inflationary bias in wages. The tendency of collective bargaining to place sustained upward pressure on wages, Slichter argued, induces considerable technological progress as employers seek less labor-intensive methods of production. It also results either in unemployment increases or in price increases. But unions are, in Slichter's view, a major device for generating additional consumer income and spending, which results in increasing employment, a diminished susceptibility to economic recessions (which contributes to the long-run preservation of capitalism), and a reinforced tendency of prices to rise in booms. Because of the income-generation effect of wage increases, Slichter observed, increasing wages does not generally result in increased unemployment (though there might be such effects in certain industries or areas on a limited basis). Were the public to attempt to minimize the effect of collective bargaining in order to eliminate even moderate inflation, concluded Slichter, it would have

---

[29] From 1982 to 1984, for example, compensation under collective bargaining lagged behind compensation gains in the total private economy. This also had occurred in 1961 to 1965; see Marten Estey, "Wages and Wage Policy, 1962–71," in William Fellner, ed., *Economic Policy and Inflation in the Sixties* (Washington, D.C.: American Enterprise Institute, 1972), p. 168.

to sacrifice a rapid rate of industrial growth and accept the increased likelihood of more numerous and more severe recessions.[30] This analysis remains the most plausible and complete understanding of the aggregate impact of collective bargaining on our economy.

But increasing wages is not the only method through which collective bargaining may have an impact on inflation. Changes in work rules and working conditions can also have considerable impact on labor costs and thereby on prices. Condition changes may be negotiated with either favorable or unfavorable effects—i.e., to decrease or increase unit labor costs. It is unfortunate that we have virtually no data that apply directly to the additional costs or savings from rules and conditions changes. Historical experience suggests that periods of high economic activity generate the growth of noneconomical practices in private business, in both union and nonunion sectors, but we have little evidence of the independent impact of collective bargaining on the growth of noneconomic practices in inflationary periods.

Factors Affecting the Relationship of Collective Bargaining and Inflation

Whatever the net impact of collective bargaining on economic stability, it is certain that its impact is not the same in all industries or in all types of inflationary circumstances. Business expansions are rarely distributed evenly across the economy. In those sectors experiencing rapid growth, collective bargaining may prove to be an additional inflationary influence. In the 1970s growth was, for a period at least, especially strong in contract construction, health services, food retailing, and state and local government services. Unfortunately, these were sectors of the economy characterized by highly decentralized collective bargaining, and, in health and government services, relatively recent union organization and consequently nascent collective bargaining. Because of these characteristics, collective bargaining, instead of being a stabilizing or even a neutral influence in these sectors, became a contributor to inflationary pressures.

Can wage determination be broken down into a series of steps in order to help restrain inflation? An interesting proposal has been put forward in Italy. Wage adjustments would be broken into three parts: a bottom tier or base wage would be indexed to the inflation rate to protect the real earnings of low-paid workers, as well as of all other workers; a middle tier would gain increases tied to the individual company's profitability and productivity growth; and a third tier would be tied to occupational skills where demand for scarce skills was pressing wage levels up. On balance, the whole scheme is intended to reduce the tie of wages as a whole to inflation, with the hope of thereby breaking or moderating the price-wage spiral.[31]

---

[30] Sumner H. Slichter, "Do the Wage-Fixing Arrangements in the American Labor Market Have an Inflationary Bias?" *Proceedings* of the American Economic Association, May 1954; and "Economics and Collective Bargaining," in *Economics and the Policy Maker* (Washington, D.C.: Brookings, 1959).

[31] "CP Wants Three-Tier Pay System," *Industrial Relations Europe*, January 1982, p. 6.

Collective bargaining does not respond in the same way to different types of inflationary pressures. For example, in the boom occasioned by consumer goods shortages at the end of World War II, collective bargaining, despite serious strikes, offered little or no independent inflationary pressures.[32] Even the decentralized bargaining system in construction operated to adjust wage levels to varying economic circumstances in the country, rather than to distort wage rates and impel them upward. During the speculative boom from 1950 to 1951, collective bargaining agreements in major manufacturing reinforced a wage-price spiral, but one that probably would have occurred anyway. On the positive side, the multiple-year term of some agreements provided a stablizing influence prior to the application of controls. In the late 1950s, the end of the post-World War II period of high production in manufacturing did not bring about a retardation in wage increases negotiated in collective bargaining; large settlements continued to be negotiated. These settlements were partly responsible for the moderate inflation of the period from 1956 to 1959.[33] The role of collective bargaining in the inflation of the period from 1965 to 1970 was described above as being dominated by generalized demand pressures and by the undesirable consequences of decentralized bargaining and rapid growth in output in a few sectors of the economy. From 1973 to 1980, collective bargaining tended to follow inflationary pressures rather than to create them. From 1981 to 1985, as inflation abated, collective bargaining settlements dropped dramatically, falling behind increases for nonunion workers. There is, therefore, a complex picture of the relationship between collective bargaining and inflation—a picture in which the source of inflationary pressures and their impact on various sectors of the economy interact with the varying structures of collective bargaining and timing of agreements. Whether collective bargaining serves as a constraint on inflationary pressures or worsens them depends on the factors listed above, though the net effect is often difficult to estimate, even after the fact.

THE PUBLIC UTILITY OF COLLECTIVE BARGAINING

What impact have unions and the institution of collective bargaining had on our society? The answer may be that there has been so great an impact that we would not recognize our society if unions and collective bargaining did not exist in it. But we cannot know if this is so because we are, of course, unable to observe our society without unions. In consequence, some people believe that the impact of unions has been great, and some believe it has been small. The matter cannot be conclusively settled. We can, however, ex-

---

[32] See, for example, Albert Rees, "Wage-Price Relations in the Basic Steel Industry, 1945–1948," *Industrial and Labor Relations Review*, 6:2, January 1953, pp. 195–205.

[33] Derek Bok and John Dunlop list and characterize these periods without describing the role of collective bargaining in each, though they note that it was "not the same in each"; see D. Bok and J. T. Dunlop, *Labor in the American Community* (New York: Simon and Schuster, 1970), pp. 292–293.

plore aspects of the impact of unions and collective bargaining in specific terms. From a study of these several items, some readers may come to a generalized judgment on the impact of unions. Others will find the matter still unsettled in their minds.

In this chapter the impact of unions on two major aspects of our society has been described. What remains to be done here is to survey the general social impact of unions and collective bargaining.

1 *Unions and collective bargaining are a method by which workers participate in the governance of our society.* It would be possible, perhaps, to deny to workers these particular methods of participation, as is often done in totalitarian countries. In such countries workers' organizations (i.e., unions) either are outlawed or are controlled by the state. There are proposals made in the United States periodically to substantially restrict the activities of unions—for example, by prohibiting the strike and replacing it with a system of compulsory arbitration of labor disputes. But it is likely that in our society, where the freedom of individuals and groups is of great concern, such restrictions imposed over the objections of workers would cause great social unrest. Those who favor substantial legal restrictions on unions argue that because most American employees do not belong to unions, there is not a great deal of support for their activities among working people. But this is surely a misreading. Not all employees join unions or are represented in collective bargaining, but many of those who do are very much committed to the process and will struggle to retain it. Many of those members undoubtedly favor their freedom to participate and are glad that others do participate. To attempt to substantially restrain the activities of workers' organizations in our society would create considerable turmoil.[34]

2 *Collective bargaining reduces the role of the government in the relationships of management and labor.* The essential function of collective bargaining, wrote John R. Commons, "is the elimination, as far as possible, of a third party...whether king, legislature, governor or dictator, handing down rules and regulations from above—and the substitution of rules agreed upon collectively."[35] The American system of collective bargaining establishes rules about wages, benefits, working conditions, and the resolution of grievances and other disputes. The rules established by collective bargaining are often imitated by nonunion firms. The result is a system of rules established largely exclusive of the government. Both management and labor tend to prefer this private system of rule making and to oppose government intervention.

Would there be more or less government intervention without unions? Many managers seem to believe that the government would take little or no

---

[34] Lloyd Ulman and Elaine Sorensen, "Exit, Voice and Muscle: A Note," *Industrial Relations*, 23:3, Fall 1984, pp. 424–428.

[35] John R. Commons, *Myself* (New York: Macmillan, 1934), pp. 72–73. Commons was a great legal and social historian and a pioneer in developing social welfare programs in the United States.

interest in employee relations if unions did not exist. These managers believe that they would be left to establish employee relations policies without any outside interference, from either the unions or the government. In support of their position, they point to the United States 70 to 100 years ago, before the organization of unions, and note that there was little government involvement in labor relations then. In the years since that time both collective bargaining *and* government regulation have expanded, they point out.

What is unconvincing about this argument is the suggestion that in the absence of unions American society today would be much like it was many decades ago. This is very unlikely. Whatever it would be today without unions and collective bargaining, it would probably not be as it was long ago. Too many things have changed (including population, technology, and economics) and too many events have occurred (including two world wars). It is well to remember that unionism in this country made its greatest advances during the two great wars, when the society most needed the support of the working people. Had unions not grown, and with them the private system of labor-management relations that is collective bargaining, the likelihood is that the government would have more closely regulated employee relations, either as the champion of the workers or simply in the interest of industrial peace. Increased governmental regulation was the course of development in most nations abroad. It is highly unlikely that in the United States alone management would have been left in unilateral control of employee relations. The choice American managers faced was to bargain collectively about compensation, conditions of work, and grievance procedures or to see the government enter these fields as a regulator.

3 *Collective bargaining makes certain contributions to our society that are of lesser significance than those just mentioned, but are nonetheless important.* Among these contributions are the determination of priorities within labor and within management, the day-to-day administration of the workplace, and the resolution of problems unique to certain industries and occupations.[36] Each of these matters is ill suited to resolution by the bureaucratic procedures of governmental administrative agencies or by litigation in the courts. Yet each of these matters involves many specific problems that must be resolved. For the efficient handling of such matters, if collective bargaining did not exist, we should have to invent it.

4 *Unions and collective bargaining subject the public to the inconvenience, and sometimes the danger, of work stoppages.* Often it seems that if unions did not exist, strikes would not occur, or it may appear that unions and collective bargaining can be retained, but the strike eliminated. Certainly, from the point of view of the general public, the work stoppage is the most annoying aspect of our system of collective bargaining. Attempts of management and

---

[36] John T. Dunlop, "The Social Utility of Collective Bargaining," in Lloyd Ulman, ed., *Challenges to Collective Bargaining* (Englewood Cliffs, N.J.: Prentice-Hall, 1967), pp. 172–175.

labor to lessen the frequency of strikes in order to improve the public performance of collective bargaining have been described in previous chapters.

CHAPTER SUMMARY

Unions and collective bargaining have affected management in many important ways. Collective bargaining (1) compels management to set long-term corporate strategies regarding employees and employment practices and to establish a consistent labor relations policy, (2) tends to require senior management to become aware of day-to-day problems in the operation of the business, (3) establishes a common law of the shop which subjects management actions to scrutiny by third parties, (4) permits management in some instances to invest its compensation dollar in a way that makes most sense to employees, (5) has permitted management to better meet the needs of its employees without having to feel disloyal to the principles of cost minimization, and (6) makes changes more difficult at the workplace and production processes more rigid by establishing formal rules and causing informal practices to become precedents.

Unions are widely believed by management to restrict efficient work practices and thereby to contribute to low productivity. Several studies have shown a distinct productivity advantage in unionized firms; some studies have shown the opposite. Studies which show a productivity advantage do not say that unions actually contribute to increasing productivity, but only that they are associated with it. Unions may organize in more productive plants, attract a better-quality work force, or spur management to greater efforts to offset higher labor costs. Unions reduce profits for firms, however, and may cause companies to invest less in new technology and new products than otherwise.

Union members earn more than persons not represented by unions. Unions may also affect the earnings of nonunion workers. Several studies have investigated this issue with varied conclusions. Two possibilities have been identified. With the "threat" effect, employers in the nonunion sector increase wages to union levels as a defense against union organization. Through the "crowding" effect, unions limit the number of high-wage jobs and raise the supply of workers who can be paid low wages by nonunion employers. In the long run, the crowding effect seems to dominate over the threat effect. In the short run, in industries where there are strong unions, union wage gains are passed on to the nonunion workers. It has been concluded that unions, on balance, contribute to reducing wage inequality in the United States rather than to increasing it.

Collective bargaining, wage increases, unemployment, and inflation are mixed up in a web of causes and effects. There are many ways, however, that unions appear to contribute to inflation and unemployment. Unions and corporations are alleged to be special contributors to cost-push inflation by seeking and allowing wage increases that are greater than productivity gains. In addition, economists who base their opinion on the Phillips curve (which shows an inverse relation between wages and employment) allege that unions cause wage and price inflation by pressing the government to pursue policies of low employment. The maintenance of a floor under wages is another way collective bargaining contributes to the persistence of inflation.

Some aspects of collective bargaining are favorable to economic stability and act to restrain inflation. Collective bargaining entails fixed-term contracts so that wage rates and benefits are set for various periods of time. In inflationary booms, fixed-term agreements impart great initial resistance to a wage-price spiral. One interesting and plausible analysis suggests that while unions tend to impact a small inflationary bias to the economy, they also are a major device for generating additional consumer income and spending, which results in increasing employment and less susceptibility to economic recessions. Also, the upward pressure on wages includes technological progress as employers seek less labor-intensive methods of production.

The net effect of collective bargaining on economic stability is difficult to estimate and so unclear that no specific approach to policy is justified. It is certain that the impact of collective bargaining is not the same in all industries or in all types of inflationary circumstances.

QUESTIONS FOR THOUGHT AND DISCUSSION

1 What are the major ways in which unions have affected management in the United States? Are there major differences in the impact of unions on unionized firms and on nonunionized firms? What are the differences, if any?

2 What is the major impact of collective bargaining on the economy? Does collective bargaining cause inflation? Does collective bargaining cause unemployment?

3 What responsibility do unions have to control inflation? What responsibility does management have? What responsibility does government have?

4 What would our society be like without unions? Without management? Why?

5 Do unions tend to raise the wages of nonunion employees or to lower them? How would wages be determined if unions did not exist?

6 One reason many managers oppose unionization is their belief that unions insist on inefficient production processes and contribute to low productivity. What have studies of the impact of unions on productivity concluded? What impact do unions have on profits?

7 What effects does the strong managerial opposition to unions appear to have on union practices and demands? How does this in turn affect management? Is the situation different in countries where unions are not in a defensive position?

8 What is the impact of changes in work rules and working conditions on labor costs and thus on prices? How would you go about setting up a study of the impact of collective bargaining on the growth of noneconomical practices in inflationary periods?

SELECTED READING

Annable, James E., *The Price of Industrial Labor: The Role of Wages in Business Cycles and Economic Growth* (Lexington, Mass.: Lexington Books, 1984).

Freeman, Richard B., and James L. Medoff, *What Do Unions Do?* (New York: Basic Books, 1984).

Mills, Daniel Quinn, *Government, Labor and Inflation* (Chicago: University of Chicago Press, 1975).

Mitchell, Daniel J. B., *Unions, Wages and Inflation* (Washington, D.C.: Brookings, 1980).

Parsley, C. J., "Labor Union Effects on Wage Gains: A Survey of Recent Literature," *Journal of Economic Literature*, 18:1, March 1980, pp. 1–31.

Slichter, Sumner H., James Healy, and E. Robert Livernash, *The Impact of Collective Bargaining on Management* (Washington, D.C.: Brookings, 1960).

22

INDUSTRIAL RELATIONS ABROAD

INFLUENCE FROM ABROAD

It has become common to note that the world seems to be getting smaller as a result of improved communications, so that developments abroad now seem to affect us in the United States to a greater degree than they used to. There is increasing evidence of this in our labor-management relations. Years ago union officials in Germany began to serve on the supervisory boards of corporations. But until 1979 this was not done in the United States, except where unions had an intimate business role in the corporation (as in the case of a union-owned bank, for example). But in 1976 the UAW, citing European precedent, sought membership on Chrysler's board of directors and in 1979 obtained it.

American companies have not readily granted union leadership seats on corporate boards, however. The UAW obtained a seat at Chrysler only because of the company's extreme economic difficulties. Since 1979 union leaders have also gained board membership at several of the nation's airlines, again because of economic difficulties in which these companies found themselves.

But once established, the unions may have found a place on some corporate boards. Chrysler's financial fortunes have improved greatly since 1979. In 1984, former UAW President Douglas Fraser resigned from Chrysler's board, leaving a position open. Owen Bieber, Fraser's successor as president of the UAW, was then elected to Chrysler's board (in October 1984). Bieber's election occurred because the UAW wanted to serve on Chrysler's board of directors, and because Chrysler's management had accepted the role of a union representative on its board.

As is evident from this brief recounting of events at Chrysler, developments in labor-management relations abroad are not readily and uncritically adopted in America. But as is also evident in the Chrysler experience, when either labor or management sees a development abroad which interests it, it sometimes seizes opportunities (including economic distress) to introduce foreign concepts to the United States. Recently, the leadership of the AFL-CIO, dissatisfied with the degree of success (or lack of it) labor has had in American politics, has looked abroad, especially to European and Israeli Social Democratic and Labor parties, for new models.

For its part, American business has become more conscious of foreign industrial relations practices as a result of the internationalization of its own activities.

Finally, the recent advantage of Japanese and German firms in competition with American firms, both in the United States and abroad, has focused attention on the reasons for their success. Among the factors often pointed out as contributing to the success of Japanese and German firms are their systems of industrial relations. And some authors have begun to suggest that American firms borrow Japanese and German practices in the search for better productivity and enhanced competitiveness.

JAPAN

Japan, an island nation like Great Britain, has a population of more than 100 million. It is a major industrial power, which since World War II has had a very high rate of economic growth. For many years Japanese products were known in the United States for low quality and low cost. Both these characteristics were based in part on very low wages paid to Japanese employees. But these conditions are far less prevalent now. Today Japan sells many high-quality products in the United States, including televisions, radios, and phonographic equipment from such makers as Sony and Panasonic and automobiles from Toyota and Datsun. Japanese workers have received considerable wage increases in recent years, so that the difference between American and Japanese wage levels has been narrowed appreciably.

The Japanese industrial relations system is an interesting one for an American to study. In some ways the Japanese system is much like ours. For example, the Japanese have a diversified industrial economy, employ very modern technology, and have a largely free enterprise system. Government regulation of business and labor takes much the same form as in the United States, partly because after World War II the Japanese remodeled their labor laws on the American statutes. However, Japanese industrial relations are also different in profound ways from those in the United States.[1] The "dual" economic system and the "lifetime" employment system have no exact

---

[1] Taishiro Shirai, ed., *Contemporary Industrial Relations in Japan* (Madison, Wis.: University of Wisconsin Press, 1983).

American counterparts, and the result is a different role for unions and employers than in the United States.

The most unique characteristics of the Japanese industrial relations system arise from the duality of the Japanese economy. In the mid-1800s the Japanese discovered that they had fallen behind the Western nations in military and industrial development. Fearing for its future as an independent nation, Japan began to stimulate economic advancement through the agency of certain private trading companies. Over the years, these companies grew into very large and modern industrial enterprises.[2] Other elements of the Japanese economy did not grow as much or progress as rapidly. The result is that Japan's economy has two sectors: one made up of large firms that are technically advanced and another made up of many small firms, often with very inefficient production processes. As one might expect, the larger firms pay higher wages and provide better working conditions for their employees than do the less advanced firms.

The connection between the two sectors is through subcontracting. When large firms have more orders than they can fill, they subcontract them to small firms. But when there is a recession and orders decline, the subcontractors are cut off. This procedure allows the big firms to provide stable employment for their own employees and is a basic component of the "lifetime employment" system.

The lifetime employment system is practiced by large Japanese firms. Employees are hired when they finish school, and they remain with the same company all their lives. These workers are called "standard workers." They receive many benefits and are paid higher salaries as their length of time with the company increases.[3] Nonstandard workers are hired by the company to supplement its standard work force, but they have lesser benefits and may be laid off if business declines. A company may also hire temporary workers and may utilize the services of outside contractors' employees. Figure 22-1 is a diagrammatic representation of the employment structure of a large Japanese firm, showing the various categories of workers. The lifetime employment system applies primarily to standard workers. These workers are laid off only if the company has a major reduction in business. Nonstandard, temporary, and outside workers (who total approximately one-half of the firm's workers) are readily laid off. Deep recessions can require layoffs even of standard workers so that the agreements must be modified. In 1974, for example, the head of a Japanese union at a camera manufacturing plant agreed to a new contract that permitted layoffs. Then, when people actually

---

[2] Chie Nakane, *Japanese Society* (Berkeley: University of California Press, 1970).
[3] Makotu Sakurabayashi, "How a Japanese Firm Sets Salaries for Its Clerical Employees," *Compensation Review*, 7:2, 1975, pp. 42–49. Also, Nan Weiner, "The Japanese Wage System," *Compensation Review*, 14:1, 1982, pp. 45–56.

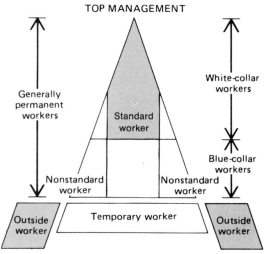

FIGURE 22-1   Employment structure of a large Japanese firm.

lost their jobs, he tried to commit suicide, since he felt responsible for their misfortune.[4]

The lifetime employment system has created among Japanese employees a degree of loyalty to the firm that is much envied by American managers.[5] The labor relations of Japanese firms also reflect this loyalty. Japanese unions are organized primarily among the permanent employees of a firm and exhibit considerable personal identification with their company, rather than with an occupation or an industry. Plant unions usually belong to a companywide federation of unions.

There are also national unions, of course, some of which are affiliated with national federations. These national federations provide general guidance to their constituent national unions, but they rarely intervene in day-to-day industrial relations. The labor movement as a whole continues to be divided on ideological grounds. The largest central federation, Sohyo, is essentially Marxist in orientation. It was formed in 1950 and identifies with the Japanese Socialist party. The second largest central federation, Domei, is anticommunist and supports the moderate Democratic Socialist party. Surprisingly to an American, the largest proportion of the membership of Sohyo, the more radical federation, is made up of government employees. Private employees are the larger group in Domei, the more moderate federation. As in the United States, Japanese unions have been losing ground.

---

[4] Fox Butterfield, "Economic Woes Imperil Lifetime Jobs in Japan," *The New York Times*, Oct. 24, 1974, p. 1.

[5] Richard T. Johnson and William G. Ouchi, "Made in America (under Japanese Management)," *Harvard Business Review*, 52:5, September–October 1974, pp. 61–69. Also, Kazutoshi Koshiro, "Lifetime Employment in Japan," *Monthly Labor Review*, 107:8, August 1984, pp. 34–35.

The unionization rate fell from 34 percent in 1975 to 29 percent in 1985. Also as in the United States, the sectors of the economy most unionized have changed from manufacturing to public services, while services are weakly organized.[6]

In the spring of each year the unions conduct a wage offensive, called Shunto. A single union is selected to try to reach an agreement with its employers, which will then become a pattern that other unions and employers can follow. Through this process, collective bargaining negotiations and strikes are concentrated in the spring months.

Employers are well organized in Japan.[7] The Japanese Federation of Employers Association (Nikkeiren) is concerned exclusively with labor relations. It coordinates labor policies among its members, expresses an employer view on labor issues and public policy in general, and disseminates information to its members. Another organization of firms that is very influential in expressing a management viewpoint on the development of national economic policy in Japan is the Federation of Economic Organizations (Keidenren). There are no comparable organizations of employers in the United States, where there are several competing employer associations, each seeking to speak for various elements of the business community. The sort of centralized and coordinated action by employers that occurs in Japan with respect to labor relations and economic policy does not occur in the United States.

GERMANY

We may identify two types of labor relations innovations that have been the subject of experimentation in Germany. These arrangements have sometimes been grouped together and referred to as developments involving "industrial democracy" or greater "worker participation in management." Discussion about which term, if either, is more appropriate need not detain us. Nor are these developments confined to Germany; counterparts exist for many of them in other European countries. However, their evolution has been carried further in Germany than elsewhere.

1 *Codetermination* involves the appointment of workers' representatives to the boards of directors of corporations. A broader definition of codetermination would stress providing workers a role in the decision-making processes of an enterprise.

2 *Works councils* are a method of providing representation for workers in

---

[6] Susan Chira, "Bitter Days for Japan's Unions," *The New York Times*, Jan. 14, 1987, pp. D1 and D5.

[7] Taishiro Shirai and Haruo Shimada, "Japan," in John T. Dunlop and Walter Galenson, eds., *Labor in the Twentieth Century* (New York: Academic Press, 1978), pp. 241–322. Also, William B. Gould, *Japan's Reshaping of American Labor Law* (Cambridge, Mass.: MIT Press, 1984).

the workplace and a chance for cooperation between workers and management on matters affecting the enterprise.

Codetermination on Supervisory Boards

The essence of codetermination is a partnership of owners and labor in the operation of an enterprise. In 1947, after World War II, the British occupation forces in the Ruhr Valley of Germany introduced codetermination into the German steel industry. In 1951 it was extended to coal also. In practice codetermination means that workers have representatives on the boards that have responsibility for the enterprise. A European firm, unlike an American enterprise, has a two-level structure of boards.[8] One level, the supervisory board, meets only a few times a year and has general responsibility for policy decisions about the enterprise. For example, the question of whether or not to acquire another company would be a matter for action by the supervisory board. There is also a management board, consisting of the top management of the enterprise, which conducts its day-to-day business. Codetermination in the German steel and coal industries affects both boards.

The supervisory boards of large companies in the steel and coal industries consist of five representatives of stockholders, five representatives of the firm's employees, and one neutral person nominated by majority vote of the other ten members of the board. Employee members of the board, or the "worker directors," are two nominees of the works councils and three nominees of the unions. (If the board has more than 11 members, the parity principle between worker and stockholder representatives applies.)[9] One member of the management board of the companies must be a labor relations manager, who cannot be chosen against the majority vote of the employee members of the supervisory board. Thus, the employees (and the unions) are represented on both the supervisory and the management boards. On the supervisory boards the structure is truly codeterminational (*mitbestimmung* in German), in that stockholders and employees have acquired an equal number of directors.

Elsewhere in German industry employees are entitled by law to just less than equal representation on the supervisory boards of corporations. Until 1976 German law gave employees one-third of the seats of supervisory boards. The unions campaigned for an increase in the proportion of employee directors to half, but they failed to acquire parity. For companies with 200 to 500 employees, shareholders elect two-thirds of the members of the board. For firms which employ 2000 or more persons, a formula permits

[8] William H. McPherson, "Codetermination in Practice," *Industrial and Labor Relations Review*, 8:4, July 1955, pp. 499–519.

[9] Bernhard Wilpert, "Research on Industrial Democracy and the German Case," *Industrial Relations Journal*, 6:1, Spring 1975, pp. 53–64.

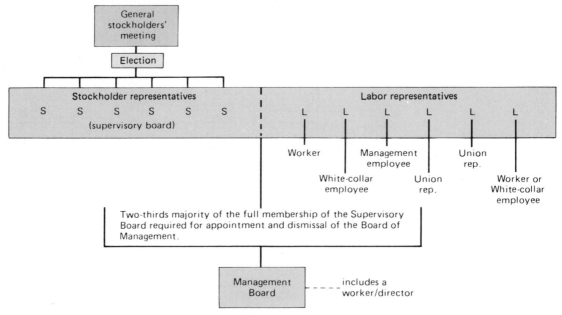

FIGURE 22-2 The organizational design of the supervisory and management board level for a corporation satisfying the German codetermination requirements outside the steel and coal industries. (*From Robert J. Kühne, "Co-Determination: A Statutory Re-Structuring of the Organization," Columbia Journal of World Business, 11:2, Summer 1976, p. 20. Also, Industrial Relations Europe, West German Supplement, 1982, March 1982, p. 3.*)

stockholders to retain a majority of directors. Briefly, the formula establishes a supervisory board that consists of representatives in the ratio of six shareholder representatives, six employee representatives, and a chairperson elected by the shareholder members. One labor representative must be an employee elected by upper-middle management, and in the event of a tie in the number of votes cast, the chairperson, ordinarily a representative of the stockholders, may cast a second vote.[10] These factors effectively guarantee stockholder control (see Figure 22-2). The formula establishes *mitbestimmung* in form but not in decision making. German law concerning the composition of the board of directors applies to all German companies, including subsidiaries of American multinationals.[11]

German unions support codetermination as providing for the participation of workers in managerial decision making and also for a greater social awareness by business. German business people have not been opposed to worker

[10] Heinz Haitman, "Managerial Employees—New Participants in Industrial Relations," *British Journal of Industrial Relations*, 12:26, July 1974, pp. 268–281.

[11] George S. McIssac and H. Henzler, "Codetermination: A Hidden Noose for MNCs," *Columbia Journal of World Business*, 9:4, Winter 1974, pp. 67–74.

representation on boards of directors.[12] They credit codetermination with helping to develop Germany's reasonably stable labor relations climate. However, they have bitterly opposed *mitbestimmung*, i.e., a board split equally between employees' and shareholders' directors. An example of the problems they foresaw occurred in 1975 when the chairman of Volkswagen, Rudolf Leiding, was removed by the combined vote of employee directors and the board members who represented the German government's 40 percent ownership of Volkswagen. Leiding was ousted because of his proposal to build a VW plant in the United States. The proposal was later given approval on November 29, 1976, by the Supervisory Board of Volkswagen, and the company is now operating production facilities in the United States.

Other European countries are now experimenting with codetermination. And there have been proposals for a Western European statute under which businesses would be incorporated and which would include codetermination provisions.[13]

Works Councils

Works councils are committees, ordinarily made up of management and employee representatives, that have certain functions in the governance of a workplace. Employee representatives are generally elected by the employees in a particular plant. If the plant is part of a larger enterprise, the plant-level works councils send delegates to a central, or enterprise, works council.

Germany has experimented with joint labor-management committees, the precursors of works councils, since 1848.[14] The most recent comprehensive legislation affecting works councils is the Works Constitution Act of 1972. The act establishes works councils as all employees' permanent representative bodies and gives them specific rights.

Works councils generally have one of four types of powers. About certain issues the council has the legal *right to be informed*. Management has a duty, in this instance, to provide information regarding certain matters to the works council. About other issues the works council has the *right to be consulted*, i.e., to offer advice to the company's management. About still other issues the council members may have the *right to investigate* matters on their own initiative. The company must cooperate in their investigation. Finally, in some instances the council has the right of *codetermination*; that is, management cannot act without the agreement of the works council.

The types of matters about which works councils may have rights are often divided in Germany into economic and social matters. *Economic matters* include mergers, transfers, closure of the firm, expansion or contraction of op-

[12] David Clutterbuck, "How Worker Directors Are Working Out," *Management Review*, 63:6, June 1974, pp. 32–34.
[13] Robert J. Kühne, *Co-Determination in Business* (New York: Praeger, 1979).
[14] Friedrich Furstenberg, "Workers' Participation in Germany," International Institute for Labor Studies, *Bulletin*, No. 6, June 1979, pp. 1–55.

erations, relocation, organizational structure, and the general trend of business and financing decisions. *Social matters* include layoffs, wage payment systems, methods of training, pensions, distribution of profits, safety and health, and holiday arrangements.[15]

The reader will note that many of the above are matters that are ordinarily left to collective bargaining in the United States. But in Germany it is the works council that negotiates arrangements with management about such issues. The works council's relationship to the unions is complex. The unions may usually nominate candidates for election to the works councils. But works council members who are also union members are apparently free to act on the council as they wish.

The works councils normally do not have the right to strike, but the unions do. It is apparently not uncommon for works council members to coordinate activities with the unions and in some instances to arrange for the unions to strike in support of employee members of a works council when there is a difference of opinion with management.[16] The unions are further removed from the workplace in Germany than in the United States, in the sense that full-time union representatives in a plant are uncommon. The unions operate primarily at the industry level, negotiating broad agreements covering wages and working conditions. The specific application of national agreements to a particular company are worked out by the works councils.

This dual structure of labor relations, the unions and the works councils, has no counterpart in the United States. The existence of works councils in all large firms is required by law in Germany. The national collective bargaining agreements apply to all firms in an industry, unless they are specifically replaced by an agreement between a particular firm and the union(s) involved. As a result, there is no such thing as the nonunion firm in the way it exists in the United States. All major firms are involved in the structure that establishes the representation rights of employees, both through works councils and through unions. In the United States, in contrast, a firm that is nonunion has no collective bargaining agreement and probably has no elected representation of its employees. (Some American nonunion firms do have elected employee staff associations, which are something like a works council, but with no rights or responsibilities established by law.)

Under German law, in all plants with at least five employees the employees may elect by secret ballot from among themselves works councils to serve for a period of 3 years. The size of the works council is dependent on the number of employees of the plant. A plant with 100 employees, for instance, has 5 works councillors. They are allowed to perform their works council duties during paid working time. The rights of the works councils are specifically described by law:

---

[15] Walter Kolvenbach, *Employee Councils in European Companies* (Deventer: Kluwer, 1978).

[16] Catherine Coffin Lindsay, "Works Councils in the Federal Republic of Germany," unpublished master's degree thesis, MIT, 1976.

- The works council is to be thoroughly informed on many labor relations matters (such as personnel planning, planned changes in workplace, and working procedure).
- The works council has a right to be consulted and to discuss with management all plans to change working conditions (including the shutdown of a plant).
- The employer is not allowed to dismiss an employee without having previously informed the works council. The works council may contest a planned dismissal.
- The works council has to be asked for its consent whenever the employer wants to employ, classify, or transfer a person. If the works council should—based on specific reasons—refuse its consent, the employer is not allowed to perform the planned action.
- Disputes are to be settled by the labor courts.
- The employer has to have the consent of the works council whenever it wants to introduce regulations concerning matters such as:

Orderly behavior
Beginning and ending of work time
Checking of conduct and efficiency by technical equipment
Social welfare institutions
Special benefit plans in connection with extensive dismissals
Wage frameworks
Suggestion systems

- The works council may on its own motion ask for the introduction of regulations.
- Disputes are settled by a conciliation board (which consists of an equal number of works councils and employees' representatives and one neutral person).

The central works council of an enterprise elects members for an economic committee that is to be informed and consulted on all important entrepreneurial plans and decisions.

Works councils have the general task of implementing the law. The councils are also the representatives of the employees in all affairs and questions that have to do with the employer-employee relationship.

The relationship between the unions and works councils is highly complex. Some observers see the unions losing ground to works councils. A survey of the attitudes of German employees taken in the mid-1980s found that works councils are believed most valuable to the individual worker, unions next significant, and the labor director(s) on corporate supervisory boards least important.[17]

---

[17] Charles J. Hobson and James B. Dworkin, "West German Labor Unrest," *Monthly Labor Review*, 69:2, February 1986, pp. 46–48.

MULTINATIONAL FIRMS

What Is a Multinational Firm?

It is an important characteristic of human societies in general and of industrial relations systems in particular that new forces for change are constantly emerging. Some of these new forces grow until they are effective in causing modifications in the industrial relations system. Others emerge briefly, then dissipate. Among the most important factors now affecting industrial relations systems in a variety of countries are the growing activities of multinational firms. What are multinationals? What has been their economic and industrial relations impact? How have the unions responded to them? What will be their impact on the shape of the future?

Multinational companies operate in more than a single nation. Often they have sales facilities, and sometimes manufacturing plants as well, in many nations. Or they may operate through subsidiary corporations in nations other than their home country. The multinationals include some of the most common names in business, including General Motors, Ford, and Exxon. Many multinationals are American-based companies, but not all are. These companies employ many thousands of people in many different countries.

Two of the most important issues raised by the emergence of multinational firms are, first, what is the current impact of multinationals on the economic and labor relations systems of various countries, including our own, and second, will the multinationals, operating as centralized units in many different countries, cause the industrial relations system in the United States to become more like that in certain countries abroad?

Economic Impact of the Multinationals

Do multinational firms[18] shift production abroad, and so lower employment opportunities in the United States?[19] Many people think so, giving estimates of jobs lost and citing examples involving certain corporations.[20] Others disagree, citing the difficulty of comparing jobs created abroad by multinational firms with those created in the United States. The balance is hard to identify quantitatively.[21] To a degree the shift of production jobs abroad has been balanced by the creation of more jobs in headquarters, service, and technical ar-

---

[18] Mira Wilkins, *The Emergence of Multinational Enterprise* (Cambridge, Mass.: Harvard University Press, 1974), two volumes.

[19] Hans Gunter, "An Overview of Some Recent Research on Multinational Corporations and Labour," *Institute for International Labour Studies Bulletin*, 12, 1974, pp. 37–46.

[20] See *Multinational Corporations*, a compendium of papers submitted to the Subcommittee on Trade, Committee on Finance, U.S. Senate (Washington, D.C.: U.S. Government Printing Office, 1973).

[21] Roger G. Hawkins, *Job Displacement and the Multinational Firm: A Methodological Review* (Washington, D.C.: Center for Multinational Studies, 1972).

eas in the United States.[22] A recent study of a particular group of overseas investments by American firms concluded that:

• United States concerns tend to build manufacturing plants abroad when they cannot profitably serve markets from plants in the United States.
• Their main foreign competitors in those markets are not local firms, but rather subsidiaries of European or Japanese multinationals.
• The net effects of the U.S. investments are, on the average, favorable to the U.S. economy.
• Employment created in the United States as a result of U.S. foreign direct investment is of a higher skill level than exists on the average in U.S. manufacturing industries.[23]

However, an interesting counterpoint to this study was provided by another observer of multinationals, who commented, "In the home countries (especially the United States), management and stockholders (of multinationals) benefit more directly than labor."[24]

Exporting American jobs is not the only criticism directed at United States–based multinationals. They are also accused of avoiding taxes and increasing imports, thereby weakening the U.S. balance of payments. Business people have attempted to refute these allegations by pointing to the advantages that foreign trade provides for the United States, especially by allowing us access to raw materials from abroad and by creating jobs at home producing goods for export.

The impact of multinationals on our economy through foreign trade and foreign investment is a complicated matter that will not soon be free from controversy. As we shall see below, the unions are particularly opposed to much that the multinationals do and are attempting to have the activities curbed both by legislation and by direct trade union action.

When operating plants abroad, the multinationals sometimes seem to be little enclaves of their home country. In the case of American firms, this involves paying American wage levels and providing close approximations to American working conditions. More often, however, American firms abroad adapt to the local labor-market conditions and pay wages and provide working conditions commensurate with local practice. Local wages and conditions are in many cases, but not all, below American levels.

---

[22] Robert B. Stobaugh et al., *The Effects of U.S. Foreign Direct Investment* (Washington, D.C.: Center for Multinational Studies, 1973); and Daniel J. B. Mitchell, *Labor Issues of American International Trade and Investment* (Baltimore: Johns Hopkins, 1976), Policy Studies in Employment and Welfare, No. 24.

[23] Robert B. Stobaugh, ed., *Nine Investments Abroad and Their Impact at Home* (Cambridge, Mass.: Harvard University Press, 1976).

[24] Raymond Vernon, "A Decade of Studying Multinational Enterprises," *Harvard Business School Bulletin*, 52:5, September–October 1976, p. 27.

Labor Relations Impact

The industrial relations systems of various countries differ considerably. How does a multinational firm adapt to these differences? Does an American firm operating abroad try to operate everywhere as if it were in America, or does it try to adapt to local conditions?

Apparently, most American multinational firms attempt to adapt to local practices in the countries in which they operate.[25] In some instances the attempt to adapt goes so far that American firms that are strictly nonunion at home recognize and deal with unions abroad. Often, however, attempts to adapt to local practices do not seem to be altogether successful, especially when management direction is centralized in the home office of the corporation, or when American managers are sent to direct foreign subsidiaries. In these instances the American managers are often ignorant of local practices, and this may cause difficulties. The fewest problems of adjustment occur when the multinational has its foreign subsidiaries directed by foreign managers who understand local practices. This may be possible where a foreign subsidiary is profitably and efficiently managed. But inefficiency and losses inevitably occasion the intervention of American management and often the attempt to import American labor relations practices in the interest, it is believed, of greater efficiency of production.

Operating subsidiaries in several countries on a basis adapted to each country can be a severe strain for a corporation. Managers must become familiar with many ways of doing things if they are to be active in the corporation as a whole. And the corporation itself must be able to pursue simultaneously quite different personnel and labor relations policies in different countries. The rapid development of multinationals in recent years has largely been based on decentralized management and considerable autonomy for foreign subsidiaries, especially in the labor relations area. Whether this pattern of development can be continued remains to be seen.

The Response of the Unions

Unions have not generally responded favorably to the expansion of the multinational firms. In the United States the labor movement has criticized the multinationals for shifting jobs to lower-paid workers abroad, thus creating unemployment in the United States.[26] Since the oil crisis of 1973, the union attack on the multinationals has grown more strident. "By 1974," said an AFL-CIO economist, "published business reports, government and academic sources began to suggest that multinationals, in fact, were guilty as charged

[25] Duane Kujawa, "The Labor Relations of United States Multinationals Abroad," *Labour and Society*, 4:1, January 1979, pp. 3–25.

[26] Gus Tyler, "Multinationals: A Global Menace," *AFL-CIO American Federationist*, 79:7, July 1972, pp. 1–7; and Andrew C. McLellan and M. C. Boggs, "Multinationals: How Quick They Jump," *AFL-CIO American Federationist*, 80:9, September 1973, pp. 21–25.

of profiteering, tax avoidance and other impacts on the U.S. economy and labor."[27]

For years the AFL-CIO had supported a national policy of free trade, i.e., allowing companies to export and import with little government restriction. But opposition to the multinationals has caused the unions now to support legislative restrictions both on trade as a whole and on the multinational firms in particular. A high official of the AFL-CIO has written:

> As we in the AFL-CIO see it, there is urgent need for an adequate U.S. trade and investment policy—for the orderly expansion of trade, including the prevention of growing adverse impacts on American workers and communities; for effective measures to regulate the operations of multinational companies; for curbs on runaway plant developments; for elimination of U.S. tax and other concessions that subsidize the foreign operations of U.S.-based multinationals; for regulations and curbs on the export of American capital and technology.[28]

Nor are American unionists alone in criticizing the multinationals. A leading European trade unionist has written, "It is...a question of the abuse of power which is exerted by the multinational corporations—disguised as an interest in profit...."[29]

The unions have only a limited capacity to respond to the multinationals. In order to restrict the activities of the firms, unions in various countries are seeking legislation to regulate the companies' activities. And, in collective bargaining, the unions are seeking to deal directly with the multinationals.

Trade union cooperation to deal collectively with the multinational firms in collective bargaining in different countries is much talked about, but as yet amounts to little. Some international trade union secretariats, cooperative bodies operating primarily in Europe, have attempted to coordinate activities, including strikes, against certain multinational companies (especially European-owned companies). Such coordination is made necessary by the alleged potential ability of a multinational corporation to shift production from a struck plant in one country to a plant that is operating in another country. If a multinational firm can effectively shift production in this way, it can very much lessen the impact of a strike against it in any single country. The unions, by international cooperation, would like to prevent this sort of transfer of production. More positively, the unions through cooperation would like to raise the standards of employment for workers in each country in which the company operates, rather than allow the company to shift produc-

---

[27] Elizabeth R. Jager, "The Changing World of Multinationals," *AFL-CIO American Federationist*, 81:9, September 1974.

[28] Lane Kirkland, "Multinationals: Impact on U.S.," *International Herald Tribune*, May 17, 1974, p. 6. Also, Stanley H. Ruttenberg, "The Union View of Multinationals: An Interpretation," in Robert J. Flanagan and Arnold R. Weber, eds., *Bargaining Without Boundaries: The Multinational Corporation and International Labor Relations* (Chicago: University of Chicago Press, 1974), pp. 179–201.

[29] Gunter Kupke, "Union Responses in Continental Europe," in Flanagan and Weber, eds., *Bargaining Without Boundaries*, pp. 203–217.

tion by new capital investment to the lower-wage countries. There have been some dramatic examples of international union cooperation against multinational firms,[30] but their real success is questionable.[31]

The factors that have limited the ability of unions in different countries to cooperate successfully in dealing with the multinationals include:

- The lack of financial and human resources needed to organize information exchange, meetings, training, and coordination of action
- The different philosophical outlooks of the trade unions in different countries, pursuing different goals
- The weakness of the trade union movement in certain areas, especially in developing countries
- The different legal obstacles hampering coordinated industrial action
- The conflict of interests between employees in the different countries in their efforts to protect employment, as shown by the difficulties encountered between the United Auto Workers in the United States and the automobile workers in Japan in seeking an agreement to reduce Japanese auto exports to the United States

Future Impact of the Multinationals

The expansion of multinational business is likely to continue, despite possible temporary setbacks in periods of economic recession. As the multinationals grow in significance, their struggle with the trade unions will assume broader proportions. A recent study by a private consulting firm in Europe included a diagram of the impact of unions on various areas of concern to multinational companies, from which Figure 22-3 is adapted. It can be seen from the figure that the union objectives are to influence a very wide range of company policies in addition to traditional concerns regarding wages and working conditions. Other policies the unions seek to affect are capital expenditures, company planning, finance, and business strategy. Tactically, the unions rely on influencing government regulation, collective bargaining, and influencing works councils and supervisory boards to obtain their objectives. The unions rely on their influence on governmental regulations as a device to control the multinationals' activities. One form of governmental intervention sought by the unions will be the laws that give workers a right to participate through representatives (union or otherwise) in corporate decisions. In dealing not with government, but directly with the companies, col-

---

[30] James N. Ellenberger, "Linking Free Unions—The Secretariats," *AFL-CIO American Federationist*, 86:8, August 1979, pp. 9–17.

[31] Richard L. Rowan, Herbert R. Northrup, and Rae Ann O'Brien, *Multinational Union Organization in the Manufacturing and Processing Industries* (Philadelphia: Industrial Research Unit, The Wharton School, University of Pennsylvania, 1980). Also, Rowan and Northrup, *Multinational Collective Bargaining Attempts* (Philadelphia: The University of Pennsylvania Press, 1979). See also Richard L. Rowan, Kenneth J. Pitterle, and Philip A. Miscimarra: *Multinational Union Organizations in the White Collar, Service, and Communication Industries* (Philadelphia: Industrial Research Unit, The Wharton School, University of Pennsylvania, 1983).

FIGURE 22-3 Union impact on multinational companies. (*Adapted from European Industrial Relations in the 1970s, Brussels: Industrial Relations Counsellors, 1972, p. 71.*)

lective bargaining will also be expanded, if possible, by unions to cover a range of company policies now generally outside its scope.

For many years European unions have been attempting to obtain a code of conduct from the European Commission (the Common Market), for multinational firms in Europe. The purpose of the proposed code, called the Vredeling Plan, is to give workers rights to balance the growth of multinational companies. The plan requires multinational companies to give information about the company to union officials and to give notice in advance of business decisions, such as plant closures or work transfers, that would have a substantial affect on the interests of employees within the Common Market. An intensely controversial proposal, the plan continues under debate in Europe.[32]

---

[32] Industrial Relations Europe, *Common Market Special Report*, 1982, pp. S-1–S-4, and *Industrial Relations Europe*, 11:127, July 1983, p. 1. Also, Duncan C. Campbell and Richard L. Rowan, *Multinational Enterprises and the OECD Industrial Relations Guidelines* (Philadelphia: Industrial Relations Unit, The Wharton School, University of Pennsylvania, 1983).

Will there be transnational collective bargaining? Will unions from different countries join in single or coordinated negotiations with and perhaps conduct strikes against, the multinationals? There has been much discussion of this possibility,[33] but actual transnational bargaining remains very rare. One example had been the coverage of all North American operations (i.e., the United States and Canada) by agreements between the large American automobile companies and the United Auto Workers in both the United States and Canada.[34] These agreements, truly transnational in scope and operation, were each between one international union and a multinational company. The agreements did not require cooperation between totally separate unions in different countries. In 1984, however, the Canadian division of the UAW left the international union to found its own national union. Whether or not the two separate national unions will bargain together in the future is uncertain.

Transnational bargaining is only at the infant stage. Whether it will progress slowly or rapidly will depend on the ability of unionists from different countries, and often with different philosophies, to cooperate and the degree to which multinationals resist the idea. These factors are not yet clear enough to be assessed.

However, despite their attempts to adapt to local conditions wherever they operate, multinationals do carry across international frontiers certain patterns of management behavior.[35] They serve, therefore, to extend labor relations practices to many nations and to cause a merging of practices.[36] Over the years, the multinationals will tend to lessen diversity among the industrial relations systems in the countries in which they operate. In this sense, the multinationals may serve to bring greater similarity to many countries, and perhaps to encourage the import of some foreign labor relations practices to the United States.

CHAPTER SUMMARY

American business has become more conscious of foreign industrial relations practices as a result of the recent successes of Japanese and German firms. Union leadership has also begun to look abroad for new models of labor-management relations. The Japanese industrial relations system is an inter-

---

[33] Lloyd Ulman, "The Rise of the International Trade Union?" in Flanagan and Weber, eds., *Bargaining Without Boundaries*, pp. 37–70. Also, "Will Unions Win International Bargaining?" *Nation's Business*, 63:6, June 1975, pp. 36ff.

[34] Malcolm Denise, "Industrial Relations and the Multinational Corporation: The Ford Experience," in Flanagan and Weber, eds., *Bargaining Without Boundaries*, pp. 135–146.

[35] Richard D. Robinson, *International Business Management: A Guide to Decision-Making* (Ninsdale, Ill.: Dryden Press, 1975).

[36] This is probably so. However, companies from different nations approach problems differently in the short run. See B. C. Roberts and Jonathan May, "The Response of Multinational Enterprises to International Trade Union Pressures," *British Journal of Industrial Relations*, 12:3, November 1974, pp. 403–416. See also John Gennard, *Multinational Corporations and British Labor* (Washington, D.C.: British-American Committee, 1972).

esting contrast to the American system. Like the United States, Japan has a diversified industrial economy, employs very modern technology, and has a largely free enterprise system. However, Japanese industrial relations are profoundly different from those in the United States. The most unique characteristics of the Japanese system arise from the duality of the Japanese economy. There is one sector made up of large, technically advanced firms and another sector of small, inefficient firms. The large firms subcontract excess orders to the smaller firms and can cut them off in a recession without disturbing their own "lifetime employment system." "Standard" workers stay in a Japanese firm all their lives and receive many benefits and high salaries. A great deal of personal responsibility and loyalty characterizes the relationship between management, standard workers, and the company. The labor relations of Japanese firms reflect these relations of loyalty. Japanese unions show considerable identification with their companies rather than with the occupation or industry.

Two types of labor relations innovations involving "industrial democracy" have been the subject of experimentation in Germany. Codetermination involves the appointment of workers' representatives to the boards of directors of corporations. The intent is to provide workers a role or even a partnership in the decision making of an enterprise. On the supervisory or policy-making boards of some large companies in the steel and coal industries, stockholders and employees have acquired an equal number of directors. Elsewhere in German industry, employees are entitled by law to just less than equal representation.

Works councils are committees ordinarily involving management and employee representatives that have functions in the governance of the workplace. They were established by law in 1972 as permanent representative bodies with specific rights. The types of rights which works councils may have are complex. They are often divided into economic and social matters and may include the right to be informed, the right to be consulted, the right to investigate, and the right to codetermine. The works councils' relationship to the unions is also complex. The unions and works councils form a kind of dual structure of labor relations which has no counterpart in the United States. All major firms in Germany are involved in the structure.

The growing activities of multinational firms are one of the most important developments now affecting industrial relations systems in many countries. Multinational firms operate in more than one nation and often have sales and manufacturing plants in different nations. They employ many thousands of people in many different nations. There are two important issues raised by the emergence of multinational firms. First, what is the current impact of multinationals on the economic and labor relations systems of the various countries, including the United States? Second, will the multinationals cause the industrial relations system in the United States to become more like that in certain countries abroad? The impact of multinationals on our economy is a complicated and highly controversial matter. Multinational firms have been criticized for exporting American jobs, avoiding taxes, and increasing imports. Unions have been particularly opposed to the expansion of the multinational firms and are attempting to have their activities curbed both by legislation and by direct trade union activity. Trade union cooperation to deal collectively with multinational firms is much talked about but as yet amounts to little. There are a number of factors which limit the ability of unions in different countries to cooperate successfully in dealing with multinationals, not least of which is the lack of financial and human resources needed to organize such an effort.

The expansion of multinational business is likely to continue, and as it does the struggle with trade unions will assume broader proportions. Transnational bargaining is a possible response, but one still in its infancy. It is likely that as multinational firms expand, they will tend to lessen the diversity between industrial relations systems.

QUESTIONS FOR THOUGHT AND DISCUSSION

1 Compare labor relations in the United States, Japan, and Germany. What are the major similarities? The major differences? What factors cause similarities? What factors cause differences?

2 What aspects of the Japanese labor relations system do you think would be worthwhile for the American industrial relations system? What aspects could never work here and why?

3 What is codetermination? How does it operate?

4 What are works councils? How do they operate?

5 Should the United States have codetermination? Works councils? Why or why not?

6 Is there any group or structure in the American labor relations system that resembles the works councils? If yes, how and how not?

7 Imagine that you have been given the task of organizing an effective worldwide strategy for developing international union cooperation in order to cope with multinational firms. What issues would you be most concerned about? What are the major problems with which you would have to deal? How would you do it?

8 What impact will multinational firms have on the worldwide labor force, especially workers in underdeveloped countries?

9 How do multinational companies affect the U.S. economy? Should the United States favor multinationals or restrict their activities? How?

10 Will multinational companies bring about the formation of multinational unions? Why or why not?

SELECTED READING

Blanpain, R., ed., *Comparative Labor Law and Industrial Relations* (Washington, D.C.: BNA Books, 1982).

Flanagan, Robert J., and Arnold R. Weber, eds., *Bargaining Without Boundaries: The Multinational Corporation and International Labor Relations* (Chicago: University of Chicago Press, 1974).

Hershfield, David C., *The Multinational Union Challenges the Multinational Company* (New York: The Conference Board, 1975), Report No. 658.

Kendall, Walter, *The Labour Movement in Europe* (London: Allen Lane, 1975).

Okuchi, Kazuo, Bernard Karsh, and Solomon B. Levine, *Workers and Employers in Japan* (Princeton, N.J.: Princeton University Press, 1974).

Stobaugh, Robert B., ed., *Nine Investments Abroad and Their Impact at Home* (Cambridge, Mass.: Harvard University Press, 1976).

Vogel, Ezra, *Japan as Number One* (New York: Random House, 1979).

CHAPTER 23

THE FUTURE OF LABOR-MANAGEMENT RELATIONS

CHANGE OR "MORE OF THE SAME"?

What does the future hold for labor-management relations? The projection most frequently made is that things will remain much as they are now. Yet no projection is more likely to be wrong. One method of examining predictions about the future is to see what our past predictions were.

Consider the question of union growth, for example. At the end of the 1920s unionism was on the decline. It seemed likely that the decline would continue, but the 1930s saw the rise of the industrial unions and the CIO. At the end of the 1930s the CIO appeared sure to replace the AFL, but World War II brought the resurgence of the AFL. The very substantial growth of unionism as a whole in the 1940s was not foreseen in the late 1930s. The experiences of the 1930s and 1940s suggested that in the 1950s the unions would continue to grow and prosper. Instead, employer resistance to unions increased in sophistication and, combined with a sluggish national economy, caused union growth to slow substantially. Unionism in the 1960s began in the stagnant mode of the 1950s, only to end in the explosive expansion of public employee unionism. The 1960s ended on a note of such growing militancy and radicalism in our society that the slower and calmer pace of the 1970s came as a surprise to most people. The 1970s were a time of wrenching economic events, including two oil crises and rapid inflation. As prices outran wage gains in the late 1970s and unemployment rose dramatically, it appeared that unions would find millions of new members. Instead, the 1980s have seen the most rapid and widespread decline of unionism since the 1920s. Thus, history suggests that what can be expected is change, not continuity.

Unfortunately, nothing is more difficult to predict than the form and magnitude of substantial change. At any given time there are many harbingers of future developments, but their message is unclear. Years later, after the facts have revealed themselves, historians are able to identify the antecedents of events, and one wonders how many people failed to see them at the time. But that is after the facts have made the direction of change apparent. In the present, the future is unclear.

Nowhere is the future as uncertain as it is in labor relations. Many factors affect the direction of labor-management relations, and often they do not appear to move in step with each other. The economic systems of the United States and the world are evolving rapidly, in directions which are difficult to perceive. The technology employed to produce goods and services is also evolving, though to most of us the specific developments remain unknown until new products and processes appear on the general market. Social and political institutions also change. Labor relations are affected by these external influences.

Furthermore, significant historical occurrences have done much to shape labor relations in this country. Both of the world wars occasioned a substantial growth of unionism. Had the two wars not occurred, it is unlikely that unions would play as great a role in our economy as they do today. Will labor relations in the United States again be significantly affected by a major military conflict? History suggests that however much we wish to avoid such a conflict, it may nonetheless occur. But when, and in what manner, it will affect American labor relations is difficult to say.

HOW WILL THE SYSTEM EVOLVE?

It is less difficult to project the internal developments of a system than to anticipate the impact of outside events on it. We are probably able to predict with some reasonable certainty the course of events in the next few years, since those events will result from the current operations of our system of labor-management relations. What impact will current developments have in the near future? Where will there be continuity, and where will there be change?

Economic Problems

Labor relations are almost certain to continue to confront difficult economic problems. Inflationary pressures are likely to rise and recede. Unemployment will sometimes be substantial and sometimes low. The business cycle, which seemed to be becoming less and less severe in the 30-year period from 1940 to 1970, has seemingly returned with a vengeance. The recession of 1970 and 1971 was more severe than those of the late 1950s and early 1960s, and the recession of the period from 1980 to 1982 was the most severe since the great depression of the 1930s. The recession of 1980 was one of the sharpest on record and followed an unusual path (the first so-called double-dip recession). The economic environment has become more unpredictable as irregular recessions have emerged.

The return of the business cycle brings with it substantial swings in the profitability of companies and the fiscal viability of government units. Dramatic fluctuations in unemployment rates also accompany the cycle. This is a more difficult economic environment for labor relations than a calmer economic setting would be. Business-cycle peaks involve labor shortages, rapidly rising labor and other costs, and associated problems. Recessions generate layoffs, unemployment, bankruptcies, and pressures for economizing. Managers and unions are required to grapple with very different types of problems in rapid succession, and the risks of failure to cope effectively with these problems become very high.

Bargaining Structure Problems

Many American industries confront substantial problems in adjusting the structure of collective bargaining to the economic environment in which they exist. The problem of bargaining structure is a major cause of industrial unrest and consequently a major characteristic of labor relations in general. Some of the most important problems of this type that now affect American labor relations are in the following industries:

• *Maritime* Labor relations are characterized by disputes between competing labor unions, despite the fact that employment declines and spokespersons for both labor and management agree that a common policy is needed to preserve the U.S. Merchant Marine.

• *Construction* Thousands of local crafts unions negotiate separate collective bargaining agreements with their counterpart employer associations; meanwhile, the unionized section of the industry loses ground to nonunion firms. The unions and unionized employers agree that a reform of collective bargaining structure is very much needed, but they are unable to agree on a method for accomplishing this.

• *Airlines* Several unions negotiate with various carriers, each separately and in a process that invites whipsawing by both sides. The industry, meanwhile, has experienced very uncertain financial health, and in some instances important provisions of collective bargaining agreements have had to be suspended because of the financial situations of various companies; with the advent of deregulation nonunion competition intensified. Again, the companies and the unions recognize a serious problem in the methods by which they conduct their relations but are unable to reach agreement on a reform of the system.

• *Supermarkets* A group of competing unions deals with a variety of supermarket chains, while nonunionized chains compete effectively with the unionized firms.

• *Automobiles*   Under the impact of changing consumer preferences and foreign competition, some American automobile companies have made major changes to adapt. Nonetheless, foreign producers are now building plants in the United States. The UAW, which has won among the best labor contracts in American history through pattern bargaining, now must consider whether there can be a single automotive pattern when some companies are financially weak and others much stronger, and when new foreign plants are sometimes unionized and sometimes not.

These few examples could be multiplied many times and extended to most of the industrial relations system. The problems described are not simply the issue over which negotiations occur in any particular year. These are deep-seated problems, unique to each industry, that have lasted a decade or more and are well recognized by both labor and management. But they are problems that labor and management have been unable to solve and may, in fact, be unable to solve in the future. What is certain is that they will continue to absorb the time and energy of persons in both labor and management. Whether or not they are solved will largely determine the future of the unionized firms in the various industries involved or, in some cases, the future of the industries themselves in the United States.

The Climate of Labor Relations

There has been a lessening frequency of strikes, and shorter strikes on the average, in the private sector. Strikes are rarely as violent or bitter as they have been in the past. There is an increased acceptance of mediation as a method to help resolve negotiations disputes and of binding arbitration to resolve grievances. There has even been a movement toward acceptance of voluntary binding arbitration to resolve contract disputes. In public employment and in the health industry, where labor relations had been in increasing turmoil in the 1960s, the 1970s brought a calming of relations. And even in industries such as maritime, construction, airlines, automobiles, and supermarkets, where fundamental problems in bargaining structure exist, the climate of labor relations has nonetheless been less agitated recently.

It is not easy to identify the causes of this improvement in the labor relations climate. Some observers have ascribed it to the maturing of labor relations.[1] In their view, where unions have become established and fear less for their survival, they are able to behave less aggressively. Conversely, as management accepts unions where they now are and ceases to challenge their very existence, relations between the companies and the unions can become more normal. Both these factors, the unions' increasing maturity and

---

[1] Richard A. Lester, *As Unions Mature* (Princeton, N.J.: Princeton University Press, 1958). Also William E. Simkin, "The Trend to Maturity in Industrial Relations," *Industrial Relations*, 3:1, February 1964, pp. 1–4.

the employers' lessened hostility to unions, seem to have been important in improving the climate of labor relations.

Recently, observers have focused less on maturity in labor relations and more on an adverse economic climate in explaining a trend toward labor-management cooperation. A combination of lower productivity, high unemployment, and the threat of high-quality foreign imports is forcing management and labor to abandon confrontation. "The adversary-versus-adversary type of relation seems to be fading," said one government official, concluding that the era of total confrontation at the bargaining table of the last 30 years is over.[2]

The establishment of unions in the 1930s and 1940s in the private sectors and in the 1960s in the public sectors has removed a cause of social unrest, and the spotlight of controversy has moved to other issues. The civil and job rights of minority groups and women have replaced union recognition as a central social issue, and labor relations turmoil has subsided. Liberals have, of course, criticized the trade unions for not adopting a more militant stance toward employers in support of the rights of minorities and women. They would like to use the trade union movement as a weapon in the civil rights struggle, and this seems to require labor relations turmoil.

An example of liberal criticism of the relatively calm industrial relations climate is offered by William Serrin's characterization of the 1970 negotiations between the UAW and GM, which involved a lengthy strike, as a *partnership* of the company and the union against the workers and the public.[3] Even political conservatives sometimes criticize union-management cooperation. Former Senator Sam Ervin of North Carolina in 1976 described the cooperation of various manufacturers and unions to support a power project on the New River in the Carolinas as a plot against the public.

In general, because labor unions tend to support liberal political objectives and managers tend to be conservative, peaceful relations between labor and management subject both to the criticism of disloyalty. An especially contentious political atmosphere can, therefore, disrupt the labor relations climate, and often threatens to do so. The trend of recent years toward a lessening of overt conflict in labor-management relations seems likely to continue for the near future. General political and social circumstances, as well as the potential for conflict in the direct relationship of the parties, however, will constrain the degree to which the labor relations climate can be improved.

HOW WILL THE ENVIRONMENT CHANGE?

The economic system has been placing some long-term and deep strains on collective bargaining. These occurred because the rate of productivity growth

---

[2] Kenneth E. Moffett, quoted in Bureau of National Affairs, *Daily Labor Report* No. 170, Aug. 29, 1980, p. A8.

[3] William Serrin, *The Company and the Union* (New York: Knopf, 1973).

TABLE 23-1   ANNUAL RATE OF INCREASE IN
REAL OUTPUT PER WORKER HOUR

Year	Percent change
1955	3.2
1955–1965	2.7
1965–1970	2.4
1970–1975	1.0
1976–1980	− 0.4
1981–1985	1.8
1986	1.9

Source: U.S. Council of Economic Advisors, *Current Economic Indicators,* monthly.

in the American economy was on a long-term decline between 1955 and 1980 (see Table 23-1). Since higher living standards are primarily the result of increased productivity, this caused living standards to improve more slowly, or even decline. This was a matter of great significance for labor relations. Labor unions exist to a large degree for the purpose of improving the living standards of the people they represent. As the growth of productivity in our economy slowed, it became more difficult for the labor organizations to win increases in purchasing power, especially at the pace they achieved in the past. This suggested increasing conflict between management and labor over economic issues. Yet in 1980 to 1986, productivity increases rebounded in America. For some employees, the opportunity for improved living standards emerged. For others, particularly in industries hard hit by foreign competition, pressures on wage levels, and thence on collective bargaining, continued.

In 1980, one prominent labor leader, Sol Chaikin, described the American work force as increasingly split into "upper and lower tiers that grow more and more apart." He identified the "haves" as working in industries characterized by capital-intensive, oligopoly-like firms and the "have-nots" as working for small, highly competitive, labor-intensive companies. The compensation of the haves was keeping ahead of price inflation, permitting continued improvements in living standards. But the earnings of the have-nots were not keeping up, so that they fell behind the haves and experienced falling living standards. This division of the work force would be, Chaikin predicted, a source of "unnoticed agony" within the labor movement in the 1980s.[4]

Manufacturing has, since the 1930s, been at the heart of the U.S. labor relations process. Yet today manufacturing employment seems on a long-term

[4] Sol C. Chaikin, "Labor's Critical Issue: The Two-Tiered Society," *The Journal of the Institute for Socioeconomic Studies,* 5:3, Autumn 1980, pp. 1–17.

downward trend.[5] Millions of new jobs are created during upturns in our economy, but the great majority are in services—a sector of the economy which is lightly unionized at best. This change in the types of jobs our economy is generating has posed a great challenge to management and labor.

LEGAL REGULATION: IS IT AN ANACHRONISM?

The current body of American labor law is not well suited in a technical sense to our changing economy. Our current law presumes a manufacturing-type employment environment—one in which the employee has a stable job, in which the employer has substantial capital invested and cannot move its facility or change its employees readily, and in which the employer has substantial net worth in a particular corporate identity and cannot readily abandon it for another corporate identity.

Yet service firms, which are increasing in importance as manufacturing employment declines, often lack these characteristics. Hence, law which is intended to provide employees a free choice about unionism has come to the unions and some observers to seem biased against union organization.[6] Manufacturing employers are increasingly able to avoid unionization of new facilities, while service employers readily change corporate identities, move locations, and replace employees as necessary to avoid unions.

The result is that top union leaders now are calling for the reform or abolition of the nation's labor laws—a major reversal of position for them. Lane Kirkland, president of the AFL-CIO, broached the idea publicly in 1984 in newspaper interviews.[7] Union leaders testifying to Congress describe the laws as hindering the advancement of organized workers.[8]

Management spokespersons, accustomed to decades of protest that the nation's labor laws unfairly favor unions,[9] have apparently been caught off guard by the unions' sudden attack on the labor laws. Few management voices have been raised in defense of the laws. If the unions are committed, perhaps the nation's labor laws will be repealed. A more significant modification of our country's industrial relations system would be difficult to imagine.

Why would the unions want the labor laws repealed? The answer is to be found in the declining success rate which unions have in NLRB elections.

---

[5] D. Quinn Mills and Malcolm R. Lovell, "Competitiveness: The Labor Dimension," in Bruce Scott and George Lodge, eds., *U.S. Competitiveness in the U.S. Economy* (Boston: Harvard Business School Press, 1984), pp. 429–478.

[6] Paul Weiler, "Promises to Keep," *Harvard Law Review*, 96:8, June 1983.

[7] Leonard M. Apcar, "Kirkland's Call to Void Labor Laws," *The Wall Street Journal*, Nov. 6, 1984, p. 31.

[8] Richard L. Trumka, president, United Mine Workers, statement before House Labor Subcommittee on Labor-Management Relations, *Daily Labor Report* No. 121, June 22, 1984, pp. F1–F4.

[9] Morgan D. Roberts, *Power and Privilege: Labor Unions in America* (New York: Universe, 1984).

The law provides predictability, orderliness, and the potential for delay. These characteristics may be seen as favorable to management, which, in a stable and predictable environment, may bring its greater resources into play against a union.

What would labor relations be like without the labor laws? There would be no NLRB elections, no unfair labor practices. Unions would be free to strike employers and related companies (suppliers or customers). The potential power of the strike would be used whenever employees were prepared to support a work stoppage.

On the other hand, employers would be free to discharge union activists, to threaten employees favorable to a union, and to promise benefits to those who oppose unionization.

On balance, who would benefit? Would employers break unions, or would unions have a more effective strike weapon? Would union membership rise or fall?

We do not know the answers to these questions today. But as the discussion about repeal of the nation's labor laws sparked by Kirkland's comment continues, answers may emerge.

WHAT FUNCTION FOR MANAGEMENT?

Developments with respect to employee and union participation in management in Europe have been dramatic in recent years. Among the most important of the developments have been:

• Employees and unions acquiring greater rights to participate in decision making
• Employees and unions receiving more information about the firm as a business enterprise, especially with respect to matters affecting personnel
• Employees and unions participating with government and business in decisions made about a wide range of social and economic matters[10]

Will the European emphasis on increased employee and union participation in management be transferred to the United States? There has been an outpouring in recent years of books and articles whose purpose is to acquaint American managers with developments abroad.[11] Some observers see a rapid progress of European concepts into American industrial relations.[12] Others, however, doubt that the impact will be great at all.[13]

---

[10] Solomon Barkin, "Redesigning Collective Bargaining and Capitalism," in Solomon Barkin, ed., *Worker Militancy and Its Consequences, 1965–75* (New York: Praeger, 1975).

[11] Thomas Kennedy, *European Labor Relations: Text and Cases* (Lexington, Mass: Lexington Books, 1980).

[12] Lee E. Preston and James E. Post, "The Third Managerial Revolution," *Academy of Management Journal*, 17:3, September 1974, pp. 476–486.

[13] Walter Galenson, "Labor and Productivity," paper given at World Management Conference, National Management Association, Washington, D.C., October 1975.

The major reason for the view that European developments will have an impact here is the belief that there is a worldwide movement toward greater employee participation in business management, which America will be unable to resist. Proponents of industrial democracy see the United States as headed toward a planned economy:

> Over the coming decade, the economy can be planned for full employment, price stability and resource conservation—or it can be planned for continued inflationary growth and a worsening distribution of income and wealth among the population. The next years will see a clear tendency toward increasing concentration of economic power in the hands of public and private bureaucracies. We may not like it, but we must face it. Otherwise we will not be able to deal with its consequences. The answer lies not in pining for a long gone economic era of small firms and free markets (though in *some* areas antitrust does make sense). It lies in making economic democracy and decentralization a major goal of economic policy.
>
> It means encouraging employee ownership and participation in management.[14]

Those who believe that workers' councils will remain confined to Western Europe do so for two reasons. First, American workers under collective bargaining already have many of the rights that works councils provide abroad. "Ironically," reports one observer, "the American worker, who does not seek control as an end in itself, exercises more control over matters in the plant that are important to him than does his counterpart in many European countries who is ideologically committed to the concept of worker's control."[15] Second, associated with the role of collective bargaining at the plant level in the American system is the opposition of most American unions to works councils. The unions perceive the councils as competitors at the workplace and evidence no interest in them. Since management in the United States also opposes works councils, it is hard to imagine what political circumstance could result in their establishment.

In 1973 Douglas Soutar, vice president for industrial relations of ASARCO (formerly American Smelting and Refining Company), served as first president from a business corporation of the Industrial Relations Research Association, a professional association of business, labor, and academic representatives. Soutar chose as the topic of his presidential address the European experiments in worker participation. Soutar commented that "it would be unrealistic to discount the extent, sophistication, and support" of worker participation programs abroad and in America. But, he suggested, "Collective bargaining [in the United States] has de facto and pragmatically matched most of the claimed accomplishments of the more formal systems [abroad]." He concluded, "In sum, my comments add up quite clearly to an

[14] Gar Alperovitz and Jeff Faux, *An Economic Program for the Coming Decade* (Washington, D.C.: Exploratory Project for Economic Alternatives, 1975).

[15] A. S. Tannenbaum, "Systems of Formal Participation," in George Strauss et al., eds., *Organizational Behavior* (Madison, Wis.: Industrial Relations Research Association, 1974), pp. 90–91.

endorsement of our own American approach to these problems of participative decision-making. . . ."[16]

In 1976 R. Heath Larry, vice chairman of the board of U.S. Steel, turned to the same topic. "Surely," Larry began, "one of the more critical problems which business management must face today relates to the fact that various constituencies which have not traditionally been a part of management are asserting that they should have a larger role in it." At the forefront of these constituencies he placed the unions: "I deplore the efforts of those in unions, in consumer groups and in government—whether here—or abroad—to become a greater part of the management process." Larry went on to explain why:

> *First:* I am not asserting that leaders within management circles are necessarily wiser than leaders in government or in labor unions or in sundry other organizations and constituencies.
>
> *Second:* I am not arguing that management is entitled to exercise any God-given prerogatives or that its decisions must be accepted by others with an attitude of unquestioning reverence.
>
> *Third:* I am not arguing against the existence of a duty or a responsibility on the part of management to explain to or to account to its many constituencies—and to do so more fully and comprehensively than it has in the past—or against the wisdom of management's listening to and seeking the counsel of appropriate representatives of such constituencies.
>
> *Fourth:* I am not arguing against acceptance and recognition of unions duly chosen by employees; for they have a very vital and legitimate role as parties to collective bargaining. But even more, they are important—very important, in fact—constituencies within the body politic—constituencies with whom management must cultivate a recognition of interdependence—even while acknowledging the difference—indeed, at times, a necessarily adversary difference—in their respective roles.
>
> *Fifth:* I am not trying to argue that capital is more important than labor—because neither is worth anything without the other.
>
> My purpose rather is to emphasize my belief that there is a distinctive role to be played by management, just as there is for labor, and government, and certain other constituencies within our country. It is the role of making plans for the future, initiating and implementing these plans with decisions when they need to be made. *It is the role of making those decisions with first recognition for the trust which the management exercises on behalf of the owners of the business.*[17]

Behind the concern of American business people about European trends toward greater employee participation in management is concern for the decision-making process or, stated otherwise, concern for management prerogatives or authority. American managers fear that employee participation is a method of advancing group decision making, or decision making by con-

---

[16] Douglas H. Soutar, "Codetermination, Industrial Democracy and the Role of Management," *Proceedings*, Industrial Relations Research Association, 1973, pp. 1–7.
[17] R. Heath Larry, "Must Management Move Over?" 1976 (mimeographed).

sensus. They regard this as a dangerous step backward with respect to the efficiency and profitability of business. In Soutar's words, "It's difficult to run a ship by committee."[18]

These concerns address fundamental issues and raise the question of what the function of management should be. Historians describe the shift away from group decision making (the outcome of appeals to ancient custom) to decision making based on authority as a fundamental precondition to the growth of modern technological society. "The appeal to reason [as a basis for decisions]...invariably implied...that men could be expected to obey rapid and trenchant decisions," the outcome of logic and experience, or authoritative written text.[19] Managers are concerned that under the banner of allowing the worker greater participation in management, business decisions will be diluted by political and social concerns, reflecting customs, fears, and other irrational factors, to the detriment of progress and efficiency.

WHAT TYPE OF LABOR MOVEMENT?

The American labor movement has been characterized as business unionism, to contrast it with the more political unionism of many labor movements abroad. The basic features of business unionism, as described in Chapter 8, constitute an acceptance of the American free enterprise system and an emphasis in union activity on wages, hours, and procedures for handling disputes at the workplace. These characteristics of the American labor movement have had an important impact on American society, imparting to our political and social processes a degree of stability that would otherwise be absent.[20] It is, therefore, a question of major importance to American society what the direction of our labor movement will be.[21]

Not for many years has the American labor movement taken so searching a look at itself. The AFL–CIO in the mid-1980s established a Committee on the Evolution of Work, and charged it with examining the status of workers and unions in America.

Out of this effort there emerged in 1985 some startling recommendations.

First, the committee urged the unions to look beyond traditional issues of wages and conditions of work to new concerns of workers, including those of women workers especially.

Second, the committee recommended going beyond the tie between collective bargaining and union membership by establishing new categories for membership. For the first time, major American unions envisioned recruiting

---

[18] Soutar, "Codetermination," p. 6.

[19] Peter Brown, "Society and the Supernatural: A Medieval Change," *Daedalus*, 104:2, Spring 1975, p. 143.

[20] Tim Bornstein, "Unions, Critics and Collective Bargaining," *Labor Law Journal*, 27:10, October 1976, pp. 614–622.

[21] John T. Dunlop, "Introduction," in John T. Dunlop and Walter Galenson, eds., *Labor in the Twentieth Century* (New York: Academic Press, 1978), pp. 1–10.

members for whom they would not do collective bargaining. Instead they would provide services and broader, political representation. The committee observed that 28 percent of all nonunion workers (about 27 million people) are former union members whom the unions might wish to regain as members even if unable to organize enough workers at the companies for which they work to obtain a collective bargaining relationship.

Third, the Committee urged unions to increase the opportunities for members to participate in their unions.[22]

With this report the AFL-CIO set its eyes on the future, and the first dim outlines of a very different American labor movement became visible.

Do Numbers Matter?

Critics of the current leadership of the American labor movement charge that it has failed to expand the role of unions. The proportion of employees who are members of labor organizations has been declining rapidly, and it forms a distinct minority of all employees. To many observers, the failure of the American labor movement to gain a greater proportion of all employees implies (indeed, is evidence of) its stagnation. Only dramatic new initiatives in the policies and orientation of the unions will correct this, critics maintain. Only with the new policies and growing numbers will the labor movement be able to play the progressive role in American society that it should play.[23]

While numbers are important, they are not critical, the current leadership seems to reply. Unions that represent only a minority of all employees still make gains that are often extended to workers who do not belong to unions. These extensions occur either by governmental action or by the action of nonunion employers. Unions, their leaders argue, set standards for many more employees than they actually represent. There is, therefore, no reason to pay undue attention to the size of union membership. In fact, a small, cohesive group can often achieve more than a large but unwieldy organization. A management representative has given some support for this view:

> It is a common assumption that growth in the influence of organized labor is proportioned to growth in union membership. [Yet] we have seen labor's influence in both collective bargaining activities and in the political arena grow steadily in the past, and I know of no basis to predict a decline in union influence in the future. The facts of union membership...are seemingly at variance with this growth of influence.[24]

---

[22] AFL-CIO Committee on the Evolution of Work, *The Changing Situation of Workers and Their Unions* (Washington, D.C.: AFL-CIO, February 1985). See also Charles McDonald, "Progress Report on AFL-CIO Blueprint for the Future," in Bureau of National Affairs, *Daily Labor Report* No. 6, Jan. 9, 1987, pp. E1–E2.

[23] Solomon Barkin, "Diversity in Industrial Relations Patterns," *Labor Law Journal*, 27:1, November 1976, pp. 678–685.

[24] Joseph W. Shuster, "Manpower and Labor Relations," paper given to the American Mining Congress Convention, 1975 (mimeographed).

What Role for the Union Leader?

Critics of the current leadership of the unions often contend that the leadership is dictatorial and announce themselves to be in support of greater union democracy. If the unions were run with greater attention to the individual member's needs, the critics maintain, the unions would be both more effective and more liberal, or leftist, politically. Existing union leadership does not agree.

A union leader is inevitably caught between the members of the organization on one hand and employers and the public on the other. The leader may be subjected to strong and conflicting pressures from either side.

In fact, much of the criticism of the labor movement in recent years has arisen from policies adopted not so much at the urging of union leadership, but at the urging of the membership. As John Dunlop and Derek Bok put it, "A candid appraisal compels the conclusion that the rank and file has contributed to most of the widely condemned union shortcomings: racial discrimination, excessive wage demands, featherbedding, and—in many instances—irresponsible strikes."[25] Very often union leaders are called on to influence their members as best they can to mitigate these practices.

But the position of the union leader as a force for responsible action vis-à-vis rank-and-file demands has been eroding and may continue to erode in the future unless some legislative action is taken. A major element in all this is Title I of the Landrum-Griffin Act of 1959. Title I gives union members a bill of rights regarding their relationship with the union and its leadership and allows an aggrieved individual to bring suit for damages against the union for violation of his or her rights. Union members have increasingly used, or threatened to use, lawsuits as a means of preventing union officials from exercising control over their action. At best, the union leaders believe themselves to be in a difficult rear-guard action against militant memberships.[26] The erosion of the power of union leadership may be a major destabilizing influence in labor relations.

IS THE BALANCE TIPPING IN AMERICAN INDUSTRIAL RELATIONS?

What is the balance between unions and management in American society as the 1980s come to a close? The unions are clearly on the defensive. Union membership has not kept pace with labor force growth, so that the percentage of employees who are members of unions has been declining for years. Labor failed in its efforts in the 1970s to get changes in the National Labor Relations Act to make it easier to organize workers into unions. And employers generally have become more committed to being nonunion and have be-

---

[25] John Dunlop and Derek Bok, *Labor in the American Community* (New York: Simon and Schuster, 1970), p. 474.

[26] Michael A. Pollock, "How Jack Joyce Is Rebuilding the Bricklayers' Morale," *Business Week*, Sept. 9, 1985, pp. 73–74.

come more successful at it.[27] In 1977, for example, the National Association of Manufacturers formed a national organization intended to help companies keep unions out of their factories, stores, and offices. The organization was called the "Council on a Union-Free Environment." Its formation was met with great hostility by the unions.

Throughout the 1960s and 1970s the unions sought, with substantial success, to obtain further governmental regulation of business practices in the employment area, such as regulation of health and safety (OSHA), pensions (ERISA), and discrimination (Title VII of the Civil Rights Act). For the 1980s the unions have had an agenda for further regulatory advances (for example, to regulate plant closings by management).

The strength of the labor movement has always been at the plant, or grass-roots, level in the United States. Lately the unions have been paying much attention to national politics and legislative action[28] and perhaps neglecting the grass roots. So some observers suggest that unions should instead build up the loyalty and commitment of workers at the plant level. According to one observer, in the 1980s automation will eliminate the worst jobs in factories, managers will continue to be aware of employee needs, cost-of-living escalators will protect wages, and so unions must attempt to deal with the dissatisfaction of workers with the content of their jobs.[29]

Tom Donahue, the AFL-CIO's secretary-treasurer, has identified an involved membership as the unions' best weapon. "We have to challenge those who tell us that the labor movement must lower its expectations," he said. "I say that we must raise them."[30] The major changes which are now occurring in the work force in the United States present an opportunity to the unions if they are able to identify the consequences of these changes and develop policies to respond to them.

MAKING COLLECTIVE BARGAINING WORK

Today the institution of collective bargaining is demonstrating some substantial ability to adapt to change and to cope with an increasingly challenging environment.

Still, there are major challenges. As the former research director of the United Steelworkers said, "Unless unions can help preserve jobs, they will lose members. Workers want jobs with good benefits and satisfactory working conditions—but in any case they want jobs. If unions are associated with

---

[27] D. Quinn Mills, "Management Performance," in Jack Steiber, D. Quinn Mills, and Robert McKersie, eds., *American Industrial Relations: A Critical Review* (Madison, Wis.: Industrial Relations Research Association, 1982).

[28] John T. Dunlop, "Past and Future Tendencies in American Labor Organization," *Daedalus*, 107:1, Winter 1978, pp. 79–96.

[29] Robert Schrank, "Are Unions an Anachronism?" *Harvard Business Review*, 57:5, September–October 1979, pp. 107–115.

[30] "Donahue to Service Employees International Union Convention," *AFL-CIO News*, June 28, 1980, p. 5.

strikes and noncompetitive practices that cause plants to go out of business, ordinary working people are not likely to be union enthusiasts."[31]

In the attempt to respond to the threat of foreign competition and growing nonunion competition at home, unions and management are moving toward a more cooperative relationship. Pushed into the background are the contentious labor-management relations of the recent past. Brought to the forefront are joint labor-management efforts to provide employment security to union members and business success to companies. Thrust back on their own resources by a period of economic adversity, unions and management in many instances are responding with enhanced cooperation.[32]

In these relationships the parties are able to resolve disagreements without major confrontations; the union shares responsibility for productivity; and the company shares responsibility for employment security and pay equity for employees.

Unions are learning how to help companies faced with intense competition to survive and prosper *and yet* continue to represent the interests of their members. It takes leadership qualities to do this: the ability to see potential; willingness to take risks; and an ability to communicate with and persuade others of the opportunities.

Creating a trusting relationship between union and management requires recognition of the obligations that the other side has, a feeling that the other side shares certain basic values, and personal integrity of the individuals involved. Progress on these dimensions is being made in American labor-management relations. It is good for labor, good for management, and good for the nation. Perhaps in response, the long slide in public approval of unions (which peaked in 1957 at 76 percent and reached bottom in 1981 at 55 percent) has reversed itself and that approval has started a slow ascent.[33]

SUPPLEMENTING OR REPLACING COLLECTIVE BARGAINING

Charles Heckscher has recommended that in order to improve their prospects, unions should become more flexible. He observes that the dwindling of unionism leaves a growing problem of how to protect employee rights in the nonunion workplace. The collective bargaining framework developed under the Wagner Act of 1935 no longer is sufficient to protect workers. Based on balancing the power of management and labor, the law gave unions a source of power in the corporation by granting them the exclusive right to represent all workers if a majority voted for the union. The rise of foreign competition and businesses' union-avoidance campaigns have undermined this structure. Unions no longer control the market for labor in basic

---

[31] Ben Fischer, "Labor Takes a Look at Itself," *Los Angeles Times*, Mar. 29, 1985, part II, p. 6.

[32] William E. Fulmer, "Labor-Management Relationships in the 1980s: Revolution or Evolution?" *Business Horizons*, 27:1, January–February 1984, pp. 26–31.

[33] Gallup Poll press release, May 19, 1985.

industries such as steel and autos and have great difficulty organizing employees in the growing service industries.

Moreover, the power-balancing concept tends to force unions to be as bureaucratic as corporations, leading to restrictive work rules and legalistic squabbles over grievances. To avoid these practices, growing numbers of nonunion companies are using self-managed work teams and other forms of worker involvement in decision making. Heckscher uses the word "managerialism" to designate the most advanced management systems. It is difficult to adapt the traditional union structure to this form of management.

Instead, Heckscher advocates what he calls "associational unionism." Workers would not be forced to choose either exclusive representation or no representation. Instead, unions and other interest groups could speak for various fractions of the work force. Wages and other matters would be determined by multilateral negotiations among management, several different groups of employees, and perhaps such outsiders as environmentalists and consumers.

Already the AFL-CIO and some of its affiliated unions have embraced a nascent form of associational unionism. Instead of limiting membership to workers under bargaining agreements, some unions offer group insurance plans and other services to associate members such as retirees and unorganized workers. It is a long step from this approach to multilateral negotiations.[34]

CONCLUDING COMMENT

Ultimately, through the complex combination of individual actions, legislative enactment, and court decision, the United States will determine the future direction of its labor relations and its labor movement. The labor movement may become more responsive to the desires of its membership, possibly at the cost of becoming less responsive to the needs of the public as a whole. The labor movement may also become larger and broader-based, but possibly thereby more overtly political in its orientation. One may hope that out of the adjustment of these conflicting circumstances a happy medium will emerge. In any case, the result is far from predictable.

CHAPTER SUMMARY

The future of labor-management relations is difficult to predict, especially changes that may result from the impact of outside events. It is less difficult to predict the internal developments of the system, which are already under way. The economic environment seems likely to put long-term and deep strains on labor relations. Managers and unions will need to grapple in rapid

---

[34] John Hoerr, "How More Flexibility Could Pump Up Labor's Muscles," *Business Week*, May 16, 1988, pp. 21–22; and Charles C. Heckscher, *The New Unionism* (New York: Basic Books, 1988).

succession with the very different kinds of problems caused by foreign competition, inflation, and recession.

Many American industries will confront substantial problems adjusting the structure of collective bargaining to the economic environment. The deep-seated problems which have lasted a decade or more will not easily be solved. In contrast to the continuing problems in the structure of bargaining, the climate of labor relations in the United States has been improving and seems likely to continue to do so. This change may be due to a maturing mutual acceptance between companies and unions or it may be due to the increasingly adverse economic climate, which demands labor-management cooperation for survival. High unemployment and the threat of high-quality foreign imports are forcing labor and management to abandon confrontation.

Many observers believe that there is a worldwide movement toward greater employee participation in business management and that the European emphasis on industrial democracy will be transferred to the United States in the future. Other observers say that such developments as works councils and other forms of employee inroads into the prerogatives and authority of management will remain confined to Western Europe. A general question is whether the American labor movement will continue to be characterized by business unionism or whether it will become more political.

There are many conflicting forces which are unsettling the balance between labor and management and which may lead to changes in the basic features of American industrial relations. Unions are increasingly on the defensive as union leaders face both internal and external problems. Union membership has not kept pace with labor force growth, and the percentage of union members has declined. Union leaders are torn between the need to be more responsive to grass roots sentiments and the need for more nationally centralized and socially responsible leadership. The traditional adversary relationship between management and labor seems out of date when competition in the international marketplace requires cooperation at home. On the other hand, a major contest between labor and management over government regulation of employment practices is likely to occur in the near future. Management seems likely to press to reduce government regulation or alter regulations and court decisions in its favor. In addition, employers are more committed to being nonunion and have been more successful at it than in the past. There are many dangers and opportunities for the collective bargaining process in the changing work force and the changing political climate.

Because of the declining role of unions and collective bargaining, proposals are now being made for new forms of unionism. "Associational unionism" would abandon exclusive representation but still preserve unions as an important force in our society.

QUESTIONS FOR THOUGHT AND DISCUSSION

1 What are the most important changes that will affect labor relations in the next 10 years in the area of technology? The economy? The attitudes and desires of people?

2 Should there be less government regulation of labor relations? Why or why not?

3 Should workers have a greater voice in management? What do you see as the appropriate role for management?

4 What type of labor movement should the United States have in the future? Should business unionism continue? Should the unions become more active politically in support of liberal and progressive goals? Why or why not?

5 Why is there an increasingly favorable climate in labor-management relations? Is this likely to continue if union members move toward more participation in managerial decision making? Is it likely to continue if economic conditions lead to wider splits between the haves and the have-nots? Why or why not?

6 Will the European trends toward greater employee participation in the management and ownership of business enterprises prove to be irresistible in the United States? What are the arguments for and against the possibility that the United States is headed toward industrial democracy or some form of planned economy?

7 What do you think the role of a union leader should be in relation to the rank and file and in relation to management?

8 Do you think the relationship between labor and management is likely to become less conflict-ridden and more jointly cooperative or just the opposite? Support your answer in terms of specific problems and trends.

9 What is "managerialism"? What is "associational unionism"? What do you think are the future prospects for both?

SELECTED READING

Heckscher, Charles C., *The New Unionism* (New York: Basic Books, 1988).

Kerr, Clark, *The Future of Industrial Societies: Convergence or Continuing Diversity* (Cambridge, Mass.: Harvard University Press, 1983).

Kochan, Thomas A., Harry C. Katz, and Robert B. McKersie, *The Transformation of American Industrial Relations* (New York: Basic Books, Inc., 1986).

Mills, D. Quinn, "Reforming the U.S. System of Collective Bargaining," *Monthly Labor Review*, 106:3, March 1983, pp. 18–22.

PART TWO

ARBITRATION EXERCISES

INTRODUCTION

The following are nine disputes that have been presented by labor and management to an arbitrator for resolution. Seven of these cases involve grievances submitted to an arbitrator who, acting as a judge, was asked to decide whether or not a particular action by the company, or the union, or an employee, violated the collective bargaining agreement between the company and the union. In the last two cases, the arbitrator was asked to decide if a union had violated the constitution of the AFL-CIO.

In these disputes it would appear that there must be a "right" answer to the problem: Either the action was permitted by the agreement or it was not. Therefore, it may be thought that the purpose of analysis and discussion is to find the right answer: that answer which the arbitrator would give. However, in grievance arbitration, while reaching a conclusion about whether or not the action was permitted by the collective bargaining agreement is an important aspect of the analysis, it is not all that is involved. The reader should also consider the following questions and others of this type that may occur in the process of analysis. What alternative decisions might the arbitrator make, if any? Did the company handle the situation well? How did the union handle it? Should the company (or the union) have permitted the matter to go to arbitration? Why did they permit it to do so? Was arbitration a good way to settle this dispute? What other alternatives existed? Why weren't those alternatives used? And if in discussion one person suggests a decision, someone else might ask, "Was it the correct decision? Was it the one I would have made?"

In analyzing issues submitted to arbitration, there is a tendency to concentrate on the question of whether the company's position or the union's position in the dispute was correct. But equally important is the matter of the remedy designed by the arbitrator if a violation of the contract is found to have occurred. And if the decision on whether a violation exists appears to be somewhat cut and dried, the issue of what remedy should be fashioned is rarely so. In a discharge case, should the grievant be reinstated? With back pay? Should there be a further penalty against the company for an inappropriate dismissal? If a grievant was found to have been denied an opportunity to work overtime, how much overtime should the company be required to pay the grievant? If a company subcontracted work in violation of the agreement, should the company be required to pay its own employees for the subcontracted work? Should the company be required to cancel the subcontract? Since collective bargaining agreements rarely specify the exact form of a remedy, there is much room for thought and imagination in this area.

In general, a reader should approach arbitration exercises with a critical and wide-ranging mind, not simply seeking to discover a "right" answer. The purpose of training in labor relations is to develop in students the capacity to think creatively about problems, not simply to follow rules. This is especially so because both unions and employers have the capacity to bring about changes in many of the rules that at any one time govern their relationship.

Grievance Arbitrations

THE PHANTOM STRIKE

New Jersey Raceways, Inc., operates the race track at Sidewall, N.J. Wagering is operated under the pari-mutuel system. The totalizer, which is the computing machine that records all bets and determines payoff prices, is leased from the U.S. Computer Company. Starting Saturday, March 1, 1980, the employees who operate the totalizer went on strike against U.S. Computer Company at all the tracks where it was operating throughout the country. There are approximately 80 such tracks, including the New Jersey Raceways track at Sidewall.

On February 17, 1980, at a membership meeting of local No. 341, Business Manager Robertson notified the membership (who are employees of New Jersey Raceway) of the possibility of a strike against U.S. Computer on March 1, 1980, by local No. 1621 and informed them of their obligation under the collective bargaining agreement with New Jersey Raceways to continue to work.

The union membership never took any formal action to support the strike by local No. 1621 or to honor its picket lines.

On Friday afternoon, February 29, Robertson of local No. 341 met with a Mr. Salvucci, the employer's representative. They discussed the possibility of a strike by local No. 1621, which represents employees of U.S. Computer. Robertson told Salvucci he would try to have essential services maintained at the track. Salvucci asked that all employees be required by the union to report to work.

On Saturday, March 1, the first day of the strike by local No. 1621, Robertson went to the race track. Picket lines were set up by local No. 1621 at all major entrances to the track. Robertson encountered Salvucci at a gate and was asked by him to order a group of employees to go to work. Robertson did so, in Salvucci's hearing.

At about noon on March 1, Salvucci determined that not enough employees, members of local No. 341, had reported to work, and at 12:45 p.m. he decided to cancel racing for the day. Scheduled racing was to have begun at 1:00 p.m.

During this 2-day period local No. 341 and Raceways were exchanging telegrams. On February 29, the employer telegraphed the union as follows:

> PLEASE BE ADVISED THAT IN THE EVENT THERE IS A STRIKE BY EMPLOYEES OF U.S. COMPUTER CO. REPRESENTED BY LOCAL 1621 NEW JERSEY RACEWAYS SHALL REQUIRE THAT YOUR LOCAL AND ITS MEMBERS COMPLY WITH ARTICLE 17 NO STRIKE NO LOCKOUT OF ITS COLLECTIVE BARGAINING AGREEMENT WITH NEW JERSEY RACEWAYS. FAILURE TO COMPLY WILL RESULT IN LEGAL ACTION BEING TAKEN AGAINST THE UNION AS WELL AS IMPLEMENTATION OF THE COMPANY'S RIGHTS UNDER THE CONTRACT.

A similar telegram was sent by Raceways on March 1. The union replied as follows on March 1:

> YOUR TELEGRAM OF 3/1/80 INDICATES LABOR DISPUTE EXISTS BETWEEN LOCAL 341 AND NEW JERSEY RACEWAYS. PLEASE BE ADVISED NO DISPUTE EXISTS AND I HAVE INSTRUCTED MEMBERS OF LOCAL 341 TO REPORT TO WORK ON 3/1/80.

On the afternoon of Saturday, March 1, Raceways sought a court order against local No. 341 and against Robertson. The order required the union to honor its no-strike commitment. Judge Jewett of the federal district court granted the order.

On Sunday morning, March 2, Robertson met with the executive board of local No. 341 and, according to Robertson, told them to honor the contract. Members of the executive board were stationed inside the picket lines of local No. 1621 to tell members of local No. 341 to report to work, according to Robertson.

Salvucci saw employees drive past the picket lines on Sunday and saw some cars turn back after stopping to talk with the officers of local No. 341. From this he concluded that Robertson and other officers of local No. 341 were advising employees of New Jersey Raceways not to report to work, despite Robertson's denial that this was occurring.

At noon on Sunday, Salvucci canceled the afternoon's racing program because in his judgment there were in attendance too few clerks represented by local No. 341 to permit the track to operate.

On both Saturday and Sunday management personnel from U.S. Computer were at the race track to operate the totalizer. On both days essential maintenance services were fully maintained by local No. 341.

On Monday, March 3, the track operated with a complement of about 90 percent of its employees. On Tuesday, no racing was scheduled.

During this period the employer did not contact or attempt to contact individual employees to instruct them to report to work, except that Salvucci handed out copies of the judge's temporary restraining order to employees at the picket lines on Sunday, March 2. The employer did not discipline any employee for failure to report to work.

When Raceways asked Judge Jewett on Monday, March 3, to issue a permanent restraining order against local No. 341 and Robertson, the union's attorney suggested that the matter should go to arbitration instead. The employer's attorney agreed, and an arbitrator was selected and a hearing held.

At the hearing Salvucci testified that on Sunday morning he had asked Robertson if the employees would report to work. According to Salvucci, Robertson had replied, "No." Robertson denied that this exchange had taken place. There were no other witnesses.

At the hearing the employer argued that the union had an obligation under article XVII of the agreement to compel the employees to go to work, despite local No. 1621's picket lines, by whatever powers it had, including formal disciplinary action under the union's bylaws. This obligation the union had not met, the employer's attorney argued.

The union answered that the union had not conducted or engaged in a strike. The membership of local No. 341 had not taken concerted action to stop work, and there had been no demand made of New Jersey Raceways which could be considered the objective of the alleged strike, the union representative said.

The collective bargaining agreement between local No. 341 and New Jersey Raceways had the following provisions in article XVII:

> The Local agrees that during the term of this Agreement, it will not participate in any strike, either "economic" or "unfair labor practice," against the Employer or in sympathetic or general strike whether within or outside the property of the Employer; and any such participation by an employee covered by this Agreement shall be cause for his discharge.

QUESTIONS FOR THOUGHT AND DISCUSSION

1 Why is New Jersey Raceways seeking an arbitrator's decision that the union is violating the agreement?

2 Do you think local No. 341 is striking in support of local No. 1621? Why or why not? Has New Jersey Raceways presented enough evidence to determine if local No. 341 is engaging in a strike?

3 How would you decide whether Salvucci or Robertson is telling the truth about the Sunday morning conversation?

4 The employer has asked the arbitrator to infer that when union officials talk to

union members and the members don't go to work, the officials must be telling them not to go to work, despite the union officials' denials. Would you make this inference?

5 Would the issues in question have changed appreciably if the company had pursued immediate disciplinary action against employees who failed to report to work?

THE OVERWORKED TEACHERS

Until 1964, high school English teachers at Harrison High taught five periods per day. In 1964 the superintendent introduced a new English curriculum that put more emphasis on writing skills. This change called for students to write a theme a week for the 35 weeks of the school year. In order to provide teachers with the additional time needed to read the themes and to evaluate this new program, the teachers' work load was cut from five teaching periods a day to four. As a result, English teachers had 10 preparation periods per week. This policy was in effect in 1967, when Harrison teachers first began collective bargaining, and continued in effect up until the 1975–1976 school year. In October 1975, the teachers' association filed a grievance concerning an alleged increase in the work load of the English teachers at Harrison. The grievance said there had been an increase in class size and class schedule.

The school committee, by means of a letter sent by its lawyer on November 7, 1975, indicated that the proposed changes should be brought to the table and bargained pursuant to section 2-03 of the agreement (see below). The grievance was settled. In the years following the settlement of the grievance, each English teacher taught alternating loads of four classes and five classes, for an average load of four and a half classes. According to the union, teachers accepted a fifth class in alternate years on a voluntary basis to prevent certain materials from being removed from the curriculum.

In plans for the 1979–1980 school year, one-semester courses were to be eliminated and English teachers would be required to teach five periods a day. As a result, the number of preparation periods would be reduced from 10 per week to 5. This would result in an increased time load of from 7 to 15 hours per week for each teacher since there was to be a reduction to five preparation periods and an increase in preparation incurred for the one additional class presentation each day.

In February 1979, the teachers' association became aware that an increase in the teaching load of English teachers was contemplated by the school committee. Under date of February 13, 1979, the association wrote to the superintendent asking to bargain about any such increase. There was no response from the superintendent.

In late March or April, the school committee voted to increase the English teachers' load from four to five as the superintendent had requested. The association was not notified, nor was the change bargained. The assistant superintendent communicated the change to the department head in April. The department head requested teachers in the department to list five teaching preferences for 1979–1980 at a staff meeting in April. The teachers protested this request, and some listed four preferences rather than five. The assistant superintendent made the final assignments, and he did not notify teachers of their programs before late May 1979. After receiving their 1979–1980 assignments, the English teachers filed a grievance on June 15, 1979.

The collective bargaining agreement between the school committee and the teachers' association reads as follows:

(2-03)   As to those matters, if any, not covered by this Agreement, the pre-existing rules, regulations or policy of the Committee, if any, shall control. Before the Committee adopts a change in rules, regulations, or policy which affects wages, hours or any other condition of employment and which is not covered by the terms of this Agreement, the Committee will notify the Association in writing that it is considering such a change. The Association will have the right to negotiate with the Committee, provided that it files such a request with the Committee within five (5) days after receipt of said notice. Any agreement reached with the Committee will be reduced to writing, will be signed by the Committee and the Association, and will become an addendum to this Agreement.

(5-08-01)   When scheduling permits, all teachers in the junior and senior high schools will have at least one preparation period per day during which they will not be assigned to any other duties in addition to their lunch period. At no time hereafter shall the Committee be required to hire any additional personnel to comply with the requirements of this paragraph.

(5-11)   Academic subject area junior and senior high school teachers will not be assigned more than five teaching periods per day. However, if the principal in consultation with the department heads has exhausted all scheduling possibilities and is unable to accomplish the above schedule, he may, on an emergency basis, schedule a teacher for not more than 25 instructional periods per week. Department heads will not be assigned more than two teaching periods per day. No teacher in the junior high school or senior high school will be required to teach the same academic class of students two periods in one day except where scheduling problems exist. This clause shall not apply to lab and similar situations.

(5-13-01)   Teachers in the junior high and senior high schools are requested to take additional teaching assignments will be compensated for the assignment on a pro-rata basis per class period....

Article 10: Teacher Assignment

(10-01)   Teachers with one year or more experience in the School System will be notified in writing of change in their program for the coming year, including change in the schools to which they will be assigned, the grades and/or subjects that they will teach as soon as practicable, and under normal circumstances, not later than June 1.

Both the superintendent and the attorney for the school committee met with the teachers' association about this grievance. When they were unable to resolve it, the matter went to arbitration. At the arbitration hearing, the school committee's attorney represented the employer. The superintendent attended the hearing and gave testimony. The teachers' association argued that:

> the long-standing practice of having the English teachers teach four periods is a rule, regulation or policy under the meaning of Section 2-03 of the Agreement. Teacher assignment is a mandatory subject of bargaining that the parties have negotiated over in the past.... The change in 1964 to move English teachers from five to four assignments and the change in 1979 to move them back to five were both approved by the School Committee. These voted changes affected the hours and conditions of employment in the English Department. Teachers are now required to teach one more class and maintain the writing curriculum introduced in 1964. The Committee has thus unilaterally increased the teachers' work hours by from 7 to 15 hours per week...the Committee violated the Agreement when it unilaterally changed the assignments of High School English teachers by increasing each teacher's daily assignment from four to five classes....

The school committee did not agree. Instead, the committee's attorney argued:

> Article 5-11 of the Agreement explicitly provides that junior and senior high school teachers will not be assigned more than five (5) teaching periods per day. The language only limits the Committee to assignments in excess of five classes per day. There are no limits anywhere in the Agreement up to five classes. The Agreement is clear and definite....
>
> Article 5-08-01 explicitly argues that the Committee has discretion in the assignment of teachers. This section recognizes that teachers shall have at least one preparation period per day. There is no mention anywhere in the Agreement that English teachers are to have an exception and receive two preparation periods....
>
> In the past, the Committee has changed class assignments in both English and other subject areas....
>
> There is no evidence that every time the Committee made a change it had to seek approval from the Association. The changes were made by the Committee upon recommendation of the Superintendent. The Committee argues that past practice is not really a valid argument in the present case because the Agreement clearly gives the Committee the right to assign up to five classes....

The teachers' association also requested that the arbitrator direct the superintendent

> to assign English teachers at the High School 4 periods of teaching effective September 1980 for the 1980–1981 school year, and that the English teachers compelled to teach five classes in 1979–1980 should be compensated for the extra assignment pro rata as demanded by Article 5-13-01.

QUESTIONS FOR THOUGHT AND DISCUSSION

1 What is the relationship between the school committee and the superintendent of schools?

2 Where are there disagreements between the school committee and the teachers' as-

sociation? Are these disputes over facts or over the interpretation of the agreement? How does an arbitrator resolve disputes over facts? Over contract interpretation?

3 Does the language of section 5-11 of the agreement permit the superintendent to change teacher assignments so long as they do not exceed five teaching periods per day? Why or why not?

4 How should the arbitrator answer the basic issue presented: Did the committee violate the agreement when it assigned high school English teachers five teaching periods per day commencing in the 1979–1980 school year?

5 If the arbitrator finds that the school committee violated the agreement, what remedy should the arbitrator establish?

THE IMPRISONED EMPLOYEE

Alan Johnson had been an employee of Richmond, Inc., for about 8 years. He had a work record with his supervisor initially rated as poor, but which recently had improved to good. A company official stated at the hearing described below that Johnson's attendance and performance were better and had been improving.

On or about January 19, 1979, Johnson was arrested on narcotics charges involving the sale of hard drugs to minors. On November 22, he was sentenced to the state's adult correction institution (ACI) for 3 years and fined $1000.

Meanwhile, on November 11, 1979, Johnson injured his back at work and was unable to return to work. He made a workers' compensation claim, but the claim was never settled. However, the company was aware of the injury, since Johnson filed a claim almost immediately. A letter from Dr. Waldo M. Somers stated that Johnson was injured at work and indicated he must miss at least 10 days.

Johnson did not work at Richmond after November 11, 1979. Company officials read of his being sentenced to jail in the newspaper subsequent to November 22. Johnson did not notify the company that he had been jailed.

On November 28, the company wrote to Johnson as follows: "This letter is to inform you that you have been discharged for just cause by Richmond, Inc."

Thereafter, Johnson was confined to the state ACI. On April 19, 1980, and again on April 25, 1980, he was examined by medical doctors because he was complaining of back pain.

Winston R. Bell, work release supervisor at the ACI, wrote to the local union on August 25, 1980, saying that his office had phoned Richmond, Inc., on or about May 1, 1980, seeking re-employment for Johnson under the work release program of ACI. Bell said that the call to Richmond had produced a negative response.

Since June 5, 1980, Johnson had been enrolled at the state trade shop schools in an auto-body course.

The union had filed a grievance about Johnson's discharge soon after it occurred. The delay involved in the processing of the grievance consumed several months. When the company and the union could not agree on a resolution of the matter, it was submitted to arbitration. On July 28, 1980, a hearing was held before a neutral arbitrator, at which both the union and the company were represented by attorneys.

In an arbitration hearing about a discharge, the company usually sets forth its position first. This is because the company must state its reasons for the discharge. The union thereafter presents its position.

At the hearing, company officials testified that Johnson had been discharged for two reasons: (1) the nature of the offense he had committed and for which he had been sentenced to jail and (2) nonavailability for work. The company disclaimed any intent to discharge Johnson for unsatisfactory performance.

Company officials stated that Johnson's fellow workers would not accept his return to employment in the plant. Employees called as witnesses at the hearing contradicted this assertion. They testified that Johnson had been a quiet but cooperative worker.

The company's attorney carefully cross-examined the workers who testified. He asked if they knew that Johnson had been convicted of selling drugs to young children and if that affected their view of Johnson. The employees replied that they had no personal knowledge of what Johnson had done and that he had behaved well at work.

The company argued that

> a careful review of the two medical reports revealed nothing but subjective complaints. All objective examinations resulted in negative findings. While it is not dispositive of the issue in this arbitration claim, the Employer represents that Mr. Johnson's disability is more the result of his first impending, and then existing, incarceration than it was the result of a significant injury. In any event, the Union claim appears to be that, some time in the spring of 1980, Mr. Johnson became available for work and should have been re-employed by Richmond. This claim completely overlooks the fact that Mr. Johnson never advised his employer of his impending trial or his sentence. It also ignores that fact that Mr. Johnson is not freely available for employment but is subject to a Work Release Program with many restrictions and requirements which were not subject to this Hearing. Richmond has no obligation to justify its refusal to join in the Program, rather, the Union must establish that the failure to employ Mr. Johnson under the Program or at the conclusion of his incarceration violates the Contract.

The union responded that an employer should not be allowed to discharge an employee for offenses committed off-duty.

Article VIII, section 2, of the agreement (see below) provides that "seniority shall be terminated when an employee...fails to report his absence within three (3) consecutive working days, without reasonable excuse."

Three consecutive working days from Friday, November 25, 1979, would have been Wednesday, November 30. However, the company had terminated Johnson on November 28.

The union offered evidence that Johnson was medically unfit for work until May 1, 1980. Such information had not been given to the company in November and December, at which time Johnson had already been discharged by Richmond. The union claimed that the company, by terminating Johnson in an untimely fashion, relieved him of the obligation to present a doctor's certificate as to the length of time an absence was required. Therefore, the union asked the arbitrator to reinstate Johnson with back pay.

The clauses of the collective bargaining agreement between Richmond, Inc., and the union which apply to this grievance are the following:

Article VIII, Section 2—Loss of Seniority

Continuous service and seniority shall be terminated when an employee:

(A) Quits, retires, (normal or early), or is discharged for just cause which is sustained.

(B) When an employee fails to report his absence within three (3) consecutive working days, without reasonable excuse.

(C) Fails to report for work at the termination of a leave of absence, without reasonable excuse.

(D) Fails to report for work within five working days after notification by certified mail of recall from layoff, without reasonable excuse.

(E) Has been absent from work due to layoff, non-occupational illness or disability for a period equal to the employee's prior continuous service for seniority purposes, but not more than five (5) years. Any accumulation in excess of one (1) year during such absence shall be counted only for purposes of job security and job bidding.

Article VII, Section 12—Leaves of Absence

(C) An employee who becomes ill or is injured and whose claim of illness or injury is supported by a Doctor's certificate shall be granted a leave of absence to cover the period of such illness.

QUESTION FOR THOUGHT AND DISCUSSION

1 Was Johnson discharged by the company for just cause? If not, what shall the remedy be?

THE LEADERLESS TOOLROOM

On June 27, 1972, the company established the job of group leader–Toolroom and Short-Run Department. The job rating specifications were as follows:

Performs all duties of JP-3, Toolmaker, and JMN-11, All Around Machinist. Assists, directs, instructs and maintains the work flow of up to 25 toolroom and short-run employees.

The job rating specifications of toolmaker JP-3 and all-around machinist JMN-11 are attached as appendixes.

The company then posted the job of group leader–Toolroom and Short-Run Department. Philip Weston was the successful bidder. Weston held that job from 1972 until October 1975, when the company appointed him to the position of foreman of the Toolroom and Short-Run Department, which position he held at the time of these events.

Upon the appointment of Weston as foreman in October 1975, Rene Palaci replaced Weston as group leader–Toolroom and Short-Run Department in accordance with the procedures for job posting and bidding as set forth in the agreement. Palaci held the job until his retirement on April 1, 1977. Since that date the company had not posted a vacancy for the job vacated by Palaci and had not filled the job.

On March 14, 1977, the union filed the grievance which is the subject of this arbitration (grievance No. 26). In grievance No. 26, the union charged that the company had violated the collective bargaining agreement when it did not post a group leader vacancy in the Toolroom and Short-Run Department when Palaci retired. Thereafter, on July 6, 1977, the union filed a grievance, No. 53, charging that the foreman in the toolroom, Weston, was doing bargaining-unit work. Grievance No. 53 alleged that Weston was taking parts apart. This was, in the union's view, work of the bargaining unit—either the group leader, "or if he is not in, another toolmaker who replaces him."

Grievance No. 53 was resolved at the first step of the grievance procedure. Weston agreed to get a toolmaker if one was needed in looking over work.

Thereafter the union believed that Weston was still doing bargaining-unit work. Weston denied this. He insisted that he did not as foreman do the work of toolmaker JP-3 or all-around machinist JMN-11.

In 1974 the company had decided to establish a stockroom for the pump department. The main stockroom had a group leader. The company decided not to establish a group leader position in the pump stockroom, arguing that with only three employees and a supervisor, it was unnecessary. The union filed a grievance (No. 9, dated January 11, 1974). The resolution of the grievance was "Pumps doesn't need one for four men," made by a memorandum of agreement between the company and the union, May 29, 1974.

In the Toolroom and Short-Run Department, whenever Palaci, the group leader, was absent from work, on each occasion the company replaced Palaci with Richard Marciezyk, the next-senior employee in the Toolroom and Short-Run Department. Those absences and fill-in dates were as follows:

7/7/76 to 7/19/76
10/4/76 to 10/12/76
1/3/77 to 1/10/77
1/17/77 to 1/21/77
1/31/77 to 2/7/77
2/14/77 to 2/18/77

Appendix A

Code No. _____JP-3_____

Dept. _____

Grade _____1_____

JOB RATING SPECIFICATIONS
(SHOP)

JOB NAME _____TOOLMAKER_____ CLASS _____

JOB DESCRIPTION:

A broad spectrum of skills is required to perform the function of JP-3 including such diverse abilities as:

1. Set-up and operate all machine tools necessary to perform machining such as milling, drilling, turning, boring, grinding (cylindrical and surface), sawing, and honing.

2. Work to very close tolerances and fine finishes.

3. Heat treat within the limitations of equipment available.

4. Work to very complex drawings and/or verbal instructions.

5. Determines and executes manufacturing methods.

6. Performs hand-tool work to sometimes extreme and exacting requirements. (frequent)

7. Determines by math and/or trigonometry, relative locations of features whose dimensions are not supplied on drawings or are necessary for machining purposes relative to set-up and therefore cannot be supplied by engineering department.

8. Uses all skills needed to construct or repair jigs and fixtures, punches and dies, gauges and other measuring devices.

9. Use of measuring instruments, e.g. scale micrometer, Rockwell tester, vernier, dial indicator and various gauges.

Appendix B

Code No. _____JMN-11_____

Dept. _____

Grade _____3_____

JOB RATING SPECIFICATIONS
(SHOP)

JOB NAME _____ALL AROUND MACHINIST_____ CLASS _____

JOB DESCRIPTION:

Diversified work. Works from fairly complex drawings, sketches and verbal instructions. Performs a variety of machining operations such as milling, drilling, grinding, turning, boring, sawing, burring, honing, etc. while making or repairing a variety of machined parts.

Uses a variety of precision measuring instruments, such as micrometers, verniers, depth gauges, surface plate equipment.

Performs turning to ±.0002". Holds concentricity to .0005". Makes match fits to .0001". Setups are exacting. Must be able to improvise. Must know machining characteristics of various materials. Uses shop math including trigonometry and sine bar. Performs flame soft soldering. Reports only unusual situations to supervisor.

Makes simple jigs, fixtures or tools for own work.

Maintains work area and machines in a clean and orderly condition.

The company insisted to the union that it had legitimate reasons for continuing the group leader job when Weston was made foreman and for discontinuing it now.

Oscar Rollins, the plant manager, said that the company had created the position of group leader in the toolroom in June 1972. At that time, the supervisor of the toolroom (Reggis Aspin) also had the responsibility for plant maintenance. After a period of time, it was determined by management that the toolroom could not be efficiently run with the supervisor out of the department 50 percent of the time. So the company added a group leader in the department. Rollins also said that the company did not discuss with the union or ask for the union's approval of the decision to add a group leader in this department.

Kevin Drosi, unit manager of machining, said that when Weston was made foreman, the company decided to fill the group leader job because Palaci had some skills that the company needed and the company wanted him to impart this knowledge on the repair and upkeep of punches and dies to Weston and to another toolmaker before he, Palaci, retired.

When Palaci retired, Weston had been a foreman for 17 months and he did not have any other area of responsibility. It was decided that the department could be run efficiently without a group leader at this time.

The grievance was not resolved, and the matter proceeded to arbitration. In the hearing held by the arbitrator, it was the union's contention that the job of group leader–Toolroom and Short-Run Department exists in its full scope today just as it did on April 1, 1977, when Palaci retired. It should therefore be posted for bid forthwith, and the successful bidder should be awarded the job and the contractual rate for the group leader job retroactively to April 1, 1977.

The company contended that "there has been no contract violation. The decision to fill a vacancy is the unilateral right of management."

The clauses of the collective bargaining agreement between the company and the union which apply to this grievance are the following:

Section XIV—Bid Posting

(14.08) With respect to promotion and the filling of vacancies or new jobs (caused by reasons other than layoffs and leaves of absence) it is agreed that said promotions, filling of vacancies or new jobs shall be posted for bid on the Company bulletin boards for a period of forty-four (44) consecutive hours from noon to the day of posting while the shop is working on a three-shift basis.

Section V—Rights of Management

(5.01) Subject to the provisions of this Agreement, the Company shall have the right to exercise its regular management rights and functions, including but not limited to the right to hire, transfer, discharge, layoff and discipline employees, the right to direct the efforts and assign work to its employees, the right to make and enforce reasonable rules and regulations relating to the operation of the Company's business as it shall deem advisable, the right to change or introduce methods or production facilities and to modify the sequence of operations on work performed, the right to establish proper work standards, and the right to maintain records of quantity and quality of performance of individuals. An employee and his or her steward will be allowed to review the employee's records pertinent to any areas being considered by the Company for possible disciplinary action against the employee or any other area relating to a commitment or action by the Company before or after a disciplinary action.

QUESTIONS FOR THOUGHT AND DISCUSSION

1 What has been the past practice of the union and the company with respect to toolroom absences?
2 Does the job of group leader–Toolroom and Short-Run Department still exist in its full scope, as the union argues?
3 How do you evaluate the company's stated reasons for not now filling the job of group leader? Are these reasons protected by the collective bargaining agreement?
4 What should the arbitrator do about the union's complaint that Weston is still doing bargaining-unit work?
5 How should the arbitrator rule on the issue: Did the company violate the labor agreement when it did not post a group leader vacancy in the Toolroom and Short-Run Department when Palaci retired?

THE MYSTERIOUS TIME CARDS

On February 26, 1984, Mr. William Conlin was suspended from his job without pay for 1 day by his employer for allegedly punching another employee's time card as well as his own at the end of work on February 25, 1984. Mr. Conlin denied punching any card but his own and brought a grievance against the company.

A hearing was held by an arbitrator on October 20, 1984. According to the three witnesses for the employer, on February 25, 1984, at the end of the work day, the grievant punched out two different time cards in defiance of company rules. For this the grievant was suspended.

Although certain matters were in dispute as to what occurred on February 25, 1984, others were not. The scene of the incident was documented by diagrams, photographs, and the testimony of witnesses. The office layout and the locations of the three time clocks, two time-card racks, and glass partitions indicated that an individual punching a time card can be seen from within the office where the company witnesses were located. Photographs submitted as evidence revealed that the time clocks are mounted in front of a glass partition no more than 42 inches (42") above floor level, slightly higher than the average person's waist. Time cards are placed in the top of the time clocks which can readily been seen from the office interior.

It was also undisputed that Mr. Conlin was present on February 25, approached the time clock, punched it more than once, and left the premises immediately thereafter. The company admitted that it has been unable to locate the additional time card allegedly punched by the grievant.

The facts also revealed that prior to the incident, several meetings had been held by various supervisors to inform project personnel that shop rules about clocking out would be enforced more strictly. In keeping with this change in shop policy, the project manager, assistant project manager, and floor manager were located in the office adjacent to the time clocks on February 25, 1984, for the purpose of monitoring employees punching time cards.

Mr. Conlin testified that his union representative had informed him in the weeks immediately prior to February 25, 1984, that the Company was "tightening up" on clock-related rules.

The basis of the dispute was that three management eyewitnesses contend that the grievant punched two time cards at the center time clock, while the grievant and a fellow employee eyewitness contend that the grievant punched his own time card twice.

At the union's request, each of the three company witnesses testified without the other company witnesses present and were not permitted to talk to each other between testimonies.

The three company eyewitnesses offered clear and consistent testimony concerning the incident in question. Each man testified in sufficient detail as to what he observed when the grievant punched the time clock on that date. Each man stated that the purpose of his presence in the office adjacent to the time clocks was to observe the process and to discern whether company rules regarding time-card punching were being followed.

These witnesses were consistent in their description of the grievant's shuffling of two time cards in an "end over end" fashion as he approached the time clock. This detail was revealed by the Floor Manager on direct examination when he demonstrated how the grievant was shuffling the time cards. It was further supported during a painstaking cross-examination of the company's second witness.

Further, the three company witnesses were consistent in their descriptions of the manner in which the two time cards were punched by the grievant.

The union called as a witness a fellow employee who stood next to Mr. Conlin in the punching-out line on the afternoon of February 25, 1984. According to this witness, Mr. Conlin carried only one time card and punched only one card, though he punched it several times. Mr. Conlin, testifying in his own behalf, gave the same account as his fellow employee.

QUESTIONS FOR THOUGHT AND DISCUSSION

1 How is an arbitrator to make a decision where eyewitnesses differ in their testimony?
2 How would you decide this case? What remedy, if any, is appropriate?

THE CONSTANT "TEMPORARY EMPLOYEE"

The Johnson Nursing Home is an extended health-care facility. Charles Wilson is the owner and administrator of the home and Pat McAdoo is maintenance supervisor.

The home has two patient floors and it normally assigns two housekeepers to each of these floors on each day of the week, including Saturdays and Sundays, from 8:00 a.m. to 2:00 p.m. In order to maintain this housekeeping coverage, the home indicates that it regularly employs five housekeeping employees, four full-time and one part-time. As of June 1983 the persons holding these five positions, and their regular hours of employment, were as follows:

Name	Hours of employment	Total weekly hours
B. Reardon	6 hours a day, 6 days a week	36
M. Glidden	6 hours a day, 6 days a week	36
C. Stacey	6 hours a day, 6 days a week	36
K. Anderson	6 hours a day, 6 days a week	36
V. Perkins	6 hours a day, 3 days a week	18

The home has a collective bargaining agreement with the Hospital Workers' Union. Under the home's agreement with the union, employees in the housekeeping and other departments have been permitted to take leaves of absence of up to 6 months' duration for pregnancy or other medical reasons. In any such instance, or in other instances of extended absence, the home's practice has been to hire a temporary replacement to fill in for the absent employee so that the home's normal staffing levels, many of which are mandated by regulations published by the State's Department of Public Health, will be maintained. The home's consistent practice with respect to these temporary employees has been to treat them as being outside the collective bargaining unit and not subject to the terms and conditions of the home's bargaining agreements with the union.

Susan Donovan was first employed at the home in 1976 as a housekeeper. Thereafter, Ms. Donovan resigned from her employment at the home, but subsequently, in 1979, she worked for Mr. McAdoo at another establishment in Boston.

Some time in May 1983, Ms. Donovan telephoned Mr. McAdoo at the home and asked him if he had any work he could offer her at the home. Mr. McAdoo responded that he did not have any openings at that time, but he invited her to meet Mr. Wilson and told her that he would keep her in mind if any openings did become available.

About 2 weeks later, at or about the end of May 1983, one of the full-time housekeepers working under Mr. McAdoo's direct supervision, Ms. B. Reardon, informed Mr. McAdoo that she would need to take a medical leave of absence over the next several weeks. In response to this information, Mr.

McAdoo asked Mr. Wilson if he should hire a temporary replacement for Ms. Reardon. Mr. Wilson agreed that Mr. McAdoo should hire a temporary replacement to fill in for Ms. Reardon and also for the other housekeeping employees who would be going on vacation later on in the summer.

Promptly after his conversation with Mr. Wilson, Mr. McAdoo telephoned Ms. Donovan and told her that one of his employees was going on an indefinite leave of absence, so he could hire her as a part-time fill-in. Ms. Donovan agreed to this offer and shortly thereafter, on June 2, 1983, she came to the home and submitted a written employment application to Mr. McAdoo.

Ms. Reardon commenced her leave of absence on Friday, May 30, and the next week, on June 6, 1983, Ms. Donovan commenced her employment at the home. Thereafter Ms. Reardon returned from her leave of absence on June 25, 1983, but in July, August, and September 1983 other members of the housekeeping staff, including Ms. Glidden, Ms. Stacey, Ms. Anderson, and Ms. Perkins, were away on vacation and in October 1983, Ms. Anderson took a medical leave of absence. Ms. Donovan filled in for each of these employees as well.

Throughout the foregoing period, the home, pursuant to its prior practice, treated Ms. Donovan as a temporary employee and, accordingly, paid her lesser wages and benefits than were provided by the agreement for members of the collective bargaining unit. Both Ms. Donovan and the union were aware that Ms. Donovan was not being treated as a member of the collective bargaining unit and at no time throughout this period did they present any grievance with respect to this action by the home.

Ms. Anderson returned from her leave of absence on November 11, 1983. Shortly thereafter, however, on November 21, 1983, one of the home's kitchen employees, Ms. Paris, commenced a medical leave of absence and Ms. Donovan was offered the opportunity to fill in for her. Thereafter Ms. Donovan filled in through January 1984 for Ms. Paris or, once again, for various members of the housekeeping staff who were sick or on leave of absence.

Some time in January 1984, Ms. Donovan went to see Mr. Wilson in his office and asked him about her status. At that meeting, Mr. Wilson stated to Ms. Donovan that the home had not yet had any openings in its permanent positions and that she could only be employed on a temporary basis until it did. He further stated, however, that he would keep her in mind and let her know as soon as any permanent positions did become open.

Ms. Paris did not return from her leave of absence until the first week of March 1984. Thereafter Ms. Perkins in the housekeeping department took a medical leave of absence from March 20 through May 21, 1984, and after she returned, Ms. Anderson was able to work only 1 or 2 days a week. Ms. Donovan continued to fill in for each of these persons throughout this period but, once again, she was not offered a permanent position because in the opinion of the home no such position had become available.

On May 22, 1984, the grievant filled out a dues check-off authorization and gave it to the employer.

On May 26, 1984, the union filed a grievance on behalf of Ms. Donovan. During the week of June 19, 1984, Ms. Anderson returned to full-time status. Ms. Donovan was then scheduled to work only 2 days that week.

At the arbitration hearing, Ms. Donovan testified that she then applied for welfare payments, but that a letter from the home was denied to her by Mr. McAdoo unless she resigned. Therefore, the grievant testified, she resigned on June 23, 1984.

There was no other evidence supporting the grievant's testimony in regard to the alleged cause of her resignation, and testimony of the home's bookkeeper indicated that the requested information in the form of a letter to the Welfare Department had in fact been given to the grievant by the home.

Following the testimony at the arbitration hearing, the union argued that the grievance should be sustained. "There is no just cause for the denial of her benefits or the acts that led to her forced termination. The employer should be directed to properly reinstate the grievant with full seniority and restitution of services and benefits and to make the grievant fully whole for all losses sustained because of her discharge."

"However," the union added, "if the arbitrator finds that her resignation letter of June 23, 1984, was in fact proper resignation, then we are asking that the arbitrator rule that Ms. Donovan be made whole in every way from the period of her employment to June 23, 1984, including holiday pay, sick pay, vacation pay, and the proper wage schedule."

The home in its agreement made three points:

1 The evidence established that Ms. Donovan was a temporary employee who was not covered by the terms of the agreement.

2 Nothing in the parties' agreement limits the period of time a person can be treated as a temporary employee.

3 No question regarding Ms. Donovan's resignation is properly before the arbitrator in this case.

The clauses of the agreement between the union and Johnson Nursing Home identified by the union or the employer as most relevant to the case are as follows:

Article I—Purpose and Recognition

(1.1) The intent and purpose of this Agreement is to set forth the rates of pay, hours of employment, and other conditions of employment which shall be in effect for the duration of this Agreement for the employees for whom the Union is the certified collective bargaining representative so long as such employees are employed by the Employer at its nursing home facility, in order to promote orderly and peaceful relations between the Employer and the Union and said employees and to achieve efficient operations in said nursing home facility.

(1.2) The Employer, pursuant to its legal obligations as a result of the certification of the Union by the National Labor Relations Board, recognizes the Union as the sole and exclusive bargaining agent for all regular full-time and part-time licensed practical nurses, recreation therapists, nurses aides, housekeeping employees, orderlies, and laundry employees employed by the Employer at its nursing home, excluding all other employees: dieticians, registered nurses, office clerical employees, professional employees, guards, and supervisors as defined in the Act, as amended to date.

(1.3) The words "employee" and "employees" as used hereafter in this Agreement refer only to such persons as at the time in question are within the bargaining unit described in Section 1.2. The words "full-time employee" and "full-time employees" refer only to employees employed on a permanent basis who are normally scheduled to work forty (40) hours or more per week. The words "part-time employees" refer only to employees employed on a permanent basis who are normally scheduled to work less than forty (40) hours per week but at least sixteen (16) hours per week....

Article XV

(15.5) The function of the arbitrator is to determine the interpretation and application of the specific provisions of this Agreement. There shall be no right of arbitration to obtain, and no arbitrator shall have any authority or power to award or determine, any change in, modification or alteration of, addition to, or detraction from, any of the provisions of this Agreement. No arbitrator shall have any authority or power to reverse, set aside, or modify any determination made by the Employer pursuant to the provisions of this Agreement unless he finds that such determination was arbitrary and capricious. No arbitrator shall have any power to award any back pay or other settlement to be retroactive beyond the date on which the grievance was first presented to the Employer. The award of the arbitrator on any grievance properly submitted to him hereunder, if within the scope of his authority and power, shall be final and binding upon the parties.

At the hearing the union and the employer disagreed about what the arbitrator was to decide, and left it to Ms. Donovan to state the issue as well as the answer.

QUESTIONS FOR THOUGHT AND DISCUSSION

1 How should the arbitrator frame the issue?
2 What was Susan Donovan's status under the contract?
3 How should the arbitrator rule? What remedy, if any, is proper?

WHO IS TELLING THE TRUTH?

Mr. Carl J. Hardy had been employed by the company in its Dorchester, Massachusetts, warehouse for about 2 years when, on October 3, 1987, he was discharged by the company.

The events which led to Mr. Hardy's discharge began in the spring of 1987. The agreement between the union and the company which preceded the current agreement expired at the end of January 1987. Negotiations between the company and the union failing, the union conducted a strike against the company for some 7 weeks in May, June, and July of 1987. During the strike Mr. Hardy ceased work and participated on the union's picket line.

Certain other of the employees of the company continued to work during the strike. In particular, Mr. John Leonard did so. Apparently Mr. Leonard was subjected to verbal abuse from Mr. Hardy and other strikers upon reporting to and departing from work during the period of the strike. At one point Mr. Leonard was apparently followed from work to his home by Mr. Hardy. Concerned for his safety and that of his family, Mr. Leonard moved his home and also filed a complaint against Mr. Hardy, alleging that Mr. Hardy had threatened him with a gun.

The strike ended and work resumed. Thereafter Mr. Hardy was acquitted of the charges filed against him by Mr. Leonard in a court proceeding attended, at least in part, by managers from the company. Mr. Hardy returned to work on August 20, 1987. Mr. Hardy worked on the night shift, from 2:30 p.m. until 11:10 p.m. Mr. Leonard was employed on the day shift, from 6:30 a.m. until 3:10 p.m. Thus, the shifts of the two men overlapped each working day for 40 minutes.

According to the testimony of Mr. Leonard, he was subjected to continued verbal harassment by Mr. Hardy from the date of Mr. Hardy's return to work in the warehouse. Mr. Hardy called Mr. Leonard names and made obscene gestures to him. Mr. Leonard, who is black, did not include racial epithets in the list of names Mr. Hardy, who is white, allegedly called him. Mr. Leonard testified that he ignored the provocations.

Mr. Leonard testified that on October 3, 1987, Mr. Hardy approached him while he was talking with another employee who also had worked through the strike. Mr. Hardy made an obscene gesture to Mr. Leonard and snorted at him. Mr. Leonard snorted back. Mr. Hardy walked up to Mr. Leonard and jabbing his finger at or into Mr. Leonard's left eye said to him, "Don't you ever say a [obscenity] word to me again."

Immediately thereafter Mr. Leonard and the employee with whom he had been talking reported the incident to Mr. DiSilva, the warehouse superintendent. Mr. DiSilva called Mr. Hardy to his office in the presence of the union's steward, Mr. Rinaldi. Mr. Hardy denied the incident. Mr. DiSilva sent Mr. Hardy home from work.

Mr. Leonard also went home at that time.

Prior to October 3, 1987, Mr. Hardy had received the following written warnings from the company:

January 6, 1987—warning for being in an unauthorized area of the warehouse tampering with sound system equipment. Mr. Hardy was discovered by a security guard.

January 8, 1987—warning for excessive lateness in reporting to work.

January 13, 1987—2-day suspension for not reporting to work and not calling in.

January 19, 1987—5-day suspension for unacceptable lateness in reporting to work.

February 7, 1987—warning that racial harassment of other employees would result in immediate discharge. The racial harassment was directed against the security guard, who was black, who had found Mr. Hardy in an unauthorized area of the warehouse in January.

August 27, 1987—5-day suspension for being involved on at least two occasions in serious verbal confrontation with another employee (according to testimony), one of the nonstrikers. This last suspension is being grieved by the union and has not yet been heard by an arbitrator.

Mr. DiSilva discharged Mr. Hardy by letter of October 6, 1987.

Later that evening an altercation occurred between the employee who had been with Mr. Leonard when Mr. Hardy allegedly accosted him, and another employee, a friend of Mr. Hardy who had also been a striker. Mr. Leonard's associate was discharged by the company and the other employee, who had no previous disciplinary action, was suspended from work for a day or so.

Mr. Hardy testified that the alleged incident never occurred. He said that he had not spoken nor gestured to Mr. Leonard on October 3 and that he had so informed Mr. DiSilva, who failed to investigate the matter sufficiently to determine that Mr. Hardy had not been at fault.

Both Mr. DiSilva and another member of management gave testimony that they had received harassing phone calls in the middle of the night from Mr. Hardy after his discharge.

Also, management pointed out that Mr. Hardy had once several years ago been convicted of threatening other persons with a machete.

Finally, several of Mr. Hardy's fellow workers on the late shift, and fellow strikers, testified that they had not seen any interchange between Mr. Hardy and Mr. Leonard on October 3 and that Mr. Leonard left work that day without any evident injury to his left eye. Nor was Mr. Leonard ever treated for injury to his eye.

At the hearing held before an arbitrator the representatives of the union and the company agreed that the issue to be arbitrated was: Did the company have just cause to discharge the grievant, Mr. Carl Hardy? If not, what shall be the remedy?

The attorney for the company argued that there is a pattern in Mr. Hardy's behavior which is that he retaliates against those who cross him or do what he doesn't think they should.

If Mr. Leonard were telling the truth about the incident, the company's attorney said, then the company has a right to discharge Mr. Hardy; and Mr. Leonard was telling the truth.

The union representative noted that the company in its dismissal letter to Mr. Hardy failed to cite the specific section of the contract under which he was being discharged, as it is required to do.

There had been ongoing animosity among the employees since the strike, but, said the union representative,

1 There was no racial animosity in Mr. Hardy's behavior. Indeed, one of the fellow employees and fellow strikers who testified on Mr. Hardy's behalf was black.

2 Witnesses testified that they had seen nothing wrong with Mr. Leonard's eye after the alleged incident, nor is there medical evidence of any damage to the eye.

3 There was no witness to the incident who testified other than Mr. Leonard himself.

4 Mr. DiSilva did not make a careful investigation of the incident before discharging Mr. Hardy.

In consequence of the above, the union concluded, the company has not proven its case for the discharge, and Mr. Hardy should be reinstated in his job and made whole for loss of wages and benefits.

This dispute is governed by the provisions of the collective bargaining agreement between the union and the company effective February 1, 1987, and terminating January 31, 1990.

Article VIII of the agreement is entitled "Suspension and Discharge Procedure" and includes the following language which is relevant to this case:

Section 1 ...No employee may be discharged or suspended without just cause. Prior to discharge or suspension, except as provided in Section 4 below, at least one written warning notice of a related complaint against an employee shall be given to the employee with a copy to the Steward and to the union.

 Section 4 The parties hereto also recognize that the following are some of the offenses that shall be considered as serious offenses for which the penalty may be immediate dismissal:

 d Any unprovoked assault on an employee of the Company on company property during working hours.

QUESTIONS FOR THOUGHT AND DISCUSSION

 1 How can you, or an arbitrator, determine who is telling the truth?
 2 Whose testimony do you believe? Why?
 3 Was Carl Hardy discharged for just cause? If not, what should the remedy be?

The AFL-CIO Internal Disputes Plan: Two Illustrative Cases

APPLICABLE CLAUSES OF THE AFL-CIO CONSTITUTION

Article XX—Settlement of Internal Disputes

 Section 1 The principles set forth in this Article shall be applicable to all affiliates of this Federation, and to their local unions and other subordinate bodies.

Section 2 Each affiliate shall respect the established collective bargaining relationship of every other affiliate. No affiliate shall organize or attempt to represent employees as to whom an established collective bargaining relationship exists with any other affiliate. For purposes of this Article, the term, "established collective bargaining relationship" means any situation in which an affiliate, or any local or other subordinate body thereof, has either (a) been recognized by the employer (including any governmental agency) as the collective bargaining representative for the employees involved for a period of one year or more, or (b) been certified by the National Labor Relations Board or other federal or state agency as the collective bargaining representative for the employees.

Section 3 Each affiliate shall respect the established work relationship of every other affiliate. For purposes of this Article, an "established work relationship" shall be deemed to exist as to any work of the kind which the members of an organization have customarily performed at a particular plant or work site, whether their employer is the plant operator, a contractor, or other employer. No affiliate shall by agreement or collusion with any employer or by the exercise of economic pressure seek to obtain work for its members as to which an established work relationship exists with any other affiliate, except with the consent of such affiliate. This section shall not be applicable to work in the railroad industry.

Section 20 The provisions of this Article with respect to the settlement and determination of disputes of the nature described in this Article shall constitute the sole and exclusive method for settlement and determination of such dispute and the provisions of this Article with respect to the enforcement of such settlements and determinations shall constitute the sole and exclusive method for such enforcement. No affiliate shall resort to court or other legal proceedings to settle or determine any disputes of the nature described in this Article or to enforce any settlement or determination reached hereunder.

COUNTY OF SACRAMENTO
Before the Impartial Umpire under the AFL-CIO's Internal Disputes Plan

Under date of June 18, 1979, President Wurf of the American Federation of State, County and Municipal Employees (AFSCME) wrote to President George Meany of the AFL-CIO charging that the International Union of Operating Engineers (IUOE) was interfering with AFSCME's established collective bargaining relationship for employees in the Operations-Maintenance-Inspection Unit in Sacramento County, California, in violation of section 2 of Article XX of the constitution of the AFL-CIO....

Prior to the 1970s several AFL-CIO affiliates had asserted representation rights for various employees of the County of Sacramento, California. In 1970, the county enacted an ordinance which allowed for unit determinations by an arbitrator from the American Arbitration Association.

An operations and maintenance unit was established which included mechanics, refuse collectors, heavy-equipment operators, traffic signal and communication repair workers, fire/crash workers, stock clerks, highway and bridge maintenance and repair workers, animal control officers, parks and recreation employees, janitors, and building and construction inspectors; approximately 1000 employees.

Elections were held early in 1971. AFSCME local No. 146 prevailed in the election in the operations and maintenance (O&M) unit over SOURCE, an amalgamation of IUOE local No. 3, Service Employees International Union local No. 22, and an independent, Sacramento County Employees Organization. AFSCME was certified to represent the unit.

In the early 1970s, AFSCME local No. 146 won representation rights to other employees of Sacramento County and to other local government employees in northern California. At one time AFSCME local No. 146 represented some 4000 local government employees in northern California, according to testimony at the hearing. Today AFSCME local No. 146 is said to represent less than 300 such employees.

In April 1978, Sacramento County Employees Organization (SCEO) decertified AFSCME local No. 146 as representatives of the O&M unit. On July 1, 1978, SCEO and the county signed a 1-year agreement covering the O&M unit, with a 2-year recall provision in the event of layoffs.

Late in 1978 a hiring freeze induced by the passage of Proposition 13 reduced the O&M unit to 700 employees. In December 1978, employees in the O&M unit approached IUOE local No. 39 seeking representation.

IUOE local No. 39 reports that repeated attempts to contact AFSCME local No. 146 failed; AFSCME's office was apparently closed and their phone disconnected.

So IUOE initiated a drive to decertify SCEO in the O&M unit.

In February 1979, AFSCME's international representative contacted IUOE local No. 39 and stated an interest in the O&M unit. AFSCME initiated its own petition drive in the unit.

On February 14, 1979, petitions were submitted to the county. A flaw in AFSCME's petition and too few signatures kept AFSCME off the ballot.

On February 19, the county refused to permit a recertification election, citing an alleged contract bar. IUOE petitioned the superior court to reverse the county's ruling. The superior court upheld it. On April 19, IUOE local No. 39 and members of the O&M unit appeared before the county's Board of Supervisors. On May 10, the board amended its code to permit a decertification election soon after July 1, 1979. On June 1, the election was scheduled for July 11.

In the final week of June 1979, IUOE says, it was informed by AFSCME that if IUOE won the election, AFSCME would file Article XX charges. AFSCME denies that any such contact occurred.

On June 18, AFSCME filed charges under Article XX. On July 10, Meany telegraphed the Board of Supervisors and asked for a delay in the election. The O&M unit threatened a "job action" if the election was delayed. The board refused to delay the election.

On July 11, the election was held. The ballots were impounded by court order. As of the date of hearing in this matter, the ballots had not been tallied....

AFSCME maintains that it has an established collective bargaining relationship as to employees in the O&M unit by virtue of its 1971 certification by the county to represent these employees and by virtue of several subsequent collective bargaining agreements in which the county recognized AFSCME as representative of the O&M unit.

AFSCME's decertification by an independent in 1978 does not terminate its established relationship, AFSCME argues....

IUOE argues that if it is foreclosed from representing the O&M unit, the Teamsters will do so. Also, IUOE notes that its attempts to reach AFSCME on this matter in a timely fashion in December 1978 and January 1979 were fruitless....

QUESTIONS FOR THOUGHT AND DISCUSSION

1 Why did AFSCME charge IUOE with a violation of section 2 of Article XX rather than section 3?
2 What is the significance of IUOE's reference to the Teamsters?
3 What should the impartial umpire decide in this case?

AVX CERAMICS COMPANY

Before the Impartial Umpire under the AFL-CIO Internal Disputes Plan

Under date of May 24, 1979, President Coughlin of the Office and Professional Employees International Union (OPEIU) wrote to George Meany alleging a violation of article XX of the constitution of the AFL-CIO by the International Brotherhood of Electrical Workers (IBEW), involving the AVX Ceramics Company of Buffalo, New York.

Thereafter, under date of July 17, 1979, President Pillard of the IBEW sent a telegram to Meany alleging a violation of sections 2, 3, and 20 of article XX by OPEIU at AVX Ceramics Company.

At the hearing held in this matter on July 24, 1979, the IBEW dropped its charge of a violation of section 3 of article XX by OPEIU....

IBEW local No. 1690 was certified to represent employees in production and maintenance for AVX Ceramics in 1950. The recognition clause of the IBEW collective bargaining agreements with AVX-Ceramics from 1950 to 1973 read as follows:

Section 2.01: Bargaining Unit The Company recognizes the Union as the sole collective bargaining agency with respect to rates of pay, hours and other conditions of employment in the Olean and Franklinville plants of the Company for all production and maintenance employees, including factory clerks, but excluding inspectors, timekeepers, guards, office employees and supervisors as defined in Section 2(11) of the Labor Management Relations Act of 1947, as amended.

During this period the IBEW apparently sought to bring into its area of representation certain employees whom the company had classified as inspectors. In January 1973, the IBEW filed a grievance concerning the claimed nonrepresented employees and an arbitration award placed by employees in the IBEW bargaining unit.

Also early in 1973, the International Union of Electrical, Radio and Machine Workers, AFL-CIO (IUE) filed a petition for representation with the NLRB at No. 3-RC-5652 for all unrepresented workers at the company's Seneca Avenue plant, Olean, New York. The IBEW filed as intervener but took no part in the hearing thereon. On May 15, 1973, the board held that office clerical and technical employees could maintain a single plant unit and ordered an election. In that holding, the NLRB included in the technical unit employees then known as Test Technician I and II and now known as Test Technicians. Thereafter, the IUE withdrew the petition, and no election was held.

The IBEW's recognition clause was thereafter changed, and in the collective bargaining agreement effective June 21, 1976, through June 24, 1979, the clause read as follows:

> **2.01: Bargaining Unit** The company recognizes the Union as the sole collective bargaining agency with respect to rates of pay, wages, hours and other conditions of employment in the Olean main plant and west building (on Seneca Avenue) and Franklinville plant of the Company for all production and maintenance employees, including factory clerks, stock clerks, inspectors, but excluding timekeepers, guards, office employees and supervisors as defined in Section 2(11) of the Labor Management Relations Act of 1947, as amended.

On January 14, 1974, OPEIU filed a petition for representation before the NLRB at No. 3-RC-5941 for "all office clerical and technical employees employed by the Employer at its plants in Olean, New York." Thereafter, the company stipulated to an election and on February 28, 1974, the NLRB certified OPEIU. The company and OPEIU entered into a collective bargaining agreement effective from August 21, 1976, through August 24, 1979, in which the recognition clause read as follows:

> **2.01** The Company recognizes the Union as the sole collective bargaining agency with respect to wages, hours and other conditions of employment at its plants located on Seneca Avenue, Olean, New York, for the bargaining unit described in NLRB Case No. 3-RC-5941 [as quoted above].

AVX Ceramics produces capacitors at its Olean plant. Test technicians and quality control (QC) testers are involved in testing the product manufactured by the company. QC testers generally perform five tests on the production run, which measure the capacitor's readings. These tests do not affect the product, and their findings result in rejection or in shipment to the customer. Thereafter samples of the production run are again tested by the five basic response tests. From those samples additional sampling is made for environmental testing. These are tests designed by the customer to measure the extreme responses of the product and usually result in its destruction. The product in its destroyed state is shipped to the customer. Environmental testing is performed by the test technician.

Until recently, the IBEW represented QC testers and OPEIU represented test technicians. At the time of the hearing held in this matter (July 24, 1979) there were apparently 17 QC testers and 12 test technicians employed by the company.

Until January 1976, the two groups of employees worked in separate parts of the plant. The QC testers were at a place near the end of the production line, and the test technicians were in another area. In January 1976, the test technicians were brought back to the room in which the QC testers worked. The two groups of employees worked near each other, but not intermixed, and worked under common supervision.

In April 1978, a member of the OPEIU unit complained to a supervisor that a member of the IBEW unit, a Mr. Glover, was doing OPEIU unit work. The company's supervisor apparently instructed Glover to cease doing certain types of work. On August 8, 1978, the IBEW filed a grievance on behalf of Glover, reading:

> IBEW Local 1690 Union charges that the Company violated Appendix B of the collective bargaining agreement when it misled the Union regarding work jurisdiction.
>   The Union's contention is that the full tour of duty performed historically by the tester is proper IBEW work and should not have been given to the OPEIU unit.

On September 5, 1978, the company informed OPEIU of the grievance and of its intention to go to arbitration. The company's letter informed OPEIU that the grievance "involves the issue of whether or not the Test Technicians, currently represented by your labor organization, properly belong in the unit represented by Local 1690 (IBEW)."

In January 1979, an arbitrator was appointed to hear the dispute. While discussions were under way by mail about a hearing date, OPEIU filed a petition for unit clarification with the NLRB at No. 3-UC-145. The petition asked that OPEIU be certified to represent, among others, "Q.C. testers and data clerks employed in the quality assurance lab at the employer's...plant in Olean, New York." Both QC testers and data clerks were at that time represented by IBEW.

On March 6, 1979, the NLRB held a hearing in the matter of the QC petition in which the IBEW participated.

On March 22, the arbitrator held a hearing in the matter of the IBEW grievance. OPEIU representatives attended but left the hearing when the question as to what was the issue to be arbitrated was not resolved to their satisfaction.

Also on March 22, the NLRB dismissed OPEIU's unit clarification petition.

Then, on April 18, the arbitrator in the matter of the IBEW grievance ruled as follows:

> **1** The grievance is sustained. The issues involved are whether the work performed by the Test Technician is production work or is technical work. Further, after determination of the initial issue to which bargaining unit must the work be assigned.
>
> **2** The work of Test Technician is production work.
>
> **3** The Company will assign the work performed by the Test Technician to production unit personnel.

Thereafter, the company assigned the work in dispute to production workers represented by the IBEW. The company refused to lay off the nine (then) OPEIU-represented test technicians. The IBEW agreed to accept them into membership in their existing job. The nine were given the opportunity to leave their jobs or to join the IBEW. All joined the IBEW.

Thereafter, on May 18, OPEIU filed suit in federal district court against AVX Ceramics and the IBEW....

OPEIU argues that the IBEW is now representing nine employees who were previously members of its bargaining unit and is representing test technicians of whom OPEIU is the certified collective bargaining representative. This outcome, OPEIU argues, is a violation of article XX of the constitution of the AFL-CIO by the IBEW....

The IBEW responds that OPEIU initiated the events, the outcome of which is now the subject of OPEIU's complaint. The IBEW was only acting in defense of its bargaining unit and never sought to represent OPEIU members, but was prevailed upon to do so by the company, with OPEIU's encouragement to their former members to join the IBEW.

Also, the IBEW charges that OPEIU's petition to the NLRB was in violation of section 2 of article XX and that OPEIU's suit in federal court is in violation of section 20 of article XX.

QUESTIONS FOR THOUGHT AND DISCUSSION

1 How did this situation arise?

2 Since the IBEW ended up representing former OPEIU members as a result of the arbitrator's decision and the company's action, isn't the IBEW necessarily involved in a "raid" on OPEIU?

NAME INDEX

SUBJECT INDEX